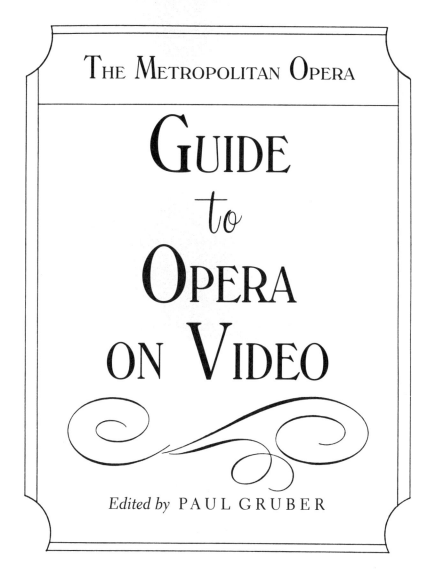

THE METROPOLITAN OPERA

GUIDE
to
OPERA
ON VIDEO

Edited by PAUL GRUBER

THE METROPOLITAN OPERA GUILD

W·W·NORTON & COMPANY·NEW YORK·LONDON

---

*The text of this book is composed in Electra, with the display set in Windsor.
Composition and manufacturing by The Maple-Vail Book Manufacturing Group.*

Library of Congress Cataloging-in-Publication Data
The Metropolitan opera guide to opera on video / edited by Paul Gruber.
p.   cm.
Includes index.
ISBN 0–393–04536–6
1. Operas—Video catalogs.   2. Video recordings—Reviews.
I. Gruber, Paul.
ML158.6.06M47   1997
016.7821′0267—dc21   97–5009
CIP

W. W. Norton & Company, Inc., 500 Fifth Avenue, New York, NY 10110
http://www.wwnorton.com

W. W. Norton & Company Ltd., 10 Coptic Street, London WC1A 1PU

1 2 3 4 5 6 7 8 9 0

Contents

JOHANN STRAUSS, JR.
Die Fledermaus
(Richard Traubner)   *301*

RICHARD STRAUSS
Salome (Jon Alan Conrad)   *304*
Elektra (Peter G. Davis)   *307*
Der Rosenkavalier
(David Hamilton)   *311*
Ariadne auf Naxos
(Jon Alan Conrad)   *316*
Die Frau ohne Schatten
(Jon Alan Conrad)   *318*
Intermezzo (Peter G. Davis)   *320*
Arabella (David Hamilton)   *322*
Capriccio (Peter G. Davis)   *325*

IGOR STRAVINSKY
Oedipus Rex (Harlow Robinson)   *327*
The Rake's Progress
(Harlow Robinson)   *330*

PIOTR ILYICH TCHAIKOVSKY
Eugene Onegin
(Harlow Robinson)   *332*
Pique Dame (The Queen of Spades)
(Harlow Robinson)   *338*

MICHAEL TIPPETT
King Priam (London Green)   *343*

GIUSEPPE VERDI
Nabucco (Harvey E. Phillips)   *345*
I Lombardi alla Prima Crociata
(Bruce Burroughs)   *348*
Ernani (Bruce Burroughs)   *350*
Giovanna d'Arco
(Harvey E. Phillips)   *353*
I Due Foscari (Bruce Burroughs)   *355*
Attila (C. J. Luten)   *357*
Macbeth (Conrad L. Osborne)   *359*
Luisa Miller (Harvey E. Phillips)   *363*
Stiffelio (C. J. Luten)   *365*
Rigoletto (London Green)   *367*
Il Trovatore (Bruce Burroughs)   *371*
La Traviata (Albert Innaurato)   *376*
I Vespri Siciliani
(Bruce Burroughs)   *383*

Simon Boccanegra
(Harvey E. Phillips)   *385*
Un Ballo in Maschera
(Harvey E. Phillips)   *389*
La Forza del Destino
(Albert Innaurato)   *393*
Don Carlo (Peter G. Davis)   *396*
Aida (Harlow Robinson)   *400*
Otello (London Green)   *406*
Falstaff (London Green)   *411*

ANTONIO VIVALDI
Orlando Furioso
(Shirley Fleming)   *415*

RICHARD WAGNER
Der Fliegende Holländer
(London Green)   *417*
Tannhäuser (C. J. Luten)   *420*
Lohengrin (C. J. Luten)   *424*
Tristan und Isolde
(London Green)   *428*
Die Meistersinger von Nürnberg
(Jon Alan Conrad)   *430*
Der Ring des Nibelungen:
Das Rheingold
(Jon Alan Conrad)   *433*
Die Walküre
(Jon Alan Conrad)   *438*
Siegfried (Jon Alan Conrad)   *441*
Götterdämmerung
(Jon Alan Conrad)   *444*
Parsifal (Conrad L. Osborne)   *448*

CARL MARIA VON WEBER
Der Freischütz (London Green)   *453*

RICCARDO ZANDONAI
Francesca da Rimini
(Peter G. Davis)   *455*

BERND ALOIS ZIMMERMANN
Die Soldaten (London Green)   *457*

Contributors   *458*

Index of Performers   *459*

Index of Directors   *479*

CONTENTS BY OPERA TITLES

PREFACE

On March 15, 1977, a new era in Metropolitan Opera history began. Puccini's *La Bohème* was telecast live from the Met stage (with a cast that included Renata Scotto, Luciano Pavarotti, Maralin Niska, and Ingvar Wixell, conducted by James Levine), and for the first time millions of viewers around the country were able to see and hear a Met performance—free of charge, and without leaving home. Regularly scheduled telecasts from the Met began the following year, but at that time few people owned videotape equipment; if you weren't at home to catch the telecast performance or its single repeat, you missed it.

But by the mid-1980s, the home video revolution had taken place, and the videocassette recorder was well established as a standard piece of home entertainment equipment. Prerecorded videotapes of films sold briskly, but tapes of opera performances were a rarity until 1985. That was the year in which Paramount Home Video offered the first Met videotapes (and Pioneer the first Met laser discs). The program was launched with four previously telecast titles: *Don Carlo, Un Ballo in Maschera, La Bohème*, and the Met's 1983 Centennial Gala; single-tape operas were priced at $59.95 and double tapes at $79.95.

At the time, I was director of the Metropolitan Opera Guild's merchandising efforts and was therefore involved with marketing the first Met videos, but my outlook on their sales was pessimistic. Yes, it was incredible that you could own a Met performance—with better picture and sound quality than you could record off the air—and play it whenever you liked. But the tapes were expensive, and I questioned how often a consumer would play an opera videotape. People had collected audio recordings of complete operas for years, but records can be (and usually are) played without demanding the complete attention of those listening. Unless one turned off the picture and used only the sound track, videotapes could be enjoyed only by those who had the time and patience to do nothing but sit and watch them. It seemed to me that the idea of owning operas on video would be attractive at first, but that buyers would soon realize they were spending a lot of money for a tape they watched once—at best— before relegating it to a shelf.

I was half wrong. While opera lovers may have found that watching an opera on tape demanded a little too much concentration, they also discovered that the format allowed them to view an opera at their leisure, with week-long intermissions if they liked. Opera on video became known as an excellent way to prepare for a live performance, especially if the work was unfamiliar. But what apparently held the greatest attraction was the idea of building an opera video library; simply having the videos available at home on the shelf evidently satisfied many collectors. (The growth of the opera video industry would have been even more robust had it not been for one practical business problem: most of the videos are very expensive to produce. The high cost is due, not to the cost of manufacturing, but to the additional contractual obligations that must be met when a performance is offered for sale.)

As video titles proliferated, consumers were soon faced with the same problem they had with audio versions of opera, that of deciding which to buy, and that is just where this volume comes in. With eight video performances of *Die Zauberflöte* and nine of *La Traviata* on store shelves, it was clear that most customers in the market for a video of one of these operas would appreciate being able to read about the different versions before making a selection. The Metropolitan Opera Guild and W. W. Norton published *The Metropolitan Opera Guide to Recorded Opera* in 1993, and several years later we decided that there was now a need for a similar volume on opera videos.

As with the earlier volume on records, we assigned operas to a group of critics, each of whom would watch every video on his or her list, review them, and try to recommend one for each opera. The major difference between the two books is one of breadth: there are far fewer opera videotapes than there are records, so that where the *Guide to Recorded Opera* had to be limited to all recordings of 150 operas, this new volume includes every video that has been commercially released in the United States. (The word "every" needs a modest qualification: a handful of out-of-print videos were simply unavailable and therefore could not be included.)

We have retained the format of the earlier volume: operas are arranged alphabetically by composer and chronologically within composer (there is an alphabetical table of contents by opera for those who haven't memorized the chronological order of Rossini's works). Each chapter, devoted to a specific opera, opens with a key to the headings used for each video, assigning a letter (and noting a voice type) for each major role in the opera, for example: A: Leonore (s); B: Marzelline (s); C: Florestan (t); D: Jacquino (t); E: Don Pizarro (bar); F: Rocco (bs); G: Don Fernando (bs).

Following an informative introduction, the videos are reviewed chronologically. Each review starts off with a heading designed to provide a great deal of information at a glance, beginning with two somewhat problematic items: a recording date and the name of the company that has released the video. As with audio recordings, recording dates are not always available; in the absence of a firm date, the copyright date is used. For the releasing com-

pany, we have tried to use the name of the label under which the recording was most recently issued. Unlike record companies, the firms that release videos usually did not make the recordings and therefore do not have permanent rights to the material. Rights are frequently bought and sold, with the result that some older performances are available on different labels simultaneously. Indeed, some of the videos reviewed here are not currently available on *any* label, but they have been included because they may well pop up again in the future. The label name is followed by the formats in which the performance has been released at one time or another: VHS for videotape and LD for laser disc. (This information, too, does not guarantee current availability, particularly on laser disc.)

The second line of the heading gives additional useful information: the kind of performance (stage, film, or studio), sound (stereo or mono), color (or black and white) and the presence (or absence) of subtitles. (On this we can only comment on the version reviewed; another company releasing the same performance may add or remove subtitles.) The length of the performance is also given on this line, followed by the cast list (using the A, B, C role designations used in the chapter headings), chorus, orchestra, and conductor. Finally, we note the producing opera company (if it is a stage performance), and, if credited, the stage director and video director. By graphically separating the videos, the headings make it possible to use the book in two ways. One can read an entire chapter to learn about all the available versions of an opera, or one can easily find a particular recording to read what the critic has to say about it.

As for the reviews themselves, the writers were encouraged to elaborate on a number of issues that don't come up in audio reviews but that are of interest to the potential buyer of a videotape. In the case of videos made from stage productions, these include not only the productions themselves (staging, design, acting), but also the way the stagings have been adapted for television. Many productions that work well in the theater don't look as good on television (and there are some—Zeffirelli's Met

La Bohème, for example—that benefit from television's ability to scale down and focus). We credit the video director because that is who determines what we see of the production and how we see it. There is also the technical quality to consider, for both picture and sound reproduction. For films of operas, the critics were encouraged to discuss the film directors' concepts (that is, if they have any).

Another technical aspect, not explored in the reviews, should be mentioned here. Most of these videos have been released on both videotape and laser disc, but were reviewed in only one format (usually tape) by the critics. Therefore, none of the reviewers were able to compare technical differences between formats. In order to give the reader some idea of these differences, I took five opera videos (from three different distributors) in both formats, synchronized the VHS and laser disc versions, and with a remove control flipped back and forth between them (a sort of operatic channel-surfing). The results were not surprising: in every case, the laser disc offered a clearer, steadier, crisper picture. The colors in the disc versions were deeper and more vivid, and blacks were blacker. On the tape versions, the picture tended to break up, whereas on disc it was sharp. Assuming one uses stereo speakers and a stereo VCR, the difference in sound quality offered by the two formats is less noticeable. Unfortunately, there are drawbacks to the laser system. Discs of operas are more expensive than the VHS versions, and there is some doubt as to the future of the format, especially if the newest format, DVD (Digital Video Discs) is successful. (At this writing, DVD is just about to go on the market, and no operas have been released in that format.)

Now that opera on television has become relatively commonplace, it's interesting to remember early critical discussions about the pros and cons of watching big productions on small screens. There was much discussion about the desirability of seeing singers in close-up (large open mouths were considered as a real turn-off) and the detriments of listening to a performance over the tiny, tinny, monophonic speakers that most television sets had at that time. Improvements in technology have made some of these points moot (both in opera houses, whose personnel now know more about televising, and in our own houses, where we have more sophisticated equipment every year), and those who like opera on television have accepted that experiencing it will always be different from experiencing the live event. (They also became accustomed to seeing subtitles on the screen, a refinement that hastened the appearance of titles in the opera house.)

If there is an overall theme to this book, it is how the creators of these videos—stage directors, video directors, designers, and performers—have attempted to meet the challenge of adapting a very old art form to a new medium. Some have succeeded, many have failed, and some haven't even tried. We think that this book offers, in addition to some expert help in selecting opera videos, an account of these attempts, and that this story in and of itself should be of interest to those who love opera, whether fresh or canned.

A multi-year project, this book represents the labor of many people, all of whom deserve formal thanks. Foremost among them are the fourteen writers, who had to sit and watch all of these videos (not to mention write about them). Several of the critics who had previously written for the *Guide to Opera on Record* thoughtlessly signed on for this volume, only to discover (and loudly complain) that watching these videos demanded more of their total attention than they had anticipated. (I had never taken the time to think of the other things a critic might do while evaluating an audio recording, but I suppose there are many.) In spite of the demands of endless video-watching, there were few defections along the way, and this is one of the few Guild books to be published as scheduled. This achievement would not have been possible without such a talented and, usually, congenial group of writers, most of whom still return my phone calls.

After contracting for the writers' services, I soon discovered that most music critics don't own videotapes and therefore had to be provided with review copies. Most of the distributing companies were very helpful, and I am glad to thank the representatives from BMG, Deutsche Grammophon, EMI, Home Vision, Kultur, London Records, Lyric, Paramount, Philips, Sony, Teldec, Video Arts International, and View Video for their help.

This book represents the fourth collaboration between the Guild and W. W. Norton. The music editor at Norton, Michael Ochs, was not only instrumental in getting the book published but was extremely patient throughout the process as we missed deadlines and continued to add material well after the book was supposed to be complete. (I just kept telling him how much more difficult the *Guide to Recorded Opera* had been, and although Michael had not been at Norton for the first book's publication, he probably heard enough horror stories from his colleagues to make him tolerant of the minor annoyances the video book offered.) Martha Graedel, Norton's ever-helpful music assistant, was also instrumental in getting the book to press.

Finally, I would be remiss if I did not acknowledge the support I have received from the Guild's board of directors and officers for this project, as well as for the many others for which I've cheerfully squandered the Guild's resources. The enthusiasm of and encouragement from the Guild's president, Alton E. Peters; its chairman, Thomas J. Hubbard, and, not the least, its managing director, Rudolph S. Rauch—booklovers all—not only make these long-term projects possible but help me wade through each one and get on to the next.

PAUL GRUBER

GUIDE
to
OPERA
ON VIDEO

BLUEBEARD'S CASTLE
(1911, revised 1918)

A: Judith (ms or s); B: Bluebeard (bs)

This haunting one-act, Bartók's only opera, has at last won a place for itself. Standard repertory will never be its status, but it is now one of those pieces that must be looked at every so often, and that has shown its power to engage an audience even when its playing problems remain substantially unsolved. *Pelléas et Mélisande* is its closest cousin, and there is no question of the influence of Maeterlinck and other French symbolists on *Bluebeard*'s librettist, Béla Balász, or of Debussy's music on that of Bartók. The young Maeterlinck, however, was a genuine mystic, steeped in ancient systems of occult knowledge and in the works of the philosophers that represent the High End of mysticism. The Symbolism of his early plays is an elaborate and precise reflection of his beliefs about the relation of fate to will, of soul to matter. Balász was a socially concerned left-wing political activist who went on to write film theory and screenplays, first in the German film industry (with Pabst, Korda, and Riefenstahl) and then the Soviet. The progression of his *Bluebeard* drama suggests less Maeterlinck's occultism, in which irresistible external forces render willed action futile, than it does the other order of symbolic language coming into vogue at that time: the Freudian, in which powerful inner forces emerge to contradict and overwhelm the conscious will. Both Balász and Bartók drew from Austro-German artistic and intellectual sources at least as much as from

French, and both were involved in developing art forms from their researches into Hungarian folk materials. Balász took from Maeterlinck the mood and force of a drama of the unseen and the basic Symbolist creed of the "representation that does not aim at being a reproduction." But his little mystery play is in the form of the ritual question-and-answer quest of old legend, introduced by a bard from folk-tale tradition and intended for austere staging given definition by then-new developments in stage lighting. Bartók's vocal line finds a correspondence between that of the mature Debussy and the *parlando rubato* of folk origin and is embedded in an astonishing setting in which a huge orchestra (full symphonic ensemble with many subdivisions, plus stage brass, organ, celesta, etc.) is mustered for predominantly delicate statements of extraordinary harmonic and rhythmic subtlety and complexity. The work casts a unique spell.

1981 LONDON (VHS / LD)

(Film, Stereo, Color, Subtitled) 58 minutes

Sylvia Sass (A), Kolos Kováts (B), London Philharmonic Orchestra—Georg Solti

Miklós Szinetár (director)

With any screen rendering of *Bluebeard*, the first question is how its two planes of action (the "real" and the symbolic) are to be shown. It is clear that the first plane can profit from sensitive camera study. The actions of its single intense relationship are simple, but the inner life of the characters is strong and the crucial transactions below the surface—good "reading" material for the camera. The problem is that it is hard to act, and in a way that is against the grain for most singers. Further, the action is preternaturally concentrated and compulsive, like that of a recurring bad dream, and leaves no room for the naturalistic flow of behavior that has become our screen norm. As for the symbolic plane, its stark, abstract imagery is almost impossible for the camera to accept: the lens itches to take us through those doors, to show us the worlds Judith sees. What we gain by this will depend on the fantasy of the director and designer. What we lose is the juxtaposition of the planes. The stage can keep both before us; the camera must choose. The tension of the stage scenario depends on keeping Bluebeard's secrets behind those doors until the former wives emerge. Slashes of colored light suggest the secrets; Judith describes them; the score evokes them. But we are repeatedly thrown back on the two people in the gloom of their "great, circular Gothic hall," and on the realization that the progression of symbolic events is not imposed on the characters, but generated by them—just like that bad dream. All this is lost the instant the camera pokes its schnozzola through the first door. In this version, we aren't really trapped to start with. The hall has become a series of vaults and passageways with lacy arched doorways, quite comfortably lit and rather fun to explore. Behind the doors lie studio sets. They aren't bad for their kind, but you can hear the platforms being hammered together, see the Mylar being stretched and the cans of spray paint being shaken, the big order from the florist arriving. Red lights and filters for that bloody haze. It's a long way from the total transport that would be the only compensation for "opening it up."

Sass is one of those fortunate performers who are inherently interesting to watch, but not in ways that are necessarily helpful here. She's on display too much, and her operatic temperament lends itself easily to that. In the early scenes she has a let's-brighten-up-the-place eagerness, and when she begins to question her husband about his former wives she suggests a kinky game being played. None of her work is lazy or empty, but the choices let the air out of the tire. Judith has one objective: to penetrate every corner of her husband's soul, against reason and good sense, against her own fears, his warnings and resistance. There's no time for dusting the furniture or smoothing the coverlet. Vocally, Sass has an important asset: a strong, colorful middle voice with a convincing chest connection. There's some harshness up top that spoils a couple of important moments, but the bulk of the role is well projected. Kováts also sings forcefully—sometimes more so than the writing's conversational style might imply, but it's good to hear a quality bass-baritone meet the higher stretches on equal terms, and in the more lyrical passages the timbre is quite lovely. His version of Bluebeard's stonewalling, though, insinuates little beneath its blank surface. Heavy eyebrow makeup and a foolish scalloped collar do nothing for his harmless, faintly comical face. Solti conducts a strong-limbed, overtly dramatized reading, building considerable excitement at the fifth door and a quite disturbing agitation leading into the seventh. Mystery is not this conductor's long suit, however. Unlike most productions and recordings, this performance uses a version of the spoken prologue. But the character of the Bard—who first pierces the dark with his lantern, then vanishes into it as Bluebeard will at the close—is present only in voice-over. It is no fault of the actor's, but his radio tone and British accent welcome us into the world of Holmes and Poirot. No, no—not *that* kind of mystery. Good video quality, excellent sound, reasonable lip-synching.

1988 TELDEC (VHS / LD)

(Film, Stereo, Color, Subtitled) 64 minutes

Elizabeth Laurence (A), Robert Lloyd (B), London Philharmonic Orchestra—Adam Fischer

Leslie Megahey (director)

Musically, this is an understated performance. Fischer's reading—with the same orchestra as Solti's—is slower and more softly contoured, less on edge but in some places richer and weightier. Laurence's pretty voice is on the light, pale side for the music; her musically tidy singing inclines to white tone and intimate inflection. Lloyd sings gently and gravely with a voice that is deeper than Kováts's, but drier and less secure above the staff. The score unfolds rather than driving forward. The production sees *Bluebeard* as a Victorian domestic drama. The husband is a polite, tight-vested chap who lights up stogies. The wife goes about her mission with a matter-of-factness and an almost timid manner, revealing nearly as little emotionally as her partner. They have a spat over the dinner table about those final doors and the ugly business of the former wives, and he finally opens the seventh door himself. The secrets are in the nature of museum exhibits which Bluebeard is forced to revisit from time to time, culminating in a rather marvelous picture of the wives in their niches, with one left empty for Judith. We're in the era of gaslight, so all this is almost brilliantly illuminated. I wouldn't make such an issue of lighting, except that it plays a significant role in the traditional scenario: As Judith opens doors one and two (torture chamber and armory—secrets that frighten), then three through five (treasure, garden, realm—secrets that delight and impress), her mission brings light to the couple's lives. But as six and seven (lake of tears, former wives—the sorrows and loves of Bluebeard's inner life) are opened, the other doors close, the light fades, and Judith becomes a part of Bluebeard, worshiped but imprisoned. Bluebeard is left in the dark, and the old story is told once more. In the London edition, some effort is made to respect this scheme; here it is chucked entirely. Still, this is a well-made film on its own terms, intelligently staged and superbly photographed. Sound quality is good, though the level is rather low, and the lip-synching as successful as it ever gets.

The Ingmar Bergman *The Seventh Seal* being no longer available, our best bet for a video *Bluebeard* is a tape of a thoughtful stage performance. For me, a bit more of the work leaks through on Teldec than on London, but it depends which set of qualities you prefer—see above.

CONRAD L. OSBORNE

LUDWIG VAN BEETHOVEN

FIDELIO

(1805; revised 1806 and 1814)

A: Leonore (s); B: Marzelline (s); C: Florestan (t); D: Jacquino (t);
E: Don Pizarro (bar); F: Rocco (bs); G: Don Fernando (bs)

*B*eethoven's only opera, his hymn to freedom, is so crammed with profound sequences that it must be regarded as a masterpiece. Like *Die Zauberflöte* and *Boris Godunov*, though, it is commonly dismissed as a hodgepodge of genius, a careless heap of magnificence. What are Jacquino and Florestan, Marzelline and Leonore doing in the same opera? Perhaps we don't really understand the Romantic tradition of sympathetic inclusiveness. When Shakespeare treats several classes in the same play (*Hamlet, Macbeth*), the intent is often satiric or sentimental, and too often that is also the aim in productions of *Fidelio*, so that the young lovers alienate and annoy us more than they attract us to the world of Leonore and Florestan. But all of these characters are intent, in their different ways, on the same idealized harmony, and the great performers realize that. Hear singers like Elisabeth Schwarzkopf and Marcel Wittrisch singing Marzelline and Jacquino, and their intimate concerns suddenly expand our understanding of the almost mythic protagonists.

The great moments in the opera are usually considered to be Leonore's aria "Abscheulicher," the Prisoners' Chorus, and Florestan's opening lament. I remember, though, what an Austrian woman told me decades ago at my initial *Fidelio*. She had gone to the very first *Fidelio* given by the Vienna State Opera after World War II. House behavior was decorous until the Act I quartet, "Mir ist so wunderbar," in which Marzelline, her father Rocco, Jacquino, and Leonore all express privately their hopes and fears for the future. It was at that point, she said, that the entire audience seemed to realize that the war was, at long last, over, and burst into tears.

1985 VAI (VHS)

(Stage Performance, Stereo, Color, Subtitled) 130 minutes

Elisabeth Söderström (A), Elizabeth Gale (B), Anton de Ridder (C), Ian Caley (D), Robert Allman (E), Curt Appelgren (F), Michael Langdon (G), Glyndebourne Festival Chorus and London Philharmonic Orchestra—Bernard Haitink

Glyndebourne Festival: Peter Hall (stage director), Dave Heather (video director)

Like so many Glyndebourne productions, this adapts splendidly to video presentation. Its characters are both human and heroic and its intimacy at once poignant and philosophically compelling—like the work itself. John Bury's sets and Peter Hall's direction reflect this complex view. The opening scene is filled with charming detail in a home obviously made with desperate care in a prison, and Florestan's cell suggests implacability even in the darkness. A single conception unites the performance, as it does the score: except for Pizarro, all of these characters seek warmth, love, and balance. With that view, even the dramatic clichés of the text retain emotional significance.

The cast is admirable. Elizabeth Gale is a warm Marzelline, more sensual than usual. There is a breathless anticipation in much of what she does, and she phrases the aria charmingly. Ian Caley's Jacquino is, for once, appealingly human; one understands what Marzelline might have seen in him. With his beard and glasses, Curt Appelgren is a comfortable, benevolent Rocco. During the money aria he tosses a coin to Fidelio: a pleasing relationship there. All of this opening scene, which can be so conventionally coy, is in fact animated with detail; the little pantomime of mutual glances before the quartet is just one example.

Elisabeth Söderström's Fidelio is a deeply moving creation. She is a lyric soprano; in a large house even her Marschallin gets a little lost. But the dark metal in her voice suits Fidelio well, and in this setting her idealism, strength, and practical wisdom are all profoundly forceful. "Abscheulicher" and other climactic moments are well enough sung, but it is the growing dramatic tension and detail of her characterization that are unforgettable. In "O namenlose Freude," for example, she expresses more than the usual musical desperation: a genuine love and admiration for her husband.

One has the impression that Anton de Ridder is giving the Florestan of his life. The voice is light, though healthy and thick enough. It lacks heroic depth, but he phrases and paces the role movingly and, like Söderström, remains fresh-voiced to the end of the opera. Robert Allman is an interestingly subdued Pizarro; his face reflects not villainy so much as determination — no cardboard villain. Bernard Haitink conducts a performance of gravity and excitement. The overture is one of his less effective moments — it occasionally loses tension — but his work with singers is musically supportive and dramatically alert.

There are occasional problems. At such close range the entrance of the prisoners in Act I loses its sublime effect. Don Fernando is a difficult role: a profoundly human *deus ex machina*. Michael Langdon is vocally rusty and looks very uncomfortable in his wig: the moment of political fantasy is not realized. In general, though, this is a just presentation of a great opera: an intimate performance, well sung, persuasively and sometimes profoundly acted, beautifully set, and directed with a fine eye for enlivening detail. Technics are generally good, and the performance is highly recommended.

1991 KULTUR (VHS) / PIONEER (LD)

(Stage Performance, Stereo, Color, Subtitled) 129 minutes

Gabriela Beňačková (A), Marie McLaughlin (B), Josef Protschka (C), Neill Archer (D), Monte Pederson (E), Robert Lloyd (F), Hans Tschammer (G), Chorus and Orchestra of the Royal Opera House—Christoph von Dohnányi

Royal Opera, Covent Garden: Adolf Dresen (stage director), Derek Bailey (video director)

Here we can experience all at once most of the artistic disadvantages of clever analysis, big-house operatic funding, international skill, and artistic ambition—an odd comment on Covent Garden, whose strengths and weaknesses usually lie in other directions. The production has some world-class singers and is full of directorial and design ideas that fail to illuminate the musical drama at hand. Conventional views of Nazism and capitalism are both suggested, but warmth of feeling and political conviction are in short supply. The settings are an unconvincing mixture of realism and what may be intended as symbolism. Little of thematic impact is transmitted, however. The opening scene is set in yellow: it may be intended to suggest family and sunlight, but the reality is bare and charmless. The courtyard is bleakly severe but without emotional force. Later the imprisoned Florestan seems to be lit, strangely, with sunlight, and there are visions of angels, underlining the obvious. Throughout, the lighting is flat—perhaps the intention is Brechtian, but with a score by Beethoven the effect is alienating in the wrong way.

Most of the characterizations are equally arbitrary and unpersuasive, despite the talents involved. Marie McLaughlin's Marzelline is dark-voiced but dressed in regulation pink. The effect is both coy and coarse. Neill Archer is asked to play Jacquino as a Nazi: this couple's unpleasantness belongs in another opera. From Robert Lloyd's Rocco we have little but resonance and humorless efficiency. When he bounces Marzelline on his knee the effect is sickening. That may be the intent, but it is not supported by anything in the music. He also provides a limp—now and then. For Fidelio Gabriela Beňačková has, of course, a wonderful voice, lyric and yet powerful throughout its range, though she lacks entirely the driving passion central to this role. There is touching commitment at times, yes, but in the great moments little command. For Florestan Josef Protschka has a sweet and full voice, but as recorded it becomes brash in the last scene. Neither singer is persuasive visually, and little of the action devised is convincing. Pizarro is amateurishly overplayed, and several of the costume decisions are unintentionally comic, however one might justify them historically. The chorus and orchestra perform well. Dohnányi is best in the big moments, though the quiet ones sometimes lack drive and focus, as does the performance as a whole.

For its warmth, conviction, and dramatic focus, the 1985 VAI performance is far superior. There are other ways to play *Fidelio*, but here we have an authentic intimacy that deepens both the incipient tragedy and the triumph. Söderström's heroine is a profound creation, and the performance as a whole transfers very well to videotape.

LONDON GREEN

VINCENZO BELLINI

LA SONNAMBULA (1831)

A: Amina (s); B: Elvino (t); C: Rodolfo (bs)

a Sonnambula is, pun intended, Bellini's sleeper. Of the composer's works still holding stage at the cusp of the millennium, it is the one to which larger-than-life dramatic passion and intensity, indispensable to *Norma* and *Il Pirata*, cannot plausibly be applied. It is the one wherein Bellini's own dictum—that "opera, through singing, must make one weep, shudder, die" (now most often thought of in reference to *I Puritani*)—appears on the surface to have been, if not bypassed, at least muted.

In its first fifty years of life, *Sonnambula* basked in approval: it was called sublime, elegiac, pathetic (in the nonpejorative, nineteenth-century sense). Later it came to be regarded merely as a vehicle for a high-voiced prima donna assoluta, the proverbial "canary," though mezzos have appropriated Amina's role, transposed down, from the outset. Labels now routinely affixed—effete, frail, flimsy—are as much epithet as evaluation and constitute critical betrayal of a piece that has always demanded of its hearers a particularly affectionate indulgence.

Given loving realization of the expressive possibilities of its deceptive, precariously balanced simplicity, *Sonnambula* blooms as an exquisite perennial among the lyric theater's few idyllic survivors from the *bel canto* era.

1949 VIEW (VHS)

(Film, Mono, Black and White, English Narration, Not Subtitled) 90 minutes

Paola Bertini (A), Gino Sinimberghi (B), Alfredo Colella (C), Chorus and Orchestra of Teatro dell'Opera, Rome—Graziano Mucci

Cesare Barlacchi (director), Carlo Carlini (film director)

An unintentionally droll narrator sets the tone for this risible memento of postwar Italian "cinematic" opera: "Although *Sonnambula*'s sprightly story has a somber implication, it *is* a comedy." It's comic, all right, but we laugh at, not with, these primitive proceedings.

Obvious drawbacks—singing that ranges from mediocre to ghastly (with one exception) and acting subdued beyond any effectiveness (as in "Don't be operatic!")—only exacerbate the underlying deficiency: nobody connected with the enterprise has the slightest notion of Bellini style generally or *Sonnambula*'s unique requirements specifically, guaranteeing a fiasco.

Thus we get—through a lens darkly!—documentation of the sorry state to which Italian *bel canto* repertory was reduced, not just musically and vocally but also *conceptually*, by the middle of the twentieth century. The handful of careful stylists then active (Tullio Serafin, Lina Pagliughi, Tito Schipa) represented an elite minority. The awful truth, here preserved, is that Italian houses, and not just provincial ones, gave the few works of Bellini, Donizetti, and Rossini still viable (that is, prior to the 1950s *bel canto* renaissance) with a ham-fisted coarseness reflecting *verismo*'s predominance.

This film offers no antidote to opinions that *Sonnambula* is musically puerile, its heroine a hapless ninny, its hero a self-important rustic blockhead, its prodigal-son nobleman a stuffed shirt, its plot line absurd. Various gimmicks—flashbacks, multiple locations, performers resolutely lip-synching to a prerecorded sound track as if only *speaking* (especially ludicrous on sustained high notes)—simply distract.

Antediluvian sonics (the already hollow-voiced Rodolfo's aria seems to emanate from Jochanaan's cistern), murky visual quality, and frequent tape hiccups constitute further deterrents.

The positive contributor to this *Sonnambula* is Gino Sinimberghi. The tenor's lyric singing is lovely, his voicing of Elvino's denunciation of Amina burnished and strong. He's even mildly dashing, in a faded Errol Flynn sort of way. Allowed to act like a singer, and not shorn of bravura elements such as high endings ("Ah! perchè non posso odiarti" is only one of many deflating anticlimaxes here), he might have lifted this exercise to another level. Otherwise, radishes to:

1. conductor Graziano Mucci, for confusing Bellini with Cilea;
2. slender, pretty Paola Bertini's narrow, shrill tone and stylistic vacuity;
3. the disfiguring cuts and near total absence of embellishment, though we're consequently spared more inadequate vocalism and anachronistic musical manners (see also 1 and 2);
4. the superannuated chorus of villagers' knee-slapping, back-pounding guffaws over Amina's plight;
5. that effusive narrator, who speaks over what recitatives aren't eliminated, addresses the dramatis personae directly ("This may be your last chance to sleep peacefully, Amina"), characterizes them (". . . our well-meaning and simple-hearted committee"), and pontificates ("The peripatetic Count is finally riding in the right direction").

Pronouncing the opening line of Rodolfo's "Vi ravviso, o luoghi ameni," the narrator rhymes *ameni* with "hominy," thereby granting the reviewer license to warn: one "grits" one's teeth through this unwitting travesty.

1956 LEGATO CLASSICS

(Film, Mono, Black and White, Not Subtitled) 123 minutes

Anna Moffo (A), Danilo Vega (B), Plinio Clabassi (C); Chorus and Orchestra of Radiotelevisione Italiana, Milan—Bruno Bartoletti

Mario Lanfranchi (director)

No burlesque distortion exists here, dear reader; this is a genuine performance. Ample rewards loom beyond the lengthy opening scene with its bustling chorister-villagers toting signs proclaiming "Viva Amina!" and "Siate felice!" and tootling unconvincingly on Alpine horns and pipes of Pan. The perks increase as the opera progresses, though patience with Bellini's ever-reappearing rustics is a prerequisite for dealing with even the most responsible of *Sonnambulas*.

Designer Luca Crippa has succeeded very well indeed at framing the mountain village's square with all the necessary sites, each opening to a functional interior: Lisa's inn, Amina's dwelling, the mill with its rotating wheel. The gangplank above the millstream, not perilously high but quite steep instead, conveniently originates at the balcony outside the heroine's bedchamber.

Regisseur Mario Lanfranchi (then the prima donna's husband) solves many dramatic problems beautifully, such as the extended Amina / Elvino duets in act one. Those situations that cannot be made credible for a modern audience are treated lovingly, not condescendingly. Deft touches abound, although a lone tethered live calf telegraphs "simple folk live here" a bit too obviously. The great virtue of Lanfranchi's direction is the fluidity of all the movement, solo and choral. This places the moment of Amina's exculpatory final sleepwalk in high relief—she moves while everyone else, for once, is static.

Bruno Bartoletti grasps the difference between *bel canto* and later styles of Italian opera and is blessed with a cast that shares his understanding.

Surely there has never been a lovelier Amina from any standpoint than Anna Moffo is here.

At twenty-four the soprano seems to have everything, including limitless potential. She provides almost unalloyed visual and aural pleasure. The qualifier takes into account several precarious high notes and intermittent previews of cloying vocal mannerisms. At this stage, however, her consistently warm, ingratiating timbre, musical accuracy, and stylistic aplomb virtually negate the chrysalid flaws.

Danilo Vega's sweet, supple lyric tenor lacks power and is a bit short on top, but it's still the right voice for Elvino. He commands the breath for Bellini's long lines and the artistry to sculpt them meaningfully. As an actor he passes muster except when expressing anger, which emerges as robotic petulance. His figure has not yet attained the proportions of a Gigli or Tagliavini that his very round face clearly predicts for him.

Everything about Plinio Clabassi's aristocratic Rodolfo is first rate: his plangent, rock-steady bass sound, smooth-as-glass emission, mastery of legato, and dignified but not stuffy bearing (he awes the townspeople but is as much considerate gentleman as intimidating nobleman). His is a complete realization of the role on every level.

Gianna Galli's pouty, devious, slightly shrill Lisa persuades, and Anna Maria Anelli contributes a fine Teresa.

You have to ask? It's RAI hands down, sound-sight synchronization problems (opera singers really are not very good mimes) and fuzzy images aside. Lanfranchi doesn't belittle the opera's slender dramatic substance; Bartoletti and his good-looking principals offer an exemplary lyric (rather than brilliant) reading.

BRUCE BURROUGHS

Norma (1831)

A: Norma (s); B: Adalgisa (s or ms); C: Pollione (t); D: Oroveso (bs)

On the basis of its powerful and often ethereal writing for the voice, Bellini's *Norma* surely deserves the affectionate regard in which it is held by opera fans. As a piece of drama, however, *Norma* can be very difficult to take seriously. Even the most accomplished directors and designers are hard-pressed to keep this druid opera from degenerating into what looks like a parody of operatic conventions. Bellini and his librettist Felice Romani provided little in the way of psychological insight into their characters, and the mythological elements of the story remain superficial and poorly developed. In the end, *Norma* is a kind of costume drama set in Roman-occupied Gaul, more an excuse for Bellini's mellifluous score than its motivation.

It's hardly surprising, then, that *Norma* has been regarded much more as a vehicle for great sopranos (including Callas and Sutherland) than as an opportunity for directors and designers to make their mark. No doubt this also helps to explain the abundance of audio recordings and the dearth of videos: most people would rather just listen to the music and not be confronted with the flimsiness (even silliness) of the story.

1978 KULTUR (VHS) / PIONEER (LD)

(Stage Performance, Stereo, Color, Not subtitled) 153 minutes

Joan Sutherland (A), Margreta Elkins (B), Ronald Stevens (C), Clifford Grant (D), Australian Opera Chorus, Elizabethan Sydney Orchestra—Richard Bonynge

Australian Opera: Sandro Sequi (stage director), William Fitzwater (video director)

Australian Opera and the Australian Broadcasting Corporation collaborated on this video for one obvious reason: Joan Sutherland. Recorded and filmed live at the Sydney Opera House in August 1978, this *Norma* was restored in 1991. Unfortunately, the restoration could do little to obscure either the fundamental flaws of the original stage production or the fact—despite claims to the contrary in the liner notes—that by 1978 Sutherland was already past her prime and looking rather elderly for a young druid priestess. (What is generally regarded as her most successful recording of *Norma* was released in 1964.)

In 1978, too, the art of recording opera on video was still in its relative infancy. Those responsible for this project do not appear to have had much camera equipment or talent at their disposal. The performers are shot almost entirely in unflattering close-ups with very harsh lighting that only accentuates their gaping mouths, perspiration, and mussed-up hair. There are few long shots and far too many extended sequences focusing on Dame Joan's square features and chin. Never an especially subtle or resourceful actor, Sutherland is hardly shown to best visual or dramatic advantage. She makes some especially nasty faces when she learns of Pollione's love for Adalgisa.

Nor do the costumes or staging help matters.

In Act I, the druids all wear bonnets that tie underneath their chins and make them look to be suffering from toothaches. Pollione is clad in a baggy tunic that resembles the recycled draperies we used to wear at high school toga parties. The stage director made no attempt to dramatize the action or emotion, instead allowing the characters and chorus to stand virtually stationary. To what the music and words already tell us, the staging adds precious little.

While no longer in fresh, youthful voice, and at times (including during the aria "Casta Diva") singing with obvious caution and deliberation, Sutherland still provides some thrilling moments, particularly in the final scene. The tone may no longer be as soft and luscious, but the power, control, and majesty are still there.

None of the other principals approaches Sutherland's vocal level. Margreta Elkins gives a conscientious, committed performance that remains pedestrian. Ronald Stevens strains mightily and not always attractively as Pollione. Clifford Grant is somewhat better as Oroveso. Under Richard Bonynge, who supervised so many of Sutherland's triumphs, including her 1964 recording of *Norma*, the Elizabethan Sydney Orchestra plays well, although the quality of the recorded orchestral and vocal sound is far from distinguished.

This *Norma* is recommended cautiously to die-hard fans of Sutherland, who may wish to view it for atmosphere while listening to one of her other recordings of the opera. Those new to the opera will no doubt be disappointed that no subtitles are provided; instead, short written summaries in English are given on-screen at the start of each scene.

HARLOW ROBINSON

WOZZECK (1925)

A: Marie (s); B: Drum Major (t); C: Andres (t); D: Captain (t);
E: Wozzeck (bar); F: Doctor (bs)

*W*ozzeck is a true rara avis—a high art, "experimental" opera of enormous difficulty that entered the repertory. *Peter Grimes* and *Dialogues des Carmélites* are more conventional musically. *The Rake's Progress* is too, but has fared less well with a large public, as have *Lulu*, the Pucciniesque *Vanessa*, or the rhapsodically tuneful *Midsummer Marriage* by Michael Tippett. Roger Sessions's thrilling but even more difficult *Montezuma* is virtually unknown. Berg's exceptional organizational ability, astounding in his manipulation of musical form, extends to the text. He did what the remarkable writer Georg Büchner (1813–1837) could not, turning the many fragments of *Woyzeck* (probably written in 1836) into a coherent, inexorable three-act structure. Some of Büchner's wilder flights are sacrificed, but his compressed, breathless dramaturgy is put into sharper focus. Berg had probably imbibed some of the overheated musical dramaturgy of Richard Strauss, Erich Korngold, and the truly remarkable Franz Shreker. Berg used their enormous orchestra and must have had their virtuoso, effect-oriented techniques in the back of his mind. But *Wozzeck* has a stringent, dense manner that remains amazing in its totality. Berg can jump from a pointilistic, pictorial atonality to a heartstopping Mahler adagio, handling each with equal force and conviction, and more, link them into a logical whole. As is true of most of the composers of his time (see Pizzetti, Montemezzi, Zandonai, Debussy in

Pelléas, Janáček, and of course, the Germans) Berg constantly challenges the singers with equivocally noted speech contours, "unvocal" intervals, and assaults on very high or very low parts of the voice. But unlike most of his contemporaries, his vocal lines "sound." Even when approximated and coarsened (as they usually are), they have force and profile. Like Puccini's dramaturgy, curiously enough, Berg's has much in common with cinema narrative. The scenes in *Wozzeck* are short, ruthlessly organized, and distinguished as much by atmosphere and pictorial writing as by content or revelation. This would seem to make the opera ideal for film or video, though as of this writing there is only one example.

1987 KULTUR (VHS) / PIONEER (LD)

(Stage Performance, Stereo, Color, Subtitled) 91 minutes

Hildegard Behrens (A), Walter Raffeiner (B), Philip Langridge (C), Heinz Zednik (D), Franz Grundheber (E), Aage Haugland (F), Chorus and Orchestra of the Vienna State Opera—Claudio Abbado

Vienna State Opera: Adolf Dresen (stage director), Brian Large (video director)

This is a skillful, starkly effective production with a very confident, well-routined cast. These performers have no trouble with Berg's elusive style and (with a couple of exceptions) are unusually accurate. Zednik's detailed, chillingly zany Captain, Langridge's boyish Andres, and Raffeiner's horrifying Drum Major—a dangerous buffoon—are all superb. Haugland (Doctor) is the only one of the leading singers to seem overly general and somewhat self-conscious.

Hildegard Behrens was highly acclaimed for her acting, and this is perhaps the most persuasive example on video. She has a fascinating presence and plays full out with emotional readiness and physical detail. It's probably carping to complain, but her wobbly tone and vague pitches falsify the often gorgeous music given the character. But where courage and abandon matter most, she is startling.

Grundheber, a very accomplished Wozzeck, has everything but charisma. This can be an ungrateful role, and he doesn't entirely escape the trap of seeming merely inclined to rant.

Abbado gets wonderful orchestral playing (not always flatteringly recorded) and has a tight, sophisticated fix on the score, but there is less humanity in his work (and in the production) than this opera can have.

Brian Large's video production is typically well organized and musical, but there are two problems. One is an apparent problem in camera setup, which, along with a very shallow set, prevents adequate coverage—Large is compelled to focus too tightly on stage pictures, missing entrances and occasionally important details (the tavern scene in Act II really suffers). The other difficulty is the many short scenes. A curtain is brought in and Large cuts away to the orchestra with an accompanying light change. It's hard to know what he could have done otherwise, but this is distracting to a home viewer.

ALBERT INNAURATO

HECTOR BERLIOZ

LES TROYENS (1863)

A: Cassandre (s); B: Didon (ms); C: Anna (c); D: Énée (t); E: Iopas (t);
F: Hylas (t); G: Chorèbe (bar); H: Narbal (bs)

*B*erlioz's operatic epic based on Virgil's *Aeneid* has only recently been certified a nineteenth-century masterpiece comparable to the operas of Verdi and Wagner—an assessment that could not be made until 1969, when Hugh Macdonald's critical edition of the score finally made it possible to perform *Les Troyens* as the composer had conceived it. Since then, most of the world's major opera companies have produced the opera, usually as a single unit rather than splitting the five acts into two parts and performing them on separate evenings. This was a compromise Berlioz was forced to make if he hoped to see a production in his lifetime—and even then only the concluding Carthage section could be staged. Although the full score is no longer than many of Wagner's operas, the work's formidable scenic and casting demands will probably always limit its appearance to special occasions and under festival conditions. These problems partially explain why a performance tradition can scarcely be said to exist; each new production is in the nature of a discovery. Even now, singers comfortable with French operatic style as Berlioz developed it—a singular amalgam of Gluckian classicism and heroic Meyerbeerian spectacle—are difficult to find.

Les Troyens arrived at the Metropolitan Opera in 1973, and the 1983 revival—which inaugurated the company's centennial season—is at present the only video representation of the work. Unlike most recent performances, which usually make judicious cuts, not a note is omitted here, and in that respect at least, the production is faithful to Berlioz's grandiose vision of Troy's destruction, the Trojan exodus to Carthage, Énée's tragic dalliance with Didon, and the hero's flight to his true destiny in Rome.

1983 PARAMOUNT (VHS) / PIONEER (LD)

(Stage Performance, Stereo, Color, Subtitled) 253 minutes

Jessye Norman (A), Tatiana Troyanos (B), Jocelyne Taillon (C), Plácido Domingo (D), Douglas Ahlstedt (E), Philip Creech (F), Allan Monk (G), Paul Plishka (H), Metropolitan Opera Chorus and Orchestra—James Levine

Metropolitan Opera: Fabrizio Melano (stage director), Brian Large (video director)

The strengths of the Met's *Les Troyens* have always been primarily musical—the production had many weaknesses when new, and although this revival reconsidered and corrected many of them, the basic problems remain, and they are even more pronounced when seen up close. Peter Wexler's set designs are often conceptually striking—the opening scenes in Troy, for instance, dominated by seven gray, mobile, plinth-like structures against which the doomed Trojan court conducts its semi-barbaric animal worship. Mostly, though, his abstractions look drab or downright ugly, neither sufficiently precise to register as powerful symbols nor colorful enough to bring the opera to life as a vivid historical pageant. Often the video direction only makes matters worse. Since there is no visual accompaniment for the "Royal Hunt and Storm" interlude (the original ineffective film sequence had been dispensed with in 1983), we are treated to the irrelevant and distracting sight of the Met Orchestra fingering and bowing like mad, as James Levine urges them on—at such moments it's best simply to close one's eyes and use one's imagination. On the whole, Fabrizio Melano's stage direction efficiently defines the public and private forces that propel the opera, but whatever dramatic tension the performance generates comes mainly from the singers themselves.

According to press reports at the time, Domingo agreed to learn Énée against his better judgment, doubting the suitability of his voice for a part pitched so high—this performance of the role was his fourth and last to date. The tenor's misgivings are not entirely unfounded, and much of the time he seems to be gingerly feeling his way and nursing his resources, particularly at the top of his range. At least Domingo has the necessary heroic presence for the part, and apart from a few awkward moments he sings with his customary conscientiousness and care for musical detail.

The two heroines are both impressive and ideally contrasted. With her imposing figure and rhetorical majesty, Norman presents Cassandre as an awesome figure of doom who pours out a flood of glorious sound. This was Norman's Met debut role, and it's good to have a memento of such a magnificent vocal talent before all the grand poses and vocal posturings degenerated into affectation and mannerism. Troyanos could also be a mannered performer, more because of an excess of nervous energy,

one feels, than an urge to put on prima-donna airs. As Didon, though, she is wonderfully focused and a specific character emerges, one hopelessly entangled in a tragic queen-versus-woman dilemma. With her emotional honesty and glamorous but controlled mezzo-soprano, Troyanos easily dominates the last half of the opera—Didon's extended immolation scene as she sings it is surely one of the most dramatically searing half hours on any opera video.

The supporting roles—Monk's firmly sung Chorèbe, Taillon's jolly Anna, Plishka's velvet-voiced Narbal, Creech's plaintive Hylas—are all on the mark (Hylas, an offstage voice, is actually made visible on the video, singing his homesick ballad aloft in the ship's rigging). Levine's conducting has its familiar virtues of musical vigor, incisive attack, and forward momentum as he savors the score's pungent sonorities, if not always capturing its lofty grandeur. In 1983 Met videos were still faithful transcriptions of a single evening rather than composites of material drawn from several performances, and the following candid admission appeared on the box of the laser-disc version that I played: "Because of a power failure during the performance of October 8th a small part of Act II is from an earlier performance, the only time a 'Live from the Met' opera has ever included material from more than one performance."

Although visually lackluster, this production is at least an honest representation of the work, and the performance's musical appeal is considerable. Those who wish to experience this extraordinary work at home need not hesitate, especially since a competing version seems unlikely to appear in the near future.

PETER G. DAVIS

TROUBLE IN TAHITI (1952)

A: Dinah (s); B: Sam (bar)

rouble in Tahiti was first heard at Brandeis University two days before the premiere of the Blitzstein version of Weill's *Die Dreigroschenoper.* That the latter became much more popular is hardly surprising. Bernstein's work (including his own libretto) is more limited in all respects and far more depressing. The two-character opera examines a failed suburban marriage, and some have seen the couple as mirroring either the recently-married composer and his wife, or else his parents, both pairs then living in Brookline, Massachusetts.

This speculation had little bearing on general audiences seeing the opera produced by the NBC Opera on television in 1952, or those seeing this PBS version done two decades later. In its small scope, it is an ideal television opera—a sour, sad complement to its contemporary, *Amahl and the Night Visitors.* Written just before Bernstein took over the composing job on the Broadway musical *Wonderful Town, Trouble in Tahiti* begins with a jazzy, Broadwayish trio that later comments on the proceedings at various times. It sings what sound like radio jingles or the ghastly themes from the fictitious film that furnishes the opera with its title. Whiffs of what sounds like something from *On the Town* or something that will turn into *West Side Story* are also heard.

But the duets are pathetically, operatically affecting, and the two extended arias for the wife, Dinah, are superb. One is ruminative, referring to the "quiet place" the heroine longs for that became the title of Bernstein's expanded opera (1983). The other, "What a Movie!" hilariously describes the South Seas epic that the wife is forced to see again in the *triste* conclusion of the opera.

1973 KULTUR (VHS)

(Film, Stereo, Color) 45 minutes

Nancy Williams (A), Julian Patrick (B)— Leonard Bernstein

Bill Hays (director)

This British-produced version of this very American opera succeeds on all fronts. The superimposed animation is amusingly done, making all the trio's music that much more fun. We see suburban trains, billboards for *Trouble in Tahiti* (the film), and rainy city sidewalks, as well as suburban living rooms and gym shower stalls. There's no need for most conventional scenery in Eileen Diss's witty design scheme, with graphics and animation by Pat Gavin.

Contrasting with this cartoony ambience are the all-too-realistic portrayals of Dinah and Sam by Nancy Williams and Julian Patrick. Plain and unglamorous, they sing and enunciate beautifully, thankfully without any star charisma—which would have killed the ordinariness of their excellent characterizations.

Bernstein conducts with obvious authority and all his well-known feeling. One can't help thinking in retrospect that this was perhaps the production that helped make him decide to expand the opera. Not a good idea; it seems just the right length, and if anything, some of the numbers, such as Sam's "There Are Men," seem to go on too long as they are.

RICHARD TRAUBNER

GEORGES BIZET

CARMEN (1875)

A: Carmen (s or ms); B: Micaela (s); C: Don José (t);
D: Escamillo (bar)

Carmen, so long a repertory staple and still among the most reliable of opera attractions, entered a new stage of life when alternative material started to turn up regularly in performance. Much of this "new" music was taken, too unthinkingly, from the edition made by Fritz Oeser, which has been repeatedly shown by knowledgeable commentators to be faulty in method and questionable in ethics (combining material from various stages of Bizet's composition and revision, adding spurious stage directions), although much of the additional music is worth hearing on occasion.

In addition, the reinvestigation prompted by such alterations has prompted widespread abandonment of the edition with recitatives created by Ernest Guiraud after Bizet's death, once standard everywhere but in France, in favor of the work's original identity as an opèra-comique—i.e., with spoken dialogue between the musical numbers. The spoken libretto, if well performed, undoubtedly offers enhanced opportunity for more interesting characterization and interaction, and greater variety of musical effect and pacing. But its execution poses great challenge to most opera companies. Few singers are comfortable when called upon to hold the stage without the support of music, and few except those born to the language really master theatrical delivery of spoken French (musical setting provides help with pacing and inflection). Believable projection of speech in a large performance space is itself a specialized skill.

Opéra-comique means opera with speaking, not "comic opera" literally; yet one of *Carmen's* most fascinating features is the way in which it does embrace light-opera format, particularly in the earlier scenes, and then transcends it in unexpected ways. Successful performances of *Carmen* need to give both the genre and the unique personal elements their due. Such considerations ultimately matter far more to the success of a performance than the admittedly fascinating textual questions.

Four of the five performances use an *opéra-comique* edition, with considerable variation in the music and dialogue chosen for inclusion (only the Hall / Haitink production includes anything close to a full rendition of the dialogue).

1967 PHILIPS (VHS / LD)

(Stage / Studio Performance, Stereo, Color, Subtitled) 164 minutes

Grace Bumbry (A), Mirella Freni (B), Jon Vickers (C), Justino Díaz (D), Vienna State Opera Chorus, Vienna Philharmonic Orchestra— Herbert von Karajan

Herbert von Karajan (director)

Seventeen years separate this *Carmen* from the next one examined here, and the philosophical gap looms even greater than the chronological. To consider and compare the four others and then turn to this (first issued by Philips in 1995) is to realize that *Carmen* used to be a different opera.

Above all, of course it was a grand opera, with recitatives rather than spoken dialogue (a very few nonstandard alternatives have invaded the musical text, most noticeably at Carmen's death). It was also a big spectacle, with room for interpolated dances if desired (traditionally in the crowd scene of Act IV, but here provided by *L'Arlesienne* excerpts in Lilias Pasta's tavern, as rendered by "Mariemma and the Ballet de España"). And in contrast to current interest in the earthy passionate side of the work, it was then a show in which all concerned were expected to look their glamorous best. This, surely more than any kind of ahistorical production concept, explains why the clothes and hair here have a pure 1960s look, with modern materials, snazzy colors, saucy hemlines, and teased hairdos much in evidence.

If none of these features particularly impress today, an advantageous one is the recruitment of high-level vocal talent. All the principals have solid, attractive voices and never fall below a satisfying level for aural pleasure (likewise the supporting players in this festival production, who include Olivera Miljakovic, Julia Hamari, Kurt Equiluz, Robert Kerns, and Anton Diakov). The same cannot be said for their acting, which seems to be a low priority. Their work is also hurt by the obvious and none-too-accurate postsynchronization of video and audio elements; little chance for suspension of disbelief here.

That said, Bumbry sings Carmen with even, lustrous tone. Freni is in her glowing prime, her lyric soprano, as yet unstretched by later adventures, providing many a pleasurable goosebump. Vickers provides intensity and meaning in his able singing, but he remains surprisingly undistinctive; probably such an intense actor is hurt even more than the others when his performance's unity is pulled apart by filming techniques. Díaz makes no discernable attempt at characterization, but he certainly sings the role well, his bass-baritone encompassing the range extremes easily. Karajan supports them all with the plushest of accompanimental cushions, easy to underrate but difficult to equal.

The production remains clearly stagebound, despite attempts at film technique (including a Karajan cameo appearance onstage) and the huge size of the settings (stage design credited to Teo Otto, costumes and sets to Georges Wakhevitch). The main principle throughout is that the best choice is the most immediately effective one—people move a certain way because it will look good. The best way to watch the production is thus for its vocal and orchestral pleasures, divorced from dramatic considerations.

1984 RCA / COLUMBIA PICTURES (VHS / LD)

(Film, Stereo, Color, Subtitled) 152 minutes

Julia Migenes-Johnson (A), Faith Esham (B), Plácido Domingo (C), Ruggero Raimondi (D), Chorus and Children's Chorus of Radio-France, French National Orchestra—Lorin Maazel

Francesco Rosi (director)

The aesthetic difficulties of making opera work on film in real settings are evident here. Rosi even highlights them, letting actual street noises overlap the orchestra and singers. This raises immediate questions—if people can chatter like this, why do they need to sing?—and the use of choreographed movement in scenes like the cigarette chorus exacerbates the problem. At such moments Rosi seems to be suggesting a transition from everyday reality to a heightened level of stylization, but the idea is never made quite clear. It is also distracting to find the chorus kept consistently off-screen; we see crowds and we hear opera choral singing, but they are not the same people. A practical decision when filming crowd scenes outdoors, this procedure nevertheless reduces choral contributions to background music, in the manner of the Hollywood heavenly choir. There are unexpected cuts, including everything after the first choral section in the Act III opening, and all of the subsequent "Quant au douanier" ensemble.

But there are scenes and whole characters that work so well the unsolved problems can be temporarily set aside. Migenes-Johnson is a Carmen to remember, one of the few to embody the multifaceted fascination we are told she possesses. Impatient, combative, fun-loving, aloof, sexy, and independent by turns, this Carmen has learned to take care of herself but remains interested in others—especially new men. Migenes-Johnson sings well too, her moment-by-moment subtleties united in a flowing line, her French full of expression and color.

Domingo's José is not on this level as a total performance: his acting is "very good for an opera singer," his French won't be mistaken for native, and accepting him as a novice corporal in this realistic environment takes some imagination. But there remain his fervent sincerity of utterance, his responsiveness to the other actors, and the dark fullness of his tenor voice to win one over; he has been one of the most satisfying Josés onstage in recent decades, and it's good to have this visual documentation of his performance. His early scenes with Carmen are enhanced by convincing cinematic alterations, allowing intimate exchanges to take place in secluded rooms.

Raimondi's elegant carriage and macho assurance combine with his reserved bass-baritone to make a convincing Escamillo. Esham's first appearance promises a Micaela of piquancy and humor, qualities she can well use; but the singing turns out labored and unvaried. (And her aria suffers from the decision to render its final stanza as her thoughts, in voice-over; again, this raises questions about the conventions of singing that are better left unasked.) Maazel's conducting, and the orchestral and choral work, are reduced to background status by the medium and the mixing; he certainly has plenty of energy, along with some rigidity, but knowing that the soloists would later have to lip-synch may have reduced the degree of flexibility attempted.

1985 CASTLE OPERA (VHS) / PIONEER (LD)

(Stage / Studio Performance, Stereo, Color, Subtitled) 175 minutes

Maria Ewing (A), Marie McLaughlin (B), Barry McCauley (C), David Holloway (D), Glyndebourne Chorus, London Philharmonic Orchestra—Bernard Haitink

Glyndebourne Festival: Peter Hall (director and video director), Robin Lough (video director)

This Glyndebourne staging was created by Sir Peter Hall for his then wife, Maria Ewing. Its priorities resemble those seen in his other opera productions: to examine the text carefully and do justice to elements often overlooked, to avoid standard opera clichés, to bring out the truth of individuals and relationships. As has happened in other videos of his productions—especially those made like this one, without an audience—much of this can seem simply inert: the singers are not doing the usual operatic thing, but they aren't doing anything else in its place except trying to be "natural." In the spoken theater, skilled actors will create life in long passages of stillness, but even well-meaning operatic performers may manage only a pained sincerity. In addition, Hall seems to want to de-emphasize the self-contained nature of individual numbers—defensible dramatically, but hurtful when so many clear applause "buttons" trickle away lamely (again, partly the no-audience situation). Still, at many points Hall's musicality shows in his realization of scenes and handling of actors, and he *is* aiming for the heart of the drama, not just effects that will get by.

The women give the more distinctive performances. Ewing does not observe the classic niceties of vocal consistency or beauty; she grabs hold of musical phrases and molds them in her own way, almost in the manner of a diseuse, caring little for evenness of scale or timbre. But she does achieve something distinctive: her Carmen is a sullen, unapproachable, humorless woman. Her self-imposed isolation from her surroundings fits many aspects of the story, but not all—at least some vivacity and friendliness seem necessary on occasion. McLaughlin makes Micaela an unusually positive and likable person, her lovely soprano at its best and perfectly fitted to the role, her acting full of lively and endearing moments.

McCauley at first makes a negative impression; although he is as committed as the others, the repression needed in the first two acts does not come easily to him, and subdued lyrical lines produce some strangled sounds and dubious pitch. But as his emotions get wilder in the later scenes, his voice responds more gratefully, and he makes a good thing of his final scene.

David Holloway has been given an unusually restrained and persuasive look for Escamillo, and he (presumably in collaboration with the director and conductor) is one of the few toreadors with the wit to sing his refrain dryly, *avec fatuité*, as marked, rather than trying to sock it to the crowd. The voice sounds a bit unsettled and nondescript, but his performance can be enjoyed nonetheless.

Haitink conducts a lithe, trim account of the score, full of delicate colors and balances and sensitive to dramatic meaning and singers' needs. He and Hall sensibly eschew nearly all Oeser's extensions and alterations, though they allow themselves the longer version of the "Fate" underscoring while Carmen first talks to José. All do well with the nearly complete dialogue text, not always linguistically faultless but with good involvement in dramatic import, so that the scenes happen. The evocative designs by John Bury further enhance the stature of this production.

1987 DEUTSCHE GRAMMOPHON (VHS / LD)

(Stage Performance, Stereo, Color, Subtitled) 172 minutes

Agnes Baltsa (A), Leona Mitchell (B), José Carreras (C), Samuel Ramey (D), Metropolitan Opera Chorus and Orchestra—James Levine

Metropolitan Opera: Paul Mills (stage director), Brian Large (video director)

This production had first been presented at the Metropolitan Opera in the previous season, an adaptation of the Glyndebourne production just described, with Hall again directing Ewing. By the time of this telecast the cast had changed, Hall's name was no longer mentioned, and the two videos don't look like the same production at all. As Bury's designs are barely recognizable (being twice as large in all dimensions, they have sprouted second floors and sundry elaborations), it is reasonable to assume that from the start this was to be no mere reproduction but a substantial reimagining: the group scenes are necessarily more populated, blocking and entrances new, and so on.

Yet other elements intrinsic to Hall's conception (avoidance of irrelevant glamour, concentration on dramatic interaction) have been jettisoned here, and an outsider cannot know what was altered at what point. All that can be described is the impression given by this particular performance: a staging in which a director seeks to make the performers and the audience happy, within existing sets and costumes. The musical text is mostly the same as before (the fight duet no longer done at full length), but the spoken text has been heavily trimmed—though not enough to prevent most of the cast from embarrassing themselves.

Baltsa's taut, pungent mezzo, in company with her arresting stage presence, could probably be the vehicle for a notable Carmen if carefully shaped and directed. That does not happen here, and her portrayal ends up as a collection of effects, some convincing (she is good at sarcastic sneers and contrasts tragic resignation and playfulness tellingly), but it is not bound together—her work looks "staged" (much of it likely retained from other productions she's done) rather than lived. Carreras's sincere and committed demeanor likewise suggests the material for a moving José, enough so as to allow the strain of his full-voiced singing to count only as a demerit, not a disqualification. When the vocal demands are more lyrical, he shapes his lines appealingly, and he even prepares a plausible falsetto ending for the Flower Song.

Micaela was one of the roles with which Mitchell initially made her name, but this heavy, choppy performance, with no individuality or charm, cannot be representative of her best earlier work; only some high phrases sail out with appropriate magic. Ramey, though lean and concentrated rather than voluminous of voice, offers the most complete portrayal among the principals, easily commanding the stage on each entrance both physically and musically. Levine conducts a bright, forceful performance marked by brilliance more than delicacy or mystery; he is especially helpful with the precise balancing and timing of ensembles that need such care, like the smugglers' quintet and the customs ensemble.

1991 KULTUR (VHS) / PIONEER (LD)

(Stage Performance, Stereo, Color, Subtitled) 164 minutes

Maria Ewing (A), Leontina Vaduva (B), Luis Lima (C), Gino Quilico (D), Chorus and Orchestra of the Royal Opera House—Zubin Mehta

Royal Opera, Covent Garden: Nuria Espert (stage director), Barrie Gavin (video director)

This production is a puzzling mixture of the polished and inept, often in the same instant. The opening scene presents a populace color-coordinated in stylish shades of taupe and beige as if they've all been to the same couturier specializing in muted good taste (scenery by Gerardo Vera, costumes by Franca Squarcia-pino). The soldiers look identical to the very elegant peasants—nobody in the show is allowed to be dirty—and it's impossible to discern what's going on. Nor do the camera work and editing help; again and again, the choice favors a pretty picture over clear drama. The overall impression is of a lavish show for the tourist trade, with such embellishments as flamenco dancers for the opening of Act II.

Ewing deserves credit for professional adaptability: in this production, so different from the Glyndebourne one (Home Vision 1985), she embodies a quite different Carmen, full of smiles and flirtation. The voice has suffered in the meantime, surely in part from attempts at such roles as this in big houses, and though she gives it all a game try she has even more trouble than before. Lima's slender tenor just barely survives the demands of José, but he manages, while molding his music in a personal and com-mitted way. And his performance is a very specific and touching one, a boy who can hardly believe his good luck in winning someone like Carmen and unable to cope with the implications of not being "man enough" to keep her. His final scene, trying one strategy after another to get her back, becomes startlingly real and immediate.

Vaduva embodies a standard sympathetic and pretty Micaela in both voice and appearance, uninteresting but pleasing in its limited terms. Quilico moves well and presents his big number with aplomb, but the voice sounds slight for the music, at least in this large-scale production. Mehta provides good crispness and color, a bit heavy on the accents but skillful at giving his soloists the support they need. He has swallowed Oeser just about whole (the edition is named in the credits), and the cumulative effect of all the extensions and lesser alternatives is deadening.

The Karajan film offers the highest vocal and orchestral level, though in so uninvolving a visual context that one might as well just listen to the audio portion. Of the others, two achieve enough power to be recommendable: the Rosi film and the Hall / Glyndebourne production. The former has an outstanding Carmen and other interesting elements, but mixed success with adapting this stage work to film. The latter is a thoughtfully conceived and conducted stage production, its cast uneven and its studio presentation somewhat detrimental. It's overall the most absorbing video *Carmen*, but nobody should miss Migenes-Johnson in the title role.

JON ALAN CONRAD

MEFISTOFELE

(1868, revised 1875)

A: Margarita (s); B: Elena (s); C: Marta (ms); D: Faust (t);
E: Mefistofele (bs)

*A*rrigo Boito is remembered chiefly as the author of perhaps the finest opera librettos of all time—*Otello* and *Falstaff*, the two Shakespearean adaptations he crafted for Verdi—and perhaps the worst opera libretto of all time—the gnarled version of Hugo's *Angelo, Tyran de Padoue*, which became Ponchielli's *La Gioconda*. But had Boito never written a word of prose, the pair of operas he composed—the brazenly ambitious *Mefistofele* and the fascinating, unwieldy *Nerone*—would ensure his place in the annals of opera.

For the twenty-six-year old Boito to attempt an operatic version of the Faust legend (particularly in the long shadows of Berlioz and Gounod) was an act of stupendous hubris, but one fully in character for this controversial bad boy of the Italian musical avant-garde. When his *Mefistofele* was first performed, at La Scala in 1868, it was in a bloated five-hour version that incited a riot. But the revised, trimmed edition presented in Bologna seven years later (with the role of Faust wisely raised from baritone to tenor), launched the opera on an international hegira propelled by star bassos like Feodor Chaliapin, Ezio Pinza, and Norman Treigle.

It's no exaggeration to say that, of the Faust story's many operatic settings, Boito's *Mefistofele* aspires most toward Goethe's mighty drama; and it's no insult to say that its reach exceeds its grasp. As a librettist, Boito served himself more poorly than he later would Verdi. In *Mefistofele*, yawning stretches of profound but torpid Philoso-babble alternate with faster-paced but more workaday verse. The music, too, is spotty, though never less than theatrically apt and well-characterized. And there are chunks of real inspiration, such as the mighty Prologue and Epilogue and the ravishing Classical Sabbath. Ultimately, in *Mefistofele* the music speaks louder than the words; though Boito was a noisy champion of pan-Europeanism, his magnum opus is a work of unmistakably Italian gesture.

1989 KULTUR (VHS)

(Stage Performance, Mono, Color, Subtitled)
159 minutes

Gabriela Beňačková (A,B), Judith Christin (C), Dennis O'Neill (D), Samuel Ramey (E), Chorus and Orchestra of the San Francisco Opera—Maurizio Arena

San Francisco Opera: Robert Carsen (stage director), Brian Large (video director)

This *Mefistofele* is a faithful record of the staging coproduced by the San Francisco Opera and the Grand Théâtre de Genève, though Brian Large's agile camera and fertile imagination go a long way toward rendering it "videomatic." Designer Michael Levine's sets are spare, letting a series of evocatively lit scrims and vibrant late 19th-century-style costumes do the lion's share of the story-telling.

To fuse the opera's tableaux-like scenes, director Robert Carsen employs a band of heavenly stragglers from the Prologue, who keep constant, stoic vigil from faux theater boxes flanking the proscenium. Carsen also captures the kinetic quality of Boito's music, particularly in the bustling Kermesse and in the Witches' Sabbath, where a mob of eccentric revellers in various stages of formal undress gyrates to Boito's proto-horror-movie music, against a Fillmore East–like light show. In the Garden Scene, a revolving platform captures the breathless, slightly zany frenzy of the finale. More problematic are the opera's oratorio-like moments; in the Epilogue, Mefistofele's defeat and Faust's salvation should pack a more visceral punch.

Opera companies mount *Mefistofele* for star bassos, and Samuel Ramey's breathtaking vocalism makes the best possible case for this. He is in optimum form here; his supple, leonine bass is seamless, virile, and death-defying, making this taxing music sound like kid stuff. And he romps through the role with just the right sinister relish, complete with fiendish guffaws and entrances from every conceivable location. (Ramey groupies will also enjoy watching him model a series of dapper, impeccably tailored outfits; and he spends half the opera bare-chested.) Ramey's Mefistofele would be well-nigh perfect were it not, frankly, rather uninflected. As the old adage says, the devil gets the best lines; but Ramey, never a text-driven singer, could get more mileage out of them.

The rest of the cast is uniformly strong, if not stellar. As Faust, Dennis O'Neill swiftly recovers from an effortful "Dai campi, dai prati" to pour out robust, Italianate sound leavened with stylish musicality. Would that his eyes were half as expressive as his voice; instead, they seem more in search of the conductor than of the Eternal Feminine. Gabriela Beňačková follows long tradition by portraying both female leads. She makes an affecting Margarita (delivering a heartfelt and musical "L'altra notte" in the Prison Scene), as well as a majestic Helen of Troy, though there is precious little chemistry between Faust and either of the two heroines.

An ebullient Judith Christin both looks and sounds voluptuous as the dotty neighbor Marta. And Daniel Harper and Emily Manhart make brief but mellifluous contributions as Wagner and Pantalis. One of the true stars of the show, though, is the superb San Francisco Opera Chorus, which sings its formidable music with precision (particularly impressive in the breakneck Witches' Sabbath), healthy and well-tuned sound, and brio. And they act up a storm in the Kermesse and Witches' Sabbath scenes. Maurizio Arena elicits a solid, if not poetic, reading from the San Francisco Opera Orchestra in the uncut *Mefistofele*, but not without some stage / pit disorder. The uncredited subtitles are accurate and helpful, if a tad earthbound.

CORI ELLISON

PRINCE IGOR (1890)

A: Yaroslavna (s); B: Konchakovna (ms); C: Vladimir (t); D: Igor (bar);
E: Galitzky (bs); F: Konchak (bs)

orodin's only opera has never lacked for recognition, even before *Kismet* turned the Polovtsian maidens into "Strangers in Paradise," but the popularity of its arias and big choral dances has only fitfully won it complete stagings outside of Russia. Unfinished at the composer's death, *Prince Igor* was rendered performable by the efforts of Rimsky-Korsakov and Glazounov, who realized sketches, composed music to fill in gaps, and also orchestrated much of what Borodin did compose. Since the libretto had never reached a coherent final form, loose ends abound (the villain Galitzky simply vanishes at the height of his villainy, never receiving his comeuppance) and the opera's proportions are peculiar—a problem that has resulted in frequent cutting (Act III, the second Polovtsian scene, is the traditional victim).

In 1941, the Russian musicologist Pavel Lamm (who first restored the Ur-forms of *Boris*) prepared a manuscript vocal score based on the original materials, which never became widely available. However, using this score, the Maryinsky Theater recently prepared a new performing edition (available in a 1993 Philips CD recording). To date, no video edition has appeared, but given the productivity of Gergeiev's company in this area, we can at least hope for one.

1972 KULTUR (VHS)

(Film, Mono, Color, Subtitled) 110 minutes

Nelli Pshennaya / Tamara Milashkina (A), Invetta Murgoyev / Irina Bogacheva (B), Boris Tokarev / Virgilius Noreika (C), Boris Khmelnitsky / Vladimir Kinyaev (D), A. Slastin / V. Malyashev (E), Bimbolat Vataev / Yevgeni Nesterenko (F), Chorus and Orchestra of the Kirov Theater—Gennadi Provatorov

Kirov Theater: Roman Tikhomirov (director)

This manifestation of Soviet cultural uplift, a Lenfilm production, gives new meaning to the phrase "horse opera": Borodin's work has been transformed into a sort of Eastern-European Western, with a prerecorded sound track on which a competent cast is heard in a mutilated and resequenced version of the standard score. The postsynchronization by actors and supernumeraries on the screen is consistently disastrous, not least in the arias, which are usually presented on the hoof: Vladimir, Yaroslavna, Konchakovna, and Igor wander across the steppes or around town, invariably at gaits wildly incongruent with the rhythm and tempo of the music they are "singing" or "thinking." (Konchak gets to do his big aria on horseback; the horse proves no better a musician than the humans.) The plot is touched up too: for example, like a loyal Russian boy, Vladimir manages to come home with Igor, rather than remaining to wallow in Asiatic delights with Konchakovna. As a film, it's about equal parts watered-down Eisenstein and secondhand John Ford—but neither of those directors was burdened with all this awkward singing business.

Cataloguing the maltreatment of the opera's text seems superfluous: sufficient to say that it goes far beyond anything justifiable by the admittedly dubious pedigree of the standard edition (even the Polovtsian Dances are re-sequenced, and virtually every number, however celebrated, is trimmed). Anyone interested in the opera as such should simply stay away. The voices on the sound track are capable enough in the Slavic manner, getting better as they descend: whitish Yaroslavna, plummy Koncha-kovna, throaty Vladimir, acceptable Galitzky, meaty Igor, and a solid Konchak from Neste-renko. (Curiously, none of them took part in the almost contemporaneous Soviet complete LP recording under Ermler.) All are distinctly more expressive than the stone-faced actors fronting for them. The sound is marginally acceptable, limited in dynamic range, with occasional overload and sibilant distortion.

1990 LONDON (VHS / LD)

(Stage Performance, Stereo, Color, Subtitled) 194 minutes

Anna Tomowa-Sintow (A), Elena Zaremba (B), Alexei Steblianko (C), Sergei Leiferkus (D), Nicola Ghiuselev (E), Paata Burchuladze (F), Royal Ballet, Chorus and Orchestra of the Royal Opera House—Bernard Haitink

Royal Opera, Covent Garden: Andrei Serban (stage director), Humphrey Burton (video director)

This Covent Garden production is an honor-able attempt to make Borodin's opera work along relatively traditional lines. The standard text is substantially complete (small cuts in Act III, larger ones in Act IV), the principals are competent in Russian, the orchestra plays well for Haitink (though the chorus is rather less satisfactory), and the Royal Ballet is brought in for what is billed as Christopher Newton's adaptation of Fokine's choreography for the Polovtsian Dances (a new version had been planned, but a labor problem prevented its execution). The stage is framed by a wooden unit set, with changing centerpieces for the several locations (Liviu Ciulei designed the scenery, Deirdre Clancy the costumes). Producer Serban doesn't succeed in enlivening the big Putivl scenes, where there is much pointless marching about and parading of banners, and in the Polovtsian camp he again shows a fondness for meander-ing extras. Though the Galitzky scenes toy with nudity, the lechery ends up seeming quite as silly as in the more straight-laced Soviet film. The video editing doesn't always orient the viewer clearly within the sets.

On the plus side in the cast are Leiferkus's sturdy Igor and Zaremba's handsome Koncha-kovna (though she never quite sends her love music spinning into some kind of ecstasy). Tomowa-Sintow, past her prime in terms of vocal refinement and precision, is rather immo-bile but manages some expressivity in Yaroslav-na's last-act lament. Beefy both physically and vocally, Steblianko is an unattractive Vladimir, and the even heftier Burchuladze tries to put across Konchak with little more than popping eyes and stock gestures; firmer tone would have helped more. Ghiuselev, also under his best form, is a creditable Galitzky, but Francis Eger-ton and Eric Garrett as his two guzla players (Eroshka and Skula) look like refugees from some British farce.

One must add that, although not much in the performance is downright bad, a good deal of it is rather boring. (The choral episodes grow increasingly trying to the ears as the tenors tire during the course of the evening.) The Polov-tsian Dances build some excitement, both on stage and in the pit, but on the whole the opera proceeds at a stately pace, enlivened by occa-sional sparks of individuality on stage. Sound and picture quality are good, and the subtitles do their job well enough. The real challenges of *Igor* have not been solved.

The Soviet film is strictly for connoisseurs of *Kitsch* and historians of Russian popular cul-ture. *Faute de mieux*, the Covent Garden pro-duction is the choice, but waiting for the Kirov is probably a better bet.

DAVID HAMILTON

PETER GRIMES (1945)

A: Ellen Orford (s); B: Mrs. Sedley (ms); C: Auntie (c);
D: Peter Grimes (t); E: Balstrode (bar)

The work that launched Britten's international reputation and inaugurated a renaissance in British opera, *Peter Grimes* was immediately recognized for its mastery of musico-dramatic structure and timing within an essentially traditional, late-Romantic esthetic. From the beginning, however, critics debated the ambiguities in the character of the protagonist, who combines ready violence with an almost Blakean visionary strain. These issues (provocatively reviewed in Philip Brett's excellent *Cambridge Opera Handbook* devoted to the work) certainly create space for differing interpretations of the title role, and such have been forthcoming in both audio and video recordings.

The opera was first videotaped by the BBC in 1969, with Peter Pears recreating Grimes nearly a quarter-century after the premiere, under the composer's baton—a significant document that has never circulated commercially; given the current exploitation of video archives, we may hope that it will eventually become available. The two home-video versions also stem from BBC productions, from each of London's major opera companies; both are theatrically stylized rather than in the romantic-realistic mode of production favored by the composer.

1981 CASTLE OPERA (VHS) / PIONEER (LD)

(Stage Performance, Stereo, Color) 150 minutes

Heather Harper (A), Patricia Payne (B), Elizabeth Bainbridge (C), Jon Vickers (D), Norman Bailey (E), Chorus and Orchestra of the Royal Opera House—Colin Davis

Royal Opera, Covent Garden: Elijah Moshinsky (stage director), John Vernon (video director)

Except for Norman Bailey's Balstrode, this cast closely matches that of the 1978 Philips audio recording, made earlier in the history of Elijah Moshinsky's production. This abstract, rather Brechtian affair is set in spare, somber sets (designed by Timothy O'Brien), the figures costumed in black, tan, and gray (by Tazeena Firth), moving across a beige platform against a gray sky. (In the video, even skin tones acquire a beige cast!) The costumes don't war with the libretto's specified date of "Towards 1830," but the action frequently departs—perhaps even detracts—from the libretto's (and music's) specifications: in the first scene of Act I, a fish market flourishes, and the dancing in Act III takes place out on the street, rather than behind the scenes in the Moot Hall.

The video treatment adds another layer of context. With its auditorium views, applause, and curtain calls, this is explicitly a filming of a performance. During the interludes, the camera generally turns to the pit, touring the orchestra as well as showing Davis on the podium—not normally a central part of the audience's experience of these interludes. Panoramic stage shots are letterboxed, but there is much medium and close camera work, generally appropriate.

The musical performance will not surprise those familiar with the Philips recording. Its most striking element is Vickers's heroic protagonist, sung with all the intensity this great artist typically commanded. His larger-than-life Grimes much resembles his other alienated heroes (Siegmund, Tristan, Florestan, Samson, Otello): aggressively mercurial, strongest at the emotional extremes. (Britten reputedly disliked this interpretation.) With enormous authority and technical craft, the singing ranges from a knife-like edge ("And God have mercy upon me!") to incredibly focused, sustained, colored, and perfectly pitched *pianissimos* in the "mad scene." (A number of textual changes have been attributed by Vickers to Britten via Tyrone Guthrie, who directed the tenor's first Grimes at the Met in 1967, though the composer's role in them has not been established; most seriously, they entail the omission of important spoken lines during Grimes's hallucination of the dying apprentice in Act II, Scene 2.) Davis is a willing accessory, following Vickers wherever he goes, even when almost total stasis threatens.

Harper's clean-lined Ellen is a little more stressed at the extremes of range than in 1978, and her words are difficult to grasp. Bailey, slightly woolly of tone, is easier to understand. Excellent characterizations are contributed by Bainbridge, Forbes Robinson (Swallow), Philip Gelling (Keene), and John Dobson (Boles). Payne sings Mrs. Sedley well enough, but her makeup, which may have sufficed for the theater audience, does not withstand camera scrutiny. The chorus and orchestra impressively carry out Davis's strong, big-gestured interpretation, though the (predigital) recorded sound is restricted in dynamic range. (In the Pioneer laser disc version, at least, the picture is slightly snowy.)

1994 LONDON (VHS / LD)

(Stage Performance, Stereo, Color) 144 minutes

Janice Cairns (A), Susan Gorton (B), Ann Howard (C), Philip Langridge (D), Alan Opie (E),

English National Opera Chorus and Orchestra—David Atherton

English National Opera: Tim Albery (stage director), Barrie Gavin (video director)

Though also based on a stage production, this performance is presented with minimal references to that fact: we never see a curtain, auditorium, orchestra, or conductor. During the interludes we see film of landscapes and seascapes (credited to John Grierson's film *Drifters*). As the opera proceeds, these are increasingly intercut with images of the corpse of Grimes's first apprentice, of Grimes himself, and flashbacks to earlier scenes; this avoids the distracting "Young Person's Guide to the Orchestra" effect in the earlier version. Aside from a tiresome fondness for uninformative overhead shots, the camera work and editing are often impressive, clarifying the structure of ensembles by picking up singers of prominent lines (e.g., the manhunt in Act III, Scene 1). Especially in the Prologue, chiaroscuro lighting is effectively exploited, and the "look and feel" of the video is distinctly cinematic.

Though not exactly realistic, the sets (by Hildegard Bechler) are less abstract than Covent Garden's, and Tim Albery's production hews much more closely to the original stage directions than Moshinsky's. The costumes (by Nicky Gillibrand) suggest the early twentieth century rather than the nineteenth, while retaining the color range used in the earlier production (this is not an opera for bright tones, whatever the style). The chorus is often treated in a regimented manner, but the camera effectively focuses on individuals within it.

A wiry, youthful Grimes, Langridge is hardly as physically prepossessing as Vickers; he sings words meaningfully and always lets us hear the line and destination of the music. (Some of the role's more melismatic passages could be cleaner, however.) He fits well into this leaner, more urgent performance without ever quite attaining the dramatic or vocal intensity of Pears or Vickers (or the mannerisms of the latter). Cairns is a sensible, unsentimental Ellen, not glamorous—nor should she be. Mrs. Sedley is presented as a lady of substance, both physical and personal, and is the better for not being as "spooky" as usual. Opie also sings strongly, and the character parts are capable; Robert Poulton presents Keene as something of a dandy.

The work of the chorus and orchestra, not quite at the Covent Garden level, is always vivid. The only episode that misses fire here is the quartet at the end of Act II, Scene 1. The sound (digital) is much superior to that of the earlier version: wider dynamic range, brighter top, and fuller, deeper bass; the picture quality is also excellent. (The laser disc edition is also more generously tracked, which might be a point of importance in educational contexts.)

The London version offers a coherent, musically powerful, theatrically compelling performance in excellent sound. The earlier version has its visual and technical drawbacks, against which must be set its inimitable if controversial protagonist and other interpretive strengths.

DAVID HAMILTON

ALBERT HERRING (1947)

A: Lady Billows (s); B: Nancy (ms); C: Mrs. Herring (ms); D: Albert (t);
E: Sid (bar)

lbert Herring is Britten's second chamber opera (small orchestra of soloists, smallish cast without chorus), written for the English Opera Group with libretto by Eric Crozier after Maupassant. Though a comedy, it has serious undertones; its story of a young man's modest rebellion against being identified as the town's model of innocence surely resonates for anyone who has had to find a way into an adulthood that goes against society's expectations. At the same time, the overall format is that of a comedy, at times veering into farce, and *Albert Herring* will seem misshapen if such values are subordinated in performance to a deadly solemnity. Its performance needs a precise balance of tone and character in order to seem neither trivial nor pretentious.

1985 KULTUR (VHS / LD)

(Stage / Studio Performance, Stereo, Color) 145 minutes

Patricia Johnson (A), Jean Rigby (B), Patricia Kern (C), John Graham-Hall (D), Alan Opie (E), Soloists of the London Philharmonic Orchestra—Bernard Haitink

Glyndebourne Festival: Peter Hall (stage director, video director)

Peter Hall's Glyndebourne production, here taken into the studio for videotaping without an audience (the settings apparently slightly adapted), excels at balancing the serious and comic sides of the piece—more precisely, making the comedy happen by taking the characters seriously.

Thus, Lady Billows is not a two-dimensional ogre but an all-too-recognizable person, someone who feels entitled to judge and control everyone else's morality. Albert himself is not a fey nitwit but an engaging young man with a sense of self-mocking humor who knows where his future lies, but who has been prevented by filial responsibility from doing anything about it as yet—he does indeed, as Sid says, just need a nudge in the right direction. Mrs. Herring is truly scary because she is so believable in her conviction that her selfishness is justified as a mother's right. And each of the village worthies who plan Albert's coronation as the May King is delineated with similar deftness.

All the singing is more than equal to the occasion as well, and if a special mention must be made of Nancy and Sid, this is because Rigby and Opie are among the handful of operatic performers anywhere who consistently combine vocal expertise with real acting finesse. To see their scenes together or with others is a joy, and they are met on equal terms by Graham-Hall, who makes of Albert an endearing and human figure.

The supporting cast is, in Glyndebourne terms, an all-star one. Johnson, a mezzo-soprano, is not ideally matched to the dramatic-soprano writing of Lady Billows, and the loss of verbal clarity diminishes her impact, but her authority and attitude are unexaggeratedly right. Felicity Palmer booms out to chillingly believable effect as a resentful and watchful Miss Pike. And as the committee that chooses the May King, Elizabeth Gale, Derek Hammond-Stroud, and Richard Van Allan could hardly be bettered vocally, visually, or histrionically.

Hall's sure direction keeps all the elements in careful balance without drawing attention to itself; events simply seem to unfold of their own accord. Haitink's attentive, alert conducting helps immeasurably in this respect too, as do John Bury's sets and costumes. The use of a strong regional accent, though not what was originally intended by the writers, also seems exactly right for this performance. There are some moments that need a live audience to come off and thus don't do so here (unfortunately including the very end, Albert flinging his May King wreath into the audience), and a few others where the premises of close-up television production conflict with the need for operatic vocal projection. But so much in the production works beyond expectation that the most sensible reaction is simple gratitude—and purchase.

JON ALAN CONRAD

BILLY BUDD

(1951; revised 1960)

A: Vere (t); B: Billy (bar); C: Claggart (bs)

*B*ritten's *Billy Budd*, its libretto by E. M. Forster and Eric Crozier based on Melville's novella, did not have an auspicious beginning. Its original production at Covent Garden elicited a mixed reaction, and productions elsewhere were rare for some years. After the composer revised the work from four to two acts, a process of rediscovery began, and the work is now a more-than-occasional visitor in the world's great opera houses. In addition to the performance featured here, two other video documents exist, neither commercially released but both of central historical importance: a 1952 NBC telecast of scenes featuring Theodor Uppman, the original Billy; and a 1966 BBC production whose cast includes the original Vere, Peter Pears, and which played a crucial role in instigating reconsideration of the work.

1988 KULTUR (VHS / LD)

(Stage Performance, Stereo, Color) 157 minutes

Philip Langridge (A), Thomas Allen (B), Richard Van Allan (C), Chorus and Orchestra of the English National Opera—David Atherton

English National Opera: Tim Albery (stage director), Barrie Gavin (video director)

The English National Opera presents an intermittently effective but curiously conceived production, preceded by a brief background

lecture (promising an intermission talk by Crozier, which fails to materialize). The aged Vere, who is supposed to appear only at the very beginning and end to present the opera as something that happened to him many years before, looks on in some of the other scenes too, watching his younger self—indicating that some or all of the video was taped without an audience present.

The production itself is very stark and dark, mostly on a bare, slanted stage representing the deck, and in a post–Industrial Revolution world of dark, slick garb unleavened by color. At first we see only what seem to be books; these turn out to be the holystones with which the sailors scrub the deck, although they are mostly crouched motionless over them, as if praying. (This is not the last religious implication of the staging; Dansker's feeding of Billy in the brig is given definite eucharistic overtones.)

Color at first seems reserved for those not doomed to the naval underclass: the principal relief from black and gray comes with the three impressed men and the officers. The scene of the encounter with the French in Act II finally fills the stage with color, possibly just because we need a visual climax. (There isn't a sufficient aural one; not enough chorus comes through in the balance at this crucial moment.)

In a work so dependent on the implications of the relationships among the three principals, the focus made possible by the camera is helpful. We see the intensity of Claggart's reaction while Billy first introduces himself, and the interaction between him and Vere as they compete for Billy's attention. Vere himself is a relatively young man, one who speaks languidly, perhaps longingly, of Billy's goodness, and Claggart's eventual accusation plays as the outcome of this unacknowledged rivalry—fortunately this undertone is kept in proportion and not overstated. The video editing doesn't allow us to see the blow that kills Claggart; this is admittedly always an awkward moment onstage, one of those actions that's easy to write in a novel but hard to make plausible onstage, but one would have hoped for an improvement on the usual effect rather than such an evasion.

Langridge sings Vere very skillfully within the framework of a sweet, monochromatic tenor and makes his inner agitation unusually clear. Van Allen acts Claggart thoughtfully, but the voice sounds in rocky shape in this performance, well below his best standard. There are several strong voices in the company, notably John Connell's substantial bass as Dansker, Neil Howlett's resonant Redburn, and Richard Reaville's clear Maintop; others, though less vocally striking, make their scenes work well (Barry Banks and Christopher Booth-Jones as the Novice and his friend).

Thomas Allen, however, is clearly the vocal star; his voice is of exceptional quality, responsive to the detailed nuances required, and used with rare artistry. The camera inevitably exposes Allen as more mature than the inexperienced youth so stressed in the libretto—and unfortunately this is not an incidental matter but central to the story, one of the dilemmas built into some operas—but he acts the role with a convincing simplicity and sincerity. Orchestra and chorus excel with dramatically and musically pointed work under Atherton's experienced and insightful leadership. Their contribution, Allen's singing, and the strong ensemble feeling make this a worthwhile if not ideal version of a fascinating opera.

JON ALAN CONRAD

GLORIANA

(1953; revised 1966)

A: Elizabeth (s); B: Penelope Rich (s); C: Essex (t)

Famous for its ill-received Royal Gala premiere in the presence of the Queen to whom it is dedicated, *Gloriana* has made a slow return to the stage, first in a concert performance, then in a 1966 Sadler's Wells (later English National Opera) production, which is the one preserved here. *Gloriana* has remained the least performed of Britten's operas (it was the last to achieve an audio recording), not entirely without reason. It presents its title character, Queen Elizabeth I, in almost the format of a Baroque *opera seria*, one facet at a time—now the wise mediator, now the woman in love, now the beloved sovereign, now the jealous termagant. The other characters, by contrast, remain shadow figures with one or two vivid moments each. And the dramaturgy encompasses scenes that (however they reflect by implication on the queen) amount to pure pageant, like the Choral Dances. The penultimate scene falls back on that last resort of the dramatist who has run out of time, a balladeer who sums up intervening events in narration (near-incomprehensibly for anyone not up on English history). For that matter, the last scene of all combines spoken excerpts from Queen Elizabeth's actual words, orchestral and choral reprises, and montage techniques to bring about some kind of conclusion.

With all these questionable points, *Gloriana* is hard to resist. In the 1950s Britten repeatedly reveled in all the wonderful things voices and orchestras could do together, and this score is one of his most exhilarating explorations of the possibilities. It amounts to a treasure chest of rich, varied, and colorful musical inspiration, dramatically focused on the point of each scene.

1984 HBO (VHS)

(Stage Performance, Stereo, Color) 146 minutes

Sarah Walker (A), Elizabeth Vaughan (B), Anthony Rolfe Johnson (C), Chorus and Orchestra of the English National Opera— Mark Elder

English National Opera: Colin Graham (stage director), Derek Bailey (video director)

Colin Graham's production uses a permanent unit set designed by him and Alix Stone, loosely reminiscent of the Elizabethan stage with its wooden balcony, colonnade, and side staircases. This allows instant transitions between scenes and has obvious practicality for repertory and touring, but it shortchanges some of the opera's effects that count on a delayed curtain rise or alternation between full-stage and "front" scenes. More centrally, it removes variety of scope and space from a work that can benefit from such contrasts and to some extent was created to allow for them. Costumes, designed by Stone, though handsome and elegant, adhere strictly to a brown-through-gold palette that harmonizes with the setting and relaxes its vigilance only for occasional accents of military red or mourning black. Fortunately, the formalized design does not preclude a more lifelike approach to the actions within it, and the better side of Graham's direction allows the talents of his cast to come through.

Most arresting, even if problematic in some ways, is the central role of Elizabeth, as portrayed by Sarah Walker. An artist of exceptional musical and dramatic imagination, she has specific ideas for each moment and the skill to make them cohere as a view of the troubled yet proud queen. What she does not have is the soprano voice required; even though her gutsy mezzo-soprano can handle the upper range without peril and tells strongly in the many low and mid-range passages, clarity of enunciation is not available to her above the staff, and one almost wishes for subtitles during some of her climactic phrases. Rolfe Johnson is an engaging Essex, his voice at its sweetest and most ductile for his beautiful Lute Song, his musicality so insightful and complete that his merely serviceable stage figure suffices. Vaughan has penetration and clarity in her tense soprano for Lady

Rich, and a fiercely combative attitude that serves the character well. Jean Rigby's well-knit mezzo and unostentatious acting skill make a most sympathetic and complete figure of Lady Essex despite a scarcity of solo opportunities. Among the others, Neil Howlett as Mountjoy and Richard Van Allan as Raleigh contribute authoritative vocal presences; Alan Opie makes more of the small role of Cecil than one would have dreamed possible, creating a gripping character while singing extremely well. The choreography for the well-known a cappella Choral Dances (by Peter Darrell, recreated by Janet Kinson) comprises decidedly twentieth-century ballet syntax rather than any gesture toward the historical period. Fortunately, Elder has a real understanding of the gestures and colors of this music, and he gives each scene a convincing line and shape, abetted by first-class work from his orchestra and chorus.

Given *Gloriana*'s marginal status in the stage repertory, we are lucky to have it on video at all, luckier still that the production is respectable dramatically and exceptional musically.

JON ALAN CONRAD

The Turn of the Screw (1954)

A: Governess (s); B: Mrs. Grose (s); C: Miss Jessel (s); D: Flora (s);
E: Miles (treb); F: Quint (t)

*B*ritten's most concentrated and evocative opera is an extremely faithful dramatization of Henry James's novella, ingeniously adapted by Myfanwy Piper into a series of short scenes. Inevitably, with the embodiment of ghosts onstage and the invention of things for them to say, much of James's ambiguity (was it all the governess's imagination?) must disappear; but some of this is reclaimed by the Prologue, in which narration presents it all as the story the governess told afterward. The cast of six and orchestra of thirteen make this an economically conceived and gripping opera: every melodic strand and timbre tells, and every element is essential. For this reason, it might be thought to lend itself to the close focus of video presentation, though in another sense its structure is so tied to theatrical realities that translation to another medium is more than usually perilous.

1982 PHILIPS (VHS / LD)

(Film, Stereo, Color) 116 minutes

Helen Donath / Magdaléna Vášáryová (A), Ava June / Dana Medřická (B), Heather Harper / Emilia Vásáryová (C), Lilian Watson / Beata Blažičková (D), Michael Ginn / Michael Gulyás (E), Robert Tear / Juraj Kukura (F), Members of the Orchestra of the Royal Opera House—Colin Davis

Petr Weigl (director)

The sound track of this Unitel film is the recording released in audio form on the Philips label. Musically it is a fine performance, not necessarily superior to other recordings available, but worthy of mention alongside them. Colin Davis conducts with sensitivity to mood and musical structure—though his orchestra does not always manage the fine-grained detail of a group primarily oriented toward chamber playing—and his cast is a strong one. Donath makes a splendid Governess, characterized with warm involvement and sung with magnetic clarity. Tear commands respect for his expressive mastery of Quint's high melismatic writing, however uningratiating his sound (the Prologue, intended to be sung by the same tenor, is done by Philip Langridge), and Harper sings with firm authority as Miss Jessel. Ginn and Watson make a strong pair of children, and only June's unsteadiness counts as a demerit.

This cast is not the cast we see, and the actors are not only not singers but are not even native speakers of English. The resultant mismatch exacerbates the already considerable problems of performers synchronizing to an existing soundtrack. Even if they make exactly the right movements at all times (and this is by no means the case here), they do not convince us that they could have produced these vocal sounds, or (the essential operatic supposition) that the act of singing is necessary for them to express themselves.

In addition, Weigl seems not to understand the most basic need for whatever ambiguity and mystery can be achieved in the opera. He presents us with a wordless and musicless prologue, more than seven minutes long, showing us a prehistory to the story: daily life at Bly, with endless half-clothed romping on the lawn by the quartet of servants and children. So much for any possibility of our wondering who the apparitions are and guessing about them along with the governess! The guardian (not young or personable as described) is on hand, either not noticing any of this or deliberately not caring. Then, when the narrative prologue takes over, we see the governess's interview as it is narrated, along with some glosses of the director's: for instance, the interview is intercut with a final visit by the governess to the guardian's city house only to find that he has abandoned it (that detail seems to belong to another mystery story), and her journey to Bly is by train, not coach as the music depicts.

Some of the later action goes better. It is certainly good to see a real tower and lake for the important action in those locations; stage designs never quite encompass these scenes believably. At the end of his schoolroom "Malo" song, Miles kisses the governess's hand, alarming her and us. The final confrontation is enhanced by effective camera work, highlighting the fight of the governess and Quint for Miles; and afterward the governess wanders off across the lawn, desolate. On the negative hand, there is no attempt at a night effect for the nighttime scenes, even though everyone has clearly been in bed. And the ghosts are presented with smoke effects—exceedingly primitive, considering all that can be done on film.

Overall the film seems to have no sense of what makes this opera effective, and to have taken no thought or care in conveying its uniqueness. Rather, it uses it as background music for a series of "visuals," some pretty or effective on their own terms, some not. I hope that time will bring a better video representation of *The Turn of the Screw* than this hard-to-recommend one.

JON ALAN CONRAD

A MIDSUMMER NIGHT'S DREAM (1960)

A: Tytania (s); B: Helena (s); C: Hermia (ms); D: Oberon (ct);
E: Lysander (t); F: Demetrius (bar); G: Bottom (bs-bar)

The libretto that Britten and Peter Pears fashioned out of Shakespeare's comedy manages miraculously to retain all of the subplots and nearly all the well-remembered lines while cutting the text to half its length (to allow for the greater expansiveness of music). Its major dramatic reshaping, postponing the appearance of Theseus and Hippolyta until the final scene, allows the fairies to assume a dominant presence throughout, and their music spreads its magic over the whole work. Likewise the work of a real operatic master is the use of a smallish orchestra to create a feast of constantly surprising and appropriate colors; the emphasis on low winds for the rustics, plucked and percussive sounds for the fairies, and a "traditional" layout for the human lovers is only the beginning. And the inspiration of using the play-within-a-play presentation of "Pyramus and Thisbe" as a breezy parody of opera itself provides the perfect diversion for the final act—only to be topped by the truly inspired fairy music at the end.

The composer authorized one cut, speeding up the awakening of the four lovers in Act III. He made it on his own recording, but Haitink restores it in his performance, to the benefit of the scene.

1981 KULTUR (VHS) / PIONEER (LD)

(Stage Performance, Stereo, Color) 196 minutes

Ileana Cotrubas (A), Felicity Lott (B), Cynthia Buchan (C), James Bowman (D), Ryland Davies (E), Dale Duesing (F), Curt Appelgren (G), Glyndebourne Chorus, London Philharmonic Orchestra—Bernard Haitink

Glyndebourne Festival: Peter Hall (stage director), Dave Heather (video director)

The Glyndebourne production preserved here is an exceptionally fine one: near perfectly cast, directed with a sure and helpful hand by a musically attuned Shakespearean, and lovingly conducted. All of these elements work easily together, eliciting the rare feeling that the instinctive decisions of all participants miraculously coincided with each other and with the suggestions of the composer.

Oberon is James Bowman, who has virtually owned the part since first undertaking it in the late 1960s. His unearthly countertenor is just right for the coloristic and decorative aspects of the part. Ileana Cotrubas is on her best behavior here, keeping the voice high and clear for Tytania's filigree and inflecting her music and words with point. Damien Nash embodies Puck (a speaking role) with energy and moments of mystery. All the fairies keep flawless balance between the attractive side of the fairy-tale plot and the occasional sinister undertones.

Appelgren makes a believable and human Bottom, musical and rightly unaware that anything about him is comical. Patrick Powers heads a strong ensemble of rustics with an individual and funny Flute. The others are Robert Bryson, Andrew Gallacher, Donald Bell, and

Adrian Thompson (respectively Quince, Snug, Starveling, and Snout).

The prize of the performance, though, is the quartet of Athenians in love. They might have been selected for appearance alone (the ladies in particular embody the dichotomy demanded by the script: Helena tall and blonde, Hermia short and dark), but in fact they all sing beautifully and meaningfully and interact enthrallingly. Their quarrel at the height of the night's misunderstanding is compellingly real. And their canonic quartet of reconcilation is a sublime high point of the performance, as it should be.

But the performance is strong throughout, from the mobile greenery in the moonlight (propelled by people inside, to give ever-changing environments) to the unusually precise capturing of personal relationships and the genuine (because humanly based) hilarity of the "Pyramus and Thisbe" sequence. John Bury's evocative designs also include aptly Elizabethan costuming: everyday for the humans lost in the forest, elegant for the court, glitteringly otherworldly with a punk accent (Puck even breakdances for a moment) for the immortals. I am suspicious of the word "definitive" in reference to any performance, but it is hard to imagine this *Midsummer Night's Dream* being bettered. It surpasses all the available audio recordings (strong though they are) and is one of the most successful video renderings of any opera.

JON ALAN CONRAD

DEATH IN VENICE (1973)

A: Apollo (ct); B: Gustav von Aschenbach (t); C: Traveller
and six other roles (bs-bar)

enjamin Britten's setting of Thomas Mann's extraordinary novella was his fifteenth and final opera: valedictory in the most exhilarating sense, since *Death in Venice* drew very heavily on elements and themes that had proven very fruitful in Britten's past and yet took them to new levels of candor and subtlety of treatment. As one samples the later twentieth-century operatic masterpieces, is there a single one that goes as far beyond a kind of *verismo* theatricality to tackle such issues as aesthetic morality, restraint, the nature of beauty, and the consequences of instinct?

Mann's work, based on his own experience, was written in 1911, in a world more circumscribed in many ways than our own, but its questions still hung over Britten throughout his life, and, even in the wake of the 1960s, they continue to hang over us. How do we cross the abyss of pain to experience beauty freely? Is art the only viable route to spirituality? Britten's opera may be in essence a spiritual monologue, but, as he and his librettist Myfanwy Piper have dramatized it, it is a highly theatrical one, and the visual elements (dance, scene design, lighting, choreography of the actors) are centrally important to its emotional and intellectual impact. All of these aspects make it strikingly apt for video presentation.

1990 KULTUR (VHS) / PIONEER (LD)

(Studio Performance, Stereo, Color) 138 minutes

Michael Chance (A), Robert Tear (B), Alan Opie (C), Glyndebourne Chorus and London Sinfonietta—Graeme Jenkins

Glyndebourne Touring Opera: Stephen Lawless, Martha Clarke (stage directors), Robin Lough (video director)

This is something of a minimalist production, but for all of its limitations, it's an extraordinarily powerful and sensitive representation of the work, necessary to anyone who might hope to understand what its effect can be in the theater.

To take Mann's novella or Britten's opera as a sexual fable only is to miss its crushing universality. At the end of a civilized life Aschenbach yearns for a kind of instinctual and spontaneous beauty: something beyond all of his study, analysis, and creative endeavor. Tadzio. That beauty eludes him forever; he dies. It is that "quiet desperation," to apply Maugham's phrase, that Robert Tear's performance captures so movingly. Peter Pears's original performance was classic in its way: gentlemanly, desiccated, frighteningly self-absorbed, relentless. Robert Tear looks slightly absurd—short and round, and, with the beard, the baldness, and the glasses, ugly in his elegant clothes, and yet sensitive, too. His voice has an unexpected sweetness, and his singing is subtle, passionate, and full of frustration: a Chekhovian characterization. Suddenly and decisively there is more than self-indulgence in this character. Graeme Jenkins conducts with extraordinary fervor. The character's passion for life, often revealed in

Britten's orchestra, makes his disintegration as personal as it is in the novella.

The staging around Tear is often strikingly suggestive: for the gondola scene just blue light, the boat, and the gondolier standing with an oar, and for a view just an atmospherically lit hotel window. A few things, though, do not work well in such a studio-bound production. A little of the editing is unrhythmical and unclear. The games of Apollo emerge as stiff, slow, and unconvincing, and a few revelations are visually overstressed, but there is good work from Alan Opie in his many roles, and there are many moments of adult illumination. It is all bound together by a strikingly sensitive and original performance of the central role, impassioned conducting, and a simple visual symbolism that is often more moving and durable than something weightier. Recommended.

LONDON GREEN

Francesco Cilea

Adriana Lecouvreur (1902)

A: Adriana (s); B: Princess de Bouillon (ms); C: Maurizio (t);
D: Michonnet (bar); E: Prince de Bouillon (bs)

The fourth and most popular of Cilea's five operas, *Adriana Lecouvreur* has long been beloved by prima donnas of a certain age, as well as being a favorite whipping post for superior music critics. Maria Callas never sang the role (perhaps she agreed with the critics), but Renata Tebaldi did, not to mention such prominent divas from the recent past as Licia Albanese, Montserrat Caballé, Renata Scotto, Joan Sutherland, and the composer's own favorite, the incomparable Magda Olivero. Apparently the urge to take center stage and impersonate this ill-fated Comédie Française actress and intimate of Voltaire is an opportunity many sopranos find irresistible. The most famous might-have-been Adriana was Rosa Ponselle, who yearned to sing the role at the Metropolitan in 1937 and promptly left the company when that favor was denied her.

It's not really enough to covet the role simply for its juicy melodramatics and melodious arias. A singer must passionately believe in the material if the opera is to be made tolerable — Olivero certainly did, possibly the last soprano to identify completely with the *verismo* style and able to convince audiences, as long as she was onstage, that the opera was more than worthy of her considerable energies. With such a potent singing actress as Adriana, even enemies of the opera might be tempted to admire Cilea's elegant melodic invention, craftsmanship, and how cleverly his charming period pastiches capture the bustling atmosphere of backstage theatrical life in eighteenth-century Paris.

1976 LEGATO CLASSICS (VHS)

(Stage Performance, Mono, Color, Japanese Subtitles) 145 minutes

Montserrat Caballé (A), Fiorenza Cossotto (B), José Carreras (C), Attilio D'Orazi (D), Ivo Vinco (E), Chorus and Orchestra of the Lirica Italiana, Tokyo—Gianfranco Masini

Opera company, stage director, and video director uncredited

This unbuttoned performance has circulated for years as a private audio-only recording, and as such is greatly prized by admirers of Caballé and Carreras, both of whom are in exceptionally fine voice. Fans of the singers will, of course, snap up the video version as well, but others should proceed cautiously—the print I viewed, afflicted by fuzzy definition and washed-out colors, is not of professional quality. Beyond that, the staging is rudimentary, the sets are taken from stock, and the Japanese subtitles will be a severe distraction for viewers without the language. The sound track, however, is clean, well-focused, and generally representative of the period.

Even before it could be seen on video, Caballé's performance surprised many with its vigorous dramatic accents, unexpected from a singer whose temperament is basically a placid one. Looking unusually trim, Caballé clearly relishes the part, and her acting is just as uninhibited as her singing. Still, it's not especially convincing acting—all the outsize gesturing and pasted-on soulful expressions often seem more comic than tragic. Anyone who wants to savor the words should forget about that, too, and simply bask in the luscious sounds of a major voice functioning in peak condition. It's also touching to see how solicitous Caballé is of her young colleague and compatriot—not that Carreras needs any encouragement. He pours out his voice with a recklessness that he would later regret, but in 1976 no tenor rejoiced in a more gorgeous instrument.

Cossotto and her real-life husband, Ivo Vinco, were frequently teamed as the Prince and Princess de Bouillon, and they are clearly enjoying themselves to the hilt as well. The mezzo has fewer opportunities to take center stage than the soprano and tenor, but when the moment arrives for Cossotto to act the villainess, she and her steely voice are more than ready to do the job. That prince of *comprimarios*, Piero de Palma, offers a wickedly witty vignette as the Abbe, and D'Orazi is more than competent as the kindly stage director, Michonnet. Masini paces the opera smartly, although the orchestra is considerably less than first class.

1985 SONY (VHS)

(Stage Performance, Stereo, Color, Subtitled)
136 minutes

Joan Sutherland (A), Heather Begg (B), Anson Austin (C), John Shaw (D), John Wegner (E); Australian Opera Chorus, Elizabethan Sydney Orchestra—Richard Bonynge

Australian Opera: John Copley (stage director), Hugh Davison (video director)

Perhaps it would be best to draw the veil of charity over this performance. Even the most careful mentor can make a wrong decision, and Bonynge's notion that Adriana would make an appropriate vehicle for his famous wife as her fabulous career drew to a close is peculiar to say the least. Nothing in Sutherland's past suggests that the role might suit her talents, vocal or dramatic. Her generalized, one-dimensional

approach to operatic acting was tolerable enough when impersonating the more formally stylized *bel canto* heroines that were her specialty, but she looks very stiff pretending to be a grand actress and downright matronly trying to convey the emotions of a passionate young woman in the midst of a melodramatic love triangle. Worse yet, although her distinctive soprano still has some lovely patches, by 1985 an audible beat had crept in and it is especially pronounced here. Sutherland performs like the seasoned professional she always was, and as usual she acts like a good sport about it all, but this unfortunate memento from one of the century's greatest vocal phenomena would have best been left under wraps.

Another enigma is why a musician as knowledgeable about voice as Bonynge so often surrounded his wife with the sort of incompetent colleagues she must deal with here. Austin's callow tenor might possibly qualify him for a Romberg operetta and Begg probably has a decent Katisha in her, but both singers are way out of their depth attempting to cope with full-throated Italian opera, and Shaw is simply too far over the hill, even for Michonnet. In its favor, the production looks appropriately lush and atmospheric, and Copley's deft direction deserves a better cast. One suspects that Bonynge instigated the whole project simply because he has a soft spot for the opera—the lovingly shaped orchestral accompaniments are by far the best element in this otherwise mistaken enterprise.

1989 HOME VISION (VHS) / PIONEER (LD)

(Stage Performance, Stereo, Color, Subtitled)
157 minutes

Mirella Freni (A), Fiorenza Cossotto (B), Peter Dvorsky (C), Alessandro Cassis (D), Ivo Vinco (E), Chorus and Orchestra of Teatro alla Scala—Gianandrea Gavazzeni

La Scala: Lamberto Puggelli (stage director)

Freni's progress toward Adriana and other high-powered *verismo* roles late in her career was probably inevitable, if not always consistent with what the basic quality of her soft-grained lyric soprano and ingenue persona may have indicated. Still, one cannot sing Susanna and Micaela forever, and Freni's voice held up too well not for her to seek new repertory. Needless to say, her Adriana is hardly the last word in riveting theatrics or unbridled passion, but by the end one has almost come to accept her restrained approach to the role, particularly in the final act. There are even touches that escape more flamboyant interpreters, such as her poignant way of caressing the poisoned violets sent her by the evil Princess de Bouillon, and the vocal points she scores in the extended death scene are often ravishing. Pugelli evidently sensed that this lovable Adriana required gentle, feminine surroundings, and his production, designed by Paolo Bregni, is dominated by soft colors, filmy drapery, and graceful, balletic movement. Best of all, Freni's Adriana is framed by Gavazzeni's lovingly shaped accompaniments and orchestral playing of remarkable polish, refinement, and care for detail—Gavazzeni lavishes the sort of affection and respect on the second-act interlude that other conductors bestow on a Mahler adagio.

The remaining important aspects of the performance are less tolerable, particularly Dvorsky's coarse Maurizio, which sounds even more grating opposite such an elegant Adriana. Thirteen years have passed since Cossotto sang the Princess in the Tokyo performance discussed above, and the wear and tear on her voice shows, although her energy level is, if anything, higher than ever. Vinco is still a more than serviceable Prince, and Cassis offers a sympathetic portrait as Michonnet—this role, like Puccini's Sharpless, seems to be baritone-proof. The enthusiastic and protracted audience love-in after the opera is over should satisfy anyone who enjoys the sight of a beloved prima donna basking in the worship of her fans.

————————

Although much of the purely theatrical essence of *Adriana* is missing in the Scala version, there are numerous musical compensations, and this performance must remain first choice for now.

PETER G. DAVIS

DOMENICO CIMAROSA

IL MATRIMONIO SEGRETO (1792)

A: Carolina (s); B: Elisetta (s); C: Fidalma (ms); D: Paolino (t);
E: Geronimo (bar); F: Count Robinson (bs)

*P*ity the poor singers—all six of them—who on February 7, 1792, presented the premiere of *Il Matrimonio Segreto* at the Vienna Burgtheater before Emperor Leopold II and were ordered by him to perform the entire opera over again, immediately after consuming an imperial supper. But the Emperor's pleasure was well founded: Cimarosa's fiftieth opera has proved the most durable of the sixty-five he wrote, and it reached such a peak of popularity that only a year after its composition it was presented in Naples for fifty-seven straight performances. Among Cimarosa's admirers were Haydn, who conducted more than a dozen of his operas at Esterháza (some of them repeatedly), and Goethe, who directed a production of *Il Matrimonio Segreto* at Weimar.

Cimarosa's undisputed place as the leading composer of Italian comic opera eventually gave way to Rossini (who, incidentally, was born just three weeks after *Il Matrimonio*'s premiere), but he still exerted his hold as late as 1824, when no less a commentator than Stendhal declared Cimarosa superior to Rossini in a number of respects: "I find more genius in Cimarosa . . . [he] is more prolific in musical ideas than Rossini, and his ideas are better, more original and imaginative. . . . The secret of Cimarosa's power to compel the imagination lies in his use of long musical phrases, which are at once fantastically rich and extraordinarily regular. There is an excellent illustration of this manner to be seen in the first two duets of *Il Matrimonio Segreto*, and more especially in the second, 'Io ti lascio perche uniti.' The human soul can know no beauty more exquisite than these two melodies." Stendhal describes Carolina's opening aria, "Se amore si gode in pace," as "one of the loveliest musical phrases in the world."

1986 HOME VISION (VHS)

(Stage Performance, Stereo, Color, Subtitled)
140 minutes

Georgine Resick (A), Barbara Daniels (B), Marta Szirmay (C), David Kuebler (D), Carlos Feller (E), Claudio Nicolai (F), Drottningholm Court Theatre Orchestra—Hilary Griffiths

Schwetzingen Festival: Michael Hampe (stage director), Claus Viller (video director)

The Cologne Opera production, filmed live at the Schwetzingen Festival in 1986, is a deft and stylish piece of work, simply but effectively staged and sure-footed in its management of the characters and their relation to one another. It has the small flaws of any live performance—a rushed phrase here, a bit of vocal strain there, fleeting moments of questionable pitch (though mainly with one singer)—but the total impression is one of grace and liveliness. The orchestra of period instruments under the taut direction of Hilary Griffiths adds a piquant touch: we are instantly aware of the special timbre of flutes (wooden) and horns (valveless) when they rise in brief solo commentary; the slightly constricted tone of the pit ensemble takes a little getting used to, but the ear quickly adjusts.

Stendhal, somewhat contradictorally, complains at one point of Cimarosa's "symmetry." But while the regularity of phrasing and form may have got on the novelist's nerves, it provides an obvious key to staging this opera, and the Cologne director takes the hint: the ensembles are arranged in neat but never stagnant patterns that follow the music's intent. The lively spat between the two sisters, Carolina and Elisetta, is carried on across the length of a table set for tea, with Aunt Fidalma sitting dead center, attempting to referee. When the Count and Geronimo bargain (at length) over marriage arrangements, they face each other in a similar situation, eventually sinking into chairs side by side, with knees crossed in opposite directions.

The recitatives (considerably cut, to no harm) are accompanied by enough amusing stage business to make them move quickly, and the musical cuts, most of them within numbers, wreak no discernible damage. The balance between close-up camera work and full-stage views is nicely maintained. The singers are a good-looking lot, and all are delightful actors.

The romantic leads are exceptionally attractive, and fine singers to boot. Georgine Resick, the very appealing Carolina, makes a touching thing of Stendhal's "loveliest musical phrase in the world," and she is really quite adorable when she is trying to persuade the Count to fall out of love with her ("Perdonate, signor mio"). She conveys a genuine sense of distress when she thinks (mistakenly) that she has been jilted, and she is also capably tart in doing battle with sister Elisetta. That rather formidable character is handsomely portrayed by soprano Barbara Daniels, robust of figure and of voice, and a good match for the Fidalma of Marta Szirmay, who sometimes shaves just a sliver off the pitch but is so comfortably amusing in the role that one hardly notices. Her husband-hunting aria, "E vero che in casa io son la padrone," is the essence of feminine worldliness.

The men are splendid. The Paolino of David Kuebler is attractive and vigorous, the exuberant social climbing of Geronimo is made quite amiable by Carlos Feller, and Claudio Nicolai's self-satisfaction as the Count is touched, finally, by just the right among of kindness.

SHIRLEY FLEMING

THE GHOSTS OF VERSAILLES (1991)

A: Marie Antoinette (s); B: Rosina, Countess Almaviva (s); C: Samira (ms); D: Count Almaviva (t); E: Bégearss (t); F: Beaumarchais (bar); G: Figaro (bar)

When the Metropolitan Opera commissioned John Corigliano to write an opera for the company's centennial, the composer decided to base his new work on characters from the Figaro plays by Beaumarchais. Since Corigliano wanted to write music in a variety of styles, librettist William M. Hoffman suggested placing the characters in the context of a contemporary ghost world in which the ghost of Beaumarchais falls in love with the ghost of Marie Antoinette. The Figaro story, which is loosely based on Beaumarchais's *La Mère Coupable*, became an opera-within-an-opera.

The action leaps from the present world of the ghosts to the eighteenth-century world of the Figaro characters and back again many times over. The music follows suit, flowing from contemporary to classical in a well-integrated mix that ranges from dissonant ghost music to love music of extraordinary lyric beauty to a patter aria complete with echoes of Mozart and Rossini. The score calls for two orchestras: a large pit orchestra provides the music of the present, while an onstage string ensemble accompanies much of the action of the past. When the plot calls for it, they play simultaneously.

The story of *Ghosts* revolves around the relationship between Marie Antoinette and Beaumarchais. She mourns the years she was deprived of by the French Revolution; he decides to turn back the clock and change the course of history in order to prevent her execution. He enters his own play and is confronted by a rebellious Figaro who has assumed a life of his own, independent of his creator-playwright.

Corigliano and Hoffman call *Ghosts* a "grand opera buffa." Although it is unabashedly entertaining, they believe it has serious implications for our time—a time they consider an age of revolution. In this opera, they envision a reconciliation between present and past, between the legitimate desire for change and the desire not to destroy the beautiful things of the past.

The Ghosts of Versailles premiered at the Metropolitan Opera on December 19, 1991. It was the first world premiere there in twenty-four years and was received enthusiastically by critics and audiences. In January 1992, performances were taped for video.

1992 DEUTSCHE GRAMMOPHON (VHS / LD)

(Stage Performance, Stereo, Color, Subtitled) 177 minutes

Teresa Stratas (A), Renée Fleming (B), Marilyn Horne (C), Peter Kazaras (D), Graham Clark (E), Håkan Hagegård (F), Gino Quilico (G), Metropolitan Opera Chorus and Orchestra—James Levine

Metropolitan Opera: Colin Graham (stage director), Brian Large (television director)

Spectral aristocrats float through the air; a madwoman descends onto the stage in a balloon; the ghost of Marie Antoinette wanders in, looking wan and pensive. So begins *The Ghosts of Versailles*, a visually splendid work that is a natural for television.

As Marie Antoinette, soprano Teresa Stratas gives one of the greatest performances of her career. Early in the opera, she sings an aria in which she relives the day of her execution, and the horror of those memories is reflected in the dark, hollow sound of her voice. She shudders as she remembers "the odor of blood on steel," her eyes open wide with terror. Then a smile flits across her face and she gently strokes her cheek as she remembers the grace of her former life. "Once there was a golden bird," she sings, spinning out a sweet *pianissimo*. Stratas plays the role with such vulnerability that even the happy moments are poignant. Her childlike delight at Figaro's antics is touching, and when Marie Antoinette finally surrenders to her fate out of love for Beaumarchais, the soprano's face and voice become incandescent, and the joy of her surrender is deeply moving.

As her lover, Beaumarchais, Håkan Hagegård acts with conviction, combining passion with dignity. His baritone is rich and full-bodied, with a ringing top range, and his elegant bearing makes Beaumarchais a commanding presence. Figaro, on the other hand, is a mercurial character in perpetual motion. Right after his entrance, he sings a witty patter aria that requires agility, impeccable diction and an exuberant personality. Gino Quilico delivers splendidly on all fronts. His warm lyric baritone remains secure, even when he is running to escape creditors or outwit villains. Quilico is totally at ease on stage and his acting can take on breadth when needed; e.g., during the trial scene when Figaro's revolutionary ardor turns into compassion for Marie Antoinette.

Count Almaviva, sung by Peter Kazaras, also learns to be more compassionate. Kazaras, whose metallic tenor suits the character, portrays a brusque aristocrat who refuses to forgive his wife for an affair she had with Cherubino twenty years earlier. But when the Revolution descends on the Almavivas and the Count

relents, Kazaras effectively conveys the character's change of heart, particularly when he consoles his family during the prison scene. Renée Fleming, whose soprano has a compelling burnished quality, portrays Rosina (the Countess) with grace and sensitivity. Her flashback love scene with Cherubino is vocally lustrous, and her confrontations with the Count ache with desperation.

The villain, Bégearss, is played by tenor Graham Clark, who began his professional life as a physical education teacher. During his aria, "Long live the worm," he slithers down the banister, crawls along the floor, does hand stands, and sings grandly in his brazen tenor, a sound that exudes villainy. Bégearss is pure camp, as is the sultry Egyptian diva, Samira, played with gusto by Marilyn Horne. The role was written for her, and it showcases both her comedic gift and her ability to toss off *fioritura* with seeming ease. Other solid performances include: James Courtney as an acerbic Louis XVI; crystalline-voiced Tracy Dahl in the ingenue role of Florestine; Judith Christin as the sensible Susanna; Stella Zambalis as an ardent Cherubino; and Wilbur Pauley in the comic speaking role of Wilhelm, servant to the infamous Bégearss.

Conductor James Levine's performance is a marvel of balance and clarity. In a score that calls for two orchestras, forty soloists, and a chorus, Levine deftly keeps the details transparent. He brings enormous vitality to the piece, capturing the drama of each scene. The revolutionary chorus following the trial, for example, is savage in its intensity, and the serene postlude after the prison scene is tenderly played.

Just as Levine keeps the musical spheres clear, so does director Colin Graham with the staging, despite the large cast and the shifting planes of reality in the opera. The ghosts move slowly; their gestures are exaggerated, their facial expressions supercilious, lending an eerie sense of unreality to their scenes. By contrast, the characters in the eighteenth-century world move naturally. Gil Wechsler's lighting further differentiates between the two spheres: the ghosts are bathed in blue light, the Figaro characters in golden hues. The fluidity of the production is largely due to John Conklin's highly original set designs. He has created a series of striking images that flow from one to the next—environments rather than sets in the conventional sense of the word.

Although the stage production of *Ghosts* is vast, television director Brian Large has skillfully adapted it to television size by selecting details that best reveal the characters and tell the story. His camera work not only elucidates relationships but enhances the staging. For the ghosts he uses slow dissolves, adding to the other-worldly atmosphere. And during chaotic crowd scenes, such as the zany Turkish Embassy reception, fast cuts from shot to shot add momentum.

The Ghosts of Versailles is well worth viewing for the imaginative score, the witty libretto, the superb cast, the inventive production, and above all, for the extraordinary performance by Teresa Stratas.

BRIDGET PAOLUCCI

PELLÉAS ET MÉLISANDE (1902)

A: Mélisande (s); B: Geneviève (ms); C: Pelléas (t or bar);
D: Golaud (bar); E: Arkel (bs)

Although the esthetic of *Pelléas* has been widely influential, the work itself remains *sui generis*. It was long regarded as an almost exclusively French preserve, because of the dominant role of the words and the almost *parlando* manner of their setting—a tradition well represented on sound recordings. As for the orchestra, the instruments were supposed, as the Debussy disciple D. E. Inghelbrecht put it, not so much to "enter" as rather to "insinuate themselves." Both these assumptions—and also the naturalistic visual style prevalent since the premiere—were conspicuously subverted in a 1969 Covent Garden production designed by Josef Svoboda and conducted by Pierre Boulez, without a single French principal (recorded on Sony CD), and the waves thereby generated are audible and visible in the present recordings.

During its long gestation period, Debussy's score underwent extensive revision; just before the premiere, he extended many of the orchestral interludes to fit the requirements of scene changing. Further revisions were made subsequently, not all of them reflected in the text that became standard. (A passage in Act III, Scene 4, referring to Mélisande's bed, was suppressed by the censors, but is now sometimes restored, as in both video editions.) Occasionally, conductors now revert to the original shorter interludes—as in the 1985 Lyons production, for which John Eliot Gardiner also undertook to restore the "original" orchestration of the manuscript score (apparently a task not as clear-cut as it may sound, however).

c. 1985 KULTUR (VHS)

(Stage Performance, Stereo, Color, Subtitled)
145 minutes

Colette Alliot-Lugaz (A), Jocelyne Taillon (B), François Le Roux (C), José van Dam (D), Roger Soyer (E), Chorus and Orchestra of Opéra de Lyon—John Eliot Gardiner

Opéra de Lyon: Pierre Strosser (stage director), Jean-François Jung (video director)

Though filmed without an audience and avoiding any conspicuous intimations of taking place in a theater, this video evidently represents the 1985 Lyon production. Strosser's staging is something of a muddle. His solitary set presents a large hall with a patterned floor, at one side a wall pierced by doors opening to a lighted space, on the other side obscurity; pieces of indoor and outdoor furniture are varied in the several scenes. The period suggested by the set and Patrice Cauchetier's costumes is that of the opera's composition. In the opening scene, a mustached, uncertain Golaud wanders about the hall and parleys with an invisible Mélisande, only to be led off at the end by a mysterious figure (who later turns out to be the family servant); since thereafter Golaud is mustacheless and younger, there's a suggestion here that everything after the first scene is a flashback, perhaps from an asylum.

Thereafter, discontinuities burgeon between what the characters sing and what they do on stage. A glass of water does duty for the fountain, and Mélisande "loses" the ring by pitching it out the door. In Act III, Scene 1, there's no tower, no long hair; when Pelléas, reclining in a chair, asks the standing Mélisande to "lean down," she says she cannot—but she does move closer. As far as I could tell, in this staging Pelléas and Mélisande hardly ever even touch—least of all at the climax of Act IV (". . . ta bouche, ta bouche!"), where it is Golaud who ends up in Pelléas' arms!

The obvious consequence of such inconsequence is that the performers often seem ridiculous—their lips continually uttering lies of a more mundane order than the significant ones they may be telling in the drama itself. In recompense, we find little illumination of the admittedly ambiguous characters and events. A shame, for significant talent is wasted on this charade, notably van Dam, a prince among Golauds, who sings forcefully and eloquently throughout. Soyer, looking like an emaciated Abe Lincoln, retains his *gravitas*, though the voice has become edgy and infirm at the top. Taillon is a competent Geneviève, who has less nonsense to put up with in her shorter role. The lovers are less effective: Alliot-Lugaz, wistful and winsome of face, is tonally bland, and the schoolboyish Le Roux sounds throaty in the upper part of the role, which for him is the "extreme upper" part.

The orchestra's tangy French wind timbres are welcome, and the playing is always respectable; in its musical aspects, this performance remains in touch with the central *Pelléas* tradition, though the lighter scoring of the manuscript version combines with the recorded balance to leave things sounding somewhat pallid.

1992 DEUTSCHE GRAMMOPHON (VHS / LD)

(Studio Performance, Stereo, Color, Subtitled) 159 minutes

Alison Hagley (A), Penelope Walker (B), Neill Archer (C), Donald Maxwell (D), Kenneth Cox (E), Welsh National Opera Chorus and Orchestra—Pierre Boulez

Welsh National Opera: Peter Stein (stage director, video director)

Boulez's career in the opera house has been limited to a few composers: Berg, Wagner, and two productions of *Pelléas*. This one, a joint venture of the Welsh National Opera and the Théâtre du Châtelet in Paris, was taped without an audience, following the Cardiff premiere. The collaboration with the German director Peter Stein was Boulez's idea, and, despite Stein's initial reservations, turns out well: the staging is both imaginative and intelligent, creating credibly impetuous and self-centered characters and coherent scenes that illuminate the action rather than obscuring it.

The video often shows us the theater proscenium, and there are many full-stage shots; staged camera-shutter dissolves replace a conventional curtain. The visual milieu (sets by Karl-Ernst Herrmann, costumes by Moidele Bickel) is stylized medieval, its clean lines modulated by lighting (Jean Kalman) that properly colors the chiaroscuro of the land of Allemonde toward the dark side, with the result that the moments of bright light count for much. In its details, this is a realistic production, with a recognizable fountain, tower, and all—not to mention real doves and a real sheep (mercifully, only one). More significantly, what one sees is attuned to the musical gestures as well as to the literal stage directions.

Though at least one reviewer of the Welsh premiere complained of "emotional distance" in the direction, this viewer found otherwise, perhaps because the camera brings us closer to the principals. Oh, yes—as in Boulez's earlier production, none of them is French (perhaps in part, a gesture of his long-standing contempt for the Parisian opera establishment), and they sometimes seem to be working overtime at mouthing the words. For all that, and the fact that several of the voices are less than ideally focused and/or pitched, this cast is always doing something with words, music, and action.

Hagley's Mélisande is both devious and anguished, Archer's Pelléas fervent and callow.

Maxwell's Golaud progresses convincingly from bluffly insecure prince to violent husband; his menace is palpable in the vault and tower scenes and in the scene with Yniold (a very skillful boy soprano), while the abuse of Mélisande makes terrifying use of her hair, the erotic significance of which has already been fully established—not only in the tower scene with Pelléas, but also in the scene with Arkel. Cox makes the latter into an almost runic figure, clad in white, immensely tall but severely stooped. The orchestra, though not of world class, plays lucidly and powerfully, in an almost Wagnerian way, but with the textural clarity and timbral refinement that have always been Boulez specialties.

The generally idiomatic Lyons performance might make an impression without the visual distractions that burden it, but as a video the preference must go to DG, preserving a strong if nontraditional musical interpretation (and an un-French but effective cast), in a staging with considerable fidelity to the work.

DAVID HAMILTON

LAKMÉ (1883)

A: Lakmé (s); B: Mallika (ms); C: Gérald (t); D: Frédéric (bar);
E: Nilakantha (bs-bar)

*D*erived from the 1882 novel *Le mariage de Loti* by Pierre Loti, the plot of *Lakmé*, Delibes's single contribution to the standard repertory, revolves around the unbridgeable cultural gap between East and West—the same rich theme that shows up later in Puccini's *Madama Butterfly* and in the Rodgers and Hammerstein musicals *The King and I* and *South Pacific*. As a product of the era of French colonial imperialism, *Lakmé* portrays India under the British as a fascinating, exotic, and erotic civilization populated by somewhat simple-minded "children" whose allure can prove dangerous to those dedicated to defending the cause of Western military and cultural superiority. Lakmé, the devout daughter of a Brahmin priest, falls in love—against her father's warnings—with the British officer Gérald. But like Pinkerton in *Madama Butterfly*, Gérald ultimately deserts his vulnerable conquest to return to his patriotic duty of subduing the rebellious natives. Like Cio-Cio San, Lakmé responds by committing suicide, although her ingestion of a poisonous flower is a considerably less gory method than hara-kiri.

With its Indian color, imperial splendor, and choreographic possibilities, *Lakmé* proved a perfect subject for Delibes, already famous for his ballets *Coppélia* and *Sylvia*. The score contains a surprisingly large number of marvelous duets and arias—most of all, of course, for the legendary coloratura role of Lakmé. Its characters and conflicts may not be drawn with a great deal of psychological insight, and the orchestra may fulfill little more than a subsidiary musical function, but *Lakmé* boasts some of the most mellifluous and charming vocal writing produced by any nineteenth-century French composer. The mix of mysterious India and British military pomp gives designers plenty of material, too.

1976 KULTUR (VHS)

(Stage Performance, Stereo, Color, Not Subtitled) 154 minutes

Joan Sutherland (A), Huguette Tourangeau (B), Henry Wilden (C), John Pringle (D), Clifford Grant (E), Elizabethan Sydney Orchestra, Australian Opera Chorus—Richard Bonynge

Australian Opera: Norman Ayrton (stage director), John Charles (video director).

This excellent version was recorded live at the Sydney Opera House in 1976, then restored and released in 1991 by The Australian Opera. The restorers have managed to bring the quality of the recorded sound and visual image to a respectable level, providing an attractive showcase for the handsomely designed stage production (awash in sheer pastel fabrics) and for Joan Sutherland's moving performance in the title role.

Given her limited acting skills and less-than-flashy onstage demeanor, Sutherland shines as the modest, devout, and two-dimensional Lakmé, costumed very successfully by designer Desmond Digby and expertly lit by Anthony

Everingham. Even with her large stature and angular features, Sutherland is surprisingly believable as Nilakantha's devout daughter; she makes the drama work by skillful and lyrical use of her voice, which is in impressive condition here—toward the end of her career, and nine years after her Decca recording of this opera. True, she does exhibit the muffled sound and mushy enunciation on which many critics have commented, but her pitch is true, the tone is light, and one feels a marvelous ease in the way she negotiates Delibes's soaring line and sonic effects (the "Bell Song").

Nearly all of the other members of the cast rise to the level of Sutherland's inspired performance. Clifford Grant looks and sounds imposing as Nilakantha; he manages to convey with unusual success both vocally and dramatically the mixture of devotion and fear Nilakantha inspires in Lakmé and others. As Lakmé's companion Mallika, Huguette Tourangeau blends well vocally with Sutherland; their "Flower Duet" is restrained and scrupulously tuned. Henri Wilden, as Gérald, gives the weakest vocal performance among the principals, showing obvious signs of strain in the upper register. The role of Gérald's military mate Frédéric fares better in the hands of John Pringle. Isobel Buchanan, Jennifer Bermingham, and Rosina Raisbeck make the most of their small roles as members of the British expatriate community, expressing prim fascination and voyeuristic shock at the licentious ways of the Indian masses. Richard Bonynge provides subtle, strong leadership in the pit, resisting the temptation to wring too much from Delibes's sweet, ingratiating orchestral writing.

While the camera work remains conventional and static, with very few close-ups or attempts at psychological revelation, the cameras are placed at a distance that is flattering to the performers, the staging, and the design.

HARLOW ROBINSON

A VILLAGE ROMEO AND JULIET (1900–01)

A: Vreli (s); B: Sali (t); C: Dark Fiddler (bar); D: Manz (bs);
E: Marti (bs)

The fourth of Delius's six operas, and the best of the lot, was composed in 1900–01 and premiered in Berlin in 1907. Delius based his libretto on a story in a collection entitled *Die Leute von Sedwyla* (1856) by the Swiss author Gottfried Keller (1819–90); his wife Jelka translated the original English into German for its first production. The opera, meant to be played without interruption, has six scenes bridged by orchestral interludes that permit movement from one setting to another.

Its scenario is strong—a tale of childhood sweethearts whose farmer fathers' feud results in the ruin of their nurturing pastoral environment and of any possibility of a happy life together elsewhere. Its text, like those of Delius's other operas, is its weakness, often sounding flat and unpoetic when sung. The opera survives by virtue of distinctive, atmospheric harmonies and picturesque orchestrations that unfailingly evoke the allure of its out-of-doors settings, registering the exact emotional temperature of each scene. By turns sad, haunting, even ecstatic (the Walk to Paradise Garden interlude and its final scene constitute an English *Liebestod*), *A Village Romeo and Juliet*, well done, can be a deeply moving experience.

1989 LONDON (VHS / LD)

(Film, Stereo, Color) 113 minutes

Helen Field (A), Arthur Davies (B), Thomas Hampson (C), Barry Mora (D), Stafford Dean

(E), Arnold Schönberg Chorus, Austrian Radio Orchestra—Charles Mackerras

Petr Weigl (film director)

This pictorially ravishing film, made in Czechoslovakia by Petr Weigl with an affection for pastoral beauty complementing that of Delius, employs the voices of English and American artists united with the faces and bodies of convincing Czech actors for all roles, excepting the Dark Fiddler, sung *and* played by Thomas Hampson.

For all its obvious advantages, such doubling is risky. Lip-synch problems are never entirely solved, and the more one knows a particular singer the more unsettling is the sound of his or her voice coming from another's body. Danger lurks in combining opera-house sonics with actual settings, a procedure just as apt to distance the viewer from the drama as to draw one closer to it.

Weigl will reward those tolerant of these built-in hazards. His casting of the actors is without flaw; each has a convincing *physique du rôle*; each is directed to perform with sensitivity and restraint. His images—apt, poetic, never at odds with Delius's ripe romanticism— are tastefully chosen, achieving a continuity rare in such undertakings.

Weigl is fortunate in his musical collaborator. Charles Mackerras, an authoritative Delian, gets a fine ensemble from Austrian instrumentalists, a chorus trained to pronounce English without an accent, and a vocal cast exceptional in the three leading roles. Both Helen Field and Arthur Davies have fresh, youthful voices and the art to convey the emotions of the doomed lovers. Thomas Hampson finds the ambiguity in the shadowy Dark Fiddler in his skillful and subtle portrayal. Only the two fathers, Barry Mora and Stafford Dean, disappoint when they are unable to make the words of their quarrel about their land tell, the crucial dialogue precipitating the ultimate tragedy.

The occasional shortcomings of this well-groomed production do not begin to outweigh its many virtues. Since *A Village Romeo and Juliet* is likely to remain on the outer fringes of the operatic repertory and is now so well represented, anyone with the smallest interest in Delius should rush to acquire this estimable video. Recordings of fringe operas, in whatever format, are seldom in print for long.

C. J. LUTEN

L'ELISIR D'AMORE (1832)

A: Adina (s); B: Nemorino (t); C: Belcore (bar); D: Dulcamara (bs)

In any competition for world's fastest composer, Gaetano Donizetti would be right out in front with Mozart and Rossini. And *L'Elisir d'Amore* itself could well win a prize for extraordinary achievement under the most stringent deadline conditions. The composer, beseeched at almost the last minute to save the day when someone else's commission didn't work out for the Teatro della Canobbiana in Milan, offered neither to complete the half-finished commissioned work of another nor to refashion something of his own. Instead, in barely more than a week he tossed off what has become one of the most enduring works in the comic-opera repertory. *L'Elisir d'Amore*, based by fecund and resourceful librettist Felice Romani on another libretto devised by Eugène Scribe for an opera buffa, *Le Philtre*, and already set by Daniel-François Auber, has seldom been out of the repertory of major lyric performing forces. It has proved a favorite of leading sopranos and tenors of all generations. What has so obviously endeared Donizetti's achievement to both singers and audiences is the wedding of a plausible classic comic situation—the gullible country oaf impossibly in love with someone above his station—and an underlying pulse of real feeling that thoroughly humanizes all characters, even those who in other hands might acquire a perhaps negatively manipulative edge. Undeniable melodic grace in tandem with formal suppleness serve further not to endanger the opera's perennial status.

1959 LEGATO CLASSICS (VHS)

(Stage Performance, Mono, Black and White, Japanese Subtitles) 96 minutes

Alda Noni (A), Ferruccio Tagliavini (B), Arturo La Porta (C), Paolo Montarsolo (D), Chorus and Orchestra of Lirica Italiana, Tokyo—Alberto Erede

Opera company, stage director, and video company uncredited

It may win no prizes for cinematography or pin back the ears of hi-fi mavens, but this *Elisir*, taken from a Tokyo performance in 1959 (subtitles in Japanese only), is of much more than passing interest, and that principally because of the participation of the late Ferruccio Tagliavini. This is the tenor in his last, quite mature phase, the period of his American stardom well behind him. Yet no allowances need be made. The voice is supple, smooth, and sweet, the *mezza voce* as seductive as ever, the unusual ability to reach out for high notes without punching them in place, the unique resonance and tone color as ingratiating as one remembers it. The singer's phrasing of the initial descending figure of "Adina, credimi," for example, has the kind of heartfelt curve of longing few artists have been able to impart to it and makes one realize what one has been missing these many years. There are occasional pitch miscalculations, but these are a small price to pay for the alternately thrilling and whispered dynamics of "Una furtiva lagrima." Tagliavini is also an altogether convincing bumpkin, believably drunk when called for, or believably in love. It's a cherishable performance.

Alda Noni, also a veteran at this point in her career, as Adina wields a somewhat heavy lyric soprano, a little unsteady at first and decidedly lower-register-talky in her opening moments. However, she bustles around bossily on high heels, using her still serviceable coloratura technique to limn a small-town smart operator who is nevertheless always sympathetic. Paolo Montarsolo's Dulcamara is not as good a fit, the basso's truly elegant bearing out of sorts with his character's essential shadiness. It must be noted, though, that Dulcamara's entrance is missing— lost because of broadcast transmission problems—so any real appraisal of his performance is hampered. There are many other cuts in the performance other than this major accidental one. The finale is a real rush job.

If one can take in stride the cuts, washed out black-and-white television kinescope definition, the minimal camera angles (the orchestra pit is so shallow, harp tops as well as energetic and ensemble-sensitive conductor Alberto Erede get in the way of stage action), tape hiss, and shallow overall sound reproduction, an enjoyable, even valuable *Elisir* experience is still possible. Not to be overlooked: a superbly fatuous Belcore with an impressive technique from baritone Arturo La Porta. Who was he?

1981 PARAMOUNT (VHS) / PIONEER (LD)

(Stage Performance, Stereo, Color, Subtitled) 132 minutes

Judith Blegen (A), Luciano Pavarotti (B), Brent Ellis (C), Sesto Bruscantini (D), Metropolitan Opera Chorus and Orchestra—Nicola Rescigno

Metropolitan Opera: Nathaniel Merrill (stage director), Kirk Browning (video director)

The earlier of the two currently available televised Met broadcasts of Donizetti's arguably most popular *opera buffa* dates from 1981. Although it shares Luciano Pavarotti with the later release, that's about all it has in common.

This O'Hearn-Merrill production, already venerable, always had a candy-coated picture-book coziness to it that seemed to suit the material acceptably and, perhaps more important, the taste of the Met audience in a mood to relax from the demands of Wagner and major Verdi. Almost everything, from Dulcamara's balloon entrance to Pavarotti's serendipitous buffoonery, is a sight gag sure to nudge approval from even the most staid patron and, also, to make its mark in the farthest reaches of the cavernous auditorium. And the broadness is really inoffensive, and the mood benign, allowing for the important segues into genuine sentiment that make this comedy so ingratiating.

Pavarotti is in wonderful, height-of-powers fresh voice and is generous with radiant tone. "Una furtiva lagrima" is gorgeous. But it's a concert performance, utterly detached from the action. The tenor focuses on sound and sound alone. In the rest of the opera his Nemorino appears similarly uninvolved or, rather, in a perpetual state of preparedness for vocal hurdles, with the important exception of those episodes that engage his personal playfulness: Pavarotti waddling as a country bumpkin, Pavarotti taking a single swig of the elixir and becoming instantly inebriated. In contrast, Judith Blegen's Adina profits from a natural and consistent alignment of temperament and role, a bubbly spirit controlled by shrewd intelligence. Apart from a somewhat colorless lower register, her vocalism is bright and accurate, firm in coloratura and sensitive to lyricism and line. The balance of the cast is somewhat less successful. Sesto Bruscantini doesn't seem to be having a lot of fun as Dulcamara except during those moments when the glimmer of seduction *vis-à-vis* Adina flares up, and vocally he's very tight. Brent Ellis can't summon up the requisite baritonal oiliness to make Belcore amusing, much less credible.

Nicola Rescigno brings idiomatic elasticity to the orchestra, but the pit has come up with more assured playing on other occasions, and there are coordination problems with the stage. Technically, too, there are problems, with too-frequent directional drop-outs in the sound. The camera work, occasionally out of focus, doesn't always avoid angles that have singers getting in each other's way. And why have bows (so important to the sense of performance actuality) and some extended applause (although not the ovation after Pavarotti's big moment) been edited out? It's an unnecessary shortchanging, even a falsification of the event.

1984 EUROPEAN VIDEO DISTRIBUTORS (VHS)

(Film, Stereo, Color, Not Subtitled) 80 minutes

Melanie Holliday (A), Miroslav Dvorsky (B), Armando Ariostini (C), Alfredo Mariotti (D), Bratislava Radio Symphony—Piero Bellugi

Lubos Zatka and Stanislav Mesaros (directors)

It's sometimes valuable to be reminded what opera transposed to screen was like before the era of live broadcasts and performance tapes, or its dimensions when deprived of the sophisticated cinematic stylistics of Bergman, Zeffirelli, Ponnelle, Losey, et al. Such a service is rendered by a videocassette from Bratislava, a *L'Elisir d'Amore* of relatively recent vintage but antique sensibilities. Unlikely to leave one pining for a return to those sensibilities, it may still leave some mouths agape that opera on film still can be handled as if Sophia Loren in *Aida* had set a never-to-be-challenged gold standard.

This abridged, somewhat reordered version of the *opera buffa* perennial, for all its energy and eagerness to entertain, is done in by a staggering onslaught of the cutes. In the picturesque Slovakian (to keep matters Slavic as up-to-date as possible) countryside, overrun by geese and peasants sent over by the local equivalent of central casting, a housepainter, Nemorino, yearns for the local schoolmarm, Adina. He yearns at a frenetic pace—milking a goat during one duet, riding a seesaw with Dulcamara during another, wrestling in a fountain with Belcore while holding up his end of an ensemble. The only time he's still comes during "Una furtiva lagrima," when he falls asleep, presumably exhausted by directorial itchiness, and dreams of loping in slow motion across fields with Adina. It's wonderful to see a Belcore who actually twirls his mustache, a corps de ballet

carrying on in the middle of haying (hay is also, of course, for rolling in), happy soldiers splashing in a stream.

For the record, Melanie Holliday comes up with a wiry Adina, Miroslav Dvorsky an effortful Nemorino. Armando Ariostini and Alfredo Mariotti strike suitable stances but sound tired as the other principal males who drop in on Adina's village, which, given the extremely wayward lip-synching settled for here, looks as if it might actually be caught in a performance of *The Bartered Bride* over which the Donizetti track has been laid. If these Bratislava forces ever decide to produce the Smetana comedy, they need only do some additional sound recording—one endowed with more buoyancy than conductor Piero Bellugi displays on this occasion.

1992 DEUTSCHE GRAMMOPHON (VHS / LD)

(Stage Performance, Stereo, Color, Subtitled) 129 minutes

Kathleen Battle (A), Luciano Pavarotti (B), Juan Pons (C), Enzo Dara (D), Metropolitan Opera Chorus and Orchestra—James Levine

Metropolitan Opera: John Copley (stage director), Brian Large (video director)

Proceeding chronologically through the three live *Elisirs* available for home viewing provides an instructive tour of production priorities: the rag-tag innocent look of the low-budget Tokyo staging (see above), the *faux naïf* manner of the long-enduring previous Metropolitan mounting, and now this latest supernova of slickness that has replaced it. Whimsy has given way to gorgeousness with a vengeance. It's a lavish village indeed one gets to visit here, inhabited by peasants got up in pastel moiré silk so that they resemble Trianon nobility playing at shepherds and shepherdesses. But perhaps "playing" is the wrong word, because most everything in this 1992 performance comes across as heavy-going drillwork, what with all the choreographically conceived movement, laser-perfect scenery changes (which gratuitously go beyond the demands of the libretto), and the emphasis on arranged tab-leaux. It's a stunningly polished visual conception by Beni Montresor, glittering and determined to please, but it overwhelms any chance of comedy and clearly inhibits stage director John Copley from doing more than getting his people into painterly poses.

Unfortunately, too, the cast, taken as an ensemble, for the most part doesn't impress as having a sufficiently strong gift for mirth to offer any kind of counterbalance. Luciano Pavarotti's Nemorino appears less involved than ever and only fitfully tries for a laugh or two: the old standby of shaking the big bottle of elixir before imbibing is about it. Vocally, however, he stakes out fine, superstar territory even if the timbre on occasion seems reedier than ideal. But phrasing and diction are immaculate and "Una furtiva lagrima" again stops the show. Complementing Pavarotti's uninvolvement is Kathleen Battle's coolness. The soft-grained contours of her soprano seem at first far from ideal for Adina, although her silken vocal style matches the visual values espoused here. In Act II, however, she does fluent, virtuoso things that are quite breathtaking. By the time the soprano reaches "Prendi, per me sei libero," assisted by the tempo-bending indulgence of conductor James Levine (who throughout mostly prefers languor to brio), her plangent stretching of phrase amounts to a ravishing lesson in *bel canto* sensitivity—as well as ability.

Juan Pons makes a ponderous generalissimo out of Sergeant Belcore, more Scarpia-in-training than rustic. *His* big joke is to bump bellies with Dulcamara, whose characterization certainly does profit from bass Enzo Dara's facility with patter and from his mobile face, if not from his quavery sound. Dara's talent for laughter is, admittedly, considerable, but it's dwarfed here by the self-importance of the stately, gilded framework that carries all before it. The mercurial and resourceful camera work, under Brian Large's meticulous hand, pleases throughout, and Levine's orchestra sounds splendid in the spacious acoustic especially available from the laser disc edition.

———————

The *Elisir* selection brings with it a difficult call. There's something so unspontaneous about the later Met performance that to say this is absolutely the one to have would have to be circumscribed by a lot of qualifications. Still, it has production-values advantages, Pavarotti in almost as good form as he was eleven years earlier, an impeccable Battle, and the virtues and deficits of the balance of both Met casts cancel each other out. For those thirsty for other lips than today's superstar tenor's around the mouth of that bottle of *bordo*, the Tagliavini tape will prove a special delight.

Harvey E. Phillips

GAETANO DONIZETTI

LUCREZIA BORGIA (1833)

A: Lucrezia Borgia (s); B: Maffio Orsini (ms); C: Gennaro (t);
D: Don Alfonso d'Este (bar)

*I*f the music of any opera has been presented with more titles than *Lucrezia Borgia*, it must hold the Guinness World Record. Felice Romani drew his libretto from Hugo's drama, a story of the Duke of Ferrara, the Borgias, and a pope's daughter, and he probably lived to regret his selection. He had to modify his text substantially and often, thanks to the objections of numerous censors. It was performed in one place or another as *Elisa da Fosco, Eustorgia da Romano, Alfonso, Duca di Ferrara, Giovanna I di Napoli,* even *Lucrezia Borgia.*

The opera, the third of three Donizetti premieres in 1833, was composed in a hurry. The composer received the libretto act by act near the end of November and composed each act within a few days to meet La Scala's December 26 deadline. If, like all of Donizetti's tragedies, *Borgia* lapses too often into routine craftsmanship, its title role is one that has attracted the interest of prima donnas. Written for Henriette-Clementine Meric-Lalande, it was picked up quickly by the likes of Giulia Grisi, Therese Tietjens, Henriette Sonntag, and Maria de Macchi. In recent years the role has tempted Monserrat Caballé, Leyla Gencer, and Joan Sutherland.

1977 KULTUR (VHS)

(Stage Performance, Stereo, Color, Not Subtitled) 138 minutes

Joan Sutherland (A), Margreta Elkins (B), Ronald Stevens (C), Robert Allman (D), Australian Opera Chorus, Elizabethan Sydney Orchestra—Richard Bonynge

Australian Opera: George Ogilvie (stage director), John Charles (video director)

This performance was filmed on July 8, 1977, released in 1991. It is not a strong advocate for the opera, even with the presence of Joan Sutherland, making a return to the first stage of her native land.

Australian Opera went all out to provide a proper setting, including bejewelled costumes, for its prodigal daughter. However handsome Kristian Fredrickson's decoration may be, most of the stage pictures, alas, are cluttered. The presentation, even with images remarkably clean for a 1977 videotape and, at least, good orchestral sonics, also leaves something to be desired. The sound from the stage is overresonant; musical climaxes are overmonitored. Both stage and video direction are rudimentary, and there are no subtitles.

Some would tolerate these shortcomings if the musical direction were not so enervated by flabby rhythm, untidy ensemble, and some plodding tempos, and above all, if the singers could meet Donizettian requirements; but far too frequently they don't. The tenor's timbre is dry and his spread tone smears pitch. Under more than ordinary stress, the unequalized scale of the mezzo's voice is evident, high notes better than those lower. The energetic baritone has better than average diction and some real metal in the voice, but he offers little tonal shading and is ill advised to attempt the optional A-flat in his first act cabaletta.

Joan Sutherland at least lives up to her reputation; hers is a characteristic outing. It takes her a while to warm up and her enunciation is seldom firm; but she hits her stride in Borgia's dialogue with Alfonso, one of the few scenes that conveys some dramatic heat. Her ample tone dominates ensembles, as it should; most, if not all, of her high notes have a gleaming purity. In the last scene, after a less than secure start, she comes through with a splendid display of virtuoso certainty.

Sad to say, this will likely be the only video *Borgia* for some time.

C. J. LUTEN

MARY STUART

(MARIA STUARDA) (1834–35)

A: Mary Stuart (Maria Stuarda) (s); B: Elizabeth I (Elisabetta) (s);
C: Leicester (t); D: Talbot (bar); E: Cecil (bs)

*L*ike Verdi, Donizetti, usually able to circumnavigate possible objections in advance, occasionally had his problems with the censors. His *Maria Stuarda* ran afoul of the Neapolitan authorities—it was scheduled for a San Carlo premiere—when, attending a rehearsal, Queen Maria Christina fainted dead away at the sight of the opera's queenly protagonist about to lay her head on the block. Although the libretto had received official approval, it was hastily recast and the story complete changed, fitted as best possible to the existing score. The cobbled-together product, rechristened *Buondelmonte*, made its debut in 1834 and was a resounding failure. Only in the following year (much of this delay caused by the caprices of the opera's new star, the willful Maria Malibran) at La Scala did *Maria Stuarda*, complete with a freshly fashioned overture, make its real world bow. Again it was not a success but this mostly because of the deficiencies of the performers, most especially Malibran herself, who was ill.

Fitfully performed over the years, *Maria Stuarda* lagged far behind many of the Bergamo master's other stage works in popularity until twentieth-century revivals brought about broad and surprised awareness of the opera's quality as both dramatic entity and astute, compelling musical realization. Loosely based on Schiller's complex drama, which in turn is loosely based on fact, Donizetti's forty-sixth lyric effort makes stunning use of the historical situation and the personages it involved, cannily ranging in mood from the most lyrical and reflective to steely denunciation. In this latter department, the fictitious confrontation between Mary and Elizabeth, the blow-up that leads directly to Mary's precipitous downfall, has to be acknowledged one of the high points in the annals of theatrical fireworks and, incidentally, a great opportunity for prima donnas to unleash pent-up arsenals of temperament.

1982 CASTLE OPERA (VHS)

(Stage Performance, Stereo, Color, in English) 135 minutes

Janet Baker (A), Rosalind Plowright (B), David Rendall (C), John Tomlinson (D), Alan Opie (E), English National Opera Chorus and Orchestra—Charles Mackerras

English National Opera: John Copley (stage director), Peter Butler (video director)

Dame Janet Baker, retiring from the stage at the rather early age of fifty, made her London operatic farewell as the heroine of Donizetti's *Maria Stuarda*. If this was Dame Janet's own idea she should have listened to herself suggesting it with more than a bit of objective skepticism. After a splendid career in concert and oratorio, as well as opera, and close identification as a mezzo-soprano with the music of Berlioz, Britten, Monteverdi, Cavalli, Purcell, Gluck, and Handel, to blossom forth as a *bel canto* personality and to do so in a role generally undertaken by dramatic coloratura sopranos — and when vocal ease is not what it once was — seems an odd and potentially self-defeating path to want to take. And so it was, if the performance taped for posterity is representative of that final London series. True, there are many affecting moments when this estimable artist's customary caressing phrasing and tonal warmth recall her at her best, but for the most part it's an uncomfortable traversal. Her upper register sounds strained and thin, the diction murky, a sense of overall stylistic command less than total. More compromising is the inability to induce a suspension of disbelief. This is a dowdy, utterly passive Mary, a queen without bite or fire. The essential disparity between singer and what needs to be accomplished may best be epitomized by the scene of execution, which fizzles utterly. The disrobing to the famous red undergarments registers as no more than a perfunctory gesture because Dame Janet, who, inexplicably, sports a new bright henna wig for the occasion, has not been able to establish a sense of Mary's defiant, burning faith, not to mention its underlying carnality. All in all, better, for those who want to witness a proper Baker good-bye, to dip into her quite moving and beautifully voiced *Orfeo ed Euridice*, which served, fortunately, as her far more suitable and satisfying absolute exit from opera at Glyndebourne the following summer.

Nothing in the rest of this *Stuarda* quite makes up for its central disappointment. The mesh of role and personality may be closer in the case of Rosalind Plowright's Elizabeth, the haughtiness of manner and imperiousness of tone convincing, but this soprano appears to tire easily and climactic cabaletta and ensemble passages turn hooty. David Rendall's Leicester, loved by Elizabeth but devoted to Mary, is ardent enough, but his merely serviceable tenor turns bleak, squally, and flat on sustained notes. Baritones John Tomlinson and Alan Opie, especially the latter, come off better. Opie even

manages to suggest a nasty sinuousness in his relatively brief moments as Cecil. The men deliver the English text with relative clarity. Otherwise, it's often difficult to determine what sentiments are being volleyed back and forth. English, despite the subject matter, is simply not the language for tragic Donizetti. To whit: that superb outburst when Mary slashes at Elizabeth and calls her a "vil bastarda" somehow loses its full complement of venom, becomes somewhat deferential in fact, when, for the phrase to scan, "vil" is transformed into "royal."

Possibly the best aspect of the entire enterprise is the look designer Desmond Heeley has devised for it: a few basic, commanding, overscaled props against dark backdrops that also put into sharp relief the mostly black, brown, russet, and silver costumes (Elizabeth's are truly opulent). Furthermore, the camera work is clean, appropriate to John Copley's simple, ungimmicky staging. Also highly commendable is Charles Mackerras's obvious carefulness of musical preparation; orchestra, however lackluster its finish, and soloists display a constant unanimity of dynamic and rhythmic subtlety. Somehow, the Overture has been lost. Perhaps this acknowledges the opera's *Buondelmonte* version; more likely it reflects a wayward tape-editing decision, since the camera first captures Mackerras already on the podium, not entering the pit of the ENO's home theater, the London Coliseum. With this relatively brief opera spread over two cassettes, the excision doesn't make much sense.

Certainly a video worth considering, especially if one is a staunch Janet Baker fan or if completeness in Donizetti representation in the home collection is a criterion. Still, on absolute grounds, the pleasures of the performance have to be declared limited, the work's quantity of excitement certainly much more readily ignited by what's available on disc through CD versions with Caballé, Gencer, and Sutherland, and, most notably, although not yet digitally transferred, the Beverly Sills–Eileen Farrell face-off from the early 1970s.

HARVEY E. PHILLIPS

GAETANO DONIZETTI

LUCIA DI LAMMERMOOR (1835)

A: Lucia (s); B: Edgardo (t); C: Enrico (bar); D: Raimondo (bs)

*L*ucia, whose standing has profited enormously from audio recording, is ill-adapted to screen formats. Its scenes progress by a structural logic that fits poorly with video or film rhythms, and its style has given rise to conventions of staging and character action that do not benefit by close inspection. That we already have five versions of the opera is a tribute to the durability of the score and the popularity of some recent sopranos.

All the available video editions of *Lucia* are cut to some degree. Since the restoration of these cuts has become customary in recording and frequent in production, and can considerably alter the work's balance and impact, the old theater excisions will be noted here, and the major restorations in the reviews below. 1) Two entire scenes, No. 7 in the score (Raimondo / Lucia, with the bass aria "Cedi, ah, cedi"); and No. 11 (Edgardo / Enrico, the "Wolf's Crag Scene"). 2) The trio with chorus between the two sections of the Mad Scene, and the recitative following the Mad Scene. 3) Many internal cuts, sometimes of only a few bars, in development and repeat sections, of which the most important is probably the ornamented repeat in Enrico's cabaletta in the opening scene.

1967 LEGATO CLASSICS (VHS)

(Stage Performance, Mono, Color, Subtitled in Japanese) 127 minutes

Renata Scotto (A), Carlo Bergonzi (B), Mario Zanasi (C), Plinio Clabassi (D), Chorus and Orchestra of Lirica Italiana, Tokyo — Bruno Bartoletti

Opera company, stage director, and video director uncredited

This is a hot performance and a valuable document, but its limitations should be understood. Both audio and video quality, while decent for the date, are of their era. The sound is compressed, the picture grainy, and the color muted. The stage lighting is dim enough to keep sets and chorus in a blue-green murk most of the time. Much of the acting consists of arm signals while singing and attitudinized poses while waiting to sing. The Japanese subtitles are large and incessant—you can forget the lower third of the picture. The costuming for Enrico & Co. strongly foreshadows the *Saturday Night Live* Samurai and Killer Bee skits, crossbred. The only cut restored is the Mad Scene trio.

Nonetheless, an honest *Lucia* experience is available here, owing to the presence of principals who know not only how to sing, but how to passionately project the drama by vocal means, through instruments of native color and linguistic set. Anyone familiar with Scotto's studio recording of the title role will be struck by the changes eight years have wrought. Gone is most of the glinty coloratura hue reminiscent of so many interwar Italian sopranos, replaced through most of the range by tone of warmer timbre and larger size. Gone as well is some of the voice's equalization: the high extension cannot be made to match the new setup, and turns sticky at points. But she has found her way into the character's predicament and mastered the vocal and musical devices for expressing it. Within the conventions of her theatrical tradition, her performance has a lived-in-the-moment quality not commonly attained by actors, let alone opera singers.

Bergonzi, too, offers something of far greater interest than his musicianly studio Edgardos. This is a little rougher, stylistically a trifle sloppier, more pointed toward the big effects—and much more compelling. Neither on records nor in the theater can I recall the top of his voice as convincingly full-throated as it is here, and in Bartoletti he has a conductor who understands the importance of letting voices expand into the music. Though his acting priorities have to do mostly with vocal positioning, he rises to the climactic moments with true engagement: the Wedding Scene curse is chilling despite being cheated by loopy shot selection, and the "Fra poco" is satisfyingly filled out.

Zanasi makes much the same impression he did at the Met in this and similar roles. His voice is warm and voluminous, capped by splendid F-sharps and G's. Technically and musically he offers nothing particularly refined or imaginative, but is solid and straightforward. As an actor, he is not a dead presence, and beyond this sensibly pleads *nolo contendere*. The Alisa (Mirella Fiorentini) and the Normanno (Giuseppe Baratti) have voices of unusually fine quality for their roles. Choral and orchestral standards are high, and Bartoletti lets out the leash for the singers without ever losing ensemble control.

This *Lucia*'s intensity builds into a gripping Mad Scene whose tone is set by Clabassi. His voice is not the most powerful or wide-ranged of bassos, but it is beautiful, and with it he fashions an eloquent, stricken "Dalle stanze," capped by a high ending sung in a melting mezza-voce. In the few moments of the succeeding scene not filled with Scotto's sweet butterball face, his helpless reception of events is most moving. Scotto hits the emotional truth

button repeatedly—rapturous, terrified, desolate—with that fusing of vocal and physical action that is uniquely operatic. The ovation after "Ardon gl'incensi" elicits a midscene curtain call, complete with acknowledgement of conductor and flutist, right up there in the Callas / Makarova class. Love of the music, love of the character, love of oneself and one's roulades, love of the audience and of the moment: it's all one thing, manifestly contrived but somehow genuine, ultrasophisticated yet almost raw with simplicity and naïveté. And neither she nor we have been pulled away, for she is at her most striking in the trio immediately following. In its way, the real stuff.

1971 VAI (VHS)

(Film, Mono, Color, Subtitled) 108 minutes

Anna Moffo (A), Lajos Kozma (B), Giulio Fioravanti (C), Paolo Washington (D), RAI Chorus, Rome Symphony Orchestra—Carlo Felice Cillario

Mario Lanfranchi (director)

On the occasionally curdled but listenable soundtrack is a perfectly tolerable, though maximally cut, *Lucia*. Moffo is in quite good voice, and that means lots of lovely, pleasurable singing. Her interpretive emphases are of a rather veristic sort for this music, but she doesn't sound uninvolved. Nor does Kozma. His lean, strong lyric tenor, with its alternating stretches of gleam and gristle and its peculiar assortment of vowels, is not a model instrument for the role. Nonetheless, he has some interesting technical strengths and some sensitivity, and pitches himself into the music in a way that keeps the listener alert. Fioravanti is a smooth vocalist and reasonably stylish musician whose sunny high baritone is comfortable in Enrico's music. Washington's Raimondo is thoroughly professional, his rendition of the aria phrased rather like Clabassi's, though a shade blunter of utterance and plainer of tone. Cillario knows the métier, and secures tidy execution with tempos that incline to the slow and weighty.

This version also wins in the swimsuit category: Moffo and Kozma are as gorgeous as Vivian Leigh and Errol Flynn (and as unruffled of coiffure and maquillage), the Bucklaw is a handsome devil, and the entire cast is remarkably presentable considering that no stand-ins are used. The costumes are nice, and I love the Wedding Scene location, a wide, low-ceilinged reception hall with hunting trophies and *tchotchkes* on the whitewashed walls. It was probably like that.

But it is impossible to take a moment of this seriously. It proceeds in that preposterous never-never land of living mannequins who open and close their mouths, facial muscles slack and eyes fixed dreamily on the middle distance, while operatic noise pours from the screen. As per ancient law, the romantic leads are the silliest. If that isn't enough to disqualify it for you, try the "Oops!" take of Moffo—as if caught smoking by the housemother—when Edgardo announces himself in the Wedding Scene, or the hockey face-off at the top of the Sextette, or the pitched swordfight in the succeeding finale while the principals line up in the foreground to calmly talk it over, or the "Spargi d'amaro pianto," wherein Moffo is made to prance outside the castle and to perform Isadora Duncan-ish wrigglings before taking a dive on the scraggly lawn.

Strictly for artifact collectors.

1981 LEGATO CLASSICS (VHS)

(Stage Performance, Mono, Color, Not Subtitled) 120 minutes

Katia Ricciarelli (A), José Carreras (B), Leo Nucci (C), John Paul Bogart (D), unidentified chorus and orchestra—Lamberto Gardelli

Opera company, stage director, and video director uncredited

The provenance of this performance is somewhat shadowy, but it could have been anywhere Instant Opera was done with enough of a budget to hire stars. "Transfer made from best available master," reads the ominous inscription on the back of the box, so don't be complaining about the faded color, the haphazard lighting, the murky, edgy sound, or the jolting cuts from

scene to scene. No whining about subtitles, either. The stage production is strictly of the get-us-out-of-here-before-the-union-rep-shows-up variety, with a couple of story-telling moments that show a probably capable director trying to cope with time and money constraints. Both the orchestra and the undersized chorus are of lower-to-middling professional quality, and bear few rehearsal welts. Gardelli is of course an experienced and thoroughly competent conductor of such repertory, but all he can do here is hold the show loosely together. There is some compensation for all this visual and musical ticky-tack in the timbral glow and rightness of the principal voices, though only one of them is under convincing technical control. That is Leo Nucci's, and to hear his fine, centered high baritone springing through a role of just the right weight is a consistent pleasure. If he discovered something to do with the part beyond ranting villainously, this would be a classical Enrico. Ricciarelli's beautiful, mournful middle octave is as moving a sound as any to emerge from Italy in the last thirty years. Unhappily, she never found a way to integrate the top of her voice with the midrange; here, everything above G is hard-edged and beset by a beat on sustained tones. But by avoidance of nearly all higher options and some clever rewriting, she is able to offer a sort of mezzo-soprano edition that has some expressive strengths. Passages of midrange cantilena like the "Soffriva nel pianto" are richly and touchingly rendered. The ending of the "Ardon gl'incensi" makes a great deal more emotional sense in this simpler, lower restoration than in the usual exhibition, and there are other similar moments. While her Lucia has not much of a character identity, her winning presence and emotive qualities serve her well interpretively until the Mad Scene, which deteriorates into a series of staging ideas and isolated moments like the one cited above. Carreras starts shakily in the opening duet, with the top of his voice unsettled and strained. But by the Wedding Scene he's in good form, and rises to real eloquence in the final two arias, where his tone is at its loveliest and his gift for individual, deeply felt phrasing finds room to bloom. This last requires, and receives, considerable cooperation from Gardelli. As an actor, Carreras is too wrapped up in the vocal side of things to find much physical freedom—a more serious drawback on video than in the opera house. Bogart is a stolid Raimondo, but one with a plush timbre and splendid low notes, if an overly covered top. This performance makes all the usual cuts and then some (Edgardo is even given the Bum's Rush to suicide between verses of "Tu che a Dio"), except for the Raimondo / Lucia interview, which is reinstated in slightly cut form.

1982 PARAMOUNT (VHS) / PIONEER (LD)

(Stage Performance, Stereo, Color, Subtitled) 128 minutes

Joan Sutherland (A), Alfredo Kraus (B), Pablo Elvira (C), Paul Plishka (D), Metropolitan Opera Chorus and Orchestra—Richard Bonynge

Metropolitan Opera: Bruce Donnell (stage director), Kirk Browning (video director)

To the musical side first: Both leads are in extraordinary Indian Summer condition. While there's no use pretending that Sutherland's voice has all the release and float, or the soaring top, of her early years, this was very much her role, and she still sings it with beauty and unmatched overall technical command—very few lumps in the legato, the trills and divisions sparkling away. The only transposition is one full tone for the first part of the Mad Scene, whose low notes gain some new chesty color and whose cadenza remains a delight. Kraus also displays his familiar virtues: fine tonal balance and focus, admirable musical taste, and mastery of the lyrical side of the writing. "Verranno a te" doesn't come any better than this. The voice is slender, though. His shrewd calculation of proportions still leaves him short of the biggest moments, and the final scene is unsatisfying, with the "Fra poco" mezzo-tinted to

death and the climax of "Tu che a Dio" rushed past.

Elvira's baritone—a lovely lyric voice with some U.S.-Certified darkening for dramatic effect—makes for a reliable, tame Enrico. The sturdy, rich bass of Plishka is at its best, and he sings Raimondo impressively. Bonynge's reading is brisk, with a good springiness to some of the rhythms. There's a perfunctory, predictable air to much of it, however, especially in recitative.

The stage production is the one mounted for Sutherland in 1964. It wasn't directed then, only posed (by Margherita Wallmann), and certainly no one was about to start in 1982. The sets (Attilio Colonello's) looked like an Ivy League campus designed by Edward Gorey, but as soft-focus background to singing heads they're quite all right. The video production is extremely sophisticated. The cameras roll us around the scenes with a seamless rhythm, each shot intelligently composed and perfectly lit (nice for us, if not the paying customers).

Yet what registers is the presentation, not the substance, of *Lucia*—emotionally, this is almost weightless. Some of it is the acting. Sutherland, likeable and earnest, is seldom spontaneous. She carefully shows us she hears that "armonia celeste," but that's different from living it, and we're left with stage madness of the ding-dong tweety-bird sort, tastefully done. Kraus is cool and courtly, gravely explaining Edgardo's troubles without allowing them to disturb his aristocratic manner. Elvira hits his marks but provides little of the antagonist drive for the drama. Plishka is committed in a generalized way. The staging is a series of conveniences, and the singers always know where the little red light is. It's all so *arranged*.

The "Dalle stanze" illustrates what goes wrong. The arioso itself is imposingly voiced by Plishka, but as a loud public announcement— he has nowhere to go except by hitting key words with an "I really mean it!" emphasis. His concluding "Ah!" draws a spatter of understandably confused applause, ruining the wonderful choral entry at "Oh! qual funesto." Then, over this ensemble so evocative of collective awe and terror, the camera begins tracking Normanno, who has no part in the scene and would logically enter later, with Enrico. Normanno biting back of hand, flinging self despairingly into chair, etc., to show guilt and / or fear of discovery. The "Gran Scena con Cori" has become a sequence of three sections: Grand Oration and Exclamation, Aborted Ovation, and Weasel Remorse. All technically expert, and all beside the point.

There is partial restoration in the baritone cabaletta, and of the Mad Scene trio and the Raimondo / Lucia scene. This last seems to have an important dramatic purpose, but its sudden turnaround for Lucy is altogether incredible, and since the music is conventional, the passage contributes nothing unless the performers find something in the relationship between tutor and ward that makes it understandable. That is not the case here, though the scene is well and sincerely sung.

1986 KULTUR (VHS)

(Stage Performance, Stereo, Color, Subtitled) 145 minutes

Joan Sutherland (A), Richard Greager (B), Malcolm Donnelly (C), Clifford Grant (D), Australian Opera Chorus, Elizabethan Sydney Orchestra—Richard Bonynge

Australian Opera: John Copley (stage director), video director uncredited

This performance embraces the Wolf's Crag Scene in addition to the main restorations of the Paramount release, making it the most complete available video *Lucia*. It has energy, for sure, and thinking, of a sort. Some of the thinking is even about the characters. Arturo, for example, is treated interestingly. Bucklaw family members, eager for the alliance for reasons of their own, have accompanied him to the wedding, and he turns to them (especially to Lady Bucklaw) for coaching at every turn. We get the sense that he has been pushed as hard as Lucy herself and is as embarrassed and miserable at the prospect as she is. This adds to the pathos of not only this scene, but subsequent ones, as well.

On the other hand, Enrico is presented as even more of a baddie than usual, which only serves to underline the melodrama. In the opening scene, Enrico and Normanno do everything but exchange high fives to indicate gleeful wickedness, and the falconer referred to by the chorus is dragged in so that Enrico may first pull his hair, then give him a thwack upside the head. Mean! This whole scene is rather a mess, with the camera jumping point-of-view on almost every chord in an effort to push the action.

Then there's Wolf's Crag. First Enrico knocks one of Edgardo's books off the table (that'll show those egghead Ravenswoods), then begins playing with a skull. No, I don't know what the skull is doing there. He fondles it during his first long solo, and then, at "Fra l'urne gelido," chucks it over to Edgardo! Throw's low, no chance for the double play, but Edgardo snags it, brandishes it aloft at "T'ucciderò!", then dumps it off camera. Now, whose noggin are we talking about here? Given the text, I'm afraid the most likely answer is that of *il tradito genitore* himself, Edgardo, Sr. But whosoever, this is high on even the operatic incredulity scale. Well. Things are more settled elsewhere, the costumes are great, the video quality is fine, and at least it's not lazy.

The music does get bashed around a bit. Greager and Donnelly both have burly voices and aggressive attacks. They give us a rude vigor, but not much in the way of tonal beauty, evenness of line or vibrato, or finish of phrase. They're at their best in Wolf's Crag, which requires strutting and roaring—Donnelly even throws in a high A in unison with the tenor at scene's end, and it's a fearsome couple of bars. Sutherland is in marginally bumpier voice than for Paramount, especially at the outset, but there's no important difference in the impact of her performance. Grant does nothing unexpected as Raimondo. His roomy *basso cantante* is pleasing, though, and he is the most stylish vocalist of the male singers. As compared with himself on Paramount, Bonynge makes some judicious adjustments for his soloists and is otherwise the same. Choral and orchestral execution is at a high level—not quite as plush as that of the Met forces, but that isn't always for the worse. The audio quality is first-rate.

———————————

The Legato Classics edition, despite technical deficiencies, is the only one to bring us close to the heart of *Lucia*. Of the two Sutherland performances, the Paramount is the more finely sung, the Kultur the livelier and more fun to watch, as well as closer to complete.

CONRAD L. OSBORNE

ROBERTO DEVEREUX (1837)

A: Queen Elizabeth (s); B: Sara, Duchess of Nottingham (ms);
C: Roberto Devereux (t); D: Duke of Nottingham (bar)

The prolific Donizetti wrote twenty-eight operas for Naples in fifteen years. Small wonder that well before he bade farewell to the city he had come to be regarded as its resident composer. *Roberto Devereux*, the fifty-third of his seventy operas and his last for Naples, was written only nineteen years after his first opera composed for a public theater. That's an average output of almost three operas a year.

Devereux's libretto, drawn from a French play, presents straightforward conflicts in the romantic manner Donizetti habitually favored for his tragedies. Elizabeth is in love with Devereux, whose heart belongs to Sara, the wife of his best friend, who, on learning of their illicit love, changes from advocate to avenger and causes Devereux's death. The sturdiness of its book notwithstanding, the opera's success largely depends on an agile spinto soprano able, as Winton Dean put it, "to discharge the vocal rockets and Roman candles set down for Queen Elizabeth."

Despite the presence of a raging cholera plague, the opera (with the admired Giuseppina Ronzi de Begnis as Elizabeth) had a successful premiere and was mounted with some frequency, especially in Italy, until 1868, when it seemingly expired. After Maria Callas awakened interest in the romantic *bel canto* opera in the 1950s, *Roberto Devereux* was revived from its long slumber in 1964 (appropriately, in Naples) by Leyla Gencer, and later by Montserrat Caballé, its most faithful and persistent champion. Beverly Sills's vivid impersonation of the title role made it a favorite at the New York City Opera from 1970 to 1974.

1975 VAI (VHS)

(Stage Performance, Stereo, Color, Subtitled)
145 minutes

Beverly Sills (A), Susanne Marsee (B), John Alexander (C), Richard Fredricks (D), Wolf Trap Company Chorus, Filene Center Orchestra—Julius Rudel

Wolf Trap: Tito Capobianco (stage director), Kirk Browning (stage director)

There is no video of Beverly Sills in her prime. This one, set down in 1975, first released in 1993, will have to do. It is worth seeing, despite numerous liabilities in performance and presentation, because Sills, even in vocal decline and in a role at least a size too large for her lyric soprano, achieves a rich, complex impersonation of the Queen. She is memorable for incisive musicianship and the unflagging concentration, commitment, and forceful dramatic projection typical throughout her career.

The video shows its age—grainy images, except in close-ups; heavily monitored sound, sometimes afflicted with noise, hum, crackle, dropouts, and always dry (there is little resonance in the Wolf Trap shed).

Tito Capobianco's direction is sensible and usually animated. Ming Cho Lee's effective, uncluttered, almost monochrome settings have been filmed in a warmer, less atmospheric color than that seen in the theater.

Julius Rudel's pacing and shaping of the score is sound, his ensemble's execution disorderly here and there. His reading is vigorous, if never as expressive as it might be. His experience tells in his support of his singers. Elizabeth enlarged Sills's fame in 1970, but hearing this video one realizes the price she paid for assuming it. Her vibrato has loosened, and she does not always trace a firm line. Like the declining Callas in her last five years on stage, Sills tackles her highest hurdles without flinching and reveals the cost of surmounting them with similar courage.

John Alexander is sturdy and stylish, at his best in his prison scene aria. Richard Fredricks offers an agreeable, hefty sound but is deficient in legato skill. Susanne Marsee is slow to warm up, her mezzo a bit quavery until the last act, when she discloses a firmer core of tone.

Roberto Devereux has, in Elizabeth, such a fat part for a good singing-actress, it deserves to be seen as well as heard. Beverly Sills brings Elizabeth to life; but one wishes her performance could have been set down five years earlier.

C. J. LUTEN

Gaetano Donizetti

La Fille du Régiment (1840)

A: Marie (s); B: Tonio (t); C: Sulpice (bs)

onizetti's regimental daughter, who does not sleepwalk, go mad, get beheaded, or immolate herself, is nonetheless a full-fledged *bel canto* prima donna role requiring just as much vocal prowess and charismatic projection as do the tragic operatic heroines of the same era.

For this reason, and despite the legacy of faint praise as "slight" fare, *La Fille du Régiment* has maintained a tenuous yet tenacious hold on public affection through the efforts of the one or two sopranos per generation who have been in a position to champion it.

The presence of a daunting tenor part should not be discounted, though only one known revival has honored a divo's impulse (Metropolitan Opera, 1995, Luciano Pavarotti). Historically, *Fille* has succeeded or failed on the degree of dazzle in the vocalism and lovability in the persona of the artist undertaking Marie.

Unfortunately, even the most brilliant singing cannot entirely immunize this vulnerable light comedy against the effects of directorial condescension. Its special qualities survive intact only when taken on their own endearing terms, leaving the simple, formulaic plot free of vulgarities and topical references. Forced hilarity and trivialized sentiment defeat the delicate balance of elements within a work of genuine finish.

1974 VAI (VHS)

(Stage Performance, Stereo, Color, in English)
118 minutes

Beverly Sills (A), William McDonald (B), Spiro Malas (C), Wolf Trap Company Chorus, Filene Center Orchestra—Charles Wendelken-Wilson

Wolf Trap: Lotfi Mansouri (stage director), Kirk Browning (television director)

In a charming pre-curtain interview, Beverly Sills dubs her own carrot-topped Marie "a Lucille Ball with high notes." What she produces onstage in this English-language *Fille* actually bears a closer resemblance to Irving Berlin's Annie Oakley, though mugging with a musket supplants skeet shooting with a rifle. To a great extent the vastly experienced Sills transcends the strawhat-circuit ambience of this provincial outing, for she never allows her musical integrity to be compromised by the lowbrow artistry surrounding her. On the other hand, often she cannot resist overplaying the "Doin' what comes natur'lly" histrionic possibilities built into this disingenuous staging.

Sills's sustained singing emerges worn and tremulous, though her *fioritura* scintillates consistently enough. Her *acuti* are unsteady, hard in tone, and flat in pitch, belying the diva's superficial show of enjoyment in their emission. She sings "Il faut partir" quite responsibly, always striving for a true legato line. Alas, Sills's search for the radiant shimmer that once was hers in cantilena proves only intermittently fruitful. She easily carries the opera, albeit with a slightly brittle and overbearing vivacity.

William McDonald's sweet, slender, not entirely secure lyric tenor is at the service of a dimwitted bumpkin characterization to which his Grady Sutton build and physiognomy doom him. He manages Tonio's bravura passages honorably if sometimes precariously and his unquestionable sincerity shines through translation inanities.

Spiro Malas's blustery bonhomie as Sulpice might appeal more if it weren't undercut by gruff, lusterless tone quality and indeterminate pitch that particularly damages ensemble tuning.

Muriel Costa-Greenspon scores few points for subtlety, fewer still for her labored, threadbare vocalism. She does convey the Marquise's underlying goodheartedness, and her melt into loving motherhood at opera's end also melts viewer resistance.

Stanley Wexler (fledgling bass rather than aging character tenor) is not believable as the Marquise's old servant Hortentius.

Charles Wendelken-Wilson shepherds his ad hoc forces (peppered with New York City Opera personnel) sensibly, eliciting no discernible sparkle or finesse, holding disaster at bay when accuracy becomes a sometime thing.

Beni Montresor's modest, lightweight (here brightly lit) production, designed to travel with Sills—Houston and San Diego were other stops on its progress—has dated poorly. Its limited proportions cramp crowd scenes and accentuate the already larger-than-life attributes of the prima donna, perhaps deliberately.

Kirk Browning's generous close-ups spotlight Sills's distress on high notes, reveal her regiment of "fathers" as the youths they are, and underscore embarrassing aspects of Lotfi Mansouri's direction: the male peasants, all gapemouthed idiots; the grotesque nobility among the Marquise's party guests, their extraordinary titles dutifully intoned by Hortentius. Two pluses: Marie's lesson from the mincing ballet master (mimed upstage of the "serious" last-act dialogue of Sulpice and the Marquise), and the Duchess of Crackentorp cameo *not* inflated into a scene ruiner.

In sum, an appealing souvenir of what endeared Sills to the American public—her irrepressible love of performing and custom of giving her all at every moment.

1986 KULTUR (VHS)

(Stage Performance, Stereo, Color, Subtitled) 122 minutes

Joan Sutherland (A), Anson Austin (B), Gregory Yurisich (C), Australian Opera Chorus, Elizabethan Sydney Orchestra—Richard Bonynge

Australian Opera: Sandro Sequi (stage director), Peter Butler (television director)

Though some things come less easily to the Joan Sutherland of 1986 than they did in earlier years, her voice remains full, round, and mellow. At the very top the tone is somewhat attenuated and more difficult to sustain than it once was, but it's still steady, dead on pitch, and possessed of a healthy percentage of its wonted crowd-pleasing amperage. "Il faut partir," no longer effortless, impresses for the clarity and voluminousness of the sound and genuineness of the delivery, not to mention a fine trill. An accomplished comedienne, Sutherland enjoys herself thoroughly without ever mocking the opera.

Anson Austin's boyish Tonio, slight enough to be picked up and carried offstage in Act 1, projects a bit of romantic hero potential within this guileless rube role. His substantial, darkish tenor of appealing quality suffers from throatiness, but though lyric passages expose tonal impurities and technical shortcomings, he shirks no challenges: the high C's of "Pour mon âme" are launched with bravado, the last one confidently protracted.

Gregory Yurisich, a baritone Sulpice, belabors the old sergeant's crustiness quotient, sometimes barking when normal volume for his sizable, sturdy instrument would suffice. His inept French grates, and the very odd notion that a Vogue model's stance demonstrates machismo in a soldier is definitely eccentric.

Heather Begg's imposing ruin of a voice serves very well for the Marquise, abetted by her easily ruffled lofty demeanor. Big and intimidating, she convinces even when dragging Dame Joan (no sylph) away at the first-act curtain.

The bit players outsing and outact their Wolf Trap counterparts, the larger chorus makes a more compelling effect, and the whole retains its authenticity in French.

Richard Bonynge leads Donizetti's *opéra comique* as one long breath of fresh air. He exercises scrupulous judgment in matters of texture, rhythmic crispness, and apposite phrasing, slighting neither orchestra nor voices, and judiciously weights the subtle gradations of farce and pathos.

The Act II minuet is but one instance where his stylistic grasp proves revelatory: its almost stifling gentility perfectly embodies Marie's feelings of being trapped.

Sandro Sequi's felicitous direction doesn't tweak the sentimentality of the piece and therefore doesn't defeat it. Though missing no element of humor and providing plenty of amusement, this staging avoids the kind of vaudevillian shtick that compromises Mansouri's version. The latter, apparently predicated on the premise that American audiences must be hit over the head to get the joke, sometimes seems to offer an apology for *Fille* itself. Sequi produces an altogether more stylish and palpably operatic experience.

Henry Bardon's rustic Tyrol and elegant Berkenfeld chateau settings and Michael Stennett's colorful, often whimsical costumes (the Marquise's extravagant coiffures / headgear, Hortensius's canary yellow long coat and top hat) are beautifully shown off in Peter Butler's apt television direction, which allots adequate long-shot time to the full stage picture.

Diva preference aside, there's no contest here: the polished, full-scale, original-language Australian production under Bonynge's expert guidance is the video of choice. Into the bargain, Sutherland at sixty is in more solid, secure vocal estate than Sills at forty-four, and neither cast offers a second important performance.

BRUCE BURROUGHS

Gaetano Donizetti

La Favorita (1840)

A: Leonora (ms); B: Fernando (t); C: Alfonso (bar)

*L*ike so many scores written by Italian composers to French librettos for Paris premieres, Donizetti's sixty-second opera survives as an artifact of reclamation, an Italian prodigal daughter.

Though the version in the composer's native tongue is corrupt, with many of the very particular stylistic choices and refinements of the French original coarsened in a variety of ways, it remains the vehicle for the work's limited but tenacious hold on repertory status in Italy and its vague familiarity elsewhere. Toscanini's strongly voiced approval of *Favorita*, especially the level of inspiration that characterizes the fourth act, was based solely on acquaintance with the back-translated, "musically adjusted" edition.

The one recording of the work in French, not quite complete, dates from 1912; in 1918 *Favorite* disappeared from the Opéra's canon. Eighty years later the words we carry in our heads for the great arias in this piece are the Italian ones, the voices we hear singing them primarily also Italian, with the occasional Spanish or American artist commanding attention as well.

Legitimate evaluation of linguistic or artistic authenticity, important where the extant audio recordings are concerned, becomes moot in view of the lamentable shortfall of the single *Favorita* video currently available.

1952 VIEW (VHS)

(Film, Mono, Black and White, English Narration, Not Subtitled) 90 minutes

Sofia Lazzaro (Sophia Loren) / Palmira Vitali Marini (A), Gino Sinimberghi / Piero Sardelli (B), Paolo Silveri (C), Chorus and Orchestra of the Rome Opera—Nicola Rucci

Cesare Barlacchi (director), Giuseppe Fieno (film director)

Faced with the juxtaposition of this unintentional mimesis, boldly labeled *La Favorita* by its producers, and the seriousness of purpose behind the Metropolitan Opera Guild's opera-on-video review project, I can only fall back upon the words of a far wiser head—the 'possum philosopher Pogo, whose wide-eyed exclamation "Laura mercy!" summed up all persons, events, and situations for which words of description could never be adequate.

That said, one can at least supply a categorical designation, in nineties terminology, for this filmic dinosaur. It is nothing more nor less than a party tape. Hard-core *bel canto* fetishists may convene to partake of the phenomenon of group hilarity, the sort in which we find ourselves prone to ridicule something that under normal circumstances we love and revere.

The draw here, if such there be, is not the art form of opera, not Donizetti's music, certainly not the sound-track vocalism, but the leading lady, the ravishingly nubile teen-aged Sophia Loren (née Scicolone), billed under her first stage name, Sofia (with an *f*) Lazzaro. She is initially seen in chapel, kneeling without expression at a prie-dieu. When she rises and exits, the figure is unmistakable, but the face is round and full, the nose original. These are not the chiseled features familiar from the post-cosmetic surgery period of recent decades. Inexperienced and stiff, Loren lip-synchs decently enough and is eminently watchable.

Listenability is another matter, for from her lips issues the tremolo-ridden, geriatric voice of mezzo Palmira Vitali Marini, who was surely at the very end of a long career when she recorded Leonora's music. Another blossoming actress, Franca Tamantini, appears as the heroine's companion, Inez, dubbed by the pinched, shrill soprano leggiero of Miriam DiGiove. When the two young women "sing" together, the effect is devastatingly funny.

The occasionally comical onscreen hero, tenor Gino Sinimberghi, fronts for the voice of Piero Sardelli. Though Schipaesque at his best, Sardelli's tendency toward nasality mars his contribution, which includes a routinely respectable "Spirto gentil." Paolo Silveri's first-class "Vien, Leonora" is especially compromised by the terrible acoustic, which places the voices in some remote shower stall. The caba-letta, cut to shreds, consists of little more than a climactic high note. Later, "A tanto amor" barely contains a full statement of its theme. None of this matters in the least. In fact, discussing the singing conscientiously may erroneously imply that this video can be taken seriously.

The film quality is uniformly bright, vividly displaying the low-budget, heavy-handed fatuity of the project: pathetically fake beards and tonsures; the fact that Alfonso's face is made up but his neck isn't; motley peasants and soldiers riding pell-mell toward the camera in the corniest battle scene ever photographed; the ludicrous ballet of prancing Saracens in hoedown formations. All this and obnoxious narration to boot.

Nothing of musical or operatic significance exists here, though for some a glimpse of the primal Loren may constitute adequate enticement.

BRUCE BURROUGHS

DON PASQUALE (1843)

A: Norina (s); B: Ernesto (t); C: Malatesta (bar); D: Pasquale (bs)

*M*ax Rudolf told me that as Fritz Busch laid down his baton after conducting the final chord of his first Metropolitan Opera *Don Pasquale* (January 5, 1946), he said in evident surprise to the concertmaster, "Already?" Indeed, given with anything near the grace and polish that it merits, the opera fairly flies by.

To many, *Pasquale* is not merely the last example of *opera buffa* to maintain a place in the repertory, but the best and most lovable as well, for it constitutes the summation and distillation of all the genre's virtues.

What had in previous *buffa* works been treated at somewhat tiresome length is here concise and economical. The familiar participants (superannuated basso suitor; strong-willed soubrette, inappropriate object of his desire; her disadvantaged tenor true love; wily baritone manipulator) are present but not overdrawn in the conventional fashion. There is seldom any lingering in the old repetition-and-variation manner even though the several delightful arias are basically strophic in design. While imbuing every episode with precisely the right balance of melodic beauty, vocal opportunity, and comic impulse, Donizetti has managed to retire those elements of the tradition that customarily made their impact through exaggeration. It is *Don Pasquale*'s birthright to bewitch its hearers.

1955 LEGATO CLASSICS

(Film, Mono, Black and White, Not Subtitled) 107 minutes

Alda Noni (A), Cesare Valletti (B), Sesto Bruscantini (C), Italo Tajo (D), Chorus and Orchestra of Radiotelevisione Italiana, Milan—Alberto Erede

Alessandro Brisson (stage director)

In the 1950s, Milan RAI, as opposed to the Rome Opera, turned out films that were not harebrained pastiches of the works they purported to be but legitimate studio performances of them. This presentation, as musically and dramatically viable as any Italian opera house *Don Pasquale* of its era, does its producers credit.

Alessandro Brisson's affectionate staging is clever within traditional bounds. Luca Crippa's fanciful, highly detailed sets and costumes, better suited to a cinema-sized viewing space, are distractingly "busy" and difficult to look at on a small screen; the innumerable simultaneous high-contrast black-and-white patterns create too hectic a visual context for this mellow comedic gem.

The uncredited film director's preference for close-ups over wide shots reduces the impact of the opera's quartet sections. There are no subtitles, but no moronic narration, either. The cast's lip-synch precision fluctuates considerably, which undermines credibility; Cesare Valletti, for instance, forgets altogether when Ernesto crashes his uncle's wedding crying "Indietro! Mascalzoni!"

Plumpish Alda Noni's Norina, round-faced and hook-nosed, is bewigged and dressed dowdily enough to be mistaken for one of Cenerentola's stepsisters. Neither her appearance nor the sound she makes is attractive enough for this fetching role, though she completely understands its every requirement. Perfect exemplar of the narrow, edgy soubrette soprano so dear to the Italian heart, Noni occasionally suggests an alternative reading of the opera's title: "Don Pasqually."

Valletti portrays a sweet, serious Ernesto. His tone constricts and turns reedy on top when he strives for volume, but the beauty and polish of his phrasing, his elegant portamento style, his fundamentally alluring timbre, and his ravishing mezza voce sweep aside all cavils. In "Tornami a dir" he is simply superb; one tunes out Noni's shrill competence and listens only to the duet's tenor line.

Sesto Bruscantini looks just right and acts with beguiling suavity (butirro wouldn't melt in this urbane Malatesta's bocca). Unfortunately, his slender leggiero baritone lacks the necessary fleetness for Donizetti's nonexpendable vocal curlicues, which leaves an aspect of the doctor's prescribed musical characterization unrealized.

Even so, Bruscantini is Battistini reincarnate next to Italo Tajo, who performed for half a century with hardly any voice. The dual disadvantages of frequently woofy approximation of the vocal line and the wrong physique du rôle would defeat anyone but such a master of intangibles, for Tajo's theatrical instincts begat expertise as well as longevity. Still, a tall, thin Pasquale misses the appeal of a short, round one, and Tajo's studied grotesquerie is too redolent of Rossini's Don Basilio. As rubber-faced and -limbed as Danny Kaye, whom he strongly resembles, the bass delivers a memorable caricature, if one unable to evoke our sympathy.

Alberto Erede conducts a forthright, somewhat inflexible performance, disallowing spurious high notes and making all the (then) customary cuts. The requisite charm is provided by Valletti and Bruscantini (and, in her tough-bird way, Noni) in this accurate documentation of opera buffa standards and practices in Italy during the decade following World War II.

BRUCE BURROUGHS

ANTONÍN DVOŘÁK

RUSALKA (1901)

A: Rusalka (s); B: Foreign Princess (s); C: Ježibaba (ms); D: Prince (t);
E: Spirit of the Lake (bs)

The legend of the Rusalka, the water-nymph who aspires to become human, has inspired many composers, but arguably the most successful opera on this theme belongs to Dvořák. With strong Wagnerian overtones (particularly in the music for the three wood-nymphs, which seems clearly modelled on the music for the Rhine maidens), lush romantic orchestration, and several arias that have become concert favorites, *Rusalka* has been slow to enter the standard repertory largely because of its story line. It's not so easy to get the audience emotionally involved in the plight of a heroine with fins.

A recent new production (1994) at the Met proved popular enough to be revived, however, and the opera's strong score, written at the height of the composer's career, is gradually winning more converts.

1986 KULTUR (VHS)

(Stage Performance, Stereo, Color, in English)
160 minutes

Eilene Hannan (A), Phyllis Cannan (B), Ann Howard (C), John Treleaven (D), Rodney Macann (E), English National Opera Chorus and Orchestra—Mark Elder

David Pountney (stage director), Derek Bailey (video director)

The always adventurous English National Opera teamed up with Channel Four Television in producing this highly imaginative version of *Rusalka*. Director David Pountney has transferred the action from the traditional forest pond (Rusalka's home) to an Edwardian nursery, a premise that works much better than one might expect. The success of this video is due largely to its creators' intense awareness of the camera and the special possibilities of the television screen. It feels like a production made specially for video, not just another plodding reproduction of a stage performance.

When the curtain rises, Rusalka, clad in a nightdress instead of a scaly costume, is lying in bed amidst a Victorian setting, staring at a candle as the overture plays. The camera zooms in on the candle, creating the impression that what follows is her dream. The three Wood-Nymphs (also in white nightdresses) reside in three beds at the far corner of the nursery. When their presence is required, they jump up, and often ride on oversized toys strewn about the room.

During the early exposition, Rusalka sits perched above the action on a swing. Ingeniously, her legs are bound with cloth so that she must crawl, a provocative image that turns Rusalka's inability to walk into a more generalized image of physical and emotional alienation. In the center of the stage is a small wading pool, into which Rusalka dips her feet. (The production further develops the theme of physical infirmity by making the all-powerful Water Spirit an old man confined to a wheelchair.) When Ježibaba finally agrees to make Rusalka "human," she unwraps her leg bindings.

The production is full of many other unexpected images, most of them successful in conveying the atmosphere of a child's dream or nightmare. The guests at the ball in Act II are lowered on swings. The kitchen staff look like puppets, with rag-doll heads obscuring their faces. The point is clear: the terrified Rusalka is actually more "human" than they are.

As Rusalka, Eilene Hannan handles this difficult staging with apparent ease and enthusiasm, all the while singing with a rich, lyrical tone and excellent diction. She looks the part of a svelte nymph and has impressive dramatic instincts. Unfortunately, her Prince, John Treleaven, does not perform on her level; he strains uncomfortably, especially in the upper register, where his pitch is often uncertain as well.

The three Wood-Nymphs are outstanding both vocally and dramatically, as are Ann Howard as the primly dressed Victorian matron Ježibaba and Rodney Macann as the Water Spirit. Phyllis Cannan sings well enough as the Foreign Princess, but seems less comfortable with the staging demands.

But what is most appealing about this version is that it sees and interprets the action through the camera. The story is told in visual imagery possible only in the film / video medium; the focus is not on the singers' faces and mouths as they sing the music. David Pountney has exploited the potential of video to show us another way of thinking about opera.

HARLOW ROBINSON

THE BEGGAR'S OPERA (1728)

A: Polly Peachum (s); B: Lucy Lockit (s); C: Mrs. Peachum (ms);
D: Macheath (t); E: Peachum (bs)

It is difficult today to imagine the effect *The Beggar's Opera* had on its original London audiences in 1728. Operaphiles then were used to mythological, pastoral, and neoclassic plots, sung in Italian, usually composed by foreigners (like Handel). Operas were greatly dependent on vocal display and scenic extravagance. Gay's travesty replaced the sultans and goddesses with then-current London underworld figures, which made salacious allusions to the scandal-tinged government that much easier. Even more daringly, he used common street songs and pop folk ballads for its score. The effect must have been like a *Saturday Night Live* skit that reworked advertising jingles, extended into a full evening's entertainment.

Gay's opera has a well-constructed plot with colorful characters and pithy, ironic dialogue, and the sixty-nine songs are invariably enchanting (some more than others, of course). But the songs *are* short, and were meant to be, in this prototypical ballad opera. Its ditties are used as musical punctuation, unlike the extended arias and ensembles in the usual opera of the times. That is why composers like Benjamin Britten or the arranger Douglas Gamley have attempted to amplify the musical quotient, to satisfy both singers and audiences expecting more of an opera.

Gay's work also suffers from comparisons with its 1920s reworking, the Brecht-Weill *Die Dreigroschenoper*, which has an advantage of a far brassier score and having its complete orchestrations available to modern producers. Only the vocal lines of the tunes chosen by Gay and the basses and overture added by the harpsichordist Johann Pepusch have survived.

1983 HOME VISION (VHS) / PIONEER (LD)

(Studio Production, Stereo, Color) 135 minutes

Carol Hall (A), Rosemary Ashe (B), Patricia Routledge (C), Roger Daltrey (D), Stratford Johns (E), English Baroque Soloists—John Eliot Gardiner

Jonathan Miller (director)

Jonathan Miller's BBC production eschews theatrical exaggeration and tries to make the eighteenth-century language comprehensible, with an easygoing, conversational style. This is quite a challenge. In its more-or-less original version, *The Beggar's Opera* just barely holds the stage today, not only because the diction remains remote, but because few now know or care about the malpractices of Walpole's administration. Furthermore, we can't imagine the surprise of hearing a song then familiar like "Oh London is a Fine Town" fitted out with the words "Our Polly is a Sad Slut!"

Nevertheless, Miller has assembled an able cast to deliver the epigrammatic text, and to sing the songs, if not exactly with a flourish, then with some juice. Stratford Johns is an officious, reasonably slimy arch-fence Peachum— it is useful for American audiences to know that he starred for years as a detective in a British TV police series. Carol Hall is a cool, level-headed Polly Peachum, and Gary Tibbs a fine, fulsome Filch.

Rosemary Ashe, well known in London for several soubrette-tart parts, is a lovely, wicked Lucy Lockit, the jailor's daughter. But it is Patricia Routledge who really shines, as Mrs. Peachum. (Now best known from the British sitcom *Keeping Up Appearances*, she has also been a major operetta / musical star in a long career.) Picking out the initials from stolen handkerchiefs, she is hugely funny as the sarcastic but concerned mother who does like a nip of a cordial, and she sings the little that's given her with plummy precision and the sure style of a musical comedienne.

One can't quite say that about Roger Daltrey, the ex-rocker chosen to portray the highwayman hero, Macheath. His cockney vowels take getting used to, as does his (not unpleasant) sandpapery tenor. For effect, Macheath ought to be, or at least seem, well-bred; Brecht understood this, wanting *his* Macheath to be a polite and businesslike thief. Daltrey is, in the end, a conscientious, but rather mild Macheath, not really charming or sexy enough to explain why Polly and the whores go mad for him.

In such an opera, the singing itself is not the most critical item on the agenda, but there is a tradition of having excellent singers in some of the parts. The original Polly, Lavinia Fenton, reputedly had a lovely voice, and many in the famous, long-running 1920 London revival (at the suburban Lyric, Hammersmith) had fine operatic careers.

Miller has opted for realism and plenty of close-ups in this TV presentation. But this is not quite a naturalist drama, and the theatrical moments want a bit more voltage, especially the tavern scene at the beginning of Act II. In the ultra-realistic Newgate scenes, the attention to detail goes overboard, with unnecessary vignettes of other prisoners and a lot of galumphing on wooden floors. This robs the famous encounter between Polly and Lucy of some of its force ("I'm Bubbled"), and similarly downgrades the effect of Macheath's celebrated complaint, "How Happy Were I. . . ." The delicious effect of having the lowest of creatures (prostitutes and thieves) speaking as decorously as possible is also something that calls for a modicum of theatrical exaggeration.

Many seeing this video will compare it to its nearest counterpart, the 1952 Peter Brook film. In that Technicolor romp (but financial fiasco), a charming Laurence Olivier did his own sweet, if shaky, singing as Macheath, while others were dubbed. Less of the music was used (arranged by Arthur Bliss), but the cast was theatrically memorable: Dorothy Tutin—perfect as Polly—Stanley Holloway, Hugh Griffith, Kenneth Williams, and Athene Seyler as an hilariously druken Mrs. Trapes. The color production (by Georges Wakhevitch) is also far more vivid than the video's subdued palette.

The new video's English Baroque Soloists under John Eliot Gardiner use a version by Gardiner and Jeremy Barlow, who reconstructed the original songs for an earlier recording. Musically, it is all one could wish for. (Unless you prefer, as I do, the Frederick Austin arrangements first used in the 1920 performances.)

Recommended for any devotees of this seminal work, British operetta, certified Routledgeans, and aging fans of The Who.

RICHARD TRAUBNER

PORGY AND BESS (1935)

A: Bess (s); B: Serena (s); C: Clara (s); D: Maria (c);
E: Sportin' Life (t); F: Porgy (bs-bar); G: Jake (bar); H: Crown (bar)

orgy and Bess has come a long way in the sixty years of its existence, though until only recently there was a considerable divergence of opinion in trying to categorize it. It was first seen, briefly, on Broadway in long, operatic form in 1935, to somewhat puzzled audiences. Slimmed down and cut up, with half of its original chorus and orchestra, and with dialogue substituting for recitative, it was transformed into an operetta of sorts (or something somewhere between an *opéra-comique* and a musical) in the early 1940s. This was its first true success. Some of the cuts and recitatives were restored ten years later for a world tour of what was billed as "America's Greatest Musical," while critics abroad called it everything from a *"Negeroper"* or an *"amerikanische Volksoper"* to "Gershwin's operetta."

The 1959 film directed by Otto Preminger had a great deal wrong with it (apart from the omission of huge hunks of the score) but had fascinating performances by Sammy Davis, Jr. and Pearl Bailey. In the mid 1970s, London/Decca recorded *Porgy and Bess* complete, and there was a large-scale production by the Houston Grand Opera. Its reputation now gilded, the opera enjoyed a mammoth Metropolitan Opera production in 1985, and a celebrated Glyndebourne mounting a year later.

1993 EMI (VHS / LD)

(Stage / Studio Performance, Stereo, Color) 184 minutes

Cynthia Haymon (A), Cynthia Clarey (B), Paula Ingram / Harolyn Blackwell (C), Marietta Simpson (D), Damon Evans (E), Willard White (F), Gordon Hawkins / Bruce Hubbard (G), Gregg Baker (H), Glyndebourne Festival Opera Chorus, London Philharmonic, Simon Rattle

Glyndebourne Festival Opera: Trevor Nunn (director—with Yves Baigneres)

Even before the fame of the Glyndebourne *Porgy and Bess* production spread like wildfire after glowing reviews, it had been impossible to accommodate all interested Britons and visitors in the small, original Sussex theatre. The BBC decided to broadcast the opera on television, but apparently it was felt that a studio version, redirected by the stage director Trevor Nunn at Shepperton Studios, would be preferable to a live or taped broadcast.

That decision, I think, is what prevents this video version from being truly riveting. One can well sympathize with the technical problems that would have been faced in taping from so small a theater and stage as Glyndebourne's, but those same cramped limitations are what made the theater version so thrilling, according to many who saw it, especially hearing Gershwin's orchestrations played by a large orchestra in a relatively small space.

The result on your television screen is thus a compromise, half an exciting, movingly-staged theater experience and more than half something resembling the old NBC Opera broadcasts. The singers lip-synch well to the prerecorded sound track, but some spontaneity is sacrificed. There are lots of close-ups when one wants the spectacle of the whole scene.

Trevor Nunn's telling touches are what make this *Porgy* so dramatically engaging from the very start: the sweaty stevedores and shifty cocaine sellers, the crap game by lanternlight, Porgy's two sticks—no little cart here, Porgy whittling during "I Got Plenty of Nuttin'." Sportin' Life is like a weaselly loan shark, the white official truly threatening in his demand to have the dead body "buried tomorrow, or it'll be turned over to the medical students." The fishermen's "Long Pull to Get There" is actually shown, in boats, and "Bess, You Is My Woman Now" is sung by the wharf. John Gunter's production design is also well-detailed, from the dingy newspaper-wallpaper of Porgy's cramped shack to the forlorn, hurricane-battered courtyard outside.

The production really gets going at the end of Act II with Crown's seduction of Bess, and it heats up even more in the final act. The storm sequence is terrifying, highlighted by the "Somebody's Knocking at the Door" chorus and Crown's brilliantly-rendered "Redheaded Woman," sung against Porgy's mounting anger. Porgy's slaying of Crown, followed by Sportin' Life's stealing the knife away, is another chilling moment. And the finale, after Porgy's return from prison, is heartbreaking: his pathetic "Bess, Where's My Bess?" and the surging "Lord, I'm On My Way" at the opera's close, when he drops his crutches to the ground and attempts to walk to New York. The final chords have never seemed so full with the hope that he might just get there, and the despair that he never will.

Simon Rattle and the London Philharmonic are dazzling, and the cast is top-notch, beginning with Willard White's heavy, brooding Porgy and Cynthia Haymon's rich, properly not-too-sympathetic Bess. Gregg Baker is a resoundingly forceful, sensual Crown; Damon Evans is more than the Apollo Theater vaudevillian one often gets as Sportin' Life.

RICHARD TRAUBNER

ANDREA CHÉNIER (1896)

A: Maddalena (s); B: Andrea Chénier (t); C: Carlo Gérard (bar)

It happens now and again that a young artist, under stress and uncertain of the future, produces a masterpiece. *Chénier* was Giordano's biggest success (though not his only one), but it is also a wonderful opera by any standard. Waiting for his lover's father to consent to their marriage, living in poverty, some early hopes dashed, the twenty-eight-year-old composer poured everything he had into this fragile vessel. Perhaps he didn't have much, but there was enough there to enliven three of the four short acts with generally memorable musical / dramatic choices. Giordano, borrowing a lot from *Otello*, some from Catalani, and a little from the early Wagner, helped create what would later be called the *verismo* style. It's truer to call *Andrea Chénier* an early and influential sample of the "new school" of Italian music. Giordano kept the first three acts moving swiftly, impatiently. He used melodic tags rather than expansive melodies, turning a weakness into a strength. Chenier's "Improviso," Maddalena's "La mama morta," both of Gérard's feverish and wonderful arias start as recitative; only at the last minute do they bloom into big Italianate melodies. Puccini was to take Giordano's notion to a higher plane in *La Boheme*; both Mimì and Rodolfo start their famous arias in a conversational tone, melodic expansion is kept to the very end of their set pieces. In *Chénier's* remarkable second act, Giordano doesn't stop for arias at all, or even for set pieces (though the duet "Ora soave" is a popular extract). He mirrors

in eloquent music precisely the flood of ever-shifting emotional and political tides that keep his characters in contact and in danger. One can forgive the final act where the composer's lack of a strong ability to develop his melodies can create a sense of anticlimax. *Andrea Chénier* is a more interesting opera than it is usually given credit for being—the composer's disinclination to use key signatures was an egalitarian choice, not ignorance. For the year or so in which he worked on this opera, Giordano was a genius.

1955 LEGATO CLASSICS (VHS)

(Film, Mono, Black and White, Not Subtitled) 115 minutes

Antonietta Stella (A), Mario del Monaco (B), Giuseppe Taddei (C), Chorus and Orchestra of RAI Milan—Angelo Questa

Franco Corradi (director)

This has the usual problem of RAI productions—the music is canned and the singers have to lip-synch. Not everyone does it easily, and strange mouth movements happen sometimes as soloists try to catch up to themselves on the sound track. Except for that, this is the best *Chénier* on video, and the sound track is thrilling to hear. The producer, Corradi, gives the opera a traditional but imaginative treatment, distinguished by a real sympathy for the idiom and these singers. So right in touch is his work and so committed are his cast one can for long stretches forget the lip-synching. Since these offerings were shot live without retakes there are some mishaps, but overall this has an infectious sweep. Corradi's handling of crowds and minor characters provides an object lesson in unobtrusive command and observation.

The caliber of these performers is rarely matched elsewhere. The many supporting singers are superb—vocally excellent for the most part, and all totally inside their parts and very inventive. This isn't opera to them, it's life. Looking at the other videos one could scarcely imagine so much detail was possible; L'Incredibile (Athos Cesarini) is played as an "exquisite," Roucher (Franco Calabrese) has an arresting dignity and a splendid voice, the lower-class characters are full of color, unction, and danger.

Del Monaco and Stella look wonderful. The tenor, youthful here with a rare vulnerability and sweetness, does almost none of the carrying on for which he was famous (and which can be seen in the Tokyo video). His Chénier is above all a person: ardent, needy, and sensitive. It's amazing to realize, but he has a real talent for camera acting. Stella matches him for tenderness and abandon. One doesn't expect to like or believe in the poet and his Maddalena, but these two are so endearing and recognizable as decent humans caught up in murderous events that the opera becomes very moving. They sound spectacular on the sound track.

Taddei was one of two great Italian baritones of his period (the other was Tito Gobbi). His is an immense voice of glorious impact, and he is a charismatic and detailed actor. He was a short, very chubby man, but like all great actors, uses and transcends his physical appearance. Not for a second is Gérard other than a complex, haunting, and unique human being. Taddei understands and projects that Gérard's actions are rooted in a profound need for love and belonging. His understanding in Act III that he can never have it, and belongs neither with the gentry nor the revolutionaries, makes his the tragic fate in the opera. He is heartbreaking there.

Legato's print is very clear.

1961 UNKNOWN COMPANY (VHS)

(Stage Performance, Mono, Black and White, Subtitled) 118 minutes

Renata Tebaldi (A), Mario del Monaco (B), Aldo Protti (c), Chorus and Orchestra, Tokyo—Franco Capuana

Opera company, stage director, and video director unknown

Starting in the mid-1950s, troupes of Italian singers went to Japan and gave staged performances, which were telecast. This is one of the best. The work of the Japanese technicians is amazing and infuriating. These were a people virtually annihilated fifteen years before, but here they are capturing great stars in full flight. That the prosperous Western democracies did not see fit to telecast performances means that great stars who did not go to Japan—Callas, Rysanek, Vickers, Crespin, Hotter—are largely undocumented in their primes. An excellent copy that sports subtitles in both Kanji and English has been in commercial circulation.

Inevitably there is something of a clash between Italian and Japanese cultures, and a certain politically incorrect humor results. But there is a great fascination in seeing people who were alive and professional before television, who have a complete command of the stage. Certainly there are the usual "old-fashioned" poses and gestures that probably go back to the beginning of opera. But there is also a thrilling, all-out commitment from everybody, not just the stars.

Del Monaco and Tebaldi were especially important in this opera. Both knew Giordano and they sang in the memorial run of this opera at La Scala the year after he died. They *own* this piece, they love every second of it, and they are never at a loss. Their huge, stupendous voices are magnificent. Del Monaco is an opera star, not a media conglomerate. His performance is on a huge scale. All right, it's hammy, but every gesture is filled with feeling. Physically he is relaxed, specific, and plausible in ways none of the "three tenors" ever are. Exiting after the last duet, he leaves so passionately he takes a header into the wings—but emerges for his triumphant curtain call like a champ. He and Tebaldi are both very handsome. She is somewhat less comfortable (at least as caught by the camera), but how beautiful she is! She is wonderfully reactive, the process of falling in love with the eccentric poet is enchantingly detailed in Act I. In Act III her reactions to Gérard are arresting. She is in typical '61 voice—not consistently effortless at the top. But in the final duet (the usual downward transposition is used) she pours out floods of loud and soft floating tone effortlessly.

Gérard is played as a born loser by Aldo Protti. He is shorter than the other men (and in this production that means *short*!), but he has a handsome and expressive face and uses his size to advantage. Gérard's impossible attempt at nobility and his gnawing consciousness of his baseness are remarkably projected. Though Protti rarely sounded impressive on LP, in actual performance one can hear this is a sizable, ripe voice under good if not immaculate control. In fact all the supporting singers—though most were third and fourth stringers in Italy—have good voices and pungent personalities.

Yes, the sets look slapped-together and unstable, the chorus is tentative and somewhat silly, and there are problems in the orchestra, but the skillful Capuana has a feverish rightness of touch that keeps everything moving. Seeing this is to love not just this opera, but *opera* all over again.

1985 HOME VISION (VHS) / PIONEER (LD)

(Stage Performance, Stereo, Color, Subtitled) 130 minutes

Eva Marton (A), José Carreras (B), Piero Cappuccilli (C), Chorus and Orchestra of Teatro alla Scala—Riccardo Chailly

La Scala: Lamberto Puggelli (stage director), Brian Large (video director)

One might title this, "A giantess and others." Poor Eva Marton towers over everybody, especially the tenor and baritone, so she is forever hurling herself to the floor. Sometimes she is made to stand against a conveniently situated trestle so the tenor can hop up and appear to be almost her height. She gives much the best performance here. Hardly Italianate and never vulnerable, she offers considerable personal force and an unwieldy but impressive voice.

One can only wonder what Giordano would have made of the rest. Everything he would have expected has vanished. The supporting singers have neither personalities nor voices—not even the added reverberation helps. The hardy troopers in Tokyo are sublime by comparison. We have the usual heavy-handed "I hate opera, don't you?" modern production. Producer Puggelli provides a clumsy gloss (chaotically photographed) but neglects the humanity that is so abundant in the opera. Pugelli uses projections and traps in a spurious attempt at "cinema," but he has done nothing with the characters. What is one to make of his choices in the first act? The countess's guests all look as if they had sheep on their heads—they have ridiculous huge wigs and death mask makeup. But why isn't Maddalena gotten up the same way? Why doesn't Chénier have a wig? An artist moving in aristocratic circles would hardly have been so rude as not to wear one. Okay, he's making a revolutionary statement—by time-travelling to a barber in the late twentieth century? Poor Carreras looks all moussed up in an all-purpose-tenor do. Had they but thought of it the Jacobins could have added this to the terror. Are we supposed to take a director seriously who plays with slides but pays no attention to his actors?

One suspects Giordano would have been upset by Carreras. He may well have been the most naturally gifted of the "three." In any earlier age he would have worked to secure his high and not-so-high notes. He might have found a teacher who would have warned him about the "drop your jaw, wag your tongue, scream, and hope for the best" school of singing. It can never be said too often—opera acting stems from opera singing. A tenor whose voice isn't working well is not going to be expressive.

Carreras is no shorter than del Monaco and was younger at the time of the taping, but he looks dyspeptic and has no presence. Though Carreras probably consciously eschewed the "hammy" old-fashioned ways of del Monaco, he ends up looking bland and stressed in comparison.

Capuccilli, rather past his best vocally, is an experienced and capable Gérard but rather dull—the ocean of added resonance swallows up his tone. The subtitles are clumsy and confusing—one suspects the translator was not an English speaker.

1985 KULTUR (VHS)

(Stage Performance, Stereo, Color, Subtitled) 120 minutes

Anna Tomowa-Sintov (A), Plácido Domingo (B), Giorgio Zancanaro (C), Chorus and Orchestra of the Royal Opera House—Julius Rudel

Royal Opera, Covent Garden: Michael Hampe (stage director), Humphrey Burton (video director)

This is a shrewd, intelligent production, with a highly competent cast. The producer, Michael Hampe, has good ideas, some of them unusual but telling (in Act III, old blind Madelon, having given her grandchild to the army, is suddenly abandoned by the crowd and left to feel her way out; we get to see the young woman Maddalena redeems from the guillotine). He handles his principals with tact, though the best stage work (if not the best singing) comes from hardy English veterans like Patricia Johnson and John Dobson. As usual in videos nowadays the sound has been "sweetened" considerably—one can hear a balance engineer working feverishly to enhance the singing. Poor Cynthia Buchan's thin voice (she sings Bersi—asking her to behave as though she had the tic douloureux in Act I is among Hampe's few missteps) comes bouncing back through various fields of artificial echo at the start of Act II. One can wonder, therefore, if history will find this a "true" document of what the stars could really do in a big house.

As always, Domingo looks good—it helps that he is tall for a tenor. He has excellent musical instincts—"Si, fu soldato" from Act III is sung with attention to its intricate rhythms, and his phrasing is consistently intelligent. I was not riveted though—his singing as singing is small-scaled and somewhat tentative, especially at the top. Though he avails himself of the standard downward transposition for the final duet, he is uneasy with the high notes and tends to scream, then truncate them. There is no question that in this period he was the most accomplished tenor the world had to offer (though Andrea Chénier was probably not his best role). In that context one may find the performance on this tape worrisome, sad, or, I suppose, wonderful. Tomowa-Sintov had a naturally resplendent voice that I find more appropriate in size and color for this music than the tenor's. She is not absolutely secure at the extremes of her range. She is highly intelligent but not transporting in the role. Zancanaro, also rather tall, is a solid, conventional Gérard.

The Tokyo performance, with some anomalies in the behavior of chorus and extras, is one of a kind—thrilling and authoritative with stunning work from two great stars. Despite lip-synching and some studio mishaps, Legato's tape of the RAI film is also thrilling, with a great Gérard (Taddei) and marvelous work from Stella and del Monaco. Neither Domingo nor Carreras inhabits the title role and it's hard not to feel that the style, fervor, and vocal and histrionic sureness of touch Giordano probably expected had vanished. Marton and Capuccilli at La Scala have some of the right stature and intent, Carreras is undeniably nice-looking and sincere. But the splashy production is irritating and neither it, the way it is photographed, nor the subtitles will help the Chénier novice. On the whole, the Covent Garden performance is probably the more persuasive and illuminating of the two.

ALBERT INNAURATO

ORFEO ED EURIDICE

(1762; revised 1769 and 1774)

A: Amor (s); B: Euridice (s);
C: Orfeo (originally male c; also ms, ct, t, or bar)

The premiere of *Orfeo* was sung in Italian, with a castrato, in Vienna. The opera was subsequently revised, and it was then further altered and augmented for a tenor and performed in French in 1774. Almost a century later Berlioz edited it for the brilliant mezzo-soprano Pauline Viardot. (For further detail see Roland Graeme's *Orfeo* chapter in *The Metropolitan Opera Guide to Recorded Opera*.) The conventional version uses varying selections from all of these editions, sung in Italian.

Over the last century mezzo-sopranos have continued to perform the opera most often, although the tenor Leopold Simoneau has recorded the French version with exquisite effect, and the lyric baritone Dietrich Fischer-Dieskau has also essayed Orfeo. Now countertenors are performing the role; a particularly striking example is discussed below. Nevertheless, the mezzo-soprano option remains central. Louise Homer (at the Met with Toscanini), Alice Raveau, Margarete Klose, Kirsten Thorborg, Risë Stevens, Kathleen Ferrier, and Shirley Verrett have all been notable Orfeos, and one of the most moving performances of the hero's climactic aria has been recorded (in French) by Maria Callas, sounding very much like a mezzo. Something in the role lends itself to this voice. There is nothing effeminate in Orfeo, but his passion is at first as much spiritu-

ally joyous as it is sensual, and later it is seen under the shadow of loss. What is needed in the role is not so much macho implacability as encompassing warmth of feeling and persuasive power, and then mature despair. The mezzo voice, guided by infinite dramatic sensitivity and musical intelligence, seems to provide all the qualities needed, and an inimitable musical grace as well. Now, as new generations of countertenors explore their expressive capacities, they may attain similar mastery.

1982 HBO (VHS) / PIONEER (LD)

(Stage Performance, Stereo, Color, Subtitled)
125 minutes

Elizabeth Gale (A), Elisabeth Speiser (B), Janet Baker (C), Glyndebourne Festival Chorus and London Symphony Orchestra—Raymond Leppard

Glyndebourne Festival: Peter Hall (stage director), Rodney Greenberg (video director)

With this series of performances in 1982, Janet Baker retired from the operatic stage. She has written that it was a time of turmoil and desolation. The trial of Orfeo was her own trial, she felt, as well: "The gods know the fatal weakness in all of us and choose the very thing they know we cannot do. Of course Orfeo fails the test. Of course everybody does." She wrote, though, of the closing of the rehearsal period that "until today, his journey has overwhelmed me; now I am able to stand aside from it, and all the emotions which the character and the score have let loose in me can be channelled into the proper source—our performances." And then, after the opening performance, "From the moment the curtain rose until it came down again I was filled with a tremendous calm."

The control and the spiritual freedom implied here are hallmarks of her performance. There are many things in the production, dramatic and musical, with which one disagrees, but *her* performance is sovereign in its intelligence, sensitivity, and musical mastery. Throughout she maintains a simple but infinitely suggestive eloquence. Even her concluding aria in Act I ("Addio, addio, mei sospiri"), though brightly sung, has an introspective edge. In Act II she does not command; she is a master of persuasion. The vocal tone is concentrated, the line impeccable, even in "Che faro senza Euridice," here staged in a way that might defeat anyone else.

The other singers are ordinary. Elisabeth Speiser has an impure sound for Euridice, though her Act III duet with Baker is filled with welcome tension. Elizabeth Gale has an earthy, somewhat juiceless voice for the god Amor. Leppard conducts disappointingly; what emerges is graceful but often disaffectingly casual. Peter Hall's production, surprisingly, imposes the awkward on the conventional. The basic concept involves flowing robes, earth colors, and areas of symbolic light. With this we get an Amor clumsily lowered from the flies and dressed in passionate purple silk—a better idea in the mind than on stage, where it suggests satire. The Gate of Hell has a red glow, and the animals do calisthenics during the dance music; not much threat there. The succeeding serenity does not escape dullness. Euridice dies again on stage, and Orfeo is forced to sit on the floor cradling her throughout his climactic aria: persuasive perhaps in a painting, but distractingly uncomfortable in real time on stage. The final dances introduce a number of other physical distractions. Despite all of this, however, Baker

seizes the opportunity to give us the essence of her art, and her Orfeo.

1991 HOME VISION (VHS)

(Stage Performance, Stereo, Color, Subtitled) 80 minutes

Jeremy Budd (A), Gillian Webster (B), Jochen Kowalski (C), Chorus and Orchestra of the Royal Opera House—Hartmut Haenchen

Royal Opera, Covent Garden: Harry Kupfer (stage director), Hans Hulscher (video director)

Originally conceived for the Komische Oper in Berlin, in London this production won the Olivier Award for the Outstanding Achievement in Opera. It's Harry Kupfer's contemporary variation on themes suggested by what's-his-name's opera. Among the theatrical devices you will find the usual suspects: mylar screens reflecting the audience, jeans and leather jackets, an electric guitar, a glass-and-steel technocracy, a madhouse, a Man with One Red Shoe (Euridice's), the television image as the reflection of a soul, the chorus in formal dress seated stage left of the orchestra, and occasional pantomime doubles for a couple of the characters. Euridice dies in a traffic accident. The brief program notes tell us that in Kupfer's view Orfeo sacrifices his life to create art out of his suffering; what we get on stage are several striking but garbled suggestions, but not that one.

Despite all of this, the production has some sequences of arresting power. The lighting is atmospheric throughout and the huge revolving glass-and-steel structures suggest at various times either entrapment or immense spiritual serenity. The countertenor Jochen Kowalski is a charismatic Orfeo and performs with agonized conviction, physically and musically, even when asked to do some unconvincing theatrical posturing. The voice seems to be of considerable size and colored for passion: the closest I have heard in emotional effect to what we are told of the male sopranos and altos of Gluck's own time. If we must have a boy soprano as Amor, Jeremy Budd is on this evidence one of the best since the old records of Ernest Lough and Derek Barsham, and Gillian Webster is a lovely Euridice. Hartmut Haenchen is the spirited but sensitive conductor. His "Che farò senza Euridice," for example, is taken at a brisk tempo; the usual effect of this is to make the lament sound inappropriately jolly, but here it sounds all the more deeply impassioned. In all, half of Kupfer's adventurous leaps fall short, but when they do not, he and his crew provide some remarkably provocative and moving sequences.

Janet Baker's moving farewell performance must be the *Orfeo* of record, although Jochen Kowalski offers a fascinating voice and performance in the context of Harry Kupfer's problematic production.

LONDON GREEN

FAUST (1859)

A: Marguerite (s); B: Siébel (ms); C: Faust (t); D: Valentin (bar);
E: Méphistophélès (bs)

The fundamental reasons for *Faust*'s banishment to the outskirts of our repertory have to do with questions of belief: what constitutes salvation? What's the nature of evil, and how can it be personified onstage? How important is the betrayal of love? But there is also the question of whether in fact the piece can be performed anymore. Forget the days of French Style, when great singers and stage temperaments issued from the native cultural milieu, and their aesthetic was alive throughout the Occident. That's seventy-five years behind us. *Faust* has been kept on life support ever since by Slavs and Italians, Spaniards and Americans, serving up culturally polyglot and often inelegant performances that at least infused the superb melodies with juicy tone and some sort of passion, and from time to time suggested a Romantic theatricality. Now, important performers and conductors seem uninterested in *Faust*, even when paid to play it, and directors poke at it with conceptual sticks. If they don't believe in it, we're certainly not going to, and the future of this grand old show is not promising.

1973 LEGATO CLASSICS (VHS)

(Stage Performance, Mono, Color, Subtitled in Japanese) 159 minutes

Renata Scotto (A), Milena Dal Piva (B), Alfredo Kraus (C), Lorenzo Saccomani (D), Nicolai Ghiaurov (E); Chorus and Orchestra of Lirica Italiana, Tokyo—Paul Ethuin

Opera company, stage director, and video director unknown

By happy coincidence, the sole video *Faust* is a splendid example of the type of international performance alluded to above, and makes a stronger case for the opera than any theater performance I've seen in decades. For much of its duration, this is simply an unusually well-sung, big-house *Faust*, and that is satisfying enough. But in the Garden Scene (especially from Marguerite's "Pauvre ange!" through to the end), and intermittently thereafter, it latches onto something quite beyond that, and all our questions of belief suddenly have very powerful answers. The opera turns on Marguerite's fate, and Scotto provides not simply modesty, charm, and vocal prettiness, but passion and strength. We see and hear her unreserved surrender to romantic intoxication, to love as a consecration, and then the force of her faith against despair and madness. She projects an innocence not of passivity, but of unedited emotion. Scotto is not, of course, the only soprano ever to understand these elements. But she creates here a rare unity of singing and acting technique: the voice pours out the life of the character, and the camera discloses that life being lived—each moment's experience being taken in, comprehended and felt, then generating the next sung line. This almost never happens in operatic performance. Only Valentin's death fails to come off for her, owing to some strange staging and a piece of hokum at the end. Except for three harsh top notes, she is in superb voice.

Kraus is also excellent. His lean tenor, so clear and well tuned, is in fresh, strong estate. Though his idea of line in this music is rather literal, it is also firm. He knows where the technical effects of the role lie, and every one of them comes off—quite breathtakingly in the first meeting and throughout Act II. Dramatically, he has dash and is serious and attentive but seldom personally urgent. He doesn't find much in the opening scene, which is the tenor's now-or-never chance to pull us in.

Ghiaurov is in spectacular voice. That means singing of power and beauty, pliable of texture but solid at the core. He rises to the big moments with an easy command and leaves indelible voiceprints on bits of transition like "Allons! a tes amours," near the end of the Kermesse. The bottom of his range, often its limitation, sits easily here. As an actor he is a divo presence, but his Mephisto is merely a big, sneering clown without a problem in the world. He's no real threat, and the character has no tension.

Neither Dal Piva nor Saccomani has much to offer as a thespian, but both have rich voices and solid techniques that give their music plausibility and importance and restore grand opera size to parts that are persistently undercast. And though Paul Ethuin is not a high-profile conductor, he leads a perfectly shipshape, well-paced *Faust*. His orchestra is good and his chorus very alive, both musically and theatrically, though occasionally odd of tone.

On the audio / visual front, there's plenty to complain of. Lighting levels are sometimes too low for good definition. There's intermittent blurring of image and bleeding of color. I couldn't entirely expunge tracking trouble in the last twenty minutes. Audio quality is only adequate. There are annoying snips at the two act breaks, where the Japanese announcer breaks in over the music, and unless you read Japanese, the subtitles are just visual flak. The production itself, however, has interest and integrity. A well-designed unit set combines with sharply defined lighting to give the action flow and impetus and to keep focus on Marguerite's descent through Acts III and IV. The edition is surprisingly complete, restoring once-customary cuts in the Kermesse chorus and Garden Scene duet, as well as the first tableau of Act III. But there are regrettable excisions to accommodate Scotto: the second verse of "Roi de Thulé" (which tells half the story?!) and all of "Il ne revient pas," so that the restored tableau comprises Siébel's second song and oddments of recitative and chorus. Some version of Walpurgis was staged, but is omitted from the tape. Despite these problems, I can't imagine any lover of the work, or of Romantic opera in general, remaining unmoved by the performance.

CONRAD L. OSBORNE

ROMÉO ET JULIETTE (1867)

A: Juliette (s); B: Stéphano (ms); C: Roméo (t); D: Mercutio (bar);
E: Frère Laurent (bs); F: Capulet (bs)

At the close of the nineteenth century Gounod's *Roméo et Juliette* was one of the two most popular works in the operatic repertory. The other was the same composer's *Faust*. During the fifteen-year period 1891–1906, *Roméo* opened the Metropolitan Opera's season on no fewer than six occasions; *Faust* did so twice.

Times have changed. Relegated to "period piece" status, *Roméo* now emerges only when a tenor and soprano materialize who approach the average cineaste's acceptable image of the doomed lovers. It was inevitable that the principal casting criterion for these roles should have become physical appearance, though the sacrifice can be considerable if visual credibility far outweighs artistic credentials.

The endomorphic figures of some great Roméos and Juliettes of yore, titter-provoking when viewed in photographs, housed voices and sensibilities that completely satisfied this work's demands: full-throated but polished lyricism, eloquent but refined expressivity, passionate but bridled intensity, and the rarefied art of projecting on a legitimately operatic scale what is essentially an intimate style. Without these specific elements that distinguish it as a French Romantic opera, *Roméo* might as well be done in translation, eliminating pronounced accents and rendering generic vigor and broad-stroke musicality bearable.

1994 KULTUR (VHS)

(Stage Performance, Stereo, Color, Subtitled)
170 minutes

Leontina Vaduva (A), Anna Maria Panzarella (B), Roberto Alagna (C), Francois LeRoux (D), Robert Lloyd (E), Peter Sidhom (F), Chorus and Orchestra of the Royal Opera House—Charles Mackerras

Royal Opera, Covent Garden: Nicolas Joël (stage director), Brian Large (television director)

Nicolas Joël's steamy post-Freudian take on Romeo and Juliet finds validation in the exceptional dramatic capabilities of Roberto Alagna and Leontina Vaduva, though not necessarily in the musical characterizations of Gounod or the seemly sensibility of the Barbier-Carré adaptation of Shakespeare's play. Joël's young lovers, despite their fixation on each other, are at bottom profoundly self-absorbed and prone to abstraction.

The sympathetic and persuasive Vaduva, a typical cart-before-the-horse singing actress of the post-Callas era, emotes splendidly but lacks an adequate vocal method. Moments owning a bit of glow or vibrancy give way to stretches of harsh, astringent tone quality, intonation problems, and rough-hewn phrasing. Vital notes above the staff, attenuated and clipped, disclose poor breath support. A lackluster waltz song, beclouded by Juliette's already encroaching neuroticism, presages the later "philtre" aria, done as a mini–mad scene. The soprano's protracted, open-mouthed crawl onto the bier before the final curtain may be the longest operatic collapse on video.

Alagna's wonderful Roméo combines an

ideal appearance, alluring if slightly-too-dark vocal timbre, aristocratic bearing, excellent French, and superior stylistic understanding with a passion and conviction that are never exaggerated. Fast-tracked to superstardom by zealous functionaries and pundits, he is not yet completely secure technically, therefore not beyond peril. His vocal center of gravity is too low, impeding comfortable tenorism at the very top of the range—which, though generally in pitch, doesn't ring out freely, tending instead toward constriction or throatiness. Nonetheless, Alagna's is the one consistently steady voice in this performance.

Robert Lloyd's believable Hal Holbrook look-alike Frère Laurent produces a cavernous, woolly tone that wobbles when sustained, and he addresses bridegroom *Ro-mé-o* with all the balefulness of Ramfis intoning "Radamès!" in *Aida's* Judgment Scene.

Francois LeRoux, no paragon of Gallic artistic virtue, deploys a tremulous, diffuse baritone of mediocre quality and cannot conjure Mercutio's bravado either vocally or dramatically. He delivers a feeble "Queen Mab" ballad and a bumbling third-act challenge and duel scene that fails to convince on any level.

Capulet, once the province of Journet and Plançon, nowadays falls to a decent second stringer (here Peter Sidhom) rather than a leading bass, an aesthetic (or fiscal) economy that diminishes the role's impact.

Anna Maria Panzarella's perky Stéphano and Sarah Walker's endearing Gertrude satisfy, but remaining cast members are either too mature or too immature vocally to do justice to their assignments.

Conductor Mackerras gets right to it with a vivid Prologue and never lets down, balancing Gounod's lyrical and dramatic accents adroitly throughout and emphasizing rhythmic vitality in the party scenes. Alagna, chorus, and orchestra are the maestro's only accomplished allies where musical accuracy and idiomatic expressivity are concerned.

Carlo Tommasi's flexible, bare-bones sets are shamed by his sumptuous costumes. Brian Large's tight close-ups capture the volatile Vaduva's anguished facial contortions and also reveal that Alagna looks good no matter what emotion he is embodying or how high he is singing.

BRUCE BURROUGHS

AGRIPPINA (1709)

A: Agrippina (s); B: Poppea (s); C: Nerone (t); D: Ottone (bar);
E: Claudio (bs)

It is to Domenico Scarlatti, so the story goes, that we owe the existence of *Agrippina*. The twenty-four-year-old Handel, in the course of his three-year sojourn in Italy, was spotted by Scarlatti playing the harpsichord at a Venetian masked ball and was (in the words of John Mainwaring, a contemporary biographer) "strongly importuned" by him to compose an opera. "But there was so little prospect of either honor or advantage from such an undertaking that he was very unwilling to engage in it. . . . At last, however, he consented and in three weeks he finished his *Agrippina*."

The speed of composition was undoubtedly aided by the fact that Handel lifted much of the material from his own earlier works and dipped into the music of other composers as well. He was also fortunate in his librettist, Cardinal Vincenzo Grimani, whose position as a church dignitary did not cause him to shrink from the erotic undercurrents that pervade the tale of Agrippina, one of history's great female schemers.

As for Handel's doubts about the "prospect of honor," when *Agrippina* opened in Venice on the day after Christmas in 1709, it ran for twenty-seven consecutive performances. Mainwaring's account is vivid: "The audience was so enchanted with this performance that a stranger who should have seen the manner in which they were affected, would have imagined they had all been distracted. The theater, at almost every pause, resounded with shouts and exclamations of 'Viva il caro Sassone!' [Saxon] and other expressions of approbation too extravagant to be mentioned. They were struck with the grandeur and sublimity of his style: for never had they known till then all the powers of harmony and modulation so closely arrayed, and so forcibly combined."

1985 HOME VISION

(Stage Performance, Stereo, Color, Subtitled) 160 minutes

Barbara Daniels (A), Janice Hall (B), David Kuebler (C), Claudio Nicolai (D), Gunter von Kannen (E), London Baroque Players—Arnold Östman

Schwetzingen Festival: Michael Hampe (stage director), Thomas Olofsson (video director)

While *Agrippina* is a comic opera in which lovers spy on one another, hypocrisies are laid bare, and there is much cavorting in the boudoir, the music itself is serious—it could be (and had been) fitted to other situations, and its arias of triumph, revenge, and despair have the Handelian ring familiar in works of much more solemn import. The Schwetzingen Festival production handles this dichotomy well, in a staging of the utmost elegance, resplendent in costumes of late-eighteenth-century velvet and gold braid, and with a cast of singers who, with the lift of an eyebrow or the tug of a bodice, convey the archness and the hidden motives of their maneuvers.

Reigning over all, not only as the puller of strings but in the effectiveness of her characterization, is soprano Barbara Daniels, who flies through Handel's coloratura vocal writing with ease and in camera close-ups lets the complex array of her thoughts pass deliciously (and maliciously) across her face. (The camera work and the absence of applause between numbers suggest that this television production was filmed without an audience present, though we see the festival crowd at the beginning and end of the performance.) Daniels embraces every nuance of her role, whether revealing a more-than-motherly attachment to her son Nero or a somewhat overheated intimacy with the pert Poppea (sensuality does not frighten the Schwetzingen folk). Her delivery of one of the opera's impressive arias, "Pensieri, voi mi tormentate," with its contrasting sections of slow lament and brilliant fireworks, is a tour de force.

She is ably balanced by the fetching and not-so-dumb Poppea of Janice Hall, whose bright soprano and flirtatious manipulation of surrounding suitors fulfill the part delightfully. The sparkling agility of her voice is in no way hampered by the fact that some of the demanding vocalism is delivered from a supine position on a very wide red bed—some of it, indeed, from beneath the sheets, where she is joined by her principal admirer.

The men, with the exception of a sluggish baritone in the role of Ottone (originally for contralto), hold their own very well in the face of the formidable ladies. The vaulting tenor of David Kuebler, a Schwetzingen regular, makes Nero more than a mere mama's boy and displays some fine athletic singing; Gunter von Kannen, as the Emperor Claudius, deports himself with appropriate pomposity and sings in a slightly bullish manner that is, in itself, fitting.

Some half-dozen arias are omitted in this performance, and not all the da capo repeats are taken. Scholarly shortcomings, perhaps; but the orchestra of period instruments, knowingly conducted by Arnold Östman, provides enough authenticity to please all but the most academically inclined.

SHIRLEY FLEMING

GIULIO CESARE (1724)

A: Cleopatra (s); B: Sesto (s or t); C: Giulio Cesare (c or bar);
D: Cornelia (c); E: Tolomeo (c or bs); F: Achille (bs)

The issue of whether Handel's Italian operas can speak directly to a present-day nonspecialist audience remains an open one. That they worked in their time, according to their conventions, is indisputable; but, despite one's fondest wishes, not all conventions travel out of their own time equally well. There is a "castrato problem," a "no ensembles" problem, a "*da capo* aria" problem.

Each of these has its historical explanation. The music for the high-pitched male roles (whether originally written for castratos or for women dressed as men) definitely does sound better, more convincing and musical, at its original treble pitch; but few countertenors command the color and variety to do justice to these long roles, and to opera audiences casting women in male roles suggests a theatrical premise of light make-believe, entertaining but not to be taken seriously. As to the near-exclusive reliance on arias, each one may be beautiful and inspired in its own right, but dozens of them in a row, separated only by lengthy harpsichord-accompanied recitative, and all in the same ABA form, do not make for the variety that opera audiences have come to expect. The difficulty becomes all the greater if the plot conflicts are not made clear and the audience is not drawn into the characters or the outcome (it cannot be assumed that this will happen; audiences must be *made* to care).

The last of these points may be the greatest reason for *Giulio Cesare*'s relative popularity.

We do not need to be told who Caesar and Cleopatra were, or why their relationship matters. And since the music Handel wrote for them (exposing one facet at a time, according to the conventions of the style, in eight arias each) is of surpassing beauty and penetration, this story can carry an audience past a great deal of intrigue involving other characters who are not instantly familiar except to history buffs. The three video versions of the opera make a fascinating comparison, as different in their dramatic and musical assumptions as they could possibly be.

1979 VIEW (VHS)

(Stage / Studio Performance, Stereo, Color, in German, Not Subtitled) 120 minutes

Celestina Casapietra (A), Eberhard Buchner (B), Theo Adam (C), Annelies Burmeister (D), Siegfried Vogel (E), Gunther Leib (F), Berlin State Opera Chorus and Orchestra—Peter Schreier

Berlin State Opera: Erhard Fischer (stage director), Georg F. Mielke (video director)

A production in German without subtitles is likely to find few takers in the English-speaking market—and a good thing too, in the case of this video, whose sole merit is as a demonstration of one historical stage of performance practice.

In fact, the "old" way of doing Handel opera probably deserves a fairer representation than this, which has not even the old-fashioned virtue of great vocalism to recommend it; one is reminded repeatedly that some aspects of performance have indeed improved over the past twenty years. Of course all the male roles are put down an octave for tenors or basses (to be fair, Handel himself made Sesto a tenor at a revival—one of the arias he added is used here—but even then there remained five treble voices; here there are two). All manner of abbreviation is practiced: omitting many whole scenes and arias, deleting the return to the A section, performing only the initial A, abbreviating even that. Once cuts had been determined, the guiding principle seems to have been that all remaining notes were sacred and not to be tampered with. Unless I dozed off for a moment, not a whisper of ornamentation is essayed at any point. Recitatives are rendered in strict notated rhythm (allowing for the effect of the translation), and the only appoggiaturas allowed into recitative are the ones printed in older vocal scores.

The visual scheme (scenery by Gustav Hoffmann, costumes by Christine Stromberg) favors black, bronze, and red, with the occasional metallic glint—not without a certain severe beauty, but heavy and monotonous. Costumes hint at ancient Rome while keeping everyone well covered; settings tend toward the severely geometrical (a pyramid of steps against curtains, and so on). Mostly singers stand and deliver, and their singing is not remotely magnetic enough to justify the procedure. Within the limitations, the best work is provided by Vogel and Leib, a solid bass and a pleasant baritone plowing dutifully through. Buchner's serviceable *spieltenor* is not the instrument to make Sesto's arias as gripping as they can be, and Burmeister hoots away boringly. As Caesar, Adam's authoritative manner only minimally offsets his dry bass-baritone and shameless barking of florid music. Casapietra's soprano is not unattractive, but unvaried and used without imagination; her limited mobility makes for some apprehension as Cleopatra's final florid showpiece approaches, but this does not daunt the soprano who deleted "Per pietà" from her *Così Fan Tutte* recording: she solves this obstacle by

omission too. Schreier conducts neatly and musically according to his lights, but with a constant deadly moderation and literalness. This environment adds the final leaden touch to a discouraging production.

1984 CASTLE OPERA (VHS) / PIONEER (LD)

(Stage / Studio Performance, Stereo, Color, in English) 179 minutes

Valerie Masterson (A), Della Jones (B), Janet Baker (C), Sarah Walker (D), James Bowman (E), John Tomlinson (F), English National Opera Chorus and Orchestra—Charles Mackerras

English National Opera: John Copley (stage director), John Michael Phillips (video director)

The English National Opera production (translation by Brian Trowell) stands as an example of the approved way of doing Handel circa 1980. Cutting is generally confined to whole arias (a great deal of the Sesto subplot is gone completely, including some arias performed on 1979 View); one of those remaining is reduced to merely an A section. Recitatives (also curtailed) are rhythmically flexible and graced with appoggiaturas, reprises of arias are ornamented, Handel's vocal registers are respected. The designs (scenery by John Pascoe, costumes by Michael Stennett) provide some beautifully tinted vistas, a late-twentieth-century slant on Baroque visions of classical times. Mackerras's conducting is that of a master musician who knows about style and drama. It is all highly admirable.

It is also a bit dull. The entrance of attendants or guards to provide some excuse and enlivening for the final A section of each aria becomes exceedingly predictable, and the restrained good manners of all the cast do not readily suggest dramatic matters of any great import. The most gripping singing comes from Jones and Walker, two superb mezzos with contrasting approaches: the former masterful at finding the point of ornamented writing while rendering it with a virtuoso's precision, the latter imaginative enough to personalize every line. Both make memorable impressions (even Cornelia's endless lamenting becomes enthralling) despite the cuts that remove more and more of their scenes as the work progresses. Baker, by contrast, has an intensity and seriousness that ensure one's attention but less to work with vocally, having at this stage neither tonal plush nor real florid command. (Some of her solos are transposed up a whole tone.) Masterson renders Cleopatra's music neatly and musically and looks suitably magnetic in her succession of gorgeous gowns. However, there is a carefulness in her vocal delivery, often pushed by the writing into hints of hardness and flutter, with little of the elasticity of phrasing and dynamics by which such music lives. Bowman's unvaried countertenor makes little of Ptolemy's music, and he is the one principal character unflatteringly costumed—possibly to deliberate dramatic purpose, but his bulbous pumpkin-colored costume and asp-circleted bald pate evoke nothing so much as a visitor from outer space. Tomlinson's stentorian delivery does little to justify Achilla's presence in the drama. All of these people are, in their way and under the right circumstances, good singers, but the demands of an opera like this make little allowance for limitations or miscasting.

1990 LONDON (VHS / LD)

(Stage / Studio Performance, Stereo, Color, Subtitled) 237 minutes

Susan Larson (A), Lorraine Hunt (B), Jeffrey Gall (C), Mary Westbrook-Geha (D), Drew Minter (E), James Maddalena (F), Dresden State Orchestra—Craig Smith

Peter Sellars (stage director, video director)

Some viewers will know immediately that this production is not for them. The setting is the terrace of the Cairo Hilton (scenery by Elaine Spatz-Rabinowitz, costumes by Dunmya Ramicova), visibly the worse for a recent military action, and Caesar is the U.S. President who has just flown in to oversee the aftermath. Curio dashes through the opening *coro* in secret-service attire, walkie-talkie at hand, securing the perimeter and organizing crowd responses. The President addresses the populace in a prepared speech, and when he mixes up his pages toward its end, his improvised filling-in is the concluding cadenza.

The thing is, all of this works. In the first five minutes we know who Caesar and Curio are in relation to the others, and even the laugh that the "cadenza" gag evokes has served (without our quite knowing it) to draw us into the aria convention and accept it as a valid means of communication. So it goes throughout: excesses and silliness there assuredly are along the way, but vivid realization of the drama through its music too. Sellars is sharp enough even to dramatize our own awareness of the eternal challenge of how to stage the return to the A section in all these arias; in lighter moments of that sort he'll throw in a little dance step, a reentry with bath toys, or some similar gesture of complicity with the audience. His performers are called on to alternate among realistic behavior, bursts of synchronized movement, and gestures that seem to sculpt the music in air. By such means Sellars keeps us shifting among different levels of reality and involvement: now taking the modern setting literally, now using it as an analogue for the historical figures, now striking through to universal feelings. He does run into a real problem at the end, when the triumphant union of the royal pair jars with his skeptical attitude toward heroism (apt enough for most of the drama) and he resorts to glosses about capitalism and other convenient targets. But at the crucial points along the way he shows how seriously he takes the situation: "Piangerò" has probably never been staged so simply (Cleopatra on the floor, blindfolded in near-darkness) or so affectingly.

Musically, the production holds its own easily with the others. These are not international names for the most part, but they all have strengths well attuned to the vocal demands, and Smith's urgent and stylish conducting spurs them to feats of virtuosity unmatched on the other productions. Gall and Minter both have velocity and tonal variety beyond that of most countertenors, and they create characters—a political Caesar who still can succumb to feminine appeal, a surly spoiled-kid-brother Ptolemy—that are true to the story and barely hinted at in the other productions. Larson's light soprano has some nice pliancy in it for Cleopatra's music; some moments push her into an edgy thinness, but she's consistently expressive and idiomatic. Hunt too, with a gutsier voice, consistently finds the point of her music and communicates it with almost frightening intensity; she is called on to carry out some of Sellars's wilder ideas (Sesto deliberately has a snake bite him) and does so without forfeiting believability for a moment. Maddalena is the sole Achilla to bring out some humanity in the man and some magnetism in his music. The others, if less distinctive, are still equal to the considerable demands, and they all utter Handel's language with the assurance of native speakers. They also follow through on their dramatic intents with rare conviction and continuity.

The text is essentially a complete rendition of the text of Handel's first production, with some of his later alternatives substituted but no numbers or recitative omitted; Nirena, lacking any solo as first conceived, even gains an aria from a later production. Ornamention is plentiful, unpredictable, and apt to the performers. Original vocal registers are preserved, and a variety of approaches is taken to the treble-male issue: two are countertenors, Sesto is a trouser role for a woman (as he was for Handel), and Nireno is turned into a female servant (as Handel did in revival). This production stands alone among these in assigning the "choral" passages correctly to the principal singers, and in having a visible onstage orchestra for the "Parnassus" scene.

The Sellars production on London is the one that shows what a strong and beautiful work this opera is, and does justice to nearly all of it. It is also the only complete one, and the only one in Italian. For those put off by its approach, the 1984 ENO production may be pretty and tasteful enough to satisfy.

JON ALAN CONRAD

XERXES

(SERSE) (1738)

A: Romilda (s); B: Atalanta (s); C: Xerxes (Serse) (ms); D: Arsamenes (Arsamene) (ms); E: Amastris (Amastre) (c); F: Elviro (bs); G: Ariodates (Ariodate) (bs)

*X*erxes (*Serse*, London, 1738), the fortieth of Handel's forty-two Italian operas, received five performances during the composer's lifetime, then languished for 186 years before reevaluation (Göttingen, 1924, in German). The very factors that precluded its success originally—numerous deviations from strict *opera seria* tradition, greatly diminished reliance on the *da capo* aria form, comic and satirical elements alongside elevated sentiment—partly account for its late-twentieth-century status as one of the most produced of all Handel's stage works. Moreover, matters of historical, political, and mythological significance have no catalytic bearing upon the action, despite the presence of a powerful and willful monarch, his volatile brother, and assorted high-strung personages in a nominally ancient Persian setting. Rather, the vagaries of the human heart propel the plot twists and turns. Never mind that the musical conventions of the piece, on the surface, seem removed from what post-*verismo* listeners deem operatically "emotional." Sophisticated modern skeptics, helpless before Handel's extraordinary powers, are drawn into caring about these flighty, pompous, scheming, self-absorbed, layered characters. To realize that this is but one of sixty (counting oratorios) examples of Handel's massive dramatic output is to glimpse the magnitude of his genius.

1988 KULTUR (VHS) / PIONEER (LD)

(Stage Performance, Stereo, Color, in English) 187 minutes

Valerie Masterson (A), Lesley Garrett (B), Ann Murray (C), Christopher Robson (D), Jean Rigby (E), Christopher Booth-Jones (F), Rodney Macann (G), Chorus and Orchestra of the English National Opera—Charles Mackerras

English National Opera: Nicholas Hytner (stage director), John Michael Phillips (video director)

The English National Opera has evolved into an organization where the quality of sound that emanates from its stage is not considered equal in importance to the visual and conceptual aspects of its performances. At ENO the director is king, the production's the thing, and, especially in the baroque and Mozart repertories, the managerial mantra is apparently "Lord deliver us from singers who sing."

Though this order of priorities does not mean that what the company offers is without value, it does preclude the kind of rarefied vocal artistry that moves, enlightens, and renews, and does keep a work like Handel's *Xerxes* from receiving its due.

Director / translator Nicholas Hytner draws multidimensional character portrayals from his hardworking cast, while simultaneously pitting them against as much distracting artificiality as the stage will hold: butlers-cum-stagehands in piano-key livery; a spray-painted chorus, musically underemployed but omnipresently obtrusive.

The Vauxhall Gardens of Handel's own day are the purported locale, though no climate or era is consistently evoked in David Fielding's elegant, eccentric sets and costumes. This emotionally distancing production lacks the powerful charm of the later one Stephen Wadsworth and associates created for Santa Fe and subsequent venues.

Sir Charles Mackerras leads an evening of endless instrumental felicity that shames much of what it accompanies. Mackerras's sense of proportion and propulsion, elegiacal line and chuckling undercurrent, provide a superb musical experience independent of any limitations onstage.

This is Handel sung without the highly developed skills prerequisite to the composer's arsenal of expressive devices. No one commands a trill (most attempts here are risible), few can sustain a properly intense legato or rattle off compelling fioritura. Worse, everybody has been persuaded that singing in English means conversational, pitched speaking rather than well-supported tone making. Larynxes rise with the pitch until throats close off completely on top notes.

The sole exception, alto Jean Rigby (Amastris), sings the text with admirable comprehensibility but broadly, fluidly, as though it were the original Italian, and thus manages both sostenuto and coloratura passages with surpassing eloquence.

Otherwise, Ann Murray's plummy, unstable mezzo cannot suggest Xerxes' strength, notwithstanding her earnest, conscientious "masculine" demeanor.

The production's 1995 Chicago visit profited immensely from superior leading ladies. Here, Lesley Garrett's spoiled brat Atalanta and Valerie Masterson's cool cucumber Romilda succeed along vocally deconstructive lines. Between them they barely possess one whole soprano voice. Garrett's peeps and squeaks are damnably annoying in themselves, apart from her character's innate obnoxiousness. The puny piping Masterson proffers instead of the bravura singing indispensable to the great "constancy" aria that closes Act II (Handel's "Come scoglio" equivalent) turns a potential audience rouser into an anticlimactic fizzle.

Countertenor Christopher Robson's hooty, aurally unendearing Arsamenes projects a tiresome air of fatuous hauteur rather than aggrieved nobility. Christopher Booth-Jones (Elviro) is appropriately droll, Rodney Macann (Ariodates) appropriately self-important.

Handel's often glorious score, uncut, survives this less-isn't-nearly-enough rendition, thanks to Mackerras, but it has been seen and heard recently to much greater advantage elsewhere.

BRUCE BURROUGHS

Hänsel und Gretel (1893)

A: Gretel (s); B: Hänsel (ms); C: Gertrude (ms); D: Witch (ms);
E: Peter (bar)

Humperdinck's fairy-tale opera is a wonderful concoction, filled with fascinating instrumental detail and expertly created atmosphere. Yet its potential joys can be hard to capture in actual performance: the need to use adult singers for the children and for them to simulate childlike glee can, except in the most expert of hands, be unbearably cloying. And children, so often taken to *Hänsel* as their first opera, are likely to have no patience with the blinders that adults have learned to wear and will point out disappointedly that the boy and the girl are both grown-up ladies and that they could see the witch getting out of the back of the oven and that everybody onstage was acting pretty silly. The difficulties may be circumvented to some extent in the video medium but are just as likely to be exposed all the more unavoidably.

A footnote to the operatic videos may be of some interest. A puppet film for children, made in 1954, is mostly spoken but uses Humperdinck for background music throughout, conducted by Franz Allers. The prize here is the witch, who gets to sing more than the others, as voiced by Anna Russell in memorably loony fashion. This film is available on VHS on the View label.

1981 LONDON (VHS / LD)

(Film, Stereo, Color, Subtitled) 109 minutes

Edita Gruberová (A), Brigitte Fassbaender (B), Helga Dernesch (C), Sena Jurinac (D), Her-

mann Prey (E), Vienna Boys Choir, Vienna Philharmonic Orchestra—Georg Solti

August Everding (director)

A film made from scratch might be thought a good medium for overcoming the inherent challenges that *Hänsel* presents: the aforementioned problems of scale and balance can be easily dealt with, and magical effects need not be limited to stage possibilities. Yet in this case it hasn't worked out terribly well. Animation is used to solve effects like the flight of angels and the materialization of the gingerbread house, and for additional effects like brooms flying out of the house. It always stands out as a separate device, never being blended with live action convincingly. Most often, the live performers will be looking wonderingly at the camera, and a reverse-angle shot will then reveal an animated effect. The children look unignorably adult—Gretel virtually middle-aged, Hänsel younger but acceptable as a boy only by those steeped in stage conventions. Such conventions are half-heartedly invoked by the presentation of the action as an opera-house entertainment for children (who then become the revived children of the last scene), even though the production follows the Busby Berkeley tradition of showing action that could not possibly be contained on a stage. The decision to show us delighted children in the audience at odd moments is as counterproductive here as in any other movie where this has been done: the obvious effort to assure us that we're having fun amounts to a guarantee that we're not.

Other oddities include the setting of the latter part of the witch's scene inside her house. The loss is obvious—she can navigate only the ceiling when flying on her broom—and it's not clear what the gain was intended to be. The film format thus created more problems than it solved, especially considering the underenergized actions of the singers while synchronizing to their sound track. In fairness to Everding, he does help the singers achieve something special in the simpler scenes of interaction: the parents' colloquy and the children's awakening are good examples. The success of some of the individual performances must owe a great deal to his help.

Solti, working with the ideal orchestra for this music, seems more involved than on his audio recording of a few years earlier but still less than careful about fine points of color and balance. Gruberová is as unconvincing aurally as visually; very accomplished in a steely way that does nothing to conjure up the character. Fassbaender comes off better, singing strongly and at least keeping things simple and sincere. The parents fare better: Prey gives a serious, convincing performance as the father, and Dernesch creates a fully realized mother: not only well sung but specific in characterization—concerned about survival rather than nasty by nature. Best of all is Jurinac as the witch. She benefits from one of the few successful pieces of cinema magic: first appearing as a nice friendly granny, she is transformed when she casts her first spell into a gruesome ogress. She also sings the role marvelously, with a voice that shows some age but still has steadiness and color and is used with great imaginative flair. The best thing about this film may be its preservation of a complete performance by this treasurable artist.

1982 PARAMOUNT (VHS) / PIONEER (LD)

(Stage Performance, Stereo, Color, in English) 104 minutes

Judith Blegen (A), Frederica von Stade (B), Jean Kraft (C), Rosalind Elias (D), Michael Devlin (E), Metropolitan Opera Chorus and Orchestra—Thomas Fulton

Metropolitan Opera: Bruce Donnell (stage director), Kirk Browning (video director)

This live telecast exhibits the problems inherent in the scale on which Humperdinck inflated this story, with domestic conversations carried on over a full and busy orchestra needing to be projected into a big house. These efforts are not minimized by the proximity of the cameras, which show us all the more clearly how hard the performers are working. Yet what this rendition does have going for it is that it *is* a stage performance, in which stage conventions like boys played by women, children played by adults, and the presence of an orchestra can all be accepted without undue fuss. This production is a traditional "pretty" one (designed by Robert O'Hearn, originally directed by Nathaniel Merrill), evocative and effective in those terms; it includes an agreeably complete staging of the dream pantomime complete with crowned and flying angels and a gingerbread house that materializes before our eyes. The cast is expanded to include forest creatures (at night and in the finale), impersonated by children. Fulton achieves considerable color and energy without quite making the ultimate magic with the piece—but then few conductors do; it's a much harder score to conduct well than is generally realized.

The children's roles are full of invitations to archness. Blegen does not altogether avoid these but more often steers clear, and she sings the role very prettily and musically with a light soprano well matched to the role's demands. Von Stade is even better, in character and full of well-directed boyish energy; a memorable experience visually as well as vocally. Kraft and Devlin deliver solid and enjoyable performances as the parents; nothing unexpected, but nothing disappointing either. Elias has a fine time with the witch and handles the role quite well, in terms of the usual cackling-and-*Sprechgesang* approach. Her veteran mezzo has problems achieving optimum verbal clarity in a role that keeps heading for soprano territory (the rest of the cast manages better with intelligibility). Audience reaction contributes to the sense of enjoyment: a round of applause when the witch is stuffed into the oven, and another when she flies in for her curtain call.

———————

A really fine *Hänsel* performance is as rare on video as it is in live performance; it's too diffi-cult for total success to be likely. Of these two, the Met production, despite obvious imperfec-tions, is preferable in every way; being in English it may be the wiser purchase for young newcomers to the work, in any case.

JON ALAN CONRAD

Jenůfa (1904)

A: Jenůfa (s); B: Kostelnička (s); C: Laca (t); D: Števa (t)

In *Jenůfa*, Janáček succeeded for the first time in combining his original technique of "speech-related melodies" with his innate dramatic talent to produce a work of great emotional and spiritual power. *Její Pastorkyňa* (Her Stepdaughter), the three-act play by Gabriela Preissová on which the opera is based, is written in local dialect and includes numerous interpolated folk verses and peasant celebrations, an ideal framework for Janáček's interest in folklore.

Not only does Janáček use the intonation of peasant speech as the basis of *Jenůfa*'s musical style, he also uses set pieces derived from folk song models. *Jenůfa* contains more such set pieces than any of Janáček's other major operas, which helps to explain its enduring popularity and accessibility. Because of its brutally realistic plot, involving extramarital sex in an unforgiving village milieu, *Jenůfa* has often been compared to *verismo* classics like *Cavalleria Rusticana* and *Pagliacci*. But as *Jenůfa*'s healing final scene makes clear, Janáček was at heart an optimist who believed that true love, compassion, and forgiveness would triumph over sin and evil.

1989 KULTUR (VHS)

(Stage Performance, Stereo, Color, Subtitled)
118 minutes

Roberta Alexander (A), Anja Silja (B), Philip Langridge (C), Mark Baker (D), Glyndebourne Chorus, London Philharmonic—Andrew Davis

Glyndebourne Festival: Nikolaus Lehnhoff (stage director), Derek Bailey (video director)

This 1989 Glyndebourne production of *Jenůfa* uses the original Brno version of the opera, which had not been seen or heard since its 1904 premiere. (Janáček revised the score for the 1916 Prague production.) It is a skillfully designed, sensitively directed, and beautifully sung production, and it has been brought to video with unusual taste by Derek Bailey. Under Andrew Davis, the London Philharmonic turns in a taut, driving performance that never overwhelms the singers but stresses the score's profound romanticism and rhythmic insistence.

The four principal roles are unusually well balanced both dramatically and vocally. As Jenůfa, Roberta Alexander gives one of her most memorable performances. Producing a warm, sensuous tone, she also finds the right balance between innocence and bitter experience in her acting. And the camera loves her mobile, expressive face. The roundness of Alexander's voice is nicely complemented by the steely, hard timbre of Anja Silja as her embittered stepmother. Their numerous duets offer considerable vocal and dramatic pleasure and convey the message of generational continuity that is so essential to Janáček's art.

Also well cast are Philip Langridge as the wildly jealous Laca and Mark Baker as the careless village stud. Both sing with great confidence and passion and join Alexander and Silja in projecting the Czech text unusually clearly and expressively.

Nikolaus Lehnhoff's staging contains many fine and startling moments. The action is confined in small walled spaces, which lends an atmosphere of claustrophobia that is entirely appropriate to this tale of small-town gossip and nosiness. At the same time, the lighting provides a sense of spaciousness, especially in the final act when bright springtime light streams into the previously shuttered windows of Kostelnička's sparely furnished house. Near the end of Act III, when the double sin of Jenůfa and Kostelnička has been made public on the day of Jenůfa's wedding to Laca, Lehnhoff adds a brilliant touch: the visiting villagers suddenly ransack and loot Kostelnička's house, then leave Jenůfa and Laca alone amidst a scene of domestic devastation for their glorious final scene of reconciliation and renewal.

In bringing the production to video, Derek Bailey has managed to preserve a sense of intimacy and has taken care to vary the camera work between revealing close-ups and full-stage shots. He has also emphasized the symbol of the rosemary plant seen in Act I and then shown flourishing at the window at the opera's end. Overall, an excellent version.

HARLOW ROBINSON

KÁŤA KABANOVÁ (1921)

A: Káťa Kabanová (s); B: Varvara (ms); C: Kabanicha (ms); D: Boris (t);
E: Tichon (t); F: Váňa Kudrjáš (t); G: Dikoj (bs)

Káťa Kabanová, the opera Janáček liked to call his *Appassionata*, is the best known of his numerous works inspired by Russian literature. The source was *The Thunderstorm*, an 1859 play by Alexander Ostrovsky (1823–1886), Russia's leading representative of realistic drama and the only important Russian writer before Chekhov to write exclusively for the stage.

With its stark portrayal of prejudice, hypocrisy, and domestic tyranny in a provincial Volga river town on the eve of the freeing of the serfs, *The Thunderstorm* gave Janáček two important ingredients he sought when creating an opera: adultery and suffering. (The composer downplays the social / political implications of Ostrovsky's play that stimulated heated discussion among Russian critics and intellectuals.) It also gave him plenty of dramatic material, including Káťa's spectacular suicidal leap into the Volga in the final scene.

Compact, intense, and filled with some of Janáček's most rapturously lyrical music, including a number of characteristically "Russian" themes, *Káťa* has appealed to divas and directors ever since its premiere. The staging of Káťa's riverbank suicide (like Liza's in Tchaikovsky's *Queen of Spades*, an apparent model for Janáček) presents a special challenge.

1988 KULTUR (VHS)

(Stage Performance, Stereo, Color, Subtitled)
110 minutes

Nancy Gustafson (A), Louise Winter (B), Felicity Palmer (C), Barry McCauley (D), Ryland Davies (E), John Graham-Hall (F), Donald Adams (G), Glyndebourne Chorus, London Philharmonic—Andrew Davis

Glyndebourne Festival: Nikolaus Lehnhoff (stage director), Derek Bailey (video director)

Stage director Nicolaus Lehnhoff and designer Tobias Hoheisel chose an excessively stark, minimalist look for this *Káťa*, which bears a strong visual resemblance to their *Jenůfa*, also produced at Glyndebourne. The Russian setting is downplayed here; the church steeple visible in distant silhouette looks Protestant rather than Orthodox, and "local color" is largely absent. The action seems to be taking place in a farming village like the one in *Jenůfa*, when in fact *Káťa* is set in an urban merchant milieu.

Most distinctive about the design is its strong use of fields of color: white, black, lurid green, and a strip of garish purple for the Volga. The effect is striking, but rather one-dimensional for an opera set in Russia around 1860.

The imagery is constructed around sharp angles, including a curtain that provides a triangular framing of the stage. As a symbol of their moral superiority and purity, only the heroine Káťa and her lover Boris wear white. All the other characters are clothed in black, indicating their joylessness and ignorance.

Nancy Gustafson is very well cast as Káťa. Young, slim, and attractive, with a flexible light soprano, Gustafson shows herself to be a most accomplished actress, conveying Káťa's sexual and emotional frustration with an aching immediacy. The director has taken advantage of her ability to move gracefully and easily about the stage, even giving her some choreography during the overture. The camera often lingers in expertly lit close-ups of her supple and expressive face, so that the fundamental psychological conflict that propels this opera comes across with unusual force.

Stand-outs in the supporting cast include Barry McCauley, who makes a pleasing physical and vocal partner for Gustafson; a ramrod-straight Felicity Palmer as the over-bearing and unbearable mother-in-law; and Ryland Davies as Káťa's wimpy husband. As in *Jenůfa*, the London Philharmonic under Andrew Davis plays with intensity and sensitivity to Janáček's style.

As for Káťa's leap into the Volga, it is something of a disappointment. She runs up what looks like a desert sand dune and jumps off into a mass of fluorescent purple. But the final visual image, of Káťa's drowned body lying alone and abandoned on the stage, limbs askew, is a memorable one.

HARLOW ROBINSON

The Makropulos Case (1926)

A: Emilia Marty (s); B: Krista (ms); C: Albert Gregor (t);
D: Hauk-Šendorf (t); E: Vítek (t); F: Janek (t); G: Jaroslav Prus (bar);
H: Dr. Kolenatý (bs-bar)

On the face of it, the convoluted story of an unhappy woman who has reached the age of 337 with the help of a magic elixir may not sound like the most promising subject for an opera. But to Leoš Janáček, the cautionary science-fiction tale of Elina Makropulos presented all sorts of intriguing philosophical and musical possibilities. The opera is based on an anti-utopian morality play (*Věc Makropulos*) written by Janáček's Czech countryman Karel Čapek and first produced in Prague in 1922.

While there are many psychological and thematic similarities between *The Makropulos Case* and Janáček's other operas, its musical style is quite distinct, modern and cosmopolitan. Most obviously, *The Makropulos Case* lacks the background of folk culture and folk music—whether Czech or Russian—central to *Jenůfa*, *Cunning Little Vixen*, *Káťa Kabanová*, and *From the House of the Dead*. Lacking both national "color" and detachable song-like or dance-like sections, *The Makropulos Case* was slow to enter the international repertory, but that situation has changed in recent years as major opera houses have been mounting ambitious new productions of this philosophical thriller.

With its backstage setting and supernatural atmosphere, *The Makropulos Case* offers plenty of visual and dramatic opportunities to enterprising directors and designers. And the role of the age-defying diva Elina Makropulos has attracted

some great performers over the years, including Elisabeth Söderström and Jessye Norman.

1990 VAI (VHS)

(Stage Performance, Stereo, Color, Subtitled) 123 minutes

Stephanie Sundine (A), Kathleen Brett (B), Graham Clark (C), Gary Rideout (D), Richard Margison (E), Benoit Butel (F), Cordelis Opthof (G), Robert Orth (H), Orchestra of the Canadian Opera—Berislav Klobucar

Canadian Opera: Lotfi Mansouri (stage director), Norman Campbell (video director)

Originally staged at the San Francisco Opera, this production gives the opera a strong 1920s atmosphere. If anything, director Lotfi Mansouri has opted for a style that is too realistic and earth-bound for this highly spiritual and supernatural piece. The stage is overloaded with draperies, scarves, and knick-knacks that tend to distract from the psychological tension. A more abstract and nonperiod approach (like the one taken by Elijah Moshinsky in the excellent 1996 Met production) works more effectively to convey the spookiness of the subject.

Ultimately all productions of *The Makropulos Case* succeed or fail on the strength of the "dramatic soprano" cast in the role of Elina Makropulos (*aka* Emilia Marty). Both musically and dramatically, she is the focus of the opera. In addition to a flexible, sensuous voice that can navigate the tricky vocal landscape, Marty must have sexual allure, glamor, and an aura of mystery.

Unfortunately, the Marty-Makropulos here, Stephanie Sundine, does not really possess any of these things. Her voice turns strident in the upper range, where so much of her singing lies, and there is little warmth to its tone. As an actress, she tends to resort to pained grimaces and obvious gestures that make her look desperate rather than seductive. Nor does the staging show her off to particular advantage: in Act I, she chases Gregor around a table hoping to retrieve the magic formula. The enigmatic Elina Makropulos would not stoop to such crude tactics.

Mansouri does come up with a provocative and moving solution for the staging of the opera's final scene, however. Sundine emerges suddenly looking like the decrepit, ancient, and bald 337-year old that she really is. We really see how ugly Elina Makropulos has become, both physically and emotionally. The close-up camera work nicely intensifies the impact of this dis-turbing image, and of the flame which then consumes the evil formula for the elixir.

There are some excellent performances from the members of the large supporting cast. Robert Orth makes the lawyer Kolenatý come vibrantly alive; Kathleen Brett sings the role of the young opera singer Kristina with impressive lyricism and control; and Gary Rideout shows fine comic timing in the role of Makropulos's now-senile former lover Count Hauk-Šendorf.

The video direction generally avoids the static and boring style too often employed by those filming opera. Instead of the same inevitable shots of musicians playing during the overture, we see stills of the principal performers and their roles, which is a help to viewers coming to this complicated work for the first time. Director Norman Campbell also keeps the camera moving about the stage, nicely varying close-ups and long shots and providing a variety of perspectives. The sound quality is acceptable, if not exceptional, and the singers' Czech pronunciation and projection are surprisingly good.

HARLOW ROBINSON

Treemonisha (1915)

A: Treemonisha (s); B: Monisha (s); C: Remus (t); D: Zodzetrick (t);
E: Luddud (bar); F: Ned (bs-bar)

*I*t would seem uncharitable indeed not to praise the efforts of Scott Joplin (1868–1917) to create a viable opera, nor to laud the ambition of the Houston Grand Opera to expend a good deal of effort to see his dream realized, sixty years later. Joplin, the black descendant of slaves who rose to musical prominence as the "Ragtime King" with his piano compositions, faced inummerable obstacles to getting an opera produced. *Treemonisha* was finally seen for one run-through performance in Harlem two years before the composer-librettist's death. He had to personally finance the production, which was given with only piano accompaniment.

In 1973, the producers of the Hollywood film *The Sting* had the brilliant idea of underscoring the exploits of Paul Newman and Robert Redford with Scott Joplin's rags, arranged for the film by Marvin Hamlisch. This launched a national craze for his music, much of which had been published a few years before. The Houston Grand Opera, obviously intrigued by the existence of a Joplin opera, raised *Treemonisha* from the shadowy vaults of forgotten operas. With a new orchestration by musicologist Gunther Schuller, it was first performed by the company in 1975 in an outdoor theatre in Houston. This was so successful that a tour and an eight-week Broadway run ensued, as well as a recording. Later, the work was revived in Houston, from which performances this video was made, in 1982.

1982 KULTUR (VHS)

(Stage Performance; Stereo, Color) 86 minutes

Carmen Balthrop (A), Delores Ivory (B), Curtis Rayam (C), Obba Babatunde (D), Cleveland Williams (E), Dorceal Duckens (F), Houston Grand Opera Chorus and Orchestra—John DeMain

Houston Grand Opera: Frank Corsaro (stage director), Sid Smith (video director)

This is the definitive production of *Treemonisha*; it could hardly be improved. The sets and costumes by Franco Colavecchia artfully evoke the rural south and pagan Africa. The choreography by Mabel Robinson is rousingly conceived and enthusiastically danced by the corps *and* the singers, reaching a climax with the final bows. The audience would prefer to keep everyone dancing on stage all night.

Frank Corsaro's well-known expertise with difficult, neglected, and folk operas (e.g., *The Immortal Hour, Hugh the Drover*) is given a thorough challenge here. He succeeds in telling this naïf moral fable in an effective way, but there will be a wide spectrum of tolerance for Joplin's simplistic libretto. The rhyming couplets are as mundane as the story, which has little dramatic force. "I'm greatly surprised to hear that you are not my mother" is not a line that will sing well, no matter who sets it. The opera's message seems to be that education will ease ignorance, but racial issues are themselves for the most part downplayed. Anyone expecting another *Porgy and Bess* will be sorely disappointed.

Yet I cannot think of another opera quite so African-American, in the positive, literal sense of the term. And the fully-orchestrated, joyously-chorused, and exuberantly-danced rags are so exciting that they forgive quite a lot of limitations. The finales to Acts II and III are simply knockouts and fantastically catchy ("Aunt Dinah Has Blowed De Horn" and "A Real Slow Drag"). Hardly the usual operatic finales. The rest of the music often sounds like hymns or Victorian parlor ballads, never unpleasant but not terribly distinctive, and really put in the shade by the ragtime moments.

The cast is superb, especially Carmen Balthorp in the title role. Small, but with a ringingly clear soprano, she shines in the moralizing aria before the final rag. Equally good are Curtis Rayam, as Treemonisha's savior, and Delores Ivory, as her adoptive mother. The hardworking chorus is wonderful, with clear diction and tremendous gusto, as in its responses to the Parson Alltalk's sermon. The orchestra under John DeMain delivers an exciting reading of this newly-instrumented score, effectively balancing its demure and brassy elements. I seem to remember the sets looking more impressive on stage at New York's Palace Theatre than they do on a small screen, but the video production conveys the excitement of a Broadway production. Not a bad approach for this opera, and one feels sure Joplin would have been happy with the results.

RICHARD TRAUBNER

Where the Wild Things Are (1980)

A: Max (s); B: Mama (ms)

Higglety Pigglety Pop! (1990)

A: Mother Goose (s); B: Jennie (ms); C: Pig (t); D: Lion (bar)

Capitalizing on a fact known very well to the Brothers Grimm—that children love to be scared—Maurice Sendak tapped a new vein of the macabre in his books for the young, inhabited by a variety of lumbering, big-eyed, big-mouthed monsters (who turn out to be unexpectedly soft-hearted), and by a fanciful assortment of animals whose real nature is often not immediately revealed. Oliver Knussen's attraction to these creatures might have seemed a surprising turn for a composer whose dense instrumental style has never been tailored for easy listening, but his susceptibility to fantasy was perhaps hinted early in his career, when at the age of eighteen he composed "Vocalise and Songs of Winnie-the-Pooh" and a work for clarinet called "The Cheshire Cat."

Where the Wild Things Are and *Higglety Pigglety Pop!*, with text, sets, monsters, and animals by Sendak, are based on his books of the same name; *Wild Things* was premiered by the Brussels National Opera in 1980 and in its present revised version by the Glyndebourne Touring Opera in London in 1984 (the production moved to the Glyndebourne Festival itself, and was premiered in the U.S. by the Minnesota Opera in 1985). It was an immediate success, in part because of the astonishing appearance and physical versatility of the Sendak creatures (occupied by humans and elec-

tronically manipulated), but also because the story is so sharply propelled by Knussen's colorful, prickly, headlong music. Early versions of *Higglety Pigglety Pop!* were introduced at Glyndebourne in 1984 and 1985, and the finished work was premiered at the Los Angeles Music Center in 1990.

1985 TELDEC (VHS / LD)

(Studio Performances, Color); 99 minutes

Wild Things: Karen Beardsley (A), Mary King (B), London Sinfonietta—Oliver Knussen
Higglety Pigglety Pop!: Deborah Rees (A), Cynthia Buchan, (B), Andrew Gallacher (C), Stephen Richardson (D), London Sinfonietta—Oliver Knussen

Glyndebourne Festival: Frank Corsaro (stage director), Christopher Swann (video director)

There are few serene moments during the adventures of Max, the obstreperous boy-hero of *Wild Things*, though we notice that he grows somewhat quieter as the opera progresses and concludes his travels in a positively angelic (and hungry) state. But he is, in general, a handful, and the opera's opening scene, in which he vents a really destructive rage, is caught completely in the music—as effective a depiction of chaos as any in opera.

The high tessitura and jagged contours of Max's vocal line, sung by a soprano, make the role a challenging vehicle; there are a few aria-like passages ("I dreamed that once I flew . . . "), but for the most part the nature of the music makes understanding the text almost impossible, and most of it is incomprehensible in the BBC television video, which has no subtitles. (A synopsis of both operas is provided.) But Karen Beardsley is wonderful nonetheless, athletic and childlike in her cavorting, unflagging in her energy, and undaunted by the vocal challenges. Her opening tantrum is splendid to behold, and her more peaceful episodes are touching. The four monsters (male) murmur indecipherable nothings very effectively until the moment they break into English ("Oh, please don't go . . . We love you so!") in barbershop close harmony. Delightful.

The video captures the magical qualities of the staging, from the misty progress of Max's gliding boat, seen through shifting lights that transform the stage picture from moment to moment, to the presence of the monsters, eyes rolling, noses twitching, heads lolling, mouths agape.

Higglety Pigglety Pop!, without benefit of monsters, doesn't quite match this charm. Although Jennie the Sealyham, a dog who swallows a mop, is endearing in her search for adventure, the more episodic story (again, difficult to follow in the singing) would be enhanced by subtitles. But an opera that offers a potted pink geranium singing advice to the unhappy heroine must be welcomed on its own terms, and Cynthia Buchan is a very sweet dog indeed. The scenes dissolve cinematically, one into the next, creating a smooth flow of events.

Conductor Knussen projects the splintered brightness of these scores with brittle energy.

SHIRLEY FLEMING

FRANZ LEHÁR

THE MERRY WIDOW

(DIE LUSTIGE WITWE) (1905)

A: Hanna Glawari (s); B: Valencienne (s); C: Count Danilo (t or bar);
D: Camille de Rosillon (t)

Though *The Merry Widow* is highly familiar today, one should realize the tidal-wave force with which it swept through the musical-theater world soon after it first conquered the Austro-Hungarian / German circuit. Then, it must have looked and sounded up-to-date, highly charged, and lushly romantic, wrapped up in the tissue of a typical French farce (which of course it is).

Die Lustige Witwe is so rich a masterpiece that one can approach it today from several angles. It is a raucous Parisian boulevard comedy, a Viennese modernist musical score, and now, through an aging process, an operetta valentine from the silvery twilight of the Habsburg capital. Its musical superiority—Lehár really did nothing better—is such that it is seen continuously in the opera house. It has, besides its two memorably flashy lead parts, rewarding music for the secondary lovers. Accolades also ought to be given to the two librettists, Victor Léon (1858–1940, born in Vienna as Hirschfeld) and Leo Stein (1866–1920, born in Galicia as Rosenstein). They gave a minor comedy by Offenbach's librettist Henri Meilhac the appeal that must have seduced Lehár.

1988 KULTUR (VHS)

(Stage Performance, Stereo, Color, in English)
151 minutes

Joan Sutherland (A), Anne-Maree McDonald (B), Anson Austin (C), Ronald Stevens (D), Australian Opera Chorus, Elizabethan Philharmonic Orchestra—Richard Bonynge

Australian Opera: Lotfi Mansouri (stage director), Virginia Lumsden (video director)

This Australian Opera production records a live 1988 performance televised from the Sydney Opera House. A good idea. Take so essentially theatrical a work as *The Merry Widow* and try to do it off the stage, without an audience, and you are asking for trouble. Even film directors as celebrated as Stroheim and Lubitsch couldn't pull that off.

The Australian Opera has always been a champion of operetta, and the Australian Ballet has even done its own full-length *Merry Widow* ballet. The operetta is performed in English, in Christopher Hassall's British translation. *The Merry Widow* has seemed an English-language property since the first London and New York performances in 1907–08; it was a hugely influential hit in both cities.

This *Widow* has an accurate look about it, with Kristian Fredrickson's glittery costumes, hats, and sets; here is a Maxim's that looks like a restaurant. Dame Joan is the icing on the cake. Wrapped in José Varona gowns, she is a matronly widow, but with a picture-postcard look that smacks of the Edwardian era. (The original Hanna, Mizzi Günther, was hardly lithe.) She even sounds Edwardian. True, words are lost, and even some notes in that wobbly jumble we all know and love. She is still very much a radiant star, picturesquely swathed in lilac feathers or Balkan national dress, and she enjoys all the dancing required of her.

She does not have quite the youthful glamour the part needs, however, thus deflating her contribution to the first- and second-act finales, in which the level of sauciness must rise. The rest of the cast is fairly humdrum, lacking any starry presence, youthful or mature. Anson Austin's Danilo is bland, the male comics lack the personal idiocies needed to distinguish them, and the Valencienne / Rosillon duo is only adequate.

The score is given virtually complete, including the often-cut "Charms of Domesticity" duet and the Act III cakewalk. Most of the ensemble movement is done by the dancers, in the old operetta style, and their climax is a terrific ballet at Maxim's. This is set to a Douglas Gamley medley that includes, among other Lehár tunes, "Bist du lachendes Glück" from *The Count of Luxembourg*. As if that weren't enough, the entire cast gets to sing, with Joan, "Liebe, du Himmel auf Erden" from the 1925 *Paganini* at the finale, accompanied by balloons and streamers dropping on the audience from *Himmel*. Just to make sure we all had a heavenly time.

RICHARD TRAUBNER

PAGLIACCI (1892)

A: Nedda (s); B: Canio (t); C: Beppe (t); D: Tonio (bar); E: Silvio (bar)

Pagliacci keeps on working, with the forces of the world's grandest opera houses and in basement workshops with piano accompaniment and tyro singers. It has earned its success, for it has no pedigree. Tonio's words near the opening of the Prologue, so vividly set in the music, remain the most succinct statement of the veristic credo: "The author has instead sought to paint you a slice of life. He takes for his maxim only that the artist is a man, and must write for men, and that the truth is his inspiration." The opera that follows is still the most powerful single example of that artistic philosophy, lovingly attentive to stage conventions and forms even as they melt in the heat of passion. It requires full-throated, wide-ranging voices that follow classical singing disciplines; a conductor who realizes that the way to respect the score is to dig into it as dramatic action; and a director who understands that all the conceptualizing has been done, leaving the relationships and behavior to be found. Unfortunately, our generation is out of practice on these essentials. The video issue is whether a piece whose essence is stage/life tension can be served by a camera, however candid. All these versions observe the still-standard forty-five-bar cut in the Nedda / Silvio duet.

1954 LEGATO CLASSICS (VHS)

(Studio Performance, Mono, Black and White, Not Subtitled) 76 minutes

Mafalda Micheluzzi (A), Franco Corelli (B), Mario Carlin (C), Tito Gobbi (D), Lino Puglisi (E), Chorus and Orchestra of RAI, Milan— Alfredo Simonetto

Franco Enriquez (director)

There is more than a historical byway to explore here. There's a strong directorial intelligence at work, some surprisingly good acting, theatrically alert conducting, and flashes of great singing. The film's weaknesses are primarily technical: the sound fights its way through some patches and burbles; the lip-synch, while not at all poor, achieves its customary decoupling of sight and sound; and though the film was intended for TV and the print is satisfactory, it looks crimped along the edges. Nonetheless, a lot comes through. The flavor is that of Italian postwar neorealism—this could almost be a De Sica or Rossellini production of that time, and not a bad one at that. The village of Montalto actually comes to life in the opening sequence, which culminates in a Bell Chorus that turns into a delightful street festival, beautifully finished except for a cue-nervous bell-tolling *ragazzo* who should have been given another take. The second-act *commedia* is wonderfully staged: the tacky little show is not condescended to; backstage points-of-view help convey the feel of troupers doing their work under high personal tension; and the audience's shifting involvement is tipped in with a sure touch. Cameo introductions of the characters during the prelude setup echoes in a performance-preparation sequence in the intermezzo—the sort of device that waves a red flag at the experienced viewer, but which in this case is given the right weight. Enriquez also accomplishes much with his interesting cast. Micheluzzi is stuck with a few posey shots that catch her in hands-on-hips clichés, but more often she's strong and alive in her behavior, and unlike most singers is able to take in what other characters are sending. In the *commedia*, she tells the story to the audience with point and clarity. Corelli, though an improbably glamorous Canio, shows a surprising freedom in his acting, and a fulfilling intensity in some of the big moments. He also has charm as the bulb-nosed, plastered Pagliaccio. Puglisi's sensibly acted Silvio suggests that Nedda is attracted by a settled-down petty-bourgeois life—not our standard picture of the *ganzo*, but plausibly presented. Carlin has a nice specificity as both Beppe and Arlecchino. The widest credibility gap comes with the most extravagantly gifted mummer, Gobbi. He contrives detailed pantomimic modeling, then tries to cram it in amongst the musical cues. It's inventive, but believable only in small bits of business, like handing Colombina a prop in the wings. It is also stubbornly separated from the often compelling Tonio described by the voice. Watch Micheluzzi receiving Silvio's pleas—that's good acting. Now watch Gobbi leaping and hand-signing his. That's not.

Musically, the performance is dominated by Corelli. At the outset there are touches of the tremulous vibrato that characterized his earliest singing, but once into the meat of the role he offers free, robust tone and a clean, firm line that carries a lucid projection of the language. Caruso's sumptuous singing and filled-to-bursting emotionality remain unique in the arias, but among the complete Canios left us, only Gigli really rivals this. Gobbi is also in good voice. We must still cope with the straight, hollow sound of his top, but the solidity and timbral burr are welcome. Micheluzzi is stylistically secure and always apt dramatically; her sound, though, is rather scrappy, and at some places she claws her way to the top with more grit than grace. Carlin makes every one of Arlecchino's points in his strong character tenor, with its oddly shaded chiaroscuro. Puglisi, unfortunately, barely lugs his darkly weighted baritone

through Silvio's altitudinous tessitura. The orchestral playing is above the RAI average, and Simonetto keeps the score perking; he conducts scenes and moments, not abstract phrases. Though the chorus (under La Scala's Roberto Benaglio) is not gloriously transmitted on the sound track, it's a full, well-balanced group. No subtitles clutter these well-composed shots.

1955 VAI (VHS)

(Studio Performance, Mono, Black and White, Subtitled) 58 minutes

Eva Likova (A), Jon Vickers (B), Pierre Boutet (C), Robert Savoie (D), Louis Quilico (E), Chorus and Orchestra of Radio-Canada, Montréal—Otto-Werner Mueller

Director unknown

This may bring a smile of nostalgia if you're old, or of generational smugness if you're young, but as a realization of *Pagliacci* it's on pretty thin ice. It does turn up a few items from the operatic attic. Here's Eva Likova, remembered from the New York City Opera and the American civic circuit, singing a strong, bright Nedda with good command of the range extremes and a nice trill. And Robert Savoie, a Canadian baritone who went on to several seasons at Covent Garden, is the Tonio, showing an interestingly dark voice that is inconsistently supported and some expressive ideas without much command of line or style. The young Jon Vickers is also uneasy with the idiom (*verismo* was never his métier, actually) and makes some bad linguistic mistakes; on the other hand, his voice sails forth with a solidity and ring, and sometimes an unpremeditated attack, that it didn't always later have. Quilico, Sr., offers the mellow, smooth baritone of his youth, and for fun interpolates a poised high A-natural at "Tutto scordiam"—tsk, tsk. But the terrors of early live TV are more in evidence than the excitements. To bring the piece in under an hour, the choral sequences are shortened or eliminated altogether (the whole of the Bell Chorus, including Canio's wonderful moment at "Ma poi, ricordatevi"), and the little that's left is an awful scramble. The entr'acte is substituted for the introduction to the Prologue, under an announcement. The studio production values are quaint and cramped. The performers, thus constrained, act in nervous little spurts. Likova is the most profesionally polished and Quilico the least, looking as if the notion that he must walk about and occasionally gesture at the other performers is very bad, and recent, news. The others have moments, but nothing hangs together for long. Presumably this is from a kinescope source, and if so it's in excellent shape: the black-and-white image is of good quality, though the subtitles are often hard to read. There is sound deterioration on a few of Likova's high notes; otherwise, it's decent mono. No director is credited. I hope he was well paid.

1961 UNKNOWN DISTRIBUTOR (VHS)

(Stage Performance, Mono, Color, Japanese and English Subtitles) 75 minutes

Gabriella Tucci (A), Mario del Monaco (B), Antonio Pirino (C), Aldo Protti (D), Attilio d'Orazi (E), Chorus and Orchestra, Tokyo—Giuseppe Morelli

Opera company, stage director, and video director unknown

There are some heavy hitters here, but the performance is strictly road-show routine. Morelli gets just the acceptable minimum from his orchestral and choral forces (presumably those of the Lirica Italiana, but they aren't 'fessing up), and the pulse lolls indolently during the *commedia*. The anonymous director has arranged for entirely traditional staging on an entirely traditional set. There is no period feel. The camera work is reasonably clear. Tucci is in good form, and it's a pleasure to hear such rich, full-bodied tone and flowing line in Nedda's music. Though her acting is of the stock melodramatic variety, some of the warmth and generosity that was always in her work comes through. 1961 was two or three seasons late to catch prime del Monaco. Plenty of exciting A's

and B-flats remain in the voice, but lower down there's too much flattened-out tone, too much chopping of the line, too many truncated phrase endings and shouted parlatos. When he does try for an honest cantabile, as at "Sperai, tanto il delirio," the results are shaky. There's still a stiff kind of energy in his portrayal, but the comportment too often suggests the stagewise veteran biding his time to hit the big effects. Protti was one of the important Italian baritones of his era, but sang very little in this country. I'm afraid he looks like he always sounded: a vocally gifted man (large, wide-ranged, monochrome sound, perfectly serviceable technique) without the imagination or artistic appetite to ever shed light on a phrase or a moment. He'll salute and report for duty, but that's about it—no problem, no Tonio. D'Orazi's voice is also the genuine article, and he sings a sturdy Silvio with some nice mezza-voce when needed, though he has a slurpy conception of legato. His acting is turn-and-sit, now sing. Pirino is well above the Beppe median vocally, and has more stage freedom than the others. The entire production bespeaks a wondrous and unanimous assurance that it's quite enough to show up. Memorable curtain calls and aria bows.

Visual quality is acceptable, but the sound has trouble with lower pitches and softer dynamics. The bottom part of the screen, with pint-sized English titles trying to horn in on Sumo-sized Japanese ones, is a grisly tangle.

1968 LONDON (VHS/LD)

(Film, Stereo, Color, Subtitled) 77 minutes

Raina Kabaivanska (A), Jon Vickers (B), Sergio Lorenzi (C), Peter Glossop (D), Rolando Panerai (E), Chorus and Orchestra of Teatro alla Scala—Herbert von Karajan

La Scala: Paul Hagar (stage director), Herbert von Karajan (director)

This filmed interment of what was possibly a fine stage production can be enjoyed through the simple expedient of not watching. There is compelling work on the sound track. The performance dates from Karajan's most interesting period as an opera conductor. True, some of the tempos are already overly deliberate, but they are inhibiting at only a few spots, such as the chorus at the players' arrival or the final section of the Nedda / Silvio duet. On the whole, the reading has an intensity, a dignity, a fatefulness of mood, and a sheer instrumental beauty that lifts the piece to its highest dramatic level. Some of this can be heard in better sound on the DG / La Scala recording of three years earlier. But here Karajan has a gutsier group of singers. Vickers now has his act together, and while some of his choices are still eccentric and his Italian still weird ("Un tal gioco, cray-*deh*-tuh-mi"), he is impressive, filling the arioso and the final confrontation with deep melancholy and a manly, contained rage. The voice has acquired depth and color, if also some leatheriness, since the earlier version. Kabaivanska's strong, tangy soprano doesn't sound quite housebroken for the Ballatella; thereafter, she settles into a rich and idiomatic Nedda that takes on real stature at the denouement. Glossop's splendid high dramatic baritone is in the top echelon of those recorded in the role, and he brings some characterful bite to his singing. Panerai is not in his best voice and phrases his music stiffly, but is still quality casting for Silvio. What puts the kibosh on all this is Karajan as film director. He hasn't much of an eye for what registers in acting, or the technical skill to create flow with the camera; the sequences emerge as a series of crude studies. The passionate, fate-filled messages that come to the ear are betrayed by the marmorealized images scanned by the eye, and the climax of the Nedda / Silvio duet, with the tightly clasped lovers marching off down an arched gallery, is a bit of parody that harks back to the Sid Caesar / Imogene Coca days. I suspect, though, that even a real film director would run into trouble shooting in cold blood from a pre-existing stage production, furnished with every appurtenance save the one that makes it happen—an audience. This performance is packaged with a *Cavalleria* "from" a Scala production by Giorgio Strehler. Its video quality is fine but its audio—oddly for the source—is only fair. Panerai, the Silvio, is given

billing over Glossop, the Tonio. Glossop should sue.

1982 PHILIPS (VHS / LD)

(Film, Stereo, Color, Subtitled) 70 minutes

Teresa Stratas (A), Plácido Domingo (B), Florindo Andreolli (C), Juan Pons (D), Alberto Rinaldi (E), Chorus and Orchestra of Teatro alla Scala—Georges Prêtre

Franco Zeffirelli (director)

This is not a successful film, but it contains flashes of the directorial brilliance that made Franco Zeffirelli a force in the operatic universe. His reputation is in eclipse now. The best of his work has vanished, and we are left with stage productions that have declined into decorative froufrou and scenic elephantiasis (though their craftsmanship should never be dismissed), with videos and films like this or the less interesting *Traviata*. Even for those of us who missed most of his best early work in Italy, the thing that was exciting about Zeffirelli was his ability to lead performers into a fresher, more active way of pursuing stage relationships, then supporting them with unusually thorough physical production in Romantic-Realist style, lit with a master painter's precision and imagination. The work with the performers is what made his productions live; the knack for tech is what won out. In retrospect, it is possible to feel that he was never more than a gifted designer who had the luck to collaborate with unusual performers, but this is far from the whole truth. The youthful urgency of the lovers in his stage *Romeo and Juliet,* and moments like the reimagined death of Mercutio, were surely thitherto undreamt of in Old Vic philosophy. Never again, at least hereabouts, did Mirella Freni or Gianni Raimondi bring to a stage relationship the complexity and continuity they brought into the Met's old *Bohème* after their work with Zeffirelli in the La Scala version. The Met has had no finer production, overall, since World War II than the Zeffirelli / Bernstein *Falstaff* in its initial seasons. And when Maria Callas sang her final Met Toscas, she embodied a woman (needful, neurotically jealous and insecure, specific and grounded in her actions) entirely rethought from the poised diva of her earlier portrayal. The Covent Garden production Zeffirelli had just mounted with her still had theatrical validity more than twenty years later. So there was more going on than fancy illustration.

The Stratas / Zeffirelli teaming looked like a natural, but it hasn't turned out well. It's become a sort of colorized rerun of the Fellini / Masina collaboration, but less shrewd and more sentimentalized. The very compatibility of their talents seems to lead them into each other's traps, more co-dependent than complementary. In her earliest roles at the Met (and Nedda was among them), Stratas showed an unusual emotional availability: she *was* sexy, she *was* primal, childlike, forlorn. As often happens with born creatures of the stage, an awareness of her most cherishable qualities, and of her audience's craving for them, has incorporated itself into her work, has framed it and partially defined it. Zeffirelli is not the sole donor to this Fund for the Irresistible Teresa, but he's certainly a major contributor. He has latched onto her identity as gamin-victim and played it for far more than it is worth, in the *Traviata* film and through four quite insufferable acts of the stage *Bohème*. For *Pagliacci*, stage and film, he's added a strong dose of Mediterranean carnality. Stratas now works assiduously at these qualities, rather than revealing them incidentally in pursuit of her characters. Two superior talents, leading each other astray.

In this film, nearly everything that works well is incidental, having to do with the physical concept or with the minor characters used as parts of the setting—it is like the Met *Bohème* in that respect. Zeffirelli has updated the action from the time of Leoncavallo's youth to that of his own. He uses this environment well in the scene of the troupe's arrival and in the audience sequences of Act II: there's good life in the shots of the crowd, the opening clown act with colored pinspots, the perambulations of the *Grapes of Wrath* truck, the ice-cream cart, the bicycles. Many of the choices here will be familiar to viewers of Zeffirelli's stage *Pagliacci*, of Fellini in his circus mode, or, rather strikingly, the

Enriquez film (see above). What does not work well—or at all, in fact—is epitomized by the Ballatella. In the Enriquez version, Nedda sings the aria to a winning curly-headed child. The idea's a cop-out: Nedda needs to be alone here, sorting out stuff she wouldn't show anyone, and we need to see her doing that. But at least the kid is really lovable, Micheluzzi tells him her story charmingly, and on its own level the scene comes off. Zeffirelli throws in more kids. He makes Nedda give one of them a tub bath. He adds roustabouts watching everything from the background. Stratas, in a great lather, physicalizes everything and leaves us to discover nothing. There is a surface realism to the scene, but the one truth we must take from it—Nedda's desperate longing for escape—is nowhere to be found. Stratas is in poor voice throughout, but especially so here, the breathing so labored that I wondered if Zeffirelli hadn't persuaded her to actually sing the piece while going through the screen antics. That would be "real," right?

As for the rest: Domingo isn't at his best, driving the voice too open above the *passaggio* and squeezing a bit, but is still a quality Canio. His acting is serious and straightforward. Pons sings Tonio fluently in his middleweight baritone, and his acting is presentable—it's just that there's not much spark or fantasy. Rinaldi's Silvio is similar in concept to Puglisi's for Enriquez, but is vocally threadbare. Andreolli, a sharp Beppe, is rushed through his serenade by Prêtre, who in general makes sure the singers are given no comfort margin—the reading is orderly, quick, and dry. Video quality is fine, audio only fair for a latterday film.

Recommendation: Sad, but true—the closest we come to *Pagliacci* is a forty-plus-years-old RAI TV-movie, the Legato Classics release. It has plenty of drawbacks, but is the only version with significant video-opera virtues. The London edition can be recommended for its sound track only. There's room at the top here.

CONRAD L. OSBORNE

CAVALLERIA RUSTICANA (1890)

A: Santuzza (s or ms); B: Lola (ms); C: Mamma Lucia (c or ms);
D: Turiddu (t); E: Alfio (bar)

Given its picture-postcard Sicilian setting, Catholic Easter ritual and peasant color, it is hardly surprising that designers and directors like *Cavalleria Rusticana* perhaps even more than the singers for whom Mascagni wrote such passionate and singable music. The opera's several extended orchestral interludes give an imaginative director plenty of opportunity for all kinds of stage business. An astute video director can make even more of the famous prelude and intermezzo, using them to fill in the atmosphere around the passionate action and to provide a human and natural portrait of the community whose rigid (and hypocritical) morality leads Santuzza and Turiddu to their ruin.

For this opera to make any real emotional sense to a modern audience, whose members are unlikely to be shocked by the premarital sex around which the overheated plot of *Cavalleria Rusticana* turns, the repressive nature of small-town Sicilian Catholic society must be clearly and graphically portrayed. Only if we truly understand how devastating Turiddu's two-timing is to the relentlessly devout "nice girl" Santuzza will we feel the full force of this simple but powerful tale.

1961 UNKNOWN DISTRIBUTOR (VHS)

(Stage Performance, Stereo, Black and White, English and Japanese subtitles) 72 minutes

Giulietta Simionato (A), Anna di Stasio (B), Amalia Pini (C), Angel Lo Forese (D), Attilio d'Orazi (E)—Giuseppe Morelli

Opera company, stage director, and video director unknown

The jacket notes and on-screen credits for this no-frills *Cavalleria* describe the contents only as "*Live* performance of October 23, 1961, Tokyo, Japan," without providing the name of the theater, orchestra, chorus, director, or producer. The motivation behind the project (which was aired on Japanese television) was to bring to screen the performance of Giulietta Simionato, "the leading Italian mezzo of her generation," in the role of Santuzza. Simionato took the role of Mamma Lucia in a 1940 studio recording conducted by Mascagni himself. Later she became a well-known Santuzza, recording the role several times and finally taking it onstage at the Met for the first time just two seasons before this Tokyo performance.

Roland Grame described (in *The Metropolitan Opera Guide to Recorded Opera*) Simionato's Santuzza for a Cetra-Soria recording made in 1950 as "dignified and deeply wounded, nursing her grief," while he found her 1960 version for Decca "more studied, less spontaneous, than before." His description also applies to her placid, walk-through performance in this video; its matronly style is really more appropriate for Mamma Lucia than for

Santuzza. (The fact that Simionato looks as old or older than Amalia Pini as Mamma Lucia does not help matters.) Simionato's singing is elegant, accurate, and generally pleasing, but emotionally underpowered.

Perhaps because this production was staged in Japan with a largely Japanese chorus at a time when Western opera was still quite new there, the opera's raw sexuality is oddly muted here. Santuzza and Turiddu (Angelo Lo Forese, who doesn't even get drunk during his drinking song) sing politely at each other, as if they were discussing the weather, rather than disastrous philandering.

The work by the chorus and orchestra is only barely professional.

1968 LONDON (VHS / LD)

(Film, Stereo, Color, Subtitled) 70 minutes

Fiorenza Cossotto (A), Adriana Martino (B), Anna di Stasio (C), Gianfranco Cecchele (D), Giangiacomo Guelfi (E), Chorus and Orchestra of Teatro alla Scala—Herbert von Karajan

La Scala: Giorgio Strehler (stage director), Ake Falck (video director)

This version was originally filmed in 1968 by UNITEL of Munich, along with an accompanying *Pagliacci* also conducted by Karajan. The liner notes make grand claims: "The performances on this film are not only powerful and moving in their own right; they are also a riveting record of the approach of one of this century's greatest conductors to two of the most popular and direct operas in the Italian repertoire."

And let there be no question about it—Karajan is the real star here, even though he remains off-camera except for a few moments during the prelude. From the Scala Orchestra and Chorus he elicits a savage and lush performance whose emotional power very nearly overwhelms the competent, though unremarkable vocal performances. It is unquestionably the best orchestral and choral performance offered on any *Cavalleria* available on video, and has retained an

impressive immediacy and sonic depth on the small screen.

Unfortunately, the video director does not possess Karajan's inspiration and imagination. Although the film is handsome and technically polished, the camera work concentrates almost entirely on two disconnected visual spheres: picture-postcard views of the Sicilian landscape and tight close-ups of the principals singing into each others' faces. Perhaps because the performers are not very accomplished actors, the director chooses to emphasize rocks, statuary, and rooftops rather than the human dimension of this tragic story. In the major arias and duets, the singers barely move as the camera dwells on their profiles. The visual style tends to isolate the characters from each other both musically and dramatically, giving us little sense of how they react to each other. Nor does it help that the lip-synching is frequently very obvious.

As Santuzza, Fiorenza Cossotto sings with accuracy, power, and careful musicianship. One feels little passion in her portrayal of the doomed village maiden, however; her manner is too placid and impassive. As the stud Turiddu, Gianfranco Cecchele also lacks sexual energy and physical expressiveness—and his singing is more coarse and labored than Cossotto's. Giangiacomo Guelfi does somewhat better as Alfio. Adriana Martino's Lola is almost as notable for her amazingly long eyelashes as for her acting and singing. As Mamma Lucia, Anna di Stasio stands by stoically and has less impact on the proceedings than is usually the case.

This version emphasizes the religious ritual of the Easter setting, but underplays the essential sexual attraction and jealousy.

1982 PHILIPS (VHS / LD)

(Film, Stereo, Color, Subtitled) 70 minutes

Elena Obraztsova (A), Axelle Gall (B), Fedora Barbieri (C), Plácido Domingo (D), Renato Bruson (E), Chorus and Orchestra of Teatro alla Scala—Georges Prêtre

Franco Zeffirelli (director)

Shot on location in Sicily in lush color, this brilliant film takes *Cavalleria* way offstage and bursts it wide open. Zeffirelli uses every single measure of the orchestral prelude to detail the psychological turmoil boiling inside Santuzza's insulted heart. As the film opens, she is spying with horror on Turiddu as he rides away—singing—from Lola's house on his horse at daybreak, within sight of the azure Mediterranean. By the time Turiddu's "backstage" serenade is over, we have a very good idea just how upset Santuzza is, and why.

Zeffirelli uses the same technique during the Intermezzo, when the stage is traditionally empty, during the Easter service attended by all the townspeople. (The direction particularly stresses the irony of the elaborate Easter rituals as indicative of the yawning gap between religion and reality.) He brings us inside the cathedral, following Santuzza as she slinks along the back wall, an outcast, and catches Turiddu in the act of exchanging postorgasmic glances with Lola during Mass. Throughout the film Zeffirelli narrates from Santuzza's point of view, so when she finally falls apart and tells Alfio what has happened her behavior is both inevitable and cathartic.

As Santuzza, Elena Obraztsova proves herself a surprisingly fine actress, and very responsive to Zeffirelli's concept. From the outset, she throws her feelings of despair and religious fervor right in our face and yet miraculously manages never to fall into bathos. Dressed in severe black, she projects a palpable physicality and heft that is entirely appropriate for this scorned village maiden. When she begs Turiddu to have mercy on her, pushing him finally to throw her aside, the scene vibrates with rage and violence.

Domingo is an excellent foil for Santuzza's fury. Handsome, careless, and cocky, this is the great tenor in his physical prime. He is able to execute all of Zeffirelli's ideas with apparent ease and skill. As for the singing, both he and Obraztsova are in magnificent and powerful form. (The sound track was recorded separately at La Scala, although the dubbing is so well done as to be nearly imperceptible.) This was that magical time before Obratzsova developed the disfiguring wide vibrato that regularly afflicts Russian mezzos, and before Domingo lost the ability to soar easily into the upper part of the tenor range.

In this version, the character of Mamma Lucia is given much more prominence than is usually the case. Zeffirelli uses Fedora Barbieri's wonderfully weathered face and earthy voice to register the premonition of fear and disaster inherent in the music. Her wine shop is gritty and cluttered, not the prettified café of too many stage versions.

As Alfio, Renato Bruson is formidable both vocally and dramatically, and an entirely credible husband to Axelle Gall's subtly flirtatious Lola. Lola, too, is more fully characterized than usual; in the prelude, Zeffirelli shows her luxuriating in bed after her passionate night with Turiddu.

Never does this version communicate the sense of five stars doing their separate turns. The ensemble is tight, polished, and exciting, like Georges Prêtre's conducting.

1991 VAI (VHS)

(Stage Performance, Stereo, Color, Not Subtitled) 80 minutes

Shirley Verrett (A), Rosy Orani (B), Ambra Vespasiani (C), Krjstian Johannson (D), Ettore Nova (E), Teatro Communate dei Rinnovati, Siena; Philharmonic Orchestra of Russe—Baldo Podic

Siena Festival: Mario Monicelli (stage director), Peter Goldfarb (video director)

In 1990, during the Siena Musical Week Festival, a new production of *Cavalleria Rusticana* was staged at the Teatro Communale dei Rinnovati as part of a celebration of the opera's centennial. Shirley Verrett made her (unfortunately, rather belated) debut in the role of Santuzza, and also acts as on-camera host for this video. In a short and self-conscious introduction shot on Siena's handsome main square, she briefly discusses the opera's background and gives a brief synopsis of the action, illustrated by still shots from the production. Those who do not know the opera well should listen closely, since the producers decided to dispense with English-language subtitles.

As Santuzza, Verrett has some good moments but all too often demonstrates her habitual pitch problems. Nor does she always have the power to project strongly enough over the orchestra. Visually, she is rather too advanced in age for the role of a sexually hungry village girl, and does not move easily around the stage. Santuzza's desperation fails to come across, since Verrett's acting style is limited—for the most part—to clenched fists and heavy sighs.

Singing opposite her is the disarmingly Nordic-looking and buttoned-up Krjstian Johannson, who sings his opening serenade from a side box in the theater, next to a harpist. He, too, generates very little excitement either as a singer or an actor, and strikes few sparks— either vocally or dramatically—with Verrett. Like most of the opera, his big duet with Santuzza is staged in a very static fashion, almost more like a concert version than a staged one. Neither the singing nor the acting of the two principals communicates the sense of looming tragedy that is so essential to a successful *Cavalleria*.

The numerous chorus scenes look crowded on the small stage, whose space is overstuffed and poorly utilized. The video direction only emphasizes the fact that the singers are not really bothering to react to each other. A particularly egregious example is the moment when Alfio hears Santuzza's denunciation of Turiddu and Lola; Ettore Nova hardly looks bothered at all. The sets and costumes are strictly conventional, and the Philharmonic Orchestra of Russe under Baldo Podic is never more than competent.

———

The clear choice here is Zefferelli's luminous, visionary, and passionate film, with its compelling vocal and orchestra performances and strong dramatic impact. Karajan fans may want his searing orchestral performance. For those in need of a *Cavalleria* with Japanese subtitles, the Simionato version can be recommended, but purely on linguistic grounds.

HARLOW ROBINSON

JULES MASSENET

MANON (1884)

A: Manon Lescaut (s); B: Chevalier des Grieux (t); C: Lescaut (bar);
D: De Brétigny (bar); E: Comte des Grieux (bs)

The loss of much of the French reper- tory can perhaps be borne, though not gladly. But to see *Manon* slide from view, flags flying and band still playing, is intolerable. True, its musico-linguis- tic style demands loving study, an absorption that cannot be rushed. Its heroine must be unreservedly believed in, her life strategy endorsed, by sopranos who imagine themselves liberated from and superior to her. They must go to her; Manon will not come to them. And though the opera's atmosphere and playing qualities are light, it's actually a "heavy show"— rather long, with an extended cast list, a detailed social canvas for chorus and extras, serious scenic and costume requirements that can't be cheated without dampening the effect, and a full ballet. These are, as my Assistant Headmaster used to say, reasons, but not excuses, for negligence. *Manon* must be res- cued. Its score is brilliant, fragrant, and moving, its stage life varied and delicious. Its title role is one of the most completely and compellingly drawn in the soprano literature, and des Grieux is much more than the tenor partner—it's a far juicier part than, for instance, Alfredo or Pinkerton. All the roles, in fact, have good opportunities for the right performers.

Several cuts—not good, but long standard— are observed in the single available *Manon* video. They include the concluding sequence of Act I, after the departure of Manon and des Grieux; choral repeats and developments in the Cours la Reine and Hôtel Transylvanie scenes;

a snippet of the last act; and, more unusually, the Minuet entr'acte to Cours la Reine. How- ever, Lescaut's second song and the complete ballet, reduced or eliminated in some produc- tions and recordings, are present.

1977 PARAMOUNT (VHS) / PIONEER (LD)

(Stage performance, Stereo, Color, Subtitled)
152 minutes

A: Beverly Sills, B: Henry Price, C: Richard Fredricks, D: Robert Hale, E: Samuel Ramey, Chorus and Orchestra of the New York City Opera—Julius Rudel

New York City Opera: Tito Capobianco (director)

Preserved here are one of the NYCO's most successful productions, and one of Beverly Sills's finest roles. Neither is in freshest estate, but enough remains to suggest the quality of the originals. Capobianco's Fragonard-derived con- cept (here staged by Gigi Denda, with sets by Marsha Louise Eck) is still handsome. The lighting is pedestrian, and the video production (uncredited, which seems a bit shabby) is best described as solid utilitarian: clearly limited in technical resources, it eschews breathtaking shots or postproduction effects, but follows the action clearly enough. Jose Varona's costumes are effective, too, though some of them read less well on camera than in the theater.

Sills had all the vocal equipment for the title

part: the agility, the high-soprano range extension, and a girlish, floating quality capable of fullness and color. Her grasp of the language and style was also secure. By this date, her vocal command was not what it had been for the production's premiere or her audio recording of the role. Though the top warms up and gains a better center as the performance proceeds, there is enough unsteadiness and fuzzy intonation to keep the listener nervous. The middle and lower range areas still respond well, the chirpy passages are in place, and of course Sills is too experienced a professional to be knocked far off course. The final scene is well sung and affecting. Theatrically, the early scenes do not come off well. This is a Manon who gives away her hidden treasure with the open, all-purpose smile, the array of little smirks, shrugs, and other such indications—which in any case are directed more at the audience than the onstage males—and who seems entirely comfortable in the great, wide world. Des Grieux is left with nothing to play against: the mysterious allure that draws him in, the sense of youthful vitality about to be lost to the convent and in need of rescue, aren't there. Close-ups don't help. Sills is better later, when she can work with a more serious kind of emotional sincerity and the grander kind of display. Henry Price, her des Grieux, has a tough assignment. Manifestly younger than his putative sixteen-year-old lover, slimmer, and less stagewise, he enters an old production opposite the star for whom the staging was originally devised. As an actor he is pretty much limited to burying his face in his hands and moving with reasonable grace, and

his singing hasn't a wide range of expression, either. But his clear, slender tenor is in good technical balance. He sings with clean line and some finish, has excellent intonation, and goes after the demands of "Ah, fuyez" with a will. Not a star performance, but an honorable one. Elsewhere, there's a musical-comedy scent to the proceedings. The actress trio suggests favorites more of Styne, Jule, than Massenet, Jules. Richard Fredricks, the Lescaut, barrels aboard straight out of *Shenandoah*. On the plus side, he sings with a security and ring that eludes the more nuanced character singers usually given the part. Ramey, in prime form, sings a most imposing Comte. Of course, he's as young as his son, and the camera reveals age lines that look like cat's whiskers. The pre-Wotan Robert Hale is unusual casting as De Brétigny, a role traditionally cast with a light baritone (though the most interesting I've seen was the fine character bass Gimi Beni). Hale gives it vocal solidity, but not much personality. The only supporting singer with much sense of style and character, Nico Castel, is an excellent Guillot, save in his first approach to Manon, upon whom he descends with the full comprimario complement of splutters, chortles, and throat-clearings. Rudel leads a brisk, plainly phrased performance, sometimes rushed (e.g., the whole Lescaut / De Brétigny incursion in Act II), that is musically clear without having much romantic magic. For some reason, we are subjected to every act curtain call, first grin to final wave.

CONRAD L. OSBORNE

THE MEDIUM (1946)

A: Monica (s); B: Mrs. Gobineau (s); C: Mrs. Nolan (ms);
D: Mme. Flora (c); E: Mr. Gobineau (bar); F: Toby (mute)

*M*ention Gian Carlo Menotti today and the discussion usually veers toward his skills as an impresario (or lack of them, as at the American Spoleto Festival). Yet in the 1940s and 1950s, he was American opera's most celebrated composer, with hit after hit, often on Broadway. There he racked up an impressive number of Pulitzer and other prizes. At the Metropolitan, *The Island God* (1942) and *The Last Savage* (1963) were less successful. But many of his other *verismo*-tinged works, often written for small casts and orchestras, marvellously evoke the dark postwar era with exceptional skill and a haunted beauty and ought to be staged more often than they are.

The Medium, written by commission from Columbia University, was first seen there in 1946 and mounted the following year on Broadway with a more lightweight companion piece, *The Telephone. The Medium* was suggested by an actual seance Menotti had attended in Austria in 1936. It may be looked at as a serious, mystical counterpart to Noël Coward's earlier, loonier *Blithe Spirit*; Menotti's Madame Flora is the sham spiritualist who becomes a victim of her fake art, while Coward's Madame Arcati is a thorough professional who *does* produce psychic manifestations, hilariously.

1950 VAI (VHS)

(Film, Mono, Black-and-White) 80 minutes

Anna Maria Alberghetti (A), Beverly Dame (B), Belva Kibler (C), Marie Powers (D), Donald Morgan (E), Leo Coleman (F), Studio Orchestra of Rome Radio Italia—Thomas Schippers
Gian Carlo Menotti (director)

This is a true rarity, a carefully produced film of a modern opera, directed by its composer-librettist. It is also—possibly accidentally—a striking example of postwar Italian neorealism *and* at the same time a sort of musical *film noir.* Menotti took his fifty-minute opera and expanded it to eighty minutes, adding, among other things, a long opening sequence with the medium walking through a small Italian village, and a sortie to a freak-filled street fair. The result, brilliantly designed by Georges Wakhevitch and with Marie Powers chillingly elaborating her star Broadway turn as the medium, almost resembles something like the chiller *Dead of Night*, had it been filmed by Roberto Rossellini as a musical.

The bleak, dusty exteriors accentuate Madame Flora's faded, Bohemian rooms, where smudged windows look out on sad, late-1940s rainscapes (I can't imagine the Broadway version being any more romantically depressing). It is a perfect milieu for this story of a medium descending into madness. As she does so, her drinking rises proportionally to her sadism toward her mute servant, Toby. Blows and screaming lead to melted wax poured on his chest, whipping, and finally, fatal gunshots. Is he responsible—in some way—for the cold hand Madame Flora felt at her throat? The film would have you believe he possibly wills it to happen.

Leo Coleman gives a stunning performance as the mute, possessed boy. Anna Maria Alberghetti—long before *Carnival*—is a touching, vulnerable daughter, Monica, though she is at times difficult to understand, with some shrill moments. The duped Gobineaus and Mrs. Nolan are properly characterized as dull, sad types without any striking voices. Marie Powers, by contrast, has a full range of vocal fireworks.

In the end, this has the atmospheric features of a film and the theatricality of a star perfor-mance, seen in close-up. Schippers's orchestra is positively spooky, especially the pianos. The video sound is often harshly metallic. Whether the opera ought to have been expanded is questionable: interest does flag at times and I think the short version might have been more incisive, set off by *The Telephone*. It's possible *The Consul* and *The Saint of Bleecker Street* might have been even better, filmed.

RICHARD TRAUBNER

THE TELEPHONE (1947)

A: Lucy (s); B: Ben (bar)

The impact and popularity of Gian Carlo Menotti's operas of the thirties, forties, and fifties remain unique. When he was twenty-six, *Amelia Goes to the Ball* was mounted at the Met, and his next opera, a comedy for radio called *The Old Maid and the Thief*, was until recently still done on college stages all over the country. *The Telephone* and *The Medium* ran together through the 1947–48 season on Broadway and later went on a State Department tour of Europe. *The Consul* and *The Saint of Bleeker Street* had similar success, and *Amahl and the Night Visitors* remains the most popular children's opera in American history. Abroad, the celebrated mezzo Gianna Pederzini sang *The Medium* with more than twenty companies, and such commanding singing actresses as Martha Mödl and Inge Borkh triumphed in *The Consul*, which was also recently revived with great success by L'Opéra de Montréal.

Menotti's style is lyrical and often intensely theatrical; the best productions play down the banal elements. Most of these works should find a happy home on video, but only *Amahl*, *The Medium*, and the comic curtain-raiser *The Telephone* seem to have been produced so far. Something to look into.

1992 LONDON (VHS / LD)

(Studio Production, Stereo, Color, in English)
20 minutes

Carole Farley (A), Russell Smythe (B), Scottish Chamber Orchestra—José Serebrier

Mike Newman (director)

The Telephone has been done most often as a fluffy curtain-raiser to *The Medium*. Its first performances, in New York, starred Marilyn Cotlow, who went on briefly to the Metropolitan as Philine in *Mignon:* a charming light soprano. Annaliese Rothenberger, a famous *Rosenkavalier* Sophie, sang its first performances in Germany. The idea of joining it with Poulenc's *La Voix Humaine*, as on this videotape, is intriguing. Aside from the telephone connection, one can imagine Denise Duval or Julia Migenes, wonderful as Elle, having tried Lucy at some earlier time, too. Oddly here, the Poulenc is very fine, but *The Telephone* is almost completely misconceived. It's the story of a girl so addicted to the telephone that her boy friend is finally forced to propose on . . . well, if you don't know, you can guess. The work is sociologically dated and probably best done in a forties or fifties setting, but that is not the primary problem. Whatever the era, Lucy is young: in her early twenties at most. One thinks of the Jane Powell or Kathryn Grayson of that era, or the Debbie Reynolds of a slightly later one—it's difficult think of anyone *that* naïvely self-absorbed after the sixties. The setting, too, should be simple—an ordinarily bachelor girl's (as they used to say) apartment. Here the Lucy is a compulsive woman in her thirties with a roomful of dated consumer fashions: zebra-striped pillows, plastic flamingos, ivy climbing the stairs, balance toys, a Coke machine, Mickey Mouse . . . and a cordless telephone.

Behavior that might have been curiously charming a decade earlier in her life looks desperate now: Norma Desmond in a condo. Carole Farley is a strong musician, but with a rather coarse voice that has been through Lulu at the Met and seems ready, at least in these intimate surroundings, for Minnie or Elektra. When she finally accepts Ben's proposal we are not happy for him. Under the circumstances Russell Smythe's Ben looks more foolish than usual. It's all tied to *La Voix Humaine*, and *that* is worth seeing.

LONDON GREEN

AMAHL AND THE NIGHT VISITORS (1951)

A: Amahl (treble); B: His Mother (ms or s); C: King Kaspar (t);
D: King Melchior (bar); E: King Balthazar (bs)

Another commissioned Menotti, this time from NBC, *Amahl and the Night Visitors* is the most popular opera ever written for television. It was also the first, and it was the very first opera seen by this writer, in 1951 (and yearly, after that). It still works its Yuletide wonders on television or on the stage, thanks to its exceedingly clever, touching plot (by the composer) and its enchanting score.

The story takes off from the carol "We Three Kings of Orient Are" and has the monarchs stopping to rest at the house of a poor shepherd boy and his mother on their way to the newborn Jesus. Although the plot's implications are thoroughly Christian, it might be argued that Amahl could be Jewish and the kings pre-Muslim (or ancient Pantheist), so the work has a pleasingly ecumenical feel about it.

Psychologically, *Amahl* is *The Medium* with a double happy ending. This story of an overbearing mother and another compromised boy (this time a cripple) ends with the real miracle of Amahl's recovery and the greater miracle of the birth of Christ. There is no sadism here, just a lot of impatient shouting. (One does begin to wonder about Menotti's own mother.)

Musically, an abundance of memorable tunes are set off with an often highly-charged, always clear recitative, and—as always with Menotti—pianos and winds offer accentuation. Brief though it may be, *Amahl* tells its dramatic and inspirational story perfectly, with many exciting moments.

1978 KULTUR (VHS)

(Film, Stereo, Color) 50 minutes

Robert Sapolsky (A), Teresa Stratas (B), Nico Castel (C), Giorgio Tozzi (D), Willard White (E), Philharmonia Orchestra of London—Jésus Lopez-Cobos

Arvin Brown (director)

This version of *Amahl* had its exteriors filmed on location in the Judean Hills of Israel, and its interiors (the bulk of the film) shot in a London studio. There are no new scenes that I can discern—as opposed to the expanded *Medium* on film. The result is a realistic, atmospheric production, though I seem to recall the NBC versions making a lot more of the kings' pomp and riches, especially "all that gold," as the Mother sings. Certainly, Amahl's dwelling is dirt-poor here.

Teresa Stratas is a very good choice to play the beleaguered Mother, with the neurotic edginess this role calls for. She has not, however, the plummier mezzo I remember vividly in the original mom (Rosemary Kuhlmann). Stratas does look appropriately Mediterranean; she could very well be the mother of Robert Sapolksy, the excellent Amahl.

The three kings are well cast. Nico Castel as Kaspar has the best chance to show off with his "This Is My Box" aria. Willard White makes a strong impression as Balthazar, who lives in a "black marble palace with black panthers," and Giorgio Tozzi is a regal but kindly Melchior.

The villagers, offering whatever food they have on short notice at a late hour, manage to lay on quite a spread. They then perform a fairly Broadwayish Middle-Eastern dance which is at least inoffensive; the kings seem to enjoy it.

The London Philharmonia under Jésus Lopez-Cobos plays well, and Arvin Brown's direction is straightforwardly pleasing, although I found the sudden cure of Amahl's lameness less arresting than it usually seems. Having the entire opera encased in pretty Israeli wrapping paper only makes this seasonal gift that much more festive.

RICHARD TRAUBNER

LES HUGUENOTS (1836)

A: Marguerite de Valois (s); B: Valentine (s); C: Urbain (ms);
D: Raoul de Nangis (t); E: Saint-Bris (bar); F: Nevers (bar);
G: Marcel (bs)

Meyerbeer's operas are seldom performed these days for a variety of reasons, the most frequently cited being their massive vocal requirements and scenic demands. To work their full magic, these works need a house as spectacular as the Paris Opéra with all its fabled onstage extravagance, plus singers like those in the first *Huguenots* who have passed into legend: Falcon, Nourrit, Duprez, Levasseur. Failing that today, we are forced to pay more attention to Meyerbeer's generous tunefulness, his vocal opportunities, and the brilliant orchestral effects, delivered by one or two stars surrounded by usually routine support. If the decor is never what one imagines it was a century and a half ago, the costumes are often splendid. And the happy surprise is that Meyerbeer's customary librettist, Eugène Scribe, has often supplied plots that are dramatically moving, once one sees through the baroque layers of historical and period fancy that have been laid on with a trowel. These operas can be presented in comparatively intimate fashion (on television), and you may improve your taste for them if you place them in historical context between, say, Rossini and Verdi.

1990 KULTUR (VHS) / PIONEER (LD)

(Stage Performance, Color, Stereo, Subtitled)
114 minutes

Joan Sutherland (A), Amanda Thane (B), Suzanne Johnston (C), Anson Austin (D), John Wegner (E), John Pringle (F), Clifford Grant (G), Australian Opera Chorus and Orchestra— Richard Bonynge

Australian Opera: Lotfi Mansouri (stage director), Virginia Lumsden (video director)

What strikes the viewer of *Les Huguenots* today is how uncannily similar to current events its central theme is: the bloody religious strife that led to the Saint Bartholomew's Day Massacre in France in 1572. Religious and ethnic violence in Ireland and the Balkans comes instantly to mind. The tension between the Catholics and Huguenots in this opera is musically apparent from the start of Act I, with the glittery, glib choruses of the Catholic nobles contrasted with the Huguenots' Lutheran hymns and their robust, smoky "Piff Paff!" battle song.

But the main tension in this performance comes from the fact that Dame Joan Sutherland is bidding farewell to her beloved Australian audience. How will she fare as Marguerite de Valois? What is the state of her voice that prompted this retirement? And how will everybody celebrate at the end?

Sutherland's role is quite short, but she is every inch the queen-to-be, and the duet with Raoul in Act II provokes such a frenzy from the audience that she has to acknowledge the cheers. As a partner for Dame Joan, Anson Austin is a far better Raoul than a Prince Danilo, coming forth with the requisite Parisian head voice from time to time and handling this long and difficult role with well-judged emphases—considering his non-star vocal status.

Suzanne Johnston is a spectacular Urbain: roguish, swaggering, an ideal *travesti* interpreter. Hers is the best Urbain I've seen, next to Jeanette MacDonald singing "Nobles Seigneurs, Salut!" in the lavishly staged excerpt from *Les Huguenots* in the 1935 film of *Maytime*. Amanda Thane has some exquisitely touching moments in the taxing part of Valentine, while the men range from acceptable to good, with varying expertise in French diction. The audience has a soft spot for Clifford Grant as Marcel, Raoul's crusty servant.

Richard Bonynge's conducting nicely propels the drama, though at times its difficult to hear the lush orchestration (at least through a normal TV set). John Stoddart's sets (from 1981) are attractive but sketchy, so that Michael Stennett's costumes become the main spectacle-suppliers. The dark lighting in some scenes obscures specific locations that were no doubt designed with lavish detail in 1836—the Pré St. Gervais, the chateau of Chenonceaux, etc. Lotfi Mansouri's production ensures that you are focused on the main political-religious conflict and the severe romantic constraints of Raoul and Valentine which dominate the final two acts. Small, nondisfiguring cuts are made throughout; more serious omissions are not being shown Raoul's anger at the end of Act III and the nonappearance of Marguerite at the grand finale.

The latter can be explained by Dame Joan changing into a sequined black gown to receive the sustained cheers of a grateful opera company and audience (including the Prime Minister). Amidst masses of streamers and balloons, Joan reprises the same "Home, Sweet Home" Dame Nellie Melba sang at her farewell, and receives a rather dull bowl with a somewhat ambiguous grimace. Be warned: the entire farewell reception takes up a good deal of the second video cassette.

RICHARD TRAUBNER

L'AFRICAINE (1865)

A: Sélika (s); B: Inès (s); C: Vasco da Gama (t); D: Nélusko (bar);
E: Don Pédro (bs)

Why, one may ask, is this opera about an Indian queen and a Portuguese explorer called *L'Africaine?* (Just as one may justifiably ask: why does Meyerbeer, a Berlin-born composer who made his career in Paris, have the first name Giacomo?) No matter; one must accept a certain artistic license in these things, beginning with librettist Eugène Scribe's fanciful retelling of the real exploits of Vasco da Gama. The opera can be seen as an excuse for lavish spectacle: the shipwreck scene in Act III must have been the equivalent of the audience-pleasing catastrophes prevalent in today's British pop operas. It also played on the nineteenth-century fascination for Oriental luxury and barbarism, and more specifically the picturesque French view of India that would later produce such works as *Les Pêcheurs de Perles* and *Lakmé.*

Tired businessmen also existed during the Second Empire, which accounts for the semi-clothed dancing girls in saris and their muscular consorts in the fourth-act ballet, which must have seemed kitschy even then. Fortunately, Scribe's plot does have its touching moments, and the character of Sélika has a sympathetic grandeur which Meyerbeer has exploited musically to great effect.

1988 KULTUR (VHS) / PIONEER (LD)

(Stage Performance, Stereo, Color, Subtitled)
105 minutes

Shirley Verrett (A), Ruth Ann Swenson (B), Plácido Domingo (C), Justino Dìaz (D), Michael Devlin (E), San Francisco Opera Chorus and Orchestra—Maurizio Arena

San Francisco Opera: Lotfi Mansouri (stage director), Brian Large (video director)

Wolfram Salicki's painted front curtain in this San Francisco Opera production promises a Victorianized *Africaine,* though what's behind it is often fairly skeletal. The shipwreck scene, which should show the entire stage for full effect, is for some reason shot in too-close close-ups. Amrei Salicki's costumes blend sixteenth-century Portuguese clothing with French 1860s dress, somewhat uneasily. Renaissancey tunics surmount long striped trousers. At least the saris are very pretty. By the time we are in the Indies, the scenery and costumes are more tasteful and graceful, particularly the giant deities and the pretty grove of manchineels, whose poisonous sap effectively ends the story.

Although Domingo has the most famous role (as Vasco da Gama) and aria ("O, paradis!"), the lasting impression is left by Shirley Verrett, whose Sélika is regal, lovely, and beautifully sung. Her invocation to the Hindu gods ("Fils du soleil") in the Act III prison scene is a precursor to the Bell Song in *Lakmé,* with Sélika trillingly calling Brahma to extinguish the flames in her heart for Vasco. Domingo is a spirited, properly egocentric explorer, and the only possible faults I can find are his final *e* syllables, which often sound less than authentically

French. But who cares with such a heroic voice? Justino Dìaz, as Sélika's shifty admirer Nélusko, does nicely in his prestorm retelling of the Legend of Adamastor, before he manages to steer the ship onto treacherous reefs.

L'Africaine may not have the modern resonance Les Huguenots has, but the issue of slavery does comes up, much as it does in Aida (seen six years later). It also has less impressive work for the chorus, until the end, when, offstage, it accompanies the moving deaths of Sél-ika and Nélusko. What L'Africaine offers is a rich plateful of semi-history and luscious exoticism, and Maurizio Arena's attempts to plumb Meyerbeer's luxurious scoring may seem more successful than the designers' efforts. As a streamlined modern version, this Africaine is perfectly, vocally acceptable. Perhaps it is ridiculous to want more of a show, but it wouldn't have hurt.

RICHARD TRAUBNER

CLAUDIO MONTEVERDI

ORFEO (1607)

A: Euridice (s); B: La Musica (s); C: Proserpina (s); D: La Messaggiera
(a); E: La Speranza (s or a); F: Orfeo (t or bar); G: Apollo (t or bar);
H: Plutone (bs); I: Caronte (bs)

One of the aims of the Florentine Camerata that invented opera in the late sixteenth century was to recreate the dramatic effect of Greek tragedy: the intent in using the other arts was to reinforce the dramatic effect of the poetry—as they felt the Greeks had done. The theatrical aim was to delight and overwhelm on several levels at once. One sees this particularly in the works of the composer Monteverdi, especially as bolder contemporary productions demonstrate to us increasing aspirations to stylistic accuracy. Monteverdi and his librettist Striggio knew Jacopo Peri's Florentine opera *Euridice,* and the composer continued to bend the available musical means more completely to the dramatic expressivity of the poetry. When they are staged and performed with emotional vitality, there can be few more wrenching sequences than Monteverdi's settings of the Messenger's recollection of Euridice's death and Orfeo's anguished appeal to Charon to cross the Styx to rescue his beloved. A performance should capture not only details of what we suppose is authentic dramatic and musical style but something of the emotional and intellectual power of the Renaissance event itself.

1978 LONDON VHS / LD

(Stage / Studio Performance, Stereo, Color, Subtitled) 102 minutes

Dietlinde Turban (A), Trudeliese Schmidt (B), Glenys Linos (C, D), Trudeliese Schmidt (E),

Philippe Huttenlocher (F), Roland Hermann (G), Werner Gröschel (H), Hans Franzen (I), Monteverdi Ensemble of Zurich Opera—Nikolaus Harnoncourt

Zurich Opera: Jean-Pierre Ponnelle (stage director)

Jean-Pierre Ponnelle's Monteverdi productions have been heavily criticized for their stylization, but I think of them as among his most convincing works, suggesting the grandeur of the ancient world as seen through the Renaissance and greatly animating the stories with a certain formal theatrical vitality. More often than not, theatrical ritual kills dramatic interest, but Ponnelle uses it, as Nikolaus Harnoncourt does the music, to call up a Shakespearean (to us) sinew and pulse often missing in other baroque opera productions.

Here we have a beautiful Renaissance theater and an opening scene mixing earthy pastoral joy and the elegant purity of Orfeo and Euridice's love for one another—as Monteverdi does in his score. Philippe Huttenlocher sings the most transcendent "Rosa del ciel" (Orfeo's wedding song of joy) since Tito Gobbi's recording, then removes his courtly vest and, dressed as a shepherd, celebrates with his friends in a dance of tremendous rhythmic verve under Harnoncourt: the "ideal" and the "real" heartbreakingly combined in a single visual image. In the balconies of the theater some of the chorus, dressed in late Renaissance style, join in celebration. Then suddenly onstage a blue curtain falls and the messenger of Euridice's death appears before it, in an attitude of agony, with her tragic narrative.

And so it goes. Along the way there are occasional excesses and confusions (the treatment of the Charon sequence is questionable), but the opera is nearly all done with enormous emotional conviction and what one can only call a Renaissance sense of largesse. At the end, Apollo, offering Orfeo the delights of immortality, appears as a Renaissance soldier, with glittering armor and a great ruff. As nearly always, the strength of the visual image matches the energy of the score.

Musically, things are generally very satisfying. Huttenlocher has the dramatic and vocal range for the role, and Glenys Linos and Trudeliese Schmidt are both vivid performers. Neither of the basses is quite flexible enough in color or phrasing, but that is not a major drawback. Harnoncourt is an unflaggingly energetic and sensitive conductor. From it all one gets, for once, a deeply theatrical sense of the Renaissance and Classical *quest*.

LONDON GREEN

IL RITORNO D'ULISSE IN PATRIA (1640)

A: Penelope (ms); B: Minerva (ms); C: Eumete (t); D: Ulisse (bar)

*M*onteverdi composed seven operas, but only three have survived. *Il Ritorno d'Ulisse in Patria* is the second of them. Like *L'Incoronazione di Poppea* (1642), it was written for a Venetian public theater (unlike its predecessor, the 1607 *Orfeo*, which was an opulent entertainment conceived for the ducal court of the Gonzagas in Mantua).

Many musical decisions are required to realize *Ulisse* in performance. Only one score exists, its instructions as to instrumentation and choral writing decidedly incomplete. Some adaptors have turned to *Orfeo* as a model by which to orchestrate and fill missing choral parts; but surely that is wrongheaded, considering the radical changes opera underwent from 1607 to 1640 and the differing venues for which the two works were imagined. No point in looking to *Poppea* for guidance either. Its two surviving scores are posthumous, probably intended for touring companies; accompaniment in one score is for two violins and a bass, in the other for a four-part ensemble.

Doubtless the absence of verifiable orchestration and the desire to play *Ulisse* in modern (read, larger) theaters account for the variety of existing adaptations, exemplified by the two versions evaluated below.

1973 VAI (VHS)

(Stage Performance, Stereo, Color, Subtitled) 152 minutes

Janet Baker (A), Anne Howells (B), Richard Lewis (C), Benjamin Luxon (D), Glynde-bourne Festival Chorus, London Philharmonic Orchestra—Raymond Leppard

Glyndebourne Festival: Peter Hall (stage director), Dave Heather (video director)

So successful was this 1972 production of *Ulisse* (directed by Peter Hall, designed by John Bury) that it returned the following year and was among the first of the festival's live presentations to be filmed. In its day, the restraint of its direction, the purity of its visual setting—an abstract grid floor plan set with minimum props and scenic units—and its flying-machine devices that allow the gods to descend, set standards for staging antique opera. Today, the production's pacing seems slower, its movement stiffer than that to which we are now accustomed (the 1985 Salzburg *Ulisse* is an example).

Raymond Leppard is responsible for the score's realization. His string-dominated textures, however harmonically perfumed, catch much of the spirit of the music, pleasing audiences and annoying purists. His version makes use of music adapted from other Monteverdi sources to fill gaps in the score. Leppard has made wholesale cuts throughout the opera. Entire numbers, such as the flirtatious Melanto-Eurimaco scene, Iro's slaughter of the lambs, and Iro's suicide, have disappeared. A number of scenes, such as those late in the opera (the Penelope-Eumete-Telemaco episode and one involving Minerva, Jove, and Neptune), are drastically abbreviated.

There are other problems. Some of the singers of minor roles are merely adequate. Although the ensemble is everywhere lively, gearing between stage and pit, mostly in the first act, leaves something to be desired. The technical liabilities include a somewhat grainy picture quality with little color intensity, uneven sound (which includes dropouts that cause the sound to wander from one speaker to the other) and, on occasion, skimpy subtitles.

No matter. This presentation's shortcomings are insufficient to pale its strongest virtues, among which the work of the four principals and that of Ugo Trama, doubling Time and the suitor Antinous, looms large.

Janet Baker offers an unforgettable portrayal of a resolute Penelope with moving, dignified sadness. Her singing is noble, graceful, elevated, and varied in expression; she is ever the mistress of restrained pathetic accent. Benjamin Luxon's Ulisse, almost as eloquent, comes across as a leader of men, conveying with subtlety the role's wide swings of emotion. Richard Lewis is the wise and gentle shepherd Eumete. Anne Howell's imaginatively projected Minerva — young, bright and attractive — is arrestingly sung and acted.

1985 KULTUR (VHS) / PIONEER (LD)

(Stage Performance, Stereo, Color, Subtitled) 179 minutes

Kathleen Kuhlmann (A), Delores Ziegler (B), Robert Tear (C), Thomas Allen (D), Ensemble Spinario and Tolzer Boys Choir, ORF Symphony Orchestra — Jeffrey Tate

Salzburg Festival: Michael Hampe (stage director), Claus Viller (video director)

As theater, this production is ahead of its rival in the fluidity of its movement, in its amplification of dramatic detail, and in its more imposing decorations. There are fewer musical cuts (the Salzburg running time is almost a half hour longer than Glyndebourne's), thereby strengthening the dramatic impact of some key scenes insufficiently prepared in the earlier, more truncated version. Moreover, the picture and sound quality of this film are much bet-

ter — except that at the beginning of most of the eight scenes of the first act one must strain to hear the words until the engineers adjust the volume level.

Ulisse is heard in a freely adapted version by Hans Werner Henze, who has spurned any attempt at period authenticity in favor of instrumentation utilizing the full resources of a modern orchestra, with dynamics to match. His lean, colorful sonorities (lots of percussion), which far more often than not point up the dramatic action, are clearly the work of a major modern composer of opera.

The Salzburg cast is better balanced than Glyndebourne's, particularly in the smaller roles — Curtis Rayam as Iro, Alejandro Ramirez as Telemaco, and James King as Giove are superior to their English counterparts.

The leading players are admirable. As Penelope, Kathleen Kuhlmann sings well, without effacing memories of the noble Janet Baker, and is even more dramatically expansive. Her rounded characterization — resolute, firm, and humane — is touching in lament, staunch in resistance, and affecting in her surrender to Ulysses. In song and action, Thomas Allen is so impressive, forceful, and passionate as Ulisse one wonders how his disguise might fool anyone. Delores Ziegler is a no-nonsense goddess who revels in her florid vocal flights. Robert Tear is ever the sympathetic good shepherd.

Conductor Jeffrey Tate paces and shapes the opera well, makes the most of Henze's instrumental colors, but his ensemble is not always shipshape.

Neither presentation will please those whose primary consideration is a realization of Monteverdi's score more in tune with 1740 performance practice, but there are rewards for those who can accept a performance of convincing period spirit. In the absence of a more "authentic" version, Kultur would seem the more satisfactory choice; one gets more of the opera Monteverdi wrote plus superior postproduction values. The question remains: how can one be without Janet Baker's Penelope?

C. J. LUTEN

L'INCORONAZIONE DI POPPEA (1642)

A: Poppea (s); B: Drusilla (s); C: Nerone (originally male s; also s, ms,
or t); D: Ottone (originally male c; also ct or bar); E: Ottavia (ms)
F: Seneca (bs)

For most of the musical world, Monteverdi's operas are a proud rediscovery by the late twentieth century. Earlier there were collegiate versions of *Orfeo* and productions at Rome and La Scala with Verdi stars, some of whom recorded it under Franco Calusio in 1939. But it was the 1962 Glyndebourne production and subsequent recording of Raymond Leppard's edition of *L'Incoronazione di Poppea* that first alerted most of us to the composer's modern sensibility. That recording is very heavily cut and now is thought to be overorchestrated, but it was the first to assault us with Monteverdi's vivid theatricality and subtle manipulation of existent musical forms in order to set forth Busanello's cynical late Renaissance text. The existing early scores both leave us massive questions of harmony and instrumentation, and there is the continuing question of how to assign the castrato roles—the answer to which changes as we discover the expressive capacities of countertenors and the more conventional great voices in early music. What *have* been validated through research and imaginative recreation are the dramatic power of certain early music performance conventions and the profound emotional force and intellectual durability of these late Renaissance entertainments.

1979 LONDON (VHS / LD)

(Stage / Studio Performance, Stereo, Color, Subtitled) 162 minutes

Rachel Yakar (A), Janet Perry (B), Eric Tappy (C), Paul Esswood (D), Trudeliese Schmidt (E), Matti Salminen (F), Monteverdi Ensemble of Zurich Opera—Nikolaus Harnoncourt

Zurich Opera: Jean-Pierre Ponnelle (stage director)

Jean-Pierre Ponnelle's production of this late Renaissance work, comparable in its cynicism and emotional extravagance to the plays of Webster and Tourneur in the period following Shakespeare, is all baroque excess and extraordinarily vivid both theatrically and musically. The sets are overrun with detail, and the costumes something of an inviting Renaissance nightmare. Virtue is whitefaced and Fortune barebreasted and greasepainted. Eric Tappy's Nerone is not merely in love but plainly besotted, maddened by it. Alexander Oliver's tenor Arnalta turns this nurse into a dirty old woman with a varicose vein of worldly wisdom, and Trudeliese Schmidt's Ottavia has not only rage and vulnerability but strength and tragic stature. When Maria Callas was once offered the role of Poppea she complained that it was Ottavia who had the great scenes: one sees here what she meant. In this atmosphere, Rachel Yakar's Poppea is oddly innocent: childishly sensuous and self-absorbed, but not the conscious manipulator that almost everyone else has found in this role—a fascinating view. The countertenor Paul Esswood is a lyrical and touching Ottone, but neither he nor anyone else can produce that piercingly anguished tone that we are told was the special possession of the castrato—and this character.

How much all of this dramatic vitality depends on the subtlety of these fine singing actors in coloring and pointing Monteverdi's vocal line is demonstrated by Matti Salminen, who for all his beautiful voice and intelligence can no more than any other modern bass make Seneca anything but a noble windbag. What might Ezio Pinza, with his beautiful diction and infinite vocal coloring, have done with the role? The supporting singers tread the line between playful and bitter comedy very well, and Ponnelle uses his varying set to great dramatic purpose. Nikolas Harnoncourt conducts a performance of tremendous vitality and theatrical tension. Of course there are controversial elements—the production has come in for heavy criticism—but this *Poppea* has an emotional immediacy and dramatic decisiveness which at least parallel what Monteverdi seems to have had in mind.

1984 HBO (VHS)

(Stage Performance, Stereo, Color, Subtitled) 148 minutes

Maria Ewing (A), Elizabeth Gale (B), Dennis Bailey (C), Dale Duesing (D), Cynthia Clarey (E), Robert Lloyd (F), Glyndebourne Festival Chorus and London Philharmonic Orchestra—Raymond Leppard

Glyndebourne Festival: Peter Hall (stage and video director)

Peter Hall's production of this harsh, decadent tragedy with its repellently happy ending is intelligent and certainly well-intentioned, but it misses the Senecan madness at the heart of the opera. John Bury's settings, for example, are coolly classical in design—though not, as might be hoped, an effective ironic comment on the vicious actions of the characters, who are here, with one brilliant exception, played as rather

nice folk simply unable to handle their instincts.

The immortals, Fortune and Virtue, are promisingly horrifying in appearance, but when we get to Rome, Nero is simply a not-very-bright ruler in love, and not a deranged tyrant damned by irrational passion. Cynthia Clarey's Ottavia is merely bereft and melancholy, without that element of desperate cruelty (nourished at court) that gives the character depth. Dale Duesing's Ottone sings and looks well, but he's essentially the boy next door on a horrible Roman holiday. Robert Lloyd's Seneca is the usual nice old man—this time with eyeglasses—and not the life-scarred philosopher who has long fought to *tamp down* the fires of passion. The supporting characters emerge in general as either pleasantly limited (Arnalta) or foolish (Valetto). Their efforts are all earnest and the singing is pleasing enough in tone, but the librettist Busenello's tragic complexity and tension have been lost. Raymond Leppard conducts his edition of the score in lively fashion. In the midst of this we have the Poppea of Maria Ewing—deadly, alternately cute and carnally beautiful, inviting and repellent—a sensual manipulator without a real political colleague in sight. Hers is a charismatic performance of profound effect.

It all ends cynically, with Nero and Poppea on thrones singing to the audience about love, against a background of the galaxy. As so often, these ideas read well, but the dramatic effect is more indifferent than involving. Any Monteverdi enthusiast, however, will want to view this performance for Maria Ewing's haunting heroine.

Jean-Pierre Ponnelle's 1979 Zurich Opera production may have its excesses but it does reflect in vivid theatrical terms the cynicism and emotional extravagance of Monteverdi's work as few other productions have.

LONDON GREEN

Mitridate, Re di Ponto (1770)

A: Aspasia (s); B: Ismene (s); C: Sifare (ms); D: Mitridate
(t); E: Farnace (male alto or ms); F: Arbate (ms)

While writing *Mitridate, Re di Ponto*, Mozart's voice changed—he was fourteen years old. That was probably the most dramatic aspect of the opera's creation. *Mitridate* is a result of the child abuse practiced by Mozart's father, Leopold. For the most part, the highly complicated text (based on an opera libretto based on an Italian translation of a play by Racine) can have made little sense to a teenager. Just perhaps, that aspect of the story involving a young son's rebellion against an overwhelming father might have resonated—there are mild pre-echoes of *Idomeneo* here. For the most part though, Mozart was stuck tailoring his music to singers far more famous than he (he had to rewrite one aria five times for the first Mitridate).

Mithridates (known as Eupator) and his sons were historical personages. He was one of the more successful, colorful, and bloodthirsty rebels against the Roman Empire. His son Pharnaces (the opera's villain, Farnace) inspired Julius Caesar's famous line, "veni, vidi, vinci!." In the opera, conventionalized amorous intrigue is more important than battles and politics. The real Mithridates was no stranger to anything vile, his exploits in the bedroom were as bloody as his strategies for dynastic survival, and of that, to its cost, *Mitridate* drops no hint.

Opera seria form, with its long arias and reams of secco recitative, was hard to work in. Mozart's skills are impressive, his youth is less in evidence technically than in the uneven way texts and emotions are reflected within the often unwieldy aria conventions. There are exceptions—the use of g minor, a significant key for the mature Mozart, to characterize Aspasia's grief and anxiety, for example, or her wonderful cavatina in E-flat major, "Pallid' ombre" (No. 21), which only Mozart could have written. Or there is the magnificent horn obbligato in Sifare's second act aria "Lungi di te," the whole aria imprinted with an intense adult grief at parting. Throughout are the fingerprints of genius. But fingerprints are most fascinating to the specialist in the lab; the challenge for performers is to make a long work in a remote style immediate and compelling to the nonspecialist viewer. Since the opera has roles for three castratos (two of them elaborate), today's singers have to struggle with vocal lines which are apt to have far less force and brilliance in the throats of "Mozart mezzos" and woebegone countertenors.

1987 LONDON (VHS / LD)

(Film, Stereo, Color, Subtitled) 124 minutes

Yvonne Kenny (A), Joan Rodgers (B), Ann Murry (C), Gösta Winbergh (D), Ann Gjevang (E), Massimiliano Roncato (F), Concenticus Musicus—Nikolaus Harnoncourt

Jean-Pierre Ponnelle (director)

This is a movie shot to a preexisting sound track; lip-synching adds to the artificiality (though some recitative sequences may be live).

Differing and distracting sonic perspectives are used for recitative and aria, and in the arias singers are fairly frequently drowned out.

Though *opera seria* conventions are strange to us, Mozart obviously expected the "reality" of lust versus love colored by ambition to be mirrored. But Jean-Pierre Ponnelle doesn't take any of that seriously. He has inventive fun with the stage conventions of Baroque and pre-Classical staging (he filmed in the Teatro Olimpico, Vicenza), playing with perspectives, drops, and quaint props. He is sophisticated in every way: different lenses, lenses coated in softening or subtly blurring substances, great skill in lighting, beautiful framing, and a striking sense of montage are all very evident. Many shots are gorgeous. Now and again, simply through editing, Ponnelle creates a sense of "music drama." For example, in the string-accompanied recitative before the duet "Se viver non deggio" (No. 18), the results are magic. Two characters are humanized, and what is haunting in the music is given a visual correlative. But far more often, characters lurk behind columns and flamboyantly skulk about. There is little sense of people interacting, and much of Ponnelle's work seems tricked up to entertain the eye at the expense of sense (such as Sifare evidently hallucinating Aspasia and Farnace in his first aria). Old distinguished Arbates is played by a choirboy who does lots of waving and grinning and later, melodramatic grimacing. (One supposes he is a stand-in for pubescent Mozart and a steal from Ingmar Bergman's *Magic Flute* film, though at least that little girl didn't sing!)

The performers, gotten up in lush fabrics, have been encouraged to pop their eyes. Yvonne Kenny, Aspasia, suffers least; she has genuine camera presence. Gösta Winbergh, though he carries on a great deal, sometimes clumsily, wields a major voice in the title role. The two manly villains, Farnace and Sifare, are entirely and emphatically feminine. The distinguished Anne Murray, very womanly, is given more rein in the Royal Opera House performance below. As that blackguard Farnace, Anne Gjevang is hilariously coltish—a cross between Gidget and Octavian. Both sing fairly well.

In the long run, Ponnelle's self-conscious over-conceptionalizing and his self-regarding techniques are distracting, not illuminating—and yet, simply as a director's artifact, this is diverting, even absorbing to watch.

The music is heavily cut, including many memorable arias. Harnoncourt uses a "period ensemble" and plays about quite a bit with rhythms. Though some tempos are very quick, he's also capable of dragging. The singers are very musical, their level of execution is high, and some of the cuts save them from cruel exposure. A very reverberant acoustic blurs one's sense that these are mostly very small voices. Sound can be blasty and congested.

1991 KULTUR (VHS) / PIONEER (LD)

(Stage Performance, Stereo, Color, Subtitled) 177 minutes

Luba Organasova (A), Lilian Watson (B), Ann Murray (C), Bruce Ford (D), Jochen Kowalski (E), Jacquelyn Fugelle (F), Chorus and Orchestra of the Royal Opera House —Paul Daniel

Royal Opera, Covent Garden: Graham Vick (stage director), Derek Bailey (video director)

Watching this video, one can only marvel at how game modern singers are. This cast poses, preens, dances, whirls, pantomimes, and gestures with a touching generosity of spirit. Graham Vick sets the piece in Never-Never Land. There is more than a hint of Kabuki in costume and sometimes makeup (Farnace sports a chalk white face and a flesh-colored neck). Masked soldiers swish around in skirts—samurai warriors were perhaps the intention, the impression in actuality is something less than martial. In Act II they do an entrance out of the Balinese Dance Drama, stamping their own rhythms— that would certainly have raised Mozart's eyebrows, if not his hackles. In Act III they prance about in blue-bedecked Roman Armor! Costumes do not reflect reality, gender, or clothes that can ever have been worn by humans; instead, half the time most characters have wide horizontal protrusions at hip level (a period "silhouette" greatly exaggerated)—it looks like everyone is travelling with his or her own divan (design is by Paul Brown). At the end (after more Balinese stamping), dying Mitridate looks like a lampshade. An elaborately stylized gestural vocabulary reflects perhaps the Kathakali theater of India (choreography and movement are by Ron Howell)—characters finger-mold space or wave semaphorically at one another. Vick is a tonier Peter Sellars, inventing a style just as remote but less static than the stiff conventional *opera seria* manner Mozart wrote for. The viewer will have to judge whether this is interesting (rather than increasingly predictable) over the long haul of the opera, and expressive of anything more than the director's considerable ingenuity.

Musically, this is far more complete than the London video, but quite a lot of recitative is cut, as are some arias. One particularly misses No. 12, Mitridate's great B-flat major aria "Tu che fidel." Paul Daniel conducts vividly, though the strings don't have impeccable intonation.

Two of these singers are very impressive: Organasova sings Aspasia with a trumpeting glint in her upper range and impressive sweep and precision in her coloratura. One forgives a hint of thinness mid-range and what appears to be less than a blazing temperament. Bruce Ford in the title role, though perhaps light in timbre, is enormously accomplished, particularly in "Ombra mia" (No. 20) with its many high C's. Lilian Watson as Ismene has charm, but her tone is spread and she's tenuous at the top.

The problem are the two leading "men," Ann Murray and the countertenor, Jochen Kowalski. Murray is intelligent, resourceful, and eloquent in intention. But her voice, flexible and wide-ranging, is ordinary in timbre, thin, and one wouldn't swear by her intonation. That great, murderously difficult aria, "Lungi di te" (No. 13), though vividly characterized, needs some-

thing—a castrato. If a woman must sing it, a young Callas is required. Murray can't quite do it. She has even more trouble with the bravura No. 22, "Se il rigor d'ingrata sorte." These problems are more serious for Kowalski. Again, there's no missing intelligence and good intentions, and he's very capable on stage. But his piping is incongruous in the role of a flamboyant warrior-villain. He is hoarse, has no tone, no color, no dynamic options, and limited coloratura skills given the demands of the writing (his trills are poor, for instance). He can barely get through his low-lying final aria, "Gia dagli occhi" (No. 24). The problem isn't his really, it's bogus authenticity. Countertenors were used solely in church in countries where castration was unpopular. This voice works best in the high-lying, narrowly cast choral lines of Bach. In no sense is this a theater voice. Neither in range, size, nor timbre can this sound suit a thrusting, powerfully conceived dramatic part—unless one hates voices. Handel used mezzos or tenors where no castratos were available; Mozart used a tenor (for Idamante) when he rewrote *Idomeneo* after the castrato vogue. This serious problem has no obvious solution in mounting these works—but it's impossible to feel capon clucking gets us even close to what the composer had in mind.

Ponnelle's film is remarkably accomplished, sometimes amusing, and now and then arresting. What it has to do with Mozart's *Mitridate* isn't clear. The Covent Garden performance has greater musical rewards and some strong singers. Graham Vick's production seems to be more about directing unwieldy operas in a vanished style than about this opera in particular.

ALBERT INNAURATO

LA FINTA GIARDINIERA (1775)

A: Sandrina (s); B: Arminda (s); C: Serpetta (s); D: Ramiro (ms);
E: Don Anchise (Podestà) (t); F: Belfiore (t); G: Nardo (bar)

*L*a Finta Giardiniera, a three-act *opera buffa* first performed in Munich on January 13, 1775, was the eighteen-year-old Mozart's eighth stage work, but only his second crack at comedy. In many ways, however, it seems to be a study for his final and consummate Italian comic operas, *Le Nozze di Figaro* (1786) and *Così Fan Tutte* (1790). Its libretto (long attributed to Gluck's librettist Raniero de Calzabigi, but now believed to be the work of Giuseppe Petrosellini) features stock *commedia dell'arte*-based characters embroiled in a tangled web of amusing romantic intrigue, complete with disguises, mistaken identities, and crossed couplings. Yet *Finta* shares with Mozart's late comedies a strikingly serious undertone. The journeyman composer was already moving toward the fusion of genres that characterizes his mature style, striving to create a new kind of comic opera that owes as much to Diderot's serio-comic *drames bourgeois* as it does to pure Italian *opera buffa*.

For this reason, *Finta*'s characters (like those of Mozart's later operatic masterworks) speak in different musical languages: the soubrettish maid Serpetta, the aging landowner Don Anchise (the Podestà), and the earnest servant Nardo are cut largely from the cloth of *opera buffa*; the rejected suitor Ramiro (originally conceived for a castrato), the highborn lady Arminda, and the slightly pompous Count Belfiore are rooted in the world of *opera seria*; while Sandrina (the eponymous "false gardengirl"), a noblewoman disguised as a peasant, has one foot in each universe. The blend—and frequent collision—of these worlds provided Mozart with just the sort of dramatic fuel he needed to progress as an opera composer.

Interestingly, the score's finest pages, the real prophetic patches of Mozart, occur chiefly when the plot darkens. The accompanied recitatives (particularly the one preceding Belfiore's Act II aria and the one in Act III in which Sandrina and Belfiore come back to their senses) are astonishingly precocious music-drama. And the ensembles, especially the compound finales which close each act, powerfully foreshadow such masterful moments as the *Don Giovanni* sextet and the Act I finale of *Così*. Small wonder that *La Finta Giardiniera* moved the critic Christian Schubart to write, "Sparks of genius flicker here and there. . . . If Mozart is not a hothouse plant he will surely become one of the greatest composers who ever lived."

1988 PHILIPS (LD)

(Stage Performance, Stereo, Color, Subtitled)
150 minutes

Britt-Marie Aruhn (A), Eva Pilat (B), Ann Christine Biel (C), Annika Skoglund (D), Stuart Kale (E), Richard Croft (F), Petteri Salomaa (G), Chorus and Orchestra of the Drottningholm Court Theatre—Arnold Östman

Drottningholm Court Theatre: Göran Järvefelt (stage director), Thomas Olofsson (video director)

The wide shots of the jewel-like Drottningholm Court Theatre that begin each act of this *Finta Giardiniera* reinforce this video's mission: to be a faithful account of a worthy, eighteenth-century style stage production. The introductory raps on the stage floor; the lovely, determinedly two-dimensional wing and drop settings; the winsome Classical period costumes and wigs (compulsory even for the orchestra); and the delightfully primitive *coups de théâtre* (toggle-switch lightning, thunder sheets) all effectively flavor the proceedings.

There is nothing two-dimensional, however, about Göran Järvefelt's sensitive, carefully rehearsed production. From the opening ensemble, the somewhat pasteboard characters and their tangled relationships are rendered clear, nuanced, and vivid. The musical details (including the many long orchestral introductions and interludes) are mirrored with telling, never gratuitous, dramatic detail. Yet Järvefelt's staging is not without its fanciful touches. During Sandrina's agitated, c-minor Act II aria, "Crudeli, fermate," for example, her spiritual turbulence is reflected as, blindfolded, she is tossed about by veiled, black-clad figures.

Järvefelt's naturalistic style is abetted by a well-fused ensemble of mostly young, fresh, attractive singing actors who thrive under the merciless scrutiny of television cameras. The singing of this mostly Scandinavian cast is accomplished and stylish if not entirely world-class.

Soprano Britt-Marie Aruhn brings dramatic depth and dignity and pastel-tinted vocal panache to the pivotal role of Sandrina. Her Act I cavatina, "Geme la tortorella," features spot-on staccato singing, and her Elvira-like set of Act II arias is especially touching.

This cast's *buffo* characters are a colorful bunch. British tenor Stuart Kale, got up to look like the love child of George Frideric Handel and Hermione Gingold, is a properly foppish Podestà, though his suavely inflected, lightweight tenor sounds drier here than usual. Ann Christine Biel's spitfire Serpetta is eighty percent élan, fifteen percent musicality, and five percent voice, and that's just fine, really. Petteri Salomaa's lyrically vocalized Nardo is an endearingly geeky bumpkin who manages, nevertheless, a convincing eleventh-hour transition into a debonair manservant. "Con un vezzo all'Italiana," his polyglot Act II showpiece, is a highlight, broadly comic without going over the top.

The *seria* characters serve as effective counterweights. The haughty Arminda is efficiently portrayed by Eva Pilat, whose rather wan timbre is bolstered by sure technique and musicianship. American tenor Richard Croft's heartfelt Belfiore finds just the right middle ground between elegant and effete. Croft is nimble of voice and figure, dispatching both the devilish triplets and the demanding acrobatics of his Act II aria, "Già divento freddo," with uncommon grace. Annika Skoglund, as the melancholy Ramiro, claims perhaps the most distinctive voice in the cast, a dusky, tremulous, aptly androgynous instrument. She offers a rather generalized dramatic intensity and physicalizes her trouser role well enough, though she is hindered by an overly feminine makeup job and hairstyle.

The admirably lean, zippy Mozart that conductor Arnold Östman draws from the Drottningholm Orchestra will be less startling to mainstream audiences in this unfamiliar work than in Drottningholm's audio and video traversals of more standard Mozart repertory. The performance is laudably complete and follows the order of the authoritative 1978 Bärenreiter edition, except for the shift of Ramiro's aria "Se l'augellin sen fugge," from Act I to Act II. The English subtitles are clear and indispensable.

CORI ELLISON

Il Re Pastore (1775)

A: Elisa (s); B: Tamiri (s); C: Aminta (ms);
D: Alessandro (t); E: Agenore (t)

This pastoral work is by a disappointed nineteen year old, unhappy to be back in Salzburg after a tour that failed to yield a lucrative permanent post elsewhere. The young composer's new employer and later enemy, the Archbishop Colloredo, demanded an opera to entertain an illustrious guest, the Archduke Max (who was Mozart's age). Mozart was handed as text a quaint, dated court entertainment by the famous Metastasio (there could be no villain, thus there is no conflict). The Abbe Varesco, soon to be working on *Idomeneo*, cut and updated it. The work is called a "musique-concert" in the Archduke's travel diary. It did not evidently excite a lot of attention. Mozart's friend and fan, the gossipy Baron Von Schiedenhofen, refers to it only briefly as a "serenade." It is best known for its famous aria, "L'amerò sara costante" with violin obbligato (sung in the first act by Aminta, originally a castrato, who, when his true name—Abdolonymus—is revealed, becomes the Shepherd King). Its haunting, elusively melancholy E-flat major key, with its episode in c minor, is quintessential Mozart. The budding theater genius is in evidence throughout with several striking accompanied recitatives and much imaginatively characterful instrumentation (one of the great stretches in early Mozart operas is Aminta's long recitative toward the end of the first act). That Mozart was composing his violin concertos at this time is often obvious in very florid vocal lines. Many of the arias have memorably beguiling tunes. The composer evidently thought so, as he sent four to one of his first serious loves, Aloysia Weber (later his sister-in-law). He also recycled the overture and Aminta's first aria into a symphony (K. 213c).

1989 PHILIPS (VHS / LD)

(Stage Performance, Stereo, Color, Subtitled) 116 minutes

Sylvia McNair (A), Iris Vermillion (B), Angela Maria Blasi (C), Jerry Hadley (D), Claes H. Ahnsjö, Academy of St. Martin's in the Field—Neville Marriner

International Mozart Foundation, Salzburg: John Cox (stage director), Brian Large (video director)

John Cox's production respects the original manner in which this work was presented. The set is a palace room with a small stage erected. Footmen are in attendance. "Servants" help with props. Modest "set changes" occur in full view (while the orchestra tunes). Design elements (by Elisabeth Dalton) are elegant, witty, and very pretty. There are large toy sheep in Act I. The singers bow to the public after some of their arias.

As one might expect in an opera mostly made up of long recitatives and longer arias, a big burden is put on the singers to fascinate and scintillate within a delicate frame, and, very importantly, to ravish the ears. Typical of their generation, these singers are pleasant looking and at ease on stage, though under the brocade the bodies are clearly those of the late Twentieth Century. The TV manners everyone uses to signal charm seem a little strange in context. The singing is decently schooled rather than consistently memorable or everywhere greatly accomplished. One must grant that the faintly musical comedy manner of Jerry Hadley (looking handsome) does not obscure good fiorature and a real trill in his difficult D major aria, "Si spande il sol." He does rather less well by the superb and murderously difficult F major aria in Act II, "Se vincendo." One is slightly annoyed by his pronouncing "se" as though it were "say" (and despite his name, he is an Italian-American!). I wonder if the Italian of the original cast would have been clearer, more consistent and expressive than it usually is here. Back in Salzburg the original Aminta (Tomaso Consoli) was an Italian, as Angela Maria Blasi is. In Blasi's case the advantages of knowing the language are obvious. The others do not generally pronounce well. Blasi is physically engaging, smaller than the ladies she's wooing (sometimes comically). She does much alluring singing but too often abuses the white tone, as indeed do all the women here. That and some flutter (nerves?) afflict her "L'amerò." Taking

the voice off its support and damping down overtones is a wearying modern mannerism. Sylvia McNair is a particular offender and her oddly Viennese pronunciation (down to the occasional "qvell") is irritating. She has a forceful presence, but I hear her tone as thin. That's true of Claes H. Ahnsjö as well. Iris Vermillion, the Tamiri, sounds as though she has real promise, particularly when she sings out in her magnificent A major second act aria, "Se tu di me fai dono". There her timbre is striking. Elsewhere she isn't invariably in tune or rock steady. Her House of Windsor manner (perhaps it's intentional) is amusing.

Sir Neville Marriner is the very decisive conductor, probably more intrusive with his big and assertive orchestra than Mozart would have expected.

Brian Large's video work is typically musical and accomplished. Perhaps perforce he keeps his camera locked for long periods close on the singers (making the occasional evidence of post performance re-dubbing more glaring). There is some congestion on the sound track.

Not the most riveting account of some wonderful music but this is a pleasant and capable stab at the work.

ALBERT INNAURATO

IDOMENEO, RÈ DI CRETA (1781)

A: Ilia (s); B: Elettra (s); C: Idamante (ms or t); D: Arbace (t);
E: Idomeneo (t)

*M*ozart's canon of familiar "mature" masterpieces—two German *Singspiele* and a trio of Italian *opere buffe*—is framed chronologically by *Idomeneo, Rè di Creta* (1781) and *La Clemenza di Tito* (1791), a pair of masterful *opere serie* which have only recently been welcomed into the standard operatic repertory. The two pieces are like majestic bookends, *Idomeneo* heralding the full blossoming of Mozart's operatic genius and *Tito* distilling a brief but remarkable lifetime's achievement in lyric theater.

Commissioned for the 1781 Munich carnival season by the liberal, music-loving Elector Karl Theodor, *Idomeneo* is no more a pure *opera seria* than *Don Giovanni* is a pure *opera buffa* or *Die Zauberflöte* is an unadulterated *singspiel*. In *Idomeneo*, as in all of his subsequent works, the twenty-four-year-old Mozart, already a seasoned and celebrated opera composer, bursts open forms that he had long since mastered. Working with a Classicized retooling of a Baroque-style libretto, he used the moribund genre of *opera seria* as a wineskin within which he brewed his own unique, heady blend of whatever he instinctively knew would best serve the drama.

Idomeneo's most salient influence is that of Gluck (whose works had impressed Mozart during his Paris sojourn in 1778)—obvious in its mighty, organic choruses, its marches, and its dance segments, as well as in its musical continuity, its striking accompanied recitatives, and its forward-looking ensembles. And the Elec-

tor's virtuosic orchestra, celebrated as Europe's finest, inspired Mozart to new heights in pictorial detail, bold harmony, and sheer amplitude. But perhaps Mozart's greatest leap forward in *Idomeneo* is in the realm of characterization; the mythic Abraham and Isaac-type tale of conflict, sacrifice, and love between a father and son undoubtedly struck a deep chord in Mozart.

There really is no such animal as a "complete" *Idomeneo*, since Mozart left a variety of textual options. In order to suit the vocal and dramatic capabilities of several singers (and, one suspects, his own unfailing theatrical instincts), Mozart cut several arias (Nos. 27, 29, and 31) from the opera's premiere in Munich on January 29, 1781. For its next performance, at the Vienna residence of Prince Johann Adam Auersperg on March 13, 1786, Mozart provided two fresh numbers, "Non temer," K. 490, a rondo with violin obbligato, and "Spiegarti non poss' io," K. 489, an alternate Act III duet, to accommodate a tenor Idamante who replaced the castrato soprano of the 1781 version. In addition, he wrote two different variants of Idomeneo's aria "Fuor del mar" (No. 12) and four versions of Neptune's oracle (No. 28). Anytime the opera is performed, there are choices to be made.

Idomeneo has had a checkered performance history; for years it pleased neither "modern" operagoers, who turned their noses up at *opera seria*, nor *opera seria* purists, who scorned its iconoclasm. *Idomeneo* never vanished entirely, but during the nineteenth and early twentieth centuries, it was presented in heavily cut, rearranged, and augmented versions tailored to suit current musical and dramatic fashion. A landmark 1951 Glyndebourne Festival production did much to rekindle interest in *Idomeneo*, but it was not until the 1970s, when the Neue Mozart Ausgabe published an authoritative critical edition of the score, that the work began to be regularly performed and properly appreciated. In recent decades, as we have begun to reclaim the first two centuries of operatic history, we can see *Idomeneo* more clearly: not as a retrogressive nod to a dying art form, or a mere study for later operas, but as an astonishingly progressive masterpiece in and of itself.

1974 VAI (VHS)

(Stage Performance, Mono, Color, Subtitled) 128 minutes

Bozena Betley (A), Josephine Barstow (B), Leo Goeke (C), Alexander Oliver (D), Richard Lewis (E), Glyndebourne Festival Chorus, London Philharmonic Orchestra—John Pritchard

Glyndebourne Festival Opera: John Cox (stage director), Dave Heather (video director)

This live performance of *Idomeneo* from the 1974 Glyndebourne Festival is not for Mozart purists. Pruned and reconfigured, it clocks in at a trim 128 minutes, beginning like a proto-*Otello* with the dramatic storm at sea (Chorus, No. 5, "Pietà, numi, pietà") rather than with the stark, unaccompanied voice of Ilia alone onstage. In fact, there is nothing left here of Act I but a little march and an accompanied recitative framed by two choruses. Though this *Idomeneo* undeniably starts with a more visceral punch than most, the excision from Act I of much recitative and five arias (*opera seria's* chief vehicles of character delineation) robs the piece of some psychological depth and dimension. Acts II and III, however, are presented nearly intact and even retain some frequently cut arias (Nos. 10, 27, and 31), as well as "Non temer," K. 490, the rondo which Mozart added to the 1786 Vienna revival for a tenor Idamante and obbligato violin (played beautifully here).

In context, this performance may be viewed less as a benighted approach to Mozart performance than as a significant step in restoring the master's earlier works to the repertory. Tenor Richard Lewis, the Idomeneo of the seminal 1951 Glyndebourne production that put *Idomeneo* back on the map, here reprises his portrayal of the legendary Cretan monarch. He makes a strong, tortured, slightly marmoreal king, sounding a tad worn, especially in the taxing fioratura of "Fuor del mar" (No. 12). His most poignant, beautifully sung moment comes in Act III's "Accogli, o re del mar" (No. 26), the majestic duet for Idomeneo and the men's chorus.

Idomeneo is the only one of Mozart's operas in which the chorus takes a central role, and the smallish Glyndebourne Festival Chorus is one of the chief virtues of this video version, delivering unfailing balance, blend, and nuance, as well as lovely tone and dramatic involvement. The London Philharmonic under John Pritchard offers a spirited, detailed rendering of the score.

Director John Cox stresses the ceremonial, *Zauberflöte*-like aspects of the piece and is remarkably able to conjure a sense of pageantry on the postage-stamp stage of the old Glyndebourne theatre. Against Roger Butlin's simple and attractive settings—a grating-like deck flanked by concentric circular arches which frame changing backdrops—Cox creates telling, arresting stage pictures. The storm which concludes Act II, with its *Jaws*-like sea monster, is particularly vivid. The uncredited, Grecian toga-style costumes offer proof that all men are not created equal.

The basically British cast is of uniformly good quality. Bozena Betley is an appealing, musicianly Ilia, with warm tone and sure technique, though her portamento in "Se il padre perdei" (No. 11) is excessive by current standards and her "Zeffiretti lusinghieri" suffers from notey passage work. The clarion-voiced American tenor Leo Goeke is handsome and earnest, if somewhat drab and stolid, as Idamante. As Arbace, Alexander Oliver is not the usual *eminence grise*, but rather a smooth, robust vocal and dramatic presence who makes one grateful to hear Arbace's rarely performed Act III aria (No. 22, "Se colà ne' fati è scritto").

Josephine Barstow, normally a musico-dramatic dynamo, here delivers a benign, positively ingenuish Elettra. In a sweet blue gown, her hair demurely pulled back and topped by a gold coronet, she seems more like a road-company Guinevere than the usual fright-wigged, Bride of Frankenstein-style Elettra. The loss of Elettra's Act I aria (No. 4) underlines this impression. Because we first encounter her in the lyrical "Idol mio" (No. 13) in Act II, her powerful (if not pretty) Act III outburst "D'Oreste, d'Ajace" (No. 29) seems to come from left field.

A final caveat: this version is not recommended for wire-heads. A souvenir of a more primitive era in video, its visuals are grainier and its sound tinnier than we've come to expect, and the performance is less a television production than a faithfully recorded stage performance. The English subtitles are good, though.

1982 PARAMOUNT (VHS) / PIONEER (LD)

(Stage Performance, Stereo, Color, Subtitled) 185 minutes

Ileana Cotrubas (A), Hildegard Behrens (B), Frederica von Stade (C), John Alexander (D), Luciano Pavarotti (E), Metropolitan Opera Chorus and Orchestra—James Levine

Metropolitan Opera: Jean-Pierre Ponnelle (stage director), Brian Large (video director)

This *Idomeneo* is another important historical document: a memento not only of the Met's long overdue premiere of the work, but also of the days when Met telecasts were live. Even the little musical gaffes, video blips, and camera goofs seem refreshing, reinforcing the exhilarating sense of live performance.

The Met's *Idomeneo* is also the most complete version on video, and the only one which preserves both of Arbace's arias (Nos. 10 and 22) and Idomenco's final aria (No. 31). The only number missing is Idamante's final aria (No. 27), cut by Mozart himself and almost never

performed. Since this is the only video version that, following current standard practice, features a treble Idamante, it is the only one to include "S'io non moro," the earlier soprano-mezzo version of the Act III love duet for Ilia and Idamante. The two tenor numbers Mozart wrote for the 1786 Vienna revival are naturally omitted.

As befits the monumental Metropolitan Opera (if not *Idomeneo*), everything about this production is grand and outsized, yet the company's affection for and faith in this work are constantly evident. Perhaps it was the Met's cavernous scale which inspired Jean-Pierre Ponnelle to focus his production on the relationship between the gods and humanity. Ponnelle's unit set—enormous, distressed monochrome steps leading to a false upstage proscenium—is dominated by a massive, fierce bas relief of Neptune's head, which literally and figuratively overshadows the action. Ponnelle's absorbing staging is liberally laced with his trademark fevered Romantic intensity. There is much bug-eyed swooning, lurching, posing, writhing, and swirling, all of which can sometimes overwhelm on a video screen. The costumes tellingly combine elements of eighteenth-century and classic Grecian garb.

The Met's *Idomeneo* boasts a luxury lineup of world-class artists not necessarily known as Mozart singers. Ileana Cotrubas's winsome frailty and plangent tone make her a touching Ilia, especially in her gracious, well sung "Zeffiretti lusinghieri" (No. 19). Frederica von Stade's Idamante is simply definitive. Though not always at her estimable vocal best here, she limns such a sweet-spirited, deeply noble, fully-realized character that Idamante's suffering is almost unbearably palpable and his ultimate salvation is positively cathartic. The love-drunk recitative leading into "S'io non moro" (No. 20), the Act III duet for Idamante and Ilia, is heart-stopping.

The big surprise here is Luciano Pavarotti, easily the best Idomeneo on video. Though this low-lying role poses challenges for him, he is in resplendent voice (trills and all), and his recitatives are models of elegant Italian declamation. Most importantly, he demonstrates a level of musicianship and dramatic commitment he has rarely displayed elsewhere, worthy enough to atone for any number of soulless Three-Tenor excesses.

An *Idomeneo* on this scale demands an Elettra of Wagnerian proportion, the Met rightly reasoned. But, alas, the company tapped the wrong Wagnerian. Hildegard Behrens is gravely miscast in a role which exposes all of her weaknesses and none of her considerable strengths. Ponnelle's silent-movie acting style seems to grate against her fine dramatic instincts. And Elettra's cruelly testing music throws harsh light on Ms. Behrens's vocal vulnerabilities. Elettra's tour-de-force exit aria, "D'Oreste, d'Ajace" (No. 29) is a particularly painful moment, revealing a voice partitioned into a raucous top, a hoarse, tremulous middle, and raw chest tones. But, perhaps because Ms. Behrens is carried offstage in a grandly histrionic swoon, the audience seems not to notice, granting her the evening's heartiest ovation.

The underappreciated American tenor John Alexander turns in a splendidly sung Arbace. The Metropolitan Opera Orchestra, under James Levine, is the kind of virtuosic ensemble for which Mozart conceived *Idomeneo*. Here they pour forth warm, hearty tone while sacrificing nothing in pictorial detail or rhythmic verve. The mighty Metropolitan Opera Chorus is at its best in moments of traction and gravity, such as Act III's "O voto tremendo" (No. 24), but can turn blowsy at forte and shaky at piano. Sonya Friedman supplied the fine English subtitles.

1983 CASTLE OPERA (VHS)

(Stage Performance, Stereo, Color, Not Subtitled) 181 minutes

Yvonne Kenny (A), Carol Vaness (B), Jerry Hadley (C), Thomas Hemsley (D), Philip Langridge (E), Glyndebourne Festival Chorus, London Philharmonic Orchestra—Bernard Haitink

Glyndebourne Festival Opera: Trevor Nunn (stage director), Christopher Swann (video director)

In little more than a decade, Glyndebourne advanced leaps and bounds in terms of textual integrity. The company's 1983-vintage *Idomeneo*, nearly an hour longer than its 1974 version, is satisfyingly unabridged, missing only Arbace's two dramatically vestigial, frequently-cut arias and the action-stopping Act III arias for Idamante and Idomeneo (Nos. 27 and 31), which Mozart himself omitted from the first performances. The tenor rondo "Non temer", K. 490, from the 1786 Vienna version, is inserted at the top of Act II.

There is much more besides completeness, though, to recommend this performance, beginning with the eloquent, moving production by Trevor Nunn. This *Idomeneo* is above all a family drama, and Nunn maintains a tight focus on the crucial father-son conflict. Even the supernatural challenges which drive the plot seem here to be divine efforts to right the balance of a dysfunctional clan, and Elettra's plight is rendered all the more painful by her "outsider" status. Nunn's vista translates into some haunting, memorable images: the horrified populace scattering at the end of Act II, leaving Idomeneo utterly alone in the dark eye of a storm; an aborted touch between the King and Idamante during the fermata preceding the allegro of the Act II Trio (No. 16); and a cleansing final chorus ("Scenda Amor", No. 32) during which Idomeneo does not skulk off into the sunset, as he often does, but is instead invited into a heart-warming reconciliatory tableau with both his family and the Cretan people. Visually spare, with changing projections on an upstage cyclorama and simple changes of scrims, panels, and furniture, this is a "less-is-more" production which puts all its trust in Mozart and his protagonists.

And Nunn has some splendid singing actors to lean on. Jerry Hadley, in top vocal form (though inexplicably blond), strikes the right balance between elegance and ardor as the best of the tenor Idamantes. Yvonne Kenny is the finest Ilia on video, unusually ripe-voiced and expressive, purling out lovely high *pianissimos* in her opening aria (No. 1) and assured coloratura and trills elsewhere; her limpid, heartfelt

"Zeffiretti lusinghieri" is a particular highlight.

Philip Langridge, as Idomeneo, cannot match his colleagues in vocal opulence, but he offers heroic sinew, musical nuance, and truthful acting in the title role. The standout in this near-perfect cast is Carol Vaness. She contributes an Elettra of boundless vocal and dramatic color and complexity, as elemental as she is regal, as vulnerable as she is imperious. And she is in rip-roaring voice, wondrously robust and clear at both ends of Elettra's vast range. She commands honeyed legato in her Act II confession of love, "Idol mio" (No. 13), filling its drooping half-steps with poignance; and she pumps out an elemental "D'Oreste, d'Ajace" (No. 29), imbuing its demented fioratura with pathos as well as venom.

Bernard Haitink coaxes full-bodied but finely detailed playing from the London Philharmonic. His tempos tend toward the expansive, even leisurely, including a rather too dirge-like "Placido è il mar" (No. 15) in Act II. The Glyndebourne Festival Chorus, sounding hearty but a bit rough at the edges, is exemplary in its deep dramatic involvement.

1991 PHILIPS (LD)

(Stage Performance, Stereo, Color, Subtitled) 142 minutes

Ann Christine Biel (A), Anita Soldh (B), David Kuebler (C), John-Eric Jacobsson (D), Stuart Kale (E), Drottningholm Court Theatre Chorus and Orchestra—Arnold Östman

Drottningholm Court Theatre: Michael Hampe (stage director), Thomas Olofsson (video director)

Hardcore audiophiles and early music fans may favor this most recent Idomeneo, from Sweden's Drottningholm Court Theatre. Available only in state-of-the-art laser disc format, it naturally promises and delivers the best video and audio quality. And conductor Arnold Östman and his periwigged pit band offer all of the familiar assets and liabilities of period-style orchestras: idiomatic tone, complete with out-of-tune natural horns; tangy double-dots; and

zestily brisk tempos, which sometimes have an unfortunate trivializing effect. By any standards, it's hard to justify Östman's lickity-split "Zeffiretti lusinghieri", which, cantering along twice as fast as it should, ends up sounding like an organ grinder's ditty.

Drottningholm's *mise-en-scène* is as determinedly eighteenth-century as the Met's is Romantic. Director Michael Hampe anchors this *Idomeneo* firmly in *opera seria* stage conventions: arias are delivered pretty much front-and-center, with much hand-wringing, and turns and exits are sweepingly theatrical. Special effects are deliberately and effectively artificial and low-tech: storms are represented by billowing white cloths and simple on-off flips of a lighting toggle-switch. Martin Rupprecht's simple, stylized unit set, modified by changing columns, chandeliers, and projections, makes good use of Drottningholm's small but deep stage. His attractive costumes, in blacks, greys, silvers, and pale blues, are strictly in eighteenth-century style, with nary a nod to Grecian antiquity.

The mostly Scandinavian cast is generally adequate, though it has a black hole at its center. As Ilia, a listless Ann-Christine Biel sleepwalks through the performance like a fugitive from Madam Tussaud's. Never do her impassive face, her stiff body, nor her anemic voice (with its flubbed coloratura) register more than the faintest of emotions. As Idamante, American tenor David Kuebler cuts a handsome figure and demonstrates a sure way with recitative, but his timbre is tight and bleaty, with a limited palette of colors. His most distinctive trait may, however, be a pair of uncommonly mobile eyebrows, each of which has an amazing life of its own.

British tenor Stuart Kale makes a noble, heartfelt, musically refined Idomeneo. Though his runs in "Fuor del mar" (No. 12) are logey, his Act III duo with the chorus (No. 26) is particularly mellifluous and touching. Anita Soldh, as Elettra, offers the strongest performance here. Her attractive welterweight voice is easy and even throughout Elettra's punishing extremes of range and dynamics, and she handles the role's fiendish coloratura impressively.

She is also remarkably able to find truth, life, and depth in the stock gestures of eighteenth-century theatre.

Drottningholm's chorus, as tiny as its stage, could naturally use more juice in the Act II storm scene. But the little group is fresh of face and voice and turns in a clean, well-balanced, dramatically committed performance.

A few unintentionally comic moments are supplied by the English subtitles, which have all the literary grace of VCR instructions. Choice excerpts include: "Idomeneo might be a meal for fish" and "He scorns and flies me."

———————

There's not really a lemon in the bunch, so choosing between these four very different *Idomeneos* is largely a matter of personal taste. Glyndebourne's solidly staged and sung 1974 production is too incomplete to claim first place, though it features the best choral singing. Drottningholm's account is interesting chiefly as a study in Classical period dramatic and musical style and a paragon of sophisticated audio-visual technology. But if fine singing is your priority, forget this one.

If you do want starry vocalism, and you like your Mozart industrial strength, grab the Met version; with its riveting drama, virtuosic orchestral playing, textual integrity, and definitive performances by von Stade and Pavarotti, it's a winner. But, all in all, the most satisfying *Idomeneo* is the 1983 Glyndebourne version, offering a nearly ideal cast, solid musical values, and an exquisite, moving, perfectly-scaled production.

CORI ELLISON

DIE ENTFÜHRUNG AUS DEM SERAIL (1782)

A: Constanze (s); B: Blonde (s); C: Belmonte (t); D: Pedrillo (t);
E: Osmin (bs)

ozart had not been in Vienna quite a year when he began composing this *Singspiel* (a play with spoken words and musical numbers) to a libretto by Gottlieb Stephanie based on a text by Christoph Friedrich Bretzner. A hit after its premiere, *Seraglio* was quickly mounted in numerous cities where German was spoken and wound up making Mozart more money than any other opera he ever wrote.

It combined expressive melodies, symphonic writing with sophisticated harmonies, variety in its set pieces, a picaresque scenario, an exotic setting, and characters from various walks of life, including the amusingly villainous Osmin, one of opera's great comic roles. *Seraglio* loosened *opera seria*'s stranglehold on the lyric theater.

It also reflected perfectly the Age of Enlightenment which gave it life. Its civilized happy ending has words that tell all: "Nothing is as hateful as revenge. To be generous, merciful, kind and selflessly forgive is the mark of a noble soul!"

Conceived for the intimate confines of Vienna's Burgtheater in 1782 and resistant to easy staging in today's large opera houses, *Seraglio* lends itself to video presentation with its many close-ups and is flattered by astute microphone placement that makes spoken dialogue as easy to hear as musical numbers and ensures pleasing balances between stage and pit.

1980 VIEW (VHS)

(Stage Performance, Stereo, Color, Not Subtitled) 129 minutes

Carolyn Smith-Meyer (A), Barbara Sternberger (B), Armin Uhde (C), Uwe Peper (D), Rolf Tomaszewski (E), Dresden State Opera Chorus and Orchestra—Peter Gülke

Dresden State Opera: Harry Kupfer (stage director, video director)

This team of little-known singers and conductor, together with the estimable Dresden

Opera orchestra and chorus, makes an admirable, always musical ensemble, often warmer in expression than its more illustrious rivals. The cast has fresh, lightweight, flexible voices of adequate color and is as attentive to spoken dialogue as to musical episode. Guided by Harry Kupfer (whose well-regulated, sunny production, for once, is happily free of his usual, often gratuitous, social commentary), the singers and Werner Haseleu, the fine actor taking the speaking part of the Pasha Selim, are filmed in mostly close-ups and some medium shots from apposite, unobtrusive camera angles.

Indeed, the entire enterprise would hold high place among competing versions were it not for its unconscionable musical cuts (and, doubtless for some, its lack of subtitles). Three arias have been excised. One might expect Belmonte's very difficult, frequently cut "Ich baue

159

ganz," to be missing, but surely neither his "Wenn der Freude Tränen fliessen" nor Constanze's "Traurigkeit" deserves a similar fate— especially since none of the singing of Carolyn Smith-Meyer and Armin Uhde suggests they could not deal honorably with the missing parts of their roles. "Traurigkeit," in particular, can hold no terrors for one who can sing "Martern aller Arten" with as much passion and confidence as Smith-Meyer.

This presentation's production values are mixed. The live-performance film was recorded in Dresden's small opera house, its home until 1985, when the company moved back to the wonderful, old Semper-designed theater, reconstructed after its damage during World War II. Images are clear without being tightly textured or color saturated. Sonics are agreeable but limited in frequency. There are a few minor sound glitches.

1980 VAI (VHS)

(Stage Performance, Stereo, Color, Subtitled) 145 minutes

Valerie Masterson (A), Lillian Watson (B), Ryland Davies (C), James Hoback (D), Willard White (E), Glyndebourne Festival Chorus, London Philharmonic—Gustav Kuhn

Glyndebourne Festival: Peter Wood (stage director), Dave Heather (video director)

In William Dudley's airy, evocative designs, this Glyndebourne production has one of the more convincing scenic investitures among video *Seraglios*. But Mozart's opera is too often victimized by action devised by Peter Wood, a leading director at the National Theater, whose lack of faith in the music to make its points is revealed as early as the overture, when he resorts to slapstick mime-shtick.

Mistaking this humane opera for superficial comedy, Wood tries to make it "relevant" by inventing action that has no basis in Stephanie's libretto or Mozart's music (e.g., having chained prisoners moving dejectedly across the stage to demonstrate the assumed cruelty of Turkish authorities). Later, one is distracted during Constanze's grandest aria, "Martern aller Arten," by direction that has the Pasha buying birds to add to his collection (kept in a large decorative cage placed in the middle of the stage), so we will realize the potentate treats Constanze and the other ladies of his harem as caged birds.

The musical performance of the uncut score led by Gustav Kuhn is a good one. The most effective cast members are Ryland Davies and Lillian Watson, whose singing and portraiture are admirable. Valerie Masterson looks well and sings accurately enough, but her impersonation and sound are a trifle bloodless. Although his bass-baritone is not that of an ideal Osmin, Willard White makes the most of what he has.

The picture quality of this video, like that of the View version, is adequate but shows its age. The overbrightened sound is not always pleasant.

1980 DEUTSCHE GRAMMOPHON (VHS / LD)

(Stage Performance, Stereo, Color, Subtitled) 146 minutes

Edita Gruberová (A), Reri Grist (B), Francisco Araiza (C), Norbert Orth (D), Martti Talvela (E), Bavarian State Opera Chorus and Orchestra—Karl Böhm

Bavarian State Opera: August Everding (stage director), Karlheinz Hundorf (video director)

Despite a cast of international luster and spirited, stylish musical leadership by Karl Böhm (marred occasionally by untidy ensemble), this is the most disappointing of video *Seraglios*. Stage action designed by Everding seems poorly planned, even haphazard, and does not help the singers with their attempts at portraiture. In the great quartet that closes the second act, the two pairs of lovers at one point lose contact with one another and simply face the audience and sing. The elegance of Max Bignens's sets is lost by moving them about the stage far too often (e.g., the Pasha's castle, constructed in two parts, separates and comes together more often than Franco Zeffirelli could have imagined).

The singers reveal the lack of a firm, guiding hand and often seem ill at ease, only on occasion giving their known best. Gruberová has more of Constanze's vocal requirements in terms of tonal weight and flexibility than her rivals, but she needs a warmer sound to be ideally sympathetic. Her coloratura is superior, but she is too often wanting in smoothness of tone and line. Her best effort is a splendidly robust "Martern aller Arten," which wins the only ovation that almost equals those greeting every appearance of Karl Böhm. Incidentally, she is permitted to return, after "Martern" and exiting the stage, to take additional bows. Araiza, a bit below form, vocally graceful but tonally somewhat undernourished, is not his usual personable self. His brightest moments occur in "O wie ängstlich." Araiza does not sing his aria "Wenn der Freude Tränen fliessen" in the second act, as is customary, but in the third, substituting it for "Ich baue ganz," which is cut. Also vocally below par is Talvela, who mainly blusters and has no fun with Osmin, not even finding the gleeful spite for "Ha, wie will ich triumphieren." Orth is a generally crude Pedrillo (he begins his Serenade too loudly); but earns applause when he carries the giant Talvela off the stage on his back after their drunken duet. It is left to Grist to provide most of the meager charm this performance has to offer.

Without a clear dramatic viewpoint onstage, the direction of this video, which has good picture quality and slight color distortion, can't have been easy. Accordingly, one gets lots of close-ups. A good thing, too. Constanze sings "Trauerigkeit" from a downstage second-floor castle window.

1987 HOME VISION (VHS) / PIONEER (LD)

(Stage Performance, Stereo, Color, Subtitled) 140 minutes

Inge Nielsen (A), Lillian Watson (B), Deon van der Walt (C), Lars Magnusson (D), Kurt Moll (E), Chorus and Orchestra of the Royal Opera House—Georg Solti

Royal Opera, Covent Garden: Elijah Moshinsky (stage director), Humphrey Burton (video director)

This film documents the first *Seraglio* given at Covent Garden in fifty years. The size of this theater and the intimate scale of the opera inspired producer Elijah Moshinsky and designers Sidney Nolan and Timothy O'Brien to trim the stage with a false proscenium. A permanent, naturalistic set of an orchard by a run-down Levantine palace is seen, contained by colorful, abstract, strikingly painted back and front cloths. Easy continuity and closer contact with the audience is ensured by placing some of the more personal action and some solo arias before the front cloth, masking stage setups for ensuing numbers. More distracting than illuminating are an unusual number of extras, presumably intended to suggest the extent of Pasha Selim's staff.

The Pasha, who makes his entrance dressed as a European rather than a Turk, is not convincing as played by Oliver Tobias, a young, mannered actor whose action and delivery belie the calm authority of the Pasha's characteristically civilized address. Conversely, the other principals are well characterized and directed.

The musical performance led by Georg Solti is grand, sparkling, even warm, most notably in the moving Constanze-Belmont duet after the lovers' aborted escape. It and some remembered encounters of Mozart and Solti (live and on disc) lead one to conclude that the conductor is probably as underrated for his Mozart as he is overpraised for his Wagner and Strauss. The vocal cast—headed by Kurt Moll, the very model of a rich-voiced, swaggering Osmin and almost reason enough to acquire this video—is above average. Deon von der Walt's impersonation of Belmont, too often played as an aristocratic prig, is refreshingly vulnerable, his light, tonally pleasing (if not colorful) tenor so accurate he can even grapple honorably with "Ich baue ganz."

Inge Nielsen, yet another vocally nonheroic Constanza, is personable, makes a sweet sound except in her lower register, sings a poignant "Traurigkeit" and a surprisingly impassioned "Martern aller Arten." Seven years after her Glyndebourne Blonde, Lillian Watson is, if anything, a more vivid ingenue than before, a few unfocused tones notwithstanding. Lars Magnusson offers a lively, not-very-bright, cleanly sung Pedrillo.

The color of this pictorially sharp video may not be ideally intense, but in every other way it maintains high standards. Its sonics are natural; dynamics are not obviously monitored. Humphrey Burton's assured video direction is effective, except for some occasional confusion in dealing with the Pasha's large household staff.

1990 PHILIPS (LD)

(Stage Performance, Stereo, Color, Subtitled) 133 minutes

Aga Winska (A), Elisabet Hellstrom (B), Richard Croft (C), Bengt-Ola Morgny (D), Tamas Szule (E), Drottningholm Court Theater Chorus and Orchestra—Arnold Östman

Drottningholm Court Theater: Harald Clemen (stage director), Thomas Olofsson (video director)

The cubic volume of Drottningholm's charming theater, as modest as Vienna's Burgtheater, is a perfect space for performing *Seraglio*. Happily, video director Thomas Olofsson lets armchair viewers see Harald Clemen's polished, agreeable, somewhat prosaic production from the same viewpoint as members of the audience. The camera maintains a head-on position, with only a tasteful selection of mid-to-close shots to confirm we are looking at a video rather than at the real thing.

Production values are superior to any other version in this survey. Images are crisp and colorful, timbres natural and true, tonal weights well balanced.

This is the only video *Seraglio* not played out in a unit set. Its stage pictures are handsome, discretely rich in decoration, and effectively lit in all but the scene of attempted abduction, which is so dark one is sometimes uncertain about who's who.

The high musical standards associated with Drottningholm and its almost-resident maestro, the increasingly internationally well-known Arnold Östman, are evident in this well prepared, period-style performance. Andantes are not late-nineteenth-century adagios but those in the style of the late eighteenth century. Gut strings are the norm; wind and brass instruments are those Mozart would have recognized.

There is a sound vocal cast, excepting Aga Winska, Polish winner of the 1988 Queen Elizabeth of Belgium competition, whose Constanze, however appealing to the eye, is erratic in firmness of tone and intonation. The best singer is Richard Croft, a trifle vague in characterizing Belmonte but at ease with the demands of his arduous vocal requirements. Tamas Szulc is an overseer who means business and has a edge of menace and a firm bass voice with the range to accommodate Osmin's lowest notes. The second pair of lovers are eager and pleasing, especially Elisabet Hellstrom, a tall, handsome viking of a Blonde, before whom any Osmin might feel overmatched. Emmerich Shaffer is a Pasha with presence and convincing dignity.

———

None of these versions is completely satisfying, but each has something to offer. Even DG has Karl Böhm. Forced to select, I should probably choose Home Vision; Solti and Kurt Moll are nearly irrestible. But I would miss not having View's Dresden production, even without subtitles, and Philips's attractive souvenir of Drottningholm.

C. J. LUTEN

Le Nozze di Figaro (1786)

A: Countess Almaviva (s); B: Susanna (s); C: Cherubino (s or ms);
D: Marcellina (s or ms); E: Barbarina (s); F: Basilio (t); G: Count
Almaviva (bar); H: Figaro (bar or bs); I: Bartolo (bs)

What would be one's Desert Island Statement about *Le Nozze di Figaro?* Despite its farcical elements it is one of the world's great human comedies, on a level of wit and understanding with Aristophanes, Shakespearean comedy, and *Don Quixote*. And yet with all its musical perception, its emotional comprehension, *there is not an ounce of sentimentality in it,* and no conventional farce either. Like the other great operas, its music reveals its characters far more fully than its text. As has often been said, Mozart's librettist, Lorenzo Da Ponte, ends the plot with brutal economy. The guilty Count says "Countess, forgive me" and she replies, in effect, "I will." That exchange is neither sentimental nor cynical; it is *nothing*. It is Mozart who, with a very few notes, turns it into one of the most deeply moving moments in all opera—more moving because of its evanescence. Da Ponte, that wise old operator, knew just what Mozart required.

1973 VAI (VHS)

(Stage Performance, Mono, Color, Subtitled)
168 minutes

Kiri Te Kanawa (A), Ileana Cotrubas (B), Frederica von Stade (C), Nucci Condò (D), Elizabeth Gale (E), John Fryatt (F), Benjamin Luxon (G), Knut Skram (H), Marius Rintzler (I), Glyndebourne Festival Chorus and London Philharmonic Orchestra—John Pritchard

Glyndebourne Festival: Peter Hall (stage director), Dave Heather (video director)

This Glyndebourne production confirms once more what an endlessly subtle and beautiful score this is: hardly a moment in it is not revealing on four or five levels, from the broadly comic to the deeply contemplative. John Pritchard is the potent conductor, vibrant even in the most thoughtful sections. Only Act IV misses a little in terms of dramatic continuity—but more of that later. The women constitute a classic cast, and the men all offer valid and provocative characterizations. With her tremulous beauty of tone and phrasing, Ileana Cotrubas creates a magnetically warm and yet witty Susanna, and her expressive face is always suggesting new unsung messages. Kiri Te Kanawa is in the superb voice of her earliest period. "Dovo sono" is, particularly, a great piece of singing, with lovely tone, phrasing, and breath control all through—and dramatic conviction for video, too. The sopranos complement each other ideally in the Letter Duet, also: Cotrubas piquant, Te Kanawa full of quiet yearning. Frederica von Stade's Cherubino has been the world's best for so long that we may forget just what a work of art it is: physically, psychologically, and musically definitive. Her practised juvenile spontaneity alone sets this performance apart.

Benjamin Luxon's Count is vivid and attractive: wonderfully self-possessed and yet hotheaded—a complex accomplishment. His third-act aria, a very difficult one in every way, is done with extraordinary energy. Indeed, its ferocity may get a little lost in his very effort to project it: a fault, if it is one, on the right side. Marius Rintzler is a Germanically heavy Bartolo, but unlike others of this type he does manage to have some fun with it. Knut Skram is a young and congenial Figaro, more disingenuous and angry than clever. We don't always get the sense of Figaro's native craft or delicacy. This is an appealingly reckless version, and he sings it well, in a fresh but rather hard voice. Altogether the cast projects admirably what Mozart seems to have had in mind: a humanistic comedy with an edge, but only an edge, of satire.

Peter Hall's production is intelligent and inventive and he uses his cast well. One provocative problem: the fourth act does not quite build in emotional tension to the release of that supreme moment of the Count's request for pardon. This is by common consent one of the most deeply moving occasions in all opera, far more so than any of its individual components would indicate. A new world should, however briefly, dawn for us and them—and it doesn't quite happen. The sound is also occasionally a little distorted. Nevertheless, the production is worthy of its subject and contains major elements that for graceful profundity have not been surpassed elsewhere. Recommended.

1976 DEUTSCHE GRAMMOPHON (VHS / LD)

(Film, Stereo, Color, Subtitled) 181 minutes

Kiri Te Kanawa (A), Mirella Freni (B), Maria Ewing (C), Heather Begg (D), Janet Perry (E), John van Kesteren (F), Dietrich Fischer-Dieskau (G), Hermann Prey (H), Paolo Montarsolo (I), Vienna Philharmonic Orchestra—Karl Böhm

Jean-Pierre Ponnelle (director)

This is a production possessing some challenging ideas, and very much a *film*, with some sense of the life of Almaviva's estate beyond the specific activities of the opera. We see kitchen activities and horses being groomed, and Cherubino first enters dishevelled, with hay in his hair; he's been in a barn with Barbarina. During "Dove sono" there's a poetic flashback to the courtly seduction of Rosina, and Act IV is deliciously staged in the forest of one's dreams.

In addition, there is Ponnelle's special view of the characters. He obviously wants to get beyond the *politesse* of conventional productions. In the opening scene Figaro and Susanna end up tussling under the sheets. Early on, Figaro is a hot-headed male chauvinist who must learn his lesson, and he is very angry with the Count in "Se vuol ballare". Fischer-Dieskau plays Almaviva as a martinet of icy elegance, almost perpetrating a rape, with Antonio's help, in Act I. In the following scene he slaps the Countess and *kicks* the closet door open. "Contessa, perdono" is sung with great beauty, but whether this Scarpia-Count can be forgiven is a troubling question—as Ponnelle, no doubt, means it to be.

Karl Böhm's treatment of the score is heavier than Pritchard's; the effect is sometimes sluggish and discontinuous. Ponnelle directs the singers incisively, regardless of what one thinks of what they have been asked to do, and musically they match the best that may be expected of them. Several of the arias are done as voice-overs, and in "Aprite un po' quegli occhi" Figaro appears by means of a double exposure to be observing himself—an awkward idea. Mirella Freni is a memorable Susanna, amusing and attractive and typically exquisite in "Deh! vieni, non tardar." Hermann Prey's Figaro is vocally oily and dramatically coercive by choice: some distance from the amusingly clever and likeable figure commonly portrayed. Kiri Te Kanawa is sensuous and in superb voice, while Fischer-Dieskau's Count is coldly elegant and exact—everywhere but at the end of his third-act aria. Maria Ewing's Cherubino is beautifully sung and played with great adolescent flair: what a talent!

Despite some overstatements and direction that contradicts the temper of the music, this production is often visually striking and dramatically provocative, and on occasion musically entrancing, though not always at the same time. For the *Nozze* aficionado, it offers both remarkable pleasures and remarkable challenges.

1981 PHILIPS (LD)

(Stage Performance, Stereo, Color, Subtitled)
176 minutes

Sylvia Lindenstrand (A), Georgine Resick (B), Ann Christine Biel (C), Karin Mang-Habashi (D), Birgitta Larsson (E), Torbjörn Lilliequist (F), Per-Arne Wahlgren (G), Mikael Samuelson (H), Erik Saedén (I), Drottningholm Court Theatre Chorus and Orchestra—Arnold Östman

Drottningholm Court Theatre: Göran Järvefelt (stage director), Thomas Olofsson (video director)

This promises to be an enchanting performance. It was taped at the Drottningholm, built near Stockholm in 1766 and, with some of the original stage machinery, still in operation. The production utilizes what looks like stock scenery from the period, and though the lighting is electric, the effect is still partly that of the pale footlights of the eighteenth century. Orchestra members wear versions of period costume, and original instruments (including, for the recitative passages, what sounds like a fortepiano) are used. Both Marcellina's and Basilio's fourth-act arias have been restored, and appoggiaturas have sometimes been added to the vocal line.

The problem is that little of this admirable effort goes toward recreation of the vivid tensions of Mozart's disturbing comedy. The net effect, here, of all of this historical savvy is pallor rather than theatrical vivacity. We know that, in the eighteenth century, stock settings were in use for nearly all productions (the church, the drawing room, the cave), and that candles and oil lamps produced a weak stage light, but also that costumes, even out of period, could make brilliantly effective dramatic statements and performers could be stunningly (and sometimes absurdly) capricious in their treatment of text and music. Some of this (romanticized or satirized, it is true) has been revealed in such films as Stanley Kubrick's *Barry Lyndon*, Ingmar Bergman's *The Magic Flute*, and Terry Gilliam's *The Adventures of Baron Munchausen*. The point is that even without the technical resources of the modern theater, the memora-

ble artists of any period have always made profound contact with psychological truth, just as, for example, Chaplin did without sound or color, or Mary Garden did without a particularly distinctive vocal tone.

So in this *Nozze*, expect some passing moments of authenticity but no extra revelation of the theatrical validity of Mozart's opera. It's a hushed and polite performance, respectable but with little dash or command. The costumes and wigs are very plain and often ugly and the stage pictures sometimes awkward. The camera angle suggests a view from about the third row center—intended to give us the theater experience, I am sure, but on video simply static and unflattering to the singers. Those singers are earnest, but except for the Susanna there is not much distinctive in their use of the words or the music. Östman's orchestra, in this performance at least, often plods from event to event without cumulative impact, and the fortepiano does seem to plonk much more than some others I have heard. One hates to be hard on a performance style—and a twentieth-century research tradition—that in other contexts has revealed a great deal about a body of music and theater that we thought we knew, but there it is.

1990 LONDON (VHS / LD)

(Studio Production, Stereo, Color, Subtitled)
183 minutes

Jayne West (A), Jeanne Ommerlé (B), Susan Larson (C), Sue Ellen Kuzma (D), Lynn Torgove (E), Frank Kelley (F), James Maddalena (G), Sanford Sylvan (H), David Evitts (I), Arnold Schönberg Chorus, Vienna Philharmonic Orchestra—Craig Smith

Peter Sellars (director)

Most modernizations refocus a classic work and at the same time trivialize it; you gain a comfy daybed but you lose the mystery of a canopied monstrosity. This one, like the Sellars versions of *Don Giovanni* and *Così Fan Tutte*, enlarges on its source for us. All of the contemporary vexations—sexual insecurity, class intimidation, strangulation by triviality, greed, self-hatred—turn out to be *explicitly* illustrated by the music in a most surprising way. One knew instinctively about the universal truths and about the psychological bonds between Figaro's world and our own, but not so much about the absolute modernity of Mozart's musical perception. With a gasp of delight we can learn about it here.

This Figaro is a chauffeur and head of staff for Count Almaviva—in Trump Tower in New York, right now. Cherubino wears a football jersey and drinks milk directly out of the carton. At one point the Count threatens the Countess with a gun, and the fourth act takes place on the apartment terrace looking out over the New York skyline. If all of that tiresome relevance makes you want to throw up, don't. Sellars's production is no egomaniacal takeoff on the work of a genius. Nearly every musical phrase and every thought in Da Ponte's libretto is made immediate and graphically effective in this version and in his cast's superb realization of the forces at stake here. The musicianship is exceptional and the voices are fine, although voice is not the only aim. The singers use their penetrating intelligence and emotional energy to dramatize the comic agony of modern existence. Just one example will have to do: the Count's very difficult third-act aria, "Vedro, mentr'io sospiro," in which he pours out his resentment of his servant Figaro's sexual success. As James Maddelena sings it, every line radiates pain, sweat, and desire. The musical repetitions produce a nightmare intensity, and the appoggiaturas are anything but decorations; they are vehicles of the growing depth of feeling. Under Sellars, all of the singers perform with similar directness and skill. The ensembles are in general wonderfully staged, the camera work is brilliantly subservient to the dramatic task at hand, and, lastly, Craig Smith's musical direction is stirringly theatrical without being in any way pretentious.

1991 SONY (VHS / LD)

(Stage Performance, Stereo, Color, Not Subtitled) 180 minutes

Cheryl Studer (A), Marie McLaughlin (B), Gabriele Sima (C), Margarita Lilowa (D),

Yvetta Tannenbergerova (E), Heinz Zednik (F), Ruggero Raimondi (G), Lucio Gallo (H), Rudolf Mazzola (I), Vienna State Opera Chorus and Orchestra—Claudio Abbado

Theater an der Wein: Jonathan Miller (stage director), Brian Large (video director)

This is a top-of-the-line production, occasionally grandiose, well sung by some rather surprising experts and some attractive newcomers to the international scene, masterfully conducted, and directed by a man of ideas. It has been very highly praised, and in truth it is often more praiseworthy than genuinely involving. The grandiosity, for one thing, is somewhat misplaced. The stage is a turntable, so that the Countess and her room revolve into view immediately after the first scene—a procedure which temporarily destroys Mozart's mood; there's always something inhuman about living characters being *rolled* into place. Then in Act IV the set revolves again, from an indoor scene at the beginning to the front of Almaviva's house after Figaro's exit, so that we have for that wondrous final scene not a garden in the moonlight but the gigantic, forbidding exterior of an old stone mansion.

There's a hard edge to the performance, too, that denies some central qualities in the score. It is true that Ruggero Raimondi's Count is among the warmest of the characters: an attractive, self-centered Almaviva, amiable on good days. Lucio Gallo is a lively and assertive Figaro with a nice lyric baritone voice, and Gabriele Sima a charming Cherubino. But for various reasons there is an iciness about the performance that prevents much more than an objective interest in most of the characters. Cheryl Studer sings here with complete control and enacts the role very completely: love, outrage, confusion, doubt, and lust are all integrated into her characterization. It's a striking performance. Her tone, however, is basically a cold one, which might do very well with another cast, but here she must sing with a somewhat cynical, worldly-wise Susanna—almost a feminine Figaro, in fact. Marie McLaughlin is a fine singing actress, but the characterization that she and Jonathan Miller have come up with seems uncomfortably close to Despina, and, along with other elements in the production, upsets the balance and lessens the variety of emotional responses found in the score.

Claudio Abbado conducts elegantly, but given the production and its participants, warmth is in short supply. The fourth act particularly suffers in this regard. As staged, "Contessa, perdono" makes little effect, though Studer is quite lovely in the passage of forgiveness which follows. If you favor a drier view of *Figaro* than usual, much of this well-crafted performance will please you.

1993 DEUTSCHE GRAMMOPHON ARCHIV (VHS / LD)

(Stage Performance, Stereo, Color, Subtitled) 170 minutes

Hillevi Martinpelto (A), Alison Hagley (B), Pamela Helen Stephen (C), Susan McCulloch (D), Constanze Backes (E), Francis Egerton (F), Rodney Gilfry (G), Bryn Terfel (H), Carlos Feller (I), Monteverdi Choir and English Baroque Soloists—John Eliot Gardiner

Théâtre du Châtelet, Paris: Jean Louis Thamin (stage director), Olivier Mille (video director)

This is an intimate and very lively performance, with simple sets against a blue sky and trees in silhouette. Original instruments are used, with some gains in sprightliness. The major losses are in the contemplative passages, which are rushed into triviality—a particular problem for the Countess. The production is perceptive and very thoroughly rehearsed; indeed, one or two passages ("Voi che sapete" is an example) are distorted by the weight of interpretive ideas. The costumes are generally plain and dull—again a problem for the Countess, who does not fare very well in this production. Among the rest of the cast, Rodney Gilfry is a young and charismatic Count, powerful in his third-act aria, and Bryn Terfel offers a fine dark voice and great conviction and variety of color, together with a bully-boy face and physical approach that are both attractive and challenging. Altogether, the production as a whole is congenial for its lively, storybook intimacy, not quite duplicated in any other performance.

For its comprehensive view of Mozart's comedy and several superb performances, the 1973 Glyndebourne production is recommended. The brilliant Peter Sellars modernization should certainly be seen as well. Special attractions of the other versions include Mirella Freni, Maria Ewing, Dietrich Fischer-Dieskau, Cheryl Studer, and Bryn Terfel, all of whom have something vital to say about these characters.

LONDON GREEN

WOLFGANG AMADEUS MOZART

DON GIOVANNI (1787)

A: Donna Anna (s); B: Donna Elvira (s); C: Zerlina (s); D: Don Ottavio (t); E: Don Giovanni (bar or bs); F: Leporello (bs); G: Masetto (bs or bar); H: Il Commendatore (bs)

*A*n opera like *Don Giovanni* (by which I mean a Western canon masterwork of venerable age and mythic blood-line) leads a perilous life. It may pose as an innocent music theater piece, a *dramma giocoso*, but by the time it's had its antecedents explored, its psychology analyzed, its place in stage history fixed halfway between Molière and Shaw, its spiritual significance claimed by religious cautionaries, Romantic skeptics, and existentialists, and its meanings pondered by literary philosophers like Kierkegaard and philosophic *littérateurs* like De Rougemont, it's staggering under some pretty weighty obligations every time that first d minor chord resounds. The resonance of all these lauds, sermons, and exegeses can deeply enrich the experience of such a work. It can also make it well-nigh impossible to sing, play, and act it for the simple sakes of its story and characters as they are expressed in music and action—its in-fact performance values. Most "important" productions quickly reveal themselves as rather self-conscious efforts to realize a selected set of these obligations, or to throw them off in search of a fresh perspective. When it comes to the screen media, *Don Giovanni* offers some intriguing possibilities. Its extensive recitative scenes lend themselves to camera / mike intimacies and realities, and the arias and ensembles so often treated as forecurtain numbers may well be flattered, even liberated, by having their

pictures taken. Plot ensembles such as the Act I quartet or the Act II sextette, usually unpersuasive in the theater, hold promise for savvy film and tape directors and editors. Only the Act I finale seems beyond camera containment, but then its stagings generally leave us in disbelief or puzzlement anyway. So we may turn to these videos in a more hopeful state than that aroused by the prospect of most screen opera. Significant departures from the now-standard performing edition (with both tenor arias, the *Mi tradì*, and the full final sextette, but without the Leporello / Zerlina duet) will be noted.

1954 VAI (VHS)

(Stage Performance, Mono, Color, Not Subtitled) 169 minutes

Elisabeth Grümmer (A), Lisa della Casa (B), Erna Berger (C), Anton Dermota (D), Cesare Siepi (E), Otto Edelmann (F), Walter Berry (G), Deszö Ernster (H), Chorus of the Vienna State Opera, Vienna Philharmonic Orchestra—Wilhelm Furtwängler

Salzburg Festival: Herbert Graf (stage director), Paul Czinner (film director)

Originally a theater-release film, this edition combines footage shot during live performances with some from separate sessions undertaken to patch in della Casa, who sang no Elviras that summer (Elisabeth Schwarzkopf did them all and sings on the audio-only versions). There is no audience presence after the welcoming applause for Furtwängler, and no "Dalla sua pace," either, although it was included in the stage performances. Audio deterioration, which intrudes intermittently in succeeding scenes, may be the problem.

I wish I liked the performance better— sainted memory, and all that. Its vocal level is high. Siepi is in sovereign voice, pouring the music forth freely and richly throughout, and with none of the over-pointing most non-Italians find necessary. Grümmer is light for Anna, but she sings with shining timbre, incisive musicality, and a warmth that makes us nearly care for the character. Della Casa's pure tone and soaring top induce charity for her weak low notes and clumsy runs. Dermota is a strong Ottavio, and Edelmann a secure Leporello with some ringing top notes. Berger's silvery soprano is still on the button for Zerlina.

But most of this is better heard in audio editions. The video's interest at this point is mainly documentary—the stage manners of the time; the stony horrors of the *Felsenreitschule*, with its ranks of arches frowning over the curtained porticoes and stairways of a nearly Elizabethan set; the performing personalities of the singers. Graf's production is a compendium of clichés and conventions, tokenisms we are meant to accept as actualities. It proffers shtick in the disguise scenes that Chaplin and Lahr together could not make funny, Ottavio as a sort of military adjutant to Anna, Zerlina as cheery-cute schoolmarm, and Masetto with the same male-ingenue foot-stomping and pouting that Graf used to inflict on Met baritones. Della Casa is understandably at sea and conveys little beyond mildly offended dignity; Edelmann pursues his appointed rounds with a stolid determination. All this close up, from performers not yet cool about cameras. Only Grümmer, in some intimate moments, and Siepi, with his physical dash and Latin playboy air, effect partial escapes.

In the Act II finale, a simple clarity in Graf's staging, the strength of Siepi's singing, and the power and rhythmic bone of Furtwängler's conducting finally coalesce, and the production takes hold. Till then, the cramped sound track and boomy acoustics conspire against what seems to have been a well-played reading of integrity and sobriety, but not much fun or theatricality. Maddeningly, the synch is off just a tic. The film direction inevitably seems limited to the contemporary eye, and the camera work is occasionally jumpy, leading or trailing exits and crosses. Since the tape isn't letterboxed, we also have slices of bodies and other framing oddities. But the shot selections are intelligent, and there are fortuitous fragments of telling composition. The film source produces much better video quality than is the norm for stage performances of this vintage. And: no subtitles! Just the picture, free and clear.

1977 VAI (VHS)

(Stage Performance, Mono, Color, Subtitled) 178 minutes

Horiana Branisteanu (A), Rachel Yakar (B), Elizabeth Gale (C), Leo Goeke (D), Benjamin Luxon (E), Stafford Dean (F), John Rawnsley (G), Pierre Thau (H), Glyndebourne Chorus, London Philharmonic Orchestra—Bernard Haitink

Glyndebourne Festival: Peter Hall (stage director), Dave Heather (video director)

Hall and his collaborators aim for something special that ought to be something ordinary: they attempt a through-played *Don Giovanni* in which all action is derived from the characters in pursuit of their goals, in which effects don't happen unless their causes have first taken place, and in which actual transactions are insisted upon, rather than the usual set of signals. And in large part, they succeed.

Here are a few things I believed on the spot during this performance: that the Don has a ruling set of drives related to power, sex, cruelty, and defiance of taboos that compel all his actions, as well as a charm and wit that keep his social surface in order; that he and Leporello, though man and servant, are like scoundrels who revel in each others' escapades; that the women are all passionate, sexual beings who, in their very different ways, find the Don thrilling and contribute to their own misfortunes; that Masetto and Zerlina have a strong attraction but an ongoing fight about jealousy and freedom, all mixed together; that the strictures and distinctions of the society force the characters to deal with these problems in ways that are specific and immediately understandable. These are all things we are *told* we should believe in most productions of *Don Giovanni*, but how often can we really accept any of them, let alone all?

The chief agent of this credibility is the acting, which is nearly always alive in a way we usually encounter in opera only momentarily. But this is a team achievement. John Bury's costumes are a brilliant mélange of nineteenth-Century European fashions, eclectic in style yet shrewdly targeted to clarify class differences, impose manners, and lend each character a defined, engaging look. Haitink's conducting is not only spirited, precise, and polished but always connected to the dramatic event. At times it seems that Haitink, Hall, and Martin Isepp (continuo) are entirely at one—often subtly so—with the performers, so that the actions are truly generating the music. Yet Haitink and several cast members were not even involved in the production premiere a few weeks earlier. That's well-used rehearsal time.

Dave Heather's video direction is also superb. Many shots read as if the staging were conceived for television, and the editing rhythms come right out of the music. The camera work is calm and trusting: if silent partners are actively listening and participating, we don't need point-of-view shifts with every line. There is some superimposition, and two Floating Heads trios. These sequences work well enough, but this sort of thing becomes a red herring. We think a thematic line is being developed, when the only dots being connected are between scenes that happen to be dark and stationary—i.e., tough to tape.

Act II is not as complete a success as Act I (it's harder to play, period), and even Hall's imagination doesn't quite solve the end: a rather cheesy levitating cross and unscary bogeymen

groping in red underlighting and stage smoke. But it all plays, it all keeps its focus. As to individual performances: Luxon plays inner compulsion against social face compellingly, and his mellow baritone (a melting serenade) has enough thrust to satisfy the music. His choices are antiheroic, their realization concentrated and consistent. Dean's theatrical animation is sometimes more than the camera needs, but his slippery survivor of a Leporello (he looks like a headwaiter in a suburban Spanish theme restaurant) is very alive and honestly sung in a solid bass-baritone. Branisteanu's lovely middleweight soprano hasn't quite the technical sophistication to put the final vocal touches on Anna's music. I admire the performance, however. She pursues a risky take on the character (a woman of breeding in a state of shock, her primal feelings pushed far below the surface) and sticks with it convincingly. Yakar has a full-bodied sound with an appropriately sensuous color, and though the voice could use more float at times, it moves well. Both her big arias are straight into the camera, but she's in touch enough to keep them alive, and her contribution helps make the "Madamina" into a believable scene. Gale is simply the best Zerlina I've ever seen, way beyond the usual adjectives like "perky" and "fetching," and she has a round, well-grounded tone, too.

Grounding is what's missing from Leo Goeke's overly heady tenor. He manages a musical "Dalla sua pace" but runs into trouble when he tries to open the voice out, and he is walking on eggshells in much of Act II. Too bad, because he's artistically sensitive and does a serious job with the role. Thau is a strong Commendatore (a splendidly dark, Napoleonic statue, by the way), and Rawnsley's sturdy baritone serves well for his aggressive, unsavory Masetto. The subtitles are direct and blessedly minimal—like the camera work, they trust the acting to convey meaning. Video quality is reasonably good, though lighting levels are awfully low in the night scenes. Audio is only decent, not always accommodating soft / loud switches, and blurring in some of the tuttis. But a *Don Giovanni* in which the characters play real actions, and every performer registers on camera! A remarkable accomplishment.

1978 KULTUR (VHS) / PIONEER (LD)

(Film, Stereo, Color, Subtitled) 177 minutes

Edda Moser (A), Kiri Te Kanawa (B), Teresa Berganza (C), Kenneth Riegel (D), Ruggero Raimondi (E), Jose van Dam (F), Malcolm King (G), John Macurdy (H), Chorus and Orchestra of the Paris Opera—Lorin Maazel

Joseph Losey (director)

Here is a landmark of sorts: an unproductive "concept" wedded to techniques that cancel one another out. Storyboard: a Dawn of Enlightenment *La Dolce Vita*. Decaying aristocracy as source of morbid vapors that envelop all, characters that fight and copulate without ever connecting, always aloof from one another—and from Da Ponte, Mozart, and us— costumes that smother, ghastly wigs that drain quarts of blood from the faces beneath, and a Venetian setting—*gondola lugubre*, skiffs bearing soliloquizing souls through the marshes, glass-blowing as the Fifth Circle of Hell. Actualization: extreme movie realism. Warbling o'er field and garden, puffs of frosty breath in cold rooms, Commendatore skewered in pouring rain. Ideas every eight bars—new point-of-view, new setting, new insight to carry us to next edit. Heavy soundscape: chickens cluck, wagons clatter, crickets chirp; distant voices waft on the breeze or echo down the hall. And all in front of the servants, the kitchen help, the villagers— mobs of them.

Conceiver Rolf Liebermann had a perfectly sound idea for some other movie. To *Don Giovanni*, it's the antimatter twin. And we could say that director Losey has decided to embrace the clash of the conventions—so what if they don't fit? Yet he wants us to believe. He wants to morph the opera into a movie and make us swallow it that way. He zigzags desperately to avoid showing us the implausibility of lip-synching singers—he keeps them at a distance, puts them behind veils and masks, turns the camera

to the scenery, anything. But he winds up with no convention. We can't buy movie reality because it's an opera, and we can't buy the opera because of the movie. There are dozens of bright thoughts; they just don't play out. And when he has to concede a close-up (Raimondi's Serenade, Te Kanawa's "Mi tradì"), the jig is up.

There is much good work that would tell if the premise were workable. Te Kanawa sings ravishingly, and not without some fire. Moser has imaginative moments both vocally and histrionically. Berganza's mezzo is right for her earthy-peasant Zerlina, and her bravura runs are a joy—however, as an actress she doesn't do much but smile her way through. Van Dam is a wry, gentleman's gentleman Leporello, singing with extraordinary suavity and beauty. Raimondi's vocalism is his usual mixture of stylish and gauche, commanding and evasive. He acts a number of the scenes persuasively, but he doesn't find any central urgency or character key to pull them together. Riegel is asked to use his efficient but gargley tenor and his propensity for illustrating with voice and gesture to create a fussy, futile prig of an Ottavio, and does so. King and Macurdy are both first-rate vocally. A few of Maazel's tempos seem too quick, but most of his work is pointed and lively, and well integrated into the ideas of the scenes. The noted Parisian coach-accompanist Janine Reiss fills in elaborately on continuo—not her fault that these cascades of cembalo sound like the scuttling of small animals in the corner of your room. Much of the photography is gorgeous, letterboxing preserves the integrity of the shots, both audio and video quality are excellent, and the subtitles are relatively undistracting, as advertised. Doubtless the big screen would help certain scenes. But there's no throughline here, and not a whiff of emotional engagement.

1987 PHILIPS (LD)

(Stage Performance, Stereo, Color, Subtitled) 155 minutes

Helena Döse (A), Birgit Nordin (B), Anita Soldh (C), Gösta Winbergh (D), Håkan Hagegård (E), Erik Saedén (F), Tord Wallström (G),

Bengt Rundgren (H), Chorus and Orchestra of the Drottningholm Court Theatre—Arnold Östman

Drottningholm Court Theatre: Göran Järvefelt (stage director), Thomas Olofsson (video director)

A kinder, gentler *Don Giovanni*. The Drottningholm productions are attempted period recreations. On the musical side they employ period instruments with their lean textures, their honky and tootly timbres, and their clarified balances, as well as lowered tuning pitch, polarized tempos, and many sforzando attacks. On the theatrical side they feature a tiny stage in a tiny auditorium, nicely painted perspective sets with forecurtain scenes on the apron during scene shifts, simple lighting (from entirely modern sources), an easy, contemporary acting style, house lights at half, and such hoary devices as the wind machine and thunder sheet.

There is much in the work that this approach does not get at. But offering the piece as a nimble, essentially goodhearted comedy with a morality-play twist and a strong Arcadian element, and with actions played for their face values rather than their subtexts, is an entirely defensible slant that can refresh. Sometimes Östman's tempos do seem pointlessly rushed (the *andante* of the overture) or slow (the *allegretto* section of "Non mi dir,") but usually they are clearly and often interestingly used to point and color the playing of the scenes. Östman and Järvefelt have found a way to allow the performers a nice sense of discovery, and there's an unforced tone to the proceedings that is winning, even when a choice is odd or the technical level less than expert. The instrumental colors and the tuning are an antidote to the tiring aggressiveness of many modern performances, but the tuning (a full half-step down) is a mixed blessing for the singers, who must reconsider all *passaggio*-related matters. And for voices like these—generally light and a bit slack—relaxed tessitura is not what's needed.

The Anna / Ottavio pairing is the most consistently successful component. Döse is a voluptuous Anna and Winbergh a genuinely ardent Ottavio; between them they bring a heat and urgency to their relationship that wakes up this oft-sleeping dog. They, along with Rundgren (an accomplished Wagnerian), are also the classiest of the vocalists. The rest of the singing, including that of the veteran Stockholm campaigners Nordin and Saedén, is never ugly, just nondescript. It serves well enough the character emphases: Elvira as a reserved, polite gentlelady who reproves Giovanni for his own good; Leporello as a seedy, crusty old family retainer; Zerlina as a warm, ingenuous farm girl. The Statue wears whiteface but behaves like any stiff-necked father who disapproves of his daughter's date—being dead has made no difference. In the middle of all this is the estimable Hagegård, with the loopiest take yet on the Don: a foppish, even effete, narcissist who's simply unaware that his boobyish behavior might have consequences, and who is flouncily helpless when he runs into obstacles. Exactly how this leads to enthusiastic female surrender is by no means clarified, and when we add the sound of a *baryton Martin* solving *basso profundo* pitch (lovely *piano*, unpleasantly edgy *forte* with a strange "say-cheese" position for open Italian vowels and snippy enunciation), we have a truly weird protagonist. Hagegård plays it through with commitment and intelligence, though.

There is good video and audio quality, clever continuo realization, discreet subtitles, and uncomplicated video direction that stays unobtrusively with the scenes. The Prague edition, uncut, is used—no "Dalla sua pace" or "Mi tradì."

1987 SONY (VHS / LD)

(Stage Performance, Stereo, Color, Not Subtitled) 193 minutes

Anna Tomowa-Sintow (A), Julia Varady (B), Kathleen Battle (C), Gösta Winbergh (D), Samuel Ramey (E), Ferruccio Furlanetto (F), Alexander Malta (G), Paata Burchuladze (H), Chorus of the Vienna State Opera, Vienna Philharmonic Orchestra—Herbert von Karajan

Salzburg Festival: (Michael Hampe stage director), Claus Viller (video director)

Don Giovanni as cultural requirement, or, why the bars in the *Altstadt* do boomtown business after the show. The execution here is on such a high professional level, the gloss on both music and production so shiny, that any description of the table of elements will have a Great Events tone. The orchestra gives us that cushioned Cadillac ride. The stage picture forms and reforms gracefully into perfectly balanced groupings, the performers fastidiously timing out their blocking in slo-mo symmetries. The musical manners are upper class, much of the singing fine. Both picture and sound quality are state-of-the-art, the video direction expert.

But it is soon apparent that the musical journey will be a pilgrimage—slow!—to the stations of the Mozartean Cross; that all stage events will transpire according to rules of ritual pretense; and that the unfailingly predictable, undisturbing whole will quickly have us in the Land of Nod, Province of Europera. It's possible to admire, but not to care. Varady, a vocally complete and polished Elvira, offers a welcome vitality till the camera snitches on the staginess of her Act II solo scene. Battle shows some winning tenderness and behavioral naturalness when she leaves herself alone, but with "Vedrai, carino" it's back to play-acting. She sings sweetly, if carefully. Tomowa-Sintow's Anna is as close as we come these days to the old-fashioned dramatic-soprano sort, and there are compelling moments at the top of the range. Her tense, leaden physicality is not viewer-friendly, though. Ramey's Don is a peculiar case. Vocally he's not quite Siepi or Ghiaurov, but probably the best since. Not a bad-looking fellow, moves well, flashes a big social smile, seems to understand the textual points. But it's hard to tell where anything's coming from. He neither discloses his own person nor takes on another, even a phony one. It's like the hole in the doughnut: we can't say much against it, but where is it? Furlanetto sings Leporello respectably. His acting is of the illustrative school, driving home all the obvious choices with great energy—a deadly combination. Winbergh, so responsive in the Drottningholm performance, here moves through Ottavio with the air of an official presenting a calling-card that's meant to impress. His singing, now up at the notoriously sharp Vienna pitch, is musically thoughtful and vocally firm, except when he slips into a croony *pianissimo*. Malta is an unusually mature Masetto with an interesting surliness he doesn't really follow through on, and a sufficient bass voice. Burchuladze's fine vocal equipment is technically too erratic to provide the centered power needed. The scenic backgrounds (red-tiled roofs, pavilions, obelisks, greenery) are handsome, and in the final scene there's a nice planetarium show, though if we're going to have the cosmos we might prefer Johannes Kepler's to Captain Kirk's. The Salzburg contra-subtitle tradition is carried on, but it's not all that hard to tell the people from the statues: the statues are the ones with the pedestals.

1989 HOME VISION (VHS / LD)

(Stage Performance, Stereo, Color, Subtitled) 177 minutes

Edita Gruberová (A), Ann Murray (B), Suzanne Mentzer (C), Francisco Araiza (D), Thomas Allen (E), Claudio Desderi (F), Natale De Carolis (G), Sergei Koptchak (H), Chorus and Orchestra of Teatro alla Scala—Riccardo Muti

La Scala: Giorgio Strehler (stage director), Carlo Battistoni (video director)

On a gleaming black deck before an ochre sky, a lavishly dressed drill team is on maneuver. Its members swirl and billow capes and cloaks the size of tarpaulins. They assume poses in profile, then open out balletically to sing. Those of baser rank prance and fling themselves about, sometimes suggesting the *lazzi* of the director's justly famed Goldoni adventures. When run through by a sword, however, the Commandant lowers himself gradually to earth, singing and counting as he goes. There are monumental columns, stonework, statuary, staircases, cypresses—all impressive and stunningly lit. When high tech runs aground (the long, troublesome heart of Act II), the heavy folds and swags of a magnificent secondary curtain take over. We've apparently signed on for an intensive workshop in stagecraft.

No doubt Strehler is a genius, but here he

drowns his baby. We gawk at the pictures and press our buzzers when we spot a new style, but there's little to draw us into the people or their fates. Muti secures some lucid and pungent textures and accompanies some of the slower numbers blandishingly, but he rams forward everything marked quicker than *andante*, savaging proportions and making Munchkins of his singers. He also becomes a principal actor—his eight-by-ten glossy floats in and out of every little opening, shorting the circuits for performers and viewers. Inexcusable.

Needless to say, the cast can make little impression: personalities cannot emerge, voices cannot expand. Araiza comes off best, bringing some fire to his Ottavio. He has a bad patch of intonation at the start of the second verse of his first aria and overblows the climax of the second, but otherwise he sings with conviction, musicality, and beauty. Mentzer (another mezzo Zerlina) sings neatly and looks pretty but is stuck with the worst of the scampery choreography. Gruberová, gamely trying to muscle an Anna out of her essentially lightweight voice, puts a bright reinforcement on her lower octave and a gummy cover on the top one. Act I is messy, but she pulls together a well-shaped "Non mi dir." She communicates some feeling between the deep breaths. Murray is serious and competent, and rather dull.

Allen suffers the most at Muti's hand. He loses vocal control of the Champagne Aria, rattles frantically through "Su, svegliatevi," and arrives at the final scenes with his baritone (which belongs higher up in any case) in noticeably frazzled condition. Desderi, on the other hand, improves in Act II, somewhat subduing the timbral rawness and tremolo that afflict his "Madamina." Both he and Allen are trapped by the direction—all sorts of stuff is played out in all sorts of ways, but it seems just to make the same point over and over again. De Carolis is a young, suavely handsome Masetto, overdoing the vehemence in an effort to project. Koptchak is imposing, though the mike picks up more of the voice's hollow buzz than its gratifying size and steadiness. Video and audio quality are top-rate, the subtitles well handled. But these are just posies on the casket.

1990 LONDON (VHS / LD)

(Studio Production, Stereo, Color, Subtitled) 190 minutes

Dominique Labelle (A), Lorraine Hunt (B), Ai Lan Zhu (C), Carroll Freeman (D), Eugene Perry (E), Herbert Perry (F), Elmore James (G), James Patterson (H), Arnold Schoenberg Chorus, Vienna Symphony—Craig Smith

Peter Sellars (director)

This is a studio remake of the production staged at the Pepsico Summerfare in the 1980s as part of the director's Mozart / Da Ponte cycle. Here it is substantially recast, somewhat rethought, and garnished with postproduction touch-ups, not to mention a house ad. To make sure we all understand: Sellars's productions are contemporizations with sociopolitical ambitions. They search for their truths by adapting works into the behavioral *lingua franca* of the audience and the performers. They don't alter texts, but create scenarios that try to justify the texts in terms of current social understandings and conflicts. Where that proves impossible, they go ahead anyway. In the action sequences, they could be taken for interwar slice-of-life dramas, but when characters deal with inner objects or the *affetti*, they embrace a stylized movement language that draws on Oriental models. At the same time, the musical collaboration heads for the performance-practice archives. So-o-o . . . here's a *Giovanni* whose characters belong to the multiethnic underclass in a devastated drug-infested urban neighborhood (the Don, Leporello, and Anna are junkies for sure), but whose musical manners are almost prissily late *settecento*: appoggiaturas by the bushel, careful recitatives with fortepiano / cello accompaniment, suspiciously Handelian ornamentation, and so on.

There are a thousand reasons why this should not work, but there are two that make it impossible to dismiss the production. The first is that much of it plays well, and the second is that some of it is affecting and powerful. The strongest argument for "modernization" is that it releases performers. Absolved from having to first don a "style," then try to locate a semblance of spontaneous behavior within it, they can cut directly to life as they know it. Of course, they (and their audiences) have to want that and be capable of it; many don't and aren't. And we should bear in mind what is lost: everything that the "otherness" of the work has to tell us about the richness of human experience. What we stand to gain is an easy flow of character action and a stage world of some immediacy. Reality, in short.

In the bitter, grinding world of this production, in which Elvira's tardy interest in Pentecostal Christianity is the only hint of the old morality, we feel the grip of a harsh truth a fair share of the time. The most successful of the performers are the Perrys, whose remarkable brother act (in both senses) shows us a petty boss and flunky surviving through amoral expediency; and Lorraine Hunt, an Elvira in desperate search of love and salvation. The others are less consistently compelling, but all are with the program. Credibility problems arise when Sellars feels he has to externalize and explain ("You can't sing this unless you shoot up first"), or when one of his worlds intrudes on another (Masetto and Zerlina may bed down together for "Vedrai, carino," and Elvira might even writhe on the ground while singing "Mi tradì," but I don't think they do so on the street—in the Così production, Sellars created distinct spaces for the characters to throw their fits in, and that helped).

Two changes from the stage production have blunted the impact of the finale. Absent is the soft-porn slide show of Giovanni's conquests during the "Madamina," as well as the brief appearance at the window of a little blonde girl in white in response to Giovanni's Serenade ("la piccina"—he's into pedophilia). These persons still turn up at the end, the former as the demons summoning the Don to Hell beneath the pavement, the little girl as the innocent who beckons him thither. But there is nothing to connect them to, and they now seem mere titillating abstractions. Also much less clear is the setup for the Commendatore's reappearance as a scam devised by the other characters. Finally, Sellars is a nervous video director, frequently undermining his own rhythms by trying to show us everything. Still, many sequences remain absorbing—try the scene between Elvira and the disguised Leporello, two messed-up folks hungry for love, huddling in the tenement doorway. Has it ever been heartbreaking before?

Musically, Smith's prevailingly slow tempos and the many creepily drawn-out recitatives create a consistent atmosphere—it's all serious and thoughtful, though on tape it induces impatience more often than in live performance. The embellishments are over the top for my taste, and the vocal level ranges from decent downward. Hunt is the most interesting singer, but she's a mezzo who must reach for the top, transpose the "Mi tradì," and omit the B-flats in the last scene. The Perrys are both highly competent, though neither has a glamorous instrument, and Zhu is a perfectly plausible light-soprano Zerlina. The others sneak by, Freeman only if one is willing to accept a sound of about the Broadway bari-tenor caliber. This is the only video Giovanni to include the Zerlina/Leporello duet. It is a superbly well-considered cut, but if you want it, it's here. The subtitles are not so much a translation as a colloquial rendering of the directorial scenario. They blithely fudge the many contradictions it raises.

Three editions play as video entertainments: 1977 VAI, 1987 Philips, and 1990 London. Of these, the VAI (Hall/Haitink) is the most consistently intriguing, as well as the best played and sung. The other two (Järvefelt/Östman and Sellars/Smith) offer complementary visions that should be seen and dealt with. The remaining versions are hulking fixed engines with some well-tooled parts. For great singers, go audio only.

CONRAD L. OSBORNE

WOLFGANG AMADEUS MOZART

COSÌ FAN TUTTE (1790)

A: Fiordiligi (s); B: Despina (s); C: Dorabella (s or ms); D: Ferrando (t);
E: Guglielmo (bs-bar); F: Don Alfonso (bs-bar)

Così Fan Tutte has accumulated an active stage history nly in this century, and sharp changes in attitude can be discerned even in the two decades documented on these videos. We can catch the tail end of the era when the opera tended to be regarded either as broad farce or as dainty rococo confection—either way, guaranteed to have no threatening human connection—and in a severely shortened performing edition. The first section to go was Ferrando's second aria ("Ah, lo veggio"), followed by the men's duet ("Al fato dàn legge"). Recitatives would probably be trimmed, the two finales might be curtailed, and Ferrando's third aria ("Tradito, schernito") and Dorabella's second ("È amore un ladroncello") were frequently missing as well. All these decisions made the piece more playable under repertory conditions, more amenable to casting with less-than-virtuoso soloists, but vastly less interesting. More recently, the tendency is to retain most formerly cut passages, and with them the chance of exploring some of the dark undercurrents of this disturbing, profound comedy—even though the chance is not often followed up in practice.

1975 VAI (VHS)

(Stage Performance, Mono, Color, Subtitled)
150 minutes

Helena Döse (A), Danièle Perriers (B), Sylvia Lindenstrand (C), Anson Austin (D), Thomas Allen (E), Franz Petri (F), Glyndebourne Festival Chorus, London Philharmonic Orchestra—John Pritchard

Glyndebourne Festival: Adrian Slack (stage director), Dave Heather (video director)

The Glyndebourne Festival has had its moments of glory, which assuredly do not include this example of the "prehistoric" era of opera on video. Caught in unpleasantly distorted mono sound and with problems of camera placement and editing during a live performance very evident, the performance offers little of a high standard, and it serves as a convenient starting point for this discussion: the sort of routine, intended-to-be-funny-but-not production that needed to be rebelled against as standard practice for this opera. All conceivable cuts are made, some of them possibly the result of editing for television: we jump from one scene to the next abruptly and often skip over recitative connections in the process.

The best aspect of the performance is Pritchard's conducting of his excellent orchestra, taut and dramatic without tending to tempo excess in either direction. Not much in the way of sensuous beauty comes across, but the sound makes it hard to tell for sure. One can hear major-league material from Allen, caught early in his career, with the liquid ease and musical imagination to make the most of his opportunities and even build a bit of a characterization. Döse's creamy, even soprano encompasses the required range with some phrasing authority and almost enough flexibility (no trill, though).

Lindenstrand sounds light and pleasant, her duet with Allen coming across as the most satisfying ensemble work in the performance. Perriers renders Despina in a thin soprano that is gargly and fluttery when she puts pressure on it. Petri is almost completely unmemorable, and Austin actively unpleasant in tone, though he emits all the notes required of him. Little thought seems to have gone into the notion of matching or blend in ensemble.

The production is of the type once thought proper for the work—perhaps it still is in some circles—cute and toylike. Everyone acts arch in that "only for opera" way, when they are not standing immobile to deliver their arias. Emanuele Luzzati's sets are most notable for the intricate patterns of the groundcloth; otherwise they are flat and plain (if elaborately accessorized) and almost amateurish-looking, yellow and green the dominant design colors. Slack's direction amounts to arranging people symmetrically onstage and leaving them alone during their solos; he had to stage this production in sets inherited from the previous Glyndebourne production, so his heart may not have been in it. Subtitles, by the way, are credited to Spike Hughes, author of a book chronicling the Glyndebourne Festival.

1984 PHILIPS (LD)

(Stage Performance, Stereo, Color, Subtitled)
141 minutes

Ann Christine Biel (A), Ulla Severin (B), Maria Höglind (C), Lars Tibell (D), Magnus Lindén (E), Enzo Florimo (F), Chorus and Orchestra of the Drottningholm Court Theatre—Arnold Östman

Drottningholm Court Theatre: Willy Decker (stage director), Thomas Olofsson (video director)

This is a more up-to-date performance than the Glyndebourne one, and it is not so annoying, but pretty deadly nonetheless. In this case, the production, rather than archly tiresome ideas, has close to none at all, and the cast affords no magnetism of its own. It would be less than fair to say that it looks like a well-prepared student production, but there is something of that feeling in it: all are earnestly doing their best, but they are unable to seize their musical and dramatic chances and make us pay attention, and evidently no imagination has been applied by the director to help them.

Östman's conducting is blindingly fast to a traditionalist ear (as on his audio recording with a bigger-name cast)—even the introspective moments whisk along. His period instrument orchestra is up to the challenge, not so his cast. All of them are light of voice and presence and don't manage to suggest that any thought has gone into the lines they rattle off so speedily in recitative. Biel earns a certain respect for her honorable stab at "Come scoglio," her very frailty perhaps adding to the poignancy of her defiance; but it can't be pretended that she really articulates the fast notes (and Östman's tempos for her virtuosic sections are among the few portions that actually go slower than tradition). Tibell's initially pleasant tonal quality does not see him through his arias or crucial ensemble lines (in which he has trouble sustaining pitch even at these fast speeds). Lindén has the most substantial vocal material in the cast, a warm dark lyric baritone. He also comports himself with some ease and believability and makes an original point by seeming genuinely unhappy to tell Ferrando about Dorabella's unfaithfulness—which makes it all the more surprising that his second aria is omitted, without any precedent that I know of. (The preceding recitative is supplied with a new conclusion, so this is not a matter of tape editing after the fact.) The others fulfill their required functions unmemorably.

The plainness in musical expression is matched by the minimalist production: not apparently out of any aesthetic intent, but just through lack of ideas. Everybody does the basic moves suggested by the text, and little more—sometimes less, as when Tibell stands stock-still for all his solos. The lovers begin in white and acquire color as they succumb to the masquerade (not the last time this idea will show up), while Despina is a frumpy sweaty drudge. The biggest surprise comes at the end, when we leave the stage and follow the singers into, apparently, the Drottningholm commissary while the final sextet plays on the sound track. The singers hang about looking unhappy or thoughtful in their street clothes—an idea so completely divorced from the interpretation that went before it that I have no idea what to make of it.

1988 LONDON (VHS / LD)

(Film, Stereo, Color, Subtitled) 176 minutes

Edita Gruberová (A), Teresa Stratas (B), Delores Ziegler (C), Luis Lima (D), Ferruccio Furlanetto (E), Paolo Montarsolo (F), Konzertvereinigung Wiener Staatsopernchor, Vienna Philharmonic Orchestra—Nikolaus Harnoncourt

Jean-Pierre Ponnelle (director)

Ponnelle's film is full of ideas, some of them startling. As the overture finishes, a curtain parts to reveal a house through whose French doors can be seen the three men, playing cards and drinking and making very free with two young ladies. As we come closer, fears that revisionism has reached the point of providing the idealistic young men with prostitutes are allayed: these are indeed Fiordiligi and Dorabella, though the flirtation goes beyond eighteenth-century manners as generally understood (and it is indeed set in that century, designs by Ponnelle himself). The sisters retire to their rooms just in time to miss the bet, but the implication seems clear that the men live here or at least stay over regularly.

This is not the last time unscripted action casts a new light on the plot. Both women discover their suitors' true identities during their duets in Act II—Dorabella tears off Guglielmo's veil, while Ferrando removes his by choice. (And in both cases the new passion is consummated on the spot—in Ferrando's case expressly as bitter revenge on Guglielmo.) Da Ponte wrote no words for such eventful crises, of course, so everyone must try to act around their lines rather than through them. And with both men openly undisguised for the wedding, it's hard to see what the subsequent revelations and consternation are about. The final tableau of isolation and discouragement for everyone except Alfonso could be valid, but here seems unearned by the preceding action.

This is another *Così* in which everyone starts out in white and gains color as the action proceeds, ending up in white again. The whole action takes place in and around the substantial house shared by this *ménage à quatre*, conveniently located by the water (which is all we see during the farewell trio); a recurring visual motif is the bottle of wine that anchors the wager money on a bench. A hint of stylization remains, which helps avoid the problems of filming opera in "real" places: it is clear that, however elaborate the *mise-en-scène*, it is a built setting, not a real place, and Guglielmo pulls the curtain across to deliver "Donne mie" to us directly (the same idea will turn up in the Sellars and Gardiner stagings).

The musical performance is a traditional one in late-twentieth-century terms; recitatives are plausibly rendered at speech tempo, and the main eccentricity of Harnoncourt's conducting is the moderation with which the faster sections are taken. The orchestra plays extremely well, and the vocal elements are mostly of good quality, but perhaps too disparate for a real ensemble. Most notable is Stratas, who is given a lot of busy activity as Despina but handles it all while creating a specific character: a sharp, intelligent servant who's seen it all and is getting a bit tired of it. Vocally, she sounds marginally dry and worn, but she is still more than equal to the part. Gruberova, whatever one thinks of her rather edgy and tense voice, uses it with skill and understanding and produces some beautiful phrases along with a few questionable ones. Ziegler, by contrast, has irreproachable vocal material but is hard to remember in any way, positive or negative. Lima is relaxed and engaging physically, very convincing in his initial naïveté and subsequent anger; vocally he finds a smooth contained Mozartian line troublesome, and he fares best in outbursts like the opening of "Tradito, schernito." Furlanetto matches him in charm and uneven vocalism—sometimes suave and warm, other times precarious. Montarsolo's long experience shows in both positive and negative ways as he fills every line with easy authority (he must often address the camera directly) along with threadbare tone.

1989 HOME VISION (VHS)

(Stage Performance, Stereo, Color, Subtitled)
186 minutes

Daniela Dessi (A), Adelina Scarabelli (B), Delores Ziegler (C), Jozef Kundlak (D), Alessandro Corbelli (E), Claudio Desderi (F), Chorus and Orchestra of Teatro alla Scala—Riccardo Muti

La Scala: Michael Hampe (stage director), Ilio Catani (video director)

Initial impressions are promising. Muti sets things sailing with a crisp, singing, pointed overture, and the curtain rises on a beautiful stage picture (scenery and costumes by Mauro Pagano), a vista of Naples seen from under a sidewalk café's canopy. Both reactions, though not invalid, get modified as the performance proceeds. Muti's control, not often truly rigid (he allows some tempo flexibility, and even some ornamention in "Per pietà"), does not permit some of the singers to blossom as they might. He has also allowed or encouraged the ego-trippery of superimposing his own image on the action (in "Soave sia il vento" and both finales) so that involvement in the action becomes impossible and we are made to see the maestro as a controlling deity, invisible to the characters but not to us.

Likewise, the scenery is often lovely in itself, evoking some of the breezes and scents suggested by the more contemplative parts of the music. But it seldom gives the singers any help in playing their scenes, and it cannot be changed without pulling a curtain across the front of the stage partway through every scene—a ploy that becomes both predictable and inimical to involvement. Hampe's direction moves the singers into plausible groupings and actions, but seldom with any feeling that the characters are pursuing their own lives—only that they are creating pleasing patterns.

The most interesting performers are Scarabelli and Corbelli. She has an individual look and presence—an unforced goofiness reminiscent

of Imogene Coca—and knows how to use them in combination with a capable light soprano to make the most of her arias with no superimposed nonsense. Corbelli's firm steady baritone and clear musical-dramatic intent make for a very live Guglielmo even in his ensemble contributions. Dessi and Ziegler both have larger, more mature voices than we tend to get in these roles these days, which is good to hear (Ziegler sings out more and makes more of an impression here than in the Ponnelle film); but neither goes much beyond this to create something personal and individual, being seemingly content to fit into the ensemble. Desderi makes a mostly decent Alfonso but has to bellow to get through some of his more exposed lines. Kundlak sounds nasal from the start and sings with a distinct bleat; he survives, and shows some good musical intent, but is hard to enjoy. The six join together in some attractive ensemble work, reminiscent more of control from above than of a group of individuals voluntarily uniting their efforts.

1990 LONDON (VHS / LD)

(Studio Production, Stereo, Color, Subtitled)
199 minutes

Susan Larson (A), Sue Ellen Kuzma (B), Janice Felty (C), Frank Kelley (D), James Maddalena (E), Sanford Sylvan (F), Arnold-Schönberg-Chor, Vienna Symphonic Orchestra—Craig Smith

Peter Sellars (director)

Despina's Diner, the all too well-known setting (by Adrianne Lobel, costumes by Dunya Ramicova) for this production first seen in Purchase, New York, is only the starting point. The establishment of place and character gives us a start on who these people are to each other (Alfonso a disillusioned veteran with a long-unresolved relationship with Despina, and so on), and where it begins—Da Ponte set the first scene in a coffeehouse after all. But we are not to think that it all literally takes place in the diner, or that the token disguises are impenetrable; we are told as much by the way the men use the public restroom to change. Perhaps it is a bit of "play therapy" undertaken by mutual agreement to bolster sagging relationships? We'll have to come to our own conclusions about this and countless other points. But one way or another, Sellars manages to find more of the savage, pained heart of the piece than any other director in my experience. These four people start out thinking it's all a lark and end up finding out some uncomfortable truths about themselves; the sequence of arias and duets in Act II is for once as painful and dismaying as it should be—and as dark (Sellars preserves Da Ponte's suggestion of a twenty-four-hour time frame, and this sequence happens after midnight). For such an achievement, I can overlook, even enjoy, the occasional jokery: having the sisters ogling photos in magazines as the pictures of demigods they compare in their first duet, or bringing on Shirley MacLaine (in a previous year it was Dr. Ruth) to revive the poisoned men with New Age gestures and a Die Hard battery. (Her second disguise is an amusing impersonation of a female yuppie lawyer complete with briefcase, dress-for-success outfit, and Reeboks.) "Donne mie" takes an idea seen in other stagings—Guglielmo goes into the audience and sings directly to the women there—and pushes it startlingly further by having him do a Phil Donahue, offering a microphone to one "member of our studio audience" after another as if to ask "What *do* women want?" until he realizes that he's out of his depth and wants to cut to commercial.

One disjuncture that must be mentioned, though, is the forgery at a point when Mozart and Da Ponte's Dorabella is still having fun, but Sellars's is beyond all that: instead of "È amore un ladroncello," she sings the aria "Vado, ma dove?", written for the same singer. (Otherwise the score is complete, uniquely including "Ah, lo veggio.") Very right is the nightmarish choreography for the final sextet with its far from serene music, even though Sellars's unhelpful insistence on choppily edited close-ups mars the effect here as elsewhere. An example of a Sellars invention that does work, brilliantly, is the troubled long-established relationship he has devised between Despina and Alfonso; she's in tears by the end of her second aria, and the

two manage to reconcile most movingly as they team up to teach the boys how to woo.

The singers do better by their roles than some of the bigger names considered here, and all are committed, perceptive actors who execute even the stretches of stylized choreography with conviction, but vocally they fall short of what one would ideally like to hear. Larson and Felty have light voices for their parts, clear in articulation and ornamentation but thin under pressure. Kuzma's comparably plain tone is put to good use for this weary, embittered conception of Despina. Kelley's pleasing lightness and quickness in his faster music balance out with a dryness in more sustained music, some of which is a bit much for him. The most substantial voices here are Maddalena and Sylvan, both of whom sing beautifully and meaningfully and enact their roles as if it were all happening for the first time—and for once the casting corresponds to the score's demands, with Guglielmo the lower, darker voice.

1990 PIONEER (LD)

(Stage Performance, Stereo, Color, Subtitled) 170 minutes

Yvonne Kenny (A), Rosamund Illing (B), Fiona Janes (C), David Hobson (D), Jeffrey Black (E), John Pringle (F), Australian Opera Chorus, State Orchestra of Victoria—Peter Robinson

Australian Opera: Göran Järvefelt (stage director), Peter Butler (video director)

The stage direction here, though credited to Järvefelt, was "realized by" Ross A. Perry, a term that usually implies the nominal director's absence; whatever the circumstances that led to the division of labor, the onstage performers look like people who have been told what blocking to execute, but not helped to make it credible and involving. The direction seems much concerned to answer vestigial semi-questions like "How does Alfonso acquire a group of actors for the deception?" (Answer: the men are apparently in the habit of doing their drinking backstage at a theater, and Alfonso hires the whole troupe at the end of the first scene) and "Why do the girls have uniforms in the house?"

(the boys left a big suitcase with them). But it constantly leaves the singers stranded when they need to make stage sense of the music's flow.

And that is a real opportunity missed, because this cast looks ready and eager to act: they all have a personal vividness and spark that could have been molded into something quite special. Even as it is, they can be enjoyed as a fine vocal ensemble, well prepared and coordinated to satisfying musical purpose. The odd one out is Hobson, whose rather narrow, nasal tenor is not unpleasant or incapable (he renders "Un' aura amorosa" very expressively and is one of the few Ferrandos to pass the test of the fioratura near the end of Act I with honors) but belongs to a different sound-world from his colleagues. All the others have voices of substantial operatic weight without compromising responsiveness to Mozart's musical demands. Pringle, though hampered by an unbecoming wig, delivers a solid ungimmicked Alfonso, Illing a hearty, earthy Despina that is sometimes vocally unpredictable but never cutesy or coy. Black initially sounds to have almost too much voice for Guglielmo, but as his dark bass-baritone continues to roll out without encountering any problems, one comes to enjoy his easy command of the role's nuance and his unforced command of the stage.

Best of all are the two sisters. Janes has a dark round mezzo that sails precisely and memorably through Dorabella's music, and she exudes an avidity and liveliness that, even undirected as she seems to have been, lifts the whole performance's spirits again and again. Kenny is a bit more placid and unvaried in demeanor, but she too can explode with conviction. Most of all, she sings up a storm. From start to finish there's hardly a note out of place or neutrally delivered, and the notes join into an expertly molded expressive line unmatched by any of the other video Fiordiligis.

Robinson conducts a well-prepared performance, unpromisingly careful in the overture but generally alert and meaningful thereafter. Most of the possible cuts are made (Dorabella's second aria is retained), and the recitative is notably abridged. The general design scheme

(set and costume designs are by Carl Friedrich Oberle) is of an open wooden-floored stage with a permanent portal and a fortepiano at one side. Servants rearrange furniture toward the ends of scenes so that the performance proceeds without pause. The discs have been tracked so as to prevent starting easily at the beginning of Act II, and a classically mismanaged side break separates the "Come scoglio" recitative from its concluding cadence.

1992 DEUTSCHE GRAMMOPHON ARCHIV (VHS / LD)

(Stage Performance, Stereo, Color, Subtitled) 193 minutes

Amanda Roocroft (A), Eirian James (B), Rosa Mannion (C), Rainer Trost (D), Rodney Gilfry (E), Claudio Nicolai (F), Monteverdi Choir, English Baroque Soloists—John Eliot Gardiner

Théâtre du Châtelet: John Eliot Gardiner (stage director), Peter Mumford (video director)

This live performance has many appealing features. Its cast is as young (Alfonso aside) as the story demands, and they all look and sound strikingly attractive. The scenic and costume designs by Carlo Tomassi are lushly evocative, especially a terrace with a romantic Neapolitan vista, in which several scenes transpire. Scene changes are handled by means of a front drop, which as it has been designed to fit in with the rest of the decor is not too distracting. And Gardiner's conducting of his crack orchestra of period instruments provides fine color, atmosphere, and energy and will not surprise traditionalists in terms of either pacing or ornamentation. The only omission is "Ah, lo veggio."

Gardiner also serves as stage director, with Stephen Medcalf credited as assistant. It cannot be said that he has spurred his cast to continuously convincing stage life, but he does no worse than many a full-time opera director in this respect. He might have done even better had he been willing to use the personal qualities of his talented cast rather than suppress them in service of his thesis that initially there is no distinction of characterization to be found between the two women. I disagree with the idea (why search for a minimum rather than a maximum of individuality?), but respect Gardiner's right to make his case in performance. Or I would—except that he falsifies the evidence outrageously. He has reallocated the vocal lines so that each sister sings a bit of the other's Act I aria, and Dorabella also takes over one of Fiordiligi's phrases in the first finale; obviously the two will seem similar (especially having been costumed and wigged as twins) if one cooks the books this way. Even so, Mannion can't help individualizing Dorabella, expressing a bit more frivolousness from the outset. Other oddities of staging pop up in the last scene: a hint (shades of Ponnelle) that Ferrando and Fiordilgi have been indulging themselves just before the wedding ceremony, and the voicing of Despina's notary disguise an octave down, apparently by an unknown man, while she mimes.

Still, the direction has its definite successes. Staging the first scene as fencing practice (though to begin *Così* all in white has become a cliché by now) supports the action aptly, and the removal of a stage-filling white dropcloth to reveal the terrace for the next scene is a neat trick. Best of all is the staging of the very end of the opera: the two couples keep turning and reforming, unable to decide between old and new loves, until finally the sextet begins and they step out of character to tell us the moral—as themselves, young people of the 1990s, undoing buttons and hairpins to get comfortable. And the casting of all four with young singers who look to be at the start of their adult lives accomplishes a certain part of the work of making the action convincing.

Both sisters are sopranos here. Mannion is pleasant if undistinctive in tone, lively in action. Roocroft has something special to offer, with her bewitching tone and skill at floating notes magically aloft. Trost's thin tenor has enough sweetness in it to make the most of his lyrical chances, and a good musical imagination in ensemble. Gilfry's poised lyric baritone reaches low enough to do justice to what is in fact bass writing, and he matches Trost in making believable, distinct characters of the two men. Nicolai too is very much an individual, and a rather human, endearing one, for all his interfering ways; his voice is equal to the role if unremarkable. I do not know whether James calls herself a soprano or mezzo, but either way her voice has a nice combination of dark color and easy handling for the role, and she strikes a good balance between earthiness and light humor.

———————————

None of the versions really captures everything I would like to see—a full exploration of the work's potential by great musicians, singers, and actors. 1990 London comes the closest, its idiosyncracies tolerable in view of its achievement. For those out of sympathy with the Sellars approach, 1992 DG Archiv can be endorsed as a musically strong and visually appealing second choice, and 1990 Pioneer for its excellent singing.

JON ALAN CONRAD

WOLFGANG AMADEUS MOZART

LA CLEMENZA DI TITO (1791)

A: Vitellia (s); B: Servilia (s); C: Sesto (ms); D: Annio (ms); E: Tito (t)

Though it retained popularity for some years after the composer's death, Mozart's final *opera seria*, commissioned to celebrate the coronation in Prague of the Emperor Leopold II, eventually dropped into almost total oblivion for about a century. A few fitful revivals, in "adaptations" more or less extreme, tended to confirm its moribund status. However, since about 1970, thanks to recordings, provocative scholarship, and above all innovative productions that took the work seriously, *La Clemenza di Tito* has come into its own. Though simpler in means and trimmer in scale than the French-inspired *Idomeneo*, it requires major virtuosos for the roles of Tito, Sesto, and Vitellia, and the pacing of the score, involving short, almost songlike pieces as well as lengthy bravura aris, is also a significant challenge.

Working under time pressure, Mozart did not compose the simple recitatives in *Tito*, leaving them to his pupil Süssmayr. As a result, these were long regarded as freely expendable, especially in countries where Italian was opaque to the audience and few listeners would notice the omission of significant information about plot and motivation. Nowadays, the cuts are less extreme; however, one of the video productions employs a modern recomposition of these recitatives.

c. 1979 DEUTSCHE GRAMMOPHON (VHS / LD)

(Film, Stereo, Color, Subtitled) 135 minutes

Carol Neblett (A), Catherine Malfitano (B), Tatiana Troyanos (C), Anne Howells (D), Eric Tappy (E), Vienna State Opera Chorus, Vienna Philharmonic Orchestra—James Levine

Jean-Pierre Ponnelle (director)

This curious hybrid is a postsynchronized film, using a sound track with the forces of Ponnelle's Salzburg production of the opera, first seen in 1976. The film, with the same actors as singers, was shot in the Roman ruins of the Baths of Caracalla, the Forum, and Hadrian's Villa—essentially outdoors, since most of the sites in question are open to the sky. The costumes are in Ponnelle's familiar version of eighteenth-century classicism. The chorus, when needed, is impersonated by rows of statues; they, at least, present no synchronization problems, whereas the singers do, despite less frequent use of close-ups than in much filmed opera.

Levine leads a strong musical performance, clean of line and texture, played with vigor and tonal beauty, and fairly well cast. Troyanos is a fervent and fluent Sesto, Neblett is fiery and generally on top of Vitellia's coloratura. The musically sensitive Malfitano betrays some registral unevenness; Kurt Rydl is an adequate Publio. Like most modern tenors, Eric Tappy is confounded by some of the *fioritura* (the role was written for the first Don Ottavio); his lack of a truly heroic voice is somewhat compensated by vivid delivery of words. Anne Howells looks and acts well as Annio, though her spirited singing is not always well tuned. The ensembles, notably the first-act finale, are impressive in their power and stride. (Unfortunately, the VHS edition has sonic distortion in some loud passages.)

Beginning with a pantomime montage during the overture, Ponnelle's hybrid creation confounds conventional conceptions of either film or opera. Locations melt into each other without their relationships being clearly established; realistic and stylized behaviors are freely mixed—including rather more body contact than eighteenth-century theatrical etiquette would have countenanced. In these wide-open spaces, the direction inclines to even more perambulation than Ponnelle espoused on the wide stage of the Salzburg Felsenreitschule: for example, Annio sings "Torna di Tito al lato" while stalking an anguished Sesto along a high wall. The overall view of the opera is darkly eccentric: Tito has the aspect of a haunted man, Vitellia of a harpy. (By various accounts, Ponnelle's *Tito* grew progressively more exaggerated after its initial presentation in Cologne, a decade prior to this film.)

c. 1986 PHILIPS (LD)

(Stage Performance, Stereo, Color, Subtitled)
128 minutes

Anita Soldh (A), Pia-Marie Nilsson (B), Lani Poulson (C), Maria Höglind (D), Stefan Dahlberg (E), Chorus and Orchestra of the Drottningholm Court Theatre—Arnold Östman

Drottningholm Court Theatre: Göran Järvefelt (stage director), Thomas Olofsson (video director)

Strangely, the accompanying liner notes tell the viewer nothing about the remarkable venue of this production. The Drottningholm Court Theatre, outside Stockholm, is a remarkably preserved eighteenth-century theater; even the stage machinery still works. In such matters as the almost instantaneous set changes (rising or falling backdrops, quick shifting of side pieces), this is close to what audiences in Mozart's day would have seen. (As no designer is credited, one assumes that the sets are based on—or may even be—period originals.) The costumes,

credited to Järvefelt and Börje Edh, suggest Swedish court dress of the late eighteenth century, and in fact the intent of the production—again, unrevealed by the annotations—was to evoke the reign of Gustav III, Sweden's great patron of the arts (unlike Tito, however, he was assassinated in 1792, as operagoers know from Verdi's *Ballo*). The orchestra plays in period costumes and wigs, and on period instruments. The camera work, with its withdrawals to the back of the auditorium to take in audience applause, clearly invites us to imagine ourselves experiencing a performance in this specific theater.

The small theater and older instruments encourage a performance on a less grand scale than Levine's Salzburg version and are also friendly to more modest voices. Östman's leadership is firm and fortunately not as driven as in his recordings of Mozart's *buffo* operas with Drottningholm forces. But smaller voices still need great agility to cope with this music, and here the cast falls short. Dahlberg sings rather stiffly in his arias, straining throatily in the upper register. Soldh is unconvincing at the extremes of Vitellia's music, especially the bottom. Neither they nor Poulson can define their coloratura with precision, though the latter's voice is superior in evenness and registral balance. Höglind sings graciously, but not always in pitch, and the wooly sounds made by Jerker Arvidson render Publio's dull aria even more trying than usual. Only Nilsson, as Servilia, is a really distinguished vocalist, and she is exceptionally convincing. If the singing here had matched the general level of musicianship and dramatic commitment, this would be a satisfying performance; alas, it misses by some distance, and many of the numbers come off as merely lightweight rather than eloquently concise.

Järvefelt's direction of the ceremonial scenes is in keeping with the period style of the visual production, but, like Ponnelle, he encourages the principals to enact their emotions in highly physical twentieth-century ways—grimacing, acting out bodily torment, clutching each other, and so forth. Yet there are curious touches of literalism: during "Non più di fiori" Vitellia actually shreds up a floral coronet! For all the emoting, the view of the opera offered here is somewhat more optimistic than in either of the alternative editions, with Tito portrayed as a basically gentle, youthful figure. Aside from recitative cuts (a bit more is retained than in Levine's text), the opening orchestral ritornello of Sesto's "Deh, per questo istante solo" is mysteriously skipped.

1991 KULTUR (VHS)

(Stage Performance, Stereo, Color, Subtitled) 150 minutes

Ashley Putnam (A), Elzbieta Szmytka (B), Diana Montague (C), Martine Mahé (D), Philip Langridge (E), Glyndebourne Chorus, London Philharmonic Orchestra—Andrew Davis

Glyndebourne Festival Opera: Nicholas Hytner (stage director), Robin Lough (video director)

From antiquity via the eighteenth century, the video trajectory of *Tito* here reaches the postmodern, in a Glyndebourne production unveiled during 1991, the bicentennial of Mozart's death as well as of the opera's premiere. David Fielding's designs offer semi-abstract sets with raked floors and swatches of Pompeian decor, along with pseudoclassic costumes (nearly everyone, male or female, is garbed in off-one-shoulder, floor-length gowns). The Glyndebourne theater itself remains invisible (and inaudible—no applause after numbers, as at Drottningholm), the spatial relationship of the set to the stage is never clarified, and scene changes are concealed from the camera. Many of the stage pictures are handsome, and they and the principals are evocatively lit, often from side angles. The big idea of Nicholas Hytner's staging is Tito's isolation from both subjects and friends, and his utter loneliness pervades the opera. In this disoriented visual environment, the kinds of physical action that disconcerted

at Drottningholm appear more plausible, and Hytner's staging certainly engages the eye and the mind.

Though this performance runs longer than the other two, timing comparisons are not particularly useful, given the different texts involved—especially since this production employs a new setting of the simple recitatives by the British composer Steven Oliver. The obvious novelty of Oliver's work is its preference for more frequent and adventurous harmonic movement than Süssmayr's version. In the end, these livelier, even melodramatic recitatives, delivered with energy by the cast, succeed in making Andrew Davis's stodgy tempos and inflections in the set numbers seem even deadlier. The problem isn't that the performance *is* long, just that it *seems* long.

The singers do some good work. Putnam may have to fake Vitellia's bottom notes, but she digs into the music with energy and makes the potentially bizarre character's capricious behaviour remarkably convincing. Langridge is a worthy musician and an expressive actor, but like Tappy and Dahlberg he makes rough work of his elaborate writing; the voice is often under severe strain even in simpler lines. Both travesty parts are well presented: Montague lacks Troyanos's sheer vocal clout but gives the role a strong profile nonetheless, and Mahé is still better as Annio. Szmytka is another fine Servilia, and Peter Rose an acceptable Publio. If the orchestra is short of the Vienna standard, the chorus fills its (mostly routine) tasks effectively. Regrettably, the tape provided distorted sound in louder upper-register passages.

In terms of a video *Tito* to live with, this trio of performances offers no clearly satisfactory choice, though each one is worth at least a one-time viewing.

DAVID HAMILTON

DIE ZAUBERFLÖTE (1791)

A: Pamina (s); B: Queen of the Night (s); C: Papagena (s); D: Tamino
(t); E: Monastatos (t); F: Papageno (bar); G: Sarastro (bs)

Although *Die Zauberflöte* was a triumph from the day of its premiere in Vienna, its fame outside German-speaking countries is largely a postwar phenomenon. Early on, the spoken dialogue, an integral part of the work, seems to have been a deterrent. The Metropolitan Opera, for example, did not play the opera from the seasons of 1904/5 through 1911/12, nor from 1917/18 through 1940/41, except for 1926/27.

For the last two generations, *Zauberflöte* has become a familiar delight, played everywhere and often. The dialogue has come to be abridged; often just enough remains to get audiences from one musical number to the next. Today, if the number of video issues indicates popularity, *Zauberflöte* must now be judged among the most beloved of operas.

For all its magic and charm, the opera is clearly inhabited by two different spirits. Around March of 1791, Emanuel Schikaneder, its librettist, persuaded Mozart to collaborate with him on an opera based on one of the stories in *Dschinnistan*, a book of Oriental fairy tales. The scenario he intended for this story *(Lulu, oder die Zauberflöte)* would include a good comic part for himself. By the summer of 1791, having set music up to the first act finale of Schikaneder's exotic, farcical text, Mozart must have decided to write an opera with larger expressive dimensions. He was inspired by his Masonic convictions in shaping the Sarastro episodes. He likely convinced Schikaneder, a

fellow Mason, that they could have their moral cake and eat it too; such seriousness would heighten the Papageno element.

The variety of the productions seen in the videos exemplifies the reactions of various producers to the conflicting elements in the text (situations set up in much of the first act are turned on their heads in the second; established motivations go awry). Whatever the confusions of the text, the opera's manner of expression is always direct, the whole ultimately ennobled by the force and sweet humanity of Mozart's sublime music.

1975 HOME VISION (VHS) / CRITERION (LD)

(Film, Stereo, Color, in Swedish, Subtitled)
134 minutes

Irma Urrila (A), Birgit Nordin (B), Elisabeth Eriksson (C), Josef Kostlinger (D), Ragnar Ulfung (E), Håkan Hagegård (F), Ulrik Cold (G), Swedish State Radio Chorus and Orchestra—Eric Ericson

Ingmar Bergman (director)

A lifelong admirer of *Zauberflöte*, Ingmar Bergman dreamed of staging it for forty-five years before he produced it for Swedish TV and radio with a personally selected, young Scandinavian cast. He called the fifty days it took to complete the project the happiest time of his life. It shows—in every joyous frame of what appears to be a live performance staged at Drottningholm, that wondrous, still-functioning eighteenth-century theater whose resources are gleefully employed to recreate the spirit of Mozart's enchanted world.

Bergman has used his cinematic mastery to make of this opera a kind of inspired family entertainment. He has succeeded, as no one else has, in clarifying its drama and making it accessible and palatable to young and old alike. He has democratized all the principals except the villainous Queen of the Night and her followers, the only characters with a supernatural aura. He has given Papageno and Papagena a status equal to that of Tamino, Pamina, and Sarastro, here decidedly humanized and largely stripped of their usual solemnity. In the final tableau, Bergman has the happy bird couple and their numerous children on hand to signify their victory against all odds, a victory seen as no less significant than that of the triumphant royal pair.

This humane vision dictated several changes in the scenario. In the first act, the offensive duet of the priests, with their advice to beware the wiles of women, is cut. Pamina is shown as the daughter of Sarastro and the Queen of the Night, which gives the former a motivation that explains his fulminations against his former wife and his desire to lead his daughter back to the straight and narrow path from which the evil Queen has encouraged her to stray. No longer the ancient, Olympian priest, Sarastro becomes the kind, solicitous parent, comforting Pamina when she is threatened—first by a wicked, unfunny Monostatos, and later by her mother, singing her aria of vengeance.

There are cuts, transpositions, and tightening of several scenes in the second act. Papageno's two meetings with Papagena, who is disguised as an old woman, are telescoped into one and occurs at the point of the original first encounter, preceded by the birdman's "Ein Mädchen oder Weibchen," transposed from its usual place in the text. That maneuver necessitates cutting the second boys' trio welcoming Tamino and Papageno. Astutely, Pamina's suicide scene with the three boys comes directly after "Ach, ich fuhl's," followed by Papageno's suicide scene, a comic mirror image of Pamina's.

The trial by fire and water ensues, followed by the defeat of the Queen and a large crowd of her followers, led by Monostatos, and then the radiant finale. These revisions unravel most of the original text's dramatic tangles and clarify the action as never before. Only purists are apt to complain.

The musical portion of the film is never less than satisfying and frequently more. Conductor Eric Ericson guides with warm authority his young, talented cast, singing in Swedish (there are very good subtitles). His pacing is simple and direct, without eccentricity; he achieves an admirably smooth ensemble. The sound track was, however, recorded in a Stockholm studio before the film was shot, so there are imperfections of lip-synch, though they are seldom annoying.

Vocally outstanding among the large cast are Ulric Cold, a friendly, sympathetic Sarastro; Håkan Hagegård, a frisky, endearing Papageno; and Josef Kostlinger and Irma Urrila, expressive, dignified lovers.

1976 VIEW (VHS)

(Stage Performance, Stereo, Color, Not Subtitled) 156 minutes

Magdalena Falewicz (A), Inge Uibel (B), Heidrun Haix (C), Horst Gebhardt (D), Guntfried Speck, (E), Dieter Schloz (F), Hermann Christian Polster (G), Leipzig Gewandhaus Chorus and Orchestra—Gert Bahner

Leipzig Gewandhaus: Joachim Herz (stage director), Georg F. Mielke (video director)

Although this video has a 1988 release date, it was put together in 1976 from film shot on stage and sound recorded in a studio, with the inevitable problems attending lip-synch. The stylized realism of the designs, with many panels of lush greenery (in some scenes too much in motion), are often handsome, but certainly not Egyptian. Neither are the oriental costumes; those for the priests have the look of a Buddhist order. The direction is generally lucid, with some unusual touches (e.g., Papageno sings "Ein Madchen" without realizing he is in the presence of Papagena).

The musical performance, shorn of the Sarastro-Pamina-Tamino terzetto, is sensibly paced, alert, and expressively warm. The cast, led by Dieter Schloz, a jolly, full-toned Papageno with splendid diction, is above average. The Sarastro (Hermann Christian Polster), with an agreeable, mellow basso cantante, sings a graceful invocation to the Egyptian gods. Although no paragon of *bel canto*, Horst Gebhardt, an attractive, impulsive prince, is a welcome throwback to the days, over a generation ago, when Tamino was sung with more robust tone. Magdalena Falewicz's soprano is a bit thin, but she looks, moves, and communicates well, especially in her solo, which is unusually touching in its grief. Inger Uibel is an uneven Queen, more pleasing in lyric than in coloratura passages, as the latter are often smudged by strain and shaky intonation. The Three Ladies, uncommonly rich in tone, are pleasing, despite their foolishly ruffed costumes.

Minimal production values: no subtitles, grainy pictures, but decent enough audio.

1978 VAI (VHS)

(Stage Performance, Stereo, Color, Subtitled) 164 minutes

Felicity Lott (A), May Sandoz (B), Elizabeth Conquet (C), Leo Goeke (D), John Fryatt (E), Benjamin Luxon (F), Thomas Thomaschke (G), Glyndebourne Chorus, London Philharmonic—Bernard Haitink

Glyndebourne Festival: John Cox (stage director), Dave Heather (video director)

This video is memorable primarily for the charm of David Hockney's witty sets and costumes and John Cox's production, which keeps comedy and sobriety in equipoise, while maintaining continuity through Schikaneder's many changes of scene. Unusually faithful to the librettist's instructions, the opera is set in ancient Egypt with pyramids, temples and gardens (in delightful colors), trap doors (frequently in use), and, for Sarastro's entrance, two lions to draw his carriage. Unfortunately, the Three Boys are played by women.

The cast leaves a mixed impression. At this point in her career, Felicity Lott is more the fledgling than the assured Pamina, pale in reaction to situation and a bit strained at the top, disclosing some unsupported tone. Leo Goeke, a manly, sympathetic Tamino, has no more than a serviceable legato. Despite a less-than-ideal *physique du rôle*, tall, big-boned Benjamin Luxon sings well and is a likable, concerned Papageno. His Papagena, Elizabeth Conquest, is adorable. May Sandoz, an accurate Queen, has an anonymous voice whose tone often turns unattractive in her highest register. An East German bass with a quick vibrato, Thomas Thomaschke, new to the West in 1978, sings Sarastro in a dignified manner but without enough resonance in his lowest notes.

Bernard Haitink offers a traditional Middle European approach to the score, ripely considered, shipshape in ensemble, but insufficiently animated.

Production values are no more than acceptable. Images and sound are not tightly focused. There is picture flicker here and there.

1983 PHILIPS (VHS/LD)

Stage Performance, Stereo, Color, Subtitled) 160 minutes

Lucia Popp (A), Edita Gruberová (B), Gudrun Sieber (C), Francisco Araiza (D), Norbert Orth (E), Wolfgang Brendel (F), Kurt Moll (G), Bavarian State Chorus and Orchestra—Wolfgang Sawallisch

Bavarian State Opera: August Everding (stage director), Peter Windgassen (video director).

Few traces of Egypt are to be found in the designs made by Jürgen Rose for August Everding's production. The sets and costumes are redolent of late eighteenth-century Vienna. In fact, each of the Three Boys, in their courtly attire, might pass for the prodigy composer himself, as seen in the presence of royalty on one of his courtstorming tours. Sarastro and his associates are dressed in the plain, black, formal everyday dress worn by Viennese clerics of the day, while their followers are well-scrubbed peasants, as rococo in appearance as many of Rose's tastefully extragavant settings.

Although this production is far from displeasing, its change of time and locale from Schikaneder's instructions creates problems in playing that are not altogether resolved; dislocation creates visual problems as well. The updated conception, which mandates an entrance on foot by Sarastro rather than by lion-drawn carriage, diminishes a first impression of nobility. Likewise, a plain ecclesiastical chamber is no substitute for the solemnity and grandeur of Egyptian pyramids as a setting for the rituals of the priests.

There is one major cut in the score (political correctness is honored in the elimination of the duet of the priests decrying women's wiles) and one major transposition (the terzetto in which Sarastro parts Tamino and Pamino is now moved up to the first scene of the second act, before the bass solo "O Isis und Osiris," from its normal position much further along). There is one staging oddity that must be noted: even before the conclusion of their mating duet, the bird couple is surrounded by a bevy of adorable offspring.

Wolfgang Sawallisch's musical direction, more notable for excellent pacing, well-groomed musical execution, and keen-edged ensemble than for expressive depth, nevertheless provides a context that gives singers the opportunity to shine. Popp and Araiza, most sympathetic and persuasive as the royal couple, have seldom been heard to equal effect elsewhere on video. Gruberová is also impressive, and especially accurate in coloratura—even more, angry and forceful in the Queen's vengeance aria. Brendel is not up to their level as a singer, but his Papageno is easy to like, natural and spontaneous, proving him a worthy advocate of the Hanswurst-Kasperle tradition of comic playing (without the ham). Best of all, however, is Moll, an ideal Sarastro in vocal size, color, range, and flexibility; in expression he is at once tender and noble. The workmanlike video direction keeps the stage action reasonably clear. The picture, not so fine-grained as one might like, betrays a lot of minimum video noise. The sound is good, except on those occasions when a singer strays too far from the microphone pickup.

1987 KULTUR (VHS)

(Stage Performance, Stereo, Color, in English)
160 minutes

Yvonne Kenny (A), Christa Leahmann (B), Peta Blyth (C), Gran Wilson (D), Graeme Ewer (E), John Fulford (F), Donald Shanks (G), Australian Opera Chorus, Elizabethan Sydney Orchestra—Richard Bonynge

Australian Opera: Göran Järvefelt (stage director), Peter Prokop (video director)

This simple, elegant production has a unit set that sensibly accommodates the action of every scene. It's wooden runway flanked by two white interior walls painted with murals of Mozart's time seems to recede into infinity (except when a backdrop or doors in the rear are employed to suggest a specific space). The direction of the players, each physically well cast, is clear and seldom fussy. If the show had musical values that matched its visual virtues, it would compete with most of the other videos. It does not.

Richard Bonynge's conducting, limp and sluggish, has only an all-purpose warmth for expression. Blunt rhythms and shallow dynamics erase the contrasts that nourish dramatic conflict. Yvonne Kenny, much the best of the singers, is a committed Pamina with a firm and shining tone. John Fulford is a personable Papageno whose English can always be understood, something that can't be said of the majority of the cast. Vocal liabilities are Gran Wilson, a good-looking prince with a tenor of insufficient size and color; Christa Leahmann, an ineffective Queen without the metal to suggest imperiousness or rage; and Donald Shanks, who is without the well-focused, burnished sound Sarastro requires.

As in some other productions, the terzetto is heard in the opening scene of the second act. The priests' duet is included.

Production values are below standard. Except for close-ups, images are not pleasingly defined. The orchestra is overresonant (perhaps the result of one of Australian Opera's many experiments in pit amplification) and tends to sound mushy.

1989 PHILIPS (LD)

(Stage Performance, Stereo, Color, Subtitled) 221 minutes

Ann Christine Biel (A), Birgit Louise Frandsen (B), Anna Tomson (C), Stefan Dahlberg (D), Magnus Kyhle (E), Mikael Samuelson (F), Laszlo Polgár (G), Chorus and Orchestra of the Drottningholm Court Theater—Arnold Östman

Drottningholm Court Theater: Goran Jarvefelt (stage director), Thomas Olofsson (video director)

Göran Järvefelt's eighteenth-century-styled production, tailored for the Drottningholm Theater, is altogether different from that which he made for Sydney. Here one finds numerous scenes framed by rows of realistic painted flats on either side of the stage and a backcloth of a Viennese cityscape, the kind of tableaux with which Mozart was well acquainted (although he well might have been surprised by the smoothness of continuity achieved by the production team in this remarkable antique theater). He may not have been comfortable with the change of venue from Egypt to Vienna, but he would have surely recognized the sound of his music. Performed on period instruments, the opera is surely as light and transparent as he intended it to be. On no other video do the singers so easily get through the most strenuous passages without forcing their voices.

The cast is musical and stylish, but only Laszlo Polgár, a noble Sarastro, has an impressive instrument. The voices of the other principals are a shade too lightweight and lacking in color, but they and an excellent chorus achieve an ensemble that attests to Arnold Östman's skill and sympathetic support. His tempos are well selected, apart from the virtual *presto* used for the Queen's second aria (surely an attempt to achieve the molten rage it should have but seldom attains). One is particularly grateful for the real *andante* selected for Pamina's aria, far too often taken so slowly it masks the agitation and distress of the heroine's situation.

Available only on laser disc, this video has steady images rich in color and excellent, well balanced sonics.

1992 DEUTSCHE GRAMMOPHON (VHS / LD)

(Stage Performance, Stereo, Color, Subtitled) 169 minutes

Kathleen Battle (A), Luciana Serra (B), Barbara Kilduff (C), Francisco Araiza (D), Heinz Zednik (E), Manfred Hemm (F), Kurt Moll (G), Metropolitan Opera Chorus and Orchestra— James Levine

Metropolitan Opera: Guus Mostart (stage director), Brian Large (video director)

It seemed unlikely that David Hockney's designs for the cozy confines of Glyndebourne would be as effective rescaled to fit the Met's enormous stage, and they aren't. Part of their charm was their intimate scale. But on video, at least, the enlargement is not as injurious as it might have been. John Cox's associate producer at Glyndebourne, Guus Mostart, has staged the show so that it has admirable continuity and a lively sense of theater, except for the trials by fire and water, which have no sense of danger.

The musical performance is an unalloyed delight. James Levine's orchestra is superb, playing with musical integrity, accuracy, and silken sonorities. No other conductor on video is so unfailingly expressive; every phrase is alive. The chorus is very good, except for a few wobblers on the distaff side. No member of the cast disappoints; three members are memorable. Kathleen Battle, tonally bright and appealing, is a Pamina to cherish, especially in the second act. Kurt Moll, as always, is an olympian and serene Sarastro, Manfred Hemm a spirited and genial Papagena. More impressive in coloratura than in lyrical passages is Luciana Serra's Queen. Francisco Araiza, less colorful vocally than earlier, shapes his phrases with commendable style. The Three Boys are particularly good, rather better than the Three Ladies.

Images and sound are first rate, the best of any other VHS.

1995 DEUTSCHE GRAMMOPHON (VHS / LD)

(Semi-staged Performance, Stereo, Color, Subtitled) 160 minutes

Christiane Oelze (A), Cyndia Sieden (B), Constanze Backes (C), Michael Schade (D), Uwe Peper (E), Gerald Finley (F), Harry Peeters (G), Monteverdi Choir, English Baroque Soloists—John Eliot Gardiner

John Eliot Gardiner and Stephen Medcalf (stage directors), Pim Marks (video director)

This semi-staged presentation, filmed in the acoustically flattering Amsterdam Concertgebouw, finds the orchestra in its usual concert position. The stage action takes place on an elevated platform behind the players and on a narrow walkway in front of them. There are costumes, but no sets and minimal props. Filling in the theatrical gaps are six mime dancers of the Pilobolus Dance Theater performing yeoman duty as beasts, birds, water, fire, trees, the two Armed Men, and the gates of Sarastro's Temple.

Like most period instrument renditions, this one rebukes the Wagnerizing of this score by such maestros as Furtwängler, Klemperer, and Walter in favor of a lighter, tauter style, more in tune with the musical comedy for a small theater that Mozart actually wrote. The performance is led with uncommon precision, animation, and transparent sonorities by John Eliot Gardiner; although, oddly, there is little of expected vocal ornamentation. In any event, its bountiful musical rewards exceed its theatrical charm and the humanity of its portrayals. Except for the Sarastro, the singing of the principals, gratifyingly secure in tone, elegant and refined, falls short of the warmth and depth of feeling found in the work of Bergman's team of period specialists. Among other roles, the Three Ladies—Susan Roberts, Carola Guber, and Maria Jonas—are especially praiseworthy.

DG's presentation is serviceable, but there were more than the usual number of sonic burbles or dropouts in my review copy.

––––––––––––

The Met video—thanks above all to James Levine and the largely successful adaptation of David Hockney's designs—and that from Munich, under Wolfgang Sawallisch, set the highest current large-opera-house standards. For something closer to the opera's original specifications, one should turn to Ingmar Bergman's thoughtful and affectionate production or, if hearing Mozart sung in Swedish proves daunting, to John Eliot Gardiner and his team's precise and spirited, if rather impersonal, account of the score.

C. J. LUTEN

Boris Godunov (1874)

A: Marina (s or ms); B: Dmitri (t); C: Shuisky (t); D: Rangoni (bar or bs); E: Boris Godunov (bar or bs); F: Pimen (bs); G: Varlaam (bs)

Because Modest Mussorgsky died in 1881 at the young age of forty-two, before his two great historical operas *Boris Godunov* and *Khovanshchina* had established themselves in the repertory even in Russia, questions of textual accuracy and intent have pursued both operas ever since. At least *Boris* (unlike *Khovanshchina*) was presented on stage during the composer's lifetime: on February 8, 1874, at the Mariinsky Theatre in St. Petersburg. The same year, a vocal score was published under Mussorgsky's supervision. But because Mussorgsky had produced three different versions, several times rearranging the order of scenes and making cuts, and because his musical style was so unconventional, his colleague Nikolai Rimsky-Korsakov later felt justified in reorchestrating and rearranging *Boris*. It was his version that Western audiences first encountered in the early years of the twentieth century, with Fyodor Chaliapin in the title role. (Chaliapin's performances as Boris in the United States in the 1920s caused near-riots.) Later, the Soviet musicologist Pavel Lamm produced a more authentic score, on the basis of Mussorgsky's manuscripts. In 1940, Dmitri Shostakovich completed a new orchestration based on Lamm's work. In 1975, David Lloyd-Jones published another critical edition of the score based on Mussorgsky's second version. Various versions of *Boris* continue to be staged today, although the ones closer to Mussorgsky's original intentions now find greater favor than Rimsky Korsakov's lush and romanticized arrangement.

Boris Godunov is based on Alexander Pushkin's episodic 1825 play in verse, itself modelled on Shakespeare's historical tragedies, particularly *Macbeth*. The protagonist is a real historical figure who ruled as the Tsar of Muscovy for a brief and turbulent few years (1598–1605). The "plot" revolves around the guilt Boris feels over having murdered the rightful heir to the throne, the Tsarevich Dmitri. (For artistic purposes, Pushkin presents Boris as guilty of Dmitri's murder, although historians disagree over whether he was actually responsible.) At the same time, Boris is being challenged by an ambitious imposter claiming to be Dmitri in order to get the throne.

Because they deal with political / ideological legitimacy, an issue that made both the Romanovs and the Soviet Communists extremely uncomfortable, Pushkin's play and Mussorgsky's opera ran into many problems with Russian censors over the years. In the West, *Boris Godunov* has become the best known of all Russian operas. Its medieval pageantry, religious mysticism, brilliant use of folk and religious musical sources, large choral scenes, and surprisingly "modern" portrayal of Boris's guilty conscience have made it a favorite of directors, too. Thanks to its visual splendor, *Boris* translates well to film and video.

1978 KULTUR (VHS)

(Stage Performance, Stereo, Color, Subtitled)
181 minutes

Irina Arkhipova (A), Vladislav Piavko (B), Andrei Sokolov (C), Evgeny Nesterenko (E), Valery Yaroslavtsev (F), Artur Eisen (G), Chorus and Orchestra of the Bolshoi Theatre—Boris Khaikin

Bolshoi Theater: Leonid Baratov (stage director)

At the Bolshoi Theater, where this production was taped "live" in 1978, the Rimsky-Korsakov version of *Boris Godunov* has long reigned unchallenged. Numerous other cuts and adjustments have been made to the libretto and the score over the years, however. In this production, the first scene of the "Polish Act," set in the boudoir of Princess Marina Mniszek, is eliminated altogether, along with the role of Rangoni, the Jesuit who urges Marina to marry Dmitri in order to convert Orthodox Russia to Catholicism. Instead, the "Polish Act" (here called Act III) begins directly with the second scene by the fountain, where Dmitri and Marina declare their love for each other. Only at the very end of this scene does a nonspeaking actor playing Rangoni descend the stairs to bless the couple. The elimination of Rangoni may not be such a bad idea, for his extended aria on the glories of the faith is not one of Mussorgsky's most inspired pieces of vocal writing. It's a shame to lose Marina's boudoir scene, however, for it fleshes out her already sketchy role and contains some charming music for her attendants.

The production filmed here by Soviet State Television has been a fixture of the Bolshoi Theater for many years now. It is highly traditional and realistic, with attractive painted backdrops and luxuriously authentic costumes for Boris and the boyars. At the end of the Kromy scene, Dmitri enters on a real white horse, galloping on his way to conquer Moscow. The opening scenes of Novodevichy Monastery, and of the Uspensky Cathedral in the Kremlin, are sprawling and colorful, with endless processions of priests and princes. The chorus, which plays a central musical and dramatic role in this opera, spills over the stage and gives the necessary impression of massiveness and expanse.

Evgeny Nesterenko, the most highly-regarded Soviet baritone-bass of his generation, takes the role of Boris. It is a refined, thoughtful, and beautifully sung performance, delivered at the height of Nesterenko's career. His voice has an impressive range, youthful lift, and elasticity, but also sufficient maturity to convey the aging and psychological exhaustion of Boris's final scenes. Like all great Borises, Nesterenko is also an accomplished actor; when he shouts *"Dovol'no!"* ("Enough!") to Shuisky after hearing a description of Tsarevich Dmitri's death, he makes you shiver. His interpretation embraces the ambiguity of this noble but fatally ambitious personality.

The rest of the cast matches Nesterenko's high level. The incomparable Irina Arkhipova, also at the height of her distinguished career, sings the role of Marina with taste and clarity. As Dmitri, Vladislav Piavko has vocal power and physical agility. Valery Yaroslavtsev makes an unusually vital Pimen, Andrei Sokolov is a marvelously fawning Shuisky, and the legendary Artur Eisen inhabits the role of the drunken Varlaam with abandon, humor, and a juicy bass that sounds as if it's been pickled in vodka. All of the character roles are also very well done.

What distinguishes this performance is its obvious engagement and spontaneity. All too often at the Bolshoi during the days of Soviet power, *Boris* became a tired ritual enacted for the tourists bused in from the foreign-currency hotels—but not here. The commitment and discipline emanate from the pit, where Boris Khaikin, chief conductor at the Bolshoi from 1954, conducts one of his last performances.

The camera work (apparently done by Soviet State Television, though no credit is given either on the film or the packaging) is also unexpectedly subtle and thoughtful, with a nice combination of close, medium, and long shots and excellent lighting. At intermissions, the cameramen give us brief tours of the glorious gold-and-red interior of the Bolshoi. Sound quality is very good.

1987 HOME VISION (VHS) / PIONEER (LD)

(Stage Performance, Stereo, Color, Subtitled)
176 minutes

Tamara Sinyavskaya (A), Vladislav Piavko (B), Vladimir Kudryashov (C), Evgeny Nesterenko (E), Alexander Vedernikov (F), Arthur Eizen (G), Chorus and Orchestra of the Bolshoi Theater—Alexander Lazarev

Bolshoi Theater: Leonid Baratov (stage director), Derek Bailey (video director)

This version, filmed at the Bolshoi in 1987, is the same production as the one seen on the Kultur video, with several casting changes: Tamara Sinyavskaya replaces Arkhipova as Marina, Vladimir Kudryashov replaces Sokolov as Shuisky, and Alexander Vedernikov replaces Yaroslavtsev as Pimen. But the most significant difference is the impact of the passage of nine years on the singing and acting of Nesterenko as Boris and Piavko as Dmitri. For both men, the aging process took away physical, dramatic, and vocal agility. While the older Nesterenko may have a deeper understanding of Boris's final death scene, his portrayal of the younger Boris is considerably less convincing. His voice shows decreased flexibility, but increased vibrato. Both Piavko and Nesterenko also seem considerably less emotionally involved in what they are doing—the result, no doubt, of too many years of repeating the same roles in the same theater in the same production. It was exactly this narrowness of repertory that led so many leading Soviet singers and dancers to defect to the West during the years of Brezhnev stagnation. This is a stagnant *Boris*.

As Pimen, sixty-year-old Alexander Vedernikov (who once played Boris himself) looks undeniably ancient enough, but his frail voice barely carries. As Marina, Sinyavskaya displays a strong voice and imperious manner, but she is not in the same exalted class as Arkhipova.

The chorus and orchestra also seem to be just going through the motions. Boris Khaikin was a hard act to follow, as Alexander Lazarev's bland conducting makes all too clear.

This was a coproduction of the National Video Corporation and Gosteleradio (Soviet State Television), but despite the apparently much larger production staff used here compared to the 1978 version, the camera work is not particularly interesting or inspired. There

are fewer close-ups, with a resulting loss of emotional intensity. The booklet enclosed with the video is also very misleading, since the plot synopsis contains the omitted scene in Marina's boudoir and the eliminated character of Rangoni.

1990 LONDON (VHS / LD)

(Stage Performance, Stereo, Color, Subtitled)
210 minutes

Olga Borodina (A), Alexei Steblianko (B), Yevgeny Boitsov (C), Sergei Leiferkus (D), Robert Lloyd (E), Alexander Morosov (F), Vladimir Ognovenko (G), Chorus and Orchestra of the Kirov Opera—Valery Gergiev

Kirov Opera: Andrei Tarkovsky (stage director), Humphrey Burton (video director)

Andrei Tarkovsky's visionary production of *Boris* comes across even more effectively on video than onstage. Tarkovsky, one of the most original and influential Soviet film directors of his generation, with such important films as *Andrei Rublev* and *Solaris* to his credit, always thought in intensely visual and symbolic terms, loading his films with vivid, thoughtful details that could exercise their full impact only in close-ups.

In the theater, Tarkovsky achieved that cinematic quality, investing selected images with striking emotional and illustrative power. In creating this *Boris* (first staged at Covent Garden in 1983, then transferred to the Kirov where it was filmed by the BBC in 1990), Tarkovsky had the brilliant idea of bringing the angelic ghost of the slaughtered Tsarevich Dmitri onstage at appropriate moments to hover at the edge of the action, embodying Boris's guilty conscience. To symbolize the weight of the time and history, Tarkovsky placed a giant pendulum at the back of the stage; it begins to swing, ominously, at turning points in the action. Although the entire opera is staged on a ramp that slopes down toward the auditorium, the production is so lavishly detailed and choreographed that it never feels abstract or barren.

There are numerous startling *coups de théâtre*—the statues lining the ramp in the Polish scenes (here presented in full) that come to life dancing; the enormous fabric map of Russia in which Boris wraps himself as he plays with his children; the two long rows of red-robed boyars in Act IV. Then there's the unforgettable final tableau, which mixes four images (nicely conveyed by the excellent camera work)—snow, the ramp covered with the prone bodies of hundreds of suffering Russian peasants, the ghost of Dmitri, and a bloody axe. This production uses the David Lloyd-Jones edition of the score, which reverses the order of the last two scenes as they are presented in the Bolshoi (Rimsky-Korsakov) production. Here, the opera ends not with Boris's death, but with the anarchy of leaderless Russia out of control.

The visual excitement of the Kirov production is enhanced by superb performances from an outstanding cast. As Boris, Robert Lloyd is harrowing but highly controlled, both vocally impeccable and dramatically persuasive. His death scene (staged here with Boris and his son, Fyodor, placed on either side of the teetering throne), played with animalistic fury, can stand comparison with Martti Talvela's memorable performances at the Met. Similarly fine are Alexander Morosov as a modest, devout Pimen and Yevgeny Boitsov as an alternately scheming and obsequious Shuisky.

As one would expect, Olga Borodina is magnificent as Marina Mniszek; she is a distinguished heir to Arkhipova, her own personal mentor and model. Opposite her, Alexei Steblianko does better than I might have anticipated from other live and recorded performances with which I am familiar, but he is the weakest of the principals. True to form, Sergei Leiferkus, malevolently bald and Machiavellian, nearly steals the show in the cameo role of Rangoni, which Tarkovsky incorporates into the opera without a loss of momentum or emotional focus. In the pit, Valery Gergiev is once again exemplary in his restraint, intelligence, and commitment.

The Bolshoi *Boris* focuses on the opera's splendor and ceremony. The Kirov version stresses the unending suffering of the Russian people at the hands of their secretive, cynical, and murderous rulers—which was the message Mussorgsky had sought to convey in his score.

The Kirov production is clearly the best choice on all grounds. Those who want the Rimsky-Korsakov orchestration and a more traditional interpretation are advised to choose the Kultur Bolshoi version over the Home Vision one.

HARLOW ROBINSON

KHOVANSHCHINA (1886)

A: Emma (s); B: Marfa (ms); C: Andrei Khovansky (t); D: Vasily
Golitsyn (t); E: Fyodor Shaklovity (bar); F: Ivan Khovansky (bs);
G: Dosifei (bs)

*I*n *Khovanshchina*, set amid the social chaos of late seventeenth-century Muscovy, Mussorgsky explored the issue that still haunts progressive Russian politicians eager to drag their country into the modern world: the country's fundamentally non-Western, even barbaric, character and traditions. "O holy Russia, you won't soon wash away the rust of the Tartars," a resigned Prince Golitsyn (a Westernizer) sings in Act II. *Khovanshchina* describes the sharp ideological and cultural conflict that separated the Westernizers (those who wanted Russia to emulate Europe, led by Peter I) and the conservative Orthodox Old Believers (led here by the commanding figure of Dosifei), who rejected change as sinful.

Left unfinished and in considerable disarray at the time of Mussorgsky's death, *Khovanshchina* (which takes its clumsy name from the Khovansky family, major players in Russian politics of the late 1600s) was first mounted in Rimsky-Korsakov's prettified version in 1886. Sergei Diaghilev enlisted Stravinsky and Ravel to restore some of the cuts for his 1913 Paris production. It was Dmitri Shostakovich, working from Mussorgsky's vocal score as prepared by the Soviet musicologist Pavel Lamm, who in 1958 finally produced the most authentic edition.

Even more than in *Boris Godunov*, the chorus (and the Russian people it represents) is the hero of *Khovanshchina*. The choral music draws on the two basic traditions of Russian music: the liturgy of the Russian Orthodox Church and the folk tradition. In the opera's concluding measures, Mussorgsky provides a brilliant musical illustration of the changes that came to Russian cultural and musical life with the ascension of Peter I ("The Great") to the throne in 1689. The Old Believers, intent on holding onto their age-old ways, sing traditional liturgical chants as they set fire to themselves in protest against the government's enforced policies of Westernization. In contrast (in the Rimsky-Korsakov orchestration), we hear the Western-style military band of Peter's victorious army as the curtain falls.

For Westerners, *Khovanshchina* can be difficult to follow, meandering as it does from character to character and episode to episode. It is almost more a historical pageant than an opera, but it contains some of Mussorgsky's greatest orchestral and vocal music and conveys the essence of Russian spirituality better than any other single work written for the stage.

1979 KULTUR (VHS) / PIONEER (LD)

(Stage Performance, Stereo, Color, Subtitled) 172 minutes

Uncredited (A), Irina Arkhipova (B), Georgy Andryushchenko (C), Evgeny Raikov (D), Vladislav Romanovsky (E), Alexander Vedernikov (F), Yevgeny Nesterenko (G), Chorus and

Orchestra of the Bolshoi Theater—Yuri Simonov

Bolshoi Theater: Director unknown

The Bolshoi has traditionally preferred the Rimsky-Korsakov version of *Khovanshchina*. Musically, Rimsky-Korsakov robbed Mussorgsky's vision of its essential starkness and otherworldliness; instead, Rimsky-Korsakov produced a more homogenized, flashy orchestral style similar to the one found in his own *Russian Easter Overture*. Dramatically, the most important difference between this version and the Shostakovich version is the ending: Shostakovich ends with the Old Believers burning themselves in their chapel. Rimsky-Korsakov, however, typically came up with something more optimistic and affirmative: the arrival of Peter I's soldiers, accompanied by their Western-style military band. Peter's men stand by incredulous as they watch these religious fanatics commit suicide rather than yield to modern ways. Shostakovich's version stresses the depth of the religious convictions of the Old Believers, while Rimsky-Korsakov's seems to view Westernization as painful but necessary.

This performance was taped "live" at the Bolshoi in 1979. Who did the taping is not stated anywhere in the packaging or on the tape, but it seems to have been Soviet State Television. Similarly, no information is provided about who staged, designed, directed, or choreographed it. This lack of attribution illustrates all too well the "communal" spirit that reigned at the Bolshoi in the late Soviet era, when no one had clear responsibility for anything, and the role of the director had been reduced to insignificance. The production filmed here has been in the Bolshoi repertory for many years and is very typical of its grandiose, realistic, "picture postcard" style, with lots of elaborate painted backdrops. The blocking is primitive both for the principals and the chorus, who move around in straight lines and stand and sing as if in concert.

No single role dominates *Khovanshchina*, but the most important characters vocally are Dosifei and Marfa. As Marfa, Irina Arkhipova sings with characteristic style and fervor; her scenes are the finest in this performance. Yevgeny Nesterenko does reasonably well as Dosifei, but the role does not seem to come as naturally to him as that of Boris Godunov. The remaining singers turn in pedestrian performances. Alexander Vedernikov does not have the vocal or dramatic power to handle the role of Ivan Khovansky, while Georgy Andryushchenko as his son Andrei Khovansky sounds tentative and often sings out of tune. His big scene with Emma in Act I lacks any sense of violence or threat.

Under Yuri Simonov, the Bolshoi orchestra sounds raucous, thin, and unrefined. Even the famous Bolshoi chorus seems tired and bored here. Perhaps after sixty years of Soviet-enforced atheism and religious persecution, the troupe found it difficult to feel the religious fervor that drives *Khovanshchina*.

Camera work and sound are competent.

1989 KULTUR (VHS) / PIONEER (LD)

(Stage Performance, Stereo, Color, Subtitled) 173 minutes

Joanna Borowska (A), Ludmila Semtschuk (B), Vladimir Atlantov (C), Yuri Marusin (D), Anatoly Kocherga (E), Nicholai Ghiaurov (F), Paata Burchuladze (G), Vienna State Opera Chorus, Slovak Philharmonic Chorus, Vienna Boys' Choir, Vienna State Opera Orchestra—Claudio Abbado

Vienna State Opera: Alfred Kirchner (stage director), Brian Large (video director)

The dominant visual image of this remarkable Vienna State Opera production is a reproduction of a famous painting by the Russian artist Vasily Vereshchagin. Called "Apotheosis of War," it depicts a pyramid of skulls and was dedicated by the artist "to all great conquerors, present, past and future." Here, the set designer Erich Wonder has placed a piece of the painting into a lighted cube suspended against a black backdrop at the back of the stage. Its presence reminds us that *Khovanshchina* is really an opera about the power of rulers (especially divinely appointed autocrats like those who reigned in Russia) to control, ruin, and end the lives of their powerless subjects.

Director Alfred Kirchner has used the innovative and richly executed design (which also features a panoramic view of Moscow from Red Square) and costumes (by Joachim Herzog) not just as "local color" for the story, however. He has succeeded in integrating the visual, emotional, dramatic, and musical aspects of this sprawling opera to an extent I would hardly have thought possible. Recognizing the importance of the chorus to the spiritual message, he has used each of its many members not only as voices, but as actors in a people's drama. Some aspects of the visual production are abstract, such as the column that serves as the chapel in which the Old Believers burn themselves at the end. The clothes and furniture, however, are historically accurate and well-chosen.

The cast is unusually well-balanced and distinguished. The most convincing performance comes from Paata Burchuladze as the cult leader Dosifei; his enormous bass is combined here with a hypnotic stage presence that makes entirely credible his spiritual power over his flock of believers. As Ivan Khovansky, Nicolai Ghiaurov sings eloquently and swaggers most convincingly. Anatoly Kocherga makes the most of the small role of Shaklovity, showing imperious disregard for the low-born. Even Vladimir Atlantov (as Andrei Khovansky), not noted for his acting skills, overcomes his fondness for stagy gestures here and yells less than usual. Joanna Borowska makes us feel deep sympathy for the the Lutheran girl Emma, who must submit to the advances of those with royal blood.

The production staff has thought each moment through visually and dramatically. Choreographer Bernd R. Beinert devised a very ingenious "Dance of the Persian Girls," clothing the slave girls in black muslim and chains, which they gradually discard as the dance progresses, much to the delight of the lecherous Ivan Khovansky.

The excellence and originality of the staging is more than matched by a superb orchestral performance under Claudio Abbado. For the final scene, Abbado chose to use Stravinsky's orchestration prepared for Diaghilev; it is even more spare and mystical than the version prepared by Shostakovich.

The camera work is sophisticated, subtle, and intense, and the sound quality is excellent. This is one of the best versions of any opera available on video.

1992 PHILIPS (VHS / LD)

(Stage Performance, Stereo, Color, Subtitled)
205 minutes

Tatiana Kravtsova (A), Olga Borodina (B), Yuri Marusin (C), Konstantin Pluzhnikov (D), Viacheslav Trofimov (E), Bulat Minjelkiev (F), Nikolai Okhotnikov (G), Chorus and Orchestra of the Kirov Theater—Valery Gergiev

Kirov Theater: Fyodor Lopukhov (stage director), Brian Large (video director)

Visually, this traditional, rather old-fashioned *Khovanshchina* is quite similar to the one produced at the Bolshoi—except that Gergiev uses the preferable Shostakovich orchestration. This production has been in the repertory at the Kirov for many years now; I saw it in the summer of 1970 while studying Russian in Leningrad.

Lacking the intense visuality of the *Boris Godunov* staged at the Kirov by Andrei Tarkovsky, this *Khovanshchina* relies heavily on hanging painted flats for realistic historic atmosphere. The final scene presents a suitably rustic country scene, with several wooden chapels on the edge of a forest lake. The costumes have been redone, and the enterprise possesses a reassuring authenticity and sincerity. Very readable English-language titles flash across a solid black space at the bottom of the screen that unfortunately also cuts off the singers' feet.

The cast is nearly identical to the one featured on a Philips CD released in 1992. A nasal and occasionally straining Yuri Marusin takes the role of Andrei Khovansky. The versatile tenor Konstantin Pluzhnikov sings not only the character role of the Scribe but also that of the doomed Westernizer, Vasily Golitsyn. As usual, Olga Borodina is in vocal and dramatic command as Marfa; with her youthful good looks and voice she makes very credible her romantic attachment to Andrei. That perennial charmer Nikolai Okhotnikov is the Old Believer pastor Dosifei, although he looks a bit too much like a kindly Santa Claus to convey the darker aspects of the preacher's magnetism. As Ivan Khovansky, Bulat Minjelkiev cannot compare either vocally or dramatically to Ghiaurov.

Valery Gergiev and his orchestra perform at the energetic level we have come to expect of them—and on a much high level than the Bolshoi orchestra on the 1979 Kultur release. The quality of the vocal recording is a disappoint-

ment, however; the miking is inconsistent, and the sound sometimes watery and thin.

——————

The Vienna State production on Kultur is in all ways the most successful version. But it should be kept in mind that each of these videos uses a different version of the score: Rimsky-Korsakov at the Bolshoi, Shostakovich at the Kirov, and Shostakovich / Stravinsky in Vienna.

HARLOW ROBINSON

LA VIE PARISIENNE (1867)

A: Gabrielle (s); B: Métella (s); C: Baroness de Gondremarck (ms);
D: Pauline (s); E: Raoul de Gardefeu (t); F: Bobinet (bar); G: Frick (t);
H: Baron de Gondremarck (bs-bar)

There is far too little Offenbach *opéra-bouffe* on video. Why this is I don't know, but I can state fairly categorically that the French certainly are not mounting these works either as regularly or as dazzlingly as I remember them doing a quarter-century ago from my visits to many Parisian theaters. In the present cost-cutting era, you are more likely to come across an Offenbach revue than an opulently-mounted full-length work done with taste and style.

La Vie Parisienne is special because it was originally more of a modern-dress *vaudeville* than the other costumed travesties by Offenbach and his librettists Meilhac and Halévy (like *La Belle Hélène* or *La Périchole*). It should play like lightning, with accomplished *farceurs* who for the most part sing only secondarily. That is why to this day people still reverently recall the famous Jean-Louis Barrault / Madeleine Renaud production that set Paris aglow in the 1950s (and which was seen briefly in New York in the 1960s).

When an opera house performs Offenbach, it is the comedy that invariably suffers, while the music is usually well performed. Sometimes it is overdone, and we can't hear the all-important lyrics with vast orchestras in very large theaters that don't really suit *opéra-bouffe*.

1991 KULTUR (VHS) / PIONEER (LD)

(Stage Performance, Stereo, Color, Subtitled)
159 minutes

Isabelle Mazin (A), Hélène Delavault (B), Claire Wauthion (C), Nathalie Joly (D), Jean-François Sivadier (E), Jacques Verzier (F), Jean-Yves Chatelais (G), Alain Hocine (H), Chorus and Orchestra of the Lyon Opera—Jean-Yves Ossonce

Lyon Opera: Alain Françon (stage director), Pierre Cavassilas (video director)

This is a realistic, fairly dour *La Vie Parisienne*, set in a Paris where lust, rather than frivolity, rules. Set and costumed well beyond the Second Empire, the music and mores of which this operetta so embodies, this version seems to take place in the more serious Third Republic, sometime around 1880. Perhaps that accounts for the cold, rather calculating men-about-town, well sung by Sivadier and Verzier, who are given a revised script by Mario Bois. Further prunings include an Act I station setting (designed by Carlo Tomassi) that is merely indicated by a wrought-iron pedestrian trestle; gone are the railway workers who open the show and the customary customs agents. The rich Brazilian enters alone and, to accentuate this production's pared-down effect, removes his clothes. (Why?) There is very little choreographed folde-rol at the finale, and when finally a smoky train does go by, it's barely seen on the video.

A wall of panelled doors are revealed in the following act, promising at least some French-farce fun. Laughter is provided in the refrain of the Gabrielle-Frick duet, but reality intrudes moments later with serious plumbing noises.

The Baron (Chatelais), interestingly not portrayed as stock Swedish buffoon, seems genuinely in love with his wife while still desiring his extracurricular activities. Ensembles are further cut in the first party finale, with its catatonic guests and a *tyrolienne* that goes basically undanced. When the Baron and Pauline have their saucy duet in Act III about the pretty cloud, they don't even face each other.

The "frou frou frou" number describing the rustling walk of the Parisienne, despite the absence of dancing, seems to wake up the audience. But the celebrated split-cost ensemble leading off the next party finale goes for naught when the guests don't even see the rip. The often-cut fourth act is included, partly, to offer the Baroness's rondo, and the last party at the Café des Anglais—just a canopy with tables and chairs—ends with the company seated as can-can dancers enter and drinks are served.

Indeed, this production takes the division between the singing and dancing operetta chorus to new extremes, a fatal maneuver in a work where everyone is supposed to be dancing with pleasure. As it is, the leading characters spend an inordinate amount of time seated in chairs, hardly proper behavior for a production of one of the first great musical comedies. In the end, operatic talents are beside the point when a director wants his Gabrielle to spend two minutes silently surveying a café before launching into her rondo, and the audience shows its nonappreciation.

Jean-Yves Ossonce seems a little slow with his conducting cues. The technical credits are OK, but I'm not sure I want to spend the overture watching the cast backstage soberly curling its hair and making up. This is an unvarnished, not too funny and not too pretty Paris. Whether fashionably deconstructionist or just chintzy, it is not really the way I imagine *La Vie Parisienne*.

Might the vaults of French television have a kinescope of the Barrault / Renaud version, assuming it was televised? . . .

RICHARD TRAUBNER

LES BRIGANDS (1869)

A: Fiorella (s); B: Fragaletto (ms); C: Falsacappa (bar); D: Pietro (bar)

Les Brigands is a pivotal work in the Offenbach canon, the last work written during the Second Empire with his irreplaceable librettist team of Meilhac and Halévy. In 1870, the Franco-Prussian War ended the frivolity-filled reign of Napoléon III, and with it Offenbach's position as its musical-theater emperor. Although he had several big hits after the Commune, none have proved as enduring as the *opéra-bouffes* he composed in the 1850s and 1860s (excluding of course the monumental *Contes d'Hoffmann*, produced posthumously in 1881).

Les Brigands must have seemed in its day remarkably prescient: the chorus announcing "les bottes, les bottes, les bottes" of the carabineers might have been a warning of the tramping boots of the forthcoming German troops. But the work is in fact a much more general satire, taking place in an operetta Mediterranean; its main thrust concerns appearances and disguises, and its main characters a band of respectable bandits. This attracted a young W. S. Gilbert, who wrote an English version of Meilhac and Halévy's book that was produced, after alterations, considerably later than his principal works with Sullivan. Remember that the pirates of Penzance are also highly respectable, and the double chorus of pirates and police has its antecedent in a very similar scene in *Les Brigands*. None of this has the slightest bearing on the interest of French audiences today, nor on the Germans who have consistently revived the work in this century.

1989 KULTUR (VHS) / PIONEER (LD)

(Stage Performance, Stereo, Color, Subtitled)
122 minutes

Valerie Chevalier (A), Colette Alliot-Lugaz (B), Michel Trempont (C), Riccardo Cassinelli (D), Chorus and Orchestra of the Lyon Opera—Claire Gibault

Lyon Opera: Louis Erlo, Alain Maratrat (stage directors); Yves André Hubert (video director)

The respectable brigands in this Lyon Opera production are the Mafia; the rocky canyons of yore are now office buildings. The time is c. 1928, and the chieftan Falsacappa appears in a dress suit. This interesting conceit—sets designed by Gian Maurizio Fercioni, costumes by Fernando Bruni—puts the crooks right in the period of *Die Dreigroschenoper*, a cousin in social satire. This is fine, provided you don't expect the usual *Fra Diavolo* approach and don't mind the frequent references to mountains.

And, indeed, all seems to go right (barring a typewriter distraction in the opening) from the entrance of Falsacappa, drily impersonated by Michel Trempont. The entire first act is a fount of Offenbach at his height: the heroic entrance of the bandit's daughter, Fiorella, gun on her shoulder (Valerie Chevalier); the introduction of her suitor, Fragoletto, sunnily sung by travesti specialist Colette Alliot-Lugaz; the sublimely catchy rondo in which Fiorella gives directions;

the even more furious saltarello ensemble in which Fragoletto overcomes a traveller ("Falsacappa, voici ma prise"); and then the famous finale involving the tramping boots of the Royal Carbineers, who always arrive too late to be of any use.

If only the rest of the operetta maintained this level of jolly inspiration. In Act II, the scaffold skyscrapers now portray, improbably, a hotel at the border between Italy and Spain. All manner of tricks are tried to distract the audience, including the ubiquitous photographer with his flash. As in so many second-tier Offenbach works, several isolated numbers are effective, like the chorus of monks and the kissing duet between Fragoletto and Fiorella that follows in Act II.

But the plot quickly palls into a series of dis-guises, an uneasy mélange of *La Périchole*'s Latin characters and *La Vie Parisienne*'s dressing up. (*Périchole*, written by the same creators one year earlier, is a much better work, and someone should get French television to put out on video its brilliant transcription of the gorgeous, hilarious production that was done at the Théâtre de Paris in 1968. *That* is a model of how Offenbach ought to be done.)

Nevertheless, this *Brigands* is quite enjoyable, providing you accept the silliness of the second half. Claire Gibault conducts with great enthusiasm, and technical credits are fine. This is not, however, as triumphant a revival as the one the same theater enjoyed earlier with Chabrier's much more intriguing *L'Étoile*.

RICHARD TRAUBNER

JACQUES OFFENBACH

LES CONTES D'HOFFMANN (1881)

A: Olympia (s); B: Giulietta (s); C: Antonia (s); D: Nicklausse (ms);
E: Hoffmann (t); F: Lindorf (bar); G: Coppelius (bar);
H: Dappertutto (bar); I: Dr. Miracle (bar)

Which edition to use, the casting of the soprano and bass roles, and the disappearance of the French style from the international musical scene are the usual focuses of any review of a new *Les Contes d'Hoffmann*. Offenbach died before finishing the score, Guiraud wrote the recitatives, and the Venetian act was not performed until 1905, so there are precedents for several editions. Which one is most effective will depend upon the dramatic force of the cast and the visual daring of the designer. The standard arrangement (Olympia, Giulietta, Antonia) progresses sensibly from the coolest to the warmest relationship, but with indifferent actors the Antonia scene can be a letdown after the theatricality of the Venetian act. As for casting the same soprano as Hoffmann's three loves and Stella, that, presumably, works when it works (never, in my experience!); the baritone / bass roles are vocally less of a problem.

The last example we had of an all-French star cast in *Hoffmann* was also the first complete recording: the 1948 Opéra-Comique version with Raoul Jobin. In its day it was thought reasonably good; today it seems a revelation. And what does that style do for the opera? It provides Hoffmann with some intellectual ability and capacity for intimacy, Olympia with piquancy, Giulietta with a delicate but commanding sensuality, Antonia with a passionate fragility, and the evil basses with elegance. Of course the best international singers—as shown below—have been able to approximate some of these things under the right conductor and to provide an (Italianate) vocal and emotional opulence that cannot be gainsaid—but in the meantime something of real value is waiting to be recaptured.

1951 HOME VISION (VHS) / CRITERION (LD)

(Film, Mono, Color, in English) 125 minutes

Moira Shearer / Dorothy Bond (A), Ludmilla Tcherina / Margherita Grandi (B), Ann Ayars (C), Pamela Brown / Monica Sinclair (D), Robert Rounseville (E), Robert Helpmann / Bruce Dargaval (F, G, H, I), Sadler's Wells Opera Chorus and Royal Philharmonic Orchestra—Thomas Beecham

Michael Powell, Emeric Pressburger (directors)

From the people responsible for A *Matter of Life and Death (Stairway to Heaven)*, *Black Narcissus*, and *The Red Shoes* came this amazing technicolor dream, the winner of a special jury prize at Cannes. For some very young artistic dreamers a few years after World War II, *The Red Shoes* and this film were uniquely exciting: imaginative, alarming, and seductive in a way unlike that of any movies they knew. Dance, opera, and film technology suddenly seemed made for each other, and the leap into the world of art appeared for once justified and effortless. Those *Chorus Line* monologues mentioning the initial impact of *The Red Shoes* are authentic.

And of course both films are complete romances: their pleasure and suffering are highly sweetened—in *Hoffmann's* case, even beyond what Offenbach adds to the original stories. Half a century later, part of the fun of watching is in figuring out just what real issues are being suggested. The triumphs of this *Hoffmann* are in the visuals and in Sir Thomas Beecham's conducting and nurturing of his singers. The musical cuts are extensive but are mainly in details of the psychology and plot; the great numbers are nearly all there and beautifully articulated and paced. The four villains have been simplified—sometimes inexplicably—but their mystery and power are amplified by the fascinating dancer-actor Robert Helpmann. The Stella framework has been cut to almost nothing, but Moira Shearer lends an unforgettable elegance to the role and to the dragonfly dance that has been added for her. The part of Nicklausse is also much shortened, but Pamela Brown's brooding irony tells us all we need to know, just as it did in her wordless performance of Jane Shore in Olivier's *Richard III*.

The singers are a mixed bag. Hoffmann himself is no longer a drunken poet, but painfully in earnest and quite without charisma in the person of the carefully coiffed and costumed Robert Rounseville, whose voice is reasonably plangent throughout. The most striking singer is Bruce Dargaval—with a fresh, full, and magisterial sound, particularly in the Diamond Aria. Dorothy Bond is a light and mostly accurate Olympia whose vocal charm is immeasurably supported by Moira Shearer's incomparable dancing of the role. As Giulietta, Margherita Grandi, a famous Lady Macbeth at Glyndebourne, has authority but also an aging vocal tone. Ann Ayars (like Rounseville an American who sang at New York's City Center) sounds healthy but lacks Antonia's fragility, so that the final tale loses its dramatic point.

The triumphs of the film—and even its failures are sometimes triumphant—are visual. Shearer, Helpmann, and Brown are all, in their various ways, incomparable, and Ludmilla Tcherina is an unapproachably gorgeous Giulietta: the mannequin as art. The settings, photography, and color remain dazzling after nearly half a century. Luther's place is a glittering tavern fantasy: nothing dirty, dishevelled, or sinister there except Kleinzach, whose story becomes a full-fledged dance. Spalanzani's establishment is an elegant nightmare of lighthearted bad taste. Even the guests are marionettes, which makes not much sense but provides some Beechamesque humour. And Hoffmann wears magic glasses that will remind some of Dame Edna's. Shearer's Olympia is definitive, and even if you disagree with their interpretations the supporting cast all perform with insuperable conviction. The Venice scene is almost equally successful. Rounseville again looks like a business man in fancy dress, but Leonid Massine's skeletal Schlemil is chilling and the visual corruption is generally delightful. The Antonia act is least successful. At last we have two real human beings in love with one another, but neither one of the singers is much of a film actor. Here the supernatural intrudes into a self-consciously middle-class setting, so that the designer's strengths are not so well used. There are provocative moments, but much of the scene is strange without being convincing, and the central sequence of Antonia's dead mother is awkwardly handled. In the Epilogue, the Muse is gone, but Stella's final appearance, wordless in this production, is touching.

As a performance of *Hoffmann*, this film is heavily cut, arbitrary, and Anglo-American in both language and style. Nevertheless, it provides us with Sir Thomas Beecham's grace and some long sequences of visual magic that can never quite be equalled in a live performance. For these it is remembered, and memorable.

1981 CASTLE OPERA (VHS) / PIONEER (LD)

(Stage Performance, Stereo, Color, Not Subtitled) 155 minutes

Luciana Serra (A), Agnes Baltsa (B), Ileana Cotrubas (C), Claire Powell (D), Plácido

Domingo (E), Robert Lloyd (F), Geraint Evans (G), Siegmund Nimsgern (H), Nicola Ghiuselev (I), Chorus and Orchestra of the Royal Opera House—Georges Prêtre

Royal Opera, Covent Garden: John Schlesinger (stage director), Brian Large (video director)

This performance uses a responsible edition of the score and features an expensive, rather "realistic" production that stresses the middle-class values against which Hoffmann struggles. Spalanzani's presentation party is mainly in black, gray, and white—neither fantastic nor particularly festive; Giulietta's Venice is rich without being attractive; and Crespel's house in Munich is regulation nineteenth-century gloomy. The sociological point is made, but the production is a good deal heavier than the score.

What makes the performance so satisfying is the singing, conducting, and much of the stage direction. The musical style is Intelligent International: the cast contains Spanish, Romanian, Greek, American, English, German, and Welsh singers—the only Frenchman is in the pit. That means that most of the Offenbach wit is in the pit, too, leaving the passion for the stage. Plácido Domingo looks fine and acts very well here—he even does an acceptable drunk—and is in glorious voice, with that warm tone, even scale, and durable freshness so important in this endless role. Luciana Serra is imperturbably accurate and enacts the doll with witty exactitude. Giulietta is an oddly passive role and awkwardly scored; even the finest singing actresses (Schwarzkopf, Stevens) have been able to make little of it, and Agnes Baltsa joins them—in a red dress, too. Ileana Cotrubas is beautifully cast as Antonia—frail and vibrant at once and always phrasing for emotional meaning. So often this role can sound wan or sophomoric; it is neither here, despite some awkward staging of her mother's appearance and what must be the Fires of Hell upstaging her death. Of the villains only Geraint Evans is a galvanic personality, but he is in dry voice; the others are decently resonant. Georges Prêtre drives this team with extraordinary élan, and as a whole the performance can be strongly recommended

as musically satisfying and emotionally invigorating. Oh, yes, John Gielgud offers a plot summary before each scene. It's rather like having God as your maître d'.

1993 KULTUR (VHS) / PIONEER (LD)

(Stage Performance, Stereo, Color, Subtitled) 150 minutes

Natalie Dessay (A), Isabelle Vernet (B), Barbara Hendricks (C), Brigitte Balleys (D), Daniel Galvez-Vallejo (E), José van Dam (F, G, H, I), Chorus and Orchestra of the Lyon Opera—Kent Nagano

Lyon Opera: Louis Erlo (stage director)

Louis Erlo's production is billed as *Des Contes d'Hoffmann*, which might be translated as *"Some Tales of Hoffmann!"* Gone are Nuremberg, Paris, Venice, and Munich; it all takes place in a lunatic asylum (the term is taken directly from the videotape box). Olympia is now a catatonic on a gurney, Antonia creates her own world of grace in a bare ward whose walls occasionally bulge with feminine anatomical shapes, Nicklausse is a lesbian, Schlemil (here very old) hurls himself on a knife, and at the end Hoffmann is left embracing a transvestite and muttering the Kleinsach song. No doubt much of this touches a contemporary nerve; it ought to, since the production draws on every modern European theatrical cliché from Büchner, the Expressionists, Wedekind, and Artaud through Sartre, Durrenmatt, Duras, Weiss, and their successors, with a dash of Brechtian alienation thrown in when the singers can't characterize their roles with consistency. So there are striking moments here but very little in the way of a deepening view of humanity. Yes, the world is a madhouse, and yes, the moral universe we have constructed has frustratingly little to do with our real needs as human beings, but we've known that bare fact since James Joyce—since Homer. It's where a performance goes *from there* that's interesting.

This production, then, gives us a sort of *Cliff's Notes* on Modern Theater Practice, and that's interesting in its way, but of real vision and new illumination there is little. The ideas bounce onto the stage and then deflate when the actors and director lose confidence in them; the eventual effect is of repetition rather than deepening profundity.

Within this difficult context there are two fascinating performances: those of Gabriel Bacquier (Crespel, Schlemil) and Jose van Dam. Each is a master of economical gesture and illuminating vocal color, and their scene together has riveting tension. Of the others, Barbara Hendricks is as usual an elegant singer; the coolness of her style is apt here. Daniel Galvez-Vallejo is earnest but can't seem to get beyond an uneasy imitation of conventional romantic passion—not enough to vitalize the production. As for the score, Kent Nagano conducts it well enough (the aural balance favors the voices), but it often seems to be a pretext for the production rather than its basis. Altogether, there are points of interest, certainly; your attitude toward the project may depend on what special passions you are bringing to a given viewing.

The 1981 Covent Garden production, international in style, is recommended for its clear direction and fine singing. Beecham's 1951 film is uneven and, with its cuts and English text, certainly not definitive, but it ought to be seen for its long stretches of Powell-Pressburger imaginative fantasy—unlike anything else in the history of filmed opera.

LONDON GREEN

Giovanni Battista Pergolesi

Lo Frate 'nnamorato (1732)

A: Nena (s); B: Ascanio (s); C: Vannella (s); D: Cardella (ms); E: Nina (c); F: Luggrezia (c); G: Carlo (t); H: Marcaniello (bar); I: Don Pietro (bar)

year before the success of his intermezzo *La Serva Padrona*, Giovanni Battista Pergolesi produced a much longer comic work that won immediate favor with the Neapolitan public. *Lo Frate 'nnamorato* solidified the composer's operatic reputation, already somewhat established by *La Sallustia* but then tarnished by its successor, *Ricimero*. The Neapolitan-dialect title, which might be translated as "The Brother in Love," in itself announced a departure from the *opera seria* genre that until then (except for the requisite accompanying intermezzos) had occupied the young composer. One can only imagine the delight audiences found in this work and the many other "commedie musicali" then current that allowed them to hear their own daily language of the streets used in the theater. Now, with the release of a punctilious La Scala production, today's opera lovers are afforded a glimpse into the sentimental musical entertainments that were all the rage in eighteenth-century Naples. Its reconstruction has been patched together by musicologist Francesco Degrada from various manuscripts (as well as trimmed by him), but, unlike some works that have been previously attributed to Pergolesi and subsequently removed from his canon (*Il Maestro di Musica*, most notably), there exists strong evidence not to doubt the authenticity of all its parts. This *Lo Frate 'nnamorato*, unlike so much else having to do with this composer, may not cause any controversies; instead it has the virtue of being the real thing—well, almost.

1990 HOME VISION (VHS / LD)

(Stage Performance, Stereo, Color, Subtitled) 171 minutes

Amelia Felle (A), Nuccia Focile (B), Elizabeth Norberg-Schulz (C), Nicoletta Curiel (D), Bernadette Manca Di Nissa (E), Luciana D'Intino (F), Ezio Di Cesare (G), Alessandro Corbelli (H), Bruno De Simone (I), chamber ensemble—Riccardo Muti

La Scala: Roberto De Simone (stage director), John Michael Phillips (video director)

If any opera can ever be described as big and little at the same time, *Lo Frate 'nnamorato* certainly is it. A tiny romp of a formal comedy whose style is as venerable as the layers of Neapolitan civilization on which it plays out, it originally took six hours to perform. The current version, a mounting for La Scala in 1990 (it had last been seen there at the Piccolo Scala in 1959), still weighs in with a playing time of nearly three hours, roughly an hour per act. That's an awful lot of recitatives and A-B-A arias (each character gets at least one per act), and not much of anything in the way of ensemble to bring variety until well into Act II. The formula is rigid, but within its boundaries the 1732 score of the short-lived Pergolesi has considerable charm, occasional unexpected complexity, and a lot of wit, almost all of it captured by the musicians, designers, and director participating here.

The plot line rests on amatory mix-ups involving the members of two holiday households, one Neapolitan, one Roman, and their servants (Neapolitan is "spoken" as much as Italian)—all closely related to their *commedia dell' arte* prototype cousins. In any event, everyone wants to marry somebody other than the person for whom he or she is intended. Imbroglios, masquerades, and hidden relationships abound, providing ample opportunity for farcical confusion, and just plain confusion, too. It goes with the territory. Suffice it to say that the servants are wisest of all and a telltale birthmark leads to the ultimate unraveling and a rather surprising, bittersweet ending, not at all the heads-up, *forte, allegro*, major-key, loose-end-knotting vaudeville resolution one might expect.

La Scala obviously spared no effort in wanting to make a major statement with this production. Conductor Riccardo Muti and an ensemble of period instruments prepare a solid, loving ground for all that goes on onstage. The cast is uniformly strong of voice, with Nuccia Focile perhaps the stand-out for her admirably impassioned delivery in the trouser role of Ascanio—although the creamy contraltos of Bernadette Manca Di Nissa and Luciana D'Intino, the authoritative soprano of Amelia Felle, and the penetrating tenor of Ezio Di Cesare are also to be enjoyed. The two servant ancestors of Despina, Elizabeth Norberg-Schulz, soprano, and Nicoletta Curiel, mezzo-soprano, are also

energetically voiced. Baritone Allessandro Corbelli is both sonorous and amusing as one of the foolish *pater familias*, Baritone Bruno De Simone at least very amusing—he is the best physical actor in this assemblage—if less vocally assured as the other.

Still, what most makes the evening a success is the gorgeous care given to how everything looks. Set designer Mauro Carosi has built a great baroque architectural unit that revolves to form the interior and exterior framework for each scene. It is a sparkling eyecatcher that elegantly compliments the off-whites and pastels of Odette Nicoletti's costumes. There are luxury and taste aplenty. A gratifying, very eyepleasing chic rules, which is all to the good because director Roberto De Simone seems intent on decorative behavior for his possibly more antic characters. The individual singers do well enough with the complicated business of delineating the action, but there doesn't appear to be room for them to run with its potential for real hilarity. Perhaps, given how long the joke has to be sustained, De Simone's reticent approach was a wise decision. But one misses the juice one suspects might have made this soigné resurrection a delicious one as well.

Beautiful to look at and immaculately performed, played, and reproduced, this treatment of Pergolesi's seldom-surfacing comic concoction will delight anyone with a curiosity about the gamut of eighteenth-century operatic forms, an eagerness to experience refined stagecraft, and with enough patience to deal with a perhaps somewhat alien sense of theatrical time.

HARVEY E. PHILLIPS

GIOVANNI BATTISTA PERGOLESI

LA SERVA PADRONA (1733)

A: Serpina (s); B: Uberto (bs); C: Vespone (mime)

iovanni Battista Pergolesi died at twenty-six and left a legacy of dispute involving what he actually composed and did not compose and how much merit should be granted any of it. He is even blamed for posthumously starting the notorious chauvinism-infused *Guerre des Bouffons*, which not only split French musical circles in the middle of the eighteenth century but eventually embroiled Rousseau and Diderot as well. The spark to this artistic conflagration was a Paris revival of *La Serva Padrona*, which for the rulers of the Parisian artistic world—not the general public—was symptomatic of a mephitic Italian influence involving too much accessibility and not enough respect for the dictates of classical elegance. What we appreciate today as an essentially small-scale, lighthearted entertainment gave the French capital a quarrel of *Sacre-du-Printemps* proportions. Pergolesi, of course, never intended his bauble to be anything *but* an entertainment. That was its function: a two part "intermezzo" to be inserted between the acts of a longer and supposedly worthier *opera seria*, in this case *Il Prigioniero Superbo*. Pergolesi's drama was respectfully received, its comic relief adored. *La Serva Padrona*, enhanced by its modest performing requirements, has gone on to do more than just start fights in Paris; it has become the work for which the composer is chiefly remembered and a mainstay of chamber opera companies everywhere.

1958 VIEW (VHS)

(Film, Mono, Black and White, Not Subtitled)
65 minutes

Anna Moffo (A), Paolo Montarsolo (B), Giancarlo Cobelli (C), Rome Philharmonic Orchestra—Franco Ferrara

Mario Lanfranchi (director)

From the same era that brought forth the eye-straining television-studio *Turandot* starring Franco Corelli (also reviewed in this volume)—the late fifties—comes a visually sparkling black and white *Serva Padrona*. With the advantage of having been recorded on film rather than kinescope, there's an enjoyable freshness here that time has not reduced. In spite of a few minor continuity blips, this Cine Lirica Italiana production is eminently watchable, especially as testimony to the stunning gifts of the young Anna Moffo. If Pergolesi's is not the original operatic *How to Marry a Millionaire*, it is still one of the earliest, and the American soprano's beauty of voice as well as her personal allure make the story of the sweetly scheming servant and the aged bachelor employer who is the target of her designs thoroughly convincing. Moffo, a year before her Met debut, reveals herself to be already a very steady actress. There's authority in her bearing and enough tastefulness in her approach to resist camping up the comedy. Perhaps her Serpina (after all, note the name) could use a bit more edge, but edge is not what this gloriously rich voice—an agile lyric soprano with a full downward lyric mezzo extension—is about. One simply has to settle for life-enhancing warmth, which in fact she does ultimately modulate with knowing subtlety in her eloquent dark eyes for her principal aria, "A Serpina penserete."

Moffo's superb foil is Paolo Montarsolo, master of the slow burn (and also of lip-synching). He's magnificently precise in his physical business, and his mobile features never leave one in doubt of what's going on in his mind. His major accomplishment may actually be that in spite of all the abuse he takes he retains the dignity of the gentleman that of course Uberto is. In contrast to his *Elisir* Dulcamara, commented on elsewhere, this is an enormously congenial *buffo* role for him, and his supple bass is always at the command of his histrionic needs.

The settings are relatively elaborate for this little post-*commedia dell' arte* romp, the interior playing area embellished by a long interpolated exterior sequence. Director Mario Lanfranchi, also responsible for the Corelli *Turandot*, has a nervous hand, though, and tries to fill in the unsung spaces with more mime episodes than are strictly necessary or that he can bring off as anything but labored. He could have more constructively worked on some stage noises so that the recorded sound track does not seem quite so distant from the postdubbed action. Still, mime Giancarlo Cobelli as the valet Vespone makes a very positive contribution to the precision of that action. Franco Ferrara conducts with appropriate, steady support. A possible hitch to full enjoyment: no English titles and no booklet with or without libretto.

The major factor in recommending this postdubbed visit to a popular one-act standard is Anna Moffo. The soprano, at the beginning of her career, revels in a charm and vocal velvet that are extraordinarily engaging. *Buffo* Montarsolo and a clean transfer from film to tape also help to make this a period piece well worth having.

HARVEY E. PHILLIPS

La Gioconda (1876)

A: La Gioconda (s); B: Laura (ms); C: La Cieca (c);
D: Enzo Grimaldo (t); E: Barnaba (bar); F: Alvise (bs)

For years, experts appearing on a Met broadcast's Texaco Opera Quiz received this counsel: "When in doubt, *Gioconda!*" The tongue-in-cheek suggestion that any query without a readily apparent answer constituted a reference to something somewhere in the four chocka-block acts of Ponchielli's *dramma lirica* was never borne out in this panelist's experience. Nonetheless, the flippancy itself defines *La Gioconda*'s status in the collective conscious-ness as the everything-but-the-kitchen-sink opera.

Expressing affection for this work is not politically correct, and one's taste gets called into question. Elitists consider *Gioconda* decadent, the red-light district of the repertory. But what's not to like? A fabulously entertaining vocal feast facilitated by a high level of melodic in-spiration; an amalgam of *bel canto*, Meyerbeer-ian, and Verdian elements with an unmistak-able preview of *verismo*; the best ballet in any Italian opera; and the affecting human drama embodied in an appealing, sympathetic protag-onist.

Though anything less than inspired singing exposes its seams and shortcomings, *Gioconda* survives doggedly, stirring listeners' primal pas-sions. We're just not willing to abandon this hardy warhorse, reminder of a grander day's more glorious accomplishments, an operatic high-cholesterol fix that voice fanciers will never stop craving.

1986 KULTUR (VHS) / PIONEER (LD)

(Stage Performance, Stereo, Color, Subtitled) 169 minutes

Eva Marton (A), Ludmila Semtschuk (B), Mar-garita Lilowa (C), Plácido Domingo (D), Matteo Manuguerra (E), Kurt Rydl (F), Chorus and Orchestra of the Vienna State Opera—Adam Fischer

Vienna State Opera: Filippo Sanjust (stage director), Hugo Käch (video director)

The only *Gioconda* available on video, a sometimes dreary affair from the vocal stand-point, features three major artists, the oldest of whom steals the honors.

At sixty-one, Matteo Manuguerra deploys his ringing, secure, unpressured baritone and sover-eign stage sense in a triumphant performance. He alone, unfailingly alive to every musical and histrionic possibility, shows no sign of discom-fort with Ponchielli's melodramatic idiom. His Mephistophelean Barnaba manipulates and incites with a puppeteer's art. Slight nasality (not inappropriate to this boo-hiss villain), an occasionally abbreviated high note, and a *forte* less full than in earlier days are discernible indi-cations of vocal aging.

Plácido Domingo, uncharacteristically tenta-tive of voice and movement in the aftermath of hernia problems, navigates the evening on auto-matic pilot, his burnished middle voice and patented generalized ardor seeing him through. The B-flats of "Cielo e mar," suddenly out of visual synch and freer than those high notes where sound matches picture, appear to be dubbed.

The year 1986 should be Eva Marton's absolute prime, but her large, impressive, relentlessly loud sound is tremolo-ridden, unreliable in pitch (especially at the top), and infected with glottal shocks. Her inability to sing softly at all from F upward, or to do so in midrange and retain focus, begets monotony. Never mind the famous sustained B-flat in Act I (a moment many have failed to master), which Marton bunts, turning her back on the audience and yelling it upstage, note value curtailed—Gioconda's music brims with markings of *piano, pianissimo, dolcissimo, morendo,* all unheeded. Ultimately, the soprano falters, fudging the first high C in the farewell trio and omitting the climactic one. Except for a curious air of detachment during the third-act concertato, Marton delivers emotional involvement along with the unmodulated decibels.

Ludmila Semtschuk, a handsome Laura, offers big, unruly, overripe tone that yields excitement without dynamic variety. Margarita Lilowa acts with dignity, but her drab mezzo provides scant satisfaction in Cieca's grand contralto phrases; she must finesse both range extremes of "Voce di donna." Competent house bass Kurt Rydl, a stolid, younger-than-traditional Alvise, manages his hard-sell aria sluggishly.

Adam Fischer leads an atmospheric prelude and flavorsome ballet, but his otherwise dilatory conducting drains the score of momentum and urgency. He does steer "Suicidio!" sympathetically where Marton's vanishing lower register is concerned. Perhaps for her comfort he makes cuts in the Act II finale, farewell trio, and final duet.

Choreographer Gerlinde Dill's "Dance of the Hours" dramatizes the Enzo-Laura-Alvise triangle. The terpsichorean doge slays the lovers, a shocking "entertainment" for the real Alvise's ball guests.

Filippo Sanjust's Venetian settings pass muster, though Enzo's insubstantial *brigantino* disappoints (and glows amusingly when torched). Sanjust's striking costumes mix epochs, with bustles and conquistador-type helmets onstage simultaneously. His spotty direction benefits the chorus more than the uneven principals. Hugo Käch's smooth video realization includes vivid touches such as close-ups superimposed over ensembles. Documentary value centers on Manuguerra and Domingo; neither recorded *Gioconda* commercially.

Bruce Burroughs

DIALOGUES DES CARMÉLITES (1957)

A: Blanche de la Force (s); B: Mme. Lidoine, New Prioress (s);
C: Sister Constance (s); D: Mme. de Croissy, Old Prioress (ms);
E: Mother Marie (ms)

*B*orn in the very last year of the nineteenth century, Francis Poulenc travelled far stylistically in the course of his long career, from the cynical faddishness of his 1924 ballet *Les Biches* (written for Diaghilev's trend-setting Ballets Russes), to numerous works for the keyboard, and finally to a cluster of moving religious compositions (a Mass, a Gloria, a Stabat Mater) inspired by his rediscovery of Catholicism in 1935. His single full-length opera, *Dialogues des Carmélites*, completed in 1953, combines Poulenc's religious feelings with a response to the suffering endured by all people of faith under the then still-recent Nazi occupation of Europe.

Although resolutely tonal in its musical language, the opera (based on a screenplay) has rather unconventional dramatic structure and casting. Since it tells the story of a group of Carmelite nuns guillotined as martyrs during the Terror following the French Revolution, *Dialogues des Carmélites* has a predominantly female cast. Indeed, the only male roles of any significance are those of the father and brother of the heroine, Blanche de la Force. Nor does the opera contain any romantic intrigue; the only love or sensual passion Blanche expresses is for Jesus, God, and her calling as their servant on earth. It is a tale of female comradeship and personal courage.

The fearful Blanche also disappears for large sections of the three acts, when the focus shifts to Madame de Croissy, the Carmelites' dying spiritual leader; to the indomitable Mother Marie of the Incarnation; and to Madame Lidoine, who becomes the new Prioress after Madame de Croissy's death. In this sense, *Dialogues des Carmélites* is a "collective opera"—like *Khovanshchina* by Modest Mussorgsky, one of Poulenc's models. Like *Khovanshchina*, *Dialogues* describes the struggle of a religious sect against political persecution, and both operas end with a scene of mass martyrdom (although Mussorgsky's Old Believers commit suicide by setting themselves on fire). Poulenc's vocal and orchestral writing for the final scene at the guillotine ranks among his greatest achievements.

Due to its absence of "plot," *Dialogues* can be somewhat static on stage; most of the scenes are extended conversations about spirituality. Vocally, the opera has no real arias or detachable set pieces, proceeding instead in a fluid and highly lyrical *arioso* style, against the background of the brilliant bitter-sweet orchestral effects for which Poulenc is famous. Poulenc is also adept at assuring that the solo voices are never overwhelmed by the ingeniously transparent orchestral accompaniment.

1984 SONY (VHS)

(Stage Performance, Stereo, Color, in English)
155 minutes

Isobel Buchanan (A), Joan Sutherland (B), Anne-Maree McDonald (C), Lone Koppel (D),

Heather Begg (E), Australian Opera Chorus, Elizabethan Sydney Orchestra—Richard Bonynge

Australian Opera: Elijah Moshinsky (stage director), Henry Prokop (video director)

This package presents a live performance given by the Australian Opera at the Sydney Opera House in September 1984 and broadcast on television by Australian Broadcasting Corporation. It is perhaps the most completely successful of the videos in the Australian Opera Series, which prominently feature the team of conductor Richard Bonynge and his wife, Joan Sutherland. Its success can be traced largely to the artistic supervision of producer Elijah Moshinsky, who presents the opera simply, clearly, and with impressive emotional impact. The quality of the television direction is also unusually high; the camera work offers a sensitive combination of intimate close-ups and group shots that deftly convey the interaction between individual and collective so essential to the opera's message. In the quality of its recorded sound, this *Dialogues* sets a high standard reached by few other opera videos available. The miking is uniform and allows each word of the (unattributed!) English translation to be clearly understood, without the aid of distracting subtitles. Only Joan Sutherland's notoriously mushy pronunciation occasionally fails to put the words across.

The packaging hype claims that the video stars Dame Joan, in yet another religious role (remember her devout pagan priestesses Norma and Lakmé). And yet Sutherland's solid, work-manlike performance is definitely overshadowed by some of the other principals, especially Danish-born Lone Koppel as the tortured Madame de Croissy. Her extended death-bed scene exhibits not only vocal discipline and power but strong dramatic skills, even when the camera is staring down her throat and examining the beads of sweat on her fevered brow. As Mother Marie, the unsentimental sister who really keeps the Carmelites together, New Zealander Heather Begg projects well and possesses a formidable stage presence. As Blanche, Isobel Buchanan, better known for her Mozart roles, makes convincing the decision of a pampered and beautiful aristocrat to dedicate her life to God. Her light voice carries well over Bonynge's highly sympathetic conducting and blends extremely well with the bell-like soprano of Anne-Maree McDonald (Sister Constance). Their final loving reunion at the guillotine is credible and cathartic, just as Poulenc intended.

This *Dialogues* impresses not only in the casting of the major roles, but in the excellence of all the important minor roles, including the other nuns and Blanche's father (Geoffrey Chard) and brother (Paul Ferris). There is a strong sense of dramatic and musical ensemble that is absolutely essential for the success of this piece. In his spare but highly evocative design and lighting, John Bury wisely resists the temptation to shift attention from the opera's essential spiritual message by overdoing the French Revolution setting. Highly recommended.

Harlow Robinson

LA VOIX HUMAINE (1959)

A: Elle (s)

*I*n this forty-five minute telephone monologue for a wealthy young woman who has lost her lover, Poulenc created a powerful expansion of Jean Cocteau's 1930 play. Its requirements are a lithe and focused soprano voice with an infinite capacity to inflect and color the words, and a graceful appearance and movement. The opera has led a charmed life. Denise Duval, its creator, provided a magnificent recording, as has Julia Migenes, and on the stage Elisabeth Söderström, Magda Olivero, and many others have had success with it. The sole video performance available continues that tradition.

1992 LONDON (VHS/LD)

(Studio Performance, Stereo, Color, Subtitled) 45 minutes

Carole Farley (A), Scottish Chamber Orchestra — José Serebrier

Mike Newman (director)

La Voix Humaine has been done so touchingly on audio recordings that one is surprised at how much a really sensitive visual production of this telephone monologue adds to its effect. This one is done, rightly, in the style of the early thirties, when the Cocteau play was produced. The woman's bedroom is full of evening shadows, rich greens and browns, and the glitter of the brass bedstead. As well, a kind of atmospheric mist hangs over images once or twice shown in a mirror: the mood of the piece is greatly enhanced. Amongst these shadows, the auburn-haired Carole Farley looks both sensual and frail. One thinks of Blanche DuBois: "I don't want realism. I want magic!" This long, desperate conversation with her former lover can be regarded as a pointless excursion into the psyche of a defenseless woman or an exploration of insuperable feelings in all of us—or both. The voice is sometimes a little harsh, but Farley realizes with great skill the range of responses—from dreamlike acceptance to panic, fear, self-hatred, and the desperate clutching at illusion. And those responses are keyed with exceptional detail to the moods of Poulenc's subtle scoring. José Serebrier's conducting is equally revealing, and the camera work seems unobtrusively perfect. Recommended.

LONDON GREEN

Love for Three Oranges (1921)

A: Ninetta (s); B: Fata Morgana (s); C: Clarissa (c); D: Prince (t);
E: Truffaldino (t); F: Leandro (bar); G: King (bs)

When Prokofiev's *Love for Three Oranges* (*Liubov' k trem apel'sinam* in Russian) received its first New York performance in early 1922, the critics were confused and hostile. Richard Aldrich's review in *The New York Times* was typical: "There are a few, but only a very few, passages that bear recognizable kinship with what has hitherto been recognized as music ... What, in fine, is the underlying purpose of this work? Is it satire? Is it burlesque? Whose withers are wrung? If it is a joke it may be a good one, but it is a long and painful one."

As was so often the case in Prokofiev's career, it took a while for this sarcastic, highly theatrical and youthfully irreverent "anti-opera" to find favor with critics and audiences. Eventually, *Oranges* became the most popular of the composer's eight operas; it is no coincidence that it is also the most fanciful and absurd. Its delightfully bumptious ceremonial March (included in the orchestral Suite arranged from the opera, and also known in a widely played piano version) is one of the most famous pieces Prokofiev ever wrote. Clumping along in a jerky rhythm punctuated by prominent eighth-note rests, leaping abruptly by wide dissonant intervals, displaying conflicting tonalities and mischievous intervals of seconds and tritones with wicked pleasure, it epitomizes the awkwardly funny "wrong note" style with which Prokofiev is most strongly identified. The March even became "household music" in America, serving

for fourteen years as the theme for the radio show "The FBI in Peace and War."

Oranges is based on an eighteenth-century *commedia dell' arte* fairy tale by Carlo Gozzi, as adapted into Russian by the brilliant avant-garde Russian director Vsevolod Meyerhold around the time of the 1917 Russian Revolution. The convoluted plot serves as little more than an excuse for a discussion of various theatrical techniques. The leading characters are pawns in a struggle between supernatural forces on the one hand and the representatives of comedy and tragedy on the other. Only the Prince has any psychological depth, growing from his chronic hypochondria to the capability of true romantic love for his sweetheart, a Princess who emerges from an orange.

A successful production of *Oranges* depends much more on clever staging and acting than on singing. The vocal music contains no arias and only a few tunes. What is needed is a tight ensemble of actor-singers, directed with a strong and imaginative hand. Because of its strongly visual character, *Oranges*—unlike so many items in the repertory—is an opera that actually works better on video than on an audio recording.

1995 PIONEER (LD)

(Stage Performance, Stereo, Color, Subtitled)
105 minutes

Catherine Dubosc (A), Michele Lagrange (B), Helene Perraguin (C), Jean-Luc Viala (D),

Georges Gautier (E), Vincent Le Texier (F), Gabriel Bacquier (G), Chorus and Orchestra of the Lyon Opera—Kent Nagano

Lyon Opera: Louis Erlo (stage director), Jean-Francois Jung (video director)

Chic, droll, and acrobatic, this updated version of Prokofiev's deconstruction of opera conventions is one of the most successful ever brought to the stage—and to the screen. (It was filmed by France Telecom in association with Antenne 2 and the French Ministry of Culture.) In June 1995, California-born Kent Nagano and his lithe, youthful troupe from Lyons displayed this juicy, sweet-and-sour *Oranges* in San Francisco as part of the fiftieth anniversary of the signing of the United Nations charter there. It was an appropriate choice, since *Oranges* was multinational from its very inception: an opera by a Russian composer on an Italian subject, composed in the United States, and first staged—in French—in Chicago in 1921.

Finding the right balance between Prokofiev's churlishness and lyricism has defeated lesser talents, but stage director Louis Erlo navigates the obstacles with an unfailingly light touch. The abstract simplicity of the set design—a series of white panels arranged in different configurations—is nicely offset by Ferdinando Bruni's modern-dress costumes, which flood the stage with color and sophistication. The large chorus, divided into squabbling factions promoting tragedy or comedy, moves in and out of the narrative with ease and humor.

Oranges needs good actors more than good singers. As the hypochondriacal Prince, the plumpish Jean-Luc Viala, with an appropriately Charlie Chaplinesque hat and manner, pouts and mugs and droops but finally saves the day. As the Prince's father, the ever-worried King of Clubs, renowned bass Gabriel Bacquier finds the perfect attitude of noble silliness. Vincent Le Texier as the scheming Leandro, Michele Lagrange as the implacable Fata Morgana, and Beatrice Uria-Monzon as the nasty Smeraldina all make deliciously bad villains. Nagano and his orchestra revel in one of Prokofiev's most colorful and inventive scores but never overwhelm the singers.

Video director Jean-Francois Jung is aggressive and imaginative, avoiding static long shots and injecting visual movement, notably into the Prince's spin on a hospital cart. Jung even ventures to take the action offstage, a gesture more than justified by Prokofiev's self-conscious theatricality. The English-language titles, though easily readable against a black background at the bottom, unfortunately crowd the screen image. Sound quality is excellent.

HARLOW ROBINSON

THE FIERY ANGEL (1927)

A: Renata (s); B: Landlady (ms); C: Fortune-teller (ms); D: Mother
Superior (ms); E: Jakob Glock (t); F: Agrippa von Nettesheim (t);
G: Mephistopheles (t); H: Ruprecht (bar); I: Johann Faust (bs);
J: Inquisitor (bs)

At first glance, Sergei Prokofiev's decision in 1919 to make an opera of Valery Bryusov's *Ognennyi angel* (*The Fiery Angel* or *The Flaming Angel*), a gloomy historical novel set in sixteenth-century Counter-Reformation Germany and saturated with the mystical atmosphere of early twentieth-century Russian decadence, might seem out of character. Rosy-cheeked, sarcastic, and full of healthy creative energy, what could Prokofiev have in common with the morbid metaphysical moods of this dense *roman à clef* and its schipzophrenic, occasionally nymphomaniacal heroine, Renata?

Finished in 1927, *Angel* was originally intended for Bruno Walter and the Berlin Staatsoper, but Walter backed out of his promise to produce it after taking a look at the score. Other European and American theaters also found what Prokofiev considered to be one of his most important works unfashionably large and dramatically incoherent. Several incomplete concert versions were given in Europe during the composer's lifetime (the first by Sergei Koussevitsky in Paris in 1928), but only in 1955, two years after Prokofiev's death, was *Angel* finally staged, at the Venice Festival. Loath to "waste" so much good music, Prokofiev recycled large sections of the opera into his Symphony No. 3 (1928).

Bringing *Angel* to the stage and to video is no easy task. In his libretto Prokofiev failed to provide a satisfying emotional resolution to the central relationship between Renata and Ruprecht. The opera's tone also veers oddly between tragedy and satire; we are never quite sure whether we should be crying or laughing. At the same time, Prokofiev made sure to include lots of spectacular "infernal" stage effects, such as Ruprecht's encounter with a child-eating Mephistopheles and the concluding wild orgy at the convent where Renata seeks unsuccessfully to find refuge from the sexual demons that torment her.

1993 PHILIPS (VHS / LD)

(Stage Performance, Stereo, Color, Subtitled)
120 minutes

Galina Gorchakova (A), Evgenia Perlaskova-Verkovich (B), Larissa Dyadkova (C), Olga Markova-Mikhailenko (D), Yevgeni Boitsov (E), Vladimir Galusin (F), Konstantin Pluzhnikov (G), Sergei Leiferkus (H), Sergei Alexashkin (I), Vladimir Ognovenko (J), Kirov Opera Chorus and Orchestra — Valery Gergiev

Kirov Opera: David Freeman (stage director), Brian Large (video director)

One of the most important of Valery Gergiev's many accomplishments as conductor and artistic director at the Kirov Opera since the late 1980s has been to bring back to the historic stage of St. Petersburg's Mariinsky Theater numerous operas by major Russian composers that had for various reasons fallen out of the company's repertory. Often, as was the case with *The Fiery Angel*, the reasons were largely political and ideological. Due to its mysticism and psychosexual decadence, *Angel* was considered inappropriate for Soviet audiences by Communist cultural bureaucrats. The opera was banned from the Soviet operatic stage for decades and was produced in Russia for the first time only in 1983, in the provincial city of Perm.

But what this imaginatively staged, brilliantly executed, authoritatively sung, and ingeniously filmed new Kirov version demonstrates is just how much this opera needs a Russian-speaking cast. This *Angel* also gains immeasurably by Gergiev's long advocacy of Prokofiev's symphonic and stage works, his obvious understanding of the composer's unique and quirky creative personality.

David Freeman, who staged the Kirov production, has dealt very effectively with the problem that bedevils any director confronting *Angel*: how to represent on stage the demons who are assaulting Renata. Are they real, physically visible creatures, or simply figments of her overactive subconsious? Here, Freeman has used the members of the St. Petersburg Mariinsky Acrobatic Troupe to represent Renata's "little ones." Appearing nearly nude, bald, and in white body makeup, the acrobats crawl, squirm, and hang about the stage. Their nearly constant presence, even in silent *tableaux* between acts, reminds us that *Angel* is an opera about obsession and fantasy, not reality. In Act V, their cavorting with the disturbed nuns (some of whom strip and appear in full frontal nudity) seems a logical climax to what has preceded, rather than the gratuitously graphic incident it does in some productions I have seen.

Wisely, Freeman and designer David Roger have rejected a "realistic" approach, providing minimal sets in abstract geometric forms. Even in the "infernal" scenes the focus remains squarely on the psychological aspects of the narrative, and especially on the sadistic-masochistic relationship between Ruprecht and Renata. In some places, Gergiev and Freeman have even chosen to expand on Prokofiev's stage directions. During the symphonic entr'acte in Act III, for example, they stage the sword fight between Ruprecht and Madiel; in Prokofiev's libretto, we only see the aftermath.

Vocally and dramatically, this is as close to a dream cast for *Angel* as we are ever likely to get. There is no finer Renata today than Galina Gorchakova, with her vocal power, warmth, supple Russian diction, and sexual allure. The lush, sensual timbre of her voice is perfectly complemented by Sergei Leiferkus's steely, stalwart quality as her hapless knight, Ruprecht. (He also manages his sword with impressive skill during the duel scene.) Together, these accomplished actor-singers make credible the passionate attraction that drives this tale of psychosexual dementia.

Various distinguished and veteran Kirov soloists take the secondary roles, singing vividly and tastefully. Vladimir Galusin manages the impossibly high tessitura of the role of Agrippa von Nettesheim (written for "high tenor") with aplomb. That old master Vladimir Ognovenko makes a wonderfully sinister Inquisitor. Konstantin Pluzhnikov makes the most of the practical joker Mephistopheles. As one would expect, Gergiev provides expert guidance to the singers from the pit and draws a subtle, intense, but never raucous performance from his orchestra. His careful attention to balance ensures that the vocal line is never overwhelmed by the often voluminous orchestration.

Television director Brian Large has overseen the camera work in this production with love and inspiration. There is an excellent mixture of close-up, medium, and long shots that convey the psychological intensity without sacrificing a sense of the wider stage context. The repeated provocative images of the demon-acrobats create a creepy—and perfectly appropriate—atmosphere.

At last Prokofiev has found a conductor, opera house, and film crew worthy of his strange and special *Angel*.

HARLOW ROBINSON

War and Peace (1945)

A: Natasha (s); B: Sonya (ms); C: Hélène (ms); D: Pierre (t); E: Anatol
(t); F: Andrei (bar); G: Napoleon (bar); H: Kutuzov (bs)

For all its considerable and unique charms, Prokofiev's *War and Peace* is not what you'd call "lite." Epic and sprawling, as big as troubled Mother Russia herself, these thirteen loosely connected scenes overwhelm even the label "opera." "Lyric-dramatic scenes" is what Prokofiev called his masterpiece, evoking Tchaikovsky's "lyric scenes" as a description for *Eugene Onegin*—which *War and Peace* consciously emulates. Others have come up with even more convoluted descriptions of just what it is that the composer composed: dramatic chronicle, lyrico-psychological drama, heroic-epic narrative, historical opera-novel.

Despite the understandable difficulties Prokofiev and his collaborator Mira Mendelson-Prokofiev encountered in turning Tolstoy's huge opus into a libretto, the score contains some of the most appealing and heartfelt pages the composer ever wrote. Like *Romeo and Juliet*, whose 1940 premiere came just a year before Prokofiev turned to Tolstoy, *War and Peace* successfully synthesizes disparate styles found throughout the composer's oeuvre. Both Shakespeare and Tolstoy required musical resources broad and vivid enough to convey intimate romantic lyricism (Juliet Capulet and Natasha Rostova), grotesque humor (the Nurse and the members of Napoleon's suite), historical cataclysms (the Montague-Capulet feud, the French invasion of Russia), personal and national tragedy (the young lovers' double sui-

cide, Andrei's death), and folk simplicity (the bawdy people of Genoa, the Russian *narod*).

Prokofiev's long experience as a composer of ballets and film scores is obvious in *War and Peace*, which contains extended ballroom scenes and cinematic battlefield episodes. For this reason, the opera also lends itself readily to a film / video format.

1995 PHILIPS (VHS / LD)

(Stage Performance, Stereo, Color, Subtitled) 248 mins.

Yelena Prokina (A), Svetlana Volkova (B), Olga Borodina (C), Gegam Grigorian (D), Yuri Marusin (E), Alexandr Gergalov (F), Vassily Gerelo (G), Nikolai Okhotnikov (H), Kirov Opera Chorus and Orchestra—Valery Gergiev

Kirov Opera: Graham Vick (stage director), Humphrey Burton (video director)

Filmed live at the Mariinsky Theater in St. Petersburg in 1991, this handsome, imaginative production was staged jointly by the Kirov Opera, the Royal Opera House, and the Opera Bastille under the shrewd artistic supervision of Valery Gergiev, who has turned his Kirov Opera into a remarkably innovative and energetic operation since the late 1980s. The stage director, Graham Vick, has produced fascinatingly unconventional stagings of Russian operas in theaters all over the world in recent years, including Tchaikovsky's *The Queen of Spades* (at Glyndebourne) and Shostakovich's *Lady Macbeth of Mtsensk* (at the Met).

Vick's collaboration with Gergiev and the Kirov on this project proves no less successful. Using a simple abstract set with movable white panels, he has avoided the picture-postcard realism so monotonously characteristic of the Russian operatic style of the Soviet era. Some of the panels serve as walls with doors allowing for entrances and exits; others rise and fall hydraulically to represent the shifting ground of the battlefield scenes. A large backdrop depicting an ancient oak tree (the one of which Andrei sings in the very first scene) serves as a unifying visual image for the production; it bursts into leaf in the final scene as a representation of Russia's ability to endure and grow.

The costumes are faithful reproductions appropriate to the Napoleonic era, and what little furniture appears on stage is similarly elegant and perfectly in style. The set also allows for fast scene changes without bringing down the curtain, a welcome feature in an opera that runs over four hours. Many of the important scenic effects (Moscow in flames, Prince Andrei on his deathbed) are accomplished through marvelous lighting design. Vick handles the many crowd scenes with flair and ingenuity. In the extended Borodino battle scene, for example, he creates a long series of memorable "shots": a Russian wolfhound wandering about the stage, the flags of the various regiments, an onstage drummer, live horses, and a glittering miniature model of Moscow's St. Basil's Cathedral borne by four peasants.

Fortunately, the excellence of the physical production is matched by a young, strong cast that knows how to act as well as sing. The singers include several established stars: Olga Boro-

dina (in fine voice and figure) as the debauched Hélène; Yuri Marusin, whose whining voice exactly suits the character of Hélène's even more depraved brother Anatol; Gegam Grigorian, who shows subtle acting skills as the philosophical Pierre; and Kirov veteran Nikolai Okhotnikov as the hardbitten, common-sensical General Kutuzov. But perhaps the most impressive vocal performance comes from Yelena Prokina as Natasha—she also gets much of the opera's most lyrical music. Playing opposite her is Alexander Gergalov as Andrei, another performer with strong dramatic and vocal skills, in the best Stanislavskian tradition. Their reconciliation scene at Andrei's deathbed has just the right touch of lyrical pathos. As superlative as some of the individual performances are, what emerges is a strong musical and emotional understanding built up over time, rather than a succession of unconnected star turns.

Maestro Gergiev provides refined but strong direction from the pit. He sticks close to the published one-evening thirteen-scene version of the opera, taking only a few judicious nips and tucks here and there to move the pace along. His decision to place the "Epigraph" chorus before Scene 8 (the first "War" scene) instead of before Scene 1, where it impedes the natural dramatic flow, is wise.

The one problem with this outstanding version of one of the twentieth century's most important and overlooked operas is the inconsistent quality of recorded sound. Miking levels vary and some singers are occasionally barely audible; the portions of spoken dialogue suffer the most. But the camera work is superb, combining close-ups, long shots, and even some flashbacks (during Andrei's deathbed scene). Highly recommended.

HARLOW ROBINSON

MANON LESCAUT (1893)

A: Manon (s); B: Chevalier des Grieux (t); C: Edmondo (t);
D: Lescaut (bar); E: Geronte (bs)

*I*t was bold of Puccini, not yet an established opera composer in 1890 when he began work on the project, to challenge Massenet's already much-staged treatment of *Manon Lescaut*. As the composer predicted, his version of the famous Prevost novella turned out to be quite different from its predecessor, and for the past century both works have led successful lives in the opera house—by now, in fact, the Italian setting even shows signs of having overtaken its French rival in popularity.

Although Puccini took care to provide his setting with plenty of period atmosphere—the eighteenth-century *pasticcio* elements in the Act II *levée* are especially elegant—he was mainly interested in portraying the dichotomies in Manon's volatile character, her love of pleasure as contrasted with her intense attraction to des Grieux, and how her changeable behavior drives the young man to acts of such desperation. Of course all the colorful scenic and musical embellishments that Puccini provided must be carefully tended to in any production, but when these niceties are stripped away, his *Manon* is essentially a tale of two mismatched people in love, tearing each other apart. In short, the opera is a superior example of the late nineteenth-century Italian *giovane scuola*, a heated examination of sexual passion at its most destructive. Despite the opera's currency, the type of full-throated voices and outgoing operatic personalities needed to encompass and express all the unbridled emotions of such

verismo operas continue to be in short supply, a fact made clear by the spotty quality of the many available audio-only recordings. The title role is particularly demanding. Like any other ill-fated Puccini heroine, Manon requires a soprano capable of projecting the delicacy of a fragile victim as well as the impassioned despair of an agonized woman in extremis. Des Grieux is in some ways even more demanding—helpless, passive, and lyrically ingratiating when coping with Manon's vagaries, but impulsive, rash, and heroically emotive when he feels their relationship threatened. But with two fiery protagonists, Puccini's generous musical invention automatically assumes its proper function and inexorably propels the drama, even making the opera's episodic structure and numerous gaping holes in the plot no longer seem like problems.

1980 PARAMOUNT (VHS) / PIONEER (LD)

(Stage Performance, Stereo, Color, Subtitled) 134 minutes

Renata Scotto (A), Plácido Domingo (B), Philip Creech (C), Pablo Elvira (D), Renato Capecchi (E); Metropolitan Opera Chorus and Orchestra—James Levine

Metropolitan Opera: Gian Carlo Menotti (stage director), Kirk Browning (video director)

Menotti's production could be taken as a model of how to present a repertory piece in a traditional, straightforward manner while avoiding any sense of stale routine. In Act I, the inn courtyard bustles with life and dramatic character, none of it distracting from the main action, which depicts the first meeting between Manon and des Grieux and their elopement. Manon's luxurious playpen in Act II at Geronte's house is filled with fascinating toys, live ones as well as inanimate objects, giving the soprano ample opportunity to act the seductive, pampered flirt. Desmond Heeley's detailed, period sets look realistic and attractive, even under the camera's close scrutiny, while the spectacular scene of Manon's embarkation for the new world in Act III could not be more practically designed to accommodate the vivid parade of fallen women as they proceed from prison to shipboard.

Scotto and Domingo were frequently paired at the Met during the seventies and early eighties, and this performance catches them in generally fine form. For some, the Scotto sound was always an acquired taste, and by 1980 she had already assumed several roles—Gioconda, for example—that had taxed her voice and taken a toll on her resources. Despite its steely edge and patches of vinegary tone, her soprano is still a flexible and expressively nuanced instrument, and she shapes Puccini's melodies with a natural instinct for following their arching contours—a welcome asset that can no longer be taken for granted, even from Italian sopranos. Scotto is also a lovely Manon to behold, always theatrically vital and engaged, her facial expressions wonderfully responsive to every word and action. The look of genuine shock and concern when des Grieux upbraids her in Act II is especially touching, as Manon seems to realize for the first time that her frivolous behavior may have consequences for other people—a lesson she promptly forgets a moment later of course, while wasting precious time gathering up her jewels before Geronte arrives with the law. And her death as Scotto acts it is truly harrowing, a slow draining away of energy (again, precisely indicated by the music) as Manon's spirit and life are gradually extinguished.

Domingo is an appropriately ardent des Grieux, although at first he looks a bit drawn and shows a few signs of strain up top. As the performance proceeds, though, the tenor warms to the music and by Act III both the adrenaline and his voice are flowing freely. Elvira's Lescaut is an effective, firmly sung character study that brings out the man's less-admirable traits—little sister is clearly considered a useful commodity to be sold, provided that the bidder also cuts him in. Capecchi's Geronte is another marvelous cameo, an amusing old roué, but one who can also be dangerously vindictive when his ego is bruised. Levine relishes the score, conducting with both brio and lyrical expansion, and the orchestral playing is of superb quality. The performance was filmed as it happened on March 29, 1980, without patching or retakes, and overall there is a spontaneity, immediacy, and sense of occasion that later composite Met videos, for all their greater technical polish, sometimes lack.

1983 CASTLE OPERA (VHS) / PIONEER (LD)

(Stage Performance, Stereo, Color, Not Subtitled) 130 minutes

Kiri Te Kanawa (A), Plácido Domingo (B), Robin Leggate (C), Thomas Allen (D), Forbes Robinson (E), Chorus and Orchestra of the Royal Opera House—Giuseppe Sinopoli

Royal Opera, Covent Garden: Götz Friedrich (stage director), Humphrey Burton (video director)

This performance is so generic and featureless that it's hard to believe it originated in Germany (at the Hamburg Opera), where conservative productions such as this, even those with genuine character and vitality, are routinely booed off the stage. Günther Schneider-Siemssen's ornate representational sets are executed in his familiar pretty-pretty manner, but they lack distinctive originality and all the fussy period detail fails to generate much atmosphere. More surprisingly, Friedrich's direction is completely perfunctory. While one is thankful to be spared a fanciful concept—the sad tale of Manon and des Grieux, perhaps, as a distorted fantasy of Edmondo's fevered adolescent imagination—the opera needs more help from a director than mere traffic supervision.

Te Kanawa, of course, looks stunning in the first two acts; she is not entirely uninvolved, and her creamy soprano was at its most liquid in the early eighties. Whatever her vocal and theatrical strengths may be, though, they were never suited to the more stressful Puccini heroines. Her poor-little-me Manon is bland to the point of utter vacuity, and it's small wonder that Domingo constantly seems to have his mind on other matters. The tenor is in good voice save for a weak top B at the end of his embarkation aria in Act III, but he gave a far more interesting performance opposite Scotto. Robinson, Leg-

gate, and the many undervoiced British comprimarios who fill in the small roles make minimal contact with the Puccini idiom, only adding to the overall artificial nature of the performance. Sinopoli yanks the score this way and that without making his unconventional ideas sound the least bit convincing.

Only the most uncritical Te Kanawa fan would prefer her lackluster *Manon Lescaut* to the Met's production, a far superior performance in every respect.

PETER G. DAVIS

GIACOMO PUCCINI

LA BOHÈME (1896)

A: Mimì (s); B: Musetta (s); C: Rodolfo (t); D: Marcello (bar);
E: Schaunard (bar); F: Colline (bs)

*A*t his height, Puccini was a tireless fanatic about shape and point in his librettos; he wanted the most effective dramatic structure possible as support for his free-flowing music. *La Bohème* is based on a very loose narrative by Henri Murger, but the opera has no moments of diffuseness. Even the tightest of the other composers' works of the period, *Andrea Chénier* (by the same librettists), has its passages of unintentional confusion, but not *Bohème*. Theatrical cunning is a basic part of *verismo*; the best music, in turn, nearly always supports the meaning and mood of the specific phrase, and *verismo* singing style at its finest reflects this. One can hear the style developing: Caruso hasn't quite got it in his noble 1906 recording of Rodolfo's aria, but from Bori and Muzio onward the best singers are combining beautiful tone with the most mobile coloring and phrasing to create drama for the ear alone; these works are very phonogenic. In our time video performances reveal that the same heartbreaking detail vivifies the great *visual* impersonations. The individual detail cannot be taught—it often loses life in the transfer—but the approach that produces the truly personal illumination can be talked about, and supported. It is in great danger of being lost.

1967 DEUTSCHE GRAMMOPHON (VHS / LD)

(Stage / Studio Performance, Stereo, Color, Subtitled) 104 minutes

Mirella Freni (A), Adriana Martino (B), Gianni Raimondi (C), Rolando Panerai (D), Gianni Maffei (E), Ivo Vinco (F), Chorus and Orchestra of Teatro alla Scala—Herbert von Karajan

La Scala: Franco Zeffirelli (stage director), Wilhelm Semmelroth (video director)

Eggshaped Bohemians, carelessly painted realism, flat lighting, warm Italian voices in all the roles, a Musetta of some charm, a Rodolfo who can't act, gooseflesh and tears at most of the climaxes: obviously it's an *old-fashioned* production! A magnificent orchestra led with both Germanic exactitude *and* Germanic sentimentality, a budding taste for grandiose sets, some loss of those expressive musical devices—portamento, rubato, color—that were the glory of the *verismo* generation: obviously it's an *early contemporary* production! In other words, its year is 1967.

For all its clumsy urgency, this may just be the most moving *Bohème* on videotape. Nearly everyone in it is in prime vocal health, and they get first-rate care from Dr. von Karajan and his sanatorium of an orchestra. If that suggests a certain sterility, so be it. Go back to Muzio, Gigli, and the young Albanese in this work and you'll find knockabout orchestras but also a posse of expressive devices hardly credible today. With that caveat, Karajan's cast is fine. Gianni Raimondi is, if not imaginative, at least earnest and rich-voiced without much strain, which puts him in the top rank immediately. The big moments go movingly. Mirella Freni, safe from tornadoes in that makeup and hair-spray, looks sixties charming and sings with great beauty: it is a dark lyric voice full of savor. As Marcello, Rolando Panerai, with the warmest baritone sound of his time, is irresistible. Adriana Martino manages to be spiteful, attractive, and amusing at the same time: so many Musettas are simply bad-tempered and coarse. Gianni Maffei is a perfect Schaunard and Ivo Vinco sings a lovely coat song. As actors, the women are persuasive, and most of the men simulate, endearingly, the spontaneity Zeffirelli obviously wants; only Maffei and Carlo Badioli as Benoit are really beyond this Senior Drama Club stage.

The director / designer is generally inventive without being bizarre, and he moves crowds well. The Act I set is painted to simulate realistic dilapidation, but it is only when we see it at some distance in Act IV that it looks at all convincing. Act II is architecturally effective and Act III atmospheric. With all of the production's incidental problems, though, many of the central challenges of the opera have still been met. The visuals are sometimes amateurish, but the music-making is not, and there are a warmth, skill, and open delight among the singers which often make this a very moving *Bohème*.

1982 CASTLE VIDEO (VHS) / PIONEER (LD)

(Stage Performance, Stereo, Color, Not subtitled) 115 minutes

Ileana Cotrubas (A), Marilyn Zschau (B), Neil Shicoff (C), Thomas Allen (D), John Rawnsley (E), Gwynne Howell (F), Chorus and Orchestra of the Royal Opera House—Lamberto Gardelli

Royal Opera, Covent Garden: John Copley (stage director), Brian Large (video director)

This is a touching, well designed, and very well performed *Bohème* which immortalizes one truly great performance: the Mimì of Romanian soprano Ileana Cotrubas. What only a few others have done on audio recordings or onstage this singer has been able to transfer to

videotape: not always possible—on film even McCormack looks pompous and Tauber endearingly silly at times. Cotrubas enacts a Mimì at once highly individual and drawing on traditions that reach back through the *verismo* period to Cesira Ferrani, the first Mimì. There are more than a dozen moods in Cotrubas's voice and demeanor, reflecting every impulse from modesty to sensuality. In her first five minutes we see all the old-time attention to vocal color, portamento, and expressive phrasing. Just one example: in the famous pause before "ma quando vien lo sgelo" (the start of the emotional climax of Mimì's first aria), there are two traditional choices to express the sudden mood of inspiration. She can portamento up to the first note and sail with the music, or she can follow the score and observe the pause, and hope it will work the magic. Cotrubas takes the pause but lengthens it as the mood overtakes her and *drives* her to stand—a split second that creates the overwhelming moment. The performance is full of such harmonious illumination.

The production is in general a fine one, well designed, accommodatingly conducted by Gardelli, and invigoratingly directed, with only a few odd decisions to disturb the focus or contradict the score. It is also one of the best acted and sung performances, full of intelligence, amusement, and clear dramatic intent, though perhaps a certain Mediterranean sweetness is a little missed. How to define this? Rolando Panerai, in the 1967 Scala performance, and Thomas Allen, in this, are both fine Marcellos, but Panerai has it and Allen, actually the better actor, has something else: analytical ability, perhaps. Neil Shicoff looks and acts well and sings with great beauty of tone and freshness. John Rawnsley is a brilliant Schaunard, responding to everything but never upstaging, and magnificent at the moment when he discovers that Mimì has died. Marilyn Zschau, who has since sung such roles as Tosca and Elektra, is a sensitive singer and actress but really has the wrong sort of voice for this effortlessly seductive role. In general this cast sounds extraordinarily rich and touching, and they all play, with great involvement, to each other's strengths: a wonderful way to experience *La Bohème*.

1982 PARAMOUNT (VHS) / PIONEER (LD)

(Stage Performance, Stereo, Color, Subtitled), 141 minutes

Teresa Stratas (A), Renata Scotto (B), José Carreras (C), Richard Stilwell (D), Allan Monk (E), James Morris (F), Metropolitan Opera Chorus and Orchestra—James Levine

Metropolitan Opera: Franco Zeffirelli (stage director), Kirk Browning (video director)

Franco Zeffirelli's Scala production, videotaped in 1967, these days is not visually very impressive, either in its poorly lit sets or most of the acting; its warmth and distinction are mainly musical. On the other hand, his famous Metropolitan Opera version, taped in 1982, is primarily a visual feast. For sheer voice, only a couple of the singers equal their Scala counterparts, but on video the sets look marvellous—sometimes irrelevantly so—and the acting is in several cases superlative. For Act I, Zeffirelli has designed a rooftop garret seen partly from the outside—indeed, some of the action takes place on the roof itself—and for Act II an immense street-and-café area holding, it has been said, 400 people. Act III is a huge barren snowscape, superb as a background for the acts of alienation that take place there. In the opera house this approach sometimes dwarfs and distances the singers, but on video, with its close-ups, we are left only with an atmosphere of bright and bleak romance, sometimes, it is true, too weighty for Puccini's evergreen opera, which is, after all, an intimate thing.

Some of the singers, it must be said, have their vocal problems. José Carreras attacks the high notes roughly; by Act III one is wondering whether he will kill the next one or simply make a stab at it. Renata Scotto, a great Mimì in the very first of the Met telecast series in 1977, is in frankly terrible voice here; anything above the staff is raucous. Richard Stilwell sounds healthy but lacks warmth of timbre. But Zeffirelli has in general directed well, and three of his cast give superlative acting performances. Allan Monk is a delightful Schaunard. Renata

Scotto has been criticized for overacting Musetta, but aside from one or two bits of business in Act II she manages to balance warmth and malicious wit, and for once the beginning of the Waltz suggests a delicate sensuousness: it recalls the Supervia recording. As a result, Marcello's final capitulation is the overwhelming moment it should be. Her entrance and prayer in Act IV are also wonderfully urgent.

And then there is the Mimì of Teresa Stratas. Her voice is in good shape here: healthy, though a little cold and restricted in color. Quite beyond that, though, is her performance as a whole. From her first entrance it is clear that Mimì is doomed but grasping at every moment of life. In the climactic phrases of her first aria, Stratas sings quite well, but her *face* does what the *voices* of only the greatest Mimìs have done: the sun seems to appear before us. Her third act is astonishing for a kind of vibrant realism that reminds one of descriptions of Eleanora Duse. The close of her "Addio" is one of the great moments in the opera house: at once intensely theatrical and utterly expressive of the conflict. Her last act is equally astonishing. James Morris's "Vecchia Zimarra," sung alone on a little balcony overlooking Paris, is moving, and Carreras and the company handle the final scene with heartbreaking effect.

James Levine conducts his fine orchestra with extraordinary energy but less poetry than some others. Included on the tape is an interesting twenty-minute commentary by Zeffirelli. On seeing this performance again, more than a decade after it had been taped, I scribbled "A great *Bohème!*" after the final scene. A more objective viewing tells me that there are a couple of major disappointments here, but also some sequences that for operatic truth and emotional impact have not been exceeded in any other taped version.

1986 KULTUR (VHS)

(Stage Performance, Mono, Color, Subtitled), 120 minutes

Fiamma Izzo D'Amico (A), Madelyn Reneé (B), Luciano Pavarotti (C), Roberto Servile (D),

Jeffrey Mattsey (E), Francesco Ellero D'Artegna (F), Chorus and Orchestra of the Municipal Opera of Genoa—Leone Magiera

Municipal Opera Theater of Genoa on tour in Beijing: Gian Carlo Menotti (director)

This performance was taped in Beijing when the Genoa Opera was on a Chinese tour in 1986. Given these circumstances, Luciano Pavarotti's Rodolfo, and Gian Carlo Menotti as stage director, the production sounds at least provocative.

It isn't. Menotti has done distinguished stage work, but his production here emerges as routine. The cast is obedient but listless, sometimes energetic but seldom convincing. Pavarotti, in fine voice, walks through his music and stands through his character, one might say, facing the audience at the most inopportune moments and hardly bothering to change vocal colors or shape a phrase for real illumination. He does come alive for some of the final moments, but the difference between this and his San Francisco performance three years later is vast. Menotti provides one or two poetic effects, but the few new directorial ideas are nearly all troublesome, and the entrances and introductions, so important in this opera, have all been handled with a minimum of effect. Franco Colavecchia's sets look promising and may travel well, but they are often unatmospherically lit.

Of the other singers, Robert Servile is the best, and his duet with Pavarotti in Act IV is a highlight. Fiamma Izzo D'Amico has a hard, dark voice and has not been treated well by the costume, makeup, and lighting designers: a Mimì without charm. And so on. Leone Magiera is the compliant conductor.

Though it cannot brook the competition on videotape, the production was undoubtedly more exciting than this in the theater. The most touching moments are when the capacity audience breaks into the performance unexpectedly with applause—directly after the high C in Rodolfo's first-act aria, and then in the midst of "O soave fanciulla." Given a gleaming tone or two, *La Bohème* is deathless.

1989 KULTUR (VHS) / PIONEER (LD)

(Stage Performance, Stereo, Color, Subtitled), 111 minutes

Mirella Freni (A), Sandra Pacetti (B), Luciano Pavarotti (C), Gino Quilico (D), Stephen Dickson (E), Nicolai Ghiaurov (F), San Francisco Opera Chorus and Orchestra—Tiziano Severini

San Francisco Opera: Francesca Zambello (stage director), Brian Large (video director)

A phenomenal production. One might think it would trade almost wholly on nostalgia, since Mirella Freni, Luciano Pavarotti, and Nicolai Ghiaurov by 1989 had been singing all over the world for a quarter of a century and Italo Tajo (Benoit and Alcindoro) for at least twice that long (in San Francisco he was Pinza's last Leporello in 1948, and in 1956 sang Colline with Gino Quilico's father, Louis, as Marcello). There is that element, but here they are all potent performers still, and they are surrounded by a production of imagination and atmosphere, for once beautifully lit. David Mitchell's Act I set is vast and bare, but impressionistically illuminated in gray and blue for a deeply poetic effect. His second act features a two-story Momus with an angled street entrance to suggest both some intimacy and a tightly packed street crowd. Act III gleams with frozen rain, and those streetsweepers are coughing and stiff with cold.

Francesca Zambello is the director, and she has inspired her famous cast to performances of greater dramatic detail and emotional effect than I have ever seen from them before. In particular Pavarotti is an incomparably more committed, generous performer than in China three years previously. In Act I the aria and duet go well, and in Act II "Questa è Mimì" is thrilling. At the customs house there is almost a fight between Rodolfo and Marcello—not the only way to do it but here handled with conviction. The urgency of Pavarotti's tone when he realizes that Mimì is leaving him is just one example of his restudy of the role. Another is his response at the close of the opera. Despite all those theatrical tears at the end, the rest has the look of spontaneity: a very moving moment.

And Mirella Freni is transformed. Granted, her voice is harder and darker, and from time to time less steady than it was twenty-two years before at La Scala, but she has filled the role with heartbreaking detail. She compels attention, from us and her colleagues. We know, for example, that she is already thinking of joining Rodolfo and his friends *before* she asks. In Act III she is *very* ill—tired, coughing, and feverish. She grips Marcello with terror, and the "Addio" is filled with suppressed suffering. Act IV is equally focused. Her death scene is eloquent and almost unbearable.

The others are worthy of the production. Italo Tajo is fascinating, and Nicolai Ghiaurov is in his best recent voice: the Coat Song is pleasant, though a little fast for the sentiment it is here meant to convey. Sandra Pacetti has a light, pretty voice with an edge. Her characterization of Musetta is standard, but she sings the Waltz slowly and lyrically and handles the final prayer with sensitivity. Gino Quilico is as usual wonderfully direct, lithe, and specific in his actions, and there is beautiful soft singing in his Act IV duet with Pavarotti. Tiziano Severini is a lively and responsive conductor. Technically, there is a little distortion on some of the highs on my tape. The production is in general exceptionally well photographed, the camera nearly always on the action or reaction one wants to see. This is a *Bohème* to experience.

1993 LONDON (VHS / LD)

(Stage Performance, Stereo, Color, Subtitled)
113 minutes

Cheryl Barker (A), Christine Douglas (B), David Hobson (C), Roger Lemke (D), David Lemke (E), Gary Rowley (F), Australian Opera Chorus and Orchestra—Julian Smith

Australian Opera: Baz Luhrmann (stage director), Geoffrey Nottage (video director)

Here is a constructivist production of Puccini's opera set in the Paris of 1957 and intended to woo a young audience. In the accompanying booklet, the director explains that the new generations of both the 1840s and the late 1950s were alike reacting against their stable middle-class origins and, incidentally, that since vaccination against tuberculosis first became widespread only in 1958, the previous year becomes the last logical one for Mimì to die of the disease!

Generational revolution must have been happening in Paris earlier than elsewhere. In England 1958 was the year of *Look Back in Anger*, in which Jimmy Porter laments that his is the *lone* voice of rebellion, and in America we were just rediscovering, from within the middle-class womb of college, the political passions of the depression of the 1930s, through the songs of those great survivors, The Weavers. The generational revolution alluded to in this *Bohème* and the fashion statements that grew out of it were much more typical of the sixties—the period of Antonioni's film *Blow Up*, and for that matter Jean-Luc Godard's *Weekend*.

For all that, the central questions are whether this production retains enough of the authentic *Bohème* experience to make an introduction worthwhile and whether it will in fact bring a new audience to the opera for more than a tourist visit. Only the young audiences themselves will really provide the answer to the first question—and only the Australian Opera will have the information for the second.

For those of us deeply acquainted with Puccini's opera, the production may be an interesting gloss on the original work, and perhaps little more. Certainly since World War II there have been innumerable updatings, perceptive and otherwise, of innumerable operas. Any opera concerned with tyranny, however marginally, eventually gets the Nazi treatment: *Tosca*, *Fidelio*, and even *Otello*, for example. And of course Wagner is prime material. Twenty years ago Patrice Chéreau's "capitalist" Ring Cycle at Bayreuth was heavily booed, but in the succeeding decade it became for some a classic. But this production of *Bohème* does not seem to reexamine and refocus the strengths of the original work. Puccini's characters are consumed by life: poetry, art, music, philosophy, love. Luhrmann's characters are more in search of conviction than exhausted by it, more interested in Bohemian fashion than truth. Luhrmann makes the point that Murger's Bohemians and his own are both middle-class young men *posturing* at being poor. Puccini, though, makes little of this. When Marcello in Act IV says "Ah, miseria!" he means it very personally, and the music consistently reinforces this view. Luhrmann's other major point is that Mimì, unlike the men, has a life of *real* poverty, hunger, and cold. Even if the distinction is accurate, the Mimì of this production is as self-possessed and fashionably dressed and coiffed as any of them—there is precious little sense of destitution anywhere. They all live in a constructivist version of a garret apartment with a neon "L'Amour" sign on the roof just outside the window. Think *Friends*. Rodolfo and Mimì as a dour Ross and Rachel.

The singers are visually appealing and musically promising and efficient—little more here, though they have sometimes been directed interestingly. When Mimì dies, Rodolfo does not rush to her but remains on his ladder alone:

a gesture in the direction of alienation, one supposes. This proclivity toward modernization extends even to the subtitles. When Marcello ironically compares Musetta with the Biblical virgin Susannah, the translation is "She's no Mary Poppins!"

So, in sum, there is a good deal that is provocative, if not entirely convincing, in this production, and you will have, in addition, the unusual and diverting exercise of testing your convictions about, of all things, *La Bohème*.

The 1982 Covent Garden set offers a beautifully sung, well acted, and charmingly set performance with the special pleasure of Ileana Cotrubas as Mimì. Among the others, Teresa Stratas is dramatically unforgettable in the lavish Met production of 1982, and there is memorable singing in the 1967 Scala set, while the 1989 San Francisco Opera performance offers the mature Pavarotti and Freni in a poetic production of unexpected sensitivity and power.

LONDON GREEN

GIACOMO PUCCINI

TOSCA (1900)

A: Floria Tosca (s); B: Mario Cavaradossi (t); C: Scarpia (bar)

*P*uccini and his librettists, Giacosa and Illica, all fell in love with movies, and the two writers worked in the fledgling Italian movie industry. The composer's lively response to shoot-'em-ups and pagan spectacles is hard to miss in *La Fanciulla del West* and *Turandot*. Perhaps, in *Tosca*, they anticipated the media's inevitable coarsening of popular culture (as elites might see it). Their reduction of Victorien Sardou's *La Tosca* anticipates what cinema adapters do to plays and novels. Sardou's work is a vast tapestry with twenty-three speaking parts and hours of exposition and incident. Composer and collaborators boil all that down to three leads and five or so well characterized *comprimarios* whose destinies unfold in about one hundred minutes. Information is essentialized. Cavaradossi's French free-thinking is glancingly referred to but not gone into in detail. We have to intuit the ambition that has brought the low-born Tosca to prominence. By leaving out mundane details about Vitellio Scarpia's political skills and obligations he is made more frightening. Movie writers learn to leave as much as possible to montage. Giacosa and Illica left everything to Puccini's music, which takes the place of the camera and the edits. Scarpia's theme, which opens the opera, is bloodcurdling because it is without conventional melodic profile, its harmony is based on unconnected parallel chords, and it never changes. Puccini's work—auteur-like—is dense, not expansive. Offstage music supports fictional "reality"—Tosca's voice soaring through a delicate "period" piece wafts into Scarpia's room, which has a torture chamber attached; precisely tuned bells become Rome and all it symbolizes; a shepherd boy's voice summons up daily life in a time when cities were encroaching on the countryside. Shrewdly designed motives combine and recombine to create a powerfully suggestive weave of associations and memories. Immense musical learning is hidden under theatrical fireworks and a swift movement forward that in turn creates a suffocating sense of inevitability. Shards of *melos* (as in the last act duet between Tosca and Cavaradossi) are substituted for conventional "operatic" expansiveness in ways that are unfailingly evocative of "real" life. Puccini even "musicalizes" inner emotions and the glances and actions that result. One of the great stretches in opera must be the f-sharp minor interlude in Act II during which Tosca finds the knife and decides to kill Scarpia. Ironically, it isn't sung. None of this redeems Puccini's sensibility. It may be a sad comment on our century that it is probably the more or less explicit sexual sadism which keeps the opera alive. That is an unfortunate kind of prescience, but it is the prescience of a genius all the same. *Tosca* was slightly ahead of its time but was made to order for the expanding stagecraft and vogue for "realism" in opera houses in the years before the first world war. It is interesting to see if its opera house verisimilitude really translates to the video and film forms it anticipates.

195? BEL CANTO SOCIETY (VHS)

(Studio Performance, Mono, Black and White, Not Subtitled) 113 minutes

Heredia Capnist (A), Franco Corelli (B), Carlo Tagliabue (C), RAI Orchestra—Silvano Blasi

Director uncredited

The point here is the young Corelli. He is improbably handsome for a person, forget a tenor. He is very athletic (executing a nimble leap off the scaffold at one point) and quite plausibly sexy. He sounds splendid on the sound track; there is more vibrato than there was to be a few years later and less fussing around with dynamics. There is one small advantage to lip-synching for him. Freed from worrying about the mechanics of singing, Corelli is a lot more natural and engaging than he often was live. There is none of the nose squeezing for which he was famous. Capnist is a pretty woman who looks to be middle-aged. She knows her way around Tosca; her voice has a vinegary middle but a good top. Tagliabue, who began his career in the thirties, is a small, poodle-faced Scarpia. He wears his own hair in Act II and looks like a pudgy grandpa. He is rather limited in facial expression, though he sounds pretty good. Both he and Capnist suffer from having to keep up with their prerecorded selves. Their solid basic impulses have been interfered with. The rationale of prerecording here eludes me. In films it facilitates retakes. But there weren't any here—there are plenty of mishaps. Scarpia treads on Tosca's dress in Act II—she simply hauls off and pushes him away! The production is standard but not always well handled. The stabbing isn't filmed, so the less attentive will think Scarpia has had a heart attack. Cavaradossi's execution is also not filmed. Sciarrone and Spoletta seem to be having a casual chat looking down over the parapet presumably at the mashed Tosca. "Get dressed!" the Sacristan commands the obstreperous boys in Act I—but they're already in their vestments. The artificiality is a pity; the supporting singers have good voices and are capable performers.

There was a problem at the upper left of the screen, and the producer of this video masks it with "Bel Canto Society" on a black background—covering faces now and then, particularly the tall Corelli's. This vanishes for "E lucevan le stelle" but returns with a vengeance afterward, as does serious wow on the sound track.

1960 LEGATO CLASSICS (VHS)

(Film, Mono, Black and White, Not Subtitled) 123 minutes

Magda Olivero (A), Alvinio Misciano (B), Giulio Fioravanti (C), Chorus and Orchestra of the RAI—Fulvio Verni

Mario Lanfranchi (director)

Magda Olivero is unique. She is still singing on TV as of this writing. She was born in 1910, so that makes hers probably the longest professional operatic career in history, at least as far as leading roles go. She is the oldest singer to make a Met debut in a starring role (Tosca, 1975). Although never a big international star and sometimes an object of critical fun, she has developed an impassioned following. She began her career five years after Puccini's death, and there is an interesting historic dimension to what she does. This film (long thought lost) is the only one of her in a complete role. Typical of RAI, the music was prerecorded. Olivero was not meant to lip-synch; she acts for God, who is farther away than the camera. She has said she studied Garbo's movies; this time it looks like she's seen Gloria Swanson once too often—there are lots of Norma Desmond-like eye aerobics. She's caught between a rock and a hard place—not able to cut loose physically, as she would have in a live performance (her singing is fantastically colorful), and without quite the mimetic confidence for a film. But there are surprises. Her conception of the role is very sophisticated. She presents Tosca, above all, as a human being: fragile, volatile, vulnerable. Few singers (or actors, for that matter) listen as expressively as she does—the way she hears "Qual occhio al mondo" establishes beyond a doubt her profound, suffering love for Cavaradossi. Her intense hearing of his agonies in Act II makes his torture more horrifying than actually seeing it would have. Her colleagues are secure pros. The director, Mario Lanfranchi, is more than competent, though there are compromises in camera positions (Scarpia gets lost during the Te Deum but his voice roars on). Misciano is light for Cavaradossi and forces, but he, Badioli (Sacristan), the wonderfully ripe Foiani (Angelotti), and the eerie Cesarini (Spoletta) give vivid characterizations. Giulio Fioravanti, a little-noticed baritone of the time, is one of the best Scarpias on these videos. He has a fine voice and is a marvelous operatic actor with magnetic eyes and a handsome presence. Legato's print is faded and bumpy but watchable. Compromised and frustrating at times, this is a valuable document of a singular artist.

1961 VAI (VHS)

(Stage Performance, Mono, Black and White, Subtitled) 126 minutes

Renata Tebaldi (A), Eugene Tobin (B), George London (C), Stuttgart State Opera Chorus and Orchestra—Franco Patanè

Stuttgart State Opera: Director uncredited

This a rare example of a film capturing two important singers near their primes in a live performance of the roles for which they were especially acclaimed. Renata Tebaldi and George London were two of the greatest singers in the immediate period following World War II. They are both "old style" creatures of the opera house and it's thrilling to see them together. They represent traditional but somewhat different notions of operatic performance. Tebaldi has worked out a small number of movements and poses which look reasonable and never interfere with her singing. And why not—it's some singing. Perhaps she was a year or two past her very freshest, but the huge, gorgeous middle range, the large scale soft and very soft tone, the marvelous phrases ("e luna piena e il notturno effluvio floreal inebria il cor," in the first act, "poscia a civitavecchia, una tartana e via pel mar" in Act III) are all here. The high C's are reasonably easy. "Vissi d'arte" may not be her

very best crack at the aria but it's pretty impressive in the context of these videos and she gets a huge screaming ovation for it. What she does is less arresting than how she sounds but she doesn't contradict or falsify the role and when London pulls her into a more immediate "reality" she is able to respond. There have always been more charismatic operatic performers (though they aren't on video), but one has to wonder if a singer more highly praised for her "acting" like Hildegarde Behrens is any better or even as good. Compared to, say, Garbo or Bette Davis or Meryl Streep, Behrens isn't much of an actress, really, nor, in this repertory, is she much of a singer. Tebaldi is a great singer, absolutely right in the style, and physically attractive. You can imagine a more totally engrossing performer, but you are unlikely to encounter one, and meanwhile the composer Puccini is magnificently served. London *was* an engrossing performer. He is a splendid figure of a man with marvelous eyes and a pantherine elegance. He is also a singer. This is a huge black voice of superb quality with a good upper extension. His words are eloquent and his phrases are those of a magnificent thinking musician. One's only hesitation involves his physical method for producing sound—his lower jaw flaps to the left and thus looks a little strange. Even so, he is mesmerizing. His Baron has a sense of sadistic fun (removing Tosca's wrap in Act II, then elaborately smelling it; gleefully running Cavaradossi's torture behind her back) and a sudden sexual ferocity all the more shocking for the epicene prancing which has gone before. He understands that Scarpia is the true sexual nexus of the opera, a vicious seducer of the audience as well as Tosca. It's slightly irritating that the film director relies too much on long shots of London and Tebaldi together—we want to see their every glance.

Otherwise, the German singers learned their roles in Italian, which was game, but the performance is very Teutonic. The Sacristan with his menacing limp is just as scary as Spoletta—who is humpbacked. The American tenor Eugene Tobin, a big star in Stuttgart, is a hearty man with a fine voice used in the German manner (overweighted, baritonal middle, squeezed-though confident top). Patanè has trouble keeping stage / orchestra coordinated in Act II.

1961 UNKNOWN DISTRIBUTOR (VHS)

(Stage Performance, Mono, Black and White, Subtitled) 124 minutes

Renata Tebaldi (A), Gianni Poggi (B), Giangiacomo Guelfi, Chorus and Orchestra of NHK, Japan—Arturo Basile

Opera company and director uncredited

Tokyo is farther from Italy than Stuttgart, but since this is an Italian company on tour, the performance is more idiomatic. Vocally, Tebaldi is less easy in the first two acts. She has phlegm and struggles for high notes—the C's in the second act are flat by a mile. There is (for her) some unusual gear shifting in "Vissi d'arte." In Act III, she suddenly recovers. The C in "io quella lama" is stunning; the glowing, blossoming tone on "Senti effluvi di rose," breathtaking. Her physical performance is much the same as in Stuttgart though she is more relaxed here. She is capable of tenderness with Poggi and is well used to Guelfi (London keeps her off-balance). This is rather too cozy a performance to serve the conflict and tension in the score. The sets are on a grander scale than in Stuttgart, but they seem slapped-together. It takes Guelfi a little while to recover when his chair gives under him at the start of Act II.

Poggi had a significant career but was much complained about by record reviewers. True, he's unglamorous to look at and sometimes to hear. On the other hand, he is the real thing, a true Italian spinto tenor with a ripe middle range and stunning top. "La vita mia costasse" and "vittoria" would knock anybody's socks off. Sure, I wish there were more sweetness and imagination, but I'd feel more comfortable complaining if there were some like him in the world today. Guelfi, likewise, has an important voice, thunderous, easily produced. He isn't much of an interpreter, still less is he a musician, though he has a firm grasp of the role and the right energy. More than Tebaldi or Poggi he has some of the gestural expansiveness that used

to be commonplace among Italian performers. The Sacristan bleats but Angelotti (Silvio Maionica) sounds very impressive. Basile more or less keeps the orchestra together, but getting the strings to play chromatic intervals cleanly was evidently impossible.

1976 LONDON (VHS / LD)

(Film, Stereo, Color, Subtitled) 116 minutes

Raina Kabaivanska (A), Plácido Domingo (B), Sherrill Milnes (C), New Philharmonia Orchestra—Bruno Bartoletti

Gianfranco De Bosio (director)

This was "filmed on location in Rome." *Tosca* is an opera, not a documentary. As with most opera films this is far more artificial than a good stage production. It starts with Angelotti escaping in silence. Music cuts in just as he reaches the facade of Sant' Andrea della Valle. Unfortunately, that music is associated with Scarpia. De Bosio's direction is generally unmusical. The last measures of Act II accompany Tosca as she runs down flights and flights of stairs—but the music is a weird requiem for Scarpia. We get to see the shepherd boy, probably in part because he is sung by Plácido Domingo, Jr. But surely the point of his song is that it is heard by those condemned to die. "E lucevan" is sung by Cavaradossi strolling around the battlements, the camera, too close, doggedly following. That might have been a reasonable place for a flashback. We get one instead to start "Recondita armonia"—the blonde lady kneeling from nowhere will probably confuse some viewers. This film shows the tension between "real" and "reel" space and time. Scarpia escorts Tosca out to her carriage, comes back into the church—and waits with his henchmen (their heads are bowed; are they praying?)—until the sound track catches up and he can tell Spoletta to follow her. It feels like an hour since she's left—any viewer will feel she is long gone. De Bosio shows us a little of Cavaradossi being tortured, but the murder of Scarpia is shot at a far distance. Tosca has picked up a butcher knife, but he looks to be dying from a puncture wound—there's just a dribble of blood. As usual in these films, foley effects (ambient sound) are inconsistent. Sometimes we hear footsteps and crowd noises, sometimes we don't. We get a glimpse of Tosca mashed far below the Castel Sant' Angelo, but we haven't heard what would have to have been a loud plop.

It's not clear why opera singers are hired for these projects. Singers look awkward lip-synching. Anyone who loves opera will want to see the famous Domingo actually produce his voice. There is something perverse in robbing us of that—just as there would be in failing to photograph Nureyev's feet and legs or in filming Jesse Owens at a distance. The muscular effort is part of the thrill for the viewer and the expressive lexicon of the singer. This is a handsome-looking trio, though. Kabaivanska is very pretty, Milnes (without a wig), uncommonly young and athletic, and Domingo is tender and sweet in face as well as voice. But they would all have been much better performing live.

1980 LEGATO CLASSICS (VHS)

(Stage Performance, Stereo, Color, Subtitled in French) 109 minutes

Montserrat Caballé (A), José Carreras (B), Juan Pons (C), Uncredited Orchestra—Jesus Etcheverry

Opera company, stage director, and video director uncredited

One value of video is documentary. What wouldn't most of us give to have film of the greats of yesterday in action onstage? Montserrat Caballé and José Carreras were two of the biggest stars of the "second wave" of opera singers after World War II. Both had impressive voices (which did not suit all the roles they tried). This somewhat fuzzy video gives a reasonable sample of what they were like on a routine night in a very respectable, if provincial, performance. Caballé had a gorgeous upper octave, the quality of which lasted. Her best roles were those in which large-scale, moderately high-lying lyric singing was called for, with a few florid gestures thrown in. She was not naturally a *verismo* performer. She never had a

strong chest register, nor was she always happy when having to carry power upwards for more than a phrase or two. As a personality she was enchanting, literally born to sing. But her natural manner was that of a comedienne. It wasn't a question of being fat (in any case she is thinner here than she could be and is flatteringly camouflaged by her costumes) but of being innately funny. Tosca is about as far from her instincts as a rap music video would be, and the style only occasionally gives her an extended chance to shine vocally. She sings fairly well and tries to execute the staging. But she is amusing in much of the byplay, most endearingly when she and Carreras twinkle at one another big sister–kid brother style in their love scenes, apparently on the brink of the giggles. In the second act, she does the *de rigueur* shrieks and gasps but perhaps isn't altogether serious—can telling Scarpia that Angelotti is in the mad woman (*pazza*) as opposed to the well (*pozzo*) be an accident? Of course, dropping consonants and changing vowels was one of her tricks for getting around heavier roles. Mid-act she has begun to have pitch problems and to sound unsteady, though there are ravishing phrases and several stunning high C's. Darkening her sound and pushing for volume results in a frayed tone for "Vissi d'arte," and the glottal attack can't have been healthy, but she does manage an impressive diminuendo (written but usually ignored) at the aria's end. Naturally she runs offstage to jump from the parapet at the finale.

By this point, Carreras's boyish good looks were giving way to pudgy early middle age, and his timbre is no longer limpid, but he is a confident if small-scaled Cavaradossi. Juan Pons, before his fame, is a very promising Scarpia, naturally commanding and with a juicy if monochromatic sound. The set designs are the only ones on video which do not ape the real sites—practical in general and a gain in the Church Scene.

1984 CASTLE OPERA (VHS)

(Stage Performance, Stereo, Color, Not Subtitled) 126 minutes

Eva Marton (A), Giacomo Aragall (B), Ingvar Wixell (C), Verona Arena Chorus and Orchestra—Daniel Oren

Verona Arena: Sylvano Bussotti (stage director); Brian Large (video director)

One is never more aware of how intimate an opera *Tosca* is than when watching these singers run around the vast spaces of the Verona Arena. Essential points of interpersonal contact are not made, and everybody yells—even their most private thoughts. Brian Large shoots this as much as he can as an "event," showing some of the nuts and bolts of opera given in a tourist trap, but sooner or later he is forced into close-ups of the singers screaming for dear life.

Eva Marton was among the most talented singers to emerge in the mid-seventies. This is a bad Marton performance—she abuses a mighty voice with so much breath pressure that she is unsteady and her tone is frayed. There is far too much chesty growling and sheer belting. Maybe it was exciting at the top of the Arena, but close up and miked it's migraine inducing. There is no characterization to speak of. Marton plays Tosca as a homicidal maniac from the first, ready to torture and kill Cavaradossi when he's slow to open the church door. She's the only Tosca to evidently enjoy disemboweling Scarpia. That's the sole sincere stretch in her performance, though she often seems to be crying. Unfortunately, since she has no color or vulnerability beforehand it looks like more of the same. She offers accented Italian and some odd phrasing, which is also true of the adequate Wixell. Aragall has the right Latin presence and sound, though he is somewhat past his very freshest and pulls rhythms around too much—to the point of making a hash of "Recondita armonia" (after which there is no applause).

Bussotti's production gives Scarpia a long purple cloak to swish around in Act I—is the Baron dressing up in homage to his patroness, Queen Maria Carolina of Naples? Scarpia also has a regiment of boy henchmen wearing identical wigs and posing. In the church they seem to be lurking for assignations. Three of them stand behind Cavaradossi while he belts "vitto-

ria," looking for all the world like signifying monkeys.

1985 PARAMOUNT (VHS) / PIONEER (LD)

(Stage Performance, Stereo, Color, Subtitled) 127 minutes

Hildegard Behrens (A), Plácido Domingo (B), Cornell MacNeil (C), Metropolitan Opera Chorus and Orchestra—Giuseppe Sinopoli

Metropolitan Opera: Franco Zeffirelli (stage director); Kirk Browning (video director)

This isn't a persuasive performance but it is a good, sad document of its period. Franco Zeffirelli seems to have understood the zeitgeist of Reagan's America and tailored his talents accordingly. An audience of yuppies (as they were called) went to the opera and the theater because they could afford it. One might call them the *Phantom of the Opera* generation. They were only interested in seeing the chandelier fall. There occurred simultaneously a collapse in critical standards, at least in America. Zeffirelli accordingly serves up a swollen pageant creaking with tons of irrelevant business. It should chill a true opera lover's heart that the biggest applause in Act I (indeed in this video) is for the flamboyantly managed Te Deum. Scarpia's blasphemous thoughts of Tosca are quite swallowed up. In Act II, the floor opens for Tosca to see her lover's torture (do upper apartments often have subbasements?).

Naturally, the start of Act III is adorned with sleepy navvies in their skivvies. Later, Zeffirelli introduces a spurious set change. We are in Cavaradossi's dungeon for "E lucevan le stelle." There is in all this a profound falseness. There are so many nuns, tourists, and priests wandering through the church at the start of Act I it's hard to believe that Cavaradossi and Angelotti can talk in the echoey church without being overheard, or indeed, that Cavaradossi is the only person who finds Angelotti. The mechanism of the plot depends on this seeming somehow inevitable—it doesn't here. When Scarpia comes on, the boys (and women *en travesti*) who have been indulging in horse play fall to the ground as though he effected gravity. People didn't fall in terror even when Hitler walked into a room—it's silly carrying-on, and it betrays a contempt for the material and for the audience as well. In Act II, Scarpia has a small regiment of henchmen. How does Tosca get away? Surely some of them are lounging around outside. Kirk Browning, the video director, deliberately fudges the set change in Act III. Even so, having Cavaradossi underground wrecks the automatic "open air" associations that justify the tenor's aria and the pathos of his situation: stars in a chilly morning sky, a shepherd boy singing about girls, death imminent—another, warmer night, bright stars, Tosca, and life.

Hildegarde Behrens was a great star of the period; she works hard and seems sincere. But she is toneless in the middle register. Most singers fudge pitches now and then, but Behrens's voice has a way of spreading north and south of the note almost simultaneously. Quite a feat, but an unedifying one. Her tone is usually preceded by a bronchial gasp or a little yelp. She doesn't have enough breath to sustain most long phrases. Her voice is too unresponsive for her to strike a wide dynamic range or to play with phrases or even (in sound) to flirt with Cavaradossi and fence with Scarpia. Her acting is a question of heaving her shoulders upward and popping her eyes—results, one feels, of a discerning singer's dilemmas, not the character's. Cornell MacNeil was a splendid baritone of the late fifties, sixties, and seventies, but here he is very wobbly and his tone is gray. He and Behrens go through the motions professionally enough in Act II, but there is not even a second's surprise, genuine response, or clear contact between them.

Sinopoli is less distinctive (or self-promoting) than on his studio recording, but he is an interesting musician and makes the most of the superb Met orchestra. Wind playing in particular is a great pleasure, with soulful solos and impeccably voiced chords.

Italo Tajo has spirit (no voice) and "italianità" as the Sacristan. Melissa Forgerty sings beautifully (and sounds a plausible boy) as the shepherd.

The greatest pleasure here is Domingo. He sounds wonderful but also shapes his music with the sophistication and love it deserves. This, one feels, is genuinely a great tenor caught live.

1986 KULTUR (VHS)

(Stage Performance, Stereo, Color, Subtitled) 123 minutes

Eva Marton (A), Lamberto Furlan (B), John Shaw (C), Australian Opera Chorus, Elizabethan Sydney Orchestra—Alberto Erede

Australian Opera: John Copley (stage director)

This is a much better Marton performance than the Verona. The outstanding quality of her voice and her strong theatrical presence are captured without as much coarseness and forcing. It's true there's an air of general menace about her. If Scarpia and Cavaradossi get too close she is apt to swat or push them away. "I'm not in the least frightened," she says in Act II—and you better believe it. She isn't capable of much color or variety of inflection, but feeling less compelled to conquer the world from the first moment frees her to suggest some emotional readiness. She is without charm, but a tough girl from a hard background isn't an utterly wrong place to start with this character, and much of what Marton does here at least seems honest. Meanwhile she is easy and at times thrilling in the big vocal moments; one registers that she belongs on the operatic stage in a starring role.

John Copley's production is well rehearsed and detailed. It's a little strange to see a washer woman scrubbing away at the church in Act I, but most of his choices are reasonable. His staging of the Tosca-Scarpia confrontations are less generalized than usual—though having Scarpia grab and fondle a wine carafe while singing 'bramo!' in Act II looks strange. The Cavaradossi gives out with hair-raising screams while he's being tortured (the only one to do so in these videos). He doesn't seem secure in Italian and is less than wonderful to hear at some points. John Shaw, Scarpia, has learned a lot from Tito Gobbi—a good model. He has a habit of singing with his eyes shut and sports a heavy Australian accent.

Not an idiomatic performance but intermittently quite effective.

1992 TELDEC (VHS / LD)

(Film, Stereo, Color, Subtitled) 115 minutes

Catherine Malfitano (A), Plácido Domingo (B), Ruggero Raimondi (C), RAI, Rome Chorus and Orchestra—Zubin Mehta

Giuseppe Patroni Griffi (director), Brian Large (video director)

This transpires at the "real" locations, at the "real" time of day (or night) when the scenes "occurred." The singing is "live" (the orchestra was in a studio). One is skeptical about some of the "live" singing—modern technology makes "sweetening" relatively easy. Technically, this is a feat. Brian Large moves his cameras with a kind of flamboyant freedom one would have thought impossible live. Superbly musical as well as a virtuoso, Large is able to realize the opera totally, both in the big moments—the amazingly intricate Te Deum—and in the small ones—Tosca's cape slowly snaking out at the end of Act II. Thanks to the rhythm of his shots and the precision of his cuts, Large makes of film a musical medium.

The director, Griffi, is very imaginative. His first image is brilliant—a barefoot and ragged Angelotti hovers near an embalmed saint in the church. His escape, his terror, his predicament, and the environment and culture in which he is going to try and survive are all powerfully and economically encapsulated. For once, the start of the third act is completely convincing. Frightened and haggard, Cavaradossi listens to the shepherd and then is manhandled through grimly plausible preparations for a state execution. Ruggero Raimondi, Scarpia, gives the great performance of the entire role on video. George London is less conventional but Raimondi really benefits from the camera. He has a fascinating face; he exudes effortless and charismatic sexuality. Griffi uses this shrewdly—

Scarpia is hateful but irresistible. There are no comic book antics here (à la Zeffirelli), but a parade of glinting, insinuating, charming evil that could lure a saint to perdition. The entire final third of Act II has genuine suspense. Rather than rushing to write the safe passage during that f-sharp minor interlude, Scarpia enfolds Tosca in a long, exploratory kiss, mixing tenderness, need, and might. In her face is something worse than anticipation of the bargain—arousal. She kills her attraction to—even, one feels, the dawning of a preference for—Scarpia. The actual stabbing is almost like violent sexual intercourse. It is shocking and earned—exactly what it isn't anywhere else.

Raimondi's vocal method has its peculiarities (he's too fond of crooning and has a way a slithering over intervals), but this is an outstanding voice; like London he is totally organic, using vocal and musical impulses to achieve an eloquence words alone could not provide.

Malfitano tries very hard and on the whole seems preferable to Behrens (she is of the same school). Her light voice sounds pressured and white and she inflates her chest, carrying it too high for comfort at times. But she does have the volatility, the "italianità" the role requires, and she responds well to Griffi. Her Tosca is a very sexy flirt, almost Scarpia's equal in courage and deceit. Maybe she carries on too much in Act III—there is more than a hint of Norma Desmond toward the end—but it never seems positively wrong.

Domingo is typically compelling—although he is more truly in his element in the live Met performance.

1993 RCA (VHS / LD)

(Stage Performance, Stereo, Color, Subtitled) 137 minutes

Raina Kabaivanska (A), Luciano Pavarotti (B), Ingvar Wixell (C), Rome Opera Chorus and Orchestra—Daniel Oren

Rome Opera: Mauro Bolognini (stage director)

The point here is Pavarotti, who gets to encore "E lucevan le stelle," but I was more moved by Raina Kabaivanska. She acts rings around Behrens, Marton, and Malfitano; she could give those ladies lessons simply in the wearing of costumes, the handling of a train. She could give them vocal lessons, too. Kabaivanska does not have the endowment of Marton, but she has a full range of skills that Marton never troubled to acquire. In comparison to Behrens and Malfitano, it is Kabaivanska who seems the full-fledged professional. She has dead-on high notes, a long breath, and an ability to sing over a wide dynamic range (the long diminuendos at the end of "Vissi d'arte" represent wonderful singing allied to strong emotion). Her middle register is flinty and sometimes ragged with age, but she can shape parlando lines and turn easily from declamation to lyricism and back—in short, create the flirtatious, temperamental, voluptuous, suffering Tosca in vocal as well as physical terms. Dramatically, her choices are big, but firmly and confidently based on a mastery of the stage rhetoric Puccini had in mind and wrote into the score. It's a "complete" performance: powerful, moving, everywhere accomplished.

As for the tenor, he began with, and by and large has kept, an outstanding lyric voice, much in evidence here, particularly in Act III. Whether he would have had the same career had he begun ten years earlier, say, when his competition would have been di Stefano, Corelli, del Monaco, Bjoerling, and Tucker (for starters) doesn't worry the fans. I find Pavarotti's manner in Act I offensive. He bites and paws at Kabaivanska and seems to be sending up Cavaradossi (he cups his hands around his mouth for "Floria io t'amo"—a camp gesture). If we don't believe he truly loves Tosca, the meaning of the opera is lost—she's a fool to risk her life for him. Famous Italian tenors have sometimes been unprepossessing and histrionically impaired (though not always—Corelli, del Monaco, and di Stefano weren't), but that does not mean they must subvert the basic make-believe of the art

form. Poggi, for example, is a fat man of a certain age, but he conveys the basic points in the plot without ridiculing them.

The surrounding production is strange. To spare the tenor a climb, his easel is put well off the scaffold downstage where it's in the way (when Pavarotti is safely gone an extra removes it). Bolognini, the director, seems to have his operas mixed up. The end of Act I is an *auto-da-fé* out of *Don Carlo*, not a Te Deum. Act II looks like a garret from *La Bohème* and Scarpia seems to have gone shopping for cheap furniture at the Bauhaus. Bolognini isn't able to move people onstage—Tosca roams or is flung right, then roams or is flung left. One hopes he ran to Sant' Andrea della Valle to thank God for old pros like Kabaivanska and Wixell.

The video director cuts too often to the soulful conductor—his mouth usually wide open making faces at the singers. There are some obvious inserts from a dress rehearsal. It looks like a fair amount of the "live" singing has been doctored after the fact—most obviously leading up to and including "la vita mia costasse."

———

The Teldec film is dazzling, though Malfitano is good rather than great as Tosca. Ruggero Raimondi is a mesmerizing Scarpia. Domingo is very good there, magnificent on the otherwise spotty, overblown Met performance. Archivists will want Tebaldi—better in Stuttgart (with the great George London) than in Tokyo—and the constrainedly lip-synching Olivero, who is fascinating. Fans may want Caballé and Pavarotti, though Raina Kabaivanska gives the special performance on the tenor's video. Anyone interested in *Tosca* or operatic acting in general will search out the amazing second act filmed live at Convent Garden in 1964 with Maria Callas and Tito Gobbi. It's available at the right pitch on EMI. For charisma, chemistry, and performing genius it is unmatched elsewhere.

ALBERT INNAURATO

GIACOMO PUCCINI

MADAMA BUTTERFLY (1904)

A: Madama Butterfly (Cio-Cio-San) (s); B: Suzuki (ms);
C: Lt. B. F. Pinkerton (t); D: Goro (t); E: Sharpless (bar)

All the *Butterflys* available on video are of the revised version of the opera, the guise in which it is now almost exclusively performed. When Puccini's sixth opera was first heard at La Scala in 1904, it was a resounding flop, the two-act format (the revised work's Acts II and III played without a break) causing particular hostility. Extreme and very vocal audience displeasure had already been expressed at the contemporary dress of the American characters, the phrases that reminded one of previous Puccini works, the bird-call effects during the orchestral interlude between the two last scenes, and the slimness of the tenor role. Puccini took the unfavorable reaction seriously and immediately restyled a three-act *Butterfly* that led to an unqualified success a few months later in Brescia. Anyone who has had the opportunity to compare both operas in performance has to admit that the gains of the second far outweigh the losses. Still, it is fascinating to have the Act I wedding reception include deft mini-portraits of Cio-Cio-San's many relatives, to encounter the full-blown caddishness of a Pinkerton unredeemed by the remorse his "new" last-act aria conveys, to hear the composer's first and, admittedly, far less satisfying thoughts about "Tu, tu piccolo Iddio," and, as some productions still strive to replicate (e.g., the Scala one reviewed below), the palpable tension of real-time expectation induced by not bringing the curtain down between the promise of Pinkerton's return and his actual, disastrous arrival.

1974 LONDON (VHS / LD)

(Film, Stereo, Color, Subtitled) 144 minutes

Mirella Freni (A), Christa Ludwig (B), Plácido Domingo (C), Michel Sénéchal (D), Robert Kerns (E), Chorus of the Vienna State Opera, Vienna Philharmonic — Herbert von Karajan

Jean-Pierre Ponnelle (director)

Jean-Pierre Ponnelle, in this 1974 studio effort, caresses and coaxes into bloom every touching moment of *morbidezza* Puccini and his librettists calculated. He cannily launches this pastel *Butterfly* with the violent and startling black and white image of Pinkerton leaping through a window, thus setting the stage for a flashback account of all that happens up to the point when this event occurs, after the death of Cio-Cio-San. Ponnelle takes full advantage of the filmic possibilities the studio approach offers, especially making many sung passages function as interior monologues. This sensitivity to what realistically might be more suitable to thought than to utterance at least partly compensates for the loss of immediacy that singers mouthing their lines seems almost always to impose. Ponnelle's camera moves freely on his purposely artificial and constrained set, establishing telling details such as newspaper headlines that provide an enriching historical context. He also effectively introduces apt, potent wish-fulfilling visions: Butterfly, now garbed in Western dress, reunited with Pinkerton, during "Un bel dì," or her entirely

241

American-style happiness with him during the long interlude at the beginning of Act III. The director's display of conceptual insight and energy in these touches gratifies, but where he goes wrong—and this kind of error seems altogether too often to have marred his best inspirations—is in Butterfly's suicide. He pays no attention to the musical cues and has Butterfly slit her throat (why this jarring change in ritual?) only at the very end, when it is intimated Pinkerton can see her making the ultimate sacrifice.

This "reinterpretation" suddenly endows Butterfly with a vengeful, even spiteful side to her nature, which does not coincide with anything we have been carefully led by Ponnelle, not to mention Puccini, to expect of her. It works especially badly for Mirella Freni, whose incandescent innocence suffuses her Cio-Cio-San. Up to this point, Ponnelle successfully exploits what has always been most winning in this soprano: a direct and honest womanliness that still commands a childlike rapport with the world. Vulnerable and touching in image and luminous sound, her Butterfly (a role she has never sung in its entirety onstage) is enormously potent in understatedly limning a heroine who is never operatically heroic but instead, except for that jarring climax, always the victim. Christa Ludwig's dignified Suzuki (a startling casting concept at any period in the recently retired mezzo's career) and Robert Kerns's confounded Sharpless fill out the intended structure, although Michel Sénéchal's Goro does push the wily Oriental cliché too insistently. Plácido Domingo, in top vocal estate, doesn't easily establish Pinkerton's duality of yearning and callowness, a failure that undercuts a full sense of Butterfly's peril. The utmost in clarity is contributed by the Vienna Philharmonic under the leadership of Herbert von Karajan who, however, does give in to his wonted late-years tendency to attenuate the musical line almost more than it can stand. The love duet loses its forward motion, lumbering from one artificial build-up to the next. It's no wonder that at its end the newlyweds appear to opt for a night of slumber rather than a night of bliss.

1983 CASTLE OPERA (VHS)

(Stage Performance, Stereo, Color, Subtitled) 150 minutes

Raina Kabaivanska (A), Eleonora Jankovic (B), Nazzareno Antinori (C), Mario Ferrara (D), Lorenzo Saccomani (E), Chorus and Orchestra of the Arena di Verona—Maurizio Arena

Verona Arena: Giulio Chazalettes (stage director), Brian Large (video director)

As so often appears the case with productions fashioned for the Arena di Verona, simply solving the logistics of the playing and audience areas' huge proportions can be a triumph in itself. Watching this 1983 *Butterfly*, one alternately admires the ingenuity of the designer (Ulisse Santicchi) and director (Giulio Chazalettes) and regrets the necessary cost in logic and intimacy. It seems clever to use the natural slope of the amphitheater as an analog for the hill associated with Butterfly's house, until one realizes that climbing *down* the hill to get to it is not quite the same as the climbing *up* the libretto calls for. Something very important in sense of relationship and mood gets lost, not to mention simply the plausibility of, for example, using a telescope to view the harbor into which Pinkerton's ship is supposed to head. (Should it be pointed up? Down? Through the thickness of earth? Should the waiting wife really be forced to desert her child for a lonely all-night vigil at the top of the path?) To avoid the confines of playing in the stipulated interior space, the performers are always out-of-doors. This almost works until Cio-Cio-San and Suzuki are meant to strip the garden of flowers to be strewn inside (they end up strewing the exterior they just denuded) and completely sabotages the last scene when Butterfly must push the world away in preparation for her suicide. All kinds of geography are topsy-turvy. Still, opera in settings such as these has a celebratory, mass participatory quality that many seem to relish. Perhaps it is unseemly to notice the unfortunate compromises.

These would possibly be less insistent if the attendant performance were in some way special or distinguished. But in this instance the spirit of solid routine rules. Raina Kabaivanska, a gifted, conscientious soprano, finds her heroine's theatrically tragic moments the most congenial. Here she can invest her voice with apposite if somewhat standard heat. She has obviously thought out many details for her characterization, but with her tall, spinsterish and overrefined bearing (imagine a vintage Geraldine Page in the role) it remains an awkward fit, the overall effect a not quite digested patchwork. Of the others in the cast, an unusually lyric Goro in Mario Ferrara commands attention and Lorenzo Saccomani as Sharpless mostly pleases, his gentlemanly manner and even baritone outweighing his inherent lack of expressiveness. The Pinkerton, Nazzareno Antinori, essentially thin and colorless of voice and a stiff actor, warms up for the implausible love duet, but the Suzuki, Eleonora Jankovic, who begins by seeming properly efficient, is eventually undermined by timbre graininess and a bothersome tremolo. Maurizio Arena consistently prods his orchestral forces, tempos always brisk and businesslike, a decision that serves the attention span of a casual summer evening crowd better than it does, among other moments, the superb scene painting Puccini calls for at the beginning of Act III.

1986 KULTUR (VHS) / PIONEER (LD)

(Stage Performance, Stereo, Color, Subtitled) 150 minutes

Yasuko Hayashi (A), Hak-Nam Kim (B), Peter Dvorsky (C), Ernesto Gavazzi (D), Giorgio Zancanaro (E), Chorus and Orchestra of Teatro alla Scala—Lorin Maazel

La Scala: Keita Asari (stage director), Derek Bailey (video director)

This 1986 Scala staging takes full advantage of the libretto's Nagasaki locale. Ichiro Takada's settings are evocatively spare, quite daring in decisions such as reducing color to tonalities of gray (followed through in the subtle costumes of Hanae Mori) and providing Butterfly's house with a stone garden rather than the expected blushing cherry tree. The stage often, as at the beginning and Butterfly's entrance, takes on the look of calligraphy or a scroll painting. This is austere beauty at its best, the kind seldom encountered in the opera house, especially of the international sort where deluxe effect reigns more generally as the highest priority.

Director Keita Asari manipulates the pictorial materials with imagination. *Kokens*, the "invisible" stagehands of Kabuki, handle props, even house walls, with cinematic fluidity. A magical transformation, for example, of the conclusion of Act II (there is no break between Acts II and III, though otherwise this is the standard revised version) instantly switches perspectives from interior to exterior. And the death of Butterfly on an unfolding band of red has gorgeous power.

All this amounts to a promising springboard to an unusual opera experience, but, alas, it does not materialize. None of the principal singers manages to establish an arresting stage presence, and the production's physical elasticity is undermined almost all the way through by performer stiffness. Particularly damaging is the uninvolved though conscientious Yasuko Hayashi as Cio-Cio-San. Her inability to seize the dramatic moment and her rather ordinary soprano lead to the possibly unkind suspicion she's at La Scala fulfilling this assignment mainly because of her nationality. And Korean mezzo Hak-Nam Kim's main virtue appears to be that she owns the vaguely correct racial heritage that evidently suffices in Milan for being cast as Suzuki. The sole real actor among the males is Ernesto Gavazzi (Goro), who manipulates his darting line with unusual accuracy and underlining bright tone. Peter Dvorsky contributes a solid but still mostly standard Pinkerton, one who manages to rise to convincing fervor only in his farewell to his "fiorito asile." The Sharpless of Giorgio Zancanaro settles plumply on dignity of a distinctly generalized sort, but Zancanaro's superbly placed, unpunched-up baritone in itself gives considerable pleasure.

For most of the opera conductor Lorin Maazel fortunately appears to be more in touch with the potential suggested by the production's visual aura than hampered by the limitations of his cast. The sound he elicits from the Scala orchestra is tensile, the pulse malleable and alive. Only in the introduction to the final act does he succumb to a self-indulgent broadness that causes a temporary loss of focus.

Choosing a studio effort over live performances offends a basic notion of what opera is all about, but the Ponnelle *Butterfly* film, in spite of its inherently overdeliberate and over-controlled genesis, is a real achievement in getting closer to this so-often seen work. The late director's probing imagination here makes for a video that merits repeated viewing, and he has a superlative cast at his command.

HARVEY E. PHILLIPS

LA FANCIULLA DEL WEST (1910)

A: Minnie (s); B: Johnson (t); C: Rance (bar); D: Wallace (bar)

The increasing popularity of Puccini's "Wild West" opera is attested to by the number of major productions in recent years and the current availability of four versions on video. Ever since the opera had its world premiere at the Met on December 10, 1910, Americans have been amused, and perhaps bemused, by the prospect of rough California goldminers drinking, fighting, and yearning for their mothers back home while singing in florid operatic Italian—"Whiskey per tutti" indeed. For some reason that doesn't seem to be such a barrier now, perhaps because the genre of shoot-'em-up movie westerns, which *Fanciulla* resembles in many respects, is itself part of the nostalgic past. In any case, what the opera has always needed are singers who understand and are equipped—vocally and temperamentally—to project the *verismo* style as exemplified by Puccini's own *Tosca*. In that respect the Met's world premiere cast must have been close to ideal: Enrico Caruso as Johnson, Emmy Destinn as Minnie, and Pasquale Amato as Rance. The conductor was Toscanini, and no less a maestro is needed to bring out the compositional beauties of a score now recognized as one of Puccini's most original and sophisticated creations.

1963 LYRIC (VHS)

(Stage Performance, Stereo, Black and White, Japanese Subtitles) 133 minutes

Antonietta Stella (a), Gastone Limarilli (B), Anselmo Colzani (C), Unknown (D), chorus and orchestra—Oliviero de Fabritiis

Opera company, stage director, and video director uncredited

This curio will have a certain historical interest for oldtimers who remember a moment back in the fifties when it seemed as though Antonietta Stella might drive a wedge between the Callas and Tebaldi feuders. She never did, but many still appreciated her all the same as a soprano who combined a bit of Callas's dramatic spirit on the one hand and Tebaldi's vocal sheen on the other. Unfortunately there was never quite enough of either asset to give Stella a truly distinctive vocal personality, and her essentially workmanlike but refreshingly idiomatic performance here may be taken as typical. She is a likable and spunkily tomboyish Minnie whose well-oiled soprano is always put to attractive uses, even if the voice continually gives the illusion of threatening to slide away from the note. If one can adjust to that chink in her technical armor, there is much to enjoy here as she fusses lovingly over the miners, wards off the sheriff, and impulsively gives her heart to Johnson.

Looking more like a balding Mafia don than a romantic cowboy outlaw, Limarilli is no more than a perfunctory Johnson, although one cannot take such vocal security for granted from an Italian tenor nowadays. Colzani is a rather faceless Rance whose bland presence would hardly make a mouse nervous, let alone send Minnie into such an hysterical tizzy during their tense poker game. The rest of the cast is uncredited, but they appear to be a practiced group of Italian *comprimarios* delighted to be in

Japan for the occasion. De Fabritiis provides solid accompaniment rather than getting to the heart of the score, and the minimal production, vaguely perceived through the dim black-and-white photography, is short on atmosphere.

1982 CASTLE OPERA (VHS) / PIONEER (LD)

(Stage Performance, Stereo, Color, Not Subtitled) 140 minutes

Carol Neblett (A), Plácido Domingo (B), Silvano Carroli (B), Gwynne Howell (C), Chorus and Orchestra of the Royal Opera House—Nello Santi

Royal Opera, Covent Garden: Piero Faggioni (stage director), John Vernon (video director)

If anyone doubts the international character of Puccini's *Girl*, this Anglo-Italian production should put the matter to rest. Perhaps simply being aware of it creates the impression, but this lively collection of sharp-featured, bewhiskered British faces in the Polka Saloon gives the opera a positively Dickensian flavor, one that is not at all inappropriate. Each miner is effectively individualized by Faggioni's eye for detail, and everyone in this male-bonding society seems to have a life of his own, right down to Francis Egerton's suggestively fey bartender. Without indulging in any fancy gimmicks, Faggioni accepts the opera at face value, as an old-fashioned but craftily made melodrama, while letting its subtext—alienation and redemption on both a personal and a more abstract social level—take care of itself. Ken Adam's friendly sets underscore the realistic tone with their look of absolute authenticity, even when the camera brings us right into the middle of the men's barroom squabbles or, along with Johnson, into Minnie's feminine but comfortably lived-in cabin in the mountains. The last act is especially effective, set on the edge of the sequoia forest near a grist mill with a huge water wheel, which later serves as the scaffold from which Johnson escapes hanging in the knick of time. Faggioni designed the costumes as well, and his fine hand is also noticeable here. The delightfully ornate "grande-dame" dress that Minnie

dons when Johnson comes to call in Act II is a particularly inspired touch, as are the sartorial symbols of Rance's power and superiority: an elaborate white fur coat topped off by a stovepipe hat that the sheriff sports as he struts about the miners' camp.

The atmosphere onstage is genuine storybook new world, but the only unmistakable "American" touch in the casting is the freshscrubbed, blonde persona of Minnie herself—Neblett, in fact, bears more than a passing resemblance to Jeanette MacDonald, the Hollywood diva who appeared in a 1938 film version of the old David Belasco play on which the opera is based. Neblett models the part to perfection, and she certainly works hard to bring the girl to life even if her acting is seldom very specific or imaginative. A more serious flaw is the rather blowsy nature of her puffed-up lyric soprano, which lacks color, flexibility, and expressive range. In the first of his three filmed Johnsons, Domingo has never looked younger, thinner, or more romantically dashing, and his singing is a dream as well—ardent, firm, and shapely. The most vivid dramatic presence on screen, though, is Carroli's Jack Rance, a baddie through and through whose bitter, selfish, even brutal character seems all the more frightening in a man who looks so dangerously attractive. If only his singing—blunt, loud, and mushy—were half as effective. Santi's slam-bang treatment of the score is also anything but subtle, but at least the high-quality orchestral playing does full justice to the score's innumerable instrumental beauties.

1991 HOME VISION (VHS / LD)

(Stage Performance, Stereo, Color, Subtitled) 145 minutes

Mara Zampieri (A), Plácido Domingo (B), Juan Pons (C), Marco Chingari (D), Chorus and Orchestra of Teatro alla Scala, Milan—Lorin Maazel

La Scala: Jonathan Miller (stage director), John Michael Phillips (video director)

At first, this production indicates that we are in for a *Fanciulla* with a heavy "concept." The curtain rises on a lofty, box-shaped three-story interior framed by paned-glass windows and iron bars that gives just a bare suggestion of a saloon—to judge from all the detritus that litters the place, the Polka also serves as the miners' industrial workshop, dormitory, and public meeting house, a bleak milieu from which there is no escape. Stefanos Lazaridis's monochrome decor does not even lighten up for Minnie's cabin, a cheerless space devoid of creature comforts, while the finale, like the Covent Garden setting described above, takes place in a grim sort of Sutter's Mill, a gray gold-rush site covered with dirt and slime. Despite the depressing decor, Miller's direction is lively and conventional enough, missing few major points and adding little extraneous invention that might contradict the music. Even so, this is a very chilly *Fanciulla*, one more concerned with rigorously reproducing a severe topical environment rather than examining how the characters might have been shaped by it. In the end we are not moved.

The cast compliments the production's overall dour tone. Nine years have passed since we last saw this Dick Johnson, and time has not been especially kind—Domingo is now an aging bandit who has seen it all and done it all, paunchier, more seedy-looking, less of a gentleman, and just as eager as Rance to get his hands on Minnie. Luckily his voice is, if anything, more ringing and dependable. Pons is a sturdy Rance, but he does little to make the part interesting or provocative. The most controversial performance comes from Zampieri, whose odd vocal texture has those spicy qualities that apparently only an Italian can love. Once the ear adjusts to its hollow timbre and cutting edge, though, her soprano actually takes on a haunting beauty of its own, a voice that commands a wide range of colors, prizes expressive declamation, and has a welcome ability to tune notes impeccably. This Minnie is obviously no ingenue, but Zampieri's wonderfully mobile, Giulietta Masina–like face is always quick to register the right emotion—it is impossible not to root for such a sympathetic heroine, particularly one who finds herself so sorely beset by the men in her life. Luckily all three principals

have loud, lusty voices, since Maazel gives them no quarter. The conductor presides over a full-blooded symphonic reading of the score, a bit overblown perhaps but one very aware of how up-to-date Puccini was in matters of harmonic and instrumental coloring.

1992 DEUTSCHE GRAMMOPHON (VHS / LD)

(Stage Performance, Stereo, Color, Subtitled)
140 minutes

Barbara Daniels (A), Plácido Domingo (B), Sherrill Milnes (C), Yanni Yannissis (D), Metropolitan Opera Chorus and Orchestra—Leonard Slatkin

Metropolitan Opera: Giancarlo del Monaco (stage director), Brian Large (video director)

Puccini's *Girl* returned home to the Metropolitan Opera with this new edition mounted in 1992. Like so many Met productions in the age of video, this one was surely designed with a film version in mind from the very first. As effectively as it played in the house, everything looks just that much more theatrical, immediate, and fluid when viewed onscreen—obviously video director Large has also learned a great deal about his craft since filming the opera a decade earlier. In Europe, del Monaco and his frequent partner, set-designer Michael Scott, are known for their radical updatings and reinterpretations of the standard repertory, but at the Met they play it safe—of the four *Fanciullas* presently available on video, this is by far the most painstakingly representational, even more so than Faggioni's for Covent Garden. Minnie rinsing glasses in a tub of water as she spars with Rance, sacks of gold stored under the bar, horses hitched outside the swinging doors to the Polka, polished spitoons—the on-location flavor here is complete and thoughtfully applied (although it's doubtful that a photograph of Abraham Lincoln would appear on any barroom wall in 1849). The huge expanses of the Met stage are used to good advantage in Act II by showing us both the interior and exterior of Minnie's cabin as well as a panoramic view of the snow-covered landscape. Only the drab ghost-town setting for Act III is miscalculated, an inappropriate alternative to the forest clearing at dawn specified by Puccini and described so poetically by his music.

That del Monaco must have worked at some length with the cast shows in Domingo's latest Johnson, a far more nuanced performance than the one he gave a year earlier at La Scala and without any loss of vocal quality. One can read the conflict on his face during the long duet with Minnie that ends Act I, truly believe in his gentleness with her when love finally blooms later on, and admire his genuine respect at the girl's earnest attempts to improve her mind. Rance's character is also softened, and Milnes makes a most convincing quasi-villain despite a voice that now sounds rather worn. He even gets the last word here after Johnson and Minnie ride off into the sunset, leaning down to pick up a six-shooter and leaving the impression that he will put a bullet in his head after the curtain falls. As the center of attention, Daniels gives the most three-dimensional performance of all, embodying all of Minnie's physical charm, tomboyish vulnerability, and unswervable devotion to her own carefully worked out and unassailable code of values. Of all the video Minnies she most completely captures the wonderful appeal of the character. Unfortunately her voice, only a utilitarian soprano at best, sounds unpleasantly stringy and pressured much of the time, especially when attempting to soar up to a grand Puccinian climax. Slatkin gives an affectionate account of the score, and the Met Orchestra is predictably superb.

Despite the heroine's vocal deficiencies, the Met's *Fanciulla* is clearly the one to have. An honest and imaginative statement of an elusive work, the performance is also an absorbing example of operatic filmmaking at its very best.

PETER G. DAVIS

IL TRITTICO (1918):
IL TABARRO

A: Giorgetta (s); B: Luigi (t); C: Michele (bar)

SUOR ANGELICA

A: Suor Angelica (s); B: La Zia Principessa (c)

GIANNI SCHICCHI

A: Lauretta (s); B: Rinuccio (t); C: Gianni Schicchi (bar)

"*L*o spettacolo é troppo lungo!" admitted Puccini some three years after the Metropolitan premiere of *Il Trittico.* He was at last coming to terms with the reality that in spite of his original creative intentions the three one-acters were beginning to show a tendency to detach and head for independent performance. At first, *Suor Angelica* found itself frequently dropped for a presumably more digestible diptych. Then *Il Tabarro* became a relative rarity as *Gianni Schicchi* forged new alliances and served as ballast for short but weighty music dramas not even remotely related to Puccini. *Schicchi* in one way or another is still the most frequently performed of the set (it's a favorite of workshops, schools, and semi-professional companies searching for operas with larger casts and a fairly even distribution of roles), but today, at least in the major opera houses, *Il Trittico* has pretty much glued itself together again. This allows audiences to experience properly the careful balance of Grand-Guignolesque realism

(*Il Tabarro*), sentimental tragedy (*Suor Angelica*), and *buffa* high jinks (*Gianni Schicchi*) the composer envisioned. If the Dante-inspired last panel still wins out because it contains some of Puccini's freshest and most mischievously inventive pages—an unexpected achievement in laughter that rates comparison with Verdi's equally unexpected *Falstaff*—it is all the richer for being experienced in context.

1983 HOME VISION (VHS) / PIONEER (LD)

(Stage Performance, Stereo, Color, Subtitled)
150 minutes

Il Tabarro: Sylvia Sass (A), Nicola Martinucci (B), Piero Cappuccilli (C)
Suor Angelica: Rosalind Plowright (A), Dunja Vejzovich (B)
Gianni Schicchi: Cecilia Gasdia (A), Yuri Marusin (B), Juan Pons (C), Chorus and Orchestra of Teatro alla Scala—Gianandrea Gavazzeni

La Scala: Sylvano Bussotti (stage director), Brian Large (video director)

There have probably been more successful assays of Puccini's triple bill: more convincing limnings of emptiness and searing jealousy than in this *Il Tabarro*, greater heights of desperation and hysteria than are reached in this *Suor Angelica*, finer honings of comedy than are attained in this *Gianni Schicchi*. Still, the Scala *Trittico* from 1983 is an honorable traversal, an evening of high-grade if not inspired professionalism. Under the reliable although sometimes somewhat lethargic musical leadership of veteran Gianandrea Gavazzeni, there are no missteps. The same could be said for the staging of Sylvano Bussotti (he is also responsible for *Schicchi*'s sets and costumes) and for all the performers. But even with such standout elements as Piero Cappuccilli's controlled portrayal of self-destructive hatred in *Tabarro*, Rosalind Plowright's incisive reading of Angelica, Juan Pons's and Cecilia Gasdia's nuanced vocalism as Schicchi father and daughter, in the end an impression of routine nevertheless manages to triumph: capable forces brought together and presented with few real challenges to their preconceived notions as to what these three small operas should be about.

Il Tabarro benefits from a nicely clarifying set that places the action precisely in the Seine at the rear of Notre Dame. Cappuccilli, no longer the owner of an opulent baritone, nevertheless resourcefully handles key points that establish the character of Michele, the unhappy bargemaster. As his simultaneously sexually restless and remorseful wife, Sylvia Sass vocalizes well enough (the top tends toward squalliness), but she overacts in an inappropriate grande-dame manner, telegraphing her every impulse with a permanently arched eyebrow and sweeping gestures. While Cappuccilli's explosion of "Squalandrina!" when he fully realizes Giorgetta's faithlessness is delivered with a bitterness choked by resignation, Sass's enunciation of the depth of her discontent, "Come difficile essere felice," is overwrought and fussy and quite unconvincing. Tenor Nicola

Martinucci, Giorgetta's young love interest Luigi, is well cast, a plausibly handsome yet grubby presence, and his strong tenor grabs at all the right opportunities. His final struggle with Michele and the strangling that ensues are damagingly awkward. The supporting cast is variable.

In fact, smaller roles for all three operas display a surprising lightness in La Scala's *comprimario* ranks. Most of the nuns in *Suor Angelica* would not make it past a cattle call for *The Sound of Music*. But British visitor Plowright reveals superb vocal qualifications for the tragic heroine of the second work in the series, her impassioned soprano of gratifying evenness throughout the role's demanding tessitura, allowing for an ardent voicing of unending yearning. Ultimately, though, her performance is not sufficiently free to suggest the hysteria and catharsis that fire the opera's final moments. Possibly a more imaginative director could have helped her in this direction. Dunja Vejzovich is appropriately baleful as the Zia Principessa, but her spread tones and tight diction get in the way.

The appealing geometrics and subtle lighting of the convent give way to the blocky fortresslike interior of the Donati household in Florence. There's no comedy in the look of this dwelling and precious little in what goes on inside it beyond a basic manipulating of the farcical situation that *Il Trittico*'s marvelous final episode presents. Everyone appears to have been given a few clues as to who his or her character is and then left alone. The clockwork precision necessary to reveal *Schicchi*'s full conceptual brilliance is nowhere in sight. Juan Pons in the title role shows only rudimentary physical aptitude for the genre at hand, but his big baritone finds many opportunities to show off a humorous command of color and agility. As Lauretta, Cecilia Gasdia supplies vocal radiance and sweetness. Her swain Rinuccio is in the unlikely hands of Russian tenor Yuri Marusin, breathy, piercing, and slippery in perhaps not the best Slavic tradition.

The verdict is about half and half on this one: solid Scala competence on the one hand and uninspired Scala competence on the other. The best of the leading singers cannot, try as they might, bring this evening off all by themselves. As the only *Trittico* on video (where is the Met broadcast with Renata Scotto as all three heroines?), it will have to do for the moment.

HARVEY E. PHILLIPS

GIACOMO PUCCINI

TURANDOT (1926)

A: Turandot (s); B: Liù (s); C: Calaf (t); D: Timur (bs)

These days it's hard to remember a time without *Turandot*. But before the arrival of Birgit Nilsson on the scene, performances, especially at the Metropolitan, were infrequent. Indeed, the opera languished there between its American premiere (following La Scala's lead by only six months)—although it did remain in the repertory for a handful of seasons thereafter—and its triumphant and apparently permanent return with the Swedish force of nature in 1961. Today, with or without a soprano who can emulate Nilsson, it enjoys a popularity on a par with Puccini's big three: *La Bohème*, *Tosca*, and *Madama Butterfly*. What seems to have won out finally is not only acceptance of the theatrically necessary finale Franco Alfano tagged on after the composer's death—Toscanini, the musical taste arbiter of the epoch, setting down his baton in Milan at the end of the score Puccini actually completed could hardly have helped matters in this respect—but also a slowly dawning awareness of the probing musical vocabulary Puccini chose to employ. Whether or not it was the opera's exotic subject and setting, he was impelled to flirt with a departure in technique and color (the effects of bitonality, for example) that are both new and immediately, viscerally riveting. Accused so often during his career of lingering self-indulgently in a comfortable idiom, Puccini in his last stage effort pointed in directions that truly fire the what-might-have-been imagination.

1958 STANDING ROOM ONLY (VHS)

(Studio Performance, Mono, Black and White, Not Subtitled) 122 minutes

Lucille Udovick (A), Renata Mattioli (B), Franco Corelli (C), Plinio Clabassi (D), Chorus and Orchestra of RAI Milan—Fernando Previtali

Mario Lanfranchi (director)

Perhaps the most curious and arcane of the many *Turandot*s on video is this studio-origin RAI broadcast from 1958. Evidently it was reshown in Italy in more recent years, and what has been issued for home consumption is copied from an off-the-air taping made at this time of rebroadcast, the performance being followed by a late eighties or early nineties news program. The many generations of reproduction involved make these two hours more than a little daunting to watch: blurry, smeary black and white images of figures that often seem to have no faces. Voices are disembodied presences, additionally divorced from the drama by postdubbing. The antithesis of a production in the yawning Verona Arena, the studio's confined space is decidedly claustrophobic. The chorus, for example, is never seen, its actions entrusted to a handful of dancer-mimes. Such compromises and constraints abound, all adding to the impression that to do *Turandot* under such conditions makes as much sense as an ocarina recital in Radio City Music Hall.

Internal technical difficulties (Turandot arrives for her first interview with Calaf via an extraordinarily jerky elevator; the clearly under-rehearsed principals sometimes seem to give each other movement cues) are not enhanced by problems like frequent sound and picture dropouts. But in spite of everything, this is a more than passable musical performance, one whose focus and obvious raison d'être is the Calaf of Franco Corelli, then at the peak of his powers and popularity. As a Corelli memento, it has been made certain that only *his* face is seen in close-up, even when his colleagues take the vocal spotlight. Yet the penetrating impact of the heroic tenor's clarion timbre is everything one recalls and really not that severely compromised by the tape's limited sonics.

American Lucille Udovick's Princess has the requisite metal for her heroine and a considerable array of soprano colors at her disposal. It's a lighter sound than one is accustomed to in the role, and while she easily maintains a forceful line, there's some pulling back on the climactic top notes. But no matter what Udovick does, attention is always brought back to Signor Corelli. It is such a star turn for him that one half expects the concert ending after "Nessun dorma" so that fans everywhere and forever may avail themselves of an opportunity to erupt in applause.

Among the supporting cast, Plinio Clabassi, with his pointed, pungent bass, stands out as Timur. Renata Mattioli's Liù is capable, sometimes quite appealing, but her soprano seems badly recorded here, its potential for shrillness magnified. The Ping, Pang, and Pong are well above standard, their Act II scene admirably precise, and, just as their counterparts do in the Nilsson studio runthrough, they win the award for best lip-synching. The orchestra, under the mostly assured direction of Fernando Previtali, exhibits sporadic raggedness in its horn and trumpet ranks. Be warned: neither the opera nor the news broadcast carries English subtitles.

1969 LEGATO CLASSICS (VHS)

(Studio Performance, Mono, Black and White, Not Subtitled) 123 minutes

Birgit Nilsson (A), Gabriella Tucci (B), Gianfranco Cecchele (C), Boris Carmeli (D), Chorus and Orchestra of RAI Turin—Georges Prêtre

Margherita Wallmann (director)

Courtesy of Radio Italiana there reaches us a more than twenty-five-year-old souvenir of Birgit Nilsson in one of her greatest roles. It is indeed just a souvenir, a grainy black-and-white postdubbed studio concoction that for the most part provides only a suggestion of what experiencing Nilsson in the theater was like. Nilsson, under these circumstances, in close-up, does not make for a better Nilsson since she was never a particularly inventive actress and her wide immobile features were capable of limited expressiveness. The RAI cameraman seems to have come to the same conclusion and does not dwell on her equitably, which in its own way is frustrating, for, after all, one will presumably be watching this video mostly for her sake. Still, the steely, bang-on attacks are there, the amazing security throughout the role's tessitura, the blazing, fearless, in-tune high notes, the ability to ride the ensemble and add unquestionable luster to it. As for characterization, Nilsson's Princess, whether by design or fortuitous accident, remains an enigma, possibly as dangerous to Calaf's future at the end of the opera as she is at the beginning. What a contrast to Marton's so contemporary seeding of motivational clues in the video made of her San Francisco performance.

The sound recording, to which the performers lip-synch with variable proficiency (Ping, Pang, and Pong are best), is outstanding in performance quality, except that the various takes are jarringly stitched together, creating peculiar alterations in miking ambience. (This particular annoyance is compounded by the failure to add any apposite live-action noises, something that might take off at least the outermost layer of the postdubbing curse.) Besides Nilsson, conductor Georges Prêtre can be praised for stirring up considerable excitement in all the right places, even if, on occasion, possibly to create contrast, he allows the energy of the Turin ensemble to sag. Gabriella Tucci makes an appealing, very special Liù that will probably be best appreciated by those who can recall first hand this artist's singular, oddly porous, haunting lyric sound. Gianfranco Cecchele offers a straightforward, controlled, easy Calaf that these days could probably stop the show. The three P's are excellent, but bass Boris Carmeli seems a tired Timur.

The Margherita Wallmann production looks, in studio terms, opulent and detailed, although it is often difficult to define those details, such as the intended specific location of certain scenes or the spatial relationships between characters. The chorus, heard but not seen, has its collective voice mouthed to inadvertently amusing effect by photogenic but very befuddled extras. They move in predictable patterns—splitting ranks at the arrival of the advancing dollied camera is a favorite conceit—just as the massed ensemble did in the Corelli studio *Turandot* made ten years earlier. (Watching these two videos back-to-back bizarrely reconstructs those legendary Met evenings of thirty-five years ago.) There are no English subtitles, but there is some pre-echo.

1983 MGM / UA (VHS)

(Stage Performance, Stereo, Color, Subtitled) 124 minutes

Eva Marton (A), José Carreras (B), Katia Ricciarelli (C) John-Paul Bogart (D), The Vienna State Opera Chorus and Orchestra—Lorin Maazel

Vienna State Opera: Harold Prince (stage director), Rodney Greenberg (video director)

This is certainly one of the stranger-looking *Turandot*s to be encountered anywhere. The production (scenery by Timothy O'Brien, costumes by Tazeena Firth) has a kind of space-age rather than legendary timelessness about it, an unspecifiable air-terminal-like setting in which at stage level the groundlings of Peking, their faces covered and their bodies layered in mirrored-mosaic fantasy clothes, splutter about in clumps like nightmare travelers marooned by cancelled flights. Rising above them is a construction consisting of a narrow airplane ramp

and lateral access gangways to be trod on by the people of the court, the whole forming the outline of a skull, presumably referring to what all would-be riddle solvers risk at the hands of the heartless *principessa*. The overall effect is at once glittery, busy, and untheatrical in its failure to provide spatial definitions that enhance either the details or the curve of the musical and dramatic structure. The only truly effective conceit is the three individual platforms on which Ping, Pang, and Pong are rolled about during their collective and individual reveries at the beginning of Act II. But even this emerges as more of a random "good idea" than something integral to a meaningful, workable concept. Furthermore, director Harold Prince seems patently ill at ease in the handling of his principals, at once denying them effective stage geometry and burdening them with awkward, hard-to-decifer tasks such as the constant donning and taking off of masks. Actions like these, though, may come across here as more meaningless than was actually the case in the theater because of a lack of video punctuation, the camera work being consistently unstylish and casual.

But the many virtues of this 1983 performance should not be overlooked. Certainly this is one of the strongest *Turandot* casts available on video: Eva Marton in steady and pliable voice, endowing steeliness with exactly the phosphorescent colors she wants to hurl out; José Carreras impassioned and, except for slight discomfort at the top, in prime estate; Katia Ricciarelli coming into her own for a beautifully gauged and moving "Tu che di gel sei cinta"; John-Paul Bogart a more than reliable Timur. Among the three P's one notes leading baritone Robert Kerns and incomparable character tenor Heinz Zednik. And giving Altoum to veteran leading tenor Waldemar Kmentt and the Mandarin to current leading base Kurt Rydl adds valuable depth to this altogether very satisfying line-up. Definitely not to be overlooked is what Lorin Maazel accomplishes with the forces of the Vienna Philharmonic, here everywhere enjoying a field day of virtuosity, the brass salvos of the Alfano final duet being a particular ear-opener. Maazel avails himself of all opportunities to batten onto interesting, usually neglected orchestral details, especially contrapuntal lines that add an unexpected relief to the overall texture of sound. It's a pity, though, that one of the definite deficits of this release is its erratic, clouded audio quality, an undermining that in a way parallels what the uncongenial staging does to the stellar cast.

1983 CASTLE OPERA (VHS) / PIONEER (LD)

(Stage Performance, Stereo, Color, Subtitled) 116 minutes

Ghena Dimitrova (A), Cecilia Gasdia (B), Nicola Martinucci (C), Ivo Vinco (D), Chorus and Orchestra of the Arena di Verona—Maurizio Arena

Verona Arena : Giuliano Montaldo (stage director), Brian Large (video director)

In the vastness of the Verona arena, a spectacular space that's inhospitable to all but the grandest of grand opera treatments, *Turandot* is a natural, or at least it has a better than fair chance of survival. This it does in a 1983 performance that, *force majeure*, relies on moving the action from one section of the playing area to another rather than on any alteration of scenery. The looming imperial palace against a massive cyclorama always dominates the action. The solution could perhaps have worked better with more precise and more subtle lighting than appears to have been available. And the open, wall-less lack of framing of each scene also results in a certain sameness in the singers' deportment and declamation, an identical tonal posture, for example, whether the multitudes or merely one other person is being addressed. But then, Puccini's score has been known to encourage hectoring, and the big voices of Ghena Dimitrova and Nicola Martinucci as riddle poser and solver and eventual stentorian lovers don't especially seem to pine for missed opportunities for nuance.

The most visually intriguing aspect of this production by Giuliano Montaldo, with stage design by Luciano Rucceri and costumes by Nana Cecchi, is the untraditional look for Turandot herself: flowing tresses uncrowned by a ramose headdress and similarly unfettered white robes of great simplicity, both emblematic of the Princess's remove from humanity and her fixation on chastity. Soprano Dimitrova—deprived of any kind of striking entrance (she just walks into view and stands next to the Emperor), as well as the traditional super-long fingernails—doesn't necessarily derive any interpretive advantage from her costume cues. Yet she belts out a solid "In questa reggia" marred only occasionally by slippery pitch, attacks, and releases. In the aggregate hers is a curious performance. It sounds exciting but looks entirely mechanical. The questions are fiercely hurled, but the eyes are on automatic pilot. And the singer simply shuts down when the vocal ball is not bouncing her way. Turandot, an essentially one-dimensional character, in the hands of this specialist in powerhouse delivery is re-one-dimensionalized.

Tenor Martinucci makes an appealing Calaf, and he even manages not to oversing his first scene. A good deal of inelastic muscle work takes over by the time "Nessun dorma" approaches, however. But it's an assured reading, the tenor's tone consistently full if not particularly warm. Oddly, he seems as anguished *after* his conquest of Turandot (a fast-forward through the Alfano ending punctuated by a truly mirth-inducing embrace) as during all the drama leading up to it.

What most ennobles that drama and, indeed, the entire evening is the delicate, credible Liù of Cecilia Gasdia. With gorgeous phrasing and dynamic finesse she contributes both an exquisite "Signor, ascolta" and a moving suicide. She also maintains everywhere a spontaneity of sound and gesture unavailable to her colleagues. There are occasional sags in pitch, and the voice, not surprisingly, gets lost in the ensembles. The Timur of Ivo Vinco is disappointingly windy, but Gianfranco Manganotti makes an unusually punchy Emperor Altoum. Conductor Maurizio Arena shows that more than just his name qualifies him for the Verona job, and his orchestra's often soft-grained lushness effectively complements the score's many lush pages. Coordination between all the forces under his command is reasonable rather than pinpoint, but the latter in this venue must be virtually impossible. Tape sound, too, is reasonable, but somewhat frayed at climaxes.

1988 DEUTSCHE GRAMMOPHON (VHS / LD)

(Stage Performance, Stereo, Color, Subtitled)
134 minutes

Eva Marton (A), Leona Mitchell (B), Plácido Domingo (C), Paul Plishka, Metropolitan Opera Chorus and Orchestra—James Levine

Metropolitan Opera: Franco Zeffirelli (stage director), Kirk Browning (video director)

Harsh words from the minority have been aimed at the Met's current expensive production of *Turandot*, many of them presumably based on experiences in the house with this box-office blockbuster. This is opera for today's lazy, quasi-comatose after-dinner audience, snipe the naysayers, opera that's too busy, too gaudy, too *Phantom of the Opera*, too *Sunset Boulevard*, the visual quantity overwhelming and flattening musical values. Indeed, some of those who manage to admit to having a good time in the theater insist they do so by surrendering to baser instincts, a kind of when-in-Rome decision permitting them to slump back and allow a wave of calculated broad sensations to engulf them.

When the opera was first telecast, what immediately impressed was the stupendous editing job Kirk Browning's camera did on Franco Zeffirelli's handiwork. What was richness and spectacle for some or tasteless bombast for others was sifted through a visual sensibility that knew when to linger on broad proscenium vistas, when to zero in on the telling detail, how to highlight a climax, underline an emotion. What seemed at first sheer profusion became, in the broadcast, meaningful and, often, sharply apropos. The conclusion that this *Turandot* actually needed the broadcast filter to make its full mark was by no means totally illogical.

Especially with the digital sound and visual clarity available from the laser disc release of that broadcast, the home audience comes close to the total operatic package originally intended and even has it enhanced by reproduction. In fact, the brilliant sound quality, the subtlety of lighting effects, and the clarity of every camera angle forcefully argue that unless one has the best seat at the Met and knows where to look at every moment, the movie, this time at least, is indeed better than the play. And with unsuppressed ambient stage noises and the palpable presence of an audience, it very much manages to comes across as a live event.

Something else happens, too, while succumbing to this video disc's sophistication: the realization that the technology involved here perfectly complements the whizz-bang glitz of the production, technology of today in synch with contemporary tastes in entertainment style. And operatic performance style follows suit: a crack, brilliant orchestra blindingly energized by a conductor's unstinting drive, hand in glove with a soprano totally at ease—in possibly her most congenial role—with hurling shards of vocal metal, and a power tenor as adept at conquering audiences as at solving riddles. It's all of a piece: vehicle, performers, the aesthetic applied, the machinery that makes it all happen—in other words, a very rewarding marriage of cooperating elements.

If by Act III certain reservations begin to tug at the viewer's sleeve, it's because the performing coalition cannot always conceal certain undermining weaknesses. For example, Leona Mitchell's moving Liù is a nagging reminder that *Turandot* is about more than a giant assault on the senses. One begins to miss a guiding directorial hand that would somehow show a particular vision regarding these characters and these events, something other than recourse to the most obvious effects and gestures, no matter how cleverly presented. When, for example, an attempt is made to weaken Calaf's resolve using the standard gyrations of the ladies of the corps de ballet, one realizes that no particular point of view other than a belief in what registers immediately has been called upon. But even with this kind of reservation occasionally bobbing up, it can't be denied that this video *Turandot* allows for an altogether stunning opportunity to participate in a big Met event and, ultimately, a Puccini one as well.

1994 KULTUR (VHS) / PIONEER (LD)

(Stage Performance, Stereo, Color, Subtitled) 123 minutes

Eva Marton (A), Michael Sylvester (B), Lucia Mazzaria (C), Kevin Langan (D), San Francisco Chorus and Orchestra—Donald Runnicles

San Francisco Opera: Peter McClintock (stage director), Brian Large (video director)

If one is experiencing via video disc this 1994 San Francisco production of Puccini's coming-up-hot-on-the-rail front-runner, the initial hurdles come courtesy of Pioneer's production priorities. While this company can't quite see its way to supplying a cast list or a performance date for its package, it starts off things rousingly enough once the laser gets going with a blast of self-aggrandizing logo noise that should send all non-heavy-metal fans straight to the volume control. Luckily, Pioneer has David Hockney to palliate brewing annoyance. And the artist–set designer does more than that. He enchants. His conception accomplishes something rare in the *Turandot* tradition of major opera houses. He makes the work into a true fairy tale and is willing to do so even at the expense of grandeur. Instead of monumental staircases and endless overdressed panoply, he offers color and light, occasionally in primary stark contrast (the bewitching switch from a pervasive orange to a blue suffusion at the rising of the moon in Act I), at other times mystically juxtaposed (the progressions of cut-outs and scrims at the beginning of Act III). Hockney's gentler, more engaging, less presentational mode has an individualistic validity and vitality that are truly refreshing, and it invites involving speculation as to the dimensions of just what the opera is about, even and up to its metaphorical implications. This is no mean accomplishment with a stage piece that seems to be heading for slotting as mere slam-bang entertainment.

If the Ian Falconer costumes seamlessly reassert the decorative impulses, and Donald Runnicles's sensible, clean, deliberately unshowy support in the pit seem very much in synch, stage director Peter McClintock doesn't entirely fill out the visual possibilities with which Hockney has presented him. His major accomplishment seems to be devising a most workable character motivation that today's ubiquitous Turandot, Eva Marton, effectively exploits—to whit, that from her very first sighting of Calaf her resolve is shaken by unidentifiable, disturbing emotions. Throughout, her will to vanquish the nameless intruder fights her wish to submit to his domination. It's the key concept around which all else should center. But the other singers don't appear fired by any ideas about how they might fit into the scheme of things, nor really does Marton find anything else to enrich this strong structural clue. Faces tend toward inexpressiveness, movement and specific stage business to awkwardness, most notably the last-act seizing and torture of Liù. On the plus side, there is little clutter, and the outlines of the plot are never obscured, although those outlines are insufficiently filled in to endow transitional moments with much life. If the stage director has provided them, they aren't captured by Brian Large's otherwise alert camera.

Soprano Marton, in full if somewhat more quavery voice than in the recorded Met video broadcast performance, lands this side of abrasiveness in the big riddle scene but leaps to the other side in the final duet. The Calaf, Michael Sylvester, perhaps physically not the most persuasive suitor, possesses commendable if not thrilling resonance. In the relatively fool-proof role of Liù, Lucia Mazzaria comes through beautifully, the reading committed, her warm, generous timbre in all registers capped by pungent and centered high notes. Kevin Langan's Timur sounds more tired than the old king need be.

———

San Francisco has Hockney, Verona has Gasdia, but the Met production's video, whatever one's level of resistance to Zeffirellian overstatement, has the edge: the better Marton, Domingo a Calaf not to be questioned, Levine in the pit, an expert supporting cast, and, most crucial for the home viewer, video director Kirk Browning's eye to pull together all the visual richness.

HARVEY E. PHILLIPS

MAURICE RAVEL

L'HEURE ESPAGNOLE (1911)

A: Concepción (s); B: Torquemada (t); C: Gonzalve (t); D: Ramiro
(bar); E: Don Inigo Gomez (bs)

*S*pain and mechanical objects, especially clocks, were both life-long obsessions of Maurice Ravel. In *L'Heure Espagnole* he managed to combine both: a comic opera whose central character is indeed a huge clock, the locus a clockmaker's shop, and most of the characters mechanically set on their course except for Concepción, the clockmaker's wife, and Ramiro, the burly muleteer. Into a delicate world of ticking and chiming Concepción and Ramiro bring an earthiness of sexual desire warmed by the Spanish sun under which this *buffa* burlesque unreels. Precision and its undoing are both at work in the play by Franc-Nohain, which Ravel set practically word for word, and in the score, which contrasts the most delicate and calculated orchestral effects with the throbbing insistence of life's rhythms, only fully liberated in the final pages of concerted singing.

Ravel's first opera (it is often paired in performance today with his later masterpiece, *L'Enfant et les Sortilèges*) was completed quickly in 1907. Because of reservations on the part of Albert Carré, the director of the Opéra Comique, about the racy text and the composer's eager vivifying of its implications, it had to wait four years for a first performance.

1987 HOME VISION (VHS) / PIONEER (LD)

(Stage Performance, Stereo, Color, Subtitled) 50 minutes

Anna Steiger (A), Remy Corazza (B), Thierry Dran (C), François Le Roux (D), François Loup (E), London Philharmonic Orchestra—Sian Edwards

Glyndebourne Festival Opera: Frank Corsaro (stage director), Dave Heather (video director)

If, unlike director Carré, an elaborate, sustained dirty joke is your thing, Maurice Ravel definitely wrote an opera for you. However, even the best dirty jokes can go astray, which is what happens in *L'Heure Espagnole* when innate Gallic wit and quirky preoccupations with both the foibles of comic characters and the mechanical elements that control them (in this case a bulky, pot-bellied clock) get in the way. In short—and oxymoronically—Ravel's masterpiece is elegant smut of the highest order and it can only offend those who want to think the worst of its enchanting heroine Concepción, a willing philandering wife pursued by a ridiculous poet and a pompous banker. She eventually chooses neither, because the muscular Ramiro eventually emerges as the best candidate for her attentions. (In the best tradition of classical farce, he ably hoists the clock that takes turns concealing—for reasons too complicated to go into under the circumstances of a brief review—the two would-be swains. Concepción does not hold back from awarding him the palm, nor, she makes it clear, does she intend to limit re-awarding it in the future.

This Glyndebourne production captured for video dates from 1987, and visitors to the New

York City Opera, which also mounted the deft Frank Corsaro–Maurice Sendak soufflé, will recognize an old friend. With cartoonish wit, designer Sendak supplies all the visual ingredients necessary to set a clear point of view, a neat framework of primary-hued exaggeration which director Corsaro brings to life. The latter exhibits many admirable ideas, notably wedding his human puppets to a mechanistic universe by introducing them as clockwork figures. His customary trope of inventing mute characters adds to the fun, and the conceit of Concepción's supposedly deceived husband Torquemada (an appropriately tremulous Remy Corazza) being the master puppeteer behind the plot, while perhaps lacking in logic, stimulates some valuable wry hypothesizing. Some of the performers rise superbly to the frequent physical challenges this kind of comedy demands, especially Thierry Dran as the loopy, vainglorious poet Gonzalve and François Loup as the banker Don Iñigo Gomez, who has to spend most of his time onstage stuck in the bowels of that clock.

Would that the others met this standard. Soprano Anna Steiger lacks the seductive charm for Concepción and has an essentially colorless voice to boot. Ramiro, baritone François Le Roux, succeeds with his limpid, easy vocal delivery, less with his requisite macho aura. Overall ensemble acting, too, in spite of uniformly exemplary French enunciation, is disparate in style, being neither especially subtle nor convincingly broad. Ensemble singing, on the other hand, most impressive in the final quintet, is superbly balanced. This is to the credit of conductor Sian Edwards, who revels in the intricate pointillism of this score but perhaps less in its underlying carnal robustness. As is usual with taped Glyndebourne performances this one lacks an audience, a real subtraction when, as here, laughter is part of the event. Still, the method allows for a greater variety of camera angles and close-ups not otherwise available. And an audience *is* superimposed at the end, so the performers can take their well-earned bows.

Even with the drawback of no unifying sense of comedy and a conductor and leading lady not terribly in sympathy with the kind of sexual energy that would have tautened the mainspring of the performance, Glyndebourne's is a meticulous effort, allowing for a treasurable glimpse into Ravel's uniquely quirky musical as well as his theatrical imagination.

HARVEY E. PHILLIPS

Maurice Ravel

L'Enfant et les Sortilèges (1925)

A: Princess (s); B: Child (ms); C: Mother (c)

Ravel collaborated with another cat-lover, the French writer Colette, on this brief and fancifully modern "Fantaisie lyrique in two parts." Like Tchaikovsky's *Nutcracker*, *L'Enfant et les Sortilèges* (which translates as something like *The Child and the Sorcerers*) focuses on the fertile world of a child's imagination, where animals (including cats) and inanimate objects come magically to life, assuming fantastic forms and sizes. For the child here, this fantasy world is a means of escape from the dreary reality of homework, as symbolized by the awful arithmetic teacher who eventually shows up in his dreams. The orchestral and vocal writing provides wonderfully evocative portraits of the various things in the room with the boy—armchairs, clocks, teapots, fire—and then of the animals wandering in the garden (cats, squirrels, bats). By the end of the piece, the boy has learned compassion and has come to understand better the effect of his actions on other living creatures.

In genre, *L'Enfant* occupies an ambiguous place somewhere between opera and ballet and needs a highly imaginative staging to succeed. One major problem is how to deal onstage with the role of the six-year-old child, which is cast for a mezzo-soprano. Ravel's brother believed an animated film like those produced by Walt Disney would be the most effective approach.

1986 PIONEER (LD)

(Stage Performance, Stereo, Color, Not Subtitled) 50 minutes

Sylvaine Gilma (A), Françoise Ogéas (B), Jeannine Collard (C), French Radio Chorus, Orchestre National, Netherlands Dance Theater—Lorin Maazel

Jiri Kylián (choreographer and stage director)

In this inventive and emotionally satisfying version created by Jiri Kylián for his Netherlands Dance Theater, dancers and choreography dominate. The singers are placed off-camera and remain invisible throughout, while the dramatic action is played onstage by a troupe of marvelously trained dancers. Top billing goes to Marly Knoben, who dances the role of the child (whose gender seems here irrelevant) with convincing wide-eyed wonder; to Roslyn Anderson as the Mother; and to Stephen Sheriff, who makes it look easy (and fun) to dance in a easy-chair costume. Kylián also makes ingenious use of props, which are forever changing shape, form, and function. Mother's giant hoop skirt becomes a cage for the animals—and then a cradle for the final scene in which the child is rocked by his newfound animal friends. The female teacup is chic and glamorous; Mr. Arithmetic is a frightening creation with an extending metal fixture for an arm. The blackboard teems with sinister living fractions and equations. John Macfarlane's scenery and costumes combine theatricality and childish fantasy with spectacular success.

Although this version has no subtitles, they are hardly necessary given how clearly Kylián's choreography tells the story. Kylián also gives an excellent short synopsis and analysis of *L'Enfant et les Sortilèges* on-camera before the actual performance. His highly personal commentary emphasizes the fanciful nature of the piece and its universality as an expression of a child's fears and emerging feelings of humanity.

The vocal performances recede into the background here because of the dominant visual-choreographic image, but the singers, who include three veterans of Maazel's 1960 recording of this piece (Gilma, Ogéas, and Col-lard), give richly textured and idiomatic performances. So does the orchestra, under Maazel's expert leadership. Kylián and his colleagues have confronted and overcome the difficult staging challenges with notable success, and they have produced what is likely to remain the definitive version of this appealing small masterpiece.

Quality of camera work and sound are high.

HARLOW ROBINSON

MLADA (1891)

A: Voislava (s); B: Morena (ms); C: Yaromir (t); D: Mstivoy (bs);
E: Mlada (dancing role)

*A*four-act "opera-ballet" based on ancient pre-Christian Slavic legends, *Mlada* contains the features found in most of Rimsky's fifteen operas: alluring "Oriental" exoticism; a remarkable pictorial sense; refinement and a subtle command of proportion; what Rimsky's student Igor Stravinsky later called "a melodic and harmonic inspiration full of freshness"; a strong feeling for the unique synthesis of visual, musical, choreographic, and verbal elements possible only on the operatic stage; and a genius for orchestration that is the hallmark of the composer's style.

Originally, *Mlada* grew out of an odd communal project commissioned in 1872 from four members of the "Mighty Handful" (Rimsky, Mussorgsky, Borodin, and Cui) by the director of the Imperial Theaters. The composers worked from a pallid libretto by V. A. Krylov about the ninth-century Elbe Slavs, each being assigned separate scenes. Not surprisingly, the collaboration soon broke down. In 1889, Rimsky returned to *Mlada* on his own. Deeply influenced by Wagner's use of ancient German legends and myths (Rimsky had just seen the *Ring* for the first time), he expanded the libretto to include even more pageantry, pan-Slavic nationalism, pagan deities, bloody revenge, demons, and spells—not to mention an extravagant environmental finale (inspired by *Götterdämmerung* and / or *Tristan and Isolde*) complete with apocalyptical flood and cathartic rainbow.

But the most unusual and "modern" feature of Rimsky's *Mlada* is the casting of a dancer in the title role of the ghost of Princess Mlada, who has been murdered before the curtain rises by the jealous Princess Voislava and her scheming father Prince Mstivoy. Mlada appears (in *Swan Lake* or *Giselle* fashion) in dreams to the romantic hero Prince Yaromir, whom Voislava hopes to marry.

Considering the great demands it makes on an opera house (oversize orchestra, enormous chorus, ballerina, large *corps de ballet*, lavish scenery, and stage machinery), it is hardly surprising that *Mlada* has rarely been produced since its stage premiere at the Mariinsky Theater in 1892. Although the sketchy and episodic libretto is poorly constructed and at times unintentionally comic, the opera contains some of Rimsky's most colorful choral, orchestral, and solo writing, and in the hands of a skilled director can make a strong impact on stage and film.

1992 TELDEC (VHS / LD)

(Stage Performance, Stereo, Color, Subtitled)
139 minutes

Maria Gavrilova (A), Galina Borisova (B), Oleg Kulko (C), Gleb Nikolsky (D), Nina Ananiashvili (E), Bolshoi Symphony Chorus and Orchestra—Alexander Lazarev

Bolshoi Theater: Barrie Gavin (video director)

Filmed at the Bolshoi Theater in June 1992, this *Mlada* is a relatively recent addition to the narrow Bolshoi repertory, and a largely unsuccessful attempt to update the theater's notoriously conservative and stodgy production style. It is indicative of the theater's currently confused artistic and administrative situation that no one receives credit as director of this extravagant but hopelessly muddled project. Boris Pokrovsky, who has been associated with the Bolshoi for more than fifty years, supervised the production, but the artistic concept came from Valery Levental, the Bolshoi's long-time resident designer.

Levental has attempted to conceal *Mlada*'s dramatic and narrative weaknesses by cluttering the stage with hundreds of singers and dancers, miles of fabric, and wooden and cloth dolls representing Russia's pagan traditions. (The romantic hero Yaromir sings one of his arias to a wooden statue representing Mlada, which looks quite ridiculous.) Even more ill-advised was his decision to "frame" the opera in an eighteenth-century classical proscenium, complete with footmen who inexplicably appear before each act. This "approach" only further confuses the wandering story line. Why adopt an eighteenth-century frame for an opera set in the ninth century and written at the end of the nineteenth century?

Another basic problem is the half-hearted attempt by the singers in the main roles (none of whom have very polished acting skills) to act "realistically" in what is a patently unrealistic—and even campy—vehicle. The best of the principals is Maria Gavrilova as the predatory Princess Voislava; she has a strong, focused voice and leers convincingly. As her heartthrob Yaro-

mir, however, Oleg Kulko sings very tentatively (often with uncertain pitch), and wanders through his primitive blocking without a hint of conviction. Gleb Nikolsky at least sings better as Mstivoy. It is all too clear that no one told the performers how to approach their roles in dramatic terms.

As Mlada's ghost, ballerina Nina Ananiashvili, one of the biggest stars produced by the Bolshoi Ballet in recent years, steals the show from the singers. Using only her body, she creates by far the most rounded and emotionally affecting psychological portrait. She also dances seductively as Cleopatra in Act III, when the forces of evil attempt to break Mlada's hold over Yaromir by tempting him with an appearance by the famous Egyptian queen. Unfortunately, the choreography (by Andrey Petrov) for the *corps de ballet* never rises above conventional routine. Besides Ananiashvili, the chorus and orchestra generate this production's most memorable moments.

Producer Robin Scott has done a brilliant job of packaging *Mlada* for video. The subtitles appear against a transparent but darker background that allows for easy reading without obscuring the visual image. The recorded sound quality of the orchestra and chorus is excellent, and good for most of the soloists (with the exception of Kulko, whose weak voice often fails to reach the microphone). Particularly in the solo dance sequences, the camera work is imaginative and evocative. It's a shame that the performances and production concept are not better.

HARLOW ROBINSON

SADKO (1898)

A: Volkhova (s); B: Lyubava (ms); C: Nezhata (ms); D: Sadko (t); E: Sea King (bs)

Officially described as an *opera-bilina*, which *The New Grove Dictionary of Opera* defines as an "operatically treated heroic ballad," *Sadko* will probably strike the modern Western viewer as a sort of patriotic-mythological pageant—and is best taken in that spirit, without expectations of total dramatic logic. As Richard Taruskin has pointed out, the tale of Sadko, the gusla player who becomes a world trader through the love and assistance of the Sea King's daughter Volkhova, has resonances of the rise of capitalism and also of the triumph of Christianity over Slavic paganism. Sadko can also be viewed as a composer-creator figure, while Volkhova's transformation into a river connecting Novgorod to the Baltic evokes Russia's historic search for navigable access to the oceans.

The episodic tale is clothed by Rimsky-Korsakov in richly inventive music. Despite the frequent use of folklike material, the perils of rhythmic monotony are skillfully evaded (the first scene includes a chorus in 11 / 4 meter), and his command of harmonic and orchestral color is always absorbing. Nature is painted with Wagnerian splendor, and the proclamations of the supernatural Sea King are couched in the octatonic chromaticism that Rimsky passed on to his pupil Stravinsky. The vocal writing is demanding and also rewarding, especially for Sadko, Volkhova, and the three foreign guests whose celebrated arias ornament the fourth scene.

1993 PHILIPS (VHS / LD)

(Stage Performance, Stereo, Color, Subtitled)
175 minutes

Valentina Tsidipova (A), Marianna Tarassova (B), Larissa Diadkova (C), Vladimir Galusin (D), Sergei Alexashkin (E), Kirov Ballet, Chorus, and Orchestra—Valery Gergiev

Kirov Opera: Alexei Stepaniuk (stage director), Brian Large (video director)

The Kirov production of *Sadko* is based on designs by Konstantin Korovin for a 1910 staging, though—if the old photos in the liner notes are to be trusted—Viacheslav Okunev's recreations are somewhat free. Unlike some recent Kirov stagings, this one is intentionally old-fashioned and literal, but it rarely seems stodgy, and under Gergiev's baton the energy and conviction of both singing and playing carry the performance forward buoyantly and passionately.

Galusin, with ring in his tone and enthusiasm in his projection, is a natural as the bardic singer, even though his passage into the upper register isn't always smooth. Despite—or perhaps because of—a perceptible tremor in the voice, Tsidipova makes a lovely effect as Volkhova, while Tarassova, as Sadko's neglected wife, deploys enough tonal richness and musicianship to keep a one-key role from becoming boring. Diadkova is less successful at enlivening the blander writing for the guest singer from Kiev, and director Large works hard at finding distractions for the camera during her Scene 4 narrative. Others in the impressive list of fine singers that Gergiev seems able to summon up are Alexashkin, a firm and vigorous Sea King, and Nikolai Putilin, the offstage Pilgrim who rescues Sadko and Volkhova from the bottom of the sea. The trio of foreign visitors will not supplant in your ears the line-up that graced the old Golovanov recording (Ivan Kozlovsky, Pavel Lisitsian, and Mark Reizen!), but Gegam Grigorian's "Song of India" is very beguiling, and the other two (Alexander Gergalov as the Venetian, Bulat Minjelkiev as the Viking) are certainly adequate.

Wisely, Large does not try to conceal the staginess of the conventional direction or the obviously painted scenery (which confers on Sadko a house quite as spacious as Novgorod's civic banqueting hall). Panoramic full-stage shots are letterboxed from the bottom (Gergiev's arm occasionally rising above the artificial border), and the camera work is generally both apt and unobtrusive.

The subtitle translation is adequate, but the somewhat scanty printed synopsis will leave many viewers unclear about some matters of plot and action, as well as the identity of minor characters. The performance is not note-complete; aside from smaller cuts in Scenes 2 and 6, the opening portion of the underwater ballet in the latter scene is omitted (curiously, the Philips audio CD edition of the same performance restores two smaller cuts made in the video). These are trivial losses by comparison with the excellences of the performance, which seems consistently in contact with the opera's central lyrical and descriptive impulses.

DAVID HAMILTON

Nicolai Rimsky-Korsakov

The Tsar's Bride (1898)

A: Marfa (s); B: Lyubasha (ms); C: Bomelius (t); D: Gryaznoi (bar)

This opera, based on a drama by Lev Mei, was an interesting departure for the mature Rimsky-Korsakov. Thoroughly Russian in its subject matter and attitudes, it is of all Rimsky-Korsakov's scores the most like a French or Italian grand opera in its uses of recitative, aria, and ensemble for character and plot development. Indeed, it is something of a throwback to the Dargomizhsky and Glinka operas in this respect, complete with a soprano Mad-Scene-with-repentant-villain that draws on the much earlier models of Bellini, Donizetti, and Thomas, but also at moments suggests the Nina / Konstantin scene in Act IV of *The Seagull*, premiered the year before the opera was written. The story, set in the reign of Ivan the Terrible, is a triumph of melodramatic contrivance, and involves a love quadrangle, switched love and death philtres, and the selection of the innocent heroine, Marfa, as Tsar Ivan's bride on the very day of her betrothal to a young merchant. The drama offers little opportunity for the sort of descriptive grandiosity the composer gloried in, but there are scenes in which the writing takes on a personal intensity not often found in his work. The role of Gryaznoi's rejected mistress, Lyubasha, has been coveted by generations of Russian mezzos, and that of Marfa is full of beautiful work for a pure, strong lyric soprano with well-controlled high notes.

1966 KULTUR (VHS)

(Film, Mono, Black and White, Subtitled)
97 minutes

Raissa Nedashkovskaya / Galina Oleinichenko (A), Natalya Rudnaya / Larissa Avdeyeva (B), V. Zeldin / P. Chekin (C), Otar Koberidze / Yevgeni Kibkalo (D), Chorus and Orchestra of the Bolshoi Theater—Yevgeni Svetlanov

Vladimir Gorikker (director)

The first thing to understand about this film is that the score is heavily cut. This is not all bad. The work's most serious problem is that nearly all of Act I is background illustration—choruses of Oprichniki in praise of Ivan, of maidens in praise of picking hops; the dangers of manhood, the sorrows of womanhood, and so on. Little of it evokes Rimsky's best efforts, and the drama does not truly get underway till the superb Lyubasha / Gryaznoi confrontation, some forty-five minutes along. Later excisions, too, are hardly unthinkable, and in terms of cutting to the chase while preserving the central human conflict, this edition is intelligent. Still, fully a third of the music, some of it fine, is missing, as is the texture of the life developed around the subsidiary characters. The figures of Marfa's suitor, Lykov, and of her parents—all given substance in the score—are here left to establish themselves chiefly by visual means. As operatic filmmaking, this is a typical Soviet memento, except for the absence of color. Actors—idealized physical types who as children were no doubt taken to the opera once under government sponsorship—pretend to be the very different folks whose voices we hear, and are photographed in a manner reminiscent of poster art of the period. You might be amused: you won't be fooled. These may be

267

splendid actors; Koberidze and Rudnaya both have effective moments on their own terms, as does Zeldin, who plays the creepy German apothecary who dispenses the philtres. Even Nedashkovskaya, who alternates blankness and archness like a musical comedy ingenue, probably has something to offer. But it's a bootless task. The film's chief interest lies in what it conveys of atmosphere, social manner, and attitude. The directing and editing create a perfectly workable continuity, and there are a few sequences of interior monologue that, under these circumstances, come off better than the rest. The musical performance, while not at the level of the Bolshoi audio recording of the time, is solid. There is peppy leadership from Svetla-nov. Avdeyeva doesn't have all the vocal plush of the greatest Russian mezzos, but sings expressively and passionately. Oleinichenko, despite touches of the acidic quality common to many Russian sopranos, guides the line well and has the requisite top. Kibkalo is a good artist, but his voice is a high lyric baritone, not the *Heldenbariton* wanted for Gryaznoi. Chekin handles Bomelius well, and in what's left of the other roles there are such quality voices as Vera Klepatskaya's and Alexandr Vedernikov's. The black-and-white images are sharp, but the sound's a bit fuzzy. Functional subtitles, sometimes hard to see against the lighter backgrounds.

CONRAD L. OSBORNE

The Legend of Tsar Saltan (1900)

A: Militrissa (s); B: Swan-Queen (s); C: Prince Guidon (t);
D: Tsar Saltan (bs)

The Legend of Tsar Saltan, adopted by Byelsky from a Pushkin tale, is a mishmash of Rimskian operatic categories: the pantheistic / lyrical, the epic / folkish, the proto-modern ironic / satirical. All in all, fine fodder for an idle / foolish afternoon debate à la Turgenev or Chekhov. Its plot is a sly adaptation of folk fairy-tale themes. There are three sisters, one beautiful and industrious, the other two ugly and lazy, in league with an old crone. A booby of a Tsar chooses the pretty one as his wife and begets a son, who is the darling of the fawning court. An ugly women's ruse gets mother and son set out to sea in a barrel, but they are rescued by benign forces of nature and the guardian angel Swan-Queen, and installed as rulers of an enchanted island realm. After adventures that include the Prince's voyage back to the Tsar's court in the guise of a bumble-bee (cue for the famous "Flight of"), the family is reunited in an all-is-forgiven, happily-ever-after finale. The piece's structure is that of a series of tableaux linked by lengthy orchestral interludes. These last are in Rimsky's exotic descriptive vein, familiar to anyone who has heard *Sheherezade* or *Sadko*, and parts of it are rich indeed. Some of the vocal writing, such as that of the set pieces or the soaring line given the Swan-Queen, is also lyrically compelling if well sung. Much of it, though, is of a chattier story-telling sort, or a kind of elevated *recitativo accompagnato*, and depends heavily on the personalities and acting skills of the performers.

1987 VIEW (VHS)

(Film, Stereo, Color, Not Subtitled) 98 minutes

Lidija Rushizkaja, Barbara Hoene, Stephan Spiewok, Rolf Wollard (roles not credited), Chorus and Orchestra of the Dresden State Opera—Siegfried Kurz

Harry Kupfer (director)

For anyone in search of *Tsar Saltan*, this production poses formidable obstacles. It is sung in German, without subtitles or any accompanying material, so you'll have to dig up your own libretto or synopsis. Over a third of the music has been cut, including not only such sequences as the songs and dialogue for the Jester and Old Man in the first court scene, but sections of the set pieces and interludes as well. Though presumably based on a Dresden stage production, this has been filmed in a studio and is lip-synched. Kupfer has opted for an elaborately illustrative, mimetic acting style, such as is often seen in children's theater. Few lines pass without accompanying gestural or postural commentary. Several of the principals, and even some of the chorus, are quite skilled in the métier, and it must be conceded that to bring an entire operatic ensemble to this level of proficiency in the physical language, then shoot the resulting story (especially in the crowd scenes) with this degree of clarity, is a considerable technical achievement. The incessant signalling grows wearisome, however, and after a while it is hard to separate the behavior of the human characters from that of the pretend cats and bees and swans. There is some wit to the satirical side of the proceedings, but the potential for any serious engagement with the characters or for the story to really impress its moral is persistently undercut. This betrays the tone of the score's most persuasive writing and impoverishes our experience of the work. The special effects are risible. The evocative interlude of the barrel's voyage, for instance, shows a little cutout trinket jogging from left to right, then right to left in a sea of what looks like hair-conditioning gel, into which the Swan-Queen is finally introduced, a soprano in an all-white Papagena outfit, half-heartedly flapping her feathers in the gel. In the West we would assume this to be tacky satire, but it may just represent the limits of East German budgets and technologies. Kurz's conducting serves the lean-and-mean concept well enough, moving the show along and giving some point to the lighter side of the scoring while suggesting little of its weight or grandeur. The voices are of German middle-house caliber, sufficient in the character roles but not very satisfying when it comes to real singing. The best of them is the Tsar, a capable bass-baritone with a voice of some warmth. Video quality is fine, and the audio reasonably good. Unless your interest is highly specialized, I would counsel patience till we get something from native sources.

CONRAD L. OSBORNE

LA CAMBIALE DI MATRIMONIO (1810)

A: Fanny (s); B: Clarina (ms); C: Edoardo Milfort (t); D: Slook (bar);
E: Norton (bs); F: Sir Tobias Mill (bs)

*L*a Cambiale di Matrimonio was Rossini's first produced opera, and it is an astonishing achievement, even when viewed in the context of his later, more famous stage triumphs. Everything seemed to be in place right from the first: the bubbly instrumentation, the sure sense of comic / dramatic timing, a keen ear for what the voice can do best, and an amazing instinct for controlling large-scale musical structures. The only missing element is an individual melodic voice, although everyone will recognize the concluding measures of Fanny's aria "Vorrei spiegarvi," which found a new home in the familiar Rosina-Figaro duet in Act I of *The Barber of Seville.*

The libretto is conventional enough, already an overused text when the eighteen-year-old Rossini was asked to produce a quickie to take the place of a commission that failed to materialize for the 1810 festival season at Venice's Teatro San Moisè. The familiar formula involves an old man with a marriageable young daughter contracted to wed a wealthy stranger, but already hopelessly in love with the poor but honest tenor. The wrinkles in the overused plot are minor—Slook, the unwanted suitor, is from the wilds of Canada, a likable noble savage who eventually brings the two lovers together—but the conventional characters and situations hardly impede the young composer's dramatic imagination or musical spirit.

1989 TELDEC (VHS / LD)

(Stage Performance, Stereo, Color, Subtitled)
86 minutes

Janice Hall (A), Amelia Felle (B), David Kuebler (C), Alberto Rinaldi (D), Carlos Feller (E), John del Carlo (F), Stuttgart Radio Symphony Orchestra—Gianluigi Gelmetti

Schwetzingen Festival: Michael Hampe (stage director), Claus Viller (video director)

This production inaugurated a project that the German press at the time promptly labeled (facetiously, one hopes) the "Rossini Ring": *La Cambiale di Matrimonio, La Scala di Seta, L'Occasione Fa il Ladro,* and *Il Signor Bruschino,* four youthful one-act operas staged by Michael Hampe under the auspices of the Cologne Opera in the tiny rococo theater at the Schwetzingen Palace (a fifth farce in the series, *L'Inganno Felice,* was omitted). Of course these brief charmers have nothing to do with one another, aside from sharing the same composer and the conventions of *opera buffa* that Rossini inherited and proceeded to develop in his own inimitable way. Luckily, Hampe approaches the pieces without pretense, and his staging of *La Cambiale* is straightforward and low-keyed but lively and full of sly wit, while Carlo Tommasi's set, Tobias Mill's comfortable London town house, offers a nice panoramic view of Saint Paul's dome. The characters are sharply drawn, especially the Canadian "exotic," Slook, who

271

makes his entrance complete with fur coat, 'coonskin cap, rifle, and wooden cane with Indian carvings. "You're not among Americans now," says Edoardo, his young rival for Fanny's hand—a deliciously ironic comment under the circumstances, since Rinaldi as Slook is the only principal cast member onstage who is *not* an American.

Virtuoso Rossini singers are not necessarily needed for these pieces, nor are any present in this performance, although standards are acceptable enough. Hall, who tosses off her big number with sparkle and style, is perhaps the most polished, but all the performers are so personable that their vocal shortcomings seem more than tolerable—even Rinaldi, whose dry humor compensates for his rather shaky sense of line and chancy intonation. Del Carlo presents Mill as a lovable aging porcine cherub, amusingly contrasted with Feller's lean-and-hungry Dickensian lawyer, and Kuebler's ingenue tenorino fills the bill more than adequately. Looking like a comical foxy grandpa himself, Gelmetti presides benignly over the orchestra, which plays with ample verve and a sure grasp of the style. A brief interview with Hampe after the performance is not especially enlightening on any relevant subject, but we are vouchsafed some additional views of Schwetzingen Palace, an enchanting venue and among Germany's more closely kept festival secrets.

PETER G. DAVIS

GIOACHINO ROSSINI

LA SCALA DI SETA (1812)

A: Giulia (s); B: Lucilla (ms); C: Dorvil (t); D: Dormont (t); E: Blansac (bar); F: Germano (bs)

Rossini grew up quickly in the theater, and his masterly assurance in handling the extended formal structures of *La Scala di Seta* shows how far he had traveled in the two years since his first one-act *farsa*. The plot is much more elaborate, a variation on the old secret marriage theme in which Giulia and her young husband, Dorvil, must hide their union from the girl's ward, Dormont, who wishes his charge to wed the rake Blansac. Each night, Giulia lets down a silken ladder from her balcony in order to enjoy a well-deserved tryst with Dorvil, a ruse that soon leads to all sorts of complications, culminating in a riotous finale of comings, goings, and concealed figures in closets and under tables. The characters themselves do not have a great deal of musical individuality, except perhaps the slow-witted comic servant, Germano, and Giulia's dizzy cousin, Lucilla, who eventually manages to get her hands on Blansac. The overall melodic invention still seems a bit generic, but Rossini builds up to the insanely confused climax with his customary rhythmic energy, ability to define the moment with just the right *scenica parola*, and knack of turning musical forms to superb dramatic account.

1990 TELDEC (VHS / LD)

(Stage Performance, Stereo, Color, Subtitled)
100 minutes

Luciana Serra (A), Jane Bunnell (B), David Kuebler (C), David Griffith (D), Alberto Rinaldi (E), Alessandro Corbelli (F), Stuttgart Radio Symphony Orchestra—Gianluigi Gelmetti

Schwetzingen Festival: Michael Hampe (stage director), Claus Viller (video director)

Director Hampe responds to the frenetic activity of *La Scala di Seta* by increasing the energy level and relishing the flighty stage nonsense but, as with the other operas in this series, never overdoing things. Each character is once again neatly defined. Since Giulia is already married and clearly no ingenue, Serra portrays her as a glamourous but cuddly woman of the world (*four dress changes*), compared to Bunnell's endearingly bespectacled, slightly vacant Lucilla. Germano's befuddlement is also charmingly suggested by Corbelli as he gradually passes out from liquor while vainly trying to decide which tryst he is arranging and with whom. The sets are now designed by Hampe himself, who continues the European cityscape theme established in the earlier installments of his "Rossini Ring" tetralogy. This time we are in Paris, and Giulia's cozy boudoir looks out on a fashionable faubourg of quaint buildings and rooftops. Serra is the star of the show and knows it—she is an impressive presence, acting with flair and stage savvy, although her agile soprano has an edge and a dash of vinegar that will not please all tastes. Corbelli's bass-baritone also has a few rough patches, and Kuebler sings only passably, but Rinaldi, although he has less to do here, sounds in better voice than in *Cambiale*. Everyone eagerly enters into the spirit of the piece though, and the trim orchestra under Gelmetti's alert direction never fails to give the proceedings a buoyant lift.

PETER G. DAVIS

L'OCCASIONE FA IL LADRO (1812)

A: Berenice (s); B: Ernestina (s); C: Conte Alberto (t); D: Don Eusebio
(t); E: Don Parmenione (bar); F: Martino (bar)

L'Occasione fa il Ladro was first performed in November 1812. It was the sixth Rossini premiere that year, coming just two months after his first full-length comic opera, *La Pietra del Paragone*, had created a sensation in Milan. Naturally that success left the composer itching to stretch his talent, and his new one-act *farsa* builds on his previous work in the genre, both musically and dramatically. Like its predecessors, the piece is based on a popular French farce, this one with a screwball plot that was bound to tickle Rossini's sense of the ridiculous. Count Alberto and Don Parmenione meet in a country inn near Naples and inadvertantly leave with each other's luggage. In his "new" bag, Parmenione finds a picture of Berenice, Alberto's fiancée, promptly falls in love, and sets off to woo her pretending to be Alberto (whom, it seems, Berenice had never before met). The rest of the piece consists of madcap confusion as the two disguised suitors pursue Berenice and her maid, Ernestina, who have also changed places— most of the time no one is quite sure who anyone is, including Don Eusebio (Berenice's uncle and guardian), Martino (Parmenione's long-suffering servant), and perhaps the audience as well. There is more than a hint here that the composer may have been influenced by Mozart's *Così Fan Tutte*, especially when Berenice, like Fiordiligi, suddenly turns serious in her spacious aria and explores emotions that go well beyond the absurdity of her situation. The opera is also unusual in requiring two sets.

The opening scene at the inn takes place during a furious downpour, one of the earliest of many storm scenes that Rossini inserted into his operas whenever he could, and the basic musical materials of this one will turn up again in *Il Barbiere di Siviglia*.

1992 TELDEC (VHS / LD)

(Stage Performance, Stereo, Color, Subtitled)
90 minutes

Susan Patterson (A), Monica Bacelli (B), Robert Gambill (C), Stuart Kale (D), Natale de Carolis (E), Alessandro Corbelli (F), Stuttgart Radio Symphony Orchestra—Gianluigi Gelmetti

Schwetzingen Festival: Michael Hampe (stage director), Claus Viller (video director)

Hampe seizes on the libretto's expanded dramatic and scenic possibilities right from the start by showing the horse-drawn coaches of Parmenione and Alberto racing through the night to find shelter at the inn—a striking visual image, at least as transferred from stage to film. It makes a particularly vivid contrast to the following scene, a shallow interior that opens up onto the space where most of the frantic activity takes place, a gorgeous sun-drenched patio with a generous view of the Bay of Naples. As usual, Hampe accents character over comic shtick, all gain in this proto–Noël Coward comedy of manners. The director invariably sets the right tone, as in the delicious moment when Alberto stumbles onto the patio, suddenly notices that he is holding the wrong bag, and simultaneously catches his first sight of the right woman.

Patterson is especially effective in projecting Berenice's sense of fun as well as her hurt feelings; better still, her soprano is a quality instrument with an attractive silver glint that she uses to make many expressive points. Gambill and de Carolis are not only personable and adept comic actors, but they also possess more vocal quality and technical finesse than one might have expected from earlier installments in this series. Corbelli once again proves to be an inventive and amusing *buffo* baritone, both Bacelli and Kale are splendid ensemble players, and the spirited orchestral playing under Gelmetti is more than up to standards. The VHS / laser disc, by the way, does not include the short interview-documentary on Schwetzingen seen on the other three one-acters from the festival.

PETER G. DAVIS

IL SIGNOR BRUSCHINO (1813)

A: Sofia (s); B: Marianna (s); C: Florville (t); D: Gaudenzio (bs);
E: Bruschino (bs); F: Filiberto (bs)

Il Signor Bruschino was Rossini's last one-act *farsa giocosa* for the San Moisè in Venice, definitely the choice work of the lot and rightly the most popular of the five today—Italian opera would not see anything quite like it again until Puccini's *Gianni Schicchi* a century later. The plot contains nothing especially new, although the French *farceurs* who wrote the plays that Rossini's librettists adapted seemed able to spin endless variations on the theme of how young love continually and resourcefully outwits the older generation. Here Florville tries to pass himself off as old Bruschino's son, whom Gaudenzio Strappapuppole has chosen to wed his ward, Sofia—who, of course, will have none but Florville. Despite the overfamiliarity of the plot devices, the characters themselves have more comic dimension than usual, and Rossini rose to the occasion, not only perfecting the *buffo* style of his era, but also adding new elements of sentiment and acerbic satire to the mix. The lovers sing about their feelings with melting lyricism, and the extended comic sequences are brilliantly composed, sporting the same memorable profile and rich melodic invention that the composer would lavish on the great full-length comic operas to come.

1989 TELDEC (VHS / LD)

(Stage Performance, Stereo, Color, Subtitled) 97 minutes

Amelia Felle (A), Janice Hall (B), David Kuebler (C), Alessandro Corbelli (D), Alberto Rinaldi (E), Carlos Feller (F), Stuttgart Radio Symphony Orchestra—Gianluigi Gelmetti

Schwetzingen Festival: Michael Hampe (stage director), Claus Viller (video director)

This performance was originally paired with the production of *La Cambiale di Matrimonio* discussed above and shares many of the same cast members. This time Felle is the heroine and Hall the *seconda donna*, with marginally less felicitous results—Felle's Sofia looks fetching enough here, but neither her peaky soprano nor her stiff manner of using it charm the ear. Despite clever makeup and costuming (by Carlo Diappi), both Corbelli and Rinaldi look rather young to square off as a pair of battling old coots, and both are baritones rather than the basses Rossini stipulated. They are expert comic performers though, and they manage to generate plenty of sly humor and vocal brio. Kuebler continues to be a pleasant if somewhat generic swain in love, Feller adds a salty vignette as the crusty innkeeper, and there are several colorful minor characters, notably Bruschino's real son (Tito Gobbi), who turns up in the finale, drunk as a skunk, to clear up the confusion. Once again Gelmetti's crisp conducting and Hampe's inventive direction help cover most of the vocal deficiencies as the cast merrily enters into the ensemble spirit of the piece. The scenic motif is consistent with the other three productions, here a comfortable study in Gaudenzio's country estate with a lovely spread of the Italian *campagna* beyond the open French doors and windows.

PETER G. DAVIS

TANCREDI (1813)

A: Armenaide (s); B: Tancredi (ms); C: Argirio (t); D: Orbazzano (bs)

*A*s Rossini recalled the conversation in later years, Beethoven had said to him: *"Opera seria*—that's not the Italians' nature. They don't have enough musical science to deal with real drama; and how could they acquire it in Italy?" Rossini does not record his answer, though he could have had a good one. For he himself had, at age twenty-one, breathed remarkable vigor into a more or less exhausted art form and written an *opera seria* that belied the stereotype of arid recitatives, static action, and musical predictability.

Tancredi, which quickly became famous after its premiere at Venice's La Fenice in 1813, did not get off to an easy start: on the opening night of February 6, the two leading ladies got sick and the performance was cancelled midway into the second act (the contralto in the title role was said, in any case, to lean toward an "overuse of tobacco and brandies" and to have a voice sounding like an English horn). But with a successful launching some days later, the opera was off and running: it was given fifteen times that season in Venice alone, and Tancredi's opening aria quickly became famous all over Europe (toward the end of his life Rossini wryly referred to himself in a letter as "the author of the too-famous 'Di tanti palpiti' ").

In March 1813 *Tancredi* opened in Ferrara, with an important alteration. The play by Voltaire (after Tasso) on which it was based ended with the dying hero learning only at his last gasp that his beloved Armenaide had not betrayed him. For Venice, Rossini had contrived a happy ending, with the lovers healthily united; at Ferrara he reverted to the original, but it proved so unpopular that it fell into disuse and was thought to be lost. It surfaced in 1974. (In this connection, the production under consideration here holds a rather delightful surprise.)

1992 RCA (VHS / LD)

(Stage Performance, Stereo, Color, Subtitled)
166 minutes

Maria Bayo (A), Bernadette Manca di Nissa (B), Raul Gimenez (C), Ildebrando D'Arcangelo (D), South German Radio Chorus, Stuttgart Radio Symphony Orchestra—Gianluigi Gelmetti

Schwetzingen Festival: Pier Luigi Pizzi (stage director), Claus Viller (video director)

In 1824 Rossini's devoted biographer Stendhal notes that he had seen *Tancredi* some thirty times, which tells us a good deal about its immediate popularity—the title role, in fact, had become an important vehicle for reigning mezzos. The performance staged by the Schwetzingen Festival argues persuasively for more frequent revivals: this exceptionally strong cast is not only at home in Rossinian style but possessed of fine voices, and the music pours forth with an abundance of melodic richness.

One must suspend a little visual disbelief: mezzo-soprano Bernadette Manca di Nissa in the title role, comfortably plump and rounded of face, looks more like somebody's sympathetic grandmother than a warrior of derring-do, and any makeup that might have lent a hint of austerity in camera close-ups is notably missing. But the voice is gorgeous—rich and seamless from top to bottom, unfailingly smooth, firm, and creamy, even when negotiating elaborate ornamentation. It is pleasantly dark (without a hint of English horn!) and gives the impression, too, of considerable size. One is struck more by sheer vocal beauty than by an overwhelming heroism of delivery, but the trade-off is well worth it. The great moments of the performance are the two superb duets with the Armenaide of soprano Maria Bayo, in which the polished timbres of both women's voices glow seductively in parallel thirds and sixths.

Bayo gets along well on her own, too, agile and focused in the large leaps of her opening aria, and projecting convincing distress (in company with the orchestra's mournful oboe) when she is imprisoned. Her face often reflects the strain of delivering Rossini's acrobatic vocal line, but fortunately the voice doesn't.

Raul Gimenez, in the role of Argirio, Armenaide's father, displays a ringing, heroic tenor that he shades nicely from militancy to tenderness; he is a singer one can easily imagine in any number of large, romantic parts of later nineteenth-century operas. Bass Ildebrando D'Arcangelo as the unlikable suitor is a shade less expressive but remains thoroughly adequate, and the two sopranos in supporting roles are attractive and accomplished.

The staging is unpretentious but entirely serviceable, with a variety of backdrops (open sea and sky, a cathedral facade, a council table, and a rather endearing statuary horse) setting the scenes. There is some simple dancing, and the modest chorus—a little small for the patriotic valor it is called upon to project—conducts itself well.

And conductor Gianluigi Gelmetti, Schwetzingen's ever-active Rossini specialist, should be destined for operatic heaven as a reward for his final surprise: the presentation of both Rossini endings—first the tragic one and then, after the cast has taken its bows, an additional two-and-a-half minutes of music for the principals during which Tancredi and Armenaide fall into each other's arms, very much alive. The viewer can have his choice; this may be the latest thing in interactive video.

SHIRLEY FLEMING

L'ITALIANA IN ALGERI (1813)

A: Elvira (s); B: Isabella (c); C: Lindoro (t); D: Mustafà (bs)

Rossini kept his head: the "noisy enthusiasm" reported at the premiere of *L'Italiana in Algeri* at Venice's Teatro San Benedetto did not prevent his wry comment, "I thought that after having heard my opera, the Venetians would treat me as a crazy man; they have shown themselves to be crazier than I am." The opera opened on May 22, 1813, and stayed on the boards into June; by the third performance the Venetians were dropping verses in praise of the twenty-one-year-old composer into the orchestra pit.

Italiana had been a rush-order job: Rossini was engaged on short notice to fill a void in the theater's schedule; a local Venetian newspaper announced that he had written it in twenty-seven days, but the composer himself is reported to have said later that it was eighteen. The libretto by Angelo Anelli, based on the legend of Roxelane, slave of Suleiman the Magnificent, had already been used five years earlier by an older Neapolitan contemporary, Luigi Mosca. But Mosca was no match for Rossini, who by 1813 already had a half-dozen comic operas and the "heroic melodrama" *Tancredi* behind him. Stendhal found *L'Italiana* "perfection in the *opera buffa* style," and his warm opinion was echoed many years later when Richard Strauss heard the opera for the first time in 1927, and according to the conductor Vittorio Gui, "seemed mad with enthusiasm."

Oddly enough, this "perfect *opera buffa*" had the power to arouse political uneasiness on more than one occasion. At the Neapolitan premiere in 1815 Isabella's rallying cry for Italy ("Pensa alla patria") was cut from the finale of Act II (a little too inflammatory to suit local officials); and for the first Paris production in 1817 the oath-taking scene in which Mustafà is admitted into the order of the "pappatacci" was omitted—it was, perhaps, too similar to oath-takings required by France's Restoration government at the time.

1987 RCA (VHS / LD)

(Stage Performance, Stereo, Color, Subtitled)
149 minutes

Nuccia Focile (A), Doris Soffel (B), Robert Gambill (C), Gunther von Kannen (D), Bulgarian Male Chorus, Sofia, Stuttgart Radio Symphony Orchestra—Ralf Weikert

Stuttgart: Claus Viller (stage director), Gerhard Konzelmann (video director)

There is no weak link in this delightful and superbly cast production: the orchestral work under conductor Ralf Weikert is polished to the nines, and the set—handsome and detailed Moorish columns and arches looking out over a serene blue sea (with a very credible ship-wreck on the horizon)—is perfection. But the crowning triumph is the cast headed by the Isabella of contralto Doris Soffel, whose previous recorded work in Mahler symphonies and Haydn masses hardly gave her the chance to unleash her formidable coloratura. The full range of her capacities emerges here: a powerful, evenly produced, and lustrous voice, articulate in passages of precision staccato and able to curve fluently over the top of the most demanding phrase, shaping it with easy grace. The embellishments she adds to those written by the composer are appropriate and never overdone. There is a certain determination and authoritativeness in her stance, particularly apt in her patriotic exhortations but quite suited to other aspects of the character as well: Isabella, after all, never for a moment loses sight of her predicament and what needs to be done about it. Soffel's dressing scene, as she prepares to unleash her full feminine wiles on the men she must manipulate, is full of beguilement. The fellows haven't got a chance.

Robert Gambill's attractive Lindoro starts out a bit stiffly in his opening "Languir per una bella" (Stendhal thought this "one of the finest things that Rossini has ever composed for a pure tenor voice") but warms quickly to the task and makes a nice thing of the duet with Mustafà that immediately follows. From that point on he is in fine form—the vaulting vocal freedom in the "pappatacci" trio is but one example among many.

Gunther von Kannen's Mustafà is a big barrel of a man, projecting a well-grounded bass and proving quite agile in Rossini's rather inconsiderate demands for vocal acrobatics. He is by no means a boor, and von Kannen retains a likable softness just below the surface, especially telling while he is being so roundly hoodwinked. The earnestness of the oath-taking is touching while it is comical.

There is as much care exerted in the smaller roles as the major ones. Soprano Nuccia Focile is a confident and even imposing Elvira (those sustained high C's in the Act I septet sum it up), and Zulima (mezzo-soprano Susan McLean) is worthy of her "favorite slave" position. The bass of Enric Serra (Taddeo) is appropriately lighter than von Kannen's, and they complement each other well. When the whole gang gets together in one of Rossini's incomparable ensembles like the sneezing scene, the perfect *opera buffa* seems perfectly put together.

SHIRLEY FLEMING

IL BARBIERE DI SIVIGLIA (1816)

A: Rosina (s or ms); B: Almaviva (t); C: Figaro (bar); D: Basilio (bs);
E: Bartolo (bs)

*P*hilip Gossett, this age's Rossini authority, in *The New Grove Masters of Italian Opera* summarizes *Il Barbiere*'s musical supremacies well: "melodic elegance, rhythmic exhilaration, superb ensemble writing, original and delightful orchestration"—all, one can add, at the service of Rossini's breathtaking facility for musical characterization. As with Verdi and Wagner, to sing the score well is also to act it well: the invitations to subtlety in performance have kept the work alive for 170 years and through a couple of major revolutions in performance practice. The role of Rosina, for example, has belonged in various keys to divas from Maria Malibran to Amelita Galli-Curci to Marilyn Horne. No matter what their range, vocal weight, or degree of agility, the memorable Rosinas have always been able to color their vocal line for layers of suggestion. For a singer like Bidù Sayão that meant a sparkling piquancy, for Victoria de los Angeles an elegant sensuousness, and for Giulietta Simionato, witty determination. A great Figaro, likewise, not only possesses vocal health but also suggests that (like Rossini) he has three more plans in his mind than he can at that moment explain or execute. This quality of innuendo is what keeps Rossini's score open before singers and changing in vital ways every time we hear it. As it should.

1959 LEGATO CLASSICS (VHS)

(Stage Performance, Mono, Black and White, in German, Not Subtitled) 140 minutes

Erika Köth (A), Fritz Wunderlich (B), Hermann Prey (C), Hans Hotter (D), Max Proebstl (E), Chorus and Orchestra of Bavarian State Opera—Joseph Keilberth

Bavarian State Opera: stage director and video director uncredited

Anyone with an interest in the singers here or performance history in general will be immediately attracted to this tape. Here is a decently photographed black-and-white record of an all-star Munich repertory performance from the fifties. Erika Köth is well known on records but not on video in this country. Fritz Wunderlich has become a legend: an unequalled Mozart tenor who died in an accident in 1966 just three weeks before his scheduled Met debut. Hans Hotter was the greatest Wotan of his time, here seen in a rare comic role, and Hermann Prey, well-remembered for his Barber at the Met, is irrepressible at thirty in his first season in Munich. Leading them all is Joseph Keilberth, known here primarily as a Bayreuth Wagnerian who conducted the most exciting *Fliegende Holländer* ever recorded.

For all of these reasons the performance is fascinating; as a *Barbiere* production it is less so. At twenty-nine and in his first Munich season, Wunderlich is in resplendent voice and also, at this early stage, earnest but clumsy in Almaviva's more difficult music. Köth sings with reasonable accuracy and decorates for display in a voice of one color. In the lesson scene, she chirps Norina's aria from *Don Pasquale*. Hotter's Basilio has the same command, economy, and indestructible conviction as his Dutchman and Wotan; he provides a very subdued and rather frightening wit in a different psychological key from that of the score, but seeing his performance is an education of sorts anyway. Vocally he is blunt, not always on pitch, and occasionally wobbly. Prey is in fine voice and technically equal to the score, though he sings his opening aria as loudly as possible with all sorts of vocal distortions and pointless speed at the end—but for the remainder of the performance settles down to pleasant hyperactivity.

All of them need a stage director. The singers seem to have worked out some two-handed scenes sensibly, but the special effects (drunkenness, secrecy) are all embarrassing, and the ensemble scenes usually find them lined up across the stage singing to the audience. More important, the pivotal surprises seem to surprise no one but Prey; he is the only one who has a flair for this sort of thing. After their arias, the singers consistently bow, walk off the stage, and return for further bows—and the lights remain on in the auditorium during the performance: an attempt at nineteenth-century performance authenticity?

As recorded, the voices dominate the orchestra, but from what can be heard, Keilberth shoots down the score with deadly accuracy. Sets and costumes look like sets and costumes: at once frail, theatrical, and stylistically mixed. In its way, this is *Der Barbier* as much as the New York City Opera version (though sung in Italian) is *The Barber*. As such, the Bavarian State Opera production is intriguing and instructive, though only very intermittently satisfying.

1972 DEUTSCHE GRAMMOPHON (VHS / LD)

(Stage Performance, Stereo, Color, Subtitled) 142 minutes

Teresa Berganza (A), Luigi Alva (B), Hermann Prey (C), Paolo Montarsolo (D), Enzo Dara (E), Chorus and Orchestra of Teatro alla Scala —Claudio Abbado

La Scala: Jean-Pierre Ponnelle (stage director), Ernst Wild (video director)

Like others of Jean-Pierre Ponnelle, this video derives from his stage work. Here he has

a cast of marvellous singing actors all at their vocal peak, with a conductor eliciting wit and charm from a magnificent orchestra. Teresa Berganza is a sensuously beautiful and knowing Rosina, meltingly lovely from her first phrases onward, and as bewitching as anyone in the difficult and never quite satisfying "Contro un cor." Enzo Dara, though sometimes saddled with irrelevant comic business, is nevertheless a superb Bartolo. His long curly wig, in the style of Molière's comic protagonists, gives him a properly amusing look: vain, "fashionable," fancying himself a lady's man, perhaps—and that complements his characterization. Everything he provides is entertaining, but also in its theatrical way believable, motivated, and suggestive of a redemptive vulnerability. It is all well sung and splendidly timed to the music: this Bartolo is anything but the usual annoying automaton. Luigi Alva, a variable artist, is here at his very best: attractive, sweet in tone, and offering what seems spectacularly offhand virtuosity. His drunken soldier and music teacher are pleasant, though sometimes awkward, but that may be as much the problem of the designer / director as his. Hermann Prey is an affable Figaro and sings it well, though his closed baritone sound eliminates the variety of attitudes that others have found in this role. As Basilio, Paolo Montarsolo is accomplished, but made up and characterized as a grotesque rather than a human being. One unexpected pleasure: in the tiny role of the police officer, Luigi Roni sounds as terrifying as the Commandant in *Don Giovanni*. Claudio Abbado continually provides the score with a sensuous wit unlike any other modern conductor's.

For them all, Ponnelle produces his usual plethora of ideas, some good, but many—well, the production is plagued with bad jokes and bits of business that attempt to rival the music rather than support it. Bartolo, for example, is an amateur chemist here, with predictable results, while Basilio's "La Calunnia" has thunder and lightning at the climax, and Act I ends in a riot of irrelevant destruction. The comment is more than a matter of taste: the music makes all of its points of character with immense warmth and wit, and an involving production should expand, polish, and sharpen those. To turn the piece into farce (quite a different thing from comedy) does not improve but merely chills it: we feel we *should* laugh even as we are distanced or diverted from Rossini's (and librettist Sterbini's) focus. Here even some of the most accomplished actors provide rather a lot of desperate smiling, in lieu of simply having a good time. In addition, manic visual editing destroys the effect of several of Rossini's superbly built climaxes; he was, by acclamation, the best in the world at just this skill, and Ponnelle and his video director Ernst Wild are not better.

Altogether, then, this performance is something of a mixed bag, but beyond its cautionary lessons it certainly offers some pleasures that are, in the end, unforgettable.

1976 PARAMOUNT (VHS) / PIONEER (LD)

(Stage Performance, Stereo, Color, Subtitled) 156 minutes

Beverly Sills (A), Henry Price (B), Alan Titus (C), Samuel Ramey (D), Donald Gramm (E), New York City Opera Chorus and Orchestra—Sarah Caldwell

New York City Opera: Sarah Caldwell (stage director)

One can look at this as either a brash satire of Rossini's cultivated comedy or an attempt to realize its wit in 1970s American terms: blandly ridiculous and full of bad jokes, but all done with such agreeable commitment that for the moment it's modestly persuasive anyway. Most of the cast is young and nicely trained. Their characterizations generally lie in their costumes, though: Figaro is dressed as a barber pole, "Lindoro" is decorated with leatherbound books, Bartolo's cane is a huge key, and Basilio's hat is a church. It's a romp in the Sills NYCO style: what one *believes* is that the singers are having fun trying out period impersonations. Henry Price is personably stiff, Titus a good-humored athlete, Ramey eager, and Gramm comically skillful. Beverly Sills is an engaging mistress of the audience, and the videotape is most valuable for preserving that aspect of her

style, muted even on her "actual performance" audio records. In "Un voce" she decorates outrageously and plays her cadenzas to the audience. "Here I am," she implies with a wink, "a prima donna with a sense of humor, and I am going to entertain you. This is Rosina. Isn't she amazing, and aren't we having fun?" The approach, and the brilliantly negotiated aria, get huge applause. In the lesson scene she sings "Contra un cor" and then the "Ah, Vous Dirai-je Maman" variations with equally spectacular accuracy. One understands again the several facets of her reputation.

The others are in healthy voice, though vocal and verbal coloring, beyond the obvious, are in short supply. Henry Price has a light, sweet voice and some reassuring agility, while Ramey and Titus are full of youthful resonance. Sarah Caldwell conducts with wit. Much of the stage business, though, is on a level with the costumes. Technically the videotaping is adequate, though the picture blurs very briefly once or twice. But this is a *Barber* of a special kind, with attractive singers in a performance very much for its audience. It recalls an era.

1982 CASTLE OPERA (VHS) / PIONEER (LD)

(Stage Performance, Stereo, Color, Subtitled) 155 minutes

Maria Ewing (A), Max-René Cosotti (B), John Rawnsley (C), Ferruccio Furlanetto (D), Claudio Desderi (E), Glyndebourne Chorus and London Philharmonic Orchestra—Sylvain Cambreling

Glyndebourne Festival: John Cox (stage director), Dave Heather (video director)

A Glyndebourne production, and generally delectable. It is fervent without sentimentality and witty without gall. The settings are in lovely summery colors. The action, sometimes inventive, is nearly always timed to the score's rhythm and mood, and Sylvain Cambreling conducts with spirit, finesse, and an unique sense of the score's delicacy and arches of tension. The size of the theater prevents the cast from forcing visually or vocally, and the camera work is excellent—at nearly all points focused on relevant action and reaction.

The cast is immediately engaging. As Rosina, Maria Ewing is a dream: clever, warm, pretty, and a mistress of movement and vocal style. Only the top of this coppery voice is a little raucous. The way she gradually launches into happiness just after Almaviva reveals his true identity is just one example of her illumination of this role. John Rawnsley is for this production a complete Figaro: round, resonant, oily, amusing, and, strangely, a little naïve. Max-René Cosotti is, unlike any other Almaviva on videotape, a natural gentleman without the least stiffness. He moves elegantly and gives Almaviva a charming sense of humor, though humor is not the character's first aim. He also sings well, with particularly memorable *pianissimos*. Ferruccio Furlanetto (incorrectly identified on the box as Curt Appelgren) and Claudio Desderi sing well enough, but the first is playing a cartoon and the second seems, oddly, to lack the gift of comedy. Generally, though, this *Barbiere* is an exhilarating experience, often providing that frisson of illumination for which all great comedy aims. Highly recommended.

1988 RCA (VHS / LD)

(Stage Performance, Stereo, Color, Subtitled) 159 minutes

Cecilia Bartoli (A), David Kuebler (B), Gino Quilico (C), Robert Lloyd (D), Carlos Feller (E), Cologne City Opera Chorus and Stuttgart Radio Symphony Orchestra—Gabriele Ferro

Schwetzinger Festival: Claus Viller (director)

This *Barbiere* offers both promise and problems, though many will want it for its one or two extraordinary elements. Though as a whole it is heavy-handed, it does possess the great gifts of Cecilia Bartoli's captivating Rosina and Gino Quilico's charmingly acted Figaro. In her early twenties at the time, Bartoli sings wittily and with a sensuous color and an already phenomenal control that produces the effect of delighted spontaneity. Like others she is sometimes saddled with awkward business, which she handles with panache. Quilico's barber lacks the cyni-

cism of some others; he elects to play, successfully, a young, deft, and self-satisfied Figaro, though it must be said that his top voice is in this performance unexpectedly hollow, which destroys one or two of his great moments.

The production around them is more industrious than perceptively amusing. The sets are airy but generally gray and focused upstage center, which makes for some awkward ensemble pictures. Costumes are also somber, and Almaviva wears hats that cast shadows over his face. The direction explicates a text about love and money; what it lacks is the drollery that Bartoli and Quilico alone supply. Robert Lloyd does his Basilio business efficiently enough, but Carlos Feller is by design a deeply embittered rather than a comically self-centered Bartolo. There is nothing funny in the voice or characterization, and his painful angina in the midst of "A un dottor" is unsettling. As Almaviva, Kuebler is a plausible figure, but his voice is seldom beguiling nor is his manner more than willing. Midway in his scene as the drunken soldier he laughs and then for a moment comes comically alive. Otherwise he does best in the ensembles. After an understated overture, Ferro leads with spirit, but the performance is better as a setting for its sparkling Rosina and its charmingly acted Figaro than as a reflection of Rossini's *Barbiere* as a whole.

1989 DEUTSCHE GRAMMOPHON (VHS / LD)

(Stage Performance, Stereo, Color, Subtitled) 161 minutes

Kathleen Battle (A), Rockwell Blake (B), Leo Nucci (C), Ferruccio Furlanetto (D), Enzo Dara (E), Metropolitan Opera Chorus and Orchestra—Ralf Weikert

Metropolitan Opera: John Cox (stage director), Brian Large (video director)

Here we have another John Cox production, the charm of which has been expanded since Glyndebourne days to touch an audience of four thousand at the Metropolitan Opera. At various times there are, among other things, a horse and carriage, palm trees (the atmosphere is sultry), and a turntable stage with a shift from house to street and back again during the second act. As at Glyndebourne, we move in Act I to Figaro's shop so that he can measure Almaviva for a soldier's uniform. It's all quite pretty— a little large for video but dextrously done.

The cast, rather intimate vocally, looks and sings very well, if not always with that personal signature that marks some other performances. Leo Nucci's lyric Figaro is not Stracciari's, nor Milnes's, for size, but it is nimble, spirited, and smoothly vocalized: for once at the Met he has a role of suitable vocal weight. As Almaviva, Rockwell Blake, today's most notable Rossini tenor, is handsome and affable, though dramatically a little pallid. The voice is a tad sweeter here than I have heard it, and the agility, of course, is fabulous. The very difficult last act aria has been reinstated for him; in this enormous setting it arouses admiration rather than visceral excitement. Kathleen Battle sings with awesome beauty and control. Hers is a small voice, but it has a full range of lyric colors and carries beautifully; she knows exactly what it will and will not do: a performance of unique vocal control and charm.

As at La Scala, Enzo Dara is a captivating Bartolo, though some of the business is broader here and the costume has changed. Again he is a little younger than is often the case and fancies himself a stylish man: silly, perhaps, but not grotesque. Physically, he's brilliant: hands, arms, face, and posture are all expressive of his state of mind. The patter is delightfully handled: at one point in its midst he has a comic heart seizure but takes pills and continues babbling while dancing about the stage. He is totally delighted with himself and encourages delight in the audience. He then pops a final pill and dances out of the room. Why does this work dramatically when with another singer it would seem cheap or irrelevant? Probably because what Dara does demonstrates the character: this Bartolo, no matter how intractable, has such indomitable enthusiasm for life!

As at Glyndebourne seven years before, neither Ferruccio Furlanetto nor his director John Cox has solved the problem of Basilio; though the singer's voice is strong and *some* of the vaudeville has been cut (and some added), among all the effects the character's age, station, and dramatic objectives remain ambiguous and largely unconvincing: odd for a singer usually so aware dramatically. Though it lacks something in sensuous charm, Ralf Weikert conducts a trim, energetic performance; with this musicianly cast, all of the ensembles are strikingly effective. Altogether it's a well sung and warmly acted *Barbiere*, unique for the various talents of its Almaviva, Rosina, and Bartolo, and in a pleasant, responsible setting, too.

———————

The 1982 Glyndebourne production is a delightful performance as a whole, though the 1972 DG is also unforgettable for the contributions of Teresa Berganza, Enzo Dara, and Claudio Abbado. Other performances are memorable in various ways for the work of Cecilia Bartoli, Kathleen Battle, Dara, Rockwell Blake (who alone sings Almavivia's difficult second-act aria), and Beverly Sills.

LONDON GREEN

LA CENERENTOLA (1817)

A: Clorinda (s); B: Angelina (Cenerentola) (ms); C: Tisbe (ms);
D: Don Ramiro (t); E: Dandini (bar); F: Don Magnifico (bs)

Il Barbiere di Siviglia was only eight days old when Rossini—on his twenty-fourth birthday, February 29, 1816, with seventeen operas behind him—agreed to compose a new one for the next season at Rome's Teatro Valle. Before he began work on what was to become *La Cenerentola*, the next to last of his *opere buffe*, Rossini wrote *Otello* and *La Gazzetta*, a fiasco whose overture was borrowed for *Cenerentola*.

The opera opened in Rome on January 25, 1817, only thirty-two days after its librettist, Roman poet Jacopo Ferretti, suggested the Cinderella fable as a subject to Rossini. Its premiere was inauspicious, its cast of second-rate singers hastily rehearsed. Enthusiasm grew, however, during the opera's run of twenty performances, inspiring twenty other Italian theaters to mount it the following year. It quickly became an international hit and a repertory piece until the 1890s, when it disappeared. It was revived in 1920 in Pesaro, Rossini's hometown, and acclaimed the following year after a memorable production at Turin's Teatre Regio, with Conchita Supervia in the title role.

Cenerentola's sparkling score—in terms of musical invention perhaps the finest of his comedies—has always been admired. Its libretto, on the other hand, has often been criticized along these lines: 1) its characters are frivolous and, unlike those in *Il Barbiere*, the model *opera buffo*, more stylized than realistic; 2) how can a fairy tale not have an element of magic?; 3) how could a prince order a search to find a girl whose residence he is well aware of, having already been there? Those objections notwithstanding, *Cenerentola* creates dramatic tension by playing off a virtuous, ingenuous, dreamy heroine (unique in Rossini's comic operas) against the rest of the elaborately manipulated characters.

1948 VIEW (VHS)

(Film, Mono, Black and White, Not Subtitled)
94 minutes

Fiorella Carmen Forti (A), Fedora Barbieri (B), Fernanda Cadoni Azzolini (C), Gino del Signori (D), Afro Poli (E), Vito de Taranto (F), Rome Opera Chorus and Orchestra—Oliviero de Fabritiis

Fernando Cerchio (film director)

This 1948 Italian film, carefully restored for video release in 1987, tells a lot about how far cultivation of authentic Rossini style has progressed in the last sixty years. The cast has some attractive voices, notably that of young Fedora Barbieri, but its style and execution, adequate enough in its day, now seem heavy-handed. This manner of performing is exacerbated by weaknesses in the film's presentation: Cenerentola and Tisbe are portrayed by the actresses Lori Randi and Franca Tamantini, with the usual troublesome lip-synch problems unresolved; there are no subtitles, only an intrusive English narrator, who frequently speaks over the music; and there are some barbarous musical cuts.

This production is shot not in theatrical but in realistic settings, including the Royal Palaces of Turin and Monza and the Stupinigi and Tolcinasco castles.

1981 DEUTSCHE GRAMMOPHON (VHS / LD)

(Film, Stereo, Color, Subtitled) 152 minutes

Margherita Guglielmi (A), Frederica von Stade (B), Laura Zannini (C), Francisco Araiza (D), Claudio Desderi (E), Paolo Montarsolo (F), Chorus and Orchestra of Teatro alla Scala— Claudio Abbado

Jean-Pierre Ponnelle (director)

This is one of video opera's classics. Shot in 1981 at La Scala, it is a made-for-television film roughly duplicating the famous Ponnelle *Cenerentola*, a production mounted in so many venues it girdled the operatic world.

Although the treatment of the fairy tale is humane, often brilliantly inventive in action, and nearly always sets the proper tone for each scene, it is not entirely without blemish. Some will not take kindly to Alidoro's standing in for Rossini, nor to the wicked sisters being improperly attired (as they would not have been) when they are invited to the prince's ball, nor to the the characters being presented in silhouette in the great ensemble, "Questo e un nodo avviluppato," when one would prefer seeing their faces. These are, however, minor flaws in a triumphant presentation.

The cast, headed by an ideal fairy-tale couple, is as near perfection as could be reasonably requested. Von Stade touches the heart with her warm, velvety voice, smooth legato, bravura command, and appealing action. Araiza has a greater success in Milan than he was to have in Salzburg seven years later. Because he sings with more tone and is more impetuous in movement, his characterization has a brighter glow of robust youth.

In his lively, complex portrayal of Cenerentola's fatuous scalawag buffoon of a stepfather, Montarsolo shows why he was acclaimed in this role wherever he sang it. No other recorded bass on film or disc singing Magnifico's second act aria, "Sia qualunque delle figlie," equals his expression of glee at the thought of the money his influence-peddling will bring him. Outstanding in this dazzling ensemble of singing actors is Desderi, the most incisive and colorful of Dandinis. His controlled, explosive energy lights up every scene in which he appears, reaching incandescence in two duets—one with the prince, "Zitti, zitti, piano, piano," the other with Magnifico, "Una segreto d'importanza."

It is almost appropriate that Claudio Abbado, the chef for this musical feast, is never seen. His contribution is so graceful, spacious, and natural in the service of the music that it attains that summit of the opera conductor's art: it seems invisible. Abbado's ensemble is superb, proving yet again that under his baton in Italian opera, during his reign at La Scala, it had no equal.

Deutsche Grammophon's production values, in picture quality and in sound, are worthy of the event it preserves.

1983 HBO (VHS)

(Stage Performance, Stereo, Color, Subtitled) 152 minutes

Marta Taddei (A), Kathleen Kuhlmann (B), Laura Zannini (C), Laurence Dale (D), Alberto Rinaldi (E), Claudio Desderi (F), Glyndebourne Chorus, London Philharmonic— Donato Renzetti

Glyndebourne Festival: John Cox (stage director), John Vernon (video director)

John Cox has devised a production with a terminal case of the "cutes." He has turned Rossini's *giocosa* melodrama into an overbusy English pantomime, complete with cut-out scenery and props to match (by designer Allen Charles Klein). Clorinda and Tisbe have false putty noses (their behavior reveals well enough their character). A maze in the prince's palace undercuts Cenerentola's entrance at the ball and makes nonsense of the ensuing action.

The musical performance is more pleasing. Donato Renzetti conducts a performance based on a newly edited edition of Rossini's manuscript by Alberto Zedda that restores, among other things, all the music of the Prince's tutor, Alidoro, including his first act aria, almost always cut. His conducting is light and spirited, if without as much grace or authentic Rossinian rubato as one might desire. The vocal cast is headed by Kathleen Kuhlmann, who overcomes her unflattering costumes and wigs with a sympathetic impersonation and stylish singing impressive for creamy tone, agility, and expression. Laurence Dale deserves praise for his polished vocal technique and style, even if he is hardly a polished actor. Claudio Desderi, a baritone better suited to Dandini than to Magnifico, has, as ever, animating presence and art. Alberto Rinaldi's blustery Dandini seems crude in comparison with his colleagues. Ditto Roderick Kennedy as Alidoro.

Picture and sound are first rate.

1988 KULTUR (VHS) / PIONEER (LD)

(Stage Performance, Stereo, Color, Subtitled) 160 minutes

Angela Denning (A), Ann Murray (B), Daphne Evangelatos (C), Francisco Araiza (D), Gino Quilico (E), Walter Berry (F), Vienna State Opera Chorus, Vienna Philharmonic— Riccardo Chailly

Salzburg Festival: Michael Hampe (stage director), Claus Viller (television director)

Michael Hampe's production for Salzburg's Kleines Festspielhaus, with its many smooth, ingenious changes of scene, may be overstylized for Ferretti's humane treatment of the Cinderella fable, but it certainly looks elegant in the handsome Regency settings designed by Mauro Pagano. Special praise is due the extremely amusing storm scene with the Prince's horse-drawn carriage speeding through torrential rain and lightning.

The cast is, for the most part, brilliant and stylish. Murray is a sympathetic heroine, vocally agile and firm except for some unfocused tone upon her entrance in the ball scene. Francisco Araiza is heard at his recent best—a Rossinian prince, his tone mellifluous and effortlessly flowing. He is musical, precise, and fluent in

roulades, easy in attack, and has good high notes. The sisters are capable singers, look good, and are discreet and correct in action—vain, arrogant, and cruel, without a trace of grotesque camp. Walter Berry may be long in the tooth but is secure enough vocally to sustain a detailed characterization of a cruel Don Magnifico. Clearly relishing his role as the valet Dandini, Gino Quilico is playful and waspish. His Italian is excellent and he launches the wonderful final ensemble of the first scene with impressive vocal and musical authority.

However brilliant and stylish the singing may be, the hero of the evening is Riccardo Chailly. Thoughtful, supportive, always alert, he achieves that refinement of sonority and ensemble, clarity of detail, superfinely graded crescendos, and an effervescence of expression that defines masterful Rossini conducting.

The video direction is so reticent it's almost anonymous. Almost throughout the opera, the camera is pointed directly at the stage; only the length of the shots vary. The sound engineering and picture quality are admirable.

1996 LONDON (VHS / LD)

(Stage Performance, Stereo, Color, Subtitled). 164 minutes

Laura Knoop (A), Cecilia Bartoli (B), Jill Grove (C), Raul Gimenez (D), Alessandro Corbelli (E), Enzo Dara (F), Houston Grand Opera Chorus and Houston Symphony Orchestra— Bruno Campanella

Houston Grand Opera: Roberto De Simone (stage director), Brian Large (video director)

This video does not add up to the sum of its parts. Roberto De Simone has transferred his 1992 Bologna production to Houston. It is well dressed but has a unit set with stairs that make nonsense of much of the action in the ball scene. It also permits too much of the opera's humane comedy to slide into caricature. Further, Cecilia Bartoli's spirited portrayal of the title role is far too assured (almost impervious to neglect and abuse), altogether too spunky to suggest Cinderella's dreamy ingenuousness. So much more convincing in triumph (her account of the finale is electrifying) than in misery, Bartoli undercuts the play's dramatic tension.

What delights is the excellent musical performance led by Bruno Campanella, one of admirable lightness, grace, and sweetness, lacking only a sufficiency of vigor. The entire cast pleases for tonal purity, vocal agility, and Rossinian style, but none of its members, with the exception of Gimenez and Michele Pertusi (as Alidoro), digs quite so deeply into his or her roles as the individuals of the wonderful Scala team under Abbado (not even Corbelli and Dara, each justly celebrated for his characterization in this opera).

Production values are first rate, except for some graininess in the darker scenes.

One could be content with the Salzburg Festival production on Kultur if DG's classic version did not exist.

C. J. LUTEN

GIOACHINO ROSSINI

LA GAZZA LADRA (1817)

A: Ninetta (s); B: Pippo (ms); C: Giannetto (t); D: Fernando (bar);
(E) Gottardo (bs)

Rossini's biographer Stendhal objected (in his customary vigorous language) to the fact that *La Gazza Ladra* was based on "a disgusting little anecdote" that had once actually happened—except that the real servant girl was in fact hanged. But for all his fastidious revulsion toward what he called this "depressing and melodramatic" tale, Stendhal described the opera's hugely successful premiere at La Scala, which he attended, in vivid detail: "The triumph of the opera [May 31, 1817] created such a furor . . . that scarcely a moment passed without the entire audience rising to its feet as one man to shower Rossini with applause. That night, at the Caffe dell' Accademia, the composer declared that, notwithstanding his delight at the success of the work, he was utterly exhausted by the effort of bowing, literally hundreds of times, to an audience which, at every instant, had been interrupting the performance with its shouting and applause—bravo maestro! evviva Rossini!."

The composer was twenty-five and in the first flush of musical maturity, with nineteen operas already behind him, including such solid fare as *Tancredi*, *The Barber of Seville*, *Otello*, and *Cenerentola*. Not everyone approved of the direction his work was taking: he was criticized for his increasing attention to the orchestra (too "Germanic") and accused of becoming too complex. The use of the snare drums to open the *Gazza Ladra* overture, in fact, drove one young violinist to declare that Rossini ought to

be killed (a job for which he volunteered). But most of the opening-night audience was thrown into a "tempest of delight," and the opera remained on the Scala stage for three straight months.

1987 KULTUR (VHS) / PIONEER (LD)

(Stage Performance, Stereo, Color, Subtitled)
176 minutes

Ileana Cotrubas (A), Elena Zilio (B), David Kuebler (C), Brent Ellis (D), Alberto Rinaldi (E), Cologne Opera Chorus, Gürzenich Orchestra of Cologne—Bruno Bartoletti

Cologne Opera: Michael Hampe (stage director), José Montes-Baquer (video director)

The Cologne production makes a strong case for this wonderfully vibrant if somewhat ambivalent opera, which begins as near comedy but addresses a truly harrowing situation. The sets are splendidly realistic—from Fabrizio's sunny country courtyard to a prison that is dank, gloomy, and appropriately overpowering. And yes, one sees the Magpie fly away with the silver, quite convincingly.

The cast is strong and persuasive. Ileana Cotrubas presents a winsome Ninetta, tender in her expressions of love but mustering more than a touch of fire when she repels the advances of the Mayor; she has the requisite agility for Rossini's embellishments (her opening aria has been compared to Rosina's showstopping "Una

291

voce poco fa" in *The Barber of Seville*), and two of her duets—the first with her father in Act I, the second with her young peasant admirer, Pippo, in Act II—are particularly adept and striking.

As her lover, Giannetto, David Kuebler is somewhat strident at the start but gains in ease, eventually achieving a real sweetness of tone. Carlos Feller as Fabrizio, who seems to specialize in benign avuncular roles, is very reassuring in this one, and his pleasant and untroubled bass is consistently welcome. Brent Ellis makes an impassioned case for Fernando, wholehearted in his concern for his daughter. And since this opera revolves around the malevolent personality of the mayor, spurned and bent on revenge, a forceful basso is essential in the part: Alberto Rinaldi meets all the requirements—he is handsome, resonant, subtly threatening, and imposing. A Scarpia-like presence.

The two supporting women, Nucci Condò as Lucia and Elena Zilio in the trouser role of Pippo, come across as real human beings—the former as domineering but not hard, the latter as lively and ardent (a close kin of Cherubino). Zilio's rather bright mezzo is marked—but not marred—by a fastish vibrato, to which one quickly grows accustomed.

Conductor Bruno Bartoletti gives the opera an appropriately brisk pace, but the orchestra is at times heavy-handed in its chordal punctuation of recitatives, thumping in with unnecessary bluntness (the miking may be responsible). The chorus is lusty and accurate, with the exception of a shaky moment or two, a cappella, in the second act.

SHIRLEY FLEMING

La Donna del Lago (1819)

A: Elena (s); B: Malcom Groeme (ms); C: James V of Scotland (known as Uberto) (t); D: Rodrigo di Dhu (t); E: Douglas d'Angus (bs)

When Rossini wrote *La Donna del Lago* in 1819 for the great Spanish soprano Isabella Colbran—who was his mistress and whom he would marry in 1822—she was approaching the end of her peak years. She had been a brilliant mainstay of Naples's Teatro San Carlo, but the clock was ticking. Rossini's biographer Stendhal, in his flamboyant manner, puts it unkindly: "In the year 1820, one thing alone would have made the Neapolitans happy: not the gift of a constitution, but the elimination of Signorina Colbran."

It was not Signorina Colbran, however, who was responsible for the bad opening night on September 24, 1819 (she seems, in fact, to have been in good form), but an unlucky tenor who had to make his entrance far backstage, could not hear the orchestra, and came in resoundingly flat. The volatile Neapolitans erupted, and the evening was a rocky one. But ensuing performances put the matter right, and the original cast included, in addition to Colbran, the famous Rosamunda Pisaroni, described as the greatest mezzo-soprano in Italy and also the ugliest (she was badly pitted with smallpox). In a very short time this *opera seria*, with its forceful choruses and almost Verdian weight, became popular throughout Italy (it was presented thirty-two times in its first Scala season) and soon reached north of the Alps with equal success. It is rarely staged today (and rarely recorded), but it is rich in melody and impressive in its choral writing, and Rossini himself thought highly enough of it to lift several numbers for use in later operas.

Based on Sir Walter Scott's poem "The Lady of the Lake," *La Donna del Lago* is the first opera derived from that author, whose works were said to be "in the air" when Rossini first encountered the poem in French translation.

1992 HOME VISION (VHS)

(Stage Performance, Stereo, Color, Subtitled)
162 minutes

June Anderson (A), Martine Dupuy (B), Rockwell Blake (C), Chris Merritt (D), Giorgio Surjan (E), Chorus and Orchestra of Teatro alla Scala—Riccardo Muti

La Scala: Werner Herzog (stage director), Ilio Catani (video director)

A gift for night vision would be helpful in viewing this production, which is swallowed in darkness by La Scala's big stage and gloomy sets, making the viewer's search for significant details (the coat of arms in Elena's cottage that alerts the disguised king as to his whereabouts, for instance) mostly in vain. "Oh, happy dwelling," the king sings, glancing around at the black and sweating stones of what might be the bottom of a coal mine. Well, it takes a heap of living to make a house a home, as the old saying goes. The chorus of hunters, meanwhile, has hailed the coming of the morning light, only faintly perceived and too quickly gone. One must wait until the opera's final scene for the general murkiness to lift, when at last a golden throne beneath a high window introduces a touch of brightness. There are, however, some fine flashes of lightning at the end of Act I. Rossini called for onstage horns for the opening chorus, but they are not deployed here.

The viewer might ignore such matters if the singing took wing. But this, too, seems to wait for the coming of light. June Anderson, stepping out of her small lake-boat and apparently walking on water, is off to a shaky start in the barcarolle that should lilt but doesn't. The voice sounds thin and tentative, and in later scenes her intonation is questionable and her coloratura approximate. But she does gain steadiness eventually and seems, like the viewer, to be revived by the relative brilliance of the final scene. Her last aria is handsomely delivered, though she remains a rather rigid presence.

The standout in this often sluggish presentation is mezzo-soprano Martine Dupuy in the trouser role of Malcom, Elena's true love; she is electric in her two big arias, emotionally alive and precision-etched in florid passages. (One almost forgets her unfortunate headgear, sporting small furry ears, that might have come out of the Broadway production *Cats*.)

Rockwell Blake is a sturdy King James, and negotiates the killer aria that opens Act II with agility if not always agreeable tone. Chris Merritt as Rodrigo is hefty and loud, but projects a pervading bluster and insistent vibrato that grow trying. Giorgio Surjan, as Elena's father, fulfills his role with fitting military energy.

For his part, Muti seems unable much of the time to galvanize his soloists, and he must bear responsibility for the heavy-handed orchestral accompaniment of the recitatives and the frequent sogginess of the earlier scenes. But the choruses seem to inspire him, and the stage (and the pit) come to life when they are present.

SHIRLEY FLEMING

GIOACHINO ROSSINI

SEMIRAMIDE (1823)

A: Semiramide (s); B: Azema (s); C: Arsace (ms); D: Idreno (t)
E: Assur (bs)

Rossini crowned his Italian career with *Semiramide*, a *melodramma tragico* on a huge scale. The great spans of the set pieces are almost symphonic in their architectural scope, but that hardly interferes with the composer's ability to create scenes of considerable theatrical power or inhibits his musical and vocal invention. Until the early years of the twentieth century, the opera was very nearly as popular as *Il Barbiere di Siviglia* in the Rossini canon, and the title role was coveted by prima donnas from Isabella Colbran (the composer's first wife, who created the part) and Giuditta Pasta down to Adelina Patti and Nellie Melba. Semiramide, after all, is one of literature's great tragic heroines, a passionate, imperious, jealous woman who conspires to murder her husband and mount his throne, and later falls in love with a young officer who turns out to be her son and eventual executioner—Jocasta, Lady Macbeth, and Clytemnestra rolled into one. Also required is a virtuoso mezzo-soprano for the *travesti* role of Arsace, the Babylonian Queen's warrior son, and an agile basso to handle the bravura demands of Assur's coloratura music.

About a century ago operagoers began to lose their taste for such elaborately proportioned, leisurely paced spectacles. And since the singers who could do them justice vanished as well, *Semiramide* went into a long eclipse. The famous revival at La Scala in 1962, starring Joan Sutherland and Giulietta Simionato, was a revelation, although even that production was heavily cut, lest the audience's patience be sorely tested. As the *bel-canto* renaissance gathered momentum, though, and other singers rose to the challenge, more and more of the score was restored, until the appearance of a critical edition in 1990 gave opera companies the luxury of producing an authentic *Semiramide* for the first time in nearly a century.

1990 KULTUR (VHS)

(Stage Performance, Stereo, Color, Not Subtitled) 220 minutes

June Anderson (A), Young Ok Shin (B), Marilyn Horne (C), Stanford Olsen (D), Samuel Ramey (E), Metropolitan Opera Chorus and Orchestra—James Conlon

Metropolitan Opera: John Copley (stage director), Brian Large (video director)

The 1990 Metropolitan production, the company's first since 1894, took advantage of the new critical edition and presented the opera with only a few minor trims—some recitative passages and occasional interior repetitions. That said, there is not much else to savor here apart from the work itself. The direction (John Copley), sets (John Conklin), and costumes (Michael Stennett) have a low-budget look, a secondhand version of the approach to opera on classical themes popularized by the late Jean-Pierre Ponnelle: a suggestion of antiquity blended with the architecture and fashion styles of the period in which the opera was composed.

The result in this case is Semiramide clad in lush post–Napoleonic-era gowns and moving in stately manner over a stage framed by crumbling classical stonework with flavorless Hollywood road-to-Babylon projections serving as backdrops. That conceit had already become a cliché in Ponnelle's hands, and recycled here it looks even staler.

Understandably, none of the principals are inspired or much animated by the production team, especially Anderson. The soprano looks pretty enough modeling Semiramide's clothes, but she never manages to suggest that the queen has much on her mind except the next costume change and, of course, getting all the notes right—which she does, and often with considerable if rather chilly éclat. The main reason for mounting and filming the opera was doubtlessly to preserve Horne's Arsace, the most famous character in her celebrated gallery of florid Rossini roles, and it's a shame that the idea didn't occur to someone at least a decade earlier. By 1990 the unique Horne voice had become con-

siderably reduced: the lower register sounds hollow, top notes are rationed and carefully negotiated, and the overall tonal quality is rather parched. Still, she continues to be a singer of resource, and the undiminished zest of her singing is hard to resist.

Ramey is also seen in one of his signature parts, and the presence on the scene of a bass of his vocal quality and technical panache certainly helped spur the revival of Rossini's serious operas. As the strutting Assur his one-dimensional performance personality, while regrettable, is less of a liability, and his vibrant, flexible voice seldom disappoints. The Indian king, Idreno, is only an incidental character, but he has two difficult arias to sing, and Olsen's sweetly modulated tenor makes each one a pleasing interlude. Conlon has the score well in hand, and he accompanies efficiently, if seldom communicating much sense of the score's sweep, grandeur, or rhythmic vitality.

PETER G. DAVIS

GUILLAUME TELL (1829)

A: Mathilde (s); B: Arnoldo (t); C: Guillaume Tell (bar)

Thanks to the end of its overture, appropriated in the United States by a popular radio and, later, TV western, *Guillaume Tell* has been a famous title. Performances of any kind have been rare, those note complete and in French, rarer still. Perhaps that's because the work's great length (Rossini himself joked about it) makes it impracticable. Ensconced in Paris with a royal pension, Rossini felt he had to prove he could write a "masterpiece" (the great successes of his Paris years were largely retoolings of older Italian works). Rossini had to deal with the pressures and intrigues of the infamous Paris Opera and some, notably Giuseppe Verdi, felt *Guillaume Tell* suffered accordingly. Though this opera was to provide an example and a spur to later composers of Romantic operas, Rossini himself disliked the Romantic movement and resented being expected to "measure up" to late Beethoven and the "happening" Carl Maria von Weber. *Guillaume Tell* was also a father of "politically engaged" operas (notably those by the young Verdi). Rossini himself was largely indifferent to the high sentiments and democratic impulses of the great playwright Friedrich Schiller, whose play, *Wilhelm Tell*, was the opera's source. Somehow, critics have wanted to adore this work, the final opera of a singular genius all too frequently underestimated. Thanks to that hardy perennial, *The Barber of Seville*, Rossini was one of the most celebrated but least appreciated of "great" (and rich) composers. In a far more self-consciously ambitious work like *Guillaume Tell* his skill was greatly

appreciated but somehow less loved. By 1828, when the thirty-six-year-old composer was writing this opera, he was tired. Despite some flirting with other subjects over the next few years, *Guillaume Tell*, more or less consciously, was his last theater work, though he lived another three decades. It is a summa, and as such is multi-layered, complicated, and uneven. But as is often true in the long works of geniuses, cutting the less inspired parts tends to leave the thrilling sections unprepared and somehow unanchored. Berlioz and others saw that it was a curious quality of many of this opera's scenes that they move from less promising to eventually thrilling. That is a difficult kind of progression to make compelling and clear in performance and it's not a surprise that only one video has so far been released.

1991 HOME VISION (VHS)

(Stage Performance, Stereo, Color, Subtitled) 239 minutes

Cheryl Studer (A), Chris Merritt (B), Giorgio Zancanaro (C), Chorus and Orchestra of Teatro alla Scala—Riccardo Muti

La Scala: Luca Ronconi (stage director and video director)

Riccardo Muti chose the critical edition of this opera and it is offered complete, but in a new Italian translation. While this is more sophisticated than the standard one, closer to Rossini's sense and scansion, it seems strange to avoid the words the composer actually set, particularly since two of the stars here are no more at ease in Italian than they would have been in French.

This *William Tell* takes place in a legislative deliberation room with big screens at back (behind a small shelflike acting area) and at the sides. Occasionally characters and chorus leave posing and dozing at their legislative desks to come down and "act" in a very shallow downstage area. The characters are dressed in costumes of the 1820s. Luca Ronconi, the producer, wants us to know he's too sophisticated to take this opera, or perhaps the very notion of "opera," seriously. There is little hint of impersonation from the singers; it looks as though they've been discouraged from "becoming" the characters. The shallow acting area renders interaction difficult; singers look over each other's shoulders and roam left, then roam right. No scenes are "played," and people rarely look one another in the eye. Ronconi seems more interested in the elaborate films of real Swiss locations projected on the screens than in the personal and political dramas that are unfolding in front of them. They give the production the look of a travelogue inconveniently intruded upon by puny humans. The shallow downstage area is so obviously a long-term miscalculation one can only put the approval of this production down to the philistinism and ignorance that seem to reign in today's opera companies. For one thing, there is no room for the ballets; it's hardly surprising dancers of both sexes end up doing the can-can—forming a downstage kick line was the best the beset choreographer could think to do.

It's probably unfair to judge the performers under the circumstances. The great personalities of the past would likely have been fired during rehearsals. Everyone looks nervous because of all the steps and obstacles hidden around the dark set. The many supporting singers are poor, few have impressive voices, none have the ability to sketch an interesting character. The Tell (Zancanaro) and Mathilde (Cheryl Studer) are well-schooled singers with pleasant voices in good working order here. They are both doing their jobs with confidence. I guess it's naïve to believe Rossini might have wanted us to be interested in their destinies.

William Tell has one of the most difficult tenor parts in history. No less an opera lover than the amateur tenor James Joyce has left an inventory of high, higher, and stratospheric notes an Arnold must attempt in one evening. The American tenor Chris Merritt proves the exception in this bland performance. He is not fetching to see or always to hear, but he is lively. He is the only one of these singers who is animated and evidently invested in the "make-believe" of the piece. He was enjoying what was evidently a brief vogue at this time. He produces his voice perhaps as the first Arnold, Nourrit, did, that is with a strongly developed "head tone" using pharyngeal rather than chest resonance. The role's altitudinous tessitura is more easily coped with this way. Of course, the world-famous Nourrit probably had a more beautiful sound and perhaps was more consistently in tune. He was very likely given more latitude to shape and color his music by Rossini than Merritt is by Maestro Muti. Rossini merely composed, Muti is after all a *conductor*.

Ronconi cuts frequently to Muti, who thereupon flaunts his formidable hair. He is even juxtaposed onto the stage picture during the great ensemble that ends Act II. There was clearly good reason for that; Maestro probably signed the checks.

ALBERT INNAURATO

CAMILLE SAINT-SAËNS

SAMSON ET DALILA

(concert 1877; stage premiere 1892)

A: Dalila (ms); B: Samson (t); C: High Priest (bar); D: Abimélech (bs);
E: Old Hebrew (bs)

The French school of singing may have been killed by the Philistines, but *Samson* breathes on. Not many of its siblings do: *Faust*, *Carmen*, and *Hoffmann* spring to mind, and a few other French works of the period also stir now and then. What keeps *Samson* theatrically alive? It's filled with musical conviction. Those choruses in Act I have varying kinds of emotional power, the orchestral comments sometimes sweep us away unawares, and each of Dalila's scenes has a different kind of command: personal, political, sexual. Samson is the one religious leader in French or Italian opera who still retains for us full tragic stature, and if the director and singer take the High Priest of Dagon seriously he too emerges as a figure of complexity. The long sexual confrontation in Act II is continually provocative—compare it with anything in Meyerbeer—and it can all play brilliantly.

In addition, foreign singing styles are not as destructive here as in *Faust*, for example. Intelligent Verdians and Wagnerians have provided remarkable Samsons (see below), and even a Dalila with a big Italian vibrato but strong focus and breath control can present an image of authority. These roles can absorb international gifts better than some others of perhaps greater subtlety. So *Samson* waits with some fervor, as usual, for its next great tenor and mezzo-soprano.

1981 CASTLE OPERA (VHS) / PIONEER (LD)

(Stage Performance, Stereo, Color, Subtitled)
118 minutes

Shirley Verrett (A), Jon Vickers (B), Jonathan Summers (C), John Tomlinson (D), Gwynne Howell (E), Chorus and Orchestra of the Royal Opera House—Colin Davis

Royal Opera, Covent Garden: Elijah Moshinsky (stage director), John Vernon (video director)

There are weaknesses in this performance, in exposed places—the beginning and the ending, for example—but you can forget about them. This is, for once, more than a Biblical sex drama. These lovers are locked in competition, like Hyppolyta and Theseus. You can hear the weapons rattle when they *think* about making love. Jon Vickers enters with the intensity of a warrior-prophet and builds from that to passion and then agony. On her first entrance Shirley Verrett has such dignity and sexual poise that she and Vickers together suggest two warring forces of nature. The second act setting is a series of simple architectural forms and columns in the desert—not a plant in sight. That puts all the burden of sensual softness and manipulation on her confident shoulders. Her lithe, taut voice and expert treatment of the musical line expand an impression of sexual inevitability. In the last act Vickers's spiritual agony and Verrett's hatred get us through the trivialities of the Temple of Dagon scene to a true spiritual climax. Both John Tomlinson and Jonathan Summers are light-voiced, but Summers performs the High Priest with mesmerizing concentration, and Colin Davis conducts a performance of exciting tension and control. Sidney Nolan's sets do not always escape cliché, and the final catastrophe is an unconvincing disaster, but in general the visual atmosphere of crude strength supports the mood of the performance. This team has taken *Samson et Dalila* seriously, and the result has tragic depth.

1981 KULTUR (VHS) / PIONEER (LD)

(Stage Performance, Stereo, Color, Subtitled) 154 minutes

Shirley Verrett (A), Plácido Domingo (B), Wolfgang Brendel (C), Arnold Voketaitis (D), Kevin Langan (E), San Francisco Opera Chorus and Orchestra—Julius Rudel

San Francisco Opera: Nicolas Joël (stage director), Kirk Browning (video director)

This is a version that might have been designed for Citizen Kane's operatic wife. The color is forties TECHNICOLOR. All of those Biblical skies are VIVID, and all of those pagan costumes are SHAMELESSLY OSTENTATIOUS—these Philistines really live up to their reputation for tastelessness. Wolfgang Brendel's High Priest of Dagon, for example, is at first required to sing through a bird-beak headdress that suggests nothing so much as Dagon the Dragon, and later to sport a beard decorated with dozens of little ornaments: one would swear that they jingle. And Shirley Verrett, one of the most beautiful women on the operatic stage and video screen, is in the Spring scene decorated and moussed up enough to suggest an aging Flower Maiden. The final bacchanalia is just what one might expect: a lot of bodies bumping about in skivvies, and Christian Holder, of all people, managing to writhe ineptly—a triumph, in its way, of the choreographer's art. One keeps looking for a cameo appearance by Hope and Crosby.

The problem with all of this is not that it's bizarre, but that it's so damned dull, and that it flattens some very fine performances. Julius Rudel settles for a rather sleepy instrumental opulence; few of the scenes drive through orchestrally to the striking emotional reversals of which Saint-Saëns is here a master. Within this languorous framework, all of the leads sing well, though they are not invariably well miked. Shirley Verrett offers a performance full of leonine hatred and charismatic stillness, even when in this production she is asked to do some pointless things, given the adult strength of her characterization: to skulk around the mill while the blind Samson prays for death, for example, and later to push aside Samson's boy to lead Samson by herself to the fatal columns. Plácido Domingo looks heroic and is in splendid voice, particularly in the great duet in Act II, which the two of them handle with moving style and conviction. In his characterization there is nothing of the craggy Biblical patriarch, but there is an outsized humanity reminiscent of the tenor's Otello.

And Wolfgang Brendel manages to survive his costumes to project a charismatic and starkly convincing High Priest. He has not quite the savage vocal force for the final scene, but who in this era does? Brandishing a whip with which he is eventually, and unconvincingly, strangled, Arnold Voketaitis is a strong Abimelech. Altogether, there are some fine things in this production. And there is also a lot of Toys "R" Us nonsense.

In a stark Covent Garden production with a few problems, Jon Vickers and Shirley Verrett, under Colin Davis, nevertheless find the spiritual tragedy in this opera.

LONDON GREEN

DIE FLEDERMAUS (1874)

A: Rosalinde von Eisenstein (s); B: Adele (s); C: Prince Orlofsky (ms);
D: Alfred (t); E: Gabriel von Eisenstein (t); F: Dr. Falke (bar);
G: Frank (bar)

The most famous of Viennese operettas is by now firmly entrenched at the opera house, so much so that we rarely see it today in the *echt* boulevard-operetta manner in which it was originally performed at the Theater an der Wien. Furthermore, because the work's Parisian roots (a comedy by Offenbach's great librettists Meilhac and Halévy) tie the plot's central party to champagne-filled end-of-year festivities, the operetta has been indelibly linked to New Year's Eve and all manner of "gala" presentations. This invariably means top opera stars in guest appearances, to justify holiday ticket prices.

Whether all this ensures a cogent, racy reading of this boisterous operetta is another matter. Too often it's a long interruption, with the awkward display of very grand opera types winkingly "letting their hair down." Some really can't cross over into musical comedy.

Die Fledermaus also has plentiful dialogue. I firmly believe that operetta should be delivered in the local vernacular. But with excellent video subtitles, why not do the original German? Just choose one or the other: the most offensive versions are those which offer two (or more) tongues, alienating much of the the audience at least half the time, and leaving it with an inadequate idea of the plot. (Perhaps that's why champagne is always prescribed.)

1984 CASTLE OPERA (VHS) / PIONEER (LD)

(Stage Performance, Stereo, Color, Not Subtitled) 180 minutes

Kiri Te Kanawa (A), Hildegarde Heichele (B), Doris Soffel (C), Dennis O'Neill (D), Hermann Prey (E), Benjamin Luxon (F), Paul Crook (G), Chorus and Orchestra of the Royal Opera House—Plácido Domingo

Royal Opera, Covent Garden: Leopold Lindtberg and Richard Gregson (stage directors), Humphrey Burton (video director)

This Royal Opera, Covent Garden production is performed in German, with a first-rate international cast, an unusual conductor, Plácido Domingo, and the lovely sets and costumes of Julia Trevelyan Oman, who has furnished the house with many luscious evocations of the nineteenth century. Kiri Te Kanawa and Hermann Prey do not have to condescend to operetta: they both love it, and her creamy Rosalinde and his gruff Eisenstein make a delightful coupling. (Prey is, of course, a deeper-voiced Eisenstein than is the norm.)

Director Leopold Lindtberg had a considerable Swiss-German theatrical reputation, but as he was born in Vienna, he obviously knew this milieu. (He died the year of this production.)

Despite the Viennese setting, English lines do creep into the dialogue (for cheap audience ha-has), but at least in the second act there's a good joke on this silliness. Doris Soffel is a first-rate, traditional Orlofsky, fiercely bored and bald, to boot. The gala includes a lot of operetta: Prey and chorus with Barinkay's entrance song from Strauss's *Der Zigeunerbaron*, and the travesty comedy team of Dr. Evadne Hinge and Dame Hilda Brackett (since broken up) with their maniacally gleeful renditions of Sullivan and Messager standards. Frederick Ashton's neoclassic ballet to Strauss's "Frühlungsstimmen-Walzer" is an added attraction, danced by Merle Park and Wayne Eagling. And Charles Aznavour makes an awkward appearance as well, singing something from the distant land of pop.

The jail scene in Act III features the truely Viennese Josef Meinrad as Frosch, not making too much sense for an English audience. Hildegarde Heichele is a pleasant Adele, but her audition solo, like so much else in this evening, is paced rather slowly by Maestro Domingo. This lack of comic pointing affects the third-act scene in which Eisenstein reveals his true identity to Rosalinde, though Prey is heroically good in it.

Some of the camera work is a bit flat, in several instances catching the chorus during its dull nonsinging moments in the Act II finale.

1987 DEUTSCHE GRAMMOPHON (VHS / LD)

(Stage Performance, Stereo, Color, Subtitled) 146 minutes

Pamela Coburn (A), Janet Perry (B), Brigitte Fassbaender (C), Josef Hopferwieser (D), Eberhard Wächter (E), Wolfgang Brendel (F), Benno Kusche (G), Chorus and Orchestra of the Bavarian State Opera—Carlos Kleiber

Munich Nationaltheater: Otto Schenk (stage director), Brian Large (video director)

Otto Schenk has staged *Die Fledermaus* all over the world, and this Bavarian Staatsoper production, designed by Günther Schneider-Siemssen, will often remind Metropolitan Opera patrons of the production both men did there. But this is a thoroughly German affair, albeit a Bavarian one—not too far from Vienna. The costume designs here are perplexing, with the action advanced thirty years to just before the period of *The Merry Widow*, décor-wise; the Eisensteins' interior reeks of garish Viennese bad taste, with ugly pictures and flashy bird-cages. Orlofsky's ballroom is similarly overdone, with unsightly framed mirrors and blackamoors holding gas globes. There is a revolve into the dining room at the end of Act II (also used at the Met), which few today realize was first used by designer Ernst Stern in Max Reinhardt's famous *Fledermaus* in 1920s Berlin.

Carlos Kleiber's conducting has a satisfyingly frenetic drive, and while some might criticize the lack of a true Viennese *Herz* ticking behind it, I find the whole affair bracing. The cast is easily the best on video. Eberhard Wächter doesn't at first seem too vital an Eisenstein, with a pronounced vibrato, but by the time he is finished with the "Komm mit mir zum Souper" duet with Dr. Falke (a sexy Wolfgang Brendel), he is off and running, neatly executing a head-stand. Alfred also seems a trifle old, but he at least doesn't try to be Italian; when dressed in Eisenstein's cap and gown, he looks like Richard Wagner! Pamela Coburn is a highly spirited Rosalinde, with excellent diction, and the "So muss allein ich bleiben" trio becomes effectively a quartet, with the camera constantly showing a happy Kleiber. Benno Kusche is the ideal prison governor, Frank.

At the Orlofsky ball, Brigitte Fassbaender is a fierce host, with the passion of a Tartar rather than the by-now boring boredom. Rosalinde's csardas is properly fiery, with Tokay accents. The chorus is rollickingly involved at the ball, moving humorously to Adele's every "Marquis." By the time of the dance interpolation—the Explosions polka—it has been whipped into such an inebriated state that it tops it off with a conga before it collapses, to its and the audience's delight. (This stops the show so cold that Orlofsky's line, "Genug damit, genug!"—"Enough of this!"—gets a huge laugh.)

In Act III, the Frosch is a German comedian unknown to me, and the Adele is not perhaps as fresh as one would like, but Dr. Blind's stammering is very funny. All in all, a thoroughly likeable *Fledermaus*.

1990 KULTUR (VHS) / PIONEER (LD)

(Stage Performance, Stereo, Color, in English) 180 minutes

Nancy Gustafson (A), Judith Howarth (B), Jochen Kowalski (C), Bonaventura Bottone (D), Louis Otey (E), Anthony Michaels-Moore (F), Eric Garrett (G), Chorus and Orchestra of the Royal Opera House—Richard Bonynge

Royal Opera, Covent Garden: John Cox (stage director), Humphrey Burton (video director)

This live London version from Covent Garden uses the same sets and costumes as the 1964 version. But the director and conductor are different (John Cox and Richard Bonynge), there is an entirely new cast performing the English version of John Mortimer, and the stars appearing in the gala section are heavy-duty. Mortimer's many fans of television's *Rumpole of the Bailey* will enjoy the legal bits he obviously relished translating in Acts I and III. If his Britainized Vienna has a lot of American accents, his translation still sings reasonably well, though without the memorably silly conceits Howard Dietz gave the Metropolitan's English version in the 1950s.

Fortunately, the cast is a conscientious and attractive one, making the story comparatively believable and leaving the star turns to the gala figures: Luciano Pavarotti, Marilyn Horne, and the guest of honor, Joan Sutherland, singing farewell to Covent Garden. These are tastefully done, with little hokiness: Frederico's lament from *L'Arlesiana* (Cilea)—Pavarotti; "Serbami

ognor si fido" from *Semiramide*—Sutherland and Horne; "Mon coeur s'ouvre à ta voix" from *Samson et Dalila*—Horne; "Parigi, o cara" from *La Traviata*—Sutherland and Pavarotti. And finally, bidding goodbye to the stage from which she first electrified the world, Sutherland sings "Home, Sweet Home," by which time no eye will be dry.

Such star-quality and genuine sentiment unfortunately make the goings-on in *Die Fledermaus* seem a bit pallid, but we are briskly transported back to Johann Strauss's Vienna with the same Ashton-choreographed "Voices of Spring" ballet. (Viewing it in fast-forward mode will make this section funnier.) The Act III jail scene has the typical topical jokes, here at the expense of Covent Garden and the Prime Minister, John Major, seen laughing in the audience. Louis Otey, Nancy Gustafson, and Bonaventura Bottone have a rollicking time with the Act III revelation trio, and all ends happily, with a little speech and presentation for Dame Joan; even Richard Bonynge gets a present.

One untraditional bit of casting is Jochen Kowalski's Prince Orlofsky. His spectacular countertenor seems at odds with his deeper speaking voice. Purists will not be pleased with this male usurpation of a famous operetta trouser part, but at least they don't have to hear a bass-baritone singing the part—this has happened.

————

Although the 1987 Deutsche Grammophon production from Munich does not include gala stars, it is the one most likely to put you into a festive holiday mood.

RICHARD TRAUBNER

Richard Strauss

Salome (1905)

A: Salome (s); B: Herodias (ms); C: Herodes (t); D: Jochanaan (bar)

The opera with which Strauss really made his name as an operatic composer built its success on the same guaranteed recipe as many an opera, play, or film: show shocking activity, in a framework that professes to condemn it, and thus free the audience to enjoy it without guilt. With Wilde's play, slightly shortened, as its basis, this one-act gem fills a Biblically based story with religious mania masking sexual deviance and bits of near-incest, fetishism, and nudity—all in music of the most glowing purity and sensuousness. The trick now is to retain the shock for audiences that have lived through much more explicit entertainment; or else, more difficult, to reexamine the opera for values other than the obvious ones of going too far, such as the possibility of subtle character development and interaction.

1974 DEUTSCHE GRAMMOPHON (VHS / LD)

(Film, Stereo, Color, Subtitled) 102 minutes

Teresa Stratas (A), Astrid Varnay (B), Hans Beirer (C), Bernd Weikl (D), Vienna Philharmonic Orchestra—Karl Böhm

Götz Friedrich (director)

The film medium enables Friedrich to stage the action effectively and convincingly in a fairly realistic courtyard space, with momentary views of the palace interior. He uses the ability to focus attention on small features, sometimes to over-obvious effect (Jochanaan's eyes when Salome sings about them), but sometimes helpfully (to clarify the progress of the theological disputes). The costumes are more puzzling, with odd head coverings for the royal family, including a beaded bathing cap for Salome herself. The biggest barrier to involvement, though, is intrinsic to the medium: the combination of a prerecorded audio track with the film action. Not just the synchronization is problematic (less in timing than in simulating the physical act of singing); changes in distance and orientation are not matched in the unvarying aural setup. Of course this goes to the heart of the basic problem of removing sung theater from the theatrical "givens" that justify it (one may start to wonder where the orchestra is, or why people are singing at all). These problems may be unsolvable in the last analysis; they remain difficulties nonetheless.

They are worth dealing with in this case, for something quite riveting is happening with Salome herself. Undoubtedly with the director's help, Stratas creates a complete and original characterization of a spoiled but not purposely evil royal child, accustomed to instant gratification of her whims and intrigued by the prophet who challenges the premises of the only world she has known. Her unthinking praise of his physical beauty becomes even more disturbing than usual when delivered with such innocence: she has found a pretty new toy that she wants. When he not only denies her wish but denounces her for it, her extravagant devastation makes sense because she clearly has never been treated this way before. During the following interlude, she takes us through a transformation into defensive bitterness and determination to hurt the man who hurt her. Her motivation remains visible even during the dance (which film editing, and the judicious use of dancing attendants, helps her through), and continues with equal logic through to her complex feelings as she fondles the severed head—angry at first, then reliving her attraction to him, finally luxuriating in narcissistic sadness.

The others are on a less special level but do not hurt this central achievement. Beirer retains some remnants of dramatic-tenor strength for Herod, and Varnay brings authority to her vocally spent Herodias. Neither shrinks from excess in their physical embodiment of their characters, nor is this approach discouraged by their almost inhuman makeup. Weikl makes a resonant, solid Jochanaan, if not of the stature as an actor to face up to Stratas in the central confrontation. Wieslaw Ochman sounds marvelous as Narraboth, and Böhm stirs up his orchestra to fine effect while supporting his Salome skillfully. The others make their contributions to the overall atmosphere but do not stand out as anything special. No matter: it is the central figure who makes this production memorable.

1990 TELDEC (VHS / LD)

(Stage Performance, Stereo, Color, Subtitled)
109 minutes

Catherine Malfitano (A), Leonie Rysanek (B), Horst Hiestermann (C), Simon Estes (D), Orchestra of the Deutsche Oper, Berlin—Giuseppe Sinopoli

Deutsche Oper, Berlin: Petr Weigl (stage director), Brian Large (video director)

This is a good example of an above-average *Salome* stage production that would rightly be praised for taking pains with the blocking and characterization. All participants give evidence of care and sincerity, yet the overall result is not convincing.

The first image is a promising one: Josef Svoboda's white courtyard with a moon looming overhead, just as one pictures it from hearing the music. Not just pictorially evocative, the various clean-cut levels and shapes work rather well in organizing and clarifying the action under Weigl's direction. What he has not managed to do is turn opera singers into actors whose stage-sized poses and gestures can withstand the scrutiny of the camera.

This applies especially to Malfitano, working hard and earnestly to tell us who Salome is. She has been dressed in pure white (costumes by Josef Jelnek) and is spotlit throughout, and every move and expression has clearly been carefully thought through. But the calculation remains evident, and she never persuades us that she really is this uncomprehending princess. Like many another Salome, she is defeated by the demands of the dance: however carefully planned the choreography, there is simply too much music for someone who is not primarily a dancer to fill out, especially under the camera's scrutiny. Her voice is stretched by the demands of the role; at times she sounds coarse and overstressed, other times she comes through with the shine and float that characterized her earlier work as a lyric soprano.

Sinopoli handles the score with impressive color and flow, and the supporting cast does its job. Simon Estes sounds his best in this music, authoritative and resonant, and presents a suitably majestic figure visually (he too is isolated in a spotlight), although he is no more successful than she in generating a genuine interaction. Hiestermann and Rysanek both sound hard-pressed vocally but present relatively restrained visual interpretations of the royal couple.

1992 KULTUR (VHS) / PIONEER (LD)

(Stage Performance, Stereo, Color, Subtitled)
105 Minutes

Maria Ewing (A), Gillian Knight (B), Kenneth Riegel (C), Michael Devlin (D), Orchestra of the Royal Opera House—Edward Downes

Royal Opera, Covent Garden: Peter Hall (stage director and associate video director), Derek Bailey (video director)

This Covent Garden stage production has been thought through by Peter Hall with his customary care and attentiveness. He has considered every line of text and tried to ensure that its implications are understood and realized. Such elements as the blue dust that we are told Herodias wears in her hair have been attended to, and the scenery and costumes strike a carefully considered balance between historical Judea and the world of Strauss's music and Wilde's text, with overtones of Beardsley and possibly Klimt. Mostly the mixture of periods works unobtrusively and well, with only the quintet of Jews striking a jarring note in their European-looking costuming.

Moment by moment, one can appreciate the care of the undertaking. The moon looms appropriately, the stage is a riot of rich colors to match those in the score, and this prophet is the only one who could plausibly induce Salome's passion for his body, hair, and mouth. Devlin takes the stage in only a loincloth and sings his role with strength and passion, plus hints of an insanity of his own. Robin Leggate, oddly costumed in a green floor-length robe, establishes a memorable enough presence as Narraboth that his suicide becomes a major stage event rather than one easily overlooked. Riegel is a most successful Herod, his lyric tenor no longer pretty in sound but still expressive and controllable, and used for a more subtle characterization than usual. Likewise, Knight creates a regal, rather youthful and elegant Herodias with no hint of caricature about her, even though this weight of music sounds a bit taxing for her voice. The remainder of the cast, Covent Garden regulars, contribute strong work in their succession of brief opportunities.

The question mark is Ewing. In her way, she holds the stage rivetingly, but her way will not be to all tastes. Her visual performance isn't acting, exactly: she's suitably petulant at the start, gets progressively more excited, and has a fine frenzy at the end, but she does not create a carefully delineated person as the other leading actors are doing. Her singing likewise disdains the usual standards of evenness of scale and continuity of tone and weight; now she belts or half-speaks a low phrase, now she croons a quiet bit, now she summons up a full-voiced wail when nothing else will suffice. It's the sort of vocal performance that, as an unrepeatable live experience, might convince and even seem memorable, but does not hold up under the repeated scrutiny allowed by video recording. To her credit, she manages the dance more successfully than anyone else, with sufficient variety and building of tension to make the long sequence cohere and maintain suspense. Though some degree of nudity now seems to be mandatory at the end of the dance, and is present in all three videos, Ewing prolongs her final unveiling so unflinchingly that some of the intended shock is restored. The dance is indeed the most successful part of her portrayal, which is otherwise the most questionable part of a strong stage production, further enhanced by Downes's fine conducting of the excellent Covent Garden orchestra.

The Hall stage production is so well thought out that it seems to demand first consideration. But its problematic central portrayal compromises its success, and it is in exactly this respect that the Friedrich film shines. Stratas manages something here that might have been thought impossible; she turns the opera into high drama, even genuine tragedy. For that achievement, 1974 DG must take preference.

JON ALAN CONRAD

RICHARD STRAUSS

ELEKTRA (1909)

A: Elektra (s); B: Chrysothemis (s); C: Klytämnestra (ms);
D: Aegisth (t); E: Orest (bar)

With its masterly blend of timeless Greek tragedy and Freudian psychology, the Strauss-Hofmannsthal operatic treatment of Sophocles' *Elektra* has become an open invitation for "inventive" directors in these days of producer-dominated opera. The three video versions to date only hint at the variety of approaches that have been taken over the past few decades, and future productions are bound to offer many more. Gone forever, it seems, is the simple, uncluttered classical setting specified by the libretto: the inner courtyard of Agamemnon's palace in ancient Mycenae. More important to contemporary interpreters of the opera are symbolic representations of the principal characters' inner obsessions—Elektra's thirst for blood vengeance on her mother in particular—and the smothering atmosphere of decadence and moral decay that pervades the entire drama.

Of course the most effective performances will always stand or fall on the singers of the three leading female roles, especially the title part. Distinguished Elektras have never been plentiful, and small wonder. Not only must a soprano have the power to ride the crest of Strauss's orchestral tidal waves, but she must also give expressive color and dramatic nuance to the strange beauty of Hofmannsthal's language as well as be an actress of uncommon subtlety—qualities all the more crucial in a film where an Elektra is brought into such close contact with the viewer. Klytämnestra is in

some ways even trickier to portray on-screen. What may look effective from a distance can all too easily degenerate into grotesque mugging and over-the-top verbal exaggeration as the queen graphically describes her nightmares and guilt-ridden conscience. Chrysothemis must be the glorious, gleaming vocal foil to Elektra as she expresses her longing to escape and raise her own family with a semblance of normalcy. The perfect combination has yet to materialize on film, but each of the three videos presently available has a strong claim for attention.

1980 PARAMOUNT (VHS) / PIONEER (LD)

(Stage Performance, Stereo, Color, Subtitled) 112 minutes

Birgit Nilsson (A), Leonie Rysanek (B), Mignon Dunn (C), Robert Nagy (D), Donald McIntyre (E), Metropolitan Opera Chorus and Orchestra—James Levine

Metropolitan Opera: Herbert Graf (production), Paul Mills (stage director), Brian Large (video director)

Conceptually the least radical *Elektra* on video, the Metropolitan production seen here dates back to 1966, before directors really began to get fanciful. Graf's staging is clear and straightforward, leaving Rudolf Heinrich's brooding, rotting mausoleum to make the most vivid dramatic statement. That was best appreciated when the set could be seen in full view, but even on the small screen its threatening aspects forcefully suggest the crumbling ruins of a once strong and proud family. Four immense, striated, siliceous stone slabs fan down from upstage along the courtyard floor, mirrored by four matching boulders suspended from the ceiling and sweeping up to the proscenium. Through the decaying holes and gouges in the palace one can spy hints of the awful offstage activities: the ferocious procession of animals being led to sacrifice, the slaughter of Aegisth, and the household staff's frantic hunt for the murderous Orest.

There's no missing the celebratory aura about this Saturday matinee performance. Nilsson had been away from the Met for five years, and the vociferous demonstration that welcomes her back after the curtain falls, complete with a deluge of flowers and shredded programs, is all a beloved diva could possibly want. And the soprano is still a formidable force of nature in the role, although there are definite signs that this vocal phenomenon was reaching the end. The typical sunny brilliance of her tone often turns shrill and edgy when under pressure at top volume, resulting in a tendency to sing sharp much of the time. Nilsson's Elektra, like most every role she sang, functions at a cool emotional temperature—portraying obsessive neurotics was never this forthright artist's forte—and her blunt interpretation generates little dramatic fire or intensity. She is usually at her most effective when making a forceful stand-and-deliver statement or simply listening quietly, and threateningly, to the frantic outbursts of her mother and sister.

Dunn must be one of the most regally glamorous Klytämnestras in the opera's history. She looks almost too freshly turned out for a woman racked with guilt and suffering from chronic insomnia, but her vocal solidity, refusal to overdo, and willingness to give every note full value could not be more welcome or appropriate. Rysanek's Chrysothemis is a consistent joy as she unleashes her opulent soprano with unstinting generosity, although one sometimes wonders what psychological forces could possibly keep such a healthily feminine, aggressive

personality from fleeing this oppressive environment. McIntyre and Nagy perform their tasks competently if with no special distinction. Conductors are often tempted to treat the score as a showpiece for their orchestras, and Levine goes rather overboard in this respect, encouraging a performance that is excessively loud and hectic for all its instrumental virtuosity.

1981 LONDON (VHS / LD)

(Film, Stereo, Color, Subtitled) 117 minutes

Leonie Rysanek (A), Catarina Ligendza (B), Astrid Varnay (C), Hans Beirer (D), Dietrich Fischer-Dieskau (E), Vienna State Opera Chorus and Vienna Philharmonic Orchestra— Karl Böhm

Götz Friedrich (director)

Friedrich's bleak filmed vision of *Elektra* begins and ends with the surviving inhabitants of the house of Atreus looking pathetically grimy and bedraggled, quite literally caught in the pouring rain. Ruined Greek stonework is strewn all about Agamemnon's palace, although Josef Svoboda's industrial set mostly suggests an abandoned warehouse, located somewhere on the outskirts of modern-day Vienna and inhabited by a weird assortment of wretched homeless people. Klytämnestra and Aegisth look almost colorful in the midst of all this misery, grotesque fantasy figures who might have wandered in from a Fellini movie: she a flabby, raddled wreck with blackened eyes and a skin-tight shower cap, and he a bloated, painted monstrosity who dotes on black men and body builders. Since this is a production originally conceived for film, we are shown various scenes and objects, mostly in Elektra's fevered imagination, that are unlikely to be seen in a staged performance, such as the murder of Agamemnon in his bath and the king's bloodied, impassive dead face staring down on his daughter as she revels in her obsessions. It's all very entertaining, but in the end this stagy, self-indulgent gloss on *Elektra* seldom generates much dramatic tension.

That is a shame, since the cast is a superior

one, preserving cameos by such important veterans as Josef Greindl (Orest's Guardian) and Kurt Böhme (the Old Servant), as well as more prominent appearances by Varnay (herself a great Elektra in the fifties) and Beirer, not to mention Rysanek and Fischer-Dieskau, who never performed their roles onstage. Rysanek is stretched to her limits, but she is courageously unflinching before every vocal challenge. Beyond that, it is positively thrilling to hear Elektra's music sung so vividly and confidently by this powerful, succulent soprano, more familiar to operagoers at the time as Chrysothemis and, later in her career, portraying the agonies of Klytämnestra. True, her overall performance is somewhat compromised by having to lip-synch the part. Few singers ever combined the physical act of singing with body movement more naturally or expressively than Rysanek, and the dramatic tension produced by that characteristic element of her performing persona is missing here. Still, she seldom fails to penetrate to the heart of this miserable creature on a purely vocal level, particularly during the poignant recognition scene with Orest.

Made up like a ridiculous harridan, Varnay can do little to salvage Klytämnestra, and she overacts with gleeful enthusiasm—it's sad to see this great artist so thoroughly sabotaged by a director's "concept" and compounding the damage as she miscalculates one effect after another. Although her wiry soprano sounds a trifle squally, Ligendza is an unusually delicate and vulnerable Chrysothemis, and Fischer-Dieskau makes a light-voiced but eloquent Orest. Böhm died just after he had finished recording the sound track in August 1981, and the conductor takes one long last look at a beloved score by his old mentor. Understandably, he seems reluctant to let go of the music, and if the performance (with the customary stage cuts) tends to be excessively drawn out and rather lumbering, at least the Vienna Philharmonic plays with glowing, lava-like intensity. Purchasers of the laser discs are hereby warned that the second side change comes at the worst possible moment, just before Elektra's ecstatic cry of joy as she recognizes her brother.

1989 KULTUR (VHS) / PIONEER (LD)

(Stage Performance, Stereo, Color, Subtitled) 108 minutes

Eva Marton (A), Cheryl Studer (B), Brigitte Fassbaender (C), James King (D), Franz Grundheber (E), Vienna State Opera Chorus and Orchestra—Claudio Abbado

Vienna State Opera: Harry Kupfer (stage director), Brian Large (video director)

It's virtually impossible to figure out with any degree of accuracy what dramatic points Kupfer and his colleagues—set designer Hans Shavernoch and costumier Reinhard Heinrich—were attempting to make with this production. Like many opera videos from stage performances, this one is shrouded in Stygian darkness much of the time and very little detail is visible. One can make out a huge stone head on the ground, and the statue from which it came may well be lurking in the background, but one can't be sure. There are lots of Tarzan-like hanging ropes for the singers to swing upon whenever the mood strikes, but their significance remains obscure. As the curtain rises, the servant women might be clearing away the bones of sacrificial beasts before one maid is herself stripped naked and strung up. Looking like a washerwoman in her turban and work clothes, Chrysothemis suddenly opens her dingy gray rags to reveal a blood-red chemise, possibly to represent her yearning for motherhood. Many other scenic symbols can be faintly detected through the murk, but never clearly enough to add up to a coherent statement about the work. Whatever the message may be, the audience seems evenly divided over its meaning at the end, half shrieking in rapture and half loudly booing the production team.

What's unmistakable is the intensely physical nature of Kupfer's direction—the cast is constantly in motion, clutching and wrestling with each other when they're not twitching and writhing on their own. Again, the sense of it all is imprecise and elusive, especially since the singers mostly give the impression of diligently doing what they've been told rather than performing their parts with any inner conviction. Marton, in fact, is a dour, blunt Elektra who frowns a lot but never puts much expressive variety into her acting, let alone her singing. At least her voice is generally dependable, even if the tone tends to be opaque and monochromatic. Studer is an excellent Chrysothemis, her gleaming soprano sounding fresh and responsive, and Grundheber sings Orest's music with firmly rounded, sonorous tones. The main drawback is Fassbaender, whose bizarre Klytämnestra-in-Wonderland was soon to become even more overdone than it is here, if that's possible to imagine. She roars the entire role from the chest and wildly exaggerates every aspect of the character until one is only made painfully aware of a misconceived interpretation that is built from sheer artifice, from its over-the-top singing and acting right down to the cartoonish costume and makeup. Abbado gets his share of boos at the end, but the orchestral playing is in fact the best element of the performance—a leaner, more elegant instrumental sound than one generally hears in this music, but beautifully focused and shaped into wonderfully lyrical paragraphs.

———

If the visual production had been as effective as its musical execution, the London performance would be the recommended choice. For now, though, the Met's less radical but theatrically sound approach is more satisfying, despite a formidable Elektra somewhat past her prime.

PETER G. DAVIS

RICHARD STRAUSS

DER ROSENKAVALIER (1911)

A: Sophie (s); B: The Marschallin (s); C: Octavian (s or ms);
D: Faninal (bar); E: Baron Ochs (bs)

With *Rosenkavalier* Strauss turned his back on the psychological thriller exemplified by *Salome* and *Elektra*, and also on the adventurous musical language he had devised for them. Coaxed by his collaborator Hugo von Hofmannsthal, he began a series of explorations in period styles, idealistic mythology, and even autobiography. But this Viennese comedy of manners became his greatest success: its carefully detailed characterizations, intricate plotting, luxuriant orchestral writing, conversational vocal style that surges into cantilena at points of passion, and combination of sentiment, comedy, and spectacle have remained irresistible.

Rosenkavalier makes considerable demands on its performers. The singers need range and power, but also must be able to articulate rapid dialogue lightly and cleanly. The finely detailed orchestral writing calls for finesse, transparency, and rhythmic verve. The stage action is full of subtleties, requiring attention to period detail and to consistency of style. A considerable body of tradition has grown up around the work's staging, stemming initially from the Dresden premiere (supervised by Max Reinhardt), on which was based a production book whose influence can still be felt in the performances available on video. Some cuts in the score have become traditional, and all videos observe them to a greater or lesser degree.

1960 KULTUR (VHS)

(Film, Mono, Color, Subtitled) 186 minutes

Anneliese Rothenberger (A), Elisabeth Schwarzkopf (B), Sena Jurinac (C), Erich Kunz (D), Otto Edelmann (E), Vienna State Opera Chorus, Vienna Philharmonic Orchestra— Herbert von Karajan

Salzburg Festival: Rudolf Hartmann (stage director), Paul Czinner (film director)

Like Czinner's film of the 1954 Salzburg *Don Giovanni*, this is a postsynchronized enactment of a stage production to an audio recording by the same performers, made in takes that corresponded to the length of the reels of film then available. (According to Schwarzkopf, Karajan asked for only one retake during the audio recording, the Prelude to Act III.) Distractingly, the synchronization is far from precise. The production, designed by Teo Otto (costumes by Erni Kniepert) and staged by Rudolf Hartmann, inaugurated Salzburg's Grosses Festspielhaus, with its Cinemascope aspect ratio, in 1960 (not 1961, as given on the Kultur packaging); to fill out the breadth of the stage, Otto devised exterior balconies. Before each act we see Karajan briskly enter the pit and bow (to an unseen and probably nonexistent audience), and we watch him until the curtain rises. (The acts are preceded by crawling synopses, incomplete and even misleading.)

311

Featured are several noted postwar *Rosenkavalier* singers. Schwarzkopf's finely detailed Marschallin seems less mannered than in the famous 1956 recording, though with the perspective of time one detects cinematic notes in her theatrical *Gestalt* (sometimes Dietrich, occasionally Claudette Colbert). More spontaneous is Jurinac's passionate Octavian; despite a suspicion of tremolo, Rothenberger's Sophie is also winning. More problematic is Edelmann, who makes brave if often inaccurate noises in a broad Viennese accent but carries a heavy burden of schtick. Kunz's light-voiced Faninal is skillful, Hilde Rössl-Majdan is a firm and stylish Annina (the best in any of these performances), and the other character parts are handled by able veterans. Giuseppe Zampieri rather bawls the tenor aria, but he does so with golden tone, which is not the worst way of dealing with it. Karajan's conducting of the Vienna Philharmonic (a little below top form) is fluent in the fast parts, and sustains the slower ones to good effect.

Despite a few odd details (some rather exotic statuary in Act II, for example), the production is traditional; Hartmann worked with Strauss and Clemens Krauss in Munich and certainly knew the opera's traditions and subtleties. Whether Czinner, the film director, knew them as well is more questionable; either the camera work or the subsequent editing misses important points, and staging and montage combine to yield a cluttered, muddled effect at the Baron's final exit.

Kultur's videotape is based on a film print in which the blue tones have faded badly, giving the whole affair a pinkish cast. Some edits between the original film reels are clumsy, and the mono sound, greatly favoring the voices, is restricted in dynamic range and occasionally distorted; a better source print (or a digital restoration) might yield more faithful colors, though perhaps not greatly improved sound.

1979 DEUTSCHE GRAMMOPHON (VHS / LD)

(Stage Performance, Stereo, Color, Subtitled)
186 minutes

Lucia Popp (A), Gwyneth Jones (B), Brigitte Fassbaender (C), Benno Kusche (D), Manfred Jungwirth (E), Chorus and Orchestra of the Bavarian State Opera—Carlos Kleiber

Bavarian State Opera: Otto Schenk (stage director), Karlheinz Hundorf (video director)

The dominating presence in this performance is Carlos Kleiber, who draws from singers and orchestra a performance of great warmth and élan, precise yet always spontaneous, founded on a sure feeling for the movements of the bass line and the harmonies. The Munich orchestra may not be world class (the principal oboist, though an excellent musician, is of the bad old German quacking school), but it responds brilliantly to Kleiber's baton, vividly shaping the musical gestures: note, for example, the moment when the Marschallin realizes she has forgotten to kiss Octavian, and the orchestra leaps to seize the emotion. Throughout the work, the scrupulous dynamics—especially where Strauss asks for softness—give the performance a sharper profile than most, and at climaxes the orchestra sings so fervently as to compensate for some vocal limitations.

Despite those limitations, the cast is impressive. Gwyneth Jones has done nothing better than this Marschallin; while the intonational waywardness of her upper register is occasionally in evidence (most distractingly at the start of the final trio), she is usually comfortable with the vocal line and especially with Strauss's light conversational writing. A skilled actress, she musters a range of dignity, authority, irony, and generosity to match all the phases of the last-act exchanges with Octavian, Ochs, Sophie, and Faninal. Jungwirth, though his work exhibits a palpable wobble on longer notes and a limited dynamic variety, is also a master of the *parlando* style, with superb articulation even at very fast tempos; his genial rustic boorishness and acquisitiveness limn a more complex and interesting figure than Edelmann's clowning. Vocal reservations could be expressed about Fassbaender as well, but again the conviction and theatrical skill of her portrayal keep one enthralled despite occasional frayed tones. Values are slightly reversed in Popp's Sophie, physically too mature but sung with radiant and melting tone in the love music, and with real fire in the confrontations with Ochs; in the presentation of the rose, the chemistry between Sophie and Octavian is potent. The veteran Kusche just passes muster as Faninal, and the smaller parts are well managed, though Francisco Araiza makes heavy weather of the tenor aria.

Jürgen Rose's sumptuous sets and costumes are along traditional lines, and Schenk's direction cleanly and skillfully focuses the various elements of the drama—ceremonial, farcical, emotional. Among many nice details: in Act III, the candles are lit to match what is clearly Strauss's musical illustration of that action, a point handled rather casually in other stagings. The intent viewer will also observe that Octavian picks up the Italian intriguers as he quits Faninal's palace in Act II. As the latter point suggests, the camera work is well handled, nowhere more so than in the Baron's exit scene, often a mishmash. (Kleiber takes a few more cuts than most conductors in Act III.)

1984 SONY (VHS / LD)

(Stage Performance, Stereo, Color, Not Subtitled) 211 minutes

Janet Perry (A), Anna Tomowa-Sintow (B), Agnes Baltsa (C), Gottfried Hornik (D), Kurt Moll (E), Vienna State Opera Chorus, Vienna Philharmonic Orchestra—Herbert von Karajan

Salzburg Festival: Herbert von Karajan (stage director), Hugo Käch (video director)

Back at Salzburg in 1984, one discovers Otto's 1960 production still in use, though at first one isn't sure, since the picture quality is finer here and the colors appear quite different: in the version submitted for review (VHS), they are tipped toward mauve and gray tones. The generally capable video editing misses only a few important points: for example, the camera is late reaching the Marschallin in Act III when she recalls the phrase "Heut' oder Morgen. . . ." This time an audience is visible, and Karajan's progress to the podium is painfully slow.

Compared to the audio-only version Karajan made in Vienna with substantially the same cast a year or so earlier, this is rather more involving.

The orchestral playing is superbly refined yet not etiolated, and one has a real sense of a performance, albeit one that occasionally comes close to grinding to a halt under Karajan's excessively tender loving care, notably in the Marschallin's reflective passages in Act I. Perhaps because of Tomowa-Sintow's generous proportions, the curtain's rise finds her and Baltsa on the sofa rather than the bed; a rich-toned and often expressive singer who can turn squally in negotiating faster writing, Tomowa-Sintow is most comfortable in those meditative passages and acts with dignity and warmth if not glamour. Early in Act I, Baltsa is too often caught looking sideways at the conductor between grimaces, but she becomes more natural—and convincingly forceful—in Act II. A respectable, pretty Sophie, Perry is thin-voiced by comparison with Popp.

The prize performance here is Moll's Ochs, a masterful portrayal of a pretentious but sentimental lecher: in complete command of the notes from top F to bottom E, always observant of Strauss's dynamics, he sings and reads every line with meaning as well as accuracy. Particularly fine are his progressive grasp of the background to his humiliation and his attempt to blackmail his way back to grace, opposite which Tomowa-Sintow's dignity also plays well. (Regrettably, Karajan makes an unusual cut in the early part of Moll's *scena* at the end of Act II.) Hornik blusters well as Faninal, and Wilma Lipp, a Vienna coloratura star of the fifties, still makes good sounds as the duenna, but the Annina has a pronounced tremolo.

For many viewers, the surprising absence of subtitles will rule this recording completely out of court (nor is a libretto furnished—merely a synopsis).

1985 HOME VISION (VHS) / PIONEER (LD)

(Stage Performance, Stereo, Color, Subtitled) 204 minutes

Barbara Bonney (A), Kiri Te Kanawa (B), Anne Howells (C), Jonathan Summers (D), Aage Haugland (E), Chorus and Orchestra of the Royal Opera House—Georg Solti

Royal Opera, Covent Garden: John Schlesinger (stage director), Brian Large (video director)

Recorded at two live performances in February 1985, this video preserves the production initially staged the preceding December to celebrate the twenty-fifth anniversary of Solti's Covent Garden debut conducting the same work. According to the credits, the opera was "produced for the stage and adapted for television" by Schlesinger. William Dudley's sets may not desert the rococo, but offer a somewhat free version thereof (Faninal's palace, not quite furnished yet, has a vaguely industrial staircase, while in Act III the inn chamber is set within a box); Maria Björnson's costumes also push period boundaries. Compared to Schenk's Munich version, the staging seems fussy, though most of the necessary points are made.

The principals are an uneven lot. Anne Howells, a convincingly tomboyish Octavian, strains at the limits of a smallish voice and often shades the pitches. (Baltsa was the production's original protagonist; perhaps her contract for the Karajan video precluded remaking the opera so soon). Haugland certainly can sing Ochs's music, but neither in aspect—an immobile face, with pasty and grotesque makeup—nor in manner does he evoke the man's humor or lechery; he comes across as merely unpleasant. Bonney is a slightly brittle Sophie; she and Howells pick at the notes in their duets without generating much mutual magnetism or musical line. Te Kanawa, a handsome Marschallin on stage, suffers under the camera's close scrutiny: her eyes and blonde wig evoke memories of Carol Channing, and neither in action nor singing does she reveal spontaneity, focus, or comprehension of the words; in the third act she signals regret, but irony and regal command are not within her range.

Absent a single really convincing principal, the performance never pulls together. The Prelude—angular, energetic, brass very prominent, a plethora of details emphasized—tells us up front that this will be a characteristic Solti interpretation: punchy, insistent, overactive in the busy music, inert in the quieter passages, and only occasionally settling into a happy medium.

This has its effect on the cast—not only the principals, but several of the smaller parts (Annina, Valzacchi, Faninal, Marianne, the Tenor) who work awfully hard for their effects. The recorded sound is good, but the opera never really happens.

1994 DEUTSCHE GRAMMOPHON (VHS / LD)

(Stage Performance, Stereo, Color, Subtitled) 193 minutes

Barbara Bonney (A), Felicity Lott (B), Anne Sofie von Otter (C), Gottfried Hornik (D), Kurt Moll (E), Chorus and Orchestra of the Vienna State Opera—Carlos Kleiber

Vienna State Opera: Otto Schenk (stage director), Horant H. Hohlfeld (video director)

Kleiber's second video of *Rosenkavalier* (a work he has never recorded in audio form) is surprisingly disappointing. His conducting is as spontaneous and characterful as ever, and the Viennese orchestra is actually better than the one in Munich—but the same magic doesn't happen. Partly to blame is the sound: thinner than in the earlier set, with a less firm bass line and narrower dynamic range. Also at fault is the production. Rudolf Heinrich's decor is unconventional without good reason for being so; for example, the portable screens brought on to provide intimacy in the Sophie-Octavian chat and later used as shields for the Annina-Valzacchi ambush would not have been necessary in a less absurdly spacious set. Schenk's staging, recognizably the same in many details as before, is now and then fussier.

Lott, less glamorous than Te Kanawa, is a more resourceful actress, but she sings with limited color, luster, spin, and dynamic range—and thus gives the character less specificity, variety, and authority than Jones or Tomowa-Sintow. Nine years after singing with Solti, Bonney looks a bit old for Sophie and her sound is a tad harder. The tall, thin von Otter makes a highly plausible Octavian, with a nice line in boyish gawkiness; however, she does not yet command all of Fassbaender's intensity or Jurinac's passion. Happily, Moll still deploys his polish, articulation, and firm low notes, yet he seems on this occasion less commanding than fifteen years earlier. Most of the small parts are decent enough, though the casting of the aging Waldemar Kmentt as the Marschallin's major-domo is an example of Viennese sentiment carried to an over-optimistic extreme.

An unusual feature of the video treatment deserves mention. In opera videos, it is usually standard for the camera to remain fixed on the stage as long as the curtain is open, but here, during the big orchestral statement of Ochs's waltz tune near the end of Act II, and several times during his exit scene in Act III, the camera drops into the pit to watch Kleiber. It's actually fascinating to see what he's doing at these points (or, rather what he's *not* doing: just a gen-

eralized egging-on of the players rather than any kind of specific time-beating), but it profoundly intrudes upon the experience of the opera as a theatrical performance. The subtitles, easier to read than in the Munich version, unnecessarily render Mariandel's peasant dialect into cockney. In the (admittedly difficult) Act III trio, they are confusing because the words we read are often being sung by someone not currently on the screen.

The Kleiber Munich version is clearly superior to all the others, though the flawed 1960 film retains interest for its justifiably celebrated characterizations.

DAVID HAMILTON

RICHARD STRAUSS

ARIADNE AUF NAXOS

(1912; revised 1916)

A: Prima Donna / Ariadne (s); B: Zerbinetta (s); C: Composer (s);
D: Tenor / Bacchus (t); E: Harlekin (bar); F: Music Master (bar)

The revision of *Ariadne auf Naxos* is the version that holds the stage in opera houses around the world. Strauss's original version forms an integral part of the version he and Hugo von Hofmannsthal made of Moliere's *Le Bourgeois Gentilhomme*: extensive incidental music followed by a combination serious / comic opera for the entertainment of the play's characters. This first version of the opera might well be judged preferable on aesthetic grounds, for it closes all the frames in which the *opera seria* is presented—the comedians sign off after the departure of the serious characters, and then we return to the spectators. But the revision (which invented the Prologue in place of the preceding play) was still one of the best ideas Strauss ever had: not only enabling the opera to be performed in venues other than German theaters with full staffs of singers and actors on hand, but making the opera itself more practical—curtailing the fascinating but truly excessive length and difficulty of Zerbinetta's aria, for instance.

Even in the opera's newer, more workable format, it still needs careful handling, for it lives by the successful realization of one intricate detail after another; as an elaborate play-within-a-play concoction it keeps involvement at a distance and invites us to enjoy it precisely on that level of connoisseurship. Whether performed at a festival or not, *Ariadne auf Naxos* is

a "festival opera" in terms of the special attention it needs.

1988 DEUTSCHE GRAMMOPHON (VHS / LD)

(Stage Performance, Stereo, Color, Subtitled)
133 minutes

Jessye Norman (A), Kathleen Battle (B), Tatiana Troyanos (C), James King (D), Stephen Dickson (E), Franz Ferdinand Nentwig (F), Metropolitan Opera Orchestra—James Levine

Metropolitan Opera: Bodo Igesz (stage director), Brian Large (video director)

This performance represents an above-average but not extraordinary night at the Metropolitan Opera in the late 1980s: three of its most popular stars, a generally distinguished cast, the house's musical director conducting its great orchestra in one of the works he does best, all in a revival of a 1962 production that may have been carefully rehearsed in a logistical sense but that still comes to life only intermittently.

Part of the problem is that this is all too obviously a stage performance caught by the cameras and microphones. That need not be a problem in a work designed to project on the grand scale, but *Ariadne* is a chamber opera: not just in the size of orchestra or cast, but in the sense that its effects are those of atmosphere, texture, and charm. And yet the singers have to project its effects in a huge theater, while their efforts are being captured in close-up. So we have Norman, a presence who commands a stage regally and a voice designed for engulfing an audience in a flood of sound, done less than justice by the incessant extreme facial close-ups and the miking that gives everyone else the same aural presence. That latter feature may be helpful to Battle. One can hear that the role is a stretch for her delicate soprano (the high E's sound like the utmost limit of what she can reach, she has no real trill, and a handful of the little notes are smudged), but she makes an impressive effect anyway, and like Norman delivers the needed "star" presence with both charm and sparkle.

Troyanos, an involved and intense composer, is hurt by the close-ups in a different way, for her face seems oddly immobile and inexpressive much of the time when seen at close quarters. Certainly no such criticism could be made of her vocal performance, with her warm, urgent mezzo creating one magical moment after another. Her duet with Battle and subsequent solo in praise of music comprise the emotional high point of this performance. King recorded Bacchus very convincingly two decades earlier, and the fact that he can still handle such a notorious tenor-killer speaks volumes about his skill and durability. Many Bacchuses sound their best in their first low offstage phrases; King keeps improving as he goes along.

But the sound cannot be called beautiful, and it dries out at the very top. Nor is his veteran status disguised visually (of course, that could be part of the *opera seria* premise).

The trio of nymphs is very strong individually and in ensemble (Barbara Bonney, Gweneth Bean, and Dawn Upshaw). The quartet of comedians is less noteworthy: Dickson fails to make much of Harlekin and offers little vocal variety, and the others (Anthony Laciura, Allan Glassmann, Artur Korn) are of uneven quality, with not quite polished ensemble work. Joseph Frank and Nico Castel contribute expert character work (possibly over-stylized) as the Music Master and Major Domo. Oliver Messel's setting, revised and refurbished over the years, retains its elegance and evocative quality; Jane Greenwood's costumes (new to the production in 1975) flatter and assist the principals in their work. The stage direction seems mostly concerned to block the action efficiently; little of the special nature of the opera—the backstage intrigues and the onstage mixups taking unexpected mysterious turns—is attempted. Undeniably first rate is Levine's spirited and delicate work with the orchestra, with the singers also mindful of the chamber textures.

One might hope to see a more fully integrated and polished performance than this appear on video eventually. For now, this will have to do.

JON ALAN CONRAD

Richard Strauss

Die Frau ohne Schatten (1919)

A: Empress (s); B: Dyer's Wife (s); C: Nurse (ms); D: Emperor (t);
E: Barak (bar)

From a shadowy reputation as an unwieldy, obscure oddity, *Die Frau ohne Schatten* has become a relatively familiar and well-regarded opera—not a repertory piece, but one undertaken from time to time by most international opera companies as a demonstration of their technical capacity, their dedication to difficult masterworks, and their ability to engage the handful of singers accomplished enough to undertake its leading roles.

The upswing in this opera's reputation was to a great extent a result of Karl Böhm's advocacy in a series of productions, notably in Vienna and New York. Other conductors have since followed his lead, and the work's increased familiarity has led to greater overall conviction and comprehension in performance. Böhm's eventual performing edition, emulated by others, made extensive curtailments in the work, growing more and more severe as the opera progressed. Although two complete studio recordings have now appeared, cut performances are still the near-invariable rule in live performance. The stage production upon which the single video *Frau* is based was, however, musically complete—possibly a first in recent times. Its only cut applies to the Empress's spoken scene at her moment of refusal to profit at others' expense: a shortened version of the problematic recitation is spread out to fill the existing music.

1992 LONDON (VHS / LD)

(Stage Performance, Stereo, Color, Subtitled)
203 minutes

Cheryl Studer (A), Eva Marton (B), Marjana Lipovšek (C), Thomas Moser (D), Robert Hale (E), Vienna State Opera Chorus, Salzburg Children's Choir, Vienna Philharmonic Orchestra—Georg Solti

Salzburg Festival: Götz Friedrich (stage director), Brian Large (video director)

This performance from the Salzburg Festival assembles about as strong a cast as one is likely to encounter these days, under the baton of a conductor who knows and loves the work, and with an orchestra probably better acquainted with the intricate music than any other. Its strengths are, indeed, musical ones, with Solti more involved and dramatically alive than on his audio recording (with the same orchestra but a different cast), though equally careless about balance.

The musical assets must, however, be experienced in the context of about as bleak and unromantic a staging as this opera has ever been accorded. Götz Friedrich would seem to scorn anything so obvious as theatrical or visual magic (so much an implied part of this sprawling, luxurious score) and tends to handle moments calling for such magic either by elimination (furniture moved by hand) or with Kabuki-like stylization (the final bridge being a pair of bolts of the dyer's cloth unrolled by the imperial pair). Scenic designer Rolf Glittenberg places the action behind a stark, semi-circular proscenium, with one or two minimalistic scenic elements defining each location. Marianne Glittenberg's costumes mix an indeterminate plainness (the Empress looks more plebeian in her own palace than when disguised as a servant) with hints of exoticism and of Strauss's own period. There is sometimes a certain spare elegance to the resultant stage picture, but it (along with the stage direction) leaves the performers stranded to make their effects without help from their environment, and the close-ups reveal them emoting in solitary voids to greater or lesser effect, depending on their resources in such matters.

Studer fares best, a general sincerity and simplicity of attitude serving her well dramatically.

Vocally, the high, intense line of the Empress elicits strong and affecting work from her. Marton exhibits similar sincerity and dedication, but the aural results are less pleasurable: impure, effortful, often ill-defined as to pitch. Lipovšček's rich mezzo sits well on the Nurse's tricky music, and her mastery of the role can be admired; unfortunately she has been directed (or has resorted on her own) to clichéd, unilluminating melodramatic lurches and grimaces. Moser and Hale have unglamourous but solid voices, which they use musically and to as much dramatic purpose as they can in their visual isolation.

Although this production is regrettably one of the less colorful and apposite that the work has received, it is a satisfactory musical representation of the challenging score and can be recommended to that extent.

JON ALAN CONRAD

INTERMEZZO (1924)

A: Christine (s); B: Anna (s); C: Baron Lummer (t); D: Stroh (t);
E: Robert Storch (bar)

Strauss's two-act "domestic comedy" was itself an intermezzo in the fruitful collaboration between the composer and Hugo von Hofmannsthal. In need of a break from his colleague's fanciful poetical flights in *Die Ägyptische Helena* and *Die Frau ohne Schatten*, Strauss cast about for a down-to-earth subject that would also satisfy his desire to write a light conversation piece in the lyrical parlando style he had been developing since *Der Rosenkavalier*. He found the perfect material in an incident from his own marriage: a telegram mixup which led his wife, the prickly and hot-tempered Pauline, to assume that her innocent husband was conducting an affair with an actress. Strauss wrote the libretto himself, depicting his turbulent but always deeply loving relationship with his wife in a series of conversational scenes separated by symphonic interludes. Right from the first performance no one was fooled about the true identity of the argumentative couple onstage, even though Strauss had renamed them Christine and Robert—"The largest bouquet of flowers a composer ever threw at his own feet," as one contemporary critic wryly commented after the premiere. Perhaps, but despite the flattering self-portrait and the trivial nature of the plot, *Intermezzo* is a deftly written, swift-moving theater piece with the ring of real life about it. The truly amazing part is that Strauss was able to view his marriage so objectively and create two such lively, three-dimensional characters.

Beyond its personal significance, the text gave Strauss precisely the challenge he wanted as a composer, and as the opera has become more familiar we are beginning to appreciate the quality of his achievement. Not only is the musical dialogue a marvel of lyrical prosody that reveals underlying character traits with truth and precision in every measure, but the score also shows Strauss using the orchestra as an amazingly accurate "acoustical camera." The whizzing tobaggans sliding down the snowy mountains at Grundlsee, the snap of a deck of cards being shuffled during a game of skat, the whole artistic milieu of Strauss the composer and conductor—each moment crackles with musical vitality and theatrical energy. *Intermezzo* will always be something of a connoisseur item, in part because its intimate nature makes it unsuitable for large operatic stages. By the same token, that means the opera is ideally designed for home viewing, where one can fully savor every verbal and musical nuance.

1983 HOME VISION (VHS)

(Stage Performance, Stereo, Color, in English)
155 minutes

Felicity Lott (A), Elizabeth Gale (B), Ian Caley (C), Glenn Winslade (D), John Pringle (E), London Philharmonic Orchestra—Gustav Kuhn

Glyndebourne Festival: John Cox (stage director), David Buckton (video director)

Glyndebourne, Munich's Cuvilliés Theater, and the Santa Fe Opera have all championed *Intermezzo* in recent years, and each summer festival has produced a memorable production that has remained in the repertory. John Cox's Glyndebourne staging is perhaps the most flavorful of the three, with realistic sets and costumes (by Martin Battersby) that capture the twenties' period flavor of the piece in exquisite detail—the Strauss home in Garmisch looks comfortable enough to move into. By the time this revival was filmed, the production had become a seasoned classic, and the performance flows with the ease and natural pace of a spoken drama—precisely the effect that Strauss was aiming for. It was also an inspired idea to fill the screen during the interludes with appropriate family-album photos of the real Strausses rather than dwelling on shots of the orchestra at work.

When she sings Christine in Munich, Lott is comfortably at home with the original German text, but here she has Andrew Porter's graceful English translation to play with and gives an even more sensational performance. Lott's willowy figure looks fabulous modeling an extensive wardrobe of twenties' fashions, while her angular, mobile features convey every nuance of this exasperating woman's paradoxical nature. Most of Strauss's associates could not bear his better half and considered her a nagging scold, but the composer adored his unpredictable wife as a woman whose prickly temper and scatterbrained self-absorbtion were more than balanced by a truly nurturing, impulsively protective nature. Lott shows us all this and more in an interpretation just as delectable for its vocal precision and tonal purity as for its rapier wit and vivid theatricality.

Although Christine's protean personality dominates the opera (Strauss really tossed the biggest bouquet in his wife's direction), Pringle's Storch quietly takes command of every situation through the warm security of his baritone and strong dramatic presence. Caley is appropriately vacuous as the callow Baron Lummer, a harmless diversion for Christine while her husband is away conducting in Vienna, and Gale contributes a humorous vignette as Anna, the Storch's long-suffering maid. Kuhn accompanies the light-fingered conversations without obscuring a moment of delicious instrumental detail, unleashing the London Philharmonic with glorious results whenever the orchestra wells up between the scenes to comment eloquently on the action.

PETER G. DAVIS

RICHARD STRAUSS

ARABELLA (1933)

A: Arabella (s); B: Zdenka (s); C: Adelaide (ms); D: Matteo (t);
E: Mandryka (bar); F: Waldner (bs)

When librettist Hugo von Hofmannsthal died suddenly just after revising the first act of *Arabella*, Strauss set the remainder as it had been left, despite obvious problems. Not until the opera became better known, after 1950, did its individuality gradually take precedence over its much-touted resemblances to *Rosenkavalier*, whose spirit the collaborators had attempted to recover. A few gross contrivances (e.g., Mandryka's overhearing of the conversation in which Zdenka gives Matteo the key to Arabella's room) remain weaknesses, and so does the routine quality of some of the music (notably the latter part of Act II), but the central characters, finely drawn by the librettist, are often eloquently (and always fluently) sustained in the music and offer ample scope for gifted singing actors.

For a 1939 Munich production, director Rudolf Hartmann and conductor Clemens Krauss sought to minimize the weakness of the second-act finale by running it directly into the third act, with the composer's acquiescence. Somehow, this so-called "Munich version" subsequently acquired a number of damaging cuts in the third act, though the only cuts Krauss made—and Strauss approved—were brief trimmings in Act II (as is borne out by the recent publication on CD of Krauss's 1942 Salzburg performance).

1960 STANDING ROOM ONLY (VHS)

(Stage Performance, Mono, Black and White, Not Subtitled)

Lisa della Casa (A), Anneliese Rothenberger (B), Ira Malaniuk (C), Georg Paskuda (D), Dietrich Fischer-Dieskau (E), Karl-Christian Kohn (F), Chorus and Orchestra of the Bavarian State Opera—Joseph Keilberth

Bavarian State Opera: Rudolf Hartmann (stage director)

With a cast identical to that of the 1963 Deutsche Grammophon Munich Festival recording, this Bavarian Radio kinescope documents the most celebrated Arabella of the postwar years, the beautiful and creamy-voiced della Casa. Even through the grainy and flickering monochrome images (with occasional dropouts), the compressed, sometimes quavery and overloaded AM-quality audio (complete with hum), and the limited camera work, della Casa's warmth and vocal mastery come through. She manages to be alluring, coquettish, and sincere all at once, and she sings naturally and very physically, her body expressing the sense of the words and the line of the music. (Now and then, close-ups catch her in gestures that seems artificial, though they probably did not from a seat in the theater.)

Also aptly Straussian is Rothenberger's Zdenka, a very nearly plausible physical assumption. Fischer-Dieskau's Mandryka is problematic: though he certainly offers an impressive presence, the rustic aspect of the character completely escapes him, as do some of the more violent passages in his music; he is most convincing in the second-act love scene. As often, the tenors are hard to like: Paskuda is a fervent if hard-toned Matteo, Fritz Uhl a clumsy Elemer. Malaniuk and Kohn offer solid work as Arabella's parents, and Eva-Maria Rogner's Fiakermilli is remarkably accurate, if shrill. Keilberth gets good playing from the orchestra and goes wherever the singers want him to. Both the production (by Rudolf Hartmann, with sets by Helmut Jürgens) and the video treatment are traditional and conventional. The "Munich version" with the unauthorized third-act cuts is used.

Whatever its flaws, this tape preserves much of the look and feel of a performance in Munich's Prinzregententheater, including Keilberth's entrance, applause for the Arabella-Zdenka duet (with audience shots and bows from the stage), and a standing ovation at the end. (Intended for a German audience, it eschews subtitles.) Someday, the Bavarian Radio archives may yield a better video edition; until then, the present incarnation is probably only for the nostalgic or the historically-minded.

1979 LONDON (VHS / LD)

(Studio Performance, Stereo, Color, Subtitled)
159 minutes

Gundula Janowitz (A), Sona Ghazarian (B), Margarita Lilowa (C), René Kollo (D), Bernd Weikl (E), Hans Kraemmer (F), Vienna State Opera Chorus, Vienna Philharmonic — Georg Solti

Otto Schenk (stage director), Wolfgang Treu (video director)

At almost the opposite end of the video opera spectrum from the Munich kinescope of *Arabella* stands this Viennese studio production. In

splendid color and wide-range stereo, intelligently subtitled, uncut, strongly cast, gorgeously played, and directed with a fine hand, this in many ways approaches an ideal video production of an opera. Two basic facts must be accepted, however. First, the video was post-synchronized to the musical recording, and the result is frequently imperfect—not only in the singers' lip movements, but also in their body language, which occasionally betrays "marking" rather than full-voice singing.

At another level, the production is vastly more cinematic than theatrical, almost claustrophobic in its close focus and limited spatiality. The second-act set is a particularly confusing mélange of stairs, alcoves, and corridors, good for the one-on-one episodes, awkward for the larger group scenes. The intimacy and visual intensity is very engaging, however, and Schenk has drawn facially vivid performances from most of his cast.

The surprise in this respect is Janowitz, whose tonally gorgeous singing has often seemed to lack "face." A less obviously glamorous figure than della Casa, she is nonetheless lovely to watch, her expressive face and eyes always in play; Arabella's warmth, sincerity, and pride are all present, and the music is delineated with a cool, radiant sound. She is well partnered in Act I by Ghazarian, an uncommonly convincing travesty figure, if a less secure voice. Like Janowitz, Weikl proves unexpectedly expressive as a film actor, especially in modes of earnestness and ruefulness; he's in trim physical form, and his splendid sound, though not used with great subtlety, commands the wide tessitura rather well.

Matteo is extravagantly cast with René Kollo, whose baby-faced glamour well embodies the character's characteristic petulance; he sings with passion and a golden tone that turns to stridency when pressed. Arabella's parents are well impersonated, though neither is ideally firm of tone. Edita Gruberová is a brilliant, aggressively vulgar Fiakermilli, and the atmospheric Fortune Teller is none other than Martha Mödl. Indeed, the only weak link in the cast is the whiny Elemer (Göran Fransson). The Vienna

Philharmonic's playing is fluent and idiomatic, and Solti's direction is happily mellower, less insistent than in his 1957 audio recording.

1994 DEUTSCHE GRAMMOPHON (VHS / LD)

(Stage Performance, Stereo, Color, Subtitled) 166 minutes

Kiri Te Kanawa (A), Marie McLaughlin (B), Helga Dernesch (C), David Kuebler (D), Wolfgang Brendel (E), Donald McIntyre (F), Metropolitan Opera Chorus and Orchestra—Christian Thielemann

Metropolitan Opera: Otto Schenk (producer), Brian Large (video director)

This performance boasts several strong points: fine orchestral playing, Thielemann's vigorous but never forced leadership, a handsome physical production (sets by Günther Schneider-Siemssen, costumes by Milena Canonero), and characterful work from Dernesch and McIntyre as Arabella's parents. Schenk's canny staging has much in common with his Vienna version, and Large's video direction seconds it more than ably. A few cuts are taken in the last two acts. (The excellent sound occasionally betrays evidence of manipulated balances, and the subtitles are sometimes hard to read against Arabella's light skirts.)

The central figures are less successful. Te Kanawa's voice retains much of its bloom, but her characterization is relatively pallid. The problem is partly theatrical: her range of gesture and facial expression is limited. Equally, her singing lacks tonal variety and, above all, verbal clarity and force: she very visibly mouths the words, but doesn't really *pronounce* them. In the crunch of Act III, her Arabella doesn't deliver dignity and hurt to any degree; she looks woebegone and sounds neutral. (In the theater, this doubtless mattered less, but this medium of close-ups inevitably elevates the face to a position near that of the voice—and she is not the only cast member the camera catches looking sideways at the conductor or prompter.)

By contrast, Brendel's presence, both physical and verbal, projects Mandryka's rough and tender sides tellingly, only to be let down by an uncertain instrument, strained by the tessitura and often poorly tuned. McLaughlin, too, is stressed at the upper extremes of Zdenka's part, but she blends well with Te Kanawa in their scenes, and generally offers a convincing portrayal. David Kuebler works hard at Matteo's ungrateful writing, while Arabella's other three suitors are at least personable if not memorable. The spectacular, if idiosyncratic Fiakermilli is Natalie Dessay.

———————

Those severely allergic to faulty lip-sync may lean towards the Met performance, but even they might be won over by the significantly stronger Arabella and Mandryka of the London version. (Unavailable for viewing was the 1984 Glyndebourne production led by Bernard Haitink, formerly on Home Vision, of which it is reported that the "Munich" cuts were taken in Act III and that John Cox's staging was much admired for its elegance and perceptiveness.)

DAVID HAMILTON

RICHARD STRAUSS

CAPRICCIO (1942)

A: Countess (s); B: Clairon (ms); C: Flamand (t); D: Count (bar);
E: Olivier (bar); F: La Roche (bs-bar)

The marriage that interested Strauss most, other than his own, was the mysterious union of words and music—"one art redeemed through the other," as the Countess sings at the conclusion of *Capriccio*. The eighty-four-year-old Strauss's operatic swan song is nothing less than an uninterrupted two-and-a-half hour argument / discussion of that aesthetic possibility, symbolized by the rivalry between the poet, Olivier, and the composer, Flamand, for the favor of their muse, the beautiful young Countess Madeleine. The love triangle humanizes what could have been a dry, precious exercise on the part of the old composer, who was far too wily a man of the theater to waste his time on abstractions, however much the underlying proposition may have intrigued him. The witty, literate libretto was written mainly by his old colleague, the conductor Clemens Krauss, who also provided other colorful characters to enliven the discourse: the flamboyant theater director La Roche, the voluptuous actress Clairon, the Countess's blasé brother, and a pair of antic Italian opera singers. The aristocratic setting is eighteenth-century Paris at the time of Gluck, which allows Strauss the luxury of indulging his passion for pastiche to the full as he laces the score with delicious song-and-dance divertissements.

Compositionally, the opera is the final working out of the conversation-in-music techniques Strauss had been developing all his life—most rigorously in the prologue to *Ariadne auf Naxos*

and his real-life domestic comedy, *Intermezzo*—and purely as a piece of craftsmanship the score is a dazzling culmination. But more than that, the music is suffused with a benedictory autumnal beauty so typical of Strauss's late style. It blooms most exquisitely in the final scene as Madeleine weighs her dilemma and finds it impossible to choose between her suitors—both poet and musician have become one in Flamand's musical setting of Olivier's sonnet. And so Strauss leaves us with a question mark, although the inspired music he wrote for this concluding sequence reminds us that the operatic stage can only be brought to life by the composer's magic touch.

1993 LONDON (VHS / LD)

(Stage Performance, Stereo, Color, Subtitled) 144 minutes

Kiri Te Kanawa (A), Tatiana Troyanos (B), David Kuebler (C), Håkan Hagegård (D), Simon Keenlyside (E), Victor Braun (F), San Francisco Opera Orchestra—Donald Runnicles

San Francisco Opera: Stephen Lawless (stage director), Peter Maniura (video director)

This performance is badly hobbled by what, one assumes, was its very raison d'être: the Countess of Te Kanawa, apparently caught on a very bad day. Her soprano sounds consistently tired and unsteady, a liability during the first two hours as she converses with her guests and a positive disaster in the solo final scene. Gowned in Thierry Bosquet's flattering rococo-era toilette, she is a ravishing ornament as she moves gracefully through Mauro Pagano's elegantly appointed salon, but her bland presence, sleepy diction, and vocal uncertainty are grievously disappointing.

The other singers are generally satisfactory, although they can hardly be expected to compensate for the gaping vacuum in the middle of this performance. Keenlyside's smooth baritone and youthful virility could not be more appropriate as Olivier, and Braun's crusty La Roche commands the stage effectively, particularly while delivering his long theatrical credo that leaves the rest of the cast virtually speechless. Kuebler sounds rather rusty and looks too old as Flamand, but Hagegård's pudgy Count is a delight and Troyanos, only months before her tragic death, gives a spicy portrait of Clairon. As the elfin prompter, Monsieur Taupe, Michel Sénéchal could give the entire cast lessons in stage movement and trenchant character delineation. The orchestra under Runnicles plays efficiently, but one wants rather more than that in such a richly imagined, subtly textured score.

Rather than invest in this badly flawed performance, devotees of *Capriccio* are advised to wait for a competitor and stick with the audio-only recordings on EMI (Sawallisch) and Deutsche Grammophon (Böhm), both strongly cast and conducted by two experienced Strauss stylists.

PETER G. DAVIS

OEDIPUS REX (1927)

A: Jocasta (s); B: Oedipus (t); C: Shepherd (t); D: Creon (bar);
E: Messenger (bar); F: Tiresias (bs); G: Narrator (speaking role)

"I dislike opera," Igor Stravinsky told a newspaper reporter in London in early 1913. "Music can be married to gesture or to words—not to both without bigamy. That is why the artistic basis of opera is wrong and why Wagner sounds at his best in the concert-room. In any case opera is in a backwater. What operas have been written since *Parsifal?* Only two that count—*Elektra* and Debussy's *Pelléas.*"

Stravinsky's subsequent work for the stage illustrates his distaste (or at least ambivalence) for "pure" opera. After the "burlesque" *Renard*, completed in 1916 and first produced in Paris in 1922, the composer continued to mix genres in his works for the stage. These pieces are relatively short, employ dancers, and usually treat the singers (if present) as instruments in the pit. *Histoire du Soldat* (1918) is a dance-theater piece "to be read, played and danced," with a narrator relating a Russian folk variation of the Faust legend. *Pulcinella*, whose music "after Giambattista Pergolesi" uses soprano, tenor, and bass soloists, has been called a ballet with song in one act—although Stravinsky also referred to it as an *"action dansante."* With its four soloists and four-part chorus, *The Wedding* (1923) has strong operatic elements, but Stravinsky was notably vague about categorizing or staging it.

As an exile from his native Russia, Stravinsky was also bothered by the problem of language in opera. How could he write operas in Russian while living in France? One possibility was to use a "universal language," like Latin, which is exactly what he did in his unusual setting of the Sophocles tragedy *Oedipus Rex.* Stravinsky's friend Jean Cocteau prepared a libretto in French that Jean Danielou then translated into Latin. Cocteau suggested the device of a speaker who periodically summarizes (in whatever is the native language of the audience) the dramatic action about to occur. Though the concept of *Oedipus Rex* (labelled an "opera-oratorio") was more genuinely operatic in scale than anything Stravinsky had previously attempted, he had highly specific and stylized ideas about the staging that were anything but conventional or "realistic." There was to be a minimum of movement and action. In an explanatory note to the score Stravinsky wrote: "Except for the Tiresias, the Shepherd and the Messenger, the characters remain in their built-up costumes and masks. Only their arms and hands move. They should give the impression of living statues." Perhaps surprisingly, a tragic Verdian spirit hangs heavily over the vocal writing.

Sergei Diaghilev staged the premiere of *Oedipus Rex* in concert form in 1927, with the cast dressed in evening clothes and sitting in front of a black velvet curtain.

1984 HOME VISION (VHS)

(Stage Performance, Stereo, Color, Not Subtitled) 90 minutes (tape also includes Stravinsky's *The Flood*)

Felicity Palmer (A), Neil Rosenshein (B), Justin Lavender (C); Claudio Desderi (D); Anton Scharinger (E); Anton Scharinger (F); Alan Howard (G); NOS TV's Men's Choir, Concertgebouw Orchestra—Bernard Haitink

Carre Theater: Harry Wich (stage director), Hans Hulscher (video director)

Filmed at the Carre Theater in Amsterdam, this version of *Oedipus Rex* closely follows Stravinsky's staging instructions. The male chorus (dressed in evening clothes) sits in a long row of chairs placed on a slim platform below the stage area where the principal characters appear. Each of the soloists wears a mask. The narrator speaks in English (not in Dutch, as might be expected), and no subtitles are provided for the Latin texts sung by the soloists or chorus—an unfortunate decision, since few people understand Latin these days. There is little movement around the stage.

Of the soloists, Felicity Palmer as Jocasta has the greatest success musically, managing to convey a strongly emotional portrait of the doomed queen even from behind a mask and with minimal help from the director. As Oedipus, Neil Rosenshein also turns in a respectable performance, navigating the extremely high tessitura without incident. The other roles are handled with professionalism, if without special inspiration. In the narrator's role, Alan Howard speaks very distinctly but fails to vary his voice level or intonation, which produces an effect of monotony that is reinforced by the static staging.

Under Haitink, the Concertgebouw sounds powerful and impressive, as does the Men's Choir. Unfortunately, however, the quality of the recorded sound is not very high, and there is some distortion at higher volume levels. The television direction fails to provide much dramatic interest; this is really a concert version with masks.

Included on the tape with *Oedipus Rex* is a much more imaginative video of Stravinsky's "Musical Play" *The Flood*, which is about Noah and his ark. Originally created for television in collaboration with Robert Craft (who arranged the text from the Book of Genesis and The York and Chester Miracle Plays), *The Flood* was completed in 1962 and first broadcast by CBS the same year. This version, designed and directed by Jaap Drupsteen for Stichting Muzt in Amsterdam in 1985, uses the original 1962 sound track but features a newly conceived video interpretation that is colorful, humorous and provocative. Adam and Eve are even shown in full frontal nudity.

1992 PHILIPS (VHS / LD)

(Film, Stereo, Color, Subtitled) 57 minutes

Jessye Norman (A), Philip Langridge (B), Robert Swenson (C), Bryn Terfel (D), Michio Tatara (E), Harry Peeters (F), Kayoko Shiraishi (G), Shinyu-Kai Chorus, Tokyo Opera Singers, Saito Kinen Orchestra—Seiji Ozawa

Julie Taymor (director)

The brilliant and versatile avant-garde director Julie Taymor originally staged this *Oedipus* at the Saito Kinen Festival in Matsumoto, Japan, and subsequently oversaw its highly successful transformation into a film / video version. Taymor has gone far beyond Stravinsky's original concept of the piece, creating a vast and monumental ritualistic drama relying heavily on the conventions of traditional Japanese theatre. The soloists still wear masks, but the masks are perched on their heads so that their faces are clearly visible; this decision allows the piece to make a much stronger human and emotional impact. Another intriguing idea is the presence of a dancer who portrays Oedipus in many of the scenes. Taymor illustrates the blinding of Oedipus by having the dancer take Jocasta's two oversized hairpins and plunge them deep into the eyes of a seated doll depicting Oedipus. It is an inventive and chilling image.

Such imaginative and unexpected visions abound: Jocasta's death is depicted by the loss of her mask; the Narrator sometimes appears in black-and-white amid the surrounding color; the plague-infested populace stares at us hopelessly through faces covered with sores and scaly skin. Each moment has been completely rethought, and yet Taymor's interpretation never contradicts or upstages Stravinsky's score.

The use of Japanese ritual theatrical conventions only emphasizes the intentionally artificial nature of the work. That the narrative text is recited in Japanese by a mesmerizing actor (Kayoko Shiraishi) only heightens the sense of internationalism and timelessness so important to *Oedipus Rex*.

Such a luxuriously produced and creatively filmed production could overwhelm some performers, but Philip Langridge and Jessye Norman hold their own splendidly as Oedipus and Jocasta. Langridge has previously recorded this role and brings dramatic nobility and vocal assurance to his characterization of the tragic king. With her innate monumentality and statuesque presence, Norman makes Jocasta into an imposing and powerful symbol of fate and passion. Bryn Terfel's Creon is no less oversized and impressive, both vocally and dramatically.

Seiji Ozawa draws a tight and dynamic performance from soloists, orchestra, and chorus.

Happily, producers Peter Gelb and Pat Jaffe have also packaged this extraordinary production very well on video, with high-quality sound and superb camera work and lighting. They have wisely provided English-language subtitles for the Latin texts, thereby intensifying the narrative immediacy. This *Oedipus* won the Jury Prize of the 1993 Montreal International Festival of Films on Art, and surely deserved the honor.

The Philips version is not only the best choice here, but one of the most artistically successful filmed operas I have seen.

HARLOW ROBINSON

IGOR STRAVINSKY

THE RAKE'S PROGRESS (1951)

A: Anne Trulove (s); B: Baba the Turk (ms); C: Tom Rakewell (t);
D: Nick Shadow (bar)

Stravinsky's only full-length opera, *The Rake's Progress*, was inspired by engravings of William Hogarth on the theme of the prodigal son who leaves home and sweetheart for the big city, where he is drawn into sin and madness by the Mephistophelean character Nick Shadow. Firmly settled in America, the composer had attained what his colleague and compatriot Nicolas Nabokov called the "ripeness of style, a well-blended and well-aged stylistic perfection" that were necessary for the composition of this neoclassical opera, which blends comedy and tragedy in equal measure. The poetic libretto was prepared by Chester Kallman and by W. H. Auden, the latter another European artist who had found refuge in the United States.

In the past, Stravinsky had avoided categorizing his mixed-genre theatre pieces, but this time around he left no doubt as to his intentions. "*The Rake's Progress* is, emphatically, an opera—an opera of arias and recitatives, choruses and ensembles," he noted. "Its musical structure, the conception of the use of these forms, even to the relations of tonalities, is in the line of the classical tradition." Among the classical composers whose influence on *The Rake's Progress* is most evident are Mozart, Monteverdi, Donizetti, and Verdi, although the score has a thoroughly individual—and very modern—musical personality.

Because of the highly original style of the vocal writing, it took some time for singers to learn to perform *The Rake's Progress*, but now it

has gained a firm place in the repertory, especially in smaller companies. The opera's picturesque eighteenth-century English setting and its visual inspiration in Hogarth's paintings offer rich material for directors and designers.

1985 VAI (VHS)

(Stage Performance, Mono, Color) 146 minutes

Felicity Lott (A), Rosalind Elias (B), Leo Goeke (C), Samuel Ramey (D), Glyndebourne Festival Chorus, London Philharmonic Orchestra—Bernard Haitink

Glyndebourne Festival: John Cox (stage director), Dave Heather (video director)

Performed at the Glyndebourne Festival in 1977, this witty and superbly sung production was filmed (apparently with few resources) by Southern Television in 1985 and later released by VAI. Artist David Hockney, who subsequently became one of opera's leading designers, created the colorful sets, which lend to Hogarth's paintings and sketches a whimsical contemporary feel that suits Stravinsky's neoclassical idiom well. With Bernard Haitink in command, the London Philharmonic Orchestra confronts the challenges of the orchestral score with sophistication and an appropriately light touch.

The cast is unusually well-balanced and features several performers who were just starting out on what have turned into distinguished and important careers. As the evil Nick Shadow,

Samuel Ramey demonstrates remarkably clear diction, a strong and true voice, and a natural talent for the role of the bad guy. Leo Goeke takes a while to warm up dramatically in the role of Tom Rakewell; his early scenes suffer from a certain blandness and lack of humor, but his final scene in the madhouse reaches an impressive level of carefully controlled pathos. His singing is excellent throughout, and he proves to be an accomplished and sensitive partner in the many duets and ensembles. Felicity Lott does not have a large instrument at her disposal, but uses her small, lyrical voice with artistry and feeling. Her final duet with Rakewell is a particular highlight. In the comic role of Baba the Turk, Rosalind Elias displays considerable acting skills. The chorus makes an energetic vocal and dramatic contribution.

Unfortunately, the uneven quality of the recorded sound (in mono) does not do justice to the fine musicality of the vocal and orchestral performance. There are moments when the orchestral tone sounds poorly blended, and some instances of echo and fade-out in the voices. Similarly, the camera work emphasizes too many close-up shots; we never get a single large overview of the stage and proscenium. As a result, the visual image looks cramped and out of proportion. The cleverly designed credits use fragments from Hogarth's drawings.

Since the opera is sung in English, no subtitles are provided, but the text is not always comprehensible due both to the poor sound and to insufficiently clear diction and / or projection on the part of some of the singers.

HARLOW ROBINSON

EUGENE ONEGIN (1879)

A: Tatyana (s); B: Olga (ms); C: Lensky (t); D: Onegin (bar);
E: Gremin (bs)

For Russians, Tchaikovsky's *Eugene Onegin* is much more than an opera. It is a profound expression of the Russian national identity and a showcase for a fictional character whom novelist Fyodor Dostoyevsky called "the apotheosis of the Russian woman": the dreamy, bookish Tatyana Larina. Tatyana was one of the greatest creations of writer Alexander Pushkin (1799–1837), who still holds uncontested right to the title of "Russian national poet," and whose brilliant novel in verse, *Eugene Onegin* (completed in 1831), inspired what is generally considered to be Tchaikovsky's greatest opera, as well as his most popular, both in and outside of Russia.

Tchaikovsky's strong identification with the impulsive, romantic Tatyana—and his almost total inability to empathize with the cold, manipulative Onegin—led him to alter fundamentally the tone of Pushkin's Byronic novel. In *Eugene Onegin*, the composer replaced Pushkin's dry irony and parody, which pokes fun at everyone and everything (including Tatyana and her naive provinciality). Instead, Tchaikovsky gives us lush, serious sentimentality, turning Pushkin's vinegar into honey.

At the same time, the composer provides insightful portraits of Tatyana (especially in her famous letter-writing scene), the burnt-out socialite Onegin, the idealistic poet Lensky, and the silly flirt Olga. Their romantic interaction unfolds before a wonderfully detailed and lyrical background of Russian aristocratic culture of the post-Napoleonic era. With its psychological depth, many large choral and dance scenes, and brilliant ensembles and duets (such as the one preceeding the Onegin-Lensky duel), *Eugene Onegin* has strong dramatic values and can be transferred more successfully than many operas to film.

1958 KULTUR (VHS)

(Film, Mono, Color, Subtitled) 106 minutes

Ariadna Shengelaya / Galina Vishnevskaya (A), Svetlana Nemoliayeva / Larisa Avdeyeva (B), Igor Ozerov / Anton Grigoriev (C), Vadim Medvedev / Yevgeni Kibkalo (D), Ivan Petrov (E), Chorus and Orchestra of the Bolshoi Theater—Boris Khaikin

Roman Tikhomirov (director)

Back in the bad old days of communism, Soviet film studios spared no expense in making lavish "realistic" versions of the nineteenth-century Russian operatic classics. Like most such efforts, this beautifully designed and handsomely filmed 1958 Lenfilm adaptation of *Eugene Onegin* offers a double cast of actors and singers so that the action can be "opened out" for maximum cinematic effect. Roman Tikhomirov (1915–1984), a Leningrad stage director famous for bringing many operas to the screen (*Prince Igor, The Queen of Spades*), adapted this version "from Tchaikovsky's opera," making numerous cuts in the score and also slightly rearranging the order of a few musical episodes.

Cuts are taken in Tatyana's letter scene (about one-third), Monsieur Triquet's aria (we only get the first verse), the opening to the duel between Onegin and Lensky, the peasant choruses in Act I, the dances in Act III, and the final confrontation between Onegin and Tatyana. For the most part, however, the cuts are handled skillfully and do not interfere with the dramatic or musical flow. At several transitional points in the action, a narrator recites a few lines from Pushkin's novel, a device that works well.

Tikhomirov assembled an impressive double cast. The actors are physically perfect for their roles and conform precisely to the descriptions provided by Pushkin in his novel. Ariadna Shengelaya really does look like a shy, skinny teenager, with luminous dark eyes and hair; she also ages very convincingly for the final scene. Vadim Medvedev's Onegin is supercilious and sophisticated, with just the right touch of foppishness—and a marvelous gentleman's coiffure. As the romantic poet Lensky, Igor Ozerov has long hair and a dreamy gaze. Svetlana Nemoliayeva is appropriately blonde and vacuous as the tease Olga. Bass Ivan Petrov, the only member of the cast who sings and appears on screen, fits the ensemble like a glove. All the members of the supporting cast look exactly right as well—especially the (unfortunately unidentified) actor who portrays Monsieur Triquet, with his deliciously Frenchified Russian.

Vocally, this version boasts two of the greatest Soviet singers of the era, both in their youthful prime: Galina Vishnevskaya as Tatyana and Yevgeni Kibkalo as Onegin. Their singing is lyrical, subtle, and often thrilling. Less famous but equally accomplished are Larisa Avdeyeva as Olga (her role is cut significantly here, including her aria at the beginning of Act I) and Anton Grigoriev as Lenksy. His interpretation of the pre-duel aria, one of Tchaikovsky's greatest, brings out all the pathos of Lensky's loss of romantic illusions. Tikhomirov films this aria in an unconventional manner: he shows us Lensky at his writing desk at night, composing the

poem that is the aria's text, and then cuts to the snow-covered duel site at dawn as the two former friends arrive to settle their silly, tragic quarrel.

The film has many other intriguing visual moments. Toward the end of Tatyana's letter aria Tikhomirov cross-cuts between Tatyana writing her confession of love to Onegin and his reading it. This image is reinforced at the end, when we see Onegin writing his own confession of love to Tatyana, and then her receipt of his belated letter. As Lensky and Onegin are walking to their duel, we see flashbacks to the happy earlier days of their friendship as they sing their duet "Enemies! How long has it been that a thirst for blood has torn us asunder?" Often the actors do not dub the text of internal monologues; instead, they are thinking (in Tatyana's letter scene, for example).

Tikhomirov's direction never becomes distracting or gimmicky; it only strengthens the psychological portraits of the characters already present in Tchaikovsky's music. He chooses marvelous locations (aristocratic country homes, St. Petersburg interiors and canals, wheat fields) that create an evocative and authentic atmosphere.

Under the direction of Boris Khaikin, the orchestra, chorus, and dancers of the Bolshoi Theater, then at its artistic peak, perform with taste and gusto. For a Soviet film made in 1958, the sound quality is also surprisingly vivid, if somewhat variable.

1962 LEGATO CLASSICS (VHS)

(Stage Performance, Stereo, Black and White, in German, Not Subtitled) 135 minutes

Ingeborg Bremert (A), Brigitte Fassbaender (B), Fritz Wunderlich (C), Hermann Prey (D), Mino Yahia (E), Chorus and Orchestra of the Bavarian State Opera—Joseph Keilberth

Bavarian State Opera: Rudolf Hartmann (stage director)

It's a pity that the visual quality of this *Onegin*, recorded live in Munich in 1962, is so poor, for it boasts a marvelously well-balanced cast, with a particularly notable performance by Fritz Wunderlich as the dreamy romantic poet Lensky. Wunderlich's interpretations of Lensky's several big arias (his profession of love to Olga in Act I, and of course the pre-duel aria in Act II, are nothing short of *wunderbar*: a floating, creamy tone throughout the range; an expressive use of rubato; a seemingly effortless shift from the quietest *piano* to a heroic *forte*. Unlike so many tenors of the past and present, Wunderlich never screams. And his acting, while sometimes edging towards staginess, is surprisingly convincing. He makes us believe that he adores the silly Olga, and his death at the hands of the heartless Onegin packs a real emotional punch. And he manages to do all this in spite of a wretched black-and-white print that gives us only the vague outlines of his face. Actually, one has the sensation while viewing this video of peering through a blurry glass, or even an aquarium.

In fine vocal form too are Hermann Prey as Onegin, Ingeborg Bremert as Tatiana, and Brigitte Fassbaender as Olga. Prey brings just the right amount of cold arrogance to the role, without overdoing it; he makes us feel why the inexperienced Tatiana could fall in love with him. His singing is also precisely tuned and elegant. As Tatiana, Ingeborg Bremert is not the best physical casting choice: she is rather large and looks too matronly for a teenager. But her singing is warm, thoughtful, and highly disciplined (like all the principals'). And as Olga, Fassbaender has some of the most impressive low notes I have ever heard in this role. She resists the temptation to turn Olga in a flirtatious caricature.

But what really distinguishes the vocal performances in this version are the ensembles: the Act I quartet that expresses all the conflicting emotions of the four main characters after their first meeting together comes across harmoniously and beautifully tuned, with the voices well-blended and complementary. All in all, there is a palpable spirit of teamwork in the production that sets it apart from most *Onegins*.

Conductor Joseph Keilberth matches this high level of professionalism in his work with the Bavarian State Opera orchestra and chorus.

I especially liked his decision to take brisk tempos and to move the musical action along. This is one of the faster versions of this opera I have ever seen and heard, to very positive effect.

As far as one can tell from the often approximate visual image, stage director Rudolf Hartmann (no credits are given for television or video direction) also sought to propell the drama briskly, without unnecessary longeurs. The sets (by Helmut Jurgens) are relatively abstract, with shadows of trees against a white (at least it appears to be white) background, and not much fussy furniture. Hartmann's boldest directorial move is to alter somewhat the final scene. First of all, he specifies (in a note flashed on the screen) that "17 years have passed"—which is considerably more than Tchaikovsky implied. In the score and libretto, Tatiana leaves Onegin alone at the end, and he gets the final words ("Oh, my wretched fate!"). Here, however, Hartmann has Onegin leave Tatiana alone on stage for a minute or so, and adds some musical material from her Act I letter scene, expressing her ambivalance and anguish over how life has turned out. It's an interesting idea (if rather disrespectful towards Tchaikovsky's intentions) that serves to shift the main focus of the drama and the "message" more to the heroine than to the hero, and to stress how uncertain her feelings really still are.

The opera is sung here in German, and no subtitles (in any language!) are provided. There is also no commentary or explanatory material accompanying the video. This is not a version for those who are unacquainted with *Eugene Onegin*. But those who want to see and hear Wunderlich in his prime, to witnesss a rather unusual interpretation of the final scene, and to enjoy some marvelous quartet singing, may well find it worthwhile.

1984 KULTUR (VHS)

(Stage Performance, Stereo, Color, Subtitled) 155 minutes

Tatiana Novikova (A), Larissa Dyadkova (B), Yuri Marusin (C), Sergei Leiferkus (D), Nikolai Okhotnikov (E), Chorus and Orchestra of the Kirov Opera—Yuri Temirkanov

Kirov Opera: Alexander Barannikov (video director)

So wretched is the sound and visual quality of this version, originally filmed by Soviet Central Television at the Kirov Theater in Leningrad in 1984, that the efforts of a highly talented cast and conductor are rendered almost completely useless. Perhaps because of the poor quality of equipment available to them, the audio engineers have produced a recording that is extremely variable in volume (at times nearly inaudible) and sometimes overwhelms the singers with raucous orchestral sound. The singers are poorly miked, but even when they are audible the recorded vocal sound is watery and indistinct.

The camera work provides only distant shots of the stage, with hardly any close-ups even in climactic dramatic scenes such as Tatyana's letter aria or the duel. This results in a nearly total lack of emotional intensity. One seems to be watching a badly made film through the wrong end of a telescope.

These technical deficiencies would be less disturbing if the cast were less distinguished. By the early 1980s, when this production was filmed, Yuri Temirkanov had succeeded in building at the Kirov a polished and highly disciplined company with strong acting and musical values. Among the singers he helped to mold were Sergei Leiferkus, whose ramrod-straight bearing and steely cold tone made him a perfect Onegin, especially at this early stage of his career. Tenor Yuri Marusin, now a recognized international star, also got his start at the Kirov under Temirkanov, and turns in (as far as one can tell here) a passionate performance as Lensky, with ringing high notes and impressive power. Larissa Dyadkova as Olga, Tatiana Novikova as Tatyana, and Nikolai Okhotnikov as Gremin also appear to sing well.

Pleasantly old-fashioned and simple, the stage production offers little in the way of psychological insight or intensity. Yuri Temirkanov's typically deliberate and refined conducting is the most recognizable element of this botched project, which is all too typical of the highly inconsistent videos Kultur has placed on the market, always without any accompanying information.

1985 HOME VISION (VHS)

(Stage Performance, Stereo, Color, Subtitled)
159 minutes

Mirella Freni (A), Sandra Walker (B), Peter Dvorsky (C), Wolfgang Brendel (D), Nicolai Ghiaurov (E), Lyric Opera of Chicago Chorus and Orchestra—Bruno Bartoletti

Lyric Opera of Chicago: Pier Luigi Samaritani (stage director), Kirk Browning (video director)

Originally broadcast live on PBS in 1985, this version, staged at Lyric Opera of Chicago, features the debut of Italian soprano Mirella Freni in the role of Tatyana—also her debut in a Russian-language role. Unfortunately, the video only makes more obvious a fact hidden on her 1987 DG recording of Tatyana: she is far too old to be playing a naïve and awkward sixteen-year-old maiden. Her matronly appearance, posture, and movements seriously undermine the production's visual credibility, and her obvious lack of familiarity with the Russian words she is singing lend the proceedings a tentative atmosphere. This atmosphere is further heightened by the direction and design, which look sketchy, flimsy, and much too generalized for an opera supposedly set in Russia in the 1820s. As if in an attempt to hide the lack of resources (and imagination?) at their disposal, the production team also opted for extremely low level lighting throughout. The large chorus and dance scenes are cramped and unevocative.

Obvious, too, is the fact that the four principals come from different vocal and dramatic schools: Mirella Freni from Italy, Peter Dvorsky from Czechoslovakia, Wolfgang Brendel from Germany, and Sandra Walker from the United States. Perhaps this explains their failure to connect emotionally, musically, visually, or dramatically. Far too often they all seem to be singing their roles in isolation and not to each other. While Brendel has the appropriately cold aura for Onegin, he fails to show the nasty and necessary spleen (especially in the ball scene of Act II) that helps us to understand this unlikable character. And it was an error on the director's part to have Brendel play the part with a beard—he looks like Tchaikovsky, not Onegin. As Lensky, Dvorsky displays solid vocal command and some marvelous high notes, but he plays the poet too heavily, without the light touch of irony that makes the character come alive. Sandra Walker sings competently, if not with particular distinction, but her large size and inability to move easily make it very difficult to accept her as the cute, flirtatious Olga. And why is she dark-haired and Freni blonde, when Pushkin—and Tchaikovsky—specifically indicate just the opposite?

It was Freni who wanted to play this role, and who apparently persuaded the Lyric Opera of Chicago to mount this production around her. She has some fine moments vocally, but her performance fails to come together, in part because she sounds (as well as looks) far too mature.

Musically, the orchestral performance under Bruno Bartoletti is the highlight of this version. It is tender, romantic, and lyrical without descending into sentimental bathos. The quality of the recorded sound is excellent.

1988 LONDON (VHS / LD)

(Film, Stereo, Color, Subtitled) 116 minutes

Magdaléna Vášáryová / Teresa Kubiak (A), Kamila Magálová / Julia Hamari (B), Emil Horváth / Stuart Burrows (C), Michal Dočolomanský / Bernd Weikl (D), Přemysl Kočí / Nicolai Ghiaurov (E), John Alldis Choir, Orchestra of the Royal Opera House, Covent Garden— Georg Solti

Petr Weigl (director)

This film version was produced in 1988 by Mediascope of Munich in coproduction with WDR, ORF, La Sept, and Channel Four and released by Decca in 1990. It features a double cast, with young Czech actors on screen and a distinguished group of well-known singers on the sound track. Like the 1958 Soviet film version, it takes numerous cuts in Tchaikovsky's score, some of which are more questionable than those taken by Roman Tikhomirov. The first, and most obvious, cut comes at the very opening: the marvelous romance sung by Olga and Tatyana ("Slykhali li vy?"), which sets the atmosphere of aristocratic nostalgia, is excised. Instead, Petr Weigl begins with the peasants' chorus that follows, showing us a lush green field and a dirt road along which the peasants slowly make their way to the Larins' columned manor house. The other major change made in the score and libretto comes in the opera's last scene. Instead of waiting until the next day to appear to his rediscovered Tatyana, Onegin pursues her down the corridors of the palace where they have just renewed their acquaintance. Their final confrontation and parting take place on the steps of a grand staircase.

In terms of design, it seems that no expense has been spared to recreate the illusion of the life of the upper classes in Russia during the heady post-Napoleonic period. Historically appropriate clothes, jewelry, and hairstyles abound, although everything looks a little too new and pretty (in contrast to the more authentic visual style of the Soviet film version). The actors cast in the leading dramatic roles look appropriately young and feckless, although Emil Horvath seems rather too old and too dark for Lensky. For the most part, the dubbing of the singing is done tastefully and inobtrusively. As in the Soviet film version, Weigl occasionally uses the device of internal monologue.

Vocally, the cast is uniformly distinguished and delivers performances that are well-integrated and balanced. Not surprisingly, the recorded sound quality is on a considerably higher level than in the Soviet film version. As Tatyana, Teresa Kubiak finds a most convincing combination of girlish spontaneity and warmth; she also has the best low notes of any of the Tatyanas reviewed here. Her voice blends very well with Hamari's and with Weikl's. But perhaps the most emotionally affecting and exciting vocal performance comes from Stuart Burrows as Lensky; his Russian sounds entirely natural, and he reaches all parts of his range with ease. Ghiaurov and Michel Sénéchal (as Monsieur Triquet) do well in their small roles, too.

With Sir Georg Solti at the helm, the Covent Garden orchestra plays gloriously.

Even with cuts, the Bolshoi film version combines the best musical performance with the best dramatic interpretation and filming. The Petr Weigl version (also with cuts) comes in a close second. For those who want an uncut version, the Lyric Opera production is preferable to the Kirov on the grounds of recorded sound quality, although I cannot recommend either one of them with much enthusiasm.

HARLOW ROBINSON

Pique Dame

(The Queen of Spades) (1890)

A: Lisa (s); B: Countess (ms); C: Pauline (c); D: Gherman (t);
E: Yeletsky (bar); F: Tomsky (bar)

*I*f the only reason someone goes to the opera *Queen of Spades* is to find out whether the hero won or lost at cards," George Balanchine once observed, "he'd be better off staying home."

Balanchine was right: in this compelling, brooding masterpiece, composed just three years before the composer's death, Tchaikovsky focuses on psychology, not plot. *The Queen of Spades* is a psychological thriller and contains some of Tchaikovsky's most dramatic music for the stage. In adapting a small tale with the same title written in 1833 by Alexander Pushkin, Tchaikovsky profoundly altered the details and spirit of the original, just as he had with Pushkin's *Eugene Onegin*. In both cases Tchaikovsky sentimentalized and darkened the mood and the characters. He removed the elements of parody and irony that were central to Pushkin's aesthetic.

Tchaikovsky looks at Pushkin's characters through the distorting lens of *fin de siècle* gloom. He deepens the psychological portraits, transforming the protagonists Gherman and Lisa into tragic characters more typical of Dostoyevsky's urban nightmares than of Pushkin's self-consciously "literary" and playful fictional universe. Nervous foreboding, despair, and melancholy nostalgia reign in the libretto and score. Communicated in the very first bars of the overture, this sense of approaching personal and social catastrophe intensifies throughout

the opera, building to a powerful, tragic climax. One can also see *The Queen of Spades* as the composer's nostalgic tribute to the Russian aristocratic sensibility whose days were already numbered as the nineteenth century drew to a close.

Perhaps because of its pessimistic mood and the difficulty of finding tenors able to cope with the considerable vocal and acting demands of the role of Gherman, *The Queen of Spades* has never been as popular outside of Russia as the cozier *Eugene Onegin*, but it seems now to be regaining favor. Full of striking visual moments (lightning, lavish ballroom scenes, raucous evenings of gambling) and even scary supernatural apparitions (the Countess's return from the dead), *The Queen of Spades* also gives imaginative directors and designers plenty to work with.

1960 KULTUR (VHS)

(Film, Mono, Color, Subtitled) 102 minutes

O. Krasina / Tamara Milashkina (A), E. Polevitskaya / Sofia Preobrazhenskaya (B), I. Gubanov-Gurzo / L. Avadeyeva (C), O. Strizhenov / Zurab Andzhaparidze (D), V. Kulik / Yevgeny Kibkalo (E), V. Medvedev / V. Nechipailo (F), Chorus and Orchestra of the Bolshoi Theater — Yevgeny Svetlanov

Roman Tikhomirov (director)

In adapting *The Queen of Spades* for a Mosfilm feature in 1960, Soviet director Roman

Tikhomirov drastically cut the original score and libretto, trimming the opera's running time by more than an hour. Among the episodes cut are the entire opera-within-an-opera intermezzo ("The Tender-Hearted Shepherdess") in Act II, the opening choruses of Act I, the appearance of the Governess in Act I, and some of the choral sections in Act II. In addition, many arias, duets, and ensembles are abbreviated, including the Countess's aria, Lisa's final aria, and Tomsky's drinking song in Act III. Perhaps in deference to Soviet anti-Tsarist sentiments, Catherine II is nowhere to be seen at the end of Act II, either.

The result might be called a Queen of Spades "lite," with the emphasis placed on the growing dementia of the opera's protagonist, Gherman. Acted convincingly by O. Strizhenov and sung by the legendary Georgian tenor Zurab Andzhaparidze, Gherman emerges here in all his splendid madness, disintegrating before our eyes into the dark miasma of the Petersburg mists. With his Napoleonic hat and dishevelled demeanor, Strizhenov succeeds in turning the opera into the haunting study in psychological pathology that it really is. Tormented and wild-eyed, Gherman roams the stony, damp streets of Petersburg like Dostoyevsky's death-obsessed Raskolnikov, who was Gherman's literary and philosophical offspring.

All of the other doubling actors are also very convincing in their roles, though none are given nearly as much screen time. To Tikhomirov's credit, the dubbing of the sung voices is much less conspicuous than one might expect; often he avoids direct dubbing through the use of internal monologue and other devices. As the Countess, E. Polevitskaya uses her marvelously chiselled face to great advantage, especially when she silently stares down Gherman during their confrontation in her boudoir. As Lisa, O. Krasina is pretty and fragile. In the suicide scene, Tikhomirov has Lisa leave her scarf tied by the staircase down which she descends to a watery death in the canal. When Gherman shoots himself shortly afterward, he staggers out of the gambling den to expire on the same spot, next to the fluttering scarf. Such staging may take considerable liberties with the libretto,

but it is undeniably effective as cinema.

Vocally, the performances are universally excellent and well-balanced. When she sang the role of Lisa for this film, Tamara Milashkina was just embarking on what would be a very long career as one of the Bolshoi's leading sopranos. The voice is strong, lyrical, and highly dramatic. Mezzo Sophia Preobrazhenskaya, on the other hand, was just coming to the end of a distinguished career in Leningrad when she sang the role of the Countess.

Under the exciting and refined leadership of the great Yevgeny Svetlanov, the Bolshoi Orchestra and Chorus deliver intense and resonant performances. As in the case of Tikhomirov's 1958 film of *Eugene Onegin*, the sound quality is surprisingly good. The on-location shooting (the Summer Garden, along the Neva and canals, in brilliant palace ballrooms) gives this version vitality and authenticity, for *The Queen of Spades* is one of those operas most closely connected to the emotional atmosphere of a specific city and culture.

1983 KULTUR (VHS)

(Stage Performance, Stereo, Color, Subtitled)
174 minutes

Tamara Milashkina (A), Elena Obraztsova (B), L. Zhemchug (C), Vladimir Atlantov (D), Yuri Mazurok (E), Yuri Grigoriev (F), Chorus and Orchestra of the Bolshoi Theater—Yuri Simonov

Bolshoi Theater: L. Bartov (stage director), A. Barannikov (video director)

The casting in this version, filmed by Soviet television at the Bolshoi in 1983, demonstrates all too clearly one of the main reasons behind the sad decline of the Bolshoi over the last twenty years: the practice during the corrupt Brezhnev years of keeping established stars singing in major roles long past their prime and / or suitability. There was a time when Tamara Milashkina and Vladimir Atlantov were both wonderful as Lisa and Gherman, respectively. By 1983, however, that time had long past, especially for Milashkina, and yet here they are, struggling through another evening. The camera, alas, only accentuates how physically inappropriate they are as passionate young lovers, and Milashkina's voice is only a strident echo of the beautiful lyrical instrument heard in the 1960 Soviet film version of this opera. The staging is lazy, too. Instead of leaping into the canal in Act III as the libretto describes, Milashkina simply strides offstage as the curtain falls. Where is she going?

Another strange casting choice finds Elena Obraztsova, one of the greatest of all Soviet mezzos, in the role of the Countess. Temperamentally and physically, the robust, unrefined Obraztsova (better known for earthy roles like that of Santuzza in *Cavalleria Rusticana*) is ill-suited to play a fragile aristocrat at home in the court of Versailles. Nor can Obraztsova conceal her enormous vocal heft and power; she seems so much more formidable than Atlantov during their late-night encounter that it's easier to imagine her striking him dead than expiring of fright.

Clearly in evidence, too, are the tacky costumes that were *de rigueur* at the Bolshoi in Soviet times. Atlantov enters wearing what looks like a toga, with a platinum blond wig underneath what appears to be an upturned pail. Such attire does not increase his credibility as a sexually appealing seducer, or appropriately delineate him from the aristocratic milieu to which he yearns to belong. The clothes are somewhat better for the ball scenes in Act II, especially for the intermezzo, which is elaborately staged and choreographed.

One vocal performance rises above the prevailing pedestrian and stodgy level—that of young Yuri Mazurok as Yeletsky. L. Zhemchug also does very well as Paulina (and as Milovzor in the intermezzo). As usual, the Bolshoi chorus gives a solid performance, but Simonov elicits nothing more than workmanlike playing from the orchestra. The level of the recorded sound is much better than on many other Bolshoi videos and recordings, with good miking all over the stage.

It's also fun to see the ritual of the little old ladies in uniforms who enter at curtain call, bearing piles of bouquets for the various heavily decorated Soviet veterans assembled on stage for their bows.

1992 PHILIPS (VHS / LD)

(Stage Performance, Stereo, Color, Subtitled)
180 minutes

Maria Guleghina (A), Ludmila Filatova (B), Olga Borodina (C), Gegam Grigorian (D), Alexander Gergalov (E), Sergei Leiferkus (F), Kirov Opera Chorus and Orchestra—Valery Gergiev

Kirov Opera: Yuri Temirkanov (stage director), Brian Large (video director)

Filmed lived at the Mariinsky Theater in St. Petersburg in April 1992, this version features several of the most promising young Russian operatic performers of the moment: soprano Maria Guleghina, mezzo Olga Borodina, tenor Gegam Grigorian, baritone Sergei Leiferkus, and of course, conductor Valery Gergiev, who has turned the Kirov Opera into a remarkably productive and refined company during the last ten years. There is no longer any question either inside or outside of Russia that the Kirov has overtaken the Bolshoi as the leading Russian opera house. American audiences have also been seeing quite a bit of these singers in recent years, at the Met and elsewhere. Both Guleghina and Grigorian appeared in the new 1995 Met production of *The Queen of Spades*, which was conducted by Gergiev.

With such an impressive assemblage of vocal and orchestral talent, this video version would seem to be a guaranteed success. And yet it only partially delivers. For one thing, the production is a rather old one, staged by Yuri Temirkanov when he was the artistic director at the Kirov. It is traditional and a bit stodgy. The best staging is saved for the Act II intermezzo (with Borodina and Leiferkus playing Daphnis and Pluto), whose inventive choreography includes a living gilded statue of Cupid on a pedestal that comes to life and dances. The Countess's ghost appears to Gherman on a stage darkened except for a sickly green light that illuminates Ludmila Filatova as she sings seated at a table. This same lighting effect returns in the opera's final scene, when the Queen of Spades turns up in Gherman's hand.

As Lisa, Guleghina is dramatically appealing and has some exquisite vocal moments—like the hushed, exhausted tone she uses at the beginning of her final aria by the canal. Opposite her, Grigorian has power and high notes to spare, though his acting tends toward the bland. As expected, Borodina turns in a superlative, highly cultured performance in the small role of Pauline. Leiferkus brings nobility and just the right sense of masculine camaraderie to Count Tomsky.

But the problem here is the recorded sound quality. The miking is very inconsistent, and volume levels vary greatly from different spots on the stage. At many important moments (the beginning of Paulina's aria, the Countess's "Je crains de lui parler la nuit") the voices are nearly inaudible. This represents a very serious drawback and compromises a serious and lovingly presented intepretation.

1992 KULTUR (VHS) / PIONEER (LD)

(Stage Performance, Stereo, Color, Subtitled) 168 minutes

Nancy Gustafson (A), Felicity Palmer (B), Marie-Ange Todorovitch (C), Yuri Marusin (D), Dimitri Kharitonov (E), Sergei Leiferkus (F), Glyndebourne Chorus, London Philharmonic—Andrew Davis

Glyndebourne Festival: Graham Vick (stage director), Peter Maniura (video director)

This production was staged at Glyndebourne in 1992 by Graham Vick, whose brooding and splendidly staged "updated" interpretation wisely focuses much more on atmosphere and emotion than plot. Richard Hudson's sets convey Gherman's psychological obsession by means of a white backdrop splashed with black streaks that could be trees, shadows, or even blood. Punctuated with slanting ceilings, crooked doors, and walls askew, the unsettling design graphically symbolizes Gherman's weakening grasp of reality.

At the same time, the costumes and furniture are luxuriously faithful to the era in which the opera takes place: the very end of the reign of Catherine II ("The Great"). At the end of Act II, Scene 1, we see just the glow of Catherine's impending arrival at the top of a long staircase lined with elegantly attired footmen, each bearing a lighted candelabra. Throughout the production, one witnesses a provocative and for the most part successful dialogue between the sensibilities of Imperial Russia and the (very) post-Freudian Europe of 1992.

The cast includes both Russian and non-Russian artists. As Tomsky, Leiferkus is polished, noble, and manly. With his exquisite diction, ramrod-straight bearing, and impeccable musicality, he makes the most of his rather small vocal instrument and leaves us wishing that his small part were much bigger. Similarly impressive is another veteran, Felicity Palmer, as the aging Countess. Singing in fluent Russian and French, she brings excitement to each of her scenes; her post-ball aria is sad without being too sentimental or mannered. As Yeletsky, Lisa's rejected suitor and Gherman's rival, the handsome Dimitri Kharitonov shows an intuitive feeling for the dramatic and musical style.

But the success of any production of *The Queen of Spades* ultimately depends on the two singer-actors cast in the leading roles. The conscientious Nancy Gustafson more than holds up her end as a vulnerable, visually appealing Lisa, the most dramatically convincing portrayal of all those reviewed here. Even her heroic efforts cannot conceal the vocal and dramatic inadequacy of Yuri Marusin, however. Marusin has a large, but strangely plain tone; much more unfortunate is his tendency to sing under the pitch, painfully so in duets and ensembles. Called upon to portray Gherman's growing insanity, Marusin resorts to unintentionally campy Dracula-like grimaces whose comic quality grows when they are magnified in close-ups.

The camera work here is often very beautiful, with some wonderful lighting effects—especially the flickering reflection of the water into which Lisa will eventually leap. The sound is also excellent, vivid and uniform, though it seems at times to emanate elsewhere than from the singers' mouths.

The best choice is the Glyndebourne version, both for its excellent recorded sound quality and provocative staging concept. In second place comes the 1960 Soviet film version, despite its numerous cuts; it is worthwhile for its local color and succinct portrayal of Gherman's psyche, and the vocal performances are uniformly fine. Third place belongs to the Kirov version. The Bolshoi production can be recommended only as a historical (and occasionally unintentionally hysterical) artifact.

HARLOW ROBINSON

KING PRIAM (1962)

A: Andromache (s); B: Helen (ms); C: Paris (t); D: King Priam (bs-bar)

Throughout his long creative life, Michael Tippett's musical subject has been ambiguity: the conflicting moral aspects of often blameless human nature and action. That suggests tragedy, and indeed even his first opera, *The Midsummer Marriage*, though it ends in harmony, strongly dramatizes the irreconcilability of instinct and civilized behavior. With *King Priam* the composer examines this conflict as classic tragedy. Musically the work often proceeds by violent contrast: in moods, in tonalities, in orchestral and vocal intentions. The opera's essence is tension, and for the dedicated listener that makes repeated exposure exceptionally revealing. The real philosophic and emotional strength of this difficult, continually allusive work will only be determined by further imaginative productions, for it is very much a work of the theater—rather like Wagner in that respect.

1985 HOME VISION (VHS)

(Studio Performance, Stereo, Color) 135 minutes

Sarah Walker (A), Anne Mason (B), Howard Haskin (C), Rodney Macann (D), Kent Opera Chorus and Orchestra—Roger Norrington

Nicholas Hytner (stage director), Robin Lough (video director)

To judge an unfamiliar opera—especially one that takes such risks as this one—on the basis of a single worthy but modest performance—is perilous. There are, however, certain questions one asks about it; whether they can be answered in other productions is itself a question. Priam is already a tragic figure in Homer—the last Trojan king before the city's annihilation by the men of the future, the Greeks. Michael Tippett is after something more specific than that, however. With some help from Sophocles's Theban plays and Euripides's *The Trojan Women*, he sees tragedy in the conflict between political necessity and basic moral conviction. Told by a seer at Paris's birth that the boy will kill him, Priam decides to have his son put to death. When a decade later the ostensibly dead child is found living with a shepherd, Priam cannot kill him but takes him to be trained as a warrior prince with his brother Hector. As a result, of course, they all eventually die in a cycle of vengeance in the Trojan War, brought on by Paris's elopement with Helen. The moral decision results in the death of a civilization.

There are powerful scenes here, most of them in the latter half of the opera, but also, it seems to me, some grave errors in structure, compounded by an earnest production that often fails to provide the visual atmosphere demanded by such mythical, living but larger-than-life figures and issues. For too long— nearly three-quarters of the opera—we simply do not know what the central tragic conflict is as the events follow one another, and we're unsure what the choices are in considering those events. Even on further viewings there is not that sense of a closing trap that intensifies the tragic agony and the glory. And the settings, costumes, lighting, and camera work do little to intensify the atmosphere. Simplicity is not entirely the issue, but care with detail is. I know that when Rodney Macann is finally photographed with daring—from above, writhing in a little room—the agony that he has previously been at such pains to express personally then comes alive. There are numerous scenes that would benefit from such care.

Musically the performance is remarkably strong. Roger Norrington conducts a performance of electric energy. All of the women have powerful voices, and it is a pleasure to see at last so many singers whom one has heard with enjoyment on the Opera Rara *One Hundred Years of Italian Opera* audio series. Macann has a strong expressive voice and the right instincts for the role, and Howard Haskin, not quite as mellifluous as one would like, sings and acts with intention and looks good as Paris. Incidentally, it is helpful to buy a libretto. Though the opera is sung in English, the diction is not always clear. Riverrun Press offers one in Opera Guide 29, *The Operas of Michael Tippett. King Priam* is an important work, for Tippett, who also wrote the libretto, has not shirked the obligations of tragedy. The more you dig, the more you find.

LONDON GREEN

NABUCCO (1842)

A: Abigaille (s); B: Fenena (s); C: Ismaele (t); D: Nabucco (bar);
E: Zaccaria (bs)

Verdi owed his first critical triumph, that of his third opera, primarily to the revelation of theatrical as well as musical spontaneity, energy, and originality it provided. But joined to the emergence of a truly new voice on the stage of La Scala was the serendipitous expression of nationalistic fervor illustrated by the plight of the Hebrews, seen then as a clear metaphor for an Italy occupied by foreign powers. The centricity of the chorus of the oppressed, "Va, pensiero," acted like a call to arms and furnished a spiritual focus for the movement toward the unification of the country that was not to be attained for almost another three decades. Indeed, the impact of the hymn, later a quasi-unofficial national anthem, led Verdi to reframe a similarly nationalistic—and censor-riling—message in the big chorus of his succeeding work, I Lombardi: "O Signore, dal tetto natio."

In spite of its incendiary history, the contemporary rate of performance does not keep the Nabucco flame particularly well tended. New York, for example, has seen only one production each by its two major companies in the last thirty-five years. More than a metaphor that has perhaps lost some of its power or a lack of interest in the possibility of revisiting the excitement—and occasional crudities—inherent in the brio of the young composer's idiom, the opera's current viability problem may lie in casting matters: on the one hand, a short-changed *primo tenore* and, on the other, a soprano who is asked for a type of fierce agility that apparently makes most divas, on first sizing up Abigaille's pros and cons, think twice before saying yes.

1981 CASTLE OPERA (VHS) / PIONEER (LD)

(Stage Performance, Stereo, Color, Not Subtitled) 132 minutes

Ghena Dimitrova (A), Bruna Baglioni (B), Ottavio Garaventa (C), Renato Bruson (D), Dimiter Petkov (E), Chorus and Orchestra of the Arena di Verona—Maurizio Arena

Verona Arena: Renzo Giacchieri (stage director), Brian Large (video director)

With the same principals featured in the available Scala performance of five years later, a 1981 Verona Nabucco obviously presents more of an opportunity for close comparison than for considering the impact different timbres and temperaments might have on this early Verdi stage triumph. Of course, the arena itself looms as an enormous essential difference, and for once the Roman ruin makes convincing backdrop sense, acting as an unforced analog of ancient Jerusalem and Babylon. Stage director Renzo Giacchieri and designer Luciano Minguzzi accept this gift gracefully and impose only minimum touches to distinguish particularity of place or mood. They even get away with not even bothering to suggest anything resembling the Hanging Gardens. But to atone for this, Minguzzi has invented quite fetching calligraphic-influenced robes for the Hebrews, which can be examined at leisure since Giacchieri settles his choral forces into glued-in-place concert ranks. If the aura of the evening is indeed largely static (but punctuated by a splendid lightning bolt and a fiery destruction of the idol of Baal), it seems nevertheless agreeable to all concerned, not least of all Ghena Dimitrova and Renato Bruson.

As Abigaille, the dramatic soprano is actually perhaps more involved here than she was to be in Milan, but it's still mostly stand-and-deliver singing. Yet deliver she does: huge fistfuls of sound that she has mostly under control, especially once past the cruel demands on sustained-line spinning of "Anch'io dischiuso" and its treacherous cabaletta. There's even a plausible *pianissimo* before dying. The performance's vocal highlight comes with the Nabucco-Abigaille Act III duet in which Dimitrova and Bruson (as her now-crazed father) find common musical ground for an arresting elaboration of conflicting bitterness. Baritone Bruson, master of breath control and cantilena, pushes mellifluousness to full pay-off in his big last-act aria, "Dio di Giuda," but Nabucco is a personage of mercurial utterance, and that's a challenge this singer chooses not to meet.

Dimiter Petkov as Zaccaria contributes by-the-book bass solidity, improving in resonance—except at the very top of the role's tessitura—as the performance progresses. Less rewarding in less rewarding roles are tenor Ottavio Garaventa, a pallid Ismaele, and soprano Bruna Baglioni, an uneven if fundamentally warm-voiced Fenena. If conductor Maurizio Arena is not to blame for the loss of the overture, he can then be praised for a gratifyingly propulsive, rhythmically alert, and well coordinated reading of at least most of the score. Visual and sound quality rate an acceptable grade, the former hindered by low lighting levels, the latter by constraint in high and low frequencies.

1986 HOME VISION (VHS) / PIONEER (LD)

(Stage Performance, Stereo, Color, Subtitled)
140 minutes

Ghena Dimitrova (A), Raquel Pierotti (B), Bruno Beccaria (C), Renato Bruson (D), Paata Burchuladze (E), Chorus and Orchestra of Teatro alla Scala—Riccardo Muti

La Scala: Roberto De Simone (stage director), Brian Large (video director)

Musically high powered, visually opulent, resourcefully photographed, and furnished with a cast of indisputable international glamour, this opening-night *Nabucco* commands attention as a successfully captured live-performance event. The impetus behind the vitality so evident throughout that December evening in Milan emanates from conductor Riccardo Muti, who could be accused of sometimes driving his forces beyond what is actually needed to communicate excitement but whose parallel fiery drive for accurate articulation does fill the opera house with pay-off tautness. It is a tautness that, to Muti's great credit, holds through the opera's occasional moments of dignified repose, notably the Act III chorus, "Va, pensiero," staged here as a vast panorama of white robes and blue sky, a stately stillness of trenchant theatricality.

For this kind of achievement, director Roberto De Simone and set designer Mauro Carosi also deserve full credit. The "Va, pensiero" image is but one of many—the Hanging Gardens, deployment of the Babylonian lion motif, a ceremonial staircase on which chorus and extras are artfully arranged—that are not only rich in themselves but also interpret tradition in an arresting manner that never crosses over into self-indulgent willfulness. And television director Brian Large outdoes himself in establishing a telling camera viewpoint: close-ups at crucial dramatic climaxes and overhead shots that play expertly on Carosi's notions of what constitutes the Babylonian look and on De Simone's animated crowds.

Of the singers, the most consistently pleasing is Paata Burchuladze as Zaccaria—not the most phosphorescent assignment a singer might hunger for, but Burchuladze is always admirably keyed into its possibilities, his bass weighty enough for a credible high priest yet sufficiently flexible to manage passage intricacies. His is an evenly produced sound, very resonant, and with an interesting vibrato spin to it. What he "says" carries because he knows how to use words as a vocal jumping-off point.

Abigaille and Nabucco are again in the hands of Ghena Dimitrova and Renato Bruson. The Bulgarian soprano is generous with power but chary of conviction, and when one doesn't hear the demonic villainess in full-throated cry, all one sees is a rather placid lady wearing an odd hat. Abigaille's death, vocal fireworks extinguished, passes almost without notice. Bruson, in contrast, always looks to be in touch with at least some aspect of his role, especially in the later scenes, when his Eisenstein-monk appearance wonderfully fits the king in his piteous and then redeemed estates. The baritone's singing

here is subtle and full of inflection, but the trumpeting force needed earlier to suggest a challenge to God is not in his arsenal.

———————

With Dimitrova and Bruson leading both casts, a choice between *Nabuccos* hinges on other factors. La Scala's commanding production concept, superior orchestra handling by Muti, and a far more arresting Zaccaria all add substance to a nod in the direction of the Home Vision / Pioneer package. There's even an overture. What there may not be is widespread availability, but perhaps consumer pressure on Home Vision and / or Pioneer can put this to rights.

HARVEY E. PHILLIPS

I LOMBARDI ALLA PRIMA CROCIATA (1843)

A: Giselda (s); B: Oronte (t); C: Pagano / Hermit (bs)

A clear understanding of the plot of Verdi's fourth stage work is a goal that can elude even the most astute, determined opera lover. Not only are opportunities to become acquainted with *I Lombardi* in the theater rare indeed, but enlightenment doesn't necessarily dawn from following the printed text when listening to the opera on disc.

Trovatore's convolutions seem lucid and coherent next to this saga of intergenerational family love-hate relationships, accidental patricide, thwarted suicide, vengeful intrigues, banishment, and eremetism that takes place among Christians and "infidels" during the First Crusade, on two continents and, yes, in heaven itself.

In performance *Lombardi's* specific locations and historical era, very problematic to convey literally (the opera sprawls over eleven scenes), tend to receive the unit set / amorphous costuming treatment that makes economic sense to producers but contributes to audience befuddlement.

The spotlight therefore remains focused on the music, which can bear the glare only sporadically. The genius Verdi, still immature, sometimes matches the dramatic and textual crudity of Temistocle Solera's libretto with banalities of his own; other times, in a cantilena or concertato or choral passage, he rises to new heights of lyric expression that foretell the musical future of Italy.

1984 CASTLE OPERA (VHS) / PIONEER (LD)

(Stage Performance, Stereo, Color, Not Subtitled) 126 minutes

Ghena Dimitrova (A), José Carreras (B), Silvano Carroli (C); Chorus and Orchestra of Teatro alla Scala—Gianandrea Gavazzeni

La Scala: Gabriele Lavia (stage director), Brian Large (video director)

Superb vocal accomplishment and eloquent musicality in this erratic, rousing work can make it a cumulatively thrilling experience. Of *Lombardi's* three recent international-level revivals, La Scala's was the least well sung. The only one available on video, it achieves the status of distressingly flawed stopgap (especially without subtitles).

Virtue in this serious 1984 endeavor resides mainly in aspects of the physical production and in the devotional conducting of Gianandrea Gavazzeni, who knows where the treasure is buried in *Lombardi* and uncovers it with affection. His chorus of 114 (the evening's glory) and orchestra respond brilliantly, reaping the loudest audience acclamation. The maestro declines the *bis* demanded for the great chorus "O Signore, dal tetto natio."

Sheer willpower sustains Ghena Dimitrova's whoop-and-holler assault on Giselda. The soprano's rudimentary vocal technique isn't nearly up to Verdi's demands. Continually undone at the top (loud or soft, no matter), she omits reams of music to prepare for climactic shrieks. In midrange cantilena her basically driven, raw, harsh sound approaches something akin to euphony, but at too many great moments the voice, strung out and verging on collapse, almost evaporates. She exudes appropriate dignity when not ineluctably desperate.

José Carreras knows how to phrase. His entrance aria's middle-voice turns are accurate and genuinely expressive, the tone golden and ingratiating; but the going gets rough immediately. The tenor's top, accessible only through convulsive effort, emerges explosive and unsteady, the sound becoming stiff and intractable. The middle is then revisited in a wispy croon, doubtless for relief following the upward struggle. So it goes throughout: clearly noble intentions compromised by stentorian forays above the staff, where Verdi summons Oronte frequently. Carreras's handsome presence is vitiated by the spasmodic fidgeting essential to his strenuous vocal method.

Silvano Carroli can phonate but not resonate Pagano's low F; nowhere does his workaday baritone prove sufficiently arresting in this juicy bass role to justify the miscasting, though he possesses a strong enough stage presence.

Thick-voiced Carlo Bini, the most committed (and stagy) performer of the lot, sings the thankless second tenor lead, Arvino, forcefully but disagreeably. The remaining soloists are little more than ciphers.

Gabriele Lavia's staging doesn't challenge the opera's stand-and-sing conventions, manifesting common sense in simply lining up the chorus (stunningly costumed by Andrea Viotti) across the stage for its several big scenes. Giovanni Agostinucci's final setting, sunrise over captured Jerusalem, is his most effective. Elsewhere, having the newly deceased Oronte actually stand among the fluffy clouds of paradise to sing down to the mortal Giselda (rather than being an unseen *voce dal cielo* wafting in from offstage) seems a bit much, though perhaps that's how it was done in Verdi's day. Television director Brian Large misguidedly miniaturizes *Lombardi*'s grand scale through too much reductive framing.

If released commercially, the Metropolitan Opera's 1994 telecast will supersede the Scala version by virtue of its vocally—but not musically or histrionically—superior Oronte (Luciano Pavarotti), splendid Pagano (Samuel Ramey), and valiant Giselda (Lauren Flanigan). Gavazzeni's Milan ensemble, however, is not surpassed by the Met's under James Levine.

Lombardi enthusiasts might seek the audio tape of San Diego Opera's 1979 first twentieth-century U.S. staging, the best case yet presented for this work in our time. Cristina Deutekom, Carlo Bergonzi, and Paul Plishka, all in prime form, deliver secure, lyrically incandescent, dramatically incendiary vocalism: a milestone performance.

BRUCE BURROUGHS

ERNANI (1844)

A: Elvira (s); B: Ernani (t); C: Don Carlo (bar); D: Silva (bs)

Victor Hugo's 1830 verse drama *Hernani*, scandalous when new, now resounds in memory only because the young Giuseppe Verdi made it the subject of his fifth opera.

Ernani's sixteenth-century Pyrenean castles and tombs offer ample opportunity for grandiose stage pictures, but its characters are routinely dismissed as being irredeemably one-dimensional. That appraisal reckons without the vitality of the music composed for Elvira, Ernani, Carlo, and Silva in this robust, uneven early work. Its best pages are distinguished by considerable eloquence and intensity; all of it demands unflagging energy and passionate address.

Two important altered emphases differentiate *Ernani* from Verdi's previous successes, *Nabucco* and *I Lombardi:* more detailed treatment of volatile personal relationships and a less prominent role for the chorus, which is no longer a major force in the drama and has no memorable "solo" of its own.

Ernani, brimming with elements not only identifiably *bel canto* and Romantic but also precursory to full-blown Italian grand opera, depends upon singers capable of voicing the agonies of love requited and unrequited and the chivalrous conceit of death by witnessed suicide (to uphold sacred honor and a sworn oath) in tones resplendent enough to sweep aside all reservations.

1982 CASTLE OPERA (VHS) / PIONEER (LD)

(Stage Performance, Stereo, Color, Not Subtitled) 138 minutes

Mirella Freni (A), Plácido Domingo (B), Renato Bruson (C), Nicolai Ghiaurov (D), Chorus and Orchestra of Teatro alla Scala—Riccardo Muti

La Scala: Luca Ronconi (stage director), Preben Montell (video director)

Plácido Domingo's generously sung, eminently stageworthy Ernani upholds the tenor's self-set standard, meaning that it exceeds the possibilities of virtually any contemporary without offering individuating characteristics that might lift it from the level of supremely competent to that of boldly imaginative. However much one longs for a bit of over-the-top bravado from Domingo, something less well judged, contained, within bounds, one remains ever grateful for that compact, ringing, burnished tone and the industrious sort of intensity with which it is delivered.

A fine artist with equipment better suited to less virtuosic repertory, Mirella Freni lacks the bellows and the true head-voice spin to be able to phrase Elvira like a Verdian. She must resort to verismo vocal compromises, breathing in awkward places, and stopping to attack high notes (the B's and C's in this music are beyond her comfort zone) individually, unable to meld them into the line where they belong. Taking on heavy roles has exacted a toll on Freni's full, rich, originally radiant lyric soprano: a thickened middle voice that pulls inexorably on the top; a beefed up, raw chest register; and the need to spend vocal capital without stint, particularly with regard to producing volume. Once a lumbering, stressful "Ernani, involami" (awesome hurdle to most late-twentieth-century sopranos) has passed, there is usually something artistically interesting happening in Freni's singing. Unfortunately, the tone itself is seldom genuinely steady, poised, or wontedly lovely. Despite visible preoccupation with pumping out sound, Freni manages to relate to Domingo in a believably romantic way. Her perennially endearing persona and alertness to situation count for much.

Renato Bruson's singing—firm, focused, and pitch-true throughout—is as noble as his outstandingly acted Carlo's mien. Bruson's voice, lean and forward yet lustrous, may not possess the "baritenor" upper extension that incites the ultimate audience frenzy for "O de' verd'-anni miei," but then this artist has no need of interpolated high notes to win approval (and conductor Muti disallows all unscripted exhibitionism in any case).

Nicolai Ghiaurov, fifty-three in 1982, has a head start on the rusty wheeze syndrome that often afflicts bass voices as they age. In spite of the tonal fogginess, greater at the thinned-out top than at the cavernous bottom of his range, Ghiaurov commands a strong legato line. Moreover, he imbues Silva with tremendous, world-weary authority and emotional validity.

Riccardo Muti leads a performance of frequently frenetic energy (an apt enough approach to Verdi's myriad repeats), creating an undeniably stirring effect. He pushes his cast hard, maintaining taut control, evincing little sympathy for Freni's limitations, and not broadening phrases that Domingo and Bruson would surely expand if permitted to do so.

Luca Ronconi's production, abetted by coconspirators Ezio Frigerio (neologistic sets) and Franca Squarciapino (eclectic costumes), reeks of cynicism and distrust for, perhaps even dislike of, *Ernani*. A giant barbecue pit, stage center, holds some of the chorus hostage; formally dressed spectators peer down from an onstage balcony, resembling observers in an operating theater during surgery. The principals, upon whom television director Preben Montell wisely concentrates, often seem inhibited by their surroundings.

1983 PARAMOUNT (VHS) / PIONEER (LD)

(Stage Performance, Stereo, Color, Subtitled) 142 minutes

Leona Mitchell (A), Luciano Pavarotti (B), Sherrill Milnes (C), Ruggero Raimondi (D), Metropolitan Opera Chorus and Orchestra—James Levine

Metropolitan Opera: Pier Luigi Samaritani (stage director), Brian Large (television director)

Luciano Pavarotti, at his bulkiest and least mobile, hardly suggests a dashing *bandito* in the del Monaco / Corelli mold, nor has he their tireless-trumpet projection for Ernani's dramatic and confrontational passages. His singing nonetheless gives this conflated performance (cobbled together from several December 1983 Met *Ernanis*) its historical standing. Rhythmic alacrity, trenchant phrasing, a well-spun legato, and dulcet, silvery tone with a burgeoning spinto edge distinguish his work. He dispatches the arduous interpolated aria "Odi il voto" (Verdi's Parma premiere addendum) memorably, though looking quite terrified in the process.

Leona Mitchell, sacrificial lamb of this production (*somebody* had to be Elvira), exhibits extraordinarily limited capabilities of movement, expression, and involvement, creating a vacuum where a cynosure should be. That she circumvents disgrace is a triumph of youthful spunk and a strong lyric soprano—one done no favors by imposing this formidable role upon it—over all other factors. Her singing is generally full-throated, sometimes effulgent, always clumsy. She devotedly parrots some of the hok-ier, more amusing mannerisms of her illustrious predecessor Leontyne Price.

Sherrill Milnes limns his imperious, narcissistic Carlo in throaty, desiccated tone that is voluminous but not ringing, often pinched and nasal where fullness is indispensable, and consistently on the losing side of a role-length struggle to stay up to pitch (impressive top A-flat notwithstanding). Eventually one accepts the baritone's perpetual sneer as an integral part of his vocal production rather than a premeditated aspect of characterization; this monarch remains petulant and snarly even when magnanimously pardoning those who threatened his life.

Ruggero Raimondi, who has inordinate difficulty in properly forming the vowels of his native language, so pressures his voice (top-heavy for this genuine *basso cantante* part) that it emerges in a tedious *forte* drone, drifting in and out of semi-hoarseness. Like Milnes, Raimondi offers a measure of visual credibility. However, while convincing us completely of his obsession with Elvira, he unwittingly throws the opera's romantic quadrangle out of kilter because of his appearance and manner as the supposedly hoary Silva: younger and more desirable than Ernani, less detached and arrogant than Carlo. Charles Anthony, in Riccardo's brief lines, alone ranks with Pavarotti in pointedness of tone, Italianate quality, and verbal clarity.

James Levine drives the music vigorously, his quickstep tempos rendering the soloists breathless from time to time, his moments of lyrical expansion not always occurring at expected locations. He duplicates Muti's prime miscalculation: presenting the score uncut particularly taxes the already overparted soprano and imposes on the listener too many *da capo* repetitions of the young Verdi's not uniformly inspired *strettas*.

Designer-director Pier Luigi Samaritani's gargantuan traditional settings dwarf the singers and obscure the crux of the drama, which is fervidly emotional, not coldly political (or architectural). His torpid direction doesn't help. Costume designer Peter J. Hall merits a trip to the woodshed for Elvira's ludicrous couture. Brian Large has faithfully immortalized the stately ensemble posturing and (in close-ups) the lovers' vacant visages during solos.

With Domingo and Freni the interactive, credible protagonists, Bruson the superior Carlo, and Ghiaurov the more appropriate "vecchio misero," La Scala gets the nod. Pavarotti, however, offers admirers ample reason to acquire the Met video. As for Muti and Levine: a six-of-one, half-dozen-of-the-other draw.

BRUCE BURROUGHS

GIOVANNA D'ARCO (1845)

A: Giovanna (s); B: Carlo VII (t); C: Giacomo (bar)

Once believed by musicologists earlier in this century to have been lost except for its overture, *Giovanna d'Arco* was the first opera Verdi based on a play of Friedrich Schiller, *Die Jungfrau von Orleans.* Its librettist, Temistocle Solera, however, went to extraordinary lengths to insist this was not true, that the subject matter was only *shared* by Schiller and that he had never seen nor read the German writer's stage piece. Whoever should get the credit—or blame—for retelling the triumphs and martyrdom of France's most illustrious saint, so at variance with both commonly accepted legend and assumed historical truth, the opera itself was a great success at its La Scala premiere. It soon made the rounds of lyric stages throughout Italy, although, as might have been expected, the libretto eventually encountered considerable criticism and, on occasion, that almost constant bane of the composer's pre-Italian-unification career, official censorship. In spite of the acknowledged musical worth of *Giovanna d'Arco* and its promising beginnings, it quickly fell into obscurity. Indeed, not until it was resurrected for Renata Tebaldi in Naples (1951) did the opera world again have the opportunity—and at least from time to time since—to fit this important link into the chain of early Verdi achievements.

1989 TELDEC (VHS / LD)

(Stage Performance, Stereo, Color, Subtitled)
128 minutes

Susan Dunn (A), Vincenzo La Scola (B), Renato Bruson (C), Chorus and Orchestra of the Teatro Communale di Bologna—Riccardo Chailly

Teatro Communale di Bologna: Werner Herzog and Henning von Gierke (stage directors), Keith Cheetham and Werner Herzog (video directors)

Important but still problematic, *Giovanna d'Arco* today is impressive for its unremitting energy, probing flights of lyrical imagination, and foreshadowing of thematic material—both musical and psychological—to be mined in later Verdi operas. The libretto reduces Joan's holy passion to the level of a domestic dispute that doesn't even have the grace to end at the stake. Yet the refocusing to a contest of wills between the Maid and her father clearly must have resonated for the composer, in these pre-*Rigoletto* years, as a more workable dramatic device.

This 1989 performance from Bologna makes a forceful argument for encountering the opera more than we do these days. Conductor Riccardo Chailly, judicious in finding textural contrasts, lays out the musical matter with forthright lucidity. In German film director Werner Herzog's and Henning von Gierke's staging, equally straightforward minds are at work. Many visual motifs—such as the flames (an altogether misleading nonharbinger as it happens) and crucifixes of the prologue, the way a battlefield's bodies become an extension of a painted backdrop, a parade of tapers, the final assumption—demonstrate not only insight into the contours of the opera's essential stylistic vocabulary but also a commendable unwillingness to bully it into something it isn't.

Renato Bruson as Giacomo, Joan's father, reflects the good manners of this production: to noble smoothness of declamation he joins sensitivity to the dimensions of his character, thus ultimately capable of making the denunciation of his own child complexly logical. Susan Dunn in the title role, confident and lustrous of voice as she moves ceaselessly between registers, has the wherewithal to exult in the high-lying passages that accompany her death. Her stage deportment, however, is only efficient, rarely inspired. Still less physically persuasive is tenor Vincenzo La Scola as Carlo VII, but he atones for this shortfall with a sturdy, ringing instrument that possesses natural color variety and responds nimbly to text inflection. Matters of both sound and sight are strongly served by this release's technical crew.

The chance to be present at a performance of this Verdi rarity should not be lightly passed up. There is strong musical work from all forces involved, and the Herzog and von Gierke vision brings the opera into interesting relief, overriding misgivings caused by the low-temperature emotive setting favored by most of the cast.

HARVEY E. PHILLIPS

GIUSEPPE VERDI

I DUE FOSCARI (1844)

A: Lucrezia (s); B: Jacopo Foscari (t); C: Francesco Foscari (bar);
D: Loredano (bs)

In our time Verdi's sixth opera surfaces far less frequently than several of his earlier works, and when it does it seems unable to beguile audiences into repeated hearings in the theater.

Reasons for this are subtle but discernible. In setting Francesco Maria Piave's libretto adaptation of Byron's somber, slow-moving play *The Two Foscari* (concerning fifteenth-century Venetian intrigue), the composer produced a score that fully mirrors what is an almost uniformly oppressive dramatic atmosphere. The last-act "Introduction and Barcarolle" briefly palliates the prevailing musical heaviness but cannot dispel the great sense of gloom that pervades the opera.

Then, too, so much that propels the drama happens offstage; those onstage are primarily reactors, not actors. The imprisoned Jacopo's "crimes against Venice" have transpired before curtain's rise. His demise, unseen, is announced by his wife; the reported confession of someone who never appears proclaims his innocence posthumously.

Though Verdi later treated the principal elements here with more profound art—the noble father / doge *(Boccanegra)*; filial relationships *(Rigoletto, Aida)*; political complexities *(Vespri, Don Carlo)*; black villainy *(Otello)*—his *Due Foscari*, musically intriguing, vocally challenging, and far from devoid of eloquence, rewards close acquaintance, just the process a live-performance video can foster.

1988 CASTLE OPERA (VHS)

(Stage Performance, Stereo, Color, Not Subtitled) 120 minutes

Linda Roark-Strummer (A), Alberto Cupido (B), Renato Bruson (C), Luigi Roni (D), Chorus and Orchestra of Teatro alla Scala—Gianandrea Gavazzeni

La Scala: Pier Luigi Pizzi (stage director), Tonino Del Colle (video director)

Few performances of Verdi's works at the end of the twentieth century have succeeded as well as this one at the task that should always be, but too seldom is, the goal of any stage presentation of any opera: the revelation of the piece's essence, musical and dramatic, allowing whatever message it has to reach the audience uncompromised and unobscured.

How admirable the humility of Pier Luigi Pizzi before this weighty early work of a developing genius. Without revisionist conceptualism or directorial smoke and mirrors, Pizzi gives us the opera utterly without apology. When its energy or musical inspiration or dramatic impulse flag, nothing is foisted upon it in an attempt to divert our attention from this weak moment, that nondescript passage. Produced with such affectionate devotion, *Due Foscari* appears less primitive and problematic than some of the composer's stronger works from the same period have seemed when subjected to a deconstructionist visionary's devices. An important lesson is here, though it may be lost on all but the public.

The opera is superbly served by a movable multipartite set and Pizzi's series of gorgeous stage pictures, arresting to the eye because of the fastidious composition of groupings and tableaux and the brilliant use of color, texture, and line in the costumes. Substituting an endless flight of stairs with a throne at the summit for Verdi's "hall in the doge's palace" facilitates many stunning effects. The elderly doge (Renato Bruson in shiny gold raiment) laboriously climbs to the throne, so high that he becomes as remote as the Emperor Altoum, while his crimson-robed, black-capped councillors comment below. Later, the arduous ascent is repeated, this time with the court following the doge up the stairs in an ominous, predatory stalk.

The third-act "Introduction and Barcarolle," with colorfully garbed gondoliers rowing by at the rear and the camera panning wonderfully involved choristers' faces, is a delectable *scena.*

There is no great singing here, but these principals offer generous vocal strength and commitment. Linda Roark-Strummer lacks charisma and her secure, bland soprano tends toward edge and shrillness rather than warmth or roundness. She nonetheless manages Lucrezia's formidable demands with assurance, handling the dramatic fioritura nimbly, sustaining the fiendish top-voice writing impressively, and daring to sing softly when appropriate.

Alberto Cupido's thick, plummy tone brightens gradually and serves his sympathetic delineation of an extremely put-upon character increasingly well as he goes along.

Bruson's care-bent doge is a masterful portrayal. Though his well-worn voice has lost core and focus, he alone proffers a true legato, investing every line with compelling intensity, pathos, and understanding, all of which are reflected in his commanding physical presence.

Verdi flows through the veins of the Scala musicians and chorus, who thrive under Gianandrea Gavazzeni's spirited and spiritual leadership. Tonino Del Colle's bravura videography neatly captures the personal triumphs of the maestro, Bruson, and Pizzi, which draw from the Milanese public a far warmer response than seen in many Scala productions available on video.

BRUCE BURROUGHS

ATTILA (1846)

A: Odabella (s); B: Foresto (t); C: Ezio (bar); D: Attila (bs)

On political grounds alone, *Attila*, Verdi's ninth opera, was destined for immediate success. Written as desire for national independence was burgeoning, *Attila*, like *Nabucco* and *I Lombardi*, had a plot involving a people under oppressive, barbaric foreign domination with which Italians in 1846 could easily identify. Despite the opera's troublesome proportions—a long two-scene prologue followed by five scenes in three acts, a libretto that unfailingly arouses more sympathy for its invading tyrant than for any of the resisting patriots, and music whose style looks backward and forward—its best episodes are capable of overwhelming any audience with a penchant for Verdi.

1985 HOME VISION (VHS)

(Stage Performance, Stereo, Color, Subtitled)
120 minutes

Maria Chiara (A), Veriano Luchetti (B), Silvano Carroli (C), Evgeny Nesterenko (D), Chorus and Orchestra of the Arena di Verona—Nello Santi

Verona Arena: Giuliano Montaldo (stage director), Brian Large (video director)

Giuliano Montaldo's lively production was the hit of Verona's 1985 summer season. His designer, Luciano Ricerti, filled the Arena's vast stage with a monumental tree with eight enormous branches set before some ravaged classical masonry, thus symbolizing Rome's fall to nordic hordes. The action Montaldo devised for this setting is mostly clear and effective; one episode, the erection of the altar near a Venetian lagoon, is inspired.

The cast is strong. Nesterenko, his colorful bass not quite so opulent as in the previous decade, is, nevertheless, a forceful, noble warrior. Equally impressive are Maria Chiara in the voice-killer role of Odabella, attacking her demanding first aria and cabaletta with flair and holding her own in the big ensembles, and Silvano Carroli, a stalwart Ezio, incisive in song and expression. Veriano Luchetti, the odious Foresto, is also praiseworthy for predominantly liquid tone and supple line. Nello Santi gives his singers experienced, idiomatic, and animated support.

Home Vision's presentation is below par. Brian Large's direction is no more than workmanlike. Images are not crisp and, here and there, are distorted. The audio, afflicted by dropouts, primarily in the opening scene, is by 1985 standards only a bit better than passable.

1991 HOME VISION (VHS)

(Stage Performance, Stereo, Color, Subtitled)
118 minutes

Cheryl Studer (A), Kaludi Kaludov (B), Giorgio Zancanaro (C), Samuel Ramey (D), Chorus and Orchestra of Teatro alla Scala—Riccardo Muti

La Scala: Jerome Savary (stage director), Christopher Swann (video director)

Even with an overresonant environment that blunts the impact of the singers, this video is irresistible for Riccardo Muti's precise and enlightened musical direction and La Scala's physically handsome and sensibly staged production.

Samuel Ramey, with his soft-grained bass, would seem unlikely to triumph in the role of Attila; but that is just what he has done, thanks to his fine singing, great theatrical projection, and dramatic insight. One would not have thought Cheryl Studer, for all her many virtues, had either the vocal thrust and heft or oversized personality to bring off a suitable impersonation of the warrior maiden Odabella. But so she has done. Her unflinching attack, vocal flexibility, keen musicianship, and well-prepared characterization should win anyone's respect. Another surprise is the contribution of the little-known Kaludi Kaludov. His tenor may lack some color, but it has metal and is sufficiently well groomed to trace a firm line with dynamic interest and is capable of producing an honorable impersonation. Giorgio Zancanaro, as ever somewhat deficient in expression and vocal firepower for the heavier Verdi baritone parts, is heard at his best and is at least a passable Ezio.

The polished, spirited work of chorus and orchestra is testimony to Riccardo Muti's ability to maintain the standards at La Scala established by his predecessor Claudio Abbado. On this occasion the entire ensemble is operating at a level unsurpassed, to my knowledge, anywhere during the past decade.

This video, apart from the quality of its audio, maintains high production standards.

Each of these productions conveys the essential virtues of *Attila*. The preference here is for the Scala production with its superior visual beauty, musical distinction, and immaculate ensemble.

C. J. LUTEN

GIUSEPPE VERDI

MACBETH

(1847, revised 1865)

A: Lady Macbeth (s); B: Macduff (t); C: Macbeth (bar); D: Banquo (bs)

An irredeemably villainous married couple and a chorus of malicious hags dominate this oddest of mid-*ottocento* Italian operas. Its hero is capable only of tactical actions. Highly suspect women tell him which actions to perform. Along his way, he feels much. At the end, he realizes his predicament but still draws no moral conclusions. His wife yearns and seethes, but she depends on her husband to do the work. Along her way, she feels little except her rage, and to the end she keeps all ethical awareness locked out of consciousness. The husband is drawn to the intuitive and the female supernatural, and suffers night terrors and hysteria, while the wife cleaves to a cold, amoral *Realpolitik*—a calamitous displacement of the natural order. All this Verdi captures in his brooding, blunt, and mournful utterance for the title role, his extravagant effusions for Lady Macbeth, and the hot duets between them. But he leaves the lead performers to discover the characters' need for each other and for their malignant folly. That—not the jolly witches and murderers, or even the stylistic abrasions between 1847 and 1865—is the opera's central performance problem. All these productions are of the standard 1865 text, without the ballet and mime sequences or the 1847 death scene for Macbeth. Losing the latter is a cheat: it's powerfully set, and we badly need the closure for the title character.

1972 VAI (VHS)

(Stage Performance, Mono, Color, Subtitled) 148 minutes

Josephine Barstow (A), Keith Erwen (B), Kostas Paskalis (C), James Morris (D), Glyndebourne Chorus, London Philharmonic Orchestra—John Pritchard

Glyndebourne Festival: Michael Hadjimischev (director), Dave Heather (video director)

Barstow and Paskalis were justly respected in these roles, and their work—goodly stretches of it, at least—constitutes the chief attraction here. True, getting in close on Barstow's Lady Macbeth can be a mixed blessing. On the one hand, we see how zeroed in she is on every acting moment (not just her stuff), and lines like her suppressed asides to Macbeth in the banquet scene really register. On the other hand, her highly expressive face (lots of attitude, lots of eyebrow action, all aimed at row W) can prove wearing. The trap of the character is that she keeps repeating a single action, and in the solo scenes especially it is hard to avoid falling into a rhetorical pattern. Barstow, I think, nails it all down a little too neatly. But she's a terrific theatrical talent. She has an electric presence, a centered physicality free of distracting tensions, and a passionate dedication to her intelligent choices. Musically, she always sees point in the writing, and her well-knit soprano soars freely

359

through the daunting reaches of the part. Her relatively weak lower-middle range is a drawback in "La luce langue," and the Brindisi gives her some awkward spots, but on the whole the role is beautifully and commandingly sung, with a tonal warmth that pays off in the sleepwalking scene.

Paskalis, too, is a strong presence. He is at his best with inward actions and affects: "Pietà, rispetto, amore" puts a distinguished cap on his performance, simple and deep. The duettino with Banquo, much of the Act I duet with Lady Macbeth, and the parade of kings in the apparition scene also elicit some of this quality. When trying to show unwelcome surprise or terror he tends to flail and lurch, and in more demonstrative passages to fall back on generic operatic indicating. But the best of his work is well above this level, and he keeps his focus in the difficult banquet scene. His firmly seated baritone has the timbral variety and resonance required in midrange, and its slightly restricted top is not a major issue in this tessitura. There's too much *verismo* vehemence for my taste, but when he trusts the music and his instrument, his singing is of high quality. Morris's Banquo lacks the deep plush of a true basso; still, he's in fresh, strong voice, and while his acting offers nothing unpredictable, it's alert and functional. Keith Erwen sings Macduff with musical care and a voice that is pleasing but short on metal. He doesn't show much fire or acting instinct.

Glyndebourne's stage production is extremely simple: bare stage with cyclorama for the heaths and marches, slabs and arches for the rest. The staging is sensible and ungimmicked. A sumptuously costumed banquet scene makes a visual splash. Banquo's ghost is invisible to us all—our point-of-view is the guests', not Macbeth's, and Paskalis attacks an empty chair. The lighting for the video is remarkably sharp, and with the camera in tight most of the time, the principals stay at the center of attention. There is some lovely composition and sensitive editing for "Patria oppressa."

Allowing for a few balance problems common to all but the best live tapings, the audio is satisfactory. A few format decisions seem strange: yards of blank tape between acts, and

an aerial tour of the Christie gardens during this darkest of Verdi preludes. The subtitling is not helpful, often reverting to Shakespeare rather than translating Piave, and occasionally getting it wrong—"Quel sangue fumante mi sbalza nel volto!" is virtually the reverse of "Thy blood is cold." Pritchard's conducting, orderly and balanced, is also slow and dull. His orchestra's execution is good, the chorus's fairish.

1987 LONDON (VHS / LD)

(Film, Stereo, Color, Subtitled) 134 minutes

Shirley Verrett (A), Philippe Volter / Veriano Luchetti (B), Leo Nucci (C), Johan Leysen / Samuel Ramey (D), Chorus and Orchestra of the Teatro Comunale, Bologna—Riccardo Chailly

Claude d'Anna (director)

A high level of thought and imagination has gone into this film, and in the sequences where the medium can truly offer some advantage, d'Anna and his well-cast actors often deliver. Some examples: *The witches.* Filthy androgynous primitives, they cavort in the mud at the edge of the battlefield (we've seen striking images of the carnage during the prelude). They prance like the apes in *2001* and their makeup gives them minstrel-show lips, but it works—the women are good mimetic actors, their choreography is welded to events in the music, and the choral timbres are shrewdly matched to the actions. Strange and dangerous, they bear no trace of stage-witch cliché. In the apparition scene they crawl and hang on the cave's grilled gate like orangutans in a madhouse. *Banquo's aria and murder.* The night of "Mille affannose immagini" is a night of gibbets and bonfires—the corpses and belongings of the hanged are being burned by Macbeth's soldiers. During the postlude, the murderers emerge from the forest and silently gather around Banquo. Blackout. *Banquo's ghost.* Youngish, handsome, clean-shaven, and a talented actor. On his first appearance in the banquet scene he sits on the throne, removes his helmet, shakes out his "gory locks," and watches with calm amusement as Macbeth throws his fit. On his second, he perches on the staircase to the murder chamber, smiling mildly, puts his finger to his lips to shush Macbeth, and mimes Duncan asleep. *"Patria oppressa."* In a solemn, haunting sequence, the bodies of Macduff's slain children float in through the mists on a raft manned by shrouded figures, and the refugees gather for the funeral while singing the chorus. "Ah, la paterno mano" is sung at the graveside.

All these passages are beautifully staged and edited, and stick in the memory. Filmed in and around a Belgian castle, this *Macbeth* has a brooding, elemental, unforgiving atmosphere that recalls the Peter Brook *King Lear,* and the director's understanding of the score is evident throughout. Note, however, that none of the scenes described above involves the opera's central relationship. Here the production founders on the unresolved contradictions of filmed opera: the need for "movie-real" behavior versus the presentational conventions of the form, and the detachment of singing energy and commitment from acting intention and concentration. Verrett roams past attendants in the corridors while mouthing her arias; Nucci slogs through "Pietà, rispetto" while breaking into the boarded-up murder chamber. Verrett does well with the more violent sort of overt action, but doesn't suggest much going on inside. Nucci has the sort of affectless demeanor that *might* suggest something going on inside if the movie were not also an opera—given the sound track, it looks like he simply hasn't heard what's being said.

The dubbing isn't poorly done, but it still feels like a night at the karaoke club. Chailly does a fine job with this score, propulsive and colorfully accented without sounding revved-up. Verrett, who a few years before this film recorded her role impressively, still has some excellent passages and is never bashful about going after them. She's "managing," though— the top of the voice has started to fray and thin. Nucci sings solidly, but except for some improbable-sounding "mike mezza-voce" his dynamic and timbral span is narrow, his phrasing seldom imaginative. This lovely lyric baritone does not belong in such heavy repertory. Ramey's Ban-quo is satisfying—one of his best recorded roles. While Luchetti's voice and technique do not always fill out Macduff's music, he has a basic rightness of sound, style, and language, and brings welcome animation to his recitative and aria. This is a letterboxed edition, with excellent video quality and darkish sound.

1987 KULTUR (VHS)

(Stage Performance, Stereo, Color, Subtitled) 150 minutes

Mara Zampieri (A), Dennis O'Neill (B), Renato Bruson (C), James Morris (D), Chorus and Orchestra of the Deutsche Oper, Berlin— Giuseppe Sinopoli

Deutsche Oper: Luca Ronconi (stage director), Brian Large (video director).

Ronconi's production (sets and costumes by Luciano Damiani) is one of those color-coded affairs in which luridly bedizened principals and set pieces stand out sharply against an austere background. In Scene 1, Macbeth and Banquo look like military swells out of Delacroix. The witches wear upscale wedding party dresses and display ladies-in-waiting comportment. They also sport trick-store beards. The chorus of refugees offers not suffering, but a chic, sexily lit image of suffering—arty poses, sculptural faces. Brian Large understands the stylistic assumptions and furthers them where possible—in one sequence, he pulls the Macbeths out of the stage picture and pastes them up in half-length profile, jawing away at each other, then returns them to their out-front stage positions. Icons, not characters. There are some theatrically striking effects, but they tend to raise as many questions as they answer. Duncan's appearance is an example: he arrives unattended, sits to receive the Macbeths' obeisance (shifty glances, like Eisenstein's boyars), then disappears during a brief blackout, leaving the scheming couple with an empty chair. Pretty neat. But the music, intended for the procession of Duncan's retinue and barely tolerable for that purpose, is hung out to dry. Some viewers will find such goings-on pregnant with semiotic significance or will simply enjoy the fashionable tone. To them this production is heartily recommended. Meanwhile, back at the opera, the principals are faced with the problem always posed by this kind of staging: how to string together continuous behavior in a stage world that ignores everything that might generate it. Solution: do what you always do. In Morris's case this can be verified, for here he is, fifteen years after the Glyndebourne production, with very different colleagues and surroundings, giving the identical performance, allowing for blocking changes and a slight vocal shallowing. Bruson affords an admirable realization of an entirely traditional interpretation—nothing fresh or illuminating, but nothing shirked or dead, either. Stalwart and concentrated, he's got a strong face and an excellent scowl. The voice is rather monotonously dark, and he plows through the "Pietà, rispetto" heedlessly. But the singing is always grounded and hefty, and its timbre suited to the role. What to say of Mara Zampieri? Her vocalism is sometimes hooty, often straight-toned, not infrequently under the pitch. Her acting is enthusiastic, bug-eyed mugging that is little short of parodistic in close-up. However, even her most outlandish mistakes are the sort that only a major talent can make. In addition to its faults, her singing has power,

alacrity, and rhythmic drive. It is full of coloristic responses to moments. And only a high theatrical sensibility can go over the top with acting of this sort. I can't buy it, but maybe you *like* two-reelers. In a bizarre way, she and Bruson work rather well together. O'Neill plugs away stubbornly at Macduff; the voice is awfully knotty, though. Finally, there's a major Sinopoli overload here. The camera cuts away from stage to podium often and at length, disclosing in our maestro's face and physique the same quality we hear in his conducting: the compulsive worrying of an intelligent, talented fellow that we may hear in the music something other than his brilliant *aperçus*. He's the kid who's always raising his hand in class to make some point, and the more often he's right, the more you wish he'd shut up. The orchestra is fine, the chorus a bit ragged and edgy.

―――――――

Recommendation: The 1972 VAI is clearly the fullest representation of the opera, and the best-sung version, as well. The 1987 London film is worth a look, though, for its fresh view of many scenes.

CONRAD L. OSBORNE

GIUSEPPE VERDI

LUISA MILLER (1849)

A: Luisa (s); B: Federica (ms); C: Rodolfo (t); D: Miller (bar);
E: Wurm (bs); F: Count Walter (bs)

One of the four operas Verdi based on plays by Friedrich Schiller, *Luisa Miller* reduces the poet's lengthy but intensely romantic and idealistic *Kabale und Liebe (Intrigue and Love)* to a relatively simple story. Salvatore Cammarano, the librettist of that eternal complication, *Il Trovatore*, did the simplifying of this tale of thwarted love between maid and master that is destroyed by the dictates and attitudes of a rigid class system. But the last act of the opera, breaking new stylistic ground for the still young composer, adds a pungent exploration of father-daughter devotion that seems to place, at least partly, the more traditional theme of romantic fixation in the shadows. A basically conventional opera, in both subject and musical diction, suddenly veers into new and uniquely colored territory. Needless to say, the first night audience in Naples, while allowing Verdi a success, liked Act III the least.

Still not a sure-fire Verdi hit, in spite of what such committed sopranos as Anna Moffo, Katia Ricciarelli, and Montserrat Caballé brought to it in the late sixties and early seventies, *Luisa Miller*, with its wealth of long-lined, arching melody, still has enormous potential to move. And it may even be, rather than *Rigoletto*, the opera that earliest puts the composer in full touch with the nexus of relationships, especially those between parent and child, that are so central to his greatest inspirations.

1988 KULTUR (VHS)

(Stage Performance, Stereo, Color, Subtitled)
150 minutes

June Anderson (A), Suzanna Anselmi (B), Taro Ichihara (C), Eduard Tumagian (D), Romuald Tesarowicz (E), Paul Plishka (F), Montpelier Opera Chorus, Lyon Opera Chorus and Orchestra—Maurizio Arena

Lyon Opera: Jacques Lassalle (stage director), Claus Viller (video director)

With the right cast—a Luisa that can combine vulnerability with valorous resolve, a Miller whose range easily encompasses this role's high-lying tessitura, two solid bass villains, and an impassioned tenor seemingly self-propelled to catastrophe—*Luisa Miller* can go right to the heart and not be easily dislodged. With some weak links in a work in which the focus shifts from one key confrontation to another, all involving different combinations of characters, the impact is compromised. And, as in this 1988 Opéra de Lyon run-through, when hardly anyone really seems ideally matched with his or her particular assignment, little results but dissatisfaction.

Hampered by a bare-bones and conceptually barren production from Jacques Lassalle, with sets and costumes (updated to be contemporary with the opera's composition) by Maurizio Balo, poor Luisa on this occasion gets to be doubly betrayed. Mostly we seem to be in what used to be called neo-Bayreuth territory—formal ranked chorus placements, a cyclorama alternating with a coffered wood drop that manages to define visual tedium—and in this territory the players collide and gesture with a stylized awkwardness that illuminates very little, seldom able to endow each scene with even minimal dramatic tension. The major assets of the performance are purely musical ones and too scant even in that category—Maurizio Arena's detailed conducting of the overture and bass Romuald Tesarowicz, in the plum villain role of Wurm, whose ebony-hued voice overcomes initial roughness to gain steadily in security and impressiveness.

But June Anderson in the title role, albeit fleet in fioritura and with a mettlesome middle register (the cabaletta of "Tu puniscimi" comes off quite well), is too often beset by bloodless tone. Her several voices just do not come together. Her lover Rodolfo is unwisely entrusted to the lightweight tenor Taro Ichihara, and he is under severe stress when attempting to contort his lyrical abilities into quasi-hysterical but mandatory declamatory outbursts. In the end he simply runs out of steam. Father Miller is played by bass Eduard Tumagian, professional and adequate of voice, unprepossessing in presence. Bass Paul Plishka as Count Walter gives a reliable, workmanlike reading, some good low notes alternating with muddy, wobbly passage negotiation. Mezzo Suzanna Anselmi as the less pivotal Federica, Rodolfo's arranged intended, impresses as well-schooled but professionally raw. Scoring for the lower orders, Brigitte Desnoues as Laura and Michel Pastor as a peasant make a more pleasing impact. All in all, one wonders why this performance was thought a candidate for release, unless the opportunity of being the only *Luisa Miller* in the video store was deemed a sufficient rationale. Although it may far too negatively overstate the case, perhaps the last word should come from one of the more misguided subtitle translations: the distraught and abandoned Luisa in the last scene, as she rejects the offer of food—"I beg you. Respect my repugnance."

A *Luisa Miller* video really worth owning has still to be made. For those who love this intensely moving work, a number of admirable commercial and live-performance CDs are available. It's still an ears-only situation.

HARVEY E. PHILLIPS

STIFFELIO (1850)

A: Lina (s); B: Stiffelio (t); C: Raffaele (t); D: Stankar (bar); E: Jorg (bs)

Stiffelio, written between *Luisa Miller* and *Rigoletto*, has a libretto by Francesco Maria Piave based on a French play by Emile Souvestre and Eugene Bourgeois (about the plight of a Protestant minister who gives sermons on forgiveness but can hardly bear to forgive his adulterous wife). Very likely the most unjustly neglected of Verdi's works, *Stiffelio* is that rare opera that failed in its time, done in not by lack of urgent musical expression but by censors who found its book offensive.

Piave tinkered with the libretto after the opera's premiere in 1850 to no avail. So obdurate were the censors (how could a married religious leader consider divorce and murder?) that Verdi regretfully withdrew his opera from the stage four years later. He said, in evaluating his early operas, that among those that had had little success, *Stiffelio* was one of only two he would hate to consign to oblivion.

Verdi tried to give it new life by cannibalizing its music for *Aroldo* in 1857, but what he created was less incisive, artificial operatic theater. Happily, the vocal score of *Stiffelio* had been published; but not until hand copies of the partiture were found in Naples in the late 1960s was the opera awakened from its century-long slumber.

Stiffelio has its flaws—an uninspired overture, several conventional numbers, and a drama that offers no motivation for Lina's infidelity. On the other hand, its musical rewards are many—not least, the first act ensemble,

most of the episode in the cemetery, and the Stiffelio-Lina duet in the last act.

1993 KULTUR (VHS) / PIONEER (LD)

(Stage Performance, Stereo, Color, Subtitled) 123 minutes

Catherine Malfitano (A), José Carreras (B), Robin Leggate (C), Gregory Yurisch (D), Gwynne Howell (E), Chorus and Orchestra of the Royal Opera House—Edward Downes

Royal Opera, Covent Garden: Elijah Moshinsky (stage director), Brian Large (video director)

In this production, Lina is not Piave's countess living in a castle. Moshinsky has made her an American pastor's wife residing in a rural Nebraska chapel. Its exterior, with an adjacent cemetery, is strikingly depicted by a photograph on the front cloth. When it is raised, one finds a set used for all four interior scenes. This weakens the last scene, which should be set in a church with a pulpit and a congregation, as Piave instructed, for full theatrical impact.

The direction is clear and purposeful, but only Catherine Malfitano responds with generous spirit and commitment. She earns admiration, despite tone inconsistently firm in her middle register and likely to spread when she ascends above the staff. The ravages of singing, for too many years, roles for which his lyric tenor was never intended have added heft to José Carreras's once lovely voice but taken away its bloom. It sounds worn and strained under pressure. He is earnest and dignified in action, but his face and body remain expressively blank. The remainder of the principals make occasional favorable impression; but, here and there, each struggles with pitch, especially in softer passages.

Edward Downes achieves a good ensemble and leads with commendable musical honesty, if with no special dramatic flair.

Production values are first rate. Images are tightly focused, even in the nocturnal cemetery scene. The sound is also very good, although the miking is not perfectly even all over the stage. As an introduction to *Stiffelio*, this presentation, notwithstanding its shortcomings, is more than adequate.

1993 DEUTSCHE GRAMMOPHON (VHS / LD)

(Stage Performance, Stereo, Color, Subtitled) 115 minutes

Sharon Sweet (A), Plácido Domingo (B), Peter Riberti (C), Vladimir Chernov (D), Paul Plishka (E), Metropolitan Opera Chorus and Orchestra—James Levine

Metropolitan Opera: Giancarlo del Monaco (stage director), Brian Large (video director)

This finely engineered video is the first to document the opera Verdi composed in 1850.

The 1993 Met production, its principal interior set perhaps overly grand for a pastor of Stiffelio's means, functions well, and the direction is at least unobtrusive and not at all fussy.

All told, this performance is stronger than Covent Garden's, even with the liability of Sharon Sweet, whose lustrous tone is insufficient compensation for much unwieldy, graceless phrasing and an almost blank portrayal. Plácido Domingo's heroic assumption of the title role (in Andrew Porter's words "one of Verdi's greatest and grandest") and James Levine's pacing, shaping, and elegant pointing of the score are star turns. Their impressive contributions, together with those by the other capable cast members and by the imposing Metropolitan Opera orchestra and chorus, insure that no one may overlook the high quality of Verdi's long-neglected opera. Its most eloquent episodes—almost the whole of the act in the cemetery and the ensembles that close the first act and the first scene of the third—are brought to a dramatic boil. The finale is memorable for Domingo's moving, emotionally complex physical and vocal acting.

The Met video is not apt to be surpassed any time soon.

C. J. LUTEN

GIUSEPPE VERDI

RIGOLETTO (1851)

A: Gilda (s); B: Maddalena (ms); C: Duke (t); D: Rigoletto (bar);
E: Sparafucile (bs)

That damned hump!" said Tito Gobbi, talking about the difficulties of singing Rigoletto. But that hump, in a sense, is the cornerstone of nineteenth-century Romanticism *and* Realism. It was Victor Hugo's play *Le Roi S'Amuse (The King Enjoys Himself)* on which *Rigoletto* was based, and Hugo had earlier proclaimed that modern writers (like Shakespeare, he noted) must investigate not only the classically sublime, but also what he called "the grotesque": not only "heaven," but also "earth." It is the central tension between the two that animates Verdi's opera and makes its title role the ultimate trial of the baritone's art: the same man must essay the *bel canto* sublime in "Veglio o donna," the "grotesquely" spasmodic in "Pari siamo!", and a combination of the two in his climactic scene with the courtiers. The same ironies surround the other major characters. Gilda's capacity for love is in its way classically pure—sublime—but that she should lavish her feelings on the Duke is grotesque. His sensuality is likewise sublime—at least in her eyes—but that it should service such a shallow nature is also grotesque. The gods do play with us. And this leads straight from Romanticism to the Realism of the twentieth century. Any revealing performance of *Rigoletto* must be cognizant of both traditions.

1947 BEL CANTO (VHS)

(Film, Mono, Black and White, Not Subtitled)
101 minutes

Marcella Govoni / Lina Pagliughi (A), Anna Maria Canali (B), Mario Filippeschi (C), Tito Gobbi (D), Giulio Neri (E), Rome Opera Chorus and Orchestra—Tullio Serafin

Rome Opera: Carmine Gallone (director)

Why would one recommend this fifty-year-old film: black and white, sometimes blurred, conventionally (with one overwhelming exception) acted, boxy in sound, and lacking English subtitles? Find a libretto. With all its faults, this film cuts to the tragic nineteenth-century heart of *Rigoletto* as no other performance I have seen.

Its settings are massive and ornate: here is an old-fashioned theatrical realism that makes no social comment on the action. The conductor and singers will certainly be familiar to record collectors. We have from them all the authentic Hugo / Verdi Romanticism, with a protagonist of genuinely tragic complexity, a virginal Gilda of extraordinary passion, and a pleasant Duke with at least a soupçon of cynical self-awareness. Lina Pagliughi worshipped Galli-Curci, and Tetrazzini once called the young singer her successor. Pagliughi recorded Gilda twice elsewhere. Her soundtrack here, despite technical distortion, is the most moving of the three performances. The role is mimed pleasantly enough by Marcella Govoni, but Pagliughi sings with an easy accuracy, beauty of attack and phrasing, and simple dramatic commitment that have not been equalled since. There is none of Callas's layered psychological depth—that was unique. What there is, is a wealth of tender and passionate suggestion that vitalizes an often alienated "coloratura" character.

As the Duke, Mario Filippeschi is handsome enough, and can at least strut about without much embarrassment. In recordings he often strains in heavier roles, but here he is vocally buoyant, accurate, and even graceful: the quartet is a highlight. Giulio Neri's Sparafucile may lurch, but he sings the role well. His tone is large, threatening, and surprisingly vibrant. Maddalena is generally a trap for its singers: strongly visible but musically ineffective and dramatically underwritten. Anna Maria Canali is pleasantly pudgy and eager, and she is also one of the few in the whole history of recording to sing it as more than a demonstration of register breaks.

Central to the success of the performance, of course, are Tullio Serafin and Tito Gobbi. The conductor provides both lyricism and vitality. In fact, he rushes a few passages beyond the point of expressivity, but there are both theatrical excitement and proportion in whatever he does. Tito Gobbi is one of two or three singers in the whole history of filmed opera to transmit successfully to the medium something of the grand nineteenth-century tragic manner. Certain actors have done it (Forbes-Robertson, Marie Bell), but in opera Gobbi almost alone manages to combine the outsized realism of the theater with an attention to intimate detail demanded by the screen. He performs with immense vivacity and conscious control. His body will do whatever he wants, and his face, well-lit, is almost limitlessly expressive—of irony, terror, love, despair. At times the performance lacks something in spontaneity, for he is acting alone on his creative level. It took Maria Callas (seventeen years later, in the *Tosca* Act II videotape from Covent Garden) to allow him that further element consistently. Meanwhile, one takes equal pleasure here in his expressivity and his dramatic technique: a performance of genuine tragic stature. Vocally he is in good shape, although he often presses needlessly. Nevertheless, this is a performance that gives us, in a form adapted to film, the theatrical power of the vision shared by Hugo and Verdi.

1982 HBO (VHS)

(Stage Performance, Stereo, Color, in English) 140 minutes

Marie McLaughlin (A), Jean Rigby (B), Arthur Davies (C), John Rawnsley (D), John Tomlinson (E), English National Opera Chorus and Orchestra—Mark Elder

English National Opera: Jonathan Miller (director)

This is Jonathan Miller's famous "Mafia" production—now a decade-and-a-half old but still the popular example of an adaptation tradition that has been going on for a century or more. "Why *not* change the setting and the time?" asks Miller. With *Rigoletto* you can eliminate the discrepancy between the sixteenth-century setting and the nineteenth-century music by resetting the opera in Verdi's time, or you can forget about the discrepancies entirely and set it in some other era. What you gain, he says, is the excitement of experiencing the opera again as if for the first time.

So this is a performance to be seen in the context of those more conventional productions that still surround us. The skewed perspective of a different setting, like a funhouse mirror or somebody else's glasses, may for the moment help us to examine some things we had overlooked before. Here the Duke is a 1950s Mafia boss in New York and Rigoletto is his bartender: a joker, adviser, toady. The plot works well enough: a story of lawless personal revenge. What is added is a striking coarseness: with this Duke there is no room for Schipa's elegance, Pavarotti's good humor, or Peerce's nobility, and perhaps something of real value to the psychology of the story is gained. Rigoletto's social entrapment also becomes something more than an historical fable; there is an element of real claustrophobia here. The loss is in stature: an extra burden for singing actors who must convince us that such characters are really worth the glorious music.

The performance is paradoxical. Miller's conception reaches out for cutting-edge brutality and a twentieth-century pace, but his English cast and conductor are often more politely withdrawn than those in any ordinary rented Renaissance production. Marie McLaughlin is a conscientious but dull Gilda: Americans at the New York City Opera have provided more authentic musical and visual passion than this. Arthur Davies is a nasal Duke. His singing and acting are responsible but often uninflected: hardly galvanic. Mark Elder is, surprisingly for him, a lethargic conductor. That is particularly unfortunate since little of the score is cut. The exception to all of this is John Rawnsley, a good vocalist and an expressive actor. He manages both emotional spontaneity and contemporary relevance with breathtaking success.

There are some other difficulties. The libretto's usage is often decidedly English and the actors' diction unclear, and of course the setting deprives the opera of its essential tension between elegance and brutality. Nevertheless, this is a performance worth seeing for its implicit commentary on adaptation, some of its dramatic ideas, and Rawnsley's moving central performance.

1983 LONDON (VHS / LD)

(Film, Stereo, Color, Subtitled) 116 minutes

Edita Gruberová (A), Victoria Vergara (B), Luciano Pavarotti (C), Ingvar Wixell (D), Ferruccio Furlanetto (E), Vienna State Opera Chorus, Vienna Philharmonic Orchestra—Riccardo Chailly

Jean-Pierre Ponnelle (director)

Early in this century Sarah Bernhardt made both recordings and silent films. The records show an astonishing technique, and an electrifying energy that recalls Lilli Lehmann. The films, though, remain sadly but inescapably ridiculous; the grand manner, in general, will not translate to the screen, and operatic film directors have been breaking their backs on it for the century since. This *Rigoletto* is a desperate example from a decade ago. Since Bernhardt, only the technology and the taste have changed: one is better, the other is worse. Jean-Pierre Ponnelle was a vibrant thinker and a great inspiration: singers with whom he worked adored him. His productions, though, were often excessive without being stimulating and chaotic without genuine excitement—as here. The film is marked by garish color, gratuitously violent action, tiresome symbolism (both Monterone and Rigoletto are played by Wixell), incompetent editing, and sheer tastelessness, which, far from magnifying the tragedy, trivializes it. The film is nearly all theatrical gesture—interesting as a cockeyed encyclopedia of old-time stage devices. The important thing lacking is a genuine adult faith in the psychological truth of the opera.

Many of the tricks come from his stage *Rigolettos*. Some of the moments worked for Verdi, but many did not. I remember in his San Francisco production seeing the Duke climb into an onstage curtained bed with Gilda just before Rigoletto's magnificent Act II scene with the courtiers: surely the only time that in his greatest moment the jester has been upstaged for ten minutes by an inanimate (Thank God!) four-poster.

The film is full of such amusing moments; otherwise, it is ordinary. Visually it is wealthy-looking but often badly lit. Pavarotti looks like a handsome Henry VIII when he isn't standing behind something, and his face smiles even when his healthy (prerecorded) voice does not. Edita Gruberová phrases intelligently, but the voice is pinched; injured innocence is not her strength. Ingvar Wixell, as always, is an interesting actor. He plunges through the direction with some conviction. The courtier scene is deprived of the emotional variety that is its glory, though. Wixell's voice, typically, is grainy but it has an interesting core. An added delight: the tiny role of Giovanna is played by the great mezzo of the fifties, Fedora Barbieri. She acts for the back of the house: it's touching and unbearable at the same time.

Despite its technical shortcomings, the 1947 Serafin performance, with Gobbi offering a Rigoletto of startling theatrical fervor, is the recommendation. For those who want something technically more recent, the 1983 London offers at least Wixell's grit and Pavarotti's lyricism, in a coarse, mannered production. The 1982 HBO adaptation is interesting for Jonathan Miller's quite different goals and John Rawnsley's touching intensity.

LONDON GREEN

GIUSEPPE VERDI

IL TROVATORE (1853)

A: Leonora (s); B: Azucena (ms); C: Manrico (t); D: Count di Luna (bar); E: Ferrando (bs)

Now that the course of operatic evolution has passed forever beyond the era of great singers merely singing magnificently (if statically) in front of painted backdrops, *Il Trovatore*'s timeless emotional truths are proving increasingly elusive to those undertaking to keep them before the public.

The vocal techniques of contemporary singing actors rarely promote ease and security in negotiating Verdi's long-breathed, high-tessitura phrases. "Acting" and "expression" not arising out of the musico-dramatic impulse of the opera itself are too often substituted for genuine competence. Furthermore, late twentieth-century regisseurs manifest inadequate faith in this work's innate power to move and persuade, frequently seeking to create some visible compensation for its acknowledged plot incongruities.

Trovatore's theatrical effect has never depended upon any aspect of visual presentation, but rather on a high degree of success in meeting its exigent vocal demands with appropriate proportions of poised, beautiful tone and emotive discrimination. Performers not providing these essentials shortchange Verdi's objectives.

Worse, misguided efforts to reinvent the work by disregarding its historical preeminence as a singer's opera in favor of some fabricated significance as a music drama in which the singing takes second place forces a reverse metamorphosis — the butterfly becomes a caterpillar.

1949 BEL CANTO SOCIETY (VHS)

(Film, Mono, Black and White, Italian Narration, Not Subtitled) 102 minutes

Vittorina Collonello / Franca Sacchi (A), Gianna Pederzini (B), Gino Sinimberghi / Antonio Salvarezza (C), Enzo Mascherini (D), Cesare Polacco / Enrico Formichi (E), Chorus and Orchestra of Teatro dell'Opera, Rome — Gabriele Santini

Carmine Gallone (director), Giulio Fiaschi (film director)

Gianna Pederzini was surely just one major component of this project as originally conceived. A half century later she serves as raison d'être for its reappearance. "Pederzini in *Il Trovatore*" proclaims the videocassette box in large letters. Glowing liner-note tributes by Franco Corelli and Tito Gobbi prove difficult to reconcile with the artifact's reality, for none of the surpassing magnificence claimed for the mezzo made its way into this stilted, inhibitory exercise.

Director Giulio Fiaschi filmed not Verdi's great *Trovatore* itself but a cataclysmic "explication" of it, with Gabriele Santini as accomplice. The result of their collaboration, a self-conscious, disjointed, stylized hybrid, is the theatrical equivalent of a basket case. Santini does a wholesale cut-and-paste job on the score, dissecting, abridging, and rearranging, leaving a musical torso with stumps where once there were limbs. Nonspeakers of Italian may find themselves anesthetized by the ubiquitous explanatory narration. Those who comprehend will probably consider it irritating but innocuous.

Ferrando's first-scene aria is not sung by the bass but played as an orchestral solo under the narrator's spoken obbligato while we watch the burning of Azucena's mother, the abduction of the di Luna baby, Azucena's discovery that she hurled the wrong infant into the fire, the elder Count di Luna's deathbed charge to his son (the baritone) to find his missing sibling, the tournament where Manrico and Leonora meet, and so forth.

The proceedings continue piecemeal, with flashbacks, flashes forward, and much galloping about the countryside on horseback to indicate changes of scene and passage of time. Murky, often impenetrable visual quality renders discussion of sets, costumes, and production values impossible. Only a few exterior shots are light enough to permit determination of what is onscreen. The performers' lip-synching to the muffled sound track was apparently not intended to be anywhere near accurate—that would connote actual *singing*, after all—so the manifest incongruity is tremendous.

Tall Gino Sinimberghi "acts" Manrico to the canned troubadour of short Antonio Salvarezza, whose sweet, ineffably Italian instrument fulfills the assignment dependably. The matronly, juiceless sound of Franca Sacchi's unseen Leonora augurs convincingly for her future as the wobbly Cieca on Decca's 1957 recording of *La Gioconda*. She is spared most of the virtuoso passages one wouldn't want to hear her sing anyway: both recitative and cabaletta of "Tacea la notte"; the Act I trio; "D'amor sull'ali rosee"(!); the *stretta* of her duet with di Luna. Enzo Mascherini sings his serviceable "Il balen" in the Count's rooms *before* leaving to snatch Leonora from the convent. "Per me ora fatale" is cut.

As for Pederzini, her Azucena offers scant testimony to any particular vocal prowess. Moreover, as an expressive instrument, her voice—worn, stiff, the top shot—will not sustain any noticeable level of interpretative mastery. The reasons for her mythical status even among such peers as Barbieri, Simionato, and Stignani are not revealed by this film, for which the doctrine of *caveat emptor* obtains—it is for cultists and fanatics exclusively.

1957 BEL CANTO SOCIETY (VHS)

(Film, Mono, Black and White, Not Subtitled)
124 minutes

Leyla Gencer (A), Fedora Barbieri (B), Mario del Monaco (C), Ettore Bastianini (D), Plinio Clabassi (E), Chorus and Orchestra of Radiotelevisione Italiana, Milan—Fernando Previtali

Claudio Fino (director)

In this important video document, five qualified Verdians, all vocally suited to their tasks and to varying degrees expert at them, are up against the necessity of lip-synching to a prerecorded sound track and trying to make a cinematic experience out of an archetypally operatic one (with apparently negligible assistance from director Claudio Fino).

No lyric artist active in 1957 was trained in the wiles of celluloid thespianism and few could relate to a camera in a manner that would "read" believably up close. Leyla Gencer and Ettore Bastianini go overboard with not emoting like opera performers and not opening their mouths as if singing, which drastically reduces their onscreen energy output—she appears dazed, he is stolid and uninvolved.

Fortunately, Mario del Monaco and Fedora Barbieri were either unable or unwilling to follow suit. Their body language conveys an intense conviction that doesn't say "Somehow we must make this credible" but rather "We believe with all our hearts in what we're doing." A few endearingly amusing moments result in part from such performers' sheer uncomplicated self-confidence.

Del Monaco, compact and handsome, struts like a bantam rooster and tirelessly purveys his powerful, somewhat steely, not always pitch-true sound, more appropriate to "Di quella pira" (down a half step) than to "Ah sì, ben mio," but everywhere fearless, imposing, exciting.

Barbieri's Azucena, one of the great portrayals of its time, pours forth a steady stream of huge, bronzed tone, sings a "Condotta" of unforgettable dramatic impact, displays a superb legato line in "Ai nostri monti," and gets nearer the old gypsy's top B-flats than this listener has ever heard her manage.

Bastianini so abused his splendid baritone that by 1957 he had already barked a good bit of the nap off it. He shouts "Il balen," snarls "Per me ora fatale," and throughout spends vocal capital with appalling recklessness. The size and undisputed quality of his sound carry automatic authority, but this performance is a reminder of just how artistically primitive and vocally self-destructive he always was. Like del Monaco's, his appearance is ideal.

Gencer's supreme stylistic and musical grasp of her role places her light years ahead of the video competition. Nonetheless, the reasons for her also-ran status during the Callas / Milanov / Tebaldi years are evident: an often throaty voice of unexceptional color; a *pianissimo* that is detached and squeezed, not freely floated; a *forte* frequently boosted by dubious means, including glottal attacks so rife that they add up to clucking; pitch that sags regularly at major moments. This decidedly idiosyncratic vocalism diminishes but does not invalidate a worthy achievement.

Plinio Clabassi, by some margin the best video Ferrando, offers warm, beautiful tone, unspoiled by a single woof. Laura Londi is an outstanding Inez. Fernando Previtali leads a trim, stirring performance, allowing his soloists all the leeway they require without being in the least lax or subservient.

Low budget physical trappings (including some hilarious costumes) and consistently washed-out film quality constitute nonfatal liabilities.

1985 CASTLE OPERA (VHS) / PIONEER (LD)

(Stage Performance, Stereo, Color, Subtitled) 140 minutes

Rosalind Plowright (A), Fiorenza Cossotto (B), Franco Bonisolli (C), Giorgio Zancanaro (D), Paolo Washington (E), Chorus and Orchestra of the Arena di Verona—Reynald Giovaninetti

Verona Arena: Giuseppe Patroni Griffi (stage director), Brian Large (video director)

The daunting dimensions of Verona's Arena stage have historically driven designers to excesses of realism, up to and including *Aida*'s camels and elephants. However, for this 1985 *Trovatore*, Mario Ceroli and Gianfranco Fini opted instead for visual deconstruction, portraying a feudal society-at-arms, its serfs and soldiers pushing Leonardoesque war paraphernalia about: battering rams, open wood-frame pyramids and towers, stockpiles of munitions, even a quasi-Trojan horse. But the set sometimes impedes the drama. For instance, Leonora's dwelling, a maze of scaffolding and lead pipe, prevents her sweeping reentrance at "Anima mia!" in Act I. She must descend cautiously, to avoid bodily injury, thereby defeating the composer's intended impact.

Alas, there is no compensating sweep in Rosalind Plowright's singing. For all her studied urgency of manner, with the wrong voice—too small, too light, frigidly monochromatic—she is a Leonora by virtue of hubris rather than endowment. No hint of *slancio* intrudes in her non-Italianate vocalism, which invariably runs into heavy weather at the top. Unable to sustain Verdi's arching phrases as they wend upward, she is ever willing to derail the line in order to impose some special inflection and enlightening facial expression upon individual words or syllables. Intended to reveal how deeply she feels and comprehends the text, this merely demonstrates that she understands the music not at all. The Arena public, indifferent to postmodern "artistic subtlety," never warms to the soprano in the least.

Her Italian colleagues, genuine Verdians, operate on an entirely different aesthetic. Franco Bonisolli's Manrico, ripe prosciutto indeed, swaggers, poses, charges around with drawn sword, oversings, and generally presents a compendium of crudities touching on every primal tenorial instinct. This sturdy-voiced throwback to a more indulgent era interpolates high notes right and left (not all of them on pitch) and grants the standing, screaming audience a *bis* of "Di quella pira." His "Ah sì, ben mio" may be stentorian, but he attempts the trills and doesn't break his clinch with Leonora to acknowledge the cheers.

Not so Giorgio Zancanaro, the lean, mean, ornery Count di Luna, who bows ostentatiously after an "Il balen" that sounds angry rather than reflective. He is in prime form nonetheless, singing throughout with tensile strength and firm, steady tone marred, as usual, by his trademark intrusive aspirates.

No effort is expended to present Fiorenza Cossotto as old or haggish. Instead, this nearly glamorous Azucena's requisite age pervades her sound, now nasal and pinched, short on top (she can only feint at the B-flat and B), and difficult to support. Cossotto's vast experience, gripping presence, and powerful dramatic projection see her through.

Conductor Giovaninetti and director Griffi contrive to keep these disparate elements from self-destructing, and Brian Large, as always, gets us up close and intimate with the proceedings. Bonisolli, in his unfortunate pitch-black, overpouffed Liberace wig, may embody provincial aspects of opera's heritage, but he proves downright endearing next to Plowright's effortful evocation of a cold, lusterless future for Verdi.

1988 DEUTSCHE GRAMMOPHON (VHS / LD)

(Stage Performance, Stereo, Color, Subtitled) 133 minutes

Eva Marton (A), Dolora Zajick (B), Luciano Pavarotti (C), Sherrill Milnes (D), Jeffrey Wells (E), Metropolitan Opera Chorus and Orchestra—James Levine

Metropolitan Opera: Fabrizio Melano (stage director), Brian Large (video director)

Luciano Pavarotti's offstage serenade, the first engaging sound (but fifth solo voice) heard in this performance, penetrates the prevailing gloom like a ray of sunshine. The gleam never dims. Pavarotti's troubadour has style and spirit and provides both pleasure and excitement through healthy, bright, even, steady tone and splendid diction (everybody else mushes the words to one degree or another). The tenor's impassioned, never overblown delivery carries the day even when he is being cavalier about note values and pitches (the last-act denunciation of Leonora) or eschewing full involvement in dramatic incidents requiring energetic, convincing movement (the "duel" with di Luna).

Eva Marton sings at an unvarying *forte*, barely skirting disaster in Leonora's lyrical flights. Her valiant but labored vocalism is blowsy rather than opulent, generally unsteady, flat on top, and devoid of such essential Verdian virtues as dynamic shading and clean, centered tone. She picks her way precariously through the two great arias and muffs the big phrases in the convent scene and during the moments preceding the heroine's demise. No chemistry whatever exists between her matronly Leonora and Pavarotti's corpulent Manrico.

Dolora Zajick's old crone makeup belies the youthful vitality of her singing. She traverses Azucena's wide compass (low A-flat to the oft-omitted high C) with assurance and ring, her imposing chest register booming forth impressively and her top possessing all the focus and pitch security Marton's lacks. She can rattle the rafters in the hallucination scenes but also serve up a gorgeous "Ai nostri monti" with Pavarotti, the evening's most poised and poignant music making.

Sherrill Milnes all but twirls his mustache in the Count's moments of abject villainy or lust but cannot hide the fact that his days for controlling line and maintaining pitch in Verdian cantilena are behind him. The capacious Milnes sound, loosened at the seams, emerges aurally paunchy, the lower and middle ranges almost *buffo* in character. The top, now hollow, retains some compactness. The baritone's shaky but determined "Il balen" is a triumph of experience and stage presence over wizened vocal means.

Jeffrey Wells, a Ferrando much too young to have witnessed Azucena's infanticide, and Loretta Di Franco (Inez) make positive contributions.

Superior *verdiano* James Levine understands *Trovatore* completely. His sense of propulsion without haste maximizes continuity when soprano and baritone prefer to linger or lumber yet allows everyone the full measure of expression each is capable of offering.

Ezio Frigerio's arresting painted backdrops are only dimly visible despite stage lighting that has been bolstered for the benefit of Brian Large's videography. Between backdrops and audience looms the "set": stage-width stairs and shiny movable columns that nullify Fabrizio Melano's nominal direction by constituting an impediment to the comfort and dramatic conviction of the participants rather than being a support for plausible presentation. The chorus, immobilized even during music of utmost vigor, puts all desirable animation into its sound—the tried-and-true, most appropriate approach to this work.

Neither recent performance comes near matching historic audio incarnations of *Trovatore*, but Pavarotti and Zajick give the Met's effort default status as video of choice. Experienced buffs and impartial novices alike may well find the dated film by del Monaco, Barbieri, and company a necessary, not merely a supplementary, tape.

BRUCE BURROUGHS

GIUSEPPE VERDI

LA TRAVIATA (1853)

A: Violetta (s); B: Alfredo Germont (t); C: Giorgio Germont (bar)

Curiously, *La Traviata* seems to be the first opera in which someone dies from a particular disease. That the disease is consumption goes to the shocking immediacy of the work in its own time. Violetta's tragedy is given a firm grounding in a complex gestalt. The etiology of tuberculosis was unknown until 1882. As usual with mysterious epidemics, tuberculosis was seen as rising from moral failings, or as a "mark of Cain." But there was also a sense of it as a tragic gift; "phthisis," as it was called, heightened creativity in men and, in particular, was thought to enhance the sexual appeal of young women. They would have shining eyes, pale cheeks touched with red, and wild bursts of energy. By choosing to set a story in which the illness was explicit from the first, Verdi moved into a disturbing and unusual realm for opera. Music occurs in real time; the passing of time was considered of acute importance in consumption. The phases of the disease were well known and Verdi used them for a precise musical color. This is especially evident in the last act. Death arrives slowly with the gradual thinning of breath until the thread of life softly breaks—an almost exact description of the prelude to the last act. Terminal victims of consumption could also have a last-minute and illusory revival with a sudden infusion of brilliant optimism. Violetta, dying with her lover (not a priest) nearby, has just such a ninth hour upsurge of vitality. Since tuberculosis was associated with sexuality, these realistic depictions would have had an almost pornographic impact in Italy—more so than the heroine being a "fallen" women. Little wonder *La Traviata* has retained its fascination for producers. It is probably the first opera to actually demand a verisimilitudinous representation.

1954 BEL CANTO SOCIETY (VHS)

(Film, Mono, Black and White, Not Subtitled) 116 minutes

Rosanna Carteri (A), Nicola Filacuridi (B), Carlo Tagliabue (C), Unknown Chorus and Orchestra—Nino Sazogno

Franco Enriquez (director)

The second we hear the precise and ripe tenor / bass blend at the start of Act I we know this will be vocally typical of its long-vanished time. All the singers (including those in small roles) have fine voices and a highly idiomatic feel for the vocal style. Filacuridi was a useful second stringer and Tagliabue an old timer nearing retirement, but in a time when Italy produces few decent singers they are sorely missed. Carteri, a budding star of twenty-four, very pretty and with an elegant manner, has a full-bodied lyric soprano with a distinctive, not-always-pretty tone. Sometimes her high notes have an edge and occasionally she sings flat, but hers is a full-fledged, large-scale, sincere performance. Unfortunately the sound track is "canned," and that's a disaster. Tagliabue is the only one of the principals to lip-synch with dignity. The others are clearly self-conscious trying to stay with the prerecording. Carteri gives up altogether in Act III. In the Act II, Scene 2 gypsy dance, tambourines are hit before they sound, or ostentatiously hit without sounding. Alfredo knocks over a chair to get to Violetta—but it doesn't sound. On the other hand there are coughs and scrapings on the sound track. The result is a "verfremdungs effekt" that Brecht himself would have been proud of.

Enriquez's production unfolds along traditional lines. His only strange touch is having Alfredo sing "De miei bolenti spiriti" in a swing! Sadly, he plays with his camera like a hyperactive child with a toy tank—he rolls it everywhere all the time. He's so fond of zooming close-ups that then follow the singers relentlessly it must have been frightening to perform. No wonder Carteri keeps peeking nervously at the camera in Act III. Enriquez also likes Busby Berkeley–like cuts to a ceiling camera, jumpy and silly. Lighting is touch and go—odd shadows are cast and instruments sometimes flicker. This was a good attempt seriously undercut by the technology of the time.

1968 VAI (VHS)

(Film, Color, Mono, Not Subtitled) 113 minutes

Anna Moffo (A), Franco Bonisolli (B), Gino Bechi (C), Rome Opera Chorus and Orchestra—Giuseppe Patanè

Mario Lanfranchi (director)

Anna Moffo was a memorable Violetta, genuinely beautiful onstage, vocally accomplished, touchingly girlish in the role. This film, directed by her then-husband, Mario Lanfranchi, is an homage to her good looks and a respectful treatment of the opera, but it is very dull. The problem again is lip-synching. These singers cope better than those on the RAI film, but operatic performing is organic. When singers don't sing, they don't feel, either. The eyes of Moffo, Gino Bechi (who gets second billing), and Franco Bonisolli are too often empty. It also looks as though they've been instructed not to move their faces. Lanfranchi's directing rarely quickens to life. The singers strike poses and hold them. Alfredo's denunciation of Violetta

seems to be happening under water—the film moves at the usual speed but every action is painfully deliberate. Lanfranchi is conservative—a priest consoling Violetta during the third act prelude is his only eccentric choice. However, Violetta is shown living in improbable splendor. Even in destitution she is still in so big a place she could have taken in boarders and alleviated her fiscal misery. The overall musical performance is similarly idiomatic, but less polished than the RAI film. Moffo sounds and looks lovely, a few bumpy, poorly judged close-ups aside. The rather debonair but poker-faced Bechi sounds dry; Bonisolli is very capable. One feels this cast would have been more engaging filmed in a live performance.

1973 LEGATO CLASSICS (VHS)

(Stage Performance, Mono, Color, Subtitled in Japanese) 128 minutes

Renata Scotto (A), José Carreras (B), Sesto Bruscantini (C), Orchestra and Chorus of Lirica Italiana, Tokyo—Nino Verchi

Opera company, stage director, and video director unknown

Renata Scotto was perhaps the most distinctive singer to emerge as a big star in the seventies, though she had already sung successfully for close to twenty years. Here she is captured in a provincial performance just before she became the Italian diva of the Met, a position she held with increasing controversy for about ten years, beginning in 1974. She is much pudgier and less chic than she was to become, though the hand gestures that some loved, others hated, and all imitated are in evidence. Scotto has a high, bright voice, surprisingly plangent in the big moments in the middle register. She is professional in a way which few younger sopranos are—everything is firmly and certainly controlled, her effects land. She is careful about high notes here but sings over a wide dynamic range with a lot of color. Her special way of shaping and tapering phrases is unique—probably a little mannered, but greatly accomplished. Perhaps Callas would have left a little more to chance in the heat of performance, but this is a distinguished and thorough account of the role, virtually the only completely persuasive one before Angela Gheorghiu and on a larger scale (Gruberová is technically more remarkable but not nearly as idiomatic or varied). The production has handsome backgrounds and is efficiently stage managed but leaves it up to the singers to take center stage, which Scotto has no problem doing. Scotto's Violetta is no shrinking violet and seems rather tough. Like Sills, she is defiant, puzzled, angered by Germont père in Act II. In Act III she has great tragic force, more so than Sills, with more colors. But tender vulnerability isn't one of her qualities.

Carreras is the only Alfredo to look sweetly boyish. He sings sweetly, too, though with some hints of trouble to come. Bruscantini is physically an elegant old pro; vocally the emphasis is unfortunately on old—his tone is a wobbly growl, usually out of tune. Aside from two lost-looking Japanese as Giuseppe and the Messenger, the Italian cast knows what it is about. Such vocally resourceful, firmly idiomatic support is rare on these videos. Verchi sometimes loses touch with the stage and his orchestra is poor. Picture quality is watchable but hardly crystalline.

1976 VAI (VHS)

(Stage Performance, Color, Stereo, Subtitled) 140 minutes

Beverly Sills (A), Henry Price (B), Richard Fredericks (C), Wolf Trap Company Chorus, Filene Center Orchestra—Julius Rudel

Wolf Trap: Tito Capobianco (stage director), Kirk Browning (video director)

For Americans able to see her in the sixties and early seventies, Beverly Sills was a unique and unforgettable performer. Typical of the time, American media was not interested in capturing her in her prime. Surely her stunning Cleopatra in Handel's *Giulio Cesare* and her luminous Louise in Charpentier's opera should have been documented in the late sixties. Perhaps the only performance to have been televised of her truly at her best was her incredible

Zerbinetta in the original version of *Ariadne auf Naxos* with the Boston Symphony in 1968—though it's by no means certain that it will be released commercially.

By the time her Violetta was caught on camera, Sills was past her best; nor does this really seem the most flattering context for her. In any case, she got up out of a hospital bed to give this performance, unwilling as always to disappoint those who counted on her, particularly her beloved New York City Opera (despite attributions this is basically a City Opera cast and conductor).

Of course her strong presence and distinctive performing style are obvious, but her singing is variable. Her Violetta is formidable rather than vulnerable. Sometimes that's interesting—she is unusually defiant with Germont père in Act II—but in the long run she seems mature and tough in the role. She suffers in the last act, but with an edge.

The surrounding performance is undistinguished. The production is typical of mid-seventies provincial opera in America. The unit set doesn't really serve any of the acts but is particularly preposterous in Act III. The staging is usually pro forma but chorus and supporting singers have been pushed to "act" in an emphatic, campy, and disagreeable way.

Kirk Browning, the video director, has to cope with a very wide stage, which creates awkwardness for him, particularly in the "scena della bursa." That these were the very early days of opera on video is evident. A few years later someone would have noticed and suppressed Violetta's press-on nails, Alfredo's garish eye makeup, Germont père's penciled-in and immobile eyebrows.

As a souvenir of a great singer this has a value—but an equivocal one.

1982 MCA (VHS / LD)

(Film, Stereo, Color, Subtitled) 95 minutes

Teresa Stratas (A), Plácido Domingo (B), Cornell MacNeil (C), Metropolitan Opera Chorus and Orchestra—James Levine

Franco Zeffirelli (director)

"Written, designed, and directed by Franco Zeffirelli" state the credits rather chillingly, and that tells the whole story. Zeffirelli is of course very skillful; the "scena della bursa," though arguably over-elaborated, is a good example of vivid filmmaking. The director moves his camera fluently in the style of Ophuls and Cukor, and the whole has a Hollywood feel right down to the hard-working foley operators—gowns swishing, glass clinking, carriages departing, rain falling, and pigeons cooing are all dubbed in expertly. The problem is the director's sensibility. His taste is that of a window dresser in a moderately upscale department store somewhere off Hollywood Boulevard. There is a detailed, flamboyant falseness here from the first. During the Act I prelude, a boy navvy gawks at Violetta's portrait, eventually sneaking into her bedroom, evoking her flashback of the whole opera. But is she flashing back to impress him? The same boy has a major part in the third act prelude—Violetta, dying, gazes at him with a lip-smacking longing that seems odd, the more so because he looks half her age. At one fell swoop the opera, not to mention this Violetta, is sabotaged. Even then the boy isn't done; he gets to twinkle at Alfredo's arrival, going from a seeming hustler to a young opera fan who knows the story.

Zeffirelli doctors the music, cutting bits here and there, making a hash out of the great Violetta / Germont père scene in Act II, starting Act III with "Addio del passato" and jumping through the ensuing scenes. But he extends the dance music at Flora's party to pad the parts of the Russian dancers, Maximova and Vassiliev—though nothing they do has anything to do with Alfredo and Violetta or the world they live in.

Violetta lives on a scale the Queen of England might have envied. She looks to be suffering more from terminal bric-a-brac than consumption. Where would a (supposedly) twenty-two-year-old working girl have found the time, let alone the money, to acquire it all? Flora evidently lives in an opera house. Violetta hasn't found a little place in the country; her estate looks as though she's bought half of France. "Pur tanto lusso," sneers the elder Germont. But is that the truth, or the exaggeration of a provincial bigot? In any case, a loose lady's extravagance is once thing—an expenditure worthy of profligate royal princes is something else. Zeffirelli doesn't trust the composer. Maybe flashing back to the lovers' fun in the country isn't a bad idea during "De miei bolenti spiriti"—if only it looked like fun. The lovers are stiff with one another throughout the film. Showing cute teenagers and their angst during the Germont père Violetta scene is simpleminded. Surely the point here is how Violetta receives Germont's story, and why and how he tells it. But Zeffirelli can rarely keep his mind on anything for long. During the wonderful clarinet solo during which Violetta writes the note breaking up with Alfredo, we get to see the older Germont lurking around comically, waiting in ambush for his son, and Alfredo returning from Paris. The flashbacks come fast and furious in the last act and Violetta gets to die all alone in a big ballroom. (Her dying strength got her very far indeed but why didn't the director follow his basic impulse and have her fall into the arms of the working boy?)

This is probably not the fairest way to experience the singers. Overwhelmed by all the froufrou, Stratas has no choice but to play Violetta as Edith Piaf, roaming through the sets like the little sparrow waiting for it all to end. She is not in good voice, nor is Cornell MacNeil—though that probably wasn't the reason Zeffirelli cut the second verse of his aria. Domingo, in a beard, looks handsome and sounds splendid. This is a terrific find for those who hate opera, but then they aren't likely to devote ninety minutes to savoring Zeffirelli's demolition.

1987 HOME VISION (VHS)

(Stage Performance, Stereo, Color, Subtitled) 135 minutes

Marie McLaughlin (A), Walter MacNeil (B), Brent Ellis (C), Glyndebourne Chorus, London Philharmonic Orchestra—Bernard Haitink

Glyndebourne Festival: Peter Hall (stage and video director)

"Peter Hall's production of *La Traviata*" flashes first, but thoughts of directorial hubris vanish as this performance unfolds. This is easily the most effective video realization of the opera to date. Hall's production is carefully rehearsed for the stage, performed live but without an audience—facilitating camera angles and allowing for a fastidious control of what is seen. Hall's work is striking but never pushes past the framework of a nineteenth-century opera. He starts Act I with an old lecher, money in hand, pawing a supine girl while a man in a tuxedo wearing a death mask looks on. A mural of a nude provides backing to the entrance of Violetta's drawing room. Always discretely lit, it reminds us of the subtext of the opera, despite the superficial elegance and the flowery language. Clocks, death masks, and mirrors predominate in all the acts, and furniture is chosen with an eye for exactly what a slightly pretentious girl making easy money might have found (the superb designer is John Gunter). Hall is the only director to create a disturbing sense of a death bed. Not only are there the carefully chosen period medicine bottles and medical apparatus, but there is blood on Violetta's pillow. Chorus members are individuated, and the chorus responds with relish and discipline. Flora's party is the most louche and least campy to date, precisely decadent images are both witty and wicked. Hall also excels at the sort of small glances and gestures that provide emotional continuity and the illusion of reality. Violetta coughs blood into a handkerchief then kicks it under the table as Alfredo enters from the dancing in Act I. Later she snuffs out candles during "Sempre libera," preparing the room for the Baron's arrival. The violence of the lovers' confrontation during Flora's party is shocking; so is the avidity with which the chorus watches Alfredo's denunciation—a shorter guest stuck at the back angles for a better view. Maybe Hall cuts once too often to the Baron during the Brindisi but the process by which Alfredo and Violetta fall in love—they are strangers after all—is lovingly and believably delineated, rare in these films.

Violetta's Act I *scena* is in the usual version, but tenor and baritone sing both verses of their cabalettas in Act II—tests of directorial ingenuity which Hall passes with flying colors.

At first, Marie McLaughlin seems to lack the vocal and physical glamour of a star. But in this context she is a satisfying Violetta. She is an appreciable actress with wonderfully expressive eyes. Her singing is decently schooled and expressive. She is moving in the last act (and sings both verses of "Addio del passato"). Walter MacNeil strangles a little on high notes (he does not try a high C at the end of "O mio rimorso") but has a winning sweetness in the middle and is plausibly boyish. Brent Ellis, Germont père, is less successful. He has a cherubic face smeared with old age makeup and he makes the sort of mouth movements one only sees in singers, not in people (and in his case to no great advantage). Hall and his conductor, the elegant and observant Haitink, work hand-in-glove, so that musical and dramatic impulses seem to coincide. This is not only an absorbing *Traviata* but a rare vindication of opera on video.

1992 TELDEC (VHS / LD)

(Stage Performance, Stereo, Color, Subtitled) 130 minutes

Edita Gruberová (A), Neil Shicoff (B), Giorgio Zancanaro (C), Chorus and Orchestra of the Teatro La Fenice—Carlo Rizzi

La Fenice: Pier Luigi Pizzi (stage director), Derek Bailey (video director)

The three leading singers here are much above average vocally by the prevailing standards of the eighties and early nineties, but they are not riveting to watch, at least at close quarters in a very ordinary stage production. Anyone studying voice should watch Gruberová—her vocal security does not necessitate facial contortions, her jaw and tongue are free and loose, her shoulders and neck are kept free of tension although she expresses the character's torment appropriately enough, her breathing is relaxed and deep, never forced. Vocally the results are often impressive, but she is not charismatic. Shicoff and Zancanaro are also secure—and uninvolving. Maybe there is in the medium itself something inimical to singers. I wonder if we would have found Ponselle, Gigli, and Tibbett; or Melba, Caruso, and Battistini more hypnotic on camera. (Or if perhaps opera lovers in the coming century will find this more interesting because the singers will be long vanished?)

That Pizzi's production isn't very serious is adumbrated by the opening, a gondola ride to the Fenice during the prelude. There is a unit set that looks barren in the party scenes, as anonymous as a train station in the intimate ones. Stage direction is inapt or inattentive. "Would anyone care to dance?" reads the subtitle ten minutes into Act I, but people have been whirling around Violetta since curtain rise. The invitation to Flora's party is focused on by the camera at the end of Act II, Scene 1, but Germont père ignores it. Alfredo and his father should definitely have been given wigs. Violetta sports white diva gowns in the first three scenes (they bear no resemblance to the clothes an actual person might wear) and a billowy, off-white, improbable looking shift in Act III.

Gruberová has an impressive command of breath (Rizzi's tempos are often slow), good coloratura, and a strong top (she offers an powerful E-flat in alt at the end of the first act). Her *mezza voce* and soft tone are firm and well projected. Her manner is very Viennese; she is too fond of the white tone and often sings flat deliberately. Sometimes she floats sharp (at the beginning of "Dite alla giovane"). She does an awful lot of scooping upward. Still, if not exactly *echt* Italian, she has a formidable command of the role vocally. She gives what one suspects is an invariable performance physically, considered but a trace granitic. Someone should have cautioned her against covering her ear as Alfredo whispers "Parigi o cara" into it.

Shicoff is a good if Bucky Beaverish Alfredo. He does not sing "O mio rimorso," though Zancanaro sings one verse of his cabaletta and Gruberova does two (unvaried) verses of "Addio del passato." Zancanaro is vocally very capable but looks and acts like he just sauntered off the Concorde.

Video direction is a little jumpy and sometimes lingers on the conspicuously younger and better looking supporting cast, but the sound is well above average for video.

1993 SONY (VHS / LD)

(Stage Performance, Stereo, Color, Subtitled) 147 minutes

Tiziana Fabbricini (A), Roberto Alagna (B), Paolo Coni, Chorus and Orchestra of Teatro alla Scala—Riccardo Muti

La Scala: Liliana Cavani (video and stage director)

It's rather horrifying to hear Tiziana Fabbricini and Paolo Coni and realize that this is La Scala. Were they really the best the theater could do for its first new production of *La Traviata* since the days of Maria Callas? And what happened to the audience that booed Mirella Freni (some of whom booed Callas)? Did they all go deaf?

Callas is very relevant here; Fabbricini offers an imitation. Callas was professional. Fabbricini is amateurish, unable to sing in tune or provide a firm real tone in the middle. Only when she can move upward at a climax does she support her tone, and even then the results aren't pleasant.

With the sound off, Fabbricini is affecting and sincere. But we are talking about opera here. If the idea was to find an actress who could sort of carry a tune why didn't La Scala go to Meryl Streep, who after all in her youth studied with Beverly Sills's teacher? Coni, the older Germont, also sings poorly, rarely in tune, and with a muddy, dry tone. La Scala could once field impressive singers for small roles (in fact, the RAI film has some of them). But this Flora can't even sustain one phrase at a fast tempo in one breath.

Those who watch with the sound off will miss excellent conducting from Muti, more relaxed than in his studio recording and very alert theatrically. But they will see a sophisticated and interesting production. The director, Liliana Cavani, does nothing eccentric; her work is full of shrewdly judged detail. Violetta doesn't pay much attention to Alfredo at first; she behaves like a real hostess flirting with her guests. He looks mortified to have to sing his Brindisi; his wooing has an adolescent awkwardness. Only later does Violetta realize to her shock that she has responded to him. The scene with Germont père is fully worked out and Fabbricini is very responsive. Cavani is a distinguished film director and has paid close attention to the way the characters interact. "Di provenza" and the ensuing two verses of cabaletta are played as a complex scene between father and son. The last act is moving because all concerned are able to express a full range of emotion, at least physically.

Design and lighting are splendid and the chorus and supporting principals act well. The barefoot "gypsy" girls slithering around the stage and the bare chested "toreos" rubbing against the women at Flora's party contribute to one's sense of the decadence around Violetta and Alfredo.

Muti permits Fabbricini to squeal a high E-flat, but Alagna does not get to try a high C after two verses of "O, mio rimorso," and Fabbricini isn't allowed to decorate the second verses of "Ah forse lui" and "Addio del passato," though the composer would have expected it. Alagna, who is very handsome, also sings well.

Though this is a striking production, it is apt to induce wincing in those who like singing.

1995 LONDON (VHS / LD)

(Stage Performance, Stereo, Color, Subtitled) 135 minutes

Angele Ghiorghiu (A), Frank Lopardo (B), Leo Nucci (C), Chorus and Orchestra of the Royal Opera House — Georg Solti

Royal Opera, Covent Garden: Richard Eyre (stage director), Humphrey Burton and Peter Maniura (video directors)

Too often, when "acting in opera" is discussed, the singing is viewed as irrelevant. That is philistine and false. An actor in *Hamlet* who has a speech impediment is going to be ineffective no matter his other talents; vocal authority in verse is *sine qua non*. Similarly, the vocal line in opera is the expressive center of the art form. In other media to be young and pretty may be all, but in opera one must meet vocal challenges or face aesthetic failure. Angelica Ghior-

ghiu had a triumph in these performances for good reason. She is young and attractive. She has wonderful eyes, a slim, supple body, and a great deal of skill onstage. But she is also a fine singer with a distinctive, lovely tone. She understands that vocal and histrionic impulses must meet, indeed are the same in opera. She is able to soar easily through the difficult passages, using a wide coloristic range, just as she is able to embody the doomed courtesan with telling physical and facial details. It is this organic fullness that makes her so memorable. She is the most complete Violetta on video. The surrounding performance is sensitive. Richard Eyre's major eccentricity is setting Act I in a big round room with changing colors on the walls. I like the unfinished look of Act II Scene 1, and the last act has the right somewhat Romantic desolation. Eyre excels in interactions between principals and keeping the chorus alive. He makes big choices from time to time. I wasn't entirely persuaded by the camp toreros at Flora's party. However, Ghiorghiu is equal to her big run around the room during her death throes. Lopardo and Nucci are good physical performers, but the baritone is no great pleasure to hear. Solti's work is less subtle and shapely than Muti's or Haitink's but is strongly marked and quite forceful.

Hall's production is the most thorough and involving; his cast is unspectacular but mostly satisfying. Scotto is the most accomplished Violetta, though Gheorghiu is within hailing distance and looks younger and prettier. The performance around Scotto, though very provincial, is among the more idiomatic. Gruberová is greatly accomplished vocally, and sincere, but not riveting to watch. Fans of Sills and Moffo will want their performances but will probably have to squint now and then. Zeffirelli is fingernails-on-slate kitsch, but if one can endure Fabbricini vocally (she's effective dramatically), the Cavani production from La Scala is an interesting alternative to Hall's from Glyndebourne.

ALBERT INNAURATO

Giuseppe Verdi

I Vespri Siciliani (1855)

A: Elena (s); B: Arrigo (t); C: Monforte (bar); D: Procida (bs)

Les Vêpres Siciliennes, Verdi's first "from scratch" French grand opera—*Jérusalem* (1847) was *I Lombardi* reworked—has reached modern audiences almost exclusively in an Italian translation (following its twentieth-century reemergence, in German, at Stuttgart just before Hitler's rise).

That translation, made for the opera's introduction to its composer's native land, is widely scapegoated as the Achilles' heel responsible for *Vespri*'s ostracism from the standard repertory. For Italy's premiere the censors, anxious over a libretto ennobling insurrection and massacre, ordered up a bowdlerized version christened *Giovanna de Gusman*, itself subsequently expurgated (for Naples, 1857) as *Batilde di Turenna*.

Eventually title, plot, and *personaggi* were restored, but most of Eugenio Caimi's clumsy Italianization survived, too; it alters the skillfully wrought original prosody, adding syllables, subverting accents and emphases, dismantling elements successfully French in conception and style. The erstwhile *Vêpres* thus joins opera's subcaste of linguistically disadvantaged "Italian" sideliners that includes, among others, *Medea*, *La Vestale*, *Guglielmo Tell*, and *La Favorita*. (Verdi's later *Don Carlo* was ultimately mainstreamed despite its hybridization.)

Vespri's strongly characterized duet confrontations, multimovement concertati, and intricate quartets—in any language—reveal a subtler, more discriminating, yet increasingly powerful Verdi, and constitute significant landmarks in his artistic evolution.

1989 HOME VISION (VHS)

(Stage Performance, Stereo, Color, Subtitled)
214 minutes

Cheryl Studer (A), Chris Merritt (B), Giorgio Zancanaro (C), Ferruccio Furlanetto (D), Chorus and Orchestra of Teatro alla Scala—Riccardo Muti

La Scala: Pier Luigi Pizzi (stage director), Christopher Swann (video director)

Though Elena taxes the limited stamina of Cheryl Studer's non-Verdian instrument, this performance speaks well for the soprano's industry and musicianship. Studer offers some gleaming tone here and there as well as passages of real rhythmic bite and drive. Unfortunately, she begins to run out of steam before the end, whereupon her wearisome glottal attacks increase in frequency as her sound becomes ever more parched. She knows exactly how the prison scene *romanza* should be shaped, but shaky breath support sabotages her intent; the middle voice emerges gargly and occluded, the cadenza's low ending simply evaporates. She manages a nonscintillating but accurate "Bolero" (the trills defeat her, however). Dramatically, she is serviceable.

Chris Merritt's basically unlovely sound—grainy, viscous, remarkably strong—is only intermittently firm or truly focused. Nonetheless, Arrigo's music holds no terrors for him; from full, baritonal lower register to obstreperous top, he sings indefatigably, not failing to honor Verdi's requests for *mezza voce*. Merritt's appearance and histrionic instincts are against him: his lurch-and-stagger deportment produces risible moments, and in response to Studer's soporific fourth-act aria he gives every indication of nodding off. His close resemblance to Randy Quaid as Lyndon Johnson is disconcerting, if hardly his fault.

Giorgio Zancanaro's beautifully sung, tellingly acted Monforte suffers from a destructive technical habit. The baritone's persistent aspirates constitute a real blemish on his legato and thus on his expressivity. He simply cannot guide a vowel over several pitches, even slowly, without huffs and puffs: genero-*ho*-so, regna-*ha-ha*-va. Otherwise the voice itself—forward, lean, bright—facilitates a poised, persuasive performance.

Procida need not necessarily be Rasputin-like, but something beyond Ferruccio Furlanetto's dullish declamation and stolid presence would more believably convey revolutionary fervor. The bass actually sings quite well in his unexciting way, the voice sonorous from top to bottom, with impressively orotund low notes securely anchoring the big set pieces.

The unflappable Riccardo Muti, forehead barely damp after three-and-a-half hours' exertion, accomplishes a tour de force: an incisive, propulsive, galvanic yet no-nonsense reading of this fascinating work, most of whose pitfalls he skirts in brilliant fashion, drawing both precision and passion from his committed forces. Muti includes the full Paris ballet (Carla Fracci and Wayne Eagling, soloists), a lengthy curiosity. The French text would have been a far more important revelation.

Pier Luigi Pizzi's spare but not stark production reveals a brilliant sense of color and contrast abetted by bold lighting design. Perhaps reacting against the dazzling, stage-filling-flight-of-stairs *Vespris* of John Dexter and Josef Svoboda in the 1970s (Hamburg, New York, Paris), Pizzi employs multiple playing levels with moderation and his stage isn't raked. The concept is no less apposite. Memorable touches abound, such as Act I's boatload of revelers sailing slowly by upstage in the moonlight.

Christopher Swann's mainly imaginative video direction doesn't always focus on the crucial personage in an ensemble—and *Vespri* is an ensemble opera—or move the camera there with alacrity when the realization dawns.

B R U C E   B U R R O U G H S

SIMON BOCCANEGRA

(1857, revised 1881)

A: Maria Boccanegra (Amelia) (s); B: Gabriele Adorno (t); C: Simon
Boccanegra (bar); D: Paolo Albiani (bar); E: Jacopo Fiesco (bs)

A failure at its Venice premiere—following *La Traviata* by four years, the second debacle in a row at La Fenice for Verdi—this work, based on a play by the Spanish Antonio García Gutiérrez, also the source for *Il Trovatore*, nevertheless remained close to the composer's heart. Late in his career, in fact after the Requiem, and when his creative output had considerably slowed, Giulio Riccordi, Verdi's publisher, suggested a revision. The meshing of music-business opportunism on the one hand and the master's regret at a dear operatic offspring never having got its due on the other clicked into place. Much of the libretto was rewritten, along with many pages of the score, and the pivotal, stupendous Council Chamber scene added. The project brought Verdi together with Arrigo Boito for the first time in a collaboration that led directly to *Otello* and *Falstaff*. The resulting mélange of middle- and late-period Verdi somehow manages not to jar and can be accounted one of the most successful reworkings in the repertory, certainly one that has appealed for more than a century to any baritone who has not only the voice but the theatrical imagination to bring to life the conflicted protagonist.

1984 PARAMOUNT (VHS) / PIONEER (LD)

(Stage Performance, Stereo, Color, Subtitled) 153 minutes

Anna Tomowa-Sintow (A), Vasile Moldoveanu (B), Sherrill Milnes (C), Richard J. Clark (D), Paul Plishka (E), Metropolitan Opera Chorus and Orchestra—James Levine

Metropolitan Opera: Tito Capobianco (stage director), Brian Large (video director)

Except for James Levine's conducting and, fitfully, Anna Tomowa-Sintow's Amelia, there isn't a whole lot of reason to spend much time with this 1984 Met account of Verdi's pungent and complicated traversal of late-medieval blood feuds and politics. The Tito Capobianco production, borrowed from Chicago (designed by Pier Luigi Pizzi), hits the middle-range notes of "functional," "efficient," and "highly predictable," going slightly higher only for the council chamber scene, which posits a reasonably imposing space. Here crucial conflicts can be played out and the set at least doesn't commit the howler of a totally anachronistic backdrop mural as does the current nonborrowed production to which the Met has committed itself.

lly vivid characterizations. A nonactor such as Vasile Moldoveanu, as Gabriele, is consistently embarrassed and embarrassing, and histrionically gifted Sherrill Milnes left high and dry by clumsy staging generalizations. About the only scene that contains believable interaction doesn't unroll until Fiesco and Simon reconcile at the end, but these are almost foolproof moments, ones that play so beautifully because

Verdi leaves nothing to chance: the composer provides every emotional clue and it's nearly impossible for performers to miss them.

But where this *Boccanegra* falls down even more seriously is in the vocal department. Everything that Levine manages to score in sensitivity to timbral nuance and in the Met orchestra's quicksilver response cannot conceal the inadequacies of the cast. The prologue gets off to a shaky start with Richard J. Clark's sandpapery Paolo setting a standard all the male participants fall right in line with. Paul Plishka, authoritative if not particularly aristocratic in bearing, contributes a muffled, frequently unsteady Fiesco, the black depths of "Il lacerato spirito" unavailable. Moldoveanu sets off his blank and sullen demeanor with considerable tenorial strain and uncertain pitch on sustained tones. In a way, most disappointing is Sherrill Milnes, a baritone born to play Boccanegra at perhaps an earlier point in his career but here sadly and consistently out of vocal sorts. Attacks on notes above a *mezzo-forte* come out as imprecise bleats. Yes, in the middle of his voice and in quieter passages he can relax and also impress, but a Boccanegra needs to be able to cover the gamut with more than bluntness as an alternative to introspection.

Soprano Tomowa-Sintow at first appears destined to fit right into the general shakiness, but she gathers strength until one keeps focusing on her for whatever singing rewards there are to be gleaned. Hers is a matronly Amelia, and the vibrato is troublesome (it handily doubles as a trill in the council chamber ensemble). But she does manage to involve herself in the action, and the basic tonal quality can be lovely, that vibrato handsomely transforming itself into an upper-register blaze that consistently scores. Still, considering the general unevenness on display, fellow soprano Dawn Upshaw, here almost at the very start of her Met career, wisely keeps in the background as Amelia's lady-in-waiting.

It's worth adding that in the videocassette format colors commendably ring true and the sound quality is superior. Unfortunately, image, at least in cassette number one, seems often to precede the audio. The titles are too often haphazardly inaccurate, but the occasional split-screen camera work can clarify.

1991 LONDON (VHS / LD)

(Stage Performance, Stereo, Color, Subtitled) 135 minutes

Kiri Te Kanawa (A), Michael Sylvester (B), Alexandru Agache (C), Alan Opie (D), Roberto Scandiuzzi (E), Chorus and Orchestra of the Royal Opera House—Georg Solti

Royal Opera, Covent Garden: Elijah Moshinsky (stage director), Brian Large (video director)

It's always a great pleasure to encounter a particularly satisfying release, especially when it involves an opera of great stature that is not quite in the forefront of the international repertory, certainly not at its center. If after every successful revival signals are sent up that that center could be just around the corner, *Simon Boccanegra*, with its somber, brooding moods and its lack of star-turn opportunities, stubbornly remains questionable as a surefire audience pleaser. But given the kind of leadership and cast lavished on this 1991 Covent Garden production, it has no trouble revealing its very special riches and perhaps, one can only hope, inching a few more paces in the right direction. Verdi's much revised work, arguably his most unusual, here gets from all involved exactly what it deserves. Alertly conducted by Georg Solti—alert as much to telling inwardness as to climatic hyperbole—the score's special colors and textures, its chiaroscuro and refulgence, emerge with commanding presence (especially when encountered in the digital laser disc format). Elijah Moshinsky's direction is chaste, direct, unencumbered, and helped enormously by Michael Yeargan's mobile peristyle of columns that quickly and aptly suggests both interior and exterior spaces, all sensitively and intelligibly lit for television director Brian Large's restless camera angles.

Alexandru Agache's achievement in the title role merits all superlatives. A short, burly baritone with a broad peasant face, he cannot avoid being enormously convincing physically as the plebeian Doge. He moves naturally and with acute sensitivity to the rightness of gesture. Best of all, he is a singer with an unusually responsive instrument, smooth, supple, unforced throughout the role's tessitura. He does not seem to know how to utter a hackneyed phrase. In response to his daughter's Act II pleas to save her lover's life, Boccanegra sings "Nol posso!" (I cannot) three times in quick succession. In Agache's hands each rejection has its own emotional—and very communicative—inflection. As his daughter, Kiri Te Kanawa is in her very best form, spinning Amelia's long lyric lines with ravishing ease and appropriate languor. Tenor Michael Sylvester, the lover, although some may carp at his want of innately Italianate style, still provides the important outlines of a heroic Gabriele Adorno. Alan Opie leeches all possible venom from his moments as Boccanegra's nemesis, Paolo. Only bass Roberto Scandiuzzi as the forbidding Fiesco provides minor disappointments. The voice is sonorous and attractive, but it is used in an oddly casual fashion, depriving this patrician character of his requisite weight as a force in the opera's dramatic thrust.

1995 DEUTSCHE GRAMMOPHON (VHS / LD)

(Stage Performance, Stereo, Color, Subtitled) 141 minutes

Kiri Te Kanawa (A), Plácido Domingo (B), Vladimir Chernov (C), Bruno Pola (D), Robert Lloyd (E), Metropolitan Opera Chorus and Orchestra—James Levine

Metropolitan Opera: Giancarlo del Monaco (stage director), Brian Large (video director)

No question but that the Met's more recent go-around with *Boccanegra* is, overall, a happier experience. The cast is almost uniformly stronger, the production gloss fresh and opulent, and Brian Large seems to have profited by the two earlier encounters with the opera to come up with his most sophisticated camera take on it yet, taking every opportunity to indulge in deep focus, fluid panning, and a rich variety of angles, in short an arresting deftness that elucidates the complicated story and this

opera's very special mood. He has a lot to work with in Michael Scott's elaborate and realistic, if not always historically trustworthy sets (real fire in the palace fireplace, a live falcon for the Act I hunters) and in Gil Wechsler's burnished lighting. In fact, the literalness of the stage pictures probably reads better on the TV screen than it does in the house, where this approach can impress as just another in the current series of overly pictorial, wholly uncontroversial realizations that go down so easily in New York. Indeed, the reverse may be true of the Covent Garden production: relative abstraction more enhancing in the house than when reduced for home consumption.

Of the principals Plácido Domingo is especially fine as Gabriele. The role may not seize his imagination as do those Verdian leading roles with more complex plot-crucial psyches, but certainly, apart from some slightly pinched tone at the high end of the role's tessitura, the singing is wonderfully assured. Vladimir Chernov may not yet have the measure of the Doge. His conception of the role, although promising, is small-scale at this point, and he probably was hampered by not being in the best of vocal health during this particular run of performances. Verdict postponed.

An impression of dependable solidity rather than magnetizing displays of vocalism or interpretive insight characterizes the balance of the cast. Kiri Te Kanawa's Amelia sounds dry a good deal of the time, especially in the too often unresonant middle of her voice, and director del Monaco, unlike Covent Garden's Moshinsky, has allowed her to fall back into lazy, uninflected deportment. Robert Lloyd owns the commanding presence that is so right for Fiesco, but the hollowness and nasality of his vocal timbre can become irritating. Bruno Pola, a natural *buffo* miscast in the role, makes only an adequate Paolo, his big acting opportunity at the end of the Council Chamber scene played to the hilt, although it is a fundamentally illogical hilt, as he cowers far too obviously under the curses of the assembled nobles and plebeians. This kind of dramatic shortcut is symptomatic of the facile solutions, stagy choices, and rather imprecise confrontations that are far too common in del Monaco's mise-en-scène. An impression of glassy world-standard adequacy rather than probing intelligence is what tends to remain in the memory. Maestro Levine, on the other hand, convinces for deep, total commitment to bringing out all aspects of the work's particularity. Consequently, the playing of the orchestra is not only consistently splendid but also revelatory, in lyricism and poignancy far outstripping what Solti or even the younger Levine himself provide.

Before the advent of the later Metropolitan offering on Deutsche Grammophon this would have been a no-contest choice: the Covent Garden performing forces and production and the technical sophistication of London engineering winning hands down over the earlier Met production. Now the margin narrows somewhat; Levine and the Met orchestra, tenor Domingo, and state-of-the-art video direction are notable assets for DG. But the nod still goes to London for Moshinsky's unusual stage vision, Te Kanawa's fresher Amelia, Opie's resourceful Paolo, and, most especially, for Agache's stunning vocal and stage accomplishment as the Genoese Doge.

HARVEY E. PHILLIPS

GIUSEPPE VERDI

UN BALLO IN MASCHERA (1859)

A: Amelia (s); B: Oscar (s); C: Ulrica (ms); D: Riccardo (t);
E: Renato (bar)

Not an original source for an opera, a play by Scribe based on the assassination of King Gustave III of Sweden had already been set, before Verdi, by Auber and Mercadante. Still, Verdi's version has totally eclipsed these predecessors, but not without difficulties of its own, primarily with censorship in preunified Italy (different in each city where the premiere was contemplated), which objected to portraying the murder of royalty, especially in light of a recent attempt on the life of Napoleon III. The composer's own suggestion to change the setting from the Swedish court to colonial Boston allowed the Rome first night to go ahead. Since that very successful unveiling, *Un Ballo in Maschera* has commanded critical admiration as one of Verdi's most stylistically unified works and has always remained popular with the public as well as with star singers, who find in each of the opera's five leading roles ample opportunity to display their understanding of Verdian style at its purest. Through the years, as the following video selection makes evident, opera companies have alternated between the original "real" locale and the American compromise, but whether Swedish or American, the work itself remains quintessentially, and most satisfyingly, Italian opera.

1967 STANDING ROOM ONLY (VHS)

(Stage Performance, Mono, Color, Japanese Subtitles) 132 minutes

Antonietta Stella (A), Margherita Guglielmi (B), Lucia Danieli (C), Carlo Bergonzi (D), Mario Zanasi (E), Chorus and Orchestra of Lirica Italiana, Tokyo—Oliviero De Fabritiis

Opera company, stage director, and video director uncredited

From somewhere in Japan (videocassette package notes are excruciatingly meagre) comes a *Ballo in Maschera* that reminds that in 1967 some pretty exciting singing in the old tradition, the kind that seems to be scantily honored and even more scantily practiced these days, was perhaps then the rule rather than the exception, or at least could be reasonably expected when a moderately major production or tour was being put together. While Carlo Bergonzi, the Riccardo, has only recently officially left our performing midst, his legacy still very much in our ears; soprano Antonietta Stella, the Amelia, may actually be of more interest to watch in action now, her presence on American stages having been far less frequent, her recording career more circumscribed. A true diva who had the misfortune to be overshadowed in her time by Callas and Tebaldi, Stella conducts herself with peerless authority, her application to the music and the broad outlines of the drama solidly in place. Yes, a lot of what she does is mannered, but there's a terrifically ingratiating, old-trouper quality about it. The sometimes reckless attacks, the over-prominent register breaks, the sacrifice of line for underlining, the torrents of sobs, and even the moments when she feels entitled to a bit of a glazed-over rest somehow reinforce the enjoyment of witnessing a real dramatic soprano doing the kind of job generations of Italian singers have been bred to. She hits all her marks.

Bergonzi, of course, goes beyond this standard. His lovely lyrical instrument, always plagued by a thinning out at its top and a want of solidity at its bottom, shows here just how elegantly a Verdian phrase can be handled, even caressed, and how there is always room for investigating dynamic gradations. In spite of nonexistent stage instincts when it comes to using his body (only one arm appears to express an emotion), Bergonzi nevertheless convinces through superb diction and inflection, perhaps one of the few singers of whom it could be said that acting with the voice is really sufficient.

Around these two stars a kind of bare-bones staging has been assembled, barely efficient in suggesting locale, absolutely devoid of style and mood. But the point of it all—big opera personalities at work—is not affected. The other participants ably support, as was probably the full extent of the intention: an adequate, not particularly sparkling Oscar and an amiable Ulrica who is hampered by a short top and an unfortunate turnip hat. Slightly more attention getting, Mario Zanasi delivers a rough-and-ready Renato (it's the Swedish setting, by the way, if, under the circumstances, such things are still worth mentioning), blasting his baritonal way through "Eri tu," always alert for the audience dividends that can come from a high note. Visual and sonic values are at odds—night and any low-light scenes are not easily decipherable, camera positions are strictly limited to the basics, and jerky joinings between scenes eliminate applause—but the soloists, chorus, and orchestra (occasional pre-echos aside) come through with surprising finish. The whole enterprise also benefits from the freedom and suppleness of conductor Oliviero De Fabritiis, who fears neither a leisurely tempo nor an ensemble whip-up that finds all hands gamely scrambling.

1980 PARAMOUNT (VHS) / PIONEER (LD)

(Stage Performance, Stereo, Color, Subtitled) 150 minutes

Katia Ricciarelli (A), Judith Blegen (B), Bianca Berini (C), Luciano Pavarotti (D), Louis Quilico (E), Metropolitan Opera Chorus and Orchestra—Giuseppe Patanè

Metropolitan Opera: Elijah Moshinsky (stage director), Brian Large (video director)

The Met's 1980 *Ballo* production, direction by Elijah Moshinsky, sets by Peter Wexler, and costumes by Peter J. Hall, takes the action to America at the period of the Revolution. The time and place are established by a drop curtain seen during the overture. Although this specificity fires expectations as to the potential for piquant plot seasoning, they are mostly unfulfilled, the Antonio Somma libretto, perhaps fortunately, being so tightly constructed that there is little chance for much directorial maneuvering toward fancifulness or extra-text illumination. Actually, director Moshinsky makes the opera vivid in a more available and, ultimately, more important way: alert, reactive characterizations from his cast. Luciano Pavarotti, in one of his best roles—and one he sings with a gorgeously lyrical impulse for this 1980 performance—deftly coaxes forth all the elegance, humor, and pathos native to Riccardo. The superstar tenor, as is not always the case, is *there* every moment. Louis Quilico provides an unusually moving Renato, his baritone smooth, warm, and free. Even better, he finds all the opportunities to make the betrayed husband fully sympathetic.

The women in the cast also do not disappoint. Judith Blegen, whose perkiness as Oscar could be faulted as overly generalized and also too feminine, nevertheless romps expertly through her coloratura challenges. As Ulrica, Bianca Berini uses her attractive mezzo to good effect even if some tones ring hollow or with insufficient power. Perhaps best of all, Katia Ricciarelli's Amelia builds throughout to an especially rewarding experience. Eloquent, specific and always effectively understated, the soprano delivers an extraordinary, supremely wrenching "Morrò, ma prima in grazie," almost erasing any reservations about some previous tired-sounding high-register *fortes*.

In fact, the only real reservations about this taped broadcast are technical ones: the sound quality—at least in the videocassette format—is surprisingly grainy, miking and balance frequently imprecise in ensemble passages. And, because of the consistently low lighting levels, the picture is often quite fuzzy. The somber blacks, whites, and dark naturals featured for Ulrica's lair, for example, translate poorly, and during the following midnight scene at the gallows it is sometimes difficult to see anything at all. Also, whether or not due to Giuseppe Patanè's tendency to push tempos to underarticulated glassiness, the orchestra does not have its most accurate night. The English subtitles target those well-versed in their *Ballo's*. Others may feel a little shortchanged by their skimpiness.

1991 DEUTSCHE GRAMMOPHON (VHS / LD)

(Stage Performance, Stereo, Color, Subtitled) 137 minutes

Aprile Millo (A), Harolyn Blackwell (B), Florence Quivar (C), Luciano Pavarotti (D), Leo Nucci (E), Metropolitan Opera Chorus and Orchestra—James Levine

Metropolitan Opera: Piero Faggioni (stage director), Brian Large (video director)

Like a huge, sleek limousine, the Met's 1991 *Ballo* impresses with its fine finish, luxury appointments, and solid engineering. It's an unexceptionable, even a model evening in the house that should please opera aficionados with a taste for solid and comfortable performance and, please, no unpleasant surprises along the way. James Levine imbues the score with an elastic pulse, whether drawing out melody to an almost indulgent let's-take-a-long-look-at-the-scenery degree or energizing the score's brisker moments with heads-up, pedal-to-the-metal

vigor. And the Met orchestra handles exquisitely no matters what the impulse. Piero Faggioni's production (it's back to Sweden now), is graceful, realistic, built to last, and makes only routine histrionic or interpretative demands on the singers. The last scene, with *commedia dell' arte* figures at the fatal ball miming marital deception in the background while the real-action plot reaches its catastrophic denouement, is as fresh as things are allowed to get. Instead of thrusts toward theatrical probing, the focus is, as it perhaps should be given this cast, on the voices. Certainly Luciano Pavarotti, having a fine evening as Gustavo (Riccardo), merits this kind of spotlighting. He's in first-class vocal estate, fresh, ingratiatingly sensitive to line, nuance, and word. Aprile Millo, also in superior form, delivers Amelia's two arias ardently. Lovers of old-school, mannered stage deportment will be pleased to see that tradition carried on so effortlessly by one so comparatively young at this point in her career.

Leo Nucci, the Anckarström (Renato), makes "Eri tu" the effective set piece an audience waits for. Elsewhere he succumbs occasionally to bluster and slipperiness, his tone somewhat grainier than normal. Florence Quivar sings almost too beautifully for Ulrica, her honeyed timbre belying the otherworldly powers this seeress needs to project. Most animated of all is Harolyn Blackwell's charming, intricately choreographed and blocked Oscar. What she does is winning in everything except diction, which with its too soft Italian consonants somewhat undermines the stylistic credibility needed for this ambiguous catalyst to tragedy. Deutsche Grammophon comes through with superb visual and sonic production standards; even taking into consideration minor reservations, this is definitely a release glossy enough to dress up for in the privacy of one's own home.

Although the cast of the 1980 Met *Ballo* may actually have an edge on the 1991 replacement, in the final analysis it is the newer release, with its very superior technical quality, that probably should be recommended if it is a question of only one acquisition. Truly involved Verdians or admirers of stars of the near past will of course not need to be told they have to have a look at the Bergonzi-Stella Japanese mounting.

HARVEY E. PHILLIPS

LA FORZA DEL DESTINO

(1862; revised 1869)

A: Leonora (s); B: Preziosilla (ms); C: Don Alvaro (t); D: Don Carlo
(bar); E: Fra Melitone (bar); F: Padre Guardiano (bs)

La Forza del Destino was first performed in St. Petersburg, of all places, in 1861. Though it was a success, Verdi wrote to Piave, his librettist: "we have to find a way to do something about all those dead bodies [at the end]." That dissatisfaction lead to the revision of 1869, which is now the standard version of the opera. The first version ended with Don Alvaro throwing himself off a cliff, understanding that his destiny has eradicated the entire Vargas family, including Leonora, the love of his life. The current quiet ending is perhaps more effective, but less true to Verdi. A life-long atheist and a great Romantic artist, he operated from what Miguel De Unamuno would later call the "tragic sense of life." The panoramic sweep of the first version came from his soul (and certainly influenced Mussorgsky's musical dramaturgy in *Boris Godunov*). It's easy to mock the composer's attraction to the cumbersome plot with its many coincidences. But the eloquent voice given to the despairing Alvaro and Leonora in their great arias ("La vita e inferno ed infelice" and "Pace, Pace") is profoundly original and rarely matched elscwhere in opera. *Forza* is relentlessly dark, a meditation on the malign. Among its most remarkable passages occurs when Alvaro watches as the mortally wounded Leonora is brought in by the old priest, called simply The Father Guardian. As sevenths hammer, he cries out: "And are you

not sated, even now, avenging God? I curse you, I curse you!" The composer of *Otello* is in the music, the courageous outcast Giuseppe Verdi is in the lines. World famous by the early 1860s, Verdi was writing with a historical sense of his place in Italian opera. The cagy heroines of Rossini influenced his treatment of Preziosilla—a reference backward—just as the tough comic writing for the silly monk, Melitone, promises something for the future: *Falstaff.* Verdi lavished magnificent melodies on all the characters; in stretches such as the convent scene, or the first scene of Act III, he binds long movements together with a musical and hence a dramatic inevitability Shakespeare would have been proud to own. Hardly neat and never comfortable, *Forza* must surely be ranked among the most unusual and greatest Italian operas.

1958 LYRIC or
BEL CANTO SOCIETY (VHS)

(Stage Performance, Mono, Black and White, Not Subtitled) 156 minutes

Renata Tebaldi (A), Oralia Dominguez (B), Franco Corelli (C), Ettore Bastianini (D), Renato Capecchi (E), Boris Christoff (F), Chorus and Orchestra of Teatro di San Carlo, Naples—Francesco Molinari-Pradelli

San Carlo: director unknown

This was a remarkable find. The picture quality is somewhat bleached and grainy but is certainly watchable; faces in particular are clear. As in most Italian productions of this period the "Sleale!" duet is omitted.

The consumer might want to be cautious; there are no subtitles (but "property of RAI archives" scrolls across the bottom of the screen repeatedly), and no information about the plot comes with the video. Perhaps this is a way of separating the opera lover from the channel surfer whose frame of reference stops with the Three Tenors.

This was probably a routine night by the standards of the time but those standards have disappeared so totally the video has the preciousness of a revelatory artifact from the distant past. Were too many videos of this kind to surface a lot of the writing about opera in the past forty years—all that nonsense about some of the individuals shown here and about the school they represent in general—would have to be discarded. Directors and their flacks are apt to insist all singers of this style were fat and inexpressive. But look again: one singer after another is extraordinarily good looking—cosmetically speaking, everyone here would be right at home on the big or small screen. That doesn't even begin to address the amazing quality of these voices. Conductors and their flacks will mutter about that. If there were singers like this today a good many of our "authentic" maestros would be teaching. Tebaldi, continually responsive with a beautiful face, floods the opera house with glorious tone as easily as anyone else would breathe. In the murderous tessitura of the convent scene her sound is big, magnificently focused, and utterly under control. When she floats a *mezza voce* line in "La vergine degl' angeli" she fills the theater with a soft but very present radiance. But there is no fussing, none of the tics and saves we see in so many contemporary singers. She is powerfully expressive because everything is organic; her "acting" proceeds from her singing, which is rooted in the music. Astoundingly, this may not have been everybody's ideal of a great cast at the time; radishes are thrown onstage after Corelli and Bastianini have sung "Solenne in quest'

ora" magnificently. Corelli, with his glorious sound and stunning good looks (he looks like a movie star, only taller), was no del Monaco or di Stefano. In fact Milanov fans and Callas fanatics would have complaints about Tebaldi. Dominguez, the Preziosilla, was a second stringer, and yet she is so sexy, humorous, and vocally secure in this difficult part one wants to reevaluate her immediately.

The "acting" here is of the best kind in opera, securely rooted in the music, a complement to the powerful expression of the singing. But the unanimity of style that binds everyone here, the confidence and love for this opera and for opera in general, are far more revealing than any half-dozen Oliviers or Meryl Streeps would have been.

Of course there are a few amusing touches: the somewhat wheezy-looking backdrops were not meant to be scrutinized by a camera. Corelli regularly dwarfs the painted mountains in the background. The great bass, Christoff, is wearing what looks like half the cotton output in Italy on his face, and his high white wig blends oddly with the painted clouds behind him (when he first enters, Tebaldi shoots him a look of sheer shock bordering on hilarity; the get-up must have been a last-minute improvisation). But in a way, all of that seems more human, "realer" in a stage presentation than the small screen mimetics we've been taught to endorse in the opera house.

1984 PARAMOUNT (VHS) / PIONEER (LD)

(Stage Performance, Stereo, Color, Subtitled) 179 minutes

Leontyne Price (A), Isola Jones (B), Giuseppe Giacomini (C), Leo Nucci (D), Enrico Fissore (E), Bonaldo Giaiotti (F), Metropolitan Opera Chorus and Orchestra—James Levine

Metropolitan Opera: John Dexter (stage director), Kirk Browning (video director)

Leontyne Price was one of the most acclaimed singers in the post–World War II period, so this has documentary value—particularly since this is a "Live from the Met" presentation with none of the artificial "sweetening" which has become typical in the years since. The actual performance is spotty and disappointing. Four of the leading singers are Italians, and two of them (tenor and baritone) were major singers in the eighties. But how things had changed from the Naples performance! These Italians have only serviceable voices. Their personalities, such as they are, are bland. Neither words, nor musical phrases, nor even obvious emotions count for much. For the passionate Italian style, an all-purpose international competence has been substituted. Not competence of a high order, either. Giacomini is musically at sea rather often, and his throaty voice is not flatteringly caught. Nucci is only slightly better.

Leontyne Price was a victim of the shameless disregard of the arts by American broadcasting in the sixties and seventies. By 1984 she was well past her best, her stage career was winding down, and no opera company could offer the stimulating colleagues she would have taken for granted twenty years earlier. Video is not the most flattering medium for her, but it's not that simple. Singers, even great interpreters like Callas and Fisher-Dieskau, are *singers* first. If the voice isn't working, neither are they. Very few people, in my experience, have the sort of "damn the notes" abandon that can snatch triumph out of vocal adversity. Price definitely isn't one of them. Her tone here is hooded and frayed, she has no resources at the lower end of her range, her diction is funny at times and so are some of the hooting and whooping noises she makes. She knows it. Her wonderful face is as fascinating as an exotic mask. But she keeps her heavy eyelids lowered for much of the eve-

ning, robbing the viewer of the electricity and expression carried only in the eyes.

The elegantly spare old Berman sets (from 1952) are here, but with a new staging. John Dexter was a serious director who coped seriously with the problems of this opera. Some choices will mystify the viewer (that's Don Carlo glaring mutely at Leonora while their father bids her a fond good night at the start of the opera). Others are understandable from an Anglo-Saxon perspective but rather miss the point. At the end of Verdi's first act, Don Alvaro throws his gun down, surrendering. It is meant to go off, accidentally killing the Marquis, setting the opera in motion. Dexter has a retainer wrestle with Don Alvaro. That avoids an awkward piece of business and worse, the risk the gun won't go off at all, leaving the Marquis to die of apoplexy. But the opera is called *The Force of Destiny*, not *The Force of the Meddling Servant*. By the time of this taping some of Dexter's mildly controversial byplay for Preziosilla and Melitone had been toned down.

Kirk Browning's bobbing and weaving camera may induce vertigo in the susceptible.

The thrilling Naples performance is a one-of-a-kind blend of history, tradition, and musical dramatic mastery well-caught on film—though the essentially TV-oriented will need to adjust their expectations, and the actual quality of the video transfer is hit or miss. The Met video retains interest for capturing the great Leontyne Price in one of her best roles, but she is well past her prime and the surrounding performance is mediocre and sometimes poor.

ALBERT INNAURATO

GIUSEPPE VERDI

DON CARLO

(1867, revised 1884)

A: Elisabetta / Elisabeth (s); B: Eboli (ms); C: Carlo / Carlos (t);
D: Rodrigo / Rodrigue (bar); E: Filippo / Philippe (bs); F: Inquisitor (bs)

t one time among Verdi's most infrequently performed major works, *Don Carlo* has become a repertory piece the world over. Most of the labyrinthine textual problems that beset the opera have now been sorted out, and from the various versions of the five-act score conductors have a variety of options, some composer approved and others not. To recapitulate briefly: Soon after the premiere at the Paris Opéra in 1867, Verdi devised a reduced edition that he felt would make the opera more practical for houses with less lavish resources. He also made substantial revisions in the score between 1867 and 1884, always working with the original French words, which were only later translated into the Italian text commonly performed today. The most severe loss was the entire first act, in which Carlo and Elisabetta meet in France and fall in love, but many other scenes were recomposed, abridged, or omitted. While some recent productions have reinstated much of this material as well as some of Verdi's earlier thoughts, the general practice has been to respect the composer's final revision, with or without the discarded first act, and the videos to date have followed that rule of thumb.

Each performance has also had to search for a contemporary vision that will encompass and do justice to the opera's scenic splendor, complex dramatic issues, and vocal challenges. Many Verdians hold *Don Carlo* to be, if not the composer's greatest opera, the most imposing and enduring French grand opera ever written, one that penetrates far beneath the tinsel trappings of the genre and emerges as a music drama of towering stature. Despite Verdi's attempts to make the work available to smaller opera houses, *Don Carlo* remains a formidable challenge, one that only the most generously endowed company can hope to meet.

1983 PARAMOUNT (VHS) / PIONEER (LD)

(Stage Performance, Stereo, Color, Subtitled)
214 minutes

Mirella Freni (A), Grace Bumbry (B), Plácido Domingo (C), Louis Quilico (D), Nicolai Ghiaurov (E), Ferruccio Furlanetto (F), Metropolitan Opera Chorus and Orchestra—James Levine

Metropolitan Opera: John Dexter (stage director), Brian Large (video director)

The Metropolitan Opera functioned on a tight budget when John Dexter served as the company's director of productions in the seventies, and this *Don Carlo*, first seen in 1979, is positively austere compared to what the Met might have done a decade later. Yet for all of their streamlined economy, David Reppa's sets are still handsomely evocative of sixteenth-century Spain's grand plazas, lush monastery gardens, and gloomy palace rooms, concentrating on important architectural details that powerfully suggest the church-state conflicts that lie at the heart of both the opera's political and private passions. Unfortunately the action itself has little expressive point or specificity. Dexter seldom was comfortable directing the Romantic nineteenth-century repertory—he was more successful with contemporary works—and the overall effect of his *Don Carlo*, at least in this revival, is extremely chilly, detached, and lacking any sense of strong emotional commitment. As was so often the case in star-studded Met occasions at the time, the cast seems to be functioning on its own rather than participating in a fully thought-through production animated by a compelling point of view.

Levine's textual preference has always been to perform the composer's final revision of *Don Carlo* without any cuts and including the first act—he even opts to begin the opera with the choral scene that the composer had deleted before the Paris premiere and that was only discovered a century later. The conductor and orchestra, in fact, are the stars of this performance, conveying the opera's full epic sweep while giving a lovely shade to every instrumental detail.

Despite the celebrity cast, the Met has offered far better sung *Don Carlos* in the past. Freni is the clear audience favorite, and she has never looked lovelier. Back in New York after a fourteen-year absence, a once enchanting Susanna / Micaëla / Mimi soprano had presumably been transformed during the interim into a dramatic spinto, but there is not much evidence of that here. Although her voice still makes pretty sounds, it lacks body and substance in the lower register and never blooms up top with the freedom, tonal vibrancy, and power of a true Verdi soprano. Domingo had missed the opening night of this revival, but he recovered to make the matinee telecast a month later, looking rather drawn and sounding tired—he even cracks on a note during the second Elisabetta–Don Carlo confrontation (we are back in the days of unedited Met videos). Ghiaurov's stolid Filippo became slightly more interesting toward the end of his career as the

velvet wore off his bass, but his impersonation is still very bland and never comes close to the center of this complex figure. Bumbry sails into Eboli with her customary high-power voltage, although her energy would have been more welcome if it had been better focused and disciplined. Quilico's firmly sung but blunt Rodrigo hardly suggests the ambiguous nature of this idealistic intriguer, while Furlanetto, looking properly ancient as the Inquisitor (he was only thirty-three at the time), makes quavery sounds that seem to indicate vocal problems rather than old age.

1985 CASTLE OPERA (VHS)

(Stage Performance, Stereo, Color, Not Subtitled) 204 minutes

Ileana Cotrubas (A), Bruna Baglioni (B), Luis Lima (C), Giorgio Zancanaro (D), Robert Lloyd (E), Joseph Rouleau (F), Chorus and Orchestra of the Royal Opera House—Bernard Haitink

Royal Opera, Covent Garden: Luchino Visconti (stage director), Christopher Renshaw (revival stage director), Brian Large (video director)

Luchino Visconti's famous 1958 production may not have single-handedly restored *Don Carlo* to the world, as British critics once proudly claimed (the opera had become a permanent part of the Metropolitan's repertory eight years earlier), but that does not detract from the distinction of those first performances at Covent Garden conducted by Carlo Maria Giulini, or the wonderful cast that sang them: Gre Brouwenstijn, Fedora Barbieri, Jon Vickers, Tito Gobbi, and Boris Christoff. It was no doubt in hopes of recapturing a bit of the production's legendary flavor that this revival was filmed, some twenty-seven years later, before the sets were retired.

The architectural grandeur and rich colors of Visconti's sumptuously romantic concept largely survive on this video, although naturally the overall impact is necessarily diminished by Large's selective camera, which mainly concentrates on the principals. Remnants of the original directorial ideas also bubble up here and there, as in the complex relationship between Don Carlo and Rodrigo: the latter's firm, almost obsessive resolve serves as a strong stabilizing force on the neurotic young Prince, obviously unbalanced by epilepsy as well as his hopeless love for Elisabetta. The *auto-da-fé* scene is also cunningly staged, carefully preserving (as Verdi intended) the individual motivations of each character in this tense public confrontation. Another chilling touch is the cat-and-mouse power game between Filippo and the Grand Inquisitor, as the King helplessly circles the old man and desperately tries to find ways to hide from his implacable sightless gaze. There is certainly more than enough here to indicate just why this *Don Carlo* production was truly a memorable one in its day.

The principal strength of this revival is Bernard Haitink's measured conducting of the composer's complete final revision plus the first act—a rather subdued interpretation perhaps, but keenly observant of the score's dark instrumental coloring and muscular strength. The cast, however, leaves much to be desired. Looking more mousy than tragic, Cotrubas is way out of her depth as Elisabetta, even more so than other overparted lyric sopranos (Freni, Scotto, Ricciarelli) who took on a role that requires more tonal amplitude and rhetorical force than was ever available to these light Mimì-Adina-Zerlina voices. Young and darkly handsome, Lima has the ideal *physique du rôle* for Carlo as he gamely suggests the youth's disturbed persona, but his hooded, rather throttled tenor only skirts the music's expressive possibilities. Baglioni's provincial mezzo-soprano is completely at sea in Eboli's "Veil Song," and she proceeds from there to give a conventional performance with scarcely a trace of charm, danger, or vocal allure. It's good to hear a true bass sing Filippo, and Lloyd's focused performance, if rather calculated and small-scale, always commands respect. By far the most impressive voice belongs to Zancanaro, although the pleasure of hearing a healthy Italian baritone respond to Verdi so naturally and stylishly is offset by his stiff, stand-and-deliver acting. Rouleau is a terrifying Inquisitor, even if his aging bass is hard pressed to cope with the role's register extremes.

1986 SONY (VHS / LD)

(Stage Performance, Stereo, Color, Not Subtitled) 179 minutes

Fiamma Izzo d'Amico (A), Agnes Baltsa (B), José Carreras (C), Piero Cappuccilli (D), Ferruccio Furlanetto (E), Matti Salminen (F), Chorus of the Bulgarian Natgional Opera, Sofia; Chorus of the Vienna State Opera; Salzburg Concert Chorus; Berlin Philharmonic—Herbert von Karajan

Salzburg Festival: Herbert von Karajan (stage and video director)

Don Carlo had been a Karajan specialty at Salzburg ever since 1958, but he waited too long to film the opera. Everything about this performance is heavy and lugubrious, from Günther Schneider-Siemssen's ponderous sets and their dated Hollywood glitziness to the leaden movements of the singers as they laboriously drag themselves over the stage. Karajan was always a formidable musician, but his ambitions as an opera director never produced anything of importance, and the lumbering spectaculars he produced at Salzburg over the years must stand as a classic case of egomaniacal hubris. Beyond that, his musical approach to the score also became increasingly arthritic as time passed, and the results here are even more oppressively turgid than on his 1978 EMI audio-only recording with many of the same principals. As in that performance, we are given the standard four-act revision, but this time with numerous cuts that would surely have enraged Verdi.

As he did so often in his last years, Karajan preferred to work with light-voiced singers, perversely disregarding the opera's musical realities, the capacities of the voices at his disposal, and the fact that he may have actually been shortening careers. Only twenty-two at the time, Izzo d'Amico is hopelessly overparted as Elisabetta, giving a callow performance with only a minimal grasp of the role's musical and dramatic possibilities—no wonder this soprano virtually vanished from the scene only a few years later. By 1986 Baltsa had also spent most of her vocal capital, and she practically deconstructs before our eyes and ears while attempting to scream out "O don fatale." The male contingent is not much better. After years of singing inappropriate heroic roles, the tonal beauty of Carreras's once ravishing lyric tenor has worn away; Cappuccilli's aging baritone responds sluggishly to Rodrigo's elegant music; and Salminen does little more than roar as the Inquisitor. In the midst of all this vocal flotsam, Furlanetto's Filippo, lightweight but sensitively sung, stands out like a good deed in a naughty world. Sounding far more at ease than he did as the Met's Inquisitor three years earlier, the bass also has interesting ideas about the character and he projects them with considerable theatrical imagination. On the whole, though, only an uncritical Karajan devotee could find much to enjoy in this depressing artifact.

1992 EMI (VHS / LD)

(Stage Performance, Stereo, Color, Subtitled) 182 minutes

Daniela Dessì (A), Luciana d'Intino (B), Luciano Pavarotti (C), Paolo Coni (D), Samuel Ramey (E), Alexander Anisimov (F), Chorus and Orchestra of Teatro alla Scala—Riccardo Muti

La Scala: Franco Zeffirelli (stage and video director)

This performance opened the 1992–93 opera season in Milan, an especially gala occasion since Zeffirelli's lavish productions have always been eagerly anticipated at La Scala and Pavarotti, singing the title role for the first time, was making one of his infrequent appearances in Italy. Unfortunately, the tenor broke on a high note, and the subsequent booing and yelling became an international scandal, although none of that excitement is preserved in this carefully edited composite of several evenings. Pavarotti, in fact, gives quite the finest performance of this spotty cast. His burnished tenor sounds amazingly secure and fresh at fifty-seven, while he also takes care to be on his best musical behavior, shaping phrases with unusual sensitivity and responding expressively to the Infanta's predicament. Among the famous Three Tenors who have committed Don Carlo to video, Pavarotti easily takes the prize.

Zeffirelli was clearly given everything he wanted to build one of his most elaborate costume-drama spectaculars, and the production must have cost a fortune. The designer-director pulls out all the stops for a painstakingly realistic *auto-da-fé* in front of the grandiose Cathedral of our Lady of Atocha, a cast-of-thousands mob scene with representatives from every walk of sixteenth-century Spanish life, sacred and secular, from the sumptuously robed King down to the wretched half-naked heretics. The entire conception is simply too vast to be accommodated comfortably on the home screen, and despite Zeffirelli's experience at filmmaking, it all comes across looking very stiff and cramped. Worse, Zeffirelli seems to have paid more attention to the opera's decor than to its characters, who make little contact with the complex emotions that propel this tense drama.

Aside from Pavarotti, the only other major voice onstage belongs to Ramey, whose suave, well-schooled bass sounds splendid even if his one-dimensional Filippo is a very dull dog. Hearing native Italians sing their own language is always a pleasure, but Dessì's opaque soprano and lumpish phrasing do little for Elisabetta, d'Intino's pallid Eboli is on a very small scale, and Coni's irritating Rodrigo is mostly bellowed as well as constantly lingering on the sharp side of the notes (did anyone boo him?). Anisimov's rusty Inquisitor makes a minimal impression in his one big scene. After Karajan's plodding performance, Muti's textural clarity and nicely sprung rhythms come as a relief, but even the Scala orchestra cannot save this *Don Carlo* from Zeffirelli's self-indulgent overproduction and a cast dominated by vocal mediocrities.

———

None of the four *Don Carlo* videos currently available represents the piece with consistent distinction. If the classic production preserved on the Covent Garden edition had had a better cast, it would have been the choice, but for the moment, with the advantages of a respectable visual concept, superior musical leadership, and an unabridged five-act format, the Met performance must be given preference.

PETER G. DAVIS

Aida (1871)

A: Aida (s); B: Amneris (ms); C: Radames (t); D: Amonasro (bar);
E: Ramfis (bs); F: King of Egypt (bs)

Still one of the most popular of Verdi's twenty-eight operas, *Aida* symbolizes to many people all that is grand, stirring, and exotic about the operatic stage. With its ancient Egyptian setting and lavish costume requirements, *Aida* also exercises a special appeal over designers and directors, who can let their imaginations run wild without fear of upstaging the score, characterizations, or story line. This is one opera that is hard to overproduce.

Not surprisingly, producers and filmmakers have long been attracted to the visual splendor of *Aida*. In 1954, impresario Sol Hurok sponsored and hyped a film version of the opera in which a nineteen-year-old Sophia Loren (described in the publicity brochure as "five feet, eight inches tall, 38 bust, 24 waist, 36 hips") and the less curvacious but more vocally endowed Renata Tebaldi shared acting and singing duties. (Unfortunately this version is not available on video.)

Casting *Aida* for the stage and recordings has become rather difficult in recent years. To find reasonably attractive (lots of flesh was the fashion in ancient Egypt) and vocally gifted actor-singers for video versions is even more challenging.

1949 RCA (VHS / LD)

(Concert Performance, Mono, Black and White, Not Subtitled) 149 minutes

Herva Nelli (A), Eva Gustavson (B), Richard Tucker (C), Giuseppe Valdengo (D), Norman Scott (E), Dennis Harbour (F), Robert Shaw Chorale and NBC Symphony Orchestra— Arturo Toscanini

The star of this legendary concert version— originally telecast by NBC from Studio 8-H on March 26 and April 2, 1949—is not a singer, of course, but the conductor Arturo Toscanini. The camera lingers lovingly on his noble profile, his precise, even military keeping of the beat, the flashes of expectation or impatience from his smoldering gaze. That such a physically rigorous and emotionally dynamic performance could come from a man then eighty-two years old is quite fantastic. Indeed, this performance was one of the crowning achievements of Toscanini's media career and the highlight of the televised concerts he did with the NBC Symphony Orchestra between 1948 and 1952. (The audio CD version of the performance incorporates studio patches made in 1954.)

This broadcast conveys the excitement of the early days of television, when "classical" culture regularly appeared on the networks. These were the days when executives and producers were so confident in the high intellectual level of their audience that they deemed it unnecessary to provide English-language subtitles. Instead, the melliflous voice of Martin Bookspan provides a synopsis before each act, along with introductions of the singers.

Clearly, the vocal soloists respected and feared the maestro, judging from their sidelong worried glances in his direction. This is especially true of the Norwegian mezzo Eva Gustavson, who took the role of Amneris and was working with Toscanini for the first time. Unfortunately, her worry was more than justified, since her muffled voice does not carry well over the orchestra, particularly in the lower part of her range. She labors mightily, and does some ingenious emoting with her eyebrows, but in the end she fails to do Amneris's music full justice.

Also working for the first time with Toscanini was Richard Tucker as Radames. His debut was much more auspicious, however; it is the vocal highlight of the performance. Projecting calm from his innocent babyface, Tucker sings with thrilling strength, lyricism, and ease, seeming to float down to his high notes from above. Shown to advantage by Toscanini's fast tempos, Tucker's light but substantial instrument brings Act III to a sensational conclusion.

As Aida, Herva Nelli sings inconsistently, with occasional stridency, especially on top, and she does not always succeed in making herself heard over the forceful orchestra. Her father-daughter scenes with Giuseppe Valdengo are very convincing, however.

The Robert Shaw Chorale, massed in collegiate-looking choir robes behind the orchestra, brings enormous enthusiasm and musicality to the project. The fabled NBC Symphony Orchestra responds to Toscanini's understated gestures with a unique combination of meticulousness and explosive passion. With the exception of Tucker's heroic Radames, this *Aida* does not offer exceptional vocal performances. But as a document illustrating Toscanini's enormous role in the popularization (and, some would argue, degradation) of classical music in the United States, it is a must for serious collectors.

1961 VAI (VHS)

(Stage Performance, Mono, Black and White, Subtitled in English and Japanese) 156 minutes

Gariella Tucci (A), Giulietta Simionato (B), Mario del Monaco (C), Aldo Protti (D), Paolo Washington (E), Silvano Pagliuca (F) — Franco Capuana

Opera company, stage director, and video director unknown

Japanese television filmed this performance live in Tokyo on October 13, 1961. The quality of the black-and-white visual image is poor; during the tomb scene the lighting is so dark that nothing is visible for extended periods. Two sets of subtitles (Japanese and English) also obscure the bottom third of the screen. Production and scenery are primitive, and no credit is given anywhere on the credits or packaging for the stage director, video director, or production designer. Even the orchestra goes unidentified.

The main selling points for this version are the performances of several legendary singers: Gabriella Tucci as Aida, Mario del Monaco as Radames, and Giulietta Simionato as Amneris. Despite the marginally acceptable sound quality, their talent and skill still manage to make a strong impression. Most notable is Gabriella Tucci. More a lyrical than a dramatic soprano, she creates a portrayal fascinating for its fragility, vulnerability, and delicacy — qualities not often associated with Aida. Her ability to float and sustain high notes with her small but beautiful voice, and to sing with great effect at low volume levels, produce a characterization of unusual subtlety and good taste.

Mario del Monaco does not share Tucci's refined sound, but for the most part he compensates with sheer bravado and stature for his excessive sliding and tendency to sing flat. Unfortunately he looks quite silly in a short tunic. Simionato gives a gutsy performance as Amneris, without indulging in excessive hysterics. She wears some outlandish headgear with dignity.

This *Aida* often feels more like a concert version than a staged one, since the blocking is strictly perfunctory and the principals are happy to stop in the middle of the action to smile and bow to the huge ovations.

1966 BEL CANTO SOCIETY (VHS)

(Stage Performance, Mono, Black and White, Not Subtitled) 150 minutes

Leyla Gencer (A), Fiorenza Cossotto (B), Carlo Bergonzi (C), Anselmo Colzani (D), Bonaldo

Giaiotti (E), Franco Pugliese (F), Chorus and Orchestra of the Arena di Verona—Franco Capuana

Verona Arena: Herbert Graf (stage director), Cesare Barlacchi (video director)

Given the fact that *Aida* was written to celebrate the opening of the Suez Canal and has so many vast outdoor scenes, it has always been a favorite opera for open-air performances. Some of the first were staged at the ancient Arena di Verona in the early twentieth century. This production, filmed live in Verona in 1966, is remarkable not only for its marvelous setting, whose grandeur comes through even in a poor-quality black and white print, but for its stellar cast of singers. Leyla Gencer, Fiorenza Cossotto, and Carlo Bergonzi all on stage together—and in their vocal prime! Even with primitive sound technology, the magic comes through loud and clear. Actually, the quality of the sound is surprisingly good: raw, vital, and with the vocal lines well-distinguished and balanced.

Make no mistake—this is a no-frills version. It is filmed in grainy black-and-white with bleached-out lighting. The packaging includes neither a complete cast list (given in the opening credits) nor any other information. There are no subtitles, so this is a version recommended only to those who know the opera well and want to see and hear these particular performers.

As Aida, Leyla Gencer demonstrates very clearly why she is still held in such esteem by many connoisseurs. Imperious, voluptuous, and powerful, her voice and manner are perfectly suited for the musical and dramatic demands of this role. In "O Patria mia" she shows incredible breath control, singing softly but with fierce intensity and focus.

Few tenors could hold their own against Gencer, but Bergonzi makes it look easy. He paces and prowls about the stage like an animal—and also sings like one, with a force best described as elemental. His big, true voice also blends well with Gencer's, and their duets are simply incendiary. Playing to the vast and ador-

ing throng in the arena, Bergonzi hits his high notes unerringly and holds them forever, most memorably when he hands his sword to Ramfis at the end of Act III.

Finally, there is Cossotto as Amneris, her voice burning with jealousy and indignation. Few mezzo-sopranos have commanded such consistent power and tone from bottom to top. Her intonation of "Pace t'imploro" in the opera's final measures is shattering, but also blends marvelously into the vocal and orchestral texture.

Another special treat on this video is the appearance of the Kirov Ballet from Leningrad, in choreography by the troupe's long-time artistic director Konstantin Sergeyev. So much does the Verona audience like the elaborately athletic warriors' dance from Act II, Scene 2 that the dancers repeat it in full.

If you are looking for technological perfection, this is not the *Aida* for you. But if it is passion, authenticity, and three stupendous historic performances you are after, then this one deserves your attention.

1981 CASTLE OPERA (VHS) / PIONEER (LD)

(Stage Performance, Stereo, Color, Not Subtitled) 160 minutes

Maria Chiara (A), Fiorenza Cossotto (B), Nicola Martinucci (C), Giuseppe Scandola (D), Carlo Zardo (E), Alfredo Zanazzo (F), Chorus and Orchestra of the Arena di Verona— Anton Guadagno

Verona Arena: Giancarlo Sbragia (stage director), Brian Large (video director)

Monumental, spectacular, and boasting an unusually balanced cast, this 1981 version filmed by Radiotelevisione Italiana makes the most of its historic backdrop: the ancient arena at Verona. The huge stage occupies about one-third of the arena, extending up the rows of seats and stairs, which are used in several of the epic choral processionals. At the same time, Brian Large and his camera crew wisely balanced the public and private aspects of the drama so that the principal characters and their interrelationships are never overshadowed by the enormity of the physical setting. Although there are few close-ups, the camera moves deftly between the singers to register reactions, resulting in a dramatic intensity and intimacy difficult to achieve under such circumstances. This version gives us all the splendor of *Aida* without sacrificing the story line.

The three major roles are taken by three fine singers of the era, all near the peak of their careers. As Aida, Maria Chiara sings with great conviction and agility; she has a very "natural" sound and looks very comfortable. While her voice is not one of the most beautiful ever heard in this role, she uses it skillfully and to great dramatic effect. Playing opposite her as Radames, Nicola Martinucci possesses a convincing physical presence (he is relatively lean and muscular) that gives him unusual credibility as a romantic hero. At his very first entrance he also establishes his vocal authority, holding his high notes long and confidently and rolling his consonants like dice. As Amneris, Fiorenza Cossotto thrills the audience with her brassy low notes and big sound. (Her younger performance on the 1966 Bel Canto video, also filmed at the Arena di Verona, is superior, however.) Like Chiara and Martinucci, Cossotto also displays excellent diction. Their three voices blend well in ensemble.

The choreography and blocking make excellent use of the many possibilities of the Arena setting. Audio supervisor Jay David Saks has also done a masterful job with the recorded sound. The miking is consistent and undistorted, no matter where the singers are located on the stage. Before Act I, and then during each intermission, short scenes of the enthusiatic multitudes in attendance are provided, complete with ice-cream vendors and foreign tourists. These shots help us to feel the special atmosphere of what was clearly a memorable open-air performance of one of the greatest open-air operas.

This version has only one serious drawback (at least for some viewers): no English subtitles are provided.

1986 KULTUR (VHS) / PIONEER (LD)

(Stage Performance, Stereo, Color, Subtitled) 160 minutes

Maria Chiara (A), Ghena Dimitrova (B), Luciano Pavarotti (C), Juan Pons (D), Nicolai Ghiaurov (E), Paata Burchuladze (F), Chorus and Orchestra of Teatro alla Scala—Lorin Maazel

La Scala: Gabriele Lavia (stage director), Derek Bailey (video director)

This *Aida* staged at La Scala features—surprisingly enough—Pavarotti's first performance in Italy as Radames. Unfortunately, the tenor undertook this production at a time when his weight was more than heroic, a fact that even voluminous costumes and kind camera work cannot conceal. Since it was clearly difficult for him to move easily around the stage, most of the blocking calls for him to stand still and sing. In the tomb scene that concludes the opera, Pavarotti leans on a hunk of stone for support in his duet with Aida. For all that, his singing is often magnificent, and close-ups reinforce the perception of ease in voice production. Vocally, Pavarotti delivers as promised, but dramatically his performance is a disappointment.

Joining Pavarotti is an experienced and vocally well-balanced cast, with particular brilliance in the secondary male roles. As Aida, Maria Chiara looks svelte and sexy and turns in a respectable vocal performance despite occasional sharpness and stridency. As Amneris, Aida's formidable competitor for Radames's affections, Ghena Dimitrova has plenty of power and self-confidence and projects well over the orchestra even in the lowest part of her range, although her dramatic skills are more primitive than Chiara's.

In his few appearances, Paata Burchuladze steals the show as the King of Egypt, with his resonant, penetrating voice and Chaliapin-like intensity. Juan Pons and Nicolai Ghiaurov are also outstanding, as is the work from Lorin Maazel and the Scala Orchestra.

What distinguish this version are the subtle

beauty and tasteful pageantry of the design and staging. Enormous monuments loom over the action, which is often filmed from below, emphasizing the timeless splendor of the civilization in which the drama is unfolding. Through the use of a blazing sun and a brightly glowing moon, the lighting deftly conveys the desert landscape. In the first scene of Act II, in Amneris's private apartments, the presence of scores of nude—and gorgeous—serving girls provides both authenticity and appealing sensuality. The choreography for this and other scenes is inventive and well-integrated. Lighting effects also create the convincing effect of a shimmering Nile in Act III.

The camera work is competent and unobtrusive, but for the most part unadventurous. Happily, the camera does frequently cut away from straight-on close-ups of the singers to emphasize some of the many fine details in the production, including the repeated image of oppressed slaves toiling at the whim of their omnipotent masters. Overall, the production and video manage to strike the right balance between public pageantry and private drama that a successful *Aida* requires.

1989 DEUTSCHE GRAMMOPHON (VHS / LD)

(Stage Performance, Stereo, Color, Subtitled)
158 minutes

Aprile Millo (A), Dolora Zajick (B), Plácido Domingo (C), Sherrill Milnes (D), Paata Burchuladze (E), Dimitri Kavrakos (F), Metropolitan Opera Chorus and Orchestra—James Levine

Metropolitan Opera: Sonja Frisell (stage director), Brian Large (video director)

After it was first broadcast on television in 1989, this Met production was awarded an Emmy for Outstanding Classical Program in the Performing Arts. Technically, the video is excellent, with digital sound and high-quality cinematography. But emotionally, something is missing in the performance; the singers fail to connect either musically or dramatically. There

are two main reasons: Aprile Millo is unsuitable for the role of Aida, and Plácido Domingo's voice was considerably past its prime when this production was filmed.

Both dramatically and visually, Millo is too accessible and ordinary to portray convincingly a fiercely proud and passionate slave girl. Her soft characterization fails to ignite the proceedings—or to convey the intensity of her love for Radames. At times, she seems almost uncomfortable, standing to the side smiling cheerfully at her father, Amonasro.

Vocally, too, there is a lack of bite and focus. Millo's heavy vibrato often obscures the pitch, and she seems unable to reach the high notes without pushing and hitting at full volume. (Chiara, in the Scala video, does just the opposite, consistently taking her high notes at a lustrous *piano*.) Even so, Millo does manage some memorable moments, particularly in the "O, Patria mia" aria.

Visually, Domingo is perfect as Radames: tall, noble, erect, well-proportioned, physically agile. Unlike Pavarotti, he also looks good in a tunic. But if Pavarotti soars with ease into the top part of the tenor range (where so much of this role lies), Domingo strains and often goes shrill and sharp. At times he resorts to a sort of strangled yell. His voice does not blend very well with Millo's, either.

Dolora Zajick is in better vocal shape than Millo or Domingo, but her stage presence is bland. Much more exciting is Sherrill Milnes as her father; he makes Amonasro's moral outrage leap out of the screen, while singing with impressive control and authority. Burchuladze has an easy time with the role of Ramfis, while Kavrakos is a bit too wobbly as the King of Egypt.

Less spectacular and imaginative than the Scala production, the Met version still packs plenty of pageantry, gold, and supernumeraries onto the big stage. Unfortunately, the camera work focuses mainly on small parts of the stage picture, rarely giving a sense of the overall scale. The visual image onscreen looks cramped.

As expected, the Met orchestra and chorus perform superbly under James Levine.

1994 HOME VISION (VHS) / PIONEER (LD)

(Stage Performance, Stereo, Color, Subtitled)
150 minutes

Cheryl Studer (A), Luciana d'Intino (B), Dennis O'Neill (C), Alexandru Agache (D), Robert Lloyd (E), Mark Beesley (F), Chorus and Orchestra of the Royal Opera House—Edward Downes

Royal Opera, Covent Garden: Elijah Moshinsky (stage director), Brian Large (video director)

The BBC, NHK, and the Royal Opera House joined forces to produce this latest video version of *Aida*. Its most notable feature is not the vocal performances, which are strictly routine, but the production directed by Elijah Moshinsky. More precisely, the choreography (by Kate Flatt) and the staging of the combat sequences (by William Hobbs) command attention through their use of elements of tai chi and martial arts. Why such styles of movement would be used in Egypt at the time of the Pharaohs is a question not clearly answered, but the visual impact, combined with a striking lighting design that floods the stage with yellow desert-like brilliance, is stunning.

Unfortunately, the singing is not on the same high level as the production. As Aida, Cheryl Studer looks to be working very hard, and she has some serious pitch problems whenever she ventures toward the top of her range. Luciana d'Intino is somewhat better as Amneris but still lacks power and stage presence. Like Studer and d'Intino, Dennis O'Neill has considerable body weight but it does not translate into vocal power in the role of Radames. All three move somewhat clumsily onstage and fail to project any real sense of emotional involvement or sexual magnetism.

With better singers, this could have been an exciting addition to the *Aida* video inventory.

The 1981 Arena di Verona version combines a marvelous sense of grand spectacle with excellent singing. It is the best of the lot, but does not have English subtitles. Of the subtitled versions, the Scala production is the most well-rounded; it satisfies both dramatically and vocally, with imaginative staging and an excellent orchestral performance.

HARLOW ROBINSON

GIUSEPPE VERDI

OTELLO (1887)

A: Desdemona (s); B: Emilia (ms); C: Otello (t); D: Cassio (t);
E: Iago (bar)

*O*tello was Verdi's last tragic opera. The old composer saw through with magnificent clarity to the bone of Shakepeare's character. That sort of vision is *entirely* uncommon; no English-speaking *actor* but perhaps Olivier, for example, has done equally well with Shakespeare's play in the last sixty years, so that most of our great Othellos have in fact been Otellos—opera singers: Martinelli, Vinay, Vickers, Domingo. It is they who, utilizing Verdi's vision, have been able to penetrate the character's naïveté, self-obsession, and vulnerability to that essential core of generous, noble feeling that qualifies him (despite the jealousy and homicidal mania) for tragic stature.

The music and text alone give us that stature. My own introduction to the opera was through a noisy postwar pressing on 78s of the first complete recording, with Nicola Fusati. It is certainly the weakest of the major recorded performances, but I can recall its initial impact to this day. What a vindication of Verdi's and Boito's dramatic skill that there has been more than one visual performance that has not diminished that incredible aural effect!

1958 BEL CANTO SOCIETY (VHS)

(Film, Mono, Black and White, Not Subtitled)
124 minutes

Rosanna Carteri (A), Luisella Ciaffi (B), Mario del Monaco (C), Gino Mattera (D), Renato Capecchi (E), Chorus and Orchestra of RAI Milan—Tullio Serafin

Franco Enriquez (director)

Once the list of participants has been absorbed, all that needs to be known about this production is whether they are decently visible and audible. Mostly, they are. This looks like a kinescope: sometimes blurred, and with excessive black-and-white contrast—now and then Otello can hardly be seen—but it appears that the director had been poring over Orson Welles's films of *Othello* and *Macbeth*, with their spellbinding textures of shadow and patterns of camera movement. Here, too, there are crudities, failures, and technical gaffes, but also an adventurous mind at work on a tragic vision.

Tullio Serafin, in 1901 Toscanini's assistant at La Scala, and principal conductor there less than ten years later, leads a beautifully honed performance of extraordinary tension, dramatic shape, and, yes, elegance. Mario del Monaco is in superb voice: incomparably brazen, as one might expect, but on this occasion a little more than that, too. Most of his celebrated stage appearances and all of his recordings of the role were furious—psychotic—from almost the start of Act I. Here the alienation is still dominant, but with Serafin's help he summons a modicum of tenderness in the love duet, a gram of tragic despair in the early part of Act II, and some vulnerability in the great Act III monologue. There is little of the painful intimacy with Desdemona that Martinelli, Vinay, and Vickers have given us, but, save for a few groans, del Monaco's death scene is strikingly noble. Though there is still more to Otello than this, the sheer sound and conception given us here are more than once overpowering.

Renato Capecchi's Iago is in its way even more extraordinary. In his days as a Verdi baritone he had a rather ordinary voice at the service of commanding dramatic intelligence. Here the voice sounds positively black, and he is the one Iago on tape *really* to fulfill Boito's difficult prescription for the role: ordinary in public, bottomlessly evil in private. "La morte e nulla," the penultimate line in the "Credo," is here delivered almost carelessly—a mere fact—and the effect, even for those who know the piece by heart, is newly shocking.

Rosanna Carteri is an attractive Desdemona, though the voice has the same coarse edge it had in the theater. "Ave Maria" is a well-polished moment. The others constitute what was then a living Italian tradition. For the casual viewer the film is not entirely easy to watch—it is technically crude and there are no subtitles—but if you want to plunge yourself into the experience there are lessons and sensations to be dug out of it and explored.

1969 VIEW (VHS)

(Film, Stereo, Color, in German, Not Subtitled) 121 minutes

Christa Noack-Von Kamptz (A), Hanna Schmook (B), Hans Günter Nöcker (C), Hans-Otto Rogge (D), Vladimir Bauer (E), Chorus and Orchestra of Berlin Komische Oper—Kurt Masur

Walter Felsenstein (director)

For nearly fifty years until his death in 1975 Walter Felsenstein was one of Germany's leading opera directors and filmmakers—a major influence on such famous successors as Götz Friedrich and Harry Kupfer. After World War II Felsenstein worked mainly at East Berlin's Komische Oper, rehearsing each production until he thought it had reached perfection, canceling a performance if a scheduled singer were ill, and continually re-rehearsing repertory works to maintain their freshness. He aimed for a "total work of art" in which performance, design, and music assumed equal importance. His singers were to transform themselves into the roles they played and to convince their audience that they sang only because speech and gesture were insufficiently expressive. The aim was not merely realism, but an *intensity of reality* attainable, he thought, only in the theater.

These are decrees for an ideal opera theater—or a theatrical intensity which borders on the insane. Here we have elements of both. There are precedents: anyone who has heard Helge Roswaenge in the wartime Berlin recording of *Traviata* or Elisabeth Höngen and Mathieu Ahlersmayer in their psychotic 1944 *Macbeth* will recognize the style. It's mesmerizing. Under Kurt Masur, *Otello* is finished in two hours. The stylized opening crowd scene is the most agonized I've ever seen, and the coercive Iago is an expressionist madman. The Otello resembles and performs like a violent Emil Jannings, and Cassio is not merely drunk: he becomes a maniac who should be locked up. Acts II and III are terrifying, for both us and Desdemona, and Otello's death scene is shockingly brutal. The point is that all of this is not merely amusing or overstated; we are drawn into a world that suggests *Marat / Sade*, and suggests it more chillingly than any English-language production of that play that I have seen. The sheer technique and planning are awesome. There are moments when one wants to applaud and giggle at the same time.

The filmmaking is equally adventurous, and the musical treatment supports the vision: often ugly but intense and technically exact. Hans Nöcker's voice pierces through the orchestration, steadily and in tune. Vladimir Bauer hasn't much tone, but in this production he is a master of pitch, angry color, and coercive rhythm. As Desdemona, Christa Noack-Von Kamptz plays something of an outwardly cool nymphomaniac, with one of those unsteady German-maiden soprano voices that in this case supports the conception.

Make no mistake. This may not be an Italian nor an English view of *Otello*, but it is at least a total work of technique, a Felsenstein production, and, for what it is, enthralling.

1974 DEUTSCHE GRAMMOPHON (VHS / LD)

(Studio Production, Stereo, Color, Subtitled), 141 minutes

Mirella Freni (A), Stefania Malagù (B), Jon Vickers (C), Aldo Bottion (D), Peter Glossop (E), Chorus of German Opera, Berlin; Berlin Philharmonic Orchestra—Herbert von Karajan

Herbert von Karajan (director)

Jon Vickers was one of the two or three great singing actors of recent times, and Herbert von Karajan certainly conquered at one time or another the most profound operatic repertory: his 1951 live audio version of *Tristan und Isolde* with Martha Mödl and Ramon Vinay, for example, is the most wrenching performance I have heard of that score. Both bring their formidable gifts to *Otello*, and they are supported by a beloved lyric soprano in her prime and a brilliantly expressive Iago. It is certainly a performance of tragic vision. Vickers is throughout filled with tender and then violent concern rather than mere anger; it is characteristic that in Act IV he enters more like a moral force than a jealous husband. Karajan's orchestra articulates the score with a beauty of tone that only he has equalled, and Mirella Freni finds in Desdemona one of the Verdi roles proper in weight and color for her. Peter Glossop is a physically resourceful and charismatic Iago with a voice only occasionally strained by the role, and Aldo Bottion is a fashionable, lightweight Cassio: just the sort that naïve Otello might favor and Iago detest.

And yet a number of things stand in the way of complete success. On records Karajan's slowness in this performance was ponderous; one hoped that the visuals might legitimize his tempos, but here the profound and the intimate border on the pompous, and Verdi's superb variety of effect—now furious, now tender, now mercurial, now tragically despairing—is often homogenized: the result is sometimes to make the opera "tragical" rather than tragic. This limits to an extent Vickers's profound conception and eliminates some of those lightning-like responses that have given his live performances an element of supernatural energy. Freni's heroine sounds lovely but is completely submissive: Albanese, Scotto, and even Kiri Te Kanawa have retained much more of the Shakespearean vitality that Verdi found so attractive in this character. The staging is grand but bland, like the settings and lighting.

These are problems, though, in a production that still suggests high tragedy. Vickers's Otello remains lofty in conception; his dignity, sense of dramatic shape, and profound phrasing are a constant lesson, and the others provide many moments of complementary beauty and conviction. The performance should be seen.

1982 CASTLE OPERA (VHS) / PIONEER (LD)

(Stage Performance, Stereo, Color, Subtitled), 145 minutes

Kiri Te Kanawa (A), Flora Rafanelli (B), Vladimir Atlantov (C), Antonio Bevacqua (D), Piero Cappuccilli (E), Chorus and Orchestra of Arena di Verona—Zoltan Pesko

Verona Arena: Gianfranco de Bosio (stage director), Preben Montell (video director)

We begin in the afternoon with the stagehands assembling the set on the vast banks of stone seats at one end of the arena. Then it is night, and the huge audience has assembled under the stars. With the opening blast from the orchestra some lights go up on the stage area, all steps, dotted with some ugly wedge-shaped castle segments. It's all gigantically tacky. The chorus, in what look like white sheets, mostly stand stock-still and sing directly to the audience. Roderigo is half a head taller than Iago, and awkward, balding, and dressed in spangles. Dramatically, the focus is all over the place on that huge stage. For his entrance, Vladimir Atlantov is in the dark: only his white silk (?) sleeve is lit, but with the utmost brilliance.

Among the principals there is a good deal of searching for the conductor and dashing across huge distances to insufficient music. For "Fuoco di gioia" there is no visible fire, but the dancers *are* bouncing about with extraordinary calisthenic energy.

As is the performance. With that amplification system the orchestra bubbles along like a stew, but there are plenty of carrots and potatoes and formidable chunks of meat in it, and the energy provided is enormous. Atlantov is burly and warm in characterization and voice. Nothing subtle, of course, but he is very responsive. Kiri Te Kanawa is in lovely voice and, acting for millions, comes alive with big, demonstrative gestures: she seems genuinely moved and is very vibrant.

Things continue this way in the later acts. Piero Cappuccilli is gruff and noisy but also forced to demonstrate "acting": outsized gestures and popping eyes. Some of the principals are wrapped in costumes of flowing metallic cloth: it "reads" in the arena—and so do its wrinkles. At one point Te Kanawa appears in horrifying Minute Maid metallic orange. Atlantov continues energetic, fresh-voiced, and resonant, though the bottom tones disappear and he has occasional breath-control problems. Te Kanawa remains amazingly responsive: an endearing performance.

The setting structures meanwhile grow unbelievably garish, but Te Kanawa provides a magnificently sung and expansively played last act, and Atlantov's entire final scene is touchingly simple and direct. At his death he falls beside the bed and never gets to kiss Desdemona; it's terribly moving.

So: a big, ugly, and technically absurd, but energetic, healthily sung, fun-filled, and strangely moving *Otello*. The arena experience is there for the viewing.

1986 KULTUR (VHS) / PIONEER (LD)

(Film, Stereo, Color, Subtitled) 123 minutes

Katia Ricciarelli (A), Petra Malakova (B), Plácido Domingo (C), Urbano Barberini / Ezio di Cesare (D), Justino Díaz (E), Chorus and Orchestra of Teatro alla Scala—Lorin Maazel

Franco Zeffirelli (director)

As a version of Verdi's *Otello*, this famous film is disqualified in so many serious ways that even its considerable visual merits come to seem a waste. First are the cuts made in a work universally seen as the model for superb operatic construction. The longest are the "Fuoco di Gioia" chorus in Act I, the sailors' chorus in II, the entire ensemble at the close of III, and the Willow Song and a part of the Ave Maria in IV, but there are in addition *many* other smaller excisions that destroy the dramatic continuity established with such care by Boito and Verdi. On the other hand, we get a new bit of dance in Act I and a minute and a half of the ballet added for Paris in Act III.

Then there is the sound: Domingo's voice is artificially darkened in the last half of the opera—and indeed almost everyone else seems to sing with exceptional heaviness there, too. And the story is changed: in this version Otello kills Iago—by hurling a spear across the bedroom and through him. Ah, that damnable Wagnerian influence in late Verdi!

And the strengths? They are the cast and to an extent Zeffirelli's direction and film sense. Domingo is a virile, forthright, and authoritative hero, and he enacts and sings the role with profound conviction. Justino Díaz is an athletic and plausible Iago, though his top voice does not have ideal cutting power. He plays the role with great spirit, even when required to give not one but two phony villainous laughs, one of them into some reverberating architecture. Katia Ricciarelli plays a vibrant, moving Desdemona in what is left of her role, though her voice is sometimes unsteady. The remaining chunk of the Ave Maria is her best moment. Loren Maazel conducts a lively performance (available *complete* on CDs) when the orchestra is not being submerged in storm sounds or reduced to mere accompaniment (as in the Credo and other moments). Some stretches, though ("Dio ti giocondi" is an example), are taken so broadly that Verdi's sudden changes of feeling and tempo are deprived of proportion and thus excitement.

The color qualities, as always in a Zeffirelli film, have great atmospheric value, and he knows how to edit crowd scenes for clarity and mounting tension and, when his taste will permit it, to animate dramatic scenes with inventive action. The architecture is fascinating and often dramatically supportive as the characters are driven to move from place to place. Some of the cinematic devices, however, are pointless and against the rhythm of the music. "Era la notte" is illustrated with an apparently nude Cassio lying in bed in a state of moist sexual frustration: the point of Verdi's magnificently suggestive music here is that this is a *fabrication* on Iago's part and nobody's reality. And earlier, in this version the love duet begins in bed—a nice undergraduate idea on paper: the problem is that Verdi's music here is the greatest *preparatory* love sequence in the whole history of Italian opera.

If you can get through this film without severe annoyance and a sense of mounting disappointment, you will find some sequences of profundity, excitement, or inventiveness. For *Otello*, though, look elsewhere.

1992 KULTUR (VHS) / PIONEER (LD)

(Stage Performance, Stereo, Color, Subtitled) 146 minutes

Kiri Te Kanawa (A), Claire Powell (B), Plácido Domingo (C), Robin Leggate (D), Sergei Leiferkus (E), Chorus and Orchestra of the Royal Opera House—Georg Solti

Royal Opera, Covent Garden: Elijah Moshinsky (stage director), Brian Large (video director)

Elijah Moshinsky's is a grimly military production, suggestive of the twentieth century. There is no doubt that Cyprus has been under threat of siege: cannons, armor, helmets, and gray-green uniforms are everywhere, and even the lighting appears olive-drab. Sin and sacrifice are the other visual motifs; the third act is dominated by an enormous, almost colorless (on the video, at least) painting of what appears to be the dead Christ. The initial effect of all this is brutal, and what it should do dramatically is to increase the sense of tension between the harsh discipline of military life and force of human desire which is the soul of the music and text. That happens, but the larger theatrical effect is more ambiguous. Verdi's panoply of characters becomes homogenized and often pallid; sometimes it is momentarily difficult, indeed, to identify them, and on the singers the burden of effective characterization becomes enormous. Despite the painting, the Renaissance, so brilliantly evoked by Verdi, is gone from the stage.

The cast and conductor respond variously to these challenges. Solti's orchestra is superbly disciplined but brash: the love duet lacks something in tenderness and there is little mercurial fantasy in the Act III Cassio-Iago scene, for example. Sergei Leiferkus sings well in a light voice as Iago, but the slight lisp and the Russian tone production eliminate many subtleties of emotional response. Kiri Te Kanawa and Plácido Domingo are both in resplendent voice. She is lovely and involved, if not so deeply as in the Verona performance. Despite some odd bits of business, Domingo is at his brilliant best: a characterization filled with moving musical and dramatic detail and very distinguished. Before "Dio mi potevi" he weeps, and, amazingly, the effect as he does it is noble and not at all sentimental. The many close-ups are all deeply revealing of Otello's emotional state, and his last scene is very moving. Despite its striking but somewhat reductive concept, this production represents certain humanistic aspects of the opera more fully than any other videotape.

As a well-recorded, subtitled version of the opera in color with an Otello of greatness, either the Domingo-Solti or the Vickers-Karajan version is recommended—despite their shortcomings. Other videos offer special historical or artistic illuminations for our delight: Capecchi, del Monaco, the Felsenstein concept, and the Verona Arena experience.

LONDON GREEN

GIUSEPPE VERDI

FALSTAFF (1893)

A: Alice (s); B: Nannetta (s); C: Meg (ms); D: Mistress Quickly (ms);
E: Fenton (t); F: Falstaff (bar); G: Ford (bar)

Falstaff is Verdi's final stage work, produced when he was eighty. As such it utilizes a lifetime of operatic experience and requires of its singers extraordinary vocal technique, musicianship, and textual responsiveness; even Toscanini could not always secure this last. The greatest supporting singers in this opera have been among the vocal stars of their day: people like Stignani, Tassinari, Pagliughi, Dal Monte, Tibbett, and Tagliavini. The first Falstaff had previously been the first Iago: Victor Maurel, one of the great singing actors of the late nineteenth century. A bulky, beautiful sound alone will not qualify a Falstaff, and some of the most renowned—Antonio Scotti and Mariano Stabile, for example—have been better musicians and actors than vocalists. The best, of course, combine in some measure all these powers and dexterities, and under a first-rate conductor. But then a great Falstaff, as opposed to a merely amusing or vocally pleasing one, is as rare as a great Boris.

1976 VAI (VHS)

(Stage Performance, Mono, Color, Subtitled)
112 minutes

Kay Griffel (A), Elizabeth Gale (B), Reni Penkova (C), Nucci Condò (D), Max-René Cosotti (E), Donald Gramm (F), Benjamin Luxon (F), Glyndebourne Festival Chorus and London Philharmonic Orchestra—John Pritchard

Glyndebourne Festival: Jean-Pierre Ponnelle (stage director), Dave Heather (video director)

This is the Glyndebourne version of Verdi's outrageous comedy based on Shakespeare's character, shifted from a fourteenth-century London whorehouse to a sixteenth-century Windsor, absurdity amusingly intact. Falstaff's adversaries are no longer whores, royalty, and soldiers going off to death, but witty suburban wives teaching him a moral lesson and terrifying him with fairy dances. The important thing is that old Verdi understood exactly the rough, Renaissance fantasy of the Shakespearean humor in this play. Falstaff in his various Shakespearean incarnations may be the greatest English reprobate, but his country neighbors share in his energies; they are just on the edge of civilized insanity themselves.

Glyndebourne performs it, though, as if it might be Mozart or Goldsmith—geniuses of another sort. Almost everything that intelligence, taste, study, and understated charm can do is present in one way or another: an admirable performance, ready for the final necessary leap into conviction. The sets have a certain rustic charm, though there are blocking problems at the Garter Inn and the final scene is sometimes visually static. Nucci Condo is a charming lyric Quickly but needs age and a certain vocal roughness and depth to provide a counterpoint to her colleagues. The wives and Nannetta are nimble but none has precisely the kind of penetrating lyricism that can make their scenes more than simply jovial. Bardolfo and Pistola are typical of the performance; the bulbous drunkenness and disreputable qualities are certainly understood, but they are more indicated than fully acted, as if by well-prepared college faculty members rather than fully committed actor-singers. John Pritchard conducts a polished but rather solemn performance, at its best in the mercurial opening to the final scene and superbly exact in the closing ensemble.

All of this would be a charming background for a riotous performance of the central role. Donald Gramm, a very fine artist, is musical and intelligent but lacks the good-natured vulgarity to make it all more than academically amusing. Under the circumstances, Benjamin Luxon's Ford is the most persuasive performance, though he seems to be losing his voice in the final scene. The voice, however, is nicely proportioned for the small house, and he balances charmingly the elements of rationality, blunt outrage, and wit found in the character. Jean-Pierre Ponnelle's direction is generally efficient, though a couple of the visual climaxes have not been effectively photographed. As a whole the presentation has charm and precision but is more admirable than genuinely funny.

1979 LONDON (VHS / LD)

(Studio Performance, Stereo, Color, Subtitled) 126 minutes

Karan Armstrong (A), Jutta Renate Ihloff (B), Sylvia Lindenstrand (C), Marta Szirmay (D), Max-René Cosotti (E), Gabriel Bacquier (F), Richard Stilwell (G), Vienna State Opera and Berlin German Opera Choruses and Vienna Philharmonic Orchestra—Georg Solti

Götz Friedrich (director)

This bustling opera with its frequently simultaneous scenes benefits wonderfully from the multiple sets and mobility of film. The impression here is often of a vital neighborhood rather than a room through which crowds of people happen to be rushing. In addition, Götz Friedrich's direction is sensitive; the camera and the characters move with a rhythmic élan that nearly always reflects the music. Visually it is charmingly rustic, and the singers are attractive, camera wise, and often inventive. Solti conducts with his usual verve and precision—a Shakespearean vitality at the center of Verdi's intentions. The wondrous opening music of the final scene becomes, unfortunately, background for very busy preparation in the forest, but the fairies' entrance is charmingly visualized, played, and performed. Throughout, the camera work and choreography of this exceptionally complicated work provide both clarity and delight.

And the singers are stimulating. Max-René Cosotti is a very appealing Fenton, and better recorded than in the Glyndebourne production. Karan Armstrong has a darkish, sometimes unsteady voice, but she is such a vivacious and disciplined actress that one is captivated anyway. Marta Szirmay's Quickly lacks the outspoken richness of the great Italian mezzos, but she is wonderfully insinuating; Jutta Renata Ihloff looks ravishing and sings a fine Fairy Song. As Ford, Richard Stilwell has just the right balance between rectitude and humor: for once, one can still see the young man in this character.

At the center of it all is Gabriel Bacquier's Falstaff, ripely sung and magnificently acted: an immense, wine-stained old windbag, unbearable and charming all at once, full of a terrifying energy. And superbly made up and costumed; his appearance dressed for amorous conquest is one of the great comic moments.

Some of the production is, no doubt, overdone, and a few moments are misconceived, but this is one of the two productions in which the varied energies of the score are consistently mirrored in the visual production.

1982 SONY (VHS / LD)

(Stage Performance, Stereo, Color, Not Subtitled) 135 minutes

Raina Kabaivanska (A), Janet Perry (B), Trudeliese Schmidt (C), Christa Ludwig (D), Francisco Araiza (E), Giuseppe Taddei (F), Rolando Panerai (G), Vienna State Opera Chorus and Vienna Philharmonic Orchestra—Herbert von Karajan

Salzburg Festival: Herbert von Karajan (stage and video director)

The admirable expertise of its participants produces a dispiriting performance indeed. The Vienna Philharmonic plays with unequalled elegance; of palpitating wit and rude humor there is virtually none under Herbert von Karajan, who forty years ago produced Wagner, Verdi, and Puccini performances of extraordinary subtlety *and* vitality. Here the music has a glassy smoothness that would be excessive for *Capriccio* and, however admirable in the abstract, is seldom persuasive in this work. Günther Schneider-Siemssen's sets are somber, though his Windsor Forest is, like Karajan's orchestra in that scene, full of elegant mystery. Karajan's stage direction is orderly but shows no comic flair. Of the singers only Christa Ludwig and the lovers seem to be enjoying themselves; the rest seldom look each other in the eye and in fact seem to have more fun during the curtain calls than during the performance.

As Fenton, Francisco Araiza is agile and appealing. Raina Kabaivanska acts with confident elegance but produces a squally, impure tone entirely unsuited to the charismatic Alice. Rolando Panerai had been a wonderful Ford on records for twenty-five years, but his natural amiability creates onstage a neutral effect compounded by an exceptionally uninteresting costume. Likewise Giuseppe Taddei, noted on records for the striking dramatic focus of his Rigoletto, Don Giovanni, Leporello, and Falstaff, is here remarkably ordinary: a plump man rather pleasantly in search of romance. This Falstaff is hardly on the edge of comic madness and certainly not a cause of wit in others. He sings with admirable care but he has not been well directed in the big comic moments or costumed to suggest a character much beyond the conventional. Very odd. But then so is the performance. Who would have thought that this world-class cast could be dull?

1983 CASTLE OPERA (VHS) / PIONEER (LD)

(Stage Performance, Stereo, Color, Subtitled) 141 minutes

Katia Ricciarelli (A), Barbara Hendricks (B), Brenda Boozer (C), Lucia Valentini-Terrani (D), Dalmacio Gonzales (E), Renato Bruson (F), Leo Nucci (G), Chorus and Orchestra of the Royal Opera House—Carlo Maria Giulini

Royal Opera, Covent Garden: Richard Eyre (stage director), Brian Large (video director)

Since neither the tape box nor the libretto has a complete cast list (shame!), I was frustrated not to know who the exceptional Pistola of this performance was until the cast was finally given during the curtain calls. He has remarkable presence on stage, comic talent, and a strikingly large, penetrating bass voice—the best Pistola I've ever heard. He is, it turns out, the American William Wildermann. He must have been more than sixty in 1982, for I first heard him as a striking Méphistofélès with Fortune Gallo's touring San Carlo Opera when I was a child in San Francisco in the late 1940s. He is delightful here.

The rest of the performance is a peculiar mixture of the beautiful and the bizarre. The production marked Carlo Maria Giulini's return to staged opera after more than a decade. The orchestral work is expert but oddly humorless—perhaps the rather distant recording helps to create this effect. The indoor sets are conventionally Elizabethan and, drearily, structured to prevent interesting character groupings. Windsor Forest is an unpleasant surprise: remarkably bare, with what looks like a Freudian Bayreuth tree that in no way suggests the mercurial fantasy in the music. The women's costumes are nearly all in solid colors with similar huge white collars, and Ford is in black: grimly Puritanical and pointless, since nothing in the music or in Leo Nucci's expansively Italianate performance supports this idea. Barbara Hendricks and Dalmacio Gonzales are handsome lovers; she sings well, he adequately. Lucia Valentini-Terrani is a Quickly of some charm, though she has not the voice to dominate in this role. She has been padded to look enormous around the middle: the effect is uncomfortable and unconvincing. As Alice, Katia Ricciarelli looks lovely, plays wittily, and has a voice which glitters, though occasionally it seems insubstantial and unsteady.

Leo Nucci's Ford is lively and committed—moreso than Renato Bruson's Falstaff. This is a strange impersonation. Bruson's singing is often smoothly beautiful in tone and phrasing, and his characterization rather quietly noble: except for the padding he might as well be doing a mature Roderigo in *Don Carlo*. "Va, vecchio John," for example, has grace but almost no satiric impact, and none of the great comic moments really makes its amusingly human comment. Bruson's eyes are sometimes expressive, his body—and the stage direction he has chosen to carry out—far less so. As a whole, this *Falstaff* is a performance of some discrete beauties but it seems in many ways quite consciously to skirt the essence of the opera.

1992 DEUTSCHE GRAMMOPHON (VHS / LD)

(Stage Performance, Stereo, Color, Subtitled) 126 minutes

Mirella Freni (A), Barbara Bonney (B), Susan Graham (C), Marilyn Horne (D), Frank Lopardo (E), Paul Plishka (F), Bruno Pola (G), Metropolitan Opera Chorus and Orchestra—James Levine

Metropolitan Opera: Franco Zeffirelli (stage director), Brian Large (video director)

This production arouses a house ovation at the end, and its knockabout wit and adroitness transfer beautifully from the opera house to video. James Levine and his orchestra are at their best here: rambunctious, mercurial, and always exact and exhilarating, with a fine sense of comic scene structure. The sets, as one might expect from Franco Zeffirelli, are huge but atmospheric, and designed for interesting groupings and stage business: one will not forget Bardolfo climbing the rafters at the conclusion of Scene 1, for example. At the end there is a lovely and mysterious forest. Some of the costumes are impossibly elegant and rather heavy—but the actors do have fun in them. The color and sound are excellent, and Brian Large's video direction is generally brilliant, though, as so often, the climax of Act II—the dumping of Falstaff into the river and Ford's reaction—remains visually unclear. A minor point, though.

Given these wonderful resources, the special glories of the production are its cast and Paul Mills's stage direction for the revival. Central is Paul Plishka's magnificent Falstaff: gigantic in energy and size, and yet charming and funny. He looks wonderfully grizzled and rotund, handles all of the comic business masterfully, and sings the role ripely. The comic pride, the self-satisfaction, and the age, quirks, gluttony, and sheer fun of it are all there. His cronies Bardolfo and Pistola (Anthony Laciura and James Courtney) are a delightful team, and Piero de Palma is a Caius of great energy and style. Mirella Freni is a real matron of an Alice; her sound is occasionally a little unsteady, but she has wonderfully earthy fun with the role. Marilyn Horne's roomy voice is the best of those for Quickly and her scenes with Plishka are splendidly pointed, as one might expect. Barbara Bonney and Frank Lopardo are attractive lovers, though his distinctive tenor is a little heavy for this role. Bruno Pola is an extremely rotund Ford—that fact makes an odd comment on his scene with Falstaff. There is also some wear in the voice, but, like others, he points the text aptly. Altogether this production and its Falstaff are wonderfully—and uniquely—satisfying.

The final choice is the 1992 Metropolitan Opera performance, with all its musical and dramatic satisfactions and Paul Plishka's brilliant Falstaff. An alternate is the London 1979 film, visually delightful and memorable also for *its* wonderful Falstaff, Gabriel Bacquier.

LONDON GREEN

ANTONIO VIVALDI

ORLANDO FURIOSO (1727)

A: Angelica (s); B: Orlando (ms); C: Alcina (ms); D: Bradamante (ms);
E: Ruggiero (ct); F: Medoro (t); G: Astolfo (bs)

*O*rlando Furioso was the first Vivaldi opera to be given a fully staged production in the United States. This event did not pass unnoticed: the 1980 Dallas Opera presentation drew an international audience and was the occasion for a symposium (and eventually a book) exploring the subject of Baroque opera and the Venetian operatic scene in Vivaldi's day. The present video, retaining Marilyn Horne in her Dallas title role, was taped when the production moved to San Francisco in 1989.

The staging originated in Verona, Italy, in 1978, when the opera was revived after a 250-year hiatus to celebrate the 300th anniversary of Vivaldi's birth. The original title was simply *Orlando*, so named presumably to distinguish it from an earlier (1713) *Orlando Furioso* by another Venetian composer.

Vivaldi once stated that he had written ninety-four operas, but at least one contemporary observer remarked that he was "prone to exaggeration." We do know that his operas were popular. Approximately forty-seven are accounted for, of which *Orlando* is the twenty-seventh; Vivaldi was forty-nine when he composed it in 1727 for Teatro St. Angelo, one of Venice's leading theaters and one with which he had been associated for more than a decade—even functioning as its impresario for a time. His librettist was Grazio Braccioli, a young lawyer, who drew the plot from the famous sixteenth-century epic romance by Ariosto.

An English contemporary of Vivaldi's wrote, rather tartly, that the composer "had the sense to keep violin leaps out of his vocal writing." Some of the arias in *Orlando Furioso* might challenge that statement.

1989 KULTUR (VHS) / PIONEER (LD)

(Stage Performance, Stereo, Color, Subtitled) 147 minutes

Susan Patterson (A), Marilyn Horne (B), Kathleen Kuhlmann (C), Sandra Walker (D), Jeffrey Gall (E), William Matteuzzi (F), Kevin Langan (G), San Francisco Opera Chorus and Orchestra—Randall Behr

Pier Luigi Pizzi (stage director), Brian Large (video director)

The operagoer in Vivaldi's day was a hardy specimen—operas often ran to five or six hours or even longer—and modern practicalities entail drastic cuts. Approximately one-third of *Orlando Furioso* is excised in this revival. Even so, it moves at a stately pace, with the customary A-B-A form of *da capo* arias allowing plenty of time for the viewer to ponder the action, such as it is. But the static quality inherent in this Baroque opera is nicely mitigated in a splendid production: formal white columns frame the space for a delightful set of ships that bring the protagonists to the enchanted island of the sorceress Alcina; a huge gilded horse provides transportation for the knight Ruggiero; an elaborate monument is the backdrop for Orlando's mad scene, during which he attacks the statuary with alarming ferocity. Once or twice a statue comes to life, with amusing effect. The lavish costumes are in brilliant colors—one to a customer, as it were—so that the identities of the various lovestricken ladies are easily kept sorted out.

The librettist himself summed up this opera's plot succinctly: "At its beginning, middle and end are the love, madness and recovery of Orlando." It is a role tailor-made for Marilyn Horne, and she carries it off with tremendous vitality and vocal force. The heroic stance and the demanding coloratura are second nature to her, and the ten-minute mad scene is a tour de force by any standards. The voice is in fine shape: plenty of thrust with a slight metallic edge, a golden glow at the top, and the capability of delivering the lengthy stretches of recitative with telling rhythmic emphasis. (She negotiates more than a few vocal leaps that suggest Vivaldi's fiddle-writing, whatever the contemporary comments to the contrary.)

Orlando Furioso is colored primarily by the female voice—four of its seven characters are women, and a fifth role is sung by a countertenor—and it is a blessing, therefore, that the women assembled here are so good. Susan Patterson's bright and resilient soprano is beautifully adapted to the sweet (if sometimes duplicitous) role of Angelica; the slightly husky mezzo of Kathleen Kuhlmann as the sorceress Alcina creates an evil spirit to be reckoned with; Sandra Walker's bronze-tinged mezzo contributes to a powerful image of Bradamante, a "noble woman warrior." Jeffrey Gall's countertenor is resonant, full-bodied, and mercifully unwhining. Kevin Langan, as the English prince Astolfo, displays a strong and agreeable bass; tenor William Matteuzzi, in the relatively minor role of Medoro, is bland but not unpleasant.

Much of the credit for the momentum maintained in this performance lies with conductor Randall Behr: the lengthy instrumental interludes are lively, and above all the recitatives—so substantial an element in Baroque opera—are unfailingly alert and rhythmically pointed.

SHIRLEY FLEMING

RICHARD WAGNER

DER FLIEGENDE HOLLÄNDER (1843)

A: Senta (s); B: Erik (t); C: Dutchman (bs-bar); D: Daland (bs)

With *Der Fliegende Holländer*, Wagner arrives for us. The opera has its traditional moments, but one feels that the Wagnerian voice is now *there* in a way that it had not been, even in the previous year's *Rienzi*. Wagner knew this: *Holländer* was the first of his operas that he thought suitable for Bayreuth.

What is this Wagnerian voice? A phrase will not define it, but it is obvious in the overture, and pre-eminent in the Dutchman's opening monologue. There is an inevitability, a brooding continuity of effect, a sense that one is taking in not merely some music but a man's soul—both what is hidden and what is exposed. *Holländer* provides us with the initial moments: Wagner's King Marke, Wotan, and Amfortas stretch before us, in a world of other Wagnerian heroes and heroines.

A spell is involved, and a great singer, conductor, or stage director will invoke that spell. My first Dutchman was Hans Hotter, decades ago in San Francisco. The production was typical of its time: all canvas, flatly lit. Even I, a teenager, knew it lacked poetry. But there, suddenly, was Hotter, with a voice and a presence bringing us, effortlessly it seemed, the Wagnerian spell, the Wagnerian mystery. Something of the same thing happens in a couple of the videotapes mentioned below. And without this mystery—*however* it is achieved—the Wagnerian experience is not authentic.

1985 PHILIPS (VHS / LD)

(Stage Performance, Stereo, Color, Subtitled) 136 minutes

Lisbeth Balslev (A), Robert Schunk (B), Simon Estes (C), Matti Salminen (D), Bayreuth Festival Chorus and Orchestra—Woldemar Nelsson

Bayreuth Festival: Harry Kupfer (stage director), Brian Large (video director)

Here we have a production meant to arouse intellectual participation. Jean-Pierre Ponnelle once viewed the opera as the Sailor's Dream; Kupfer sees it here as Senta's Obsession. The performance opens during the overture in what looks like an Industrial Revolution spinning room; there the Dutchman's picture falls from the wall and Senta gathers it up, seldom to let go of it during the rest of the opera, *all* of which she then calls up and observes, with growing madness. Freud and Karl Marx are evoked: Senta is the victim of a mania involving sex, power, commitment, and spiritual worth, and her father Daland has the stern vision, and appearance, of a rich merchant intent on further wealth and position. Simon Estes, sonorous and visually magnificent, appears as her visionary Dutchman. When this character appears before others he is, inconsistently, mimed by an insignificant little man in a broadbrimmed hat: presumably either the reality or all that others can see of Senta's vision. Toward the close, Senta is dragging her picture about like Ophelia's flowers, and when she is deserted by her vision she jumps out of a second-story window into the street.

All of that is a striking gloss on the opera, and of course a distortion, with attendant strains, inconsistencies, clichés, and intellectual detritus. That, whether you like it or not, is the fun:

Wagner bubbling up in an Ibsen waffle-iron. The major problem is that all of Wagner's delightful characters in this early opera—Mary, Daland, Erik, the giddy sailors and their women—become relentlessly grim aspects of Senta's madness rather than elements in a vibrant setting for her spiritual commitment.

Nonetheless, the production itself has many sequences of visual brilliance; even the clichés are sometimes strikingly realized. The sets all have a look of both weight and poetic suggestion, and the appearance of the Dutchman's ship in its various phases is quite magical, though one could do without those giant wooden fingers.

Simon Estes has splendid visionary presence and a voice that resounds in the Bayreuth theater. Kupfer requires him to roll around too much in his opening aria, which does not need that sort of visual punctuation. Estes plays and sings with extraordinary tension, but the vocal color remains the same and he does not use the words as he might. Still, it's a striking performance, and his duet with Salminen, here an authoritative, humorless Daland, is a moment of beauty. Lisbeth Balslev accomplishes her two hours and fifteen minutes of madness with unrelenting conviction; she looks the role and produces a young, fresh voice with ball bearings in it. Robert Schunk is a furious Erik; one can see Tristan looming dangerously on his horizon. Graham Clark is his interesting athletic self as the Sailor, and Anny Schlemm plays here a coercive, sharp-tongued Mary, mistress of her small empire. Though it is a bizarre, partial, and sometimes tiresome view of the opera, there are in this production several individual elements of striking quality.

1991 TELDEC (VHS)

(Stage Performance, Stereo, Color, Subtitled), 140 minutes

Hildegard Behrens (A), Raimo Sirkiä (B), Franz Grundheber (C), Matti Salminen (D), Savonlinna Opera Festival Chorus and Orchestra—Leif Segerstam

Savonlinna Opera Festival: Ilkka Bäckman (stage director), Aarno Cronvall (video director)

This Savonlinna Festival production has some elements of international reputation. The orchestra and chorus are both impressive, as is Segerstam's spirited pacing of the work. Behrens and Salminen are well known in America, and Grundheber has sung widely in Europe. Of the others, Anita Välkki (Mary) was once a major Wagnerian. Among them all, though, only Salminen is well cast. His Daland is considerably warmer here than in the Kupfer Bayreuth production, and the voice equally fresh and grand. Behrens is an artist; every moment glows with dramatic intention as she tries to create a Senta wrapped in a romantic vision. The voice, although it retains some sheen, lacks repose and purity. She is, in addition, badly costumed and lit; one must penetrate to what she is *attempting* to do to appreciate this performance. Franz Grundheber is also poorly dressed and lit, and atrociously made up for television. His voice, though it is meaty, lacks variety of color. Even at this relatively early stage he cannot manage a simple legato: attack and release are both pressured and inexact, so that the vocal line resembles a series of knots in a rope. That makes for a Dutchman more depressing than melancholy.

The production itself was probably vibrant in the theater, but it translates badly to tape. The mode is painted realism, the lighting is general, and at such close range every brush stroke on that rocky wall is visible. The editing is patternless: an endless series of extreme close-ups, with little sense of what a given setting looks like in its entirety. The taped result lacks the continuity and dramatic shape it must have had in the theater. One seldom gets beyond the sweat, the makeup, and the sheer human effort to the poetry and mystery of the opera. Neither the sinking of the Dutchman's ship nor Senta's suicide is really shown: the camera cuts away from the first, and the second is handled by an ineffective double exposure. The moments of greatest illusion are in fact the half-lit shots of the white-bearded Leif Segerstam conducting. This figure, more than anyone onstage, embodies the pulsating, thoughtful melancholy of Wagner's marvellous *Dutchman*.

1991 EMI (VHS / LD)

(Stage Performance, Stereo, Color, Subtitled) 133 minutes

Julia Varady (A), Peter Seiffert (B), Robert Hale (C), Jaakko Ryhanen (D), Bavarian State Opera Chorus and Orchestra—Wolfgang Sawallisch

Bavarian State Opera: Henning von Gierke (stage director), Rainer Mockert (video director)

The Flying Dutchman has magnificent sweep and intensity, but its staging is difficult: two realistic ships on a theatrical sea can look distractingly clever or comically inept. To dispense with the problems first, this one-act production sometimes settles for the *earnestly* inept: two expensive-looking boats slide about among the lighting effects; the spinning room is lowered summarily before our eyes from the flies; at the end, the protagonists (she first) leap into obvious stage traps (one expects to hear the "clunk" each time), etc. Thus, as often with this opera, the mystery and power of what one hears is compromised by what one sees.

Much of this, however, is redeemed by Robert Hale and Julia Varady, who emerge as fine actors who just happen to be singing. Hale looks stalwart, brooding, and sensitive, and he phrases the music and the words with extraordinary dramatic thrust. The voice is dark and lyrical, though a little undersized at both top and bottom: at the climaxes, mystery loses out in the quest for power and the result can be more querulous than despairing. Nevertheless, he provides an arresting interpretation. Julia Varady is equally riveting. She lacks the tone to suggest by itself the visionary, but she shapes the music and movement to convince us anyway, and in the final scene the top rings out with thrilling intensity: a performance to suggest the delicate fervour of Liv Ullmann.

The performance around them has its strengths. Sawallisch conducts vibrantly, though his orchestra is recorded at a rather low level. As Eric, Seiffert moves awkwardly but sings with a yearning beauty that redeems his role; as Daland, Jaakko Ryhanen sounds fresh, though he lacks something in roughness: good for him, less good for Daland. Anny Schlemm, veteran of many operatic battles, this time wobbles along happily as Mary. The chorus trudges about like a choir told to act, but it sings with spirit and finally wakes up during the party scene. The costumes are generally flattering. The camera work is quite unimaginative, but the stage direction at least has the virtue of allowing the remarkable Varady and Hale to express themselves with directness. Recommended.

The 1991 Bavarian State Opera production is conservative in concept but extraordinarily moving and perceptive in its leading performances. The 1985 Bayreuth is a distorted but occasionally provocative view with great visual impact and central performances unforgettable in quite different ways. Forced to walk the plank, I'd say buy the first and make every effort to see the second.

LONDON GREEN

TANNHÄUSER (1845)

A: Elisabeth (s); B: Venus (ms); C: Tannhäuser (t); D: Wolfram (bar);
E: Langrave Hermann (bs)

The success of *Rienzi* and *Der Flie-gende Holländer* prompted the Dresden Opera to promote their composer Richard Wagner, a member of its musical staff, to the position of court conductor in February 1843. He finished the libretto for a new opera, *Tannhäuser*, two months later and began composing its music in July. His heavy schedule of work prevented him from finishing the full score until April 1845.

In October of that year, Wagner not only conducted the premiere of his new opera but staged it as well, with as much emphasis on its action as on its musical preparation, a novel procedure for the time, and one that marks him as the progenitor of modern operatic staging. The opera's theme was one he was to employ many times during his career: love as redemption rather than pleasure (the sacred vies with and overcomes the profane), treated in the context of a strict social order.

Critics on the first night found *Tannhäuser* too long, so Wagner cut and altered it throughout its run—even after its fourth performance, when it had become a triumph. Indeed, he went on tinkering with it or thinking about it for a good part of the rest of his life. He revised it for Paris in 1861, the most notable among his changes being the rewriting of much of the Venusberg scene, including new *Tristan*esque ballet music.

Wagner was obsessed with *Tannhäuser* because for him it was the most meaningful of all his operas. Yet he was never satisfied with it.

Even late in life he toyed with the idea of revising it one more time.

The opera's various versions have posed a dilemma for producers in the latter half of our century. Before World War II, the Paris adaptation had been preferred; but afterward, unfavorable reaction to its conflicting styles of composition inspired numerous mountings of the Dresden version. At Bayreuth, Wieland Wagner decided the best solution was a conflation of the two: Paris for the first scene, Dresden, predominantly, for the rest.

1982 PHILIPS (VHS / LD)

(Stage Performance, Stereo, Color, Subtitled)
189 minutes

Gwyneth Jones (A / B), Spas Wenkoff (C), Bernd Weikl (D), Hans Sotin (E), Bayreuth Festival Chorus and Orchestra—Colin Davis

Bayreuth Festival: Götz Friedrich (stage director), Thomas Olofsson (video director)

This video is a landmark in more ways than one. By 1971, only five years after the death of Wieland Wagner, Bayreuth had lost much of its allure. In an effort to restore to Bayreuth its former reclame, Wolfgang Wagner decided that in view of the scarcity of Wagnerian superstars the play was to be the thing by which he would recapture the attention of the operatic world.

He resolved to introduce provocative productions by theatrical directors, reasoning that they alone could put a new spin on his grandfather's music dramas. That they might be inexperienced in staging opera, never mind Wagner, might turn out to be a blessing. At least they carried with them no preconceived baggage.

Tannhäuser, scheduled as the 1972 opener, was assigned to Götz Friedrich, a pupil of Walter Felsenstein, the director of East Berlin's Komische Oper, renowned for its realistic, politicized music theater. This kind of theater was typically staged in spare settings that encouraged concentration on players whose characters were sharply defined.

Thus, Tannhäuser, as Friedrich saw him, is an artist who leaves a realm of stimulating but ultimately sterile pleasure for an oppressive, coercive society with which he needs to communicate but to whose rules he cannot conform with artistic integrity. The opera, in Friedrich's words, was seen as a parable of "the journey of an artist through inner and outer worlds, in search of himself." For such an artist, the sensual and the spiritual were equal and inseparable components of love—ergo, the casting of one singer for Venus and Elisabeth, another first at Bayreuth.

Tannhäuser was the first opera filmed at Bayreuth, where dimly lit productions are the norm. It could not have been achieved if, four years earlier, Stanley Kubrick, occupied with his film *Barry Lyndon*, had not importuned Zeiss to come up with the 0.9f lens he needed to shoot two scenes in candlelight.

The *Tannhäuser* video suggests a live performance but it is not—footage outside the theater, fanfares announcing Acts II and III, and curtain calls notwithstanding. Among other things, some superimpositions (especially in the Venusberg scene) betray the film lab and the absence of an audience; the "live" stuff was simply spliced in later. No harm done: the result is in good taste, remarkably well executed technically, considering the hazards. Pictures are only slightly grainy; the sound is good, even if clearly monitored.

The performance has stunning immediacy, even though some will never accept Friedrich's, or any other director's, staging an opera's preludes. Seldom has one seen a *Tannhäuser* with all its characters so incisively delineated, each alive to every nuance of the drama.

As Venus, Gwyneth Jones copes well enough with what is, for her, an uncomfortable role, both vocally and dramatically; as Elisabeth, however, she is something of a revelation, the antithesis of the pallid heroine usually seen. Jones's Elisabeth is an impulsive, loving young woman, one who passionately receives Tannhäuser after their long separation, who suffers with him during his trial, and who dies of a broken heart when he does not return to her from Rome. She is verbally alive and in such good, often radiant, voice it is easy to forgive her when ideal purity of line and tone prove elusive.

Spas Wenkoff is a more conscientious than authoritative Tannhäuser, but he does not disappoint. His actions are clear, played with sufficient intensity to tell; his tenor has sufficient heft, and he bravely and unflinchingly confronts his role's dauntingly high tessitura. Like almost all Tannhäusers, he is at his best in the lower-lying Rome Narration.

The men of Wartburg, dressed as if they might be members of the SS, are led by Bernd Weikl, a noble, lyrical Wolfram; and Hans Sotin, abundant of bass, severe of manner. Notably stern and malevolent in the small role of Biterolf is Franz Mazura, the prototypical upholder of Warburgian family values.

Colin Davis is the able leader of the excellent Bayreuth orchestra and the magnificent chorus, trained by Norbert Balatsch, always listening to and supportive of his singers. His interpretation, merely correct in the first act, warms in the second and becomes a flame in the big ensemble in the second act. The last act, even its longeurs, is sensitively set forth.

1982 PARAMOUNT (VHS) / PIONEER (LD)

(Stage Performance, Stereo, Color, Subtitled)
176 minutes

Eva Marton (A), Tatiana Troyanos (B), Richard Cassilly (C), Bernd Weikl (D), John Macurdy (E), Metropolitan Opera Chorus and Orchestra—James Levine

Metropolitan Opera: Otto Schenk (stage director), Brian Large (video director)

This video preserves a production that cast a long shadow at the Metropolitan Opera. It was the first of the many traditional Wagnerian stagings by the team of director Otto Schenk and designer Günther Schneider-Siemssen. Although there are partisans for the team's *Ring, Parsifal,* and *Meistersinger,* most would probably count this first effort its most visually beautiful and dramatically successful.

Music director James Levine opts for the Paris version. With an orchestra superior to that in Bayreuth, he produces a warm, ingratiating sound and the most urgent first act on video. Abetted by Tatiana Troyanos, in action and tone a seductive goddess of love, the Venusberg scene is especially successful, with choreography by Norbert Vesak that works well enough and is at least less offensive than its rivals.

Richard Cassilly manages an intelligent and musical Tannhäuser despite a dry, less than heroic tenor, sometimes afflicted with an unattractive beat. His breath supply, like that of most postwar Wagnerian tenors, is not up to filling out some of his longest phrases. Eva Marton is a dignified, determined Elisabeth, more spirited than vulnerable. Her voice is youthful, generous and fervent in address, her quick vibrato less unruly than it later became. Bernd Weikl offers a sensitively sung Wolfram, even more assured here than earlier at Bayreuth. The remainder of the cast is routine and largely blank in portrayal.

Pioneer's first-rate laser disc production is accompanied by excellent notes, text, and translation.

1990 PHILIPS (VHS / LD)

(Stage Performance, Stereo, Color, Subtitled)
187 minutes

Cheryl Studer (A), Ruthild Engert-Ely (B), Richard Versalle (C), Wolfgang Brendel (D), Hans Sotin (E), Bayreuth Festival Chorus and Orchestra—Giuseppe Sinopoli

Bayreuth Festival: Wolfgang Wagner (stage director), Brian Large (film director)

This lifeless production of the Dresden version of *Tannhäuser,* with its spare settings designed in concentric circles that recall the visual style of early neo-Bayreuth, is a reminder that it is often advisable to forget the past—in Richard Wagner's words, "Children, make something new."

A critic of the day, commenting on the first showing of this production in 1985, wrote: "This was Wagnerian opera in the most slow and static vein, dumping the principals down on the stage and leaving them there until it was time to move them off again. In the end there simply was not sufficient dramatic impulse generated on stage to convince us that this opera deals with issues of any import."

Beyond the hazard of nondirection, the cast was faced with two others: Reinhard Heinrich's horrid costumes and Giuseppe Sinopoli's dramatically slack, lackadaisical, unidiomatic musical direction. His many plodding tempos (such as those for "Dich teure Halle" and the ensuing duet) might have veiled even the radiance of Flagstad and Melchior.

That may be a reason why Cheryl Studer, who sings with rich, ample, secure tone, is unable to make much of Elisabeth. The other singers make even less of an impression vocally (although Brendel's purity of line is worth noting), and each one is vague in portraiture.

Norbert Balatsch's chorus is, as usual, superb; but the engineering, clear in sound though less than ideally immediate, diminishes its impact. Pictures are crisp.

1994 KULTER (VHS) / PIONEER (LD)

(Stage Performance, Stereo, Color, Subtitled)
201 minutes

Nadine Secunde (A), Waltraud Meier (B), René Kollo (C), Bernd Weikl (D), Jan-Hendrik Rootering (E), Bavarian State Opera Chorus and Orchestra—Zubin Mehta

Bavarian State Opera: David Alden (stage director), Brian Large (video director)

This first production in Germany by David Alden, the iconoclastic director of numerous operas in Great Britain, was staged in Munich's National Theater, where it was photographed in closed sessions over three days. The music is heard in the conflation of Paris and Dresden versions that Wieland Wagner used at Bayreuth, by now the accepted way of presenting *Tannhäuser* in practically every German theater.

Alden has stated that Tannhäuser's conflict in choosing between earthly pleasures and spiritual aspirations is a metaphor for the artist's struggle to unleash his creativity. This serious, well intentioned point of view is muddled early on. Where is the contrasting choice when the scene in the Venusberg is as desolate and unsensual (except for the sexually alluring, if verbally vague, Waltraud Meier as Venus) as that in Elisabeth's *teure Halle?* There, in the room of the song contest, whose back wall is emblazoned with the inscription *Germania Nostra*, the rigid Thuringian social structure is made plain in the costumes of the guests: women are dressed exclusively in black and white, the men, except for a few colorful fops, look like Nazi thugs (lots of leather). In the final act, the wall with the inscription is in ruins, with evidence of mortar fire. One reviewer suggests that the question Alden asks is: "what [has] Tannhäuser's, or rather Wagner's art . . . done to Germany?"

If that is the director's intention, it, like so much of this concept production, is as incoherent as much of the puzzling action (e.g., why does the boy carry a heavier burden [of sin?] than any of the pilgrims) and numerous props (what is that white enameled wash basin for, used at the Virgin's shrine and, later, to aid the Landgrave in washing his hands). As with Patrice Chereau's *Ring*, what *is* strong is Alden's direction of the principal players and their skillful, dedicated responses. All of the major characters are enriched by their actions and reactions to a level well beyond any stock portrayal.

Nadine Secunde offers the most memorable portrait, illuminating Elisabeth's inner passion and faith. Although she loses an occasional bout with intonation and is uncomfortable in some of her most strenuous passages, Secunde never loses her concentration; her vocal color and fine diction make every word live.

René Kollo introduced himself to the international public a quarter century ago as Tann-

häuser in a much admired recording led by Georg Solti. Kollo's art has ripened, and his characterization is richer, but his tenor, although more forceful than before, is sadly deteriorated in tone and steadiness.

In the launching of Bernd Weikl's career, Wolfram was one of his showcase roles. His voice (not quite so much as Kollo's) has been ravaged by time and hard use. His sympathic address is no longer wedded to firm, colorful tone.

Better is Jan-Hendrik Rootering's grim, impassive Landgrave, black of bass and chilly of presence. When meeting Tannhäuser on his return to the real world, this Landgrave acts as if he doesn't believe a word the wayward minstrel says. Among minor characters, tenor Claes-Haakon Ahnsjo makes an impression with Walther von der Vogelweide's contest song and Hans Günter Nöcker gets a lot out of his belligerent, flaky Biterolf.

The excellent Bavarian orchestra and chorus perform well under the baton of Zubin Mehta, notwithstanding some rickety ensemble in the great scene at the end of the second act; but the performance is not well pointed, and the plush, undifferentiated sonorities are always heard no matter what opera Mehta is conducting.

When the big stage is well populated, there is so much going on that video director Brian Large has his hands full deciding what to film. He usually keeps things clear, but there are several moments when one wants to see more than what is being shown.

Pioneer earns admiration for the clarity of its picture and for its wide ranging sound on the laser disc version. Very few video operas boast this one's technical prowess.

The Met production, graced by memorable orchestral playing and beautiful stage pictures, will satisfy those searching for a traditional romantic approach to this opera. More urgent theater will be found in Friedrich's idiosyncratic staging at Bayreuth, with its focused attention to detailed characterization.

C. J. LUTEN

RICHARD WAGNER

LOHENGRIN (1850)

A: Elsa (s); B: Ortrud (ms); C: Lohengrin (t); D: Telramund (bar);
E: Herald (bar); F: King Heinrich (bs)

By setting the pre-Christian fable of the Swan-knight in the tenth century during the reign of King Heinrich I and the wars against the Hungarians, Wagner created an epic with pan-German overtones dominated by a self-portrait of "the absolute artist betrayed." After its premiere in 1850, *Lohengrin* not only conquered Germany, as might have been expected, but the rest of the operatic world as well. It won Wagner his first international fame, was proclaimed the quintessential German romantic opera, and for nearly a century was the favorite of his works for audiences everywhere.

During that time producers were content to stage the opera roughly as Wagner instructed. No longer. Wieland Wagner began a trend favoring visual abstraction, symbolism, and stylized acting that still has adherents.

The rigidity of the opera's social structure is often pointed up by a director who throws into relief the action of the chorus of Saxons and Brabantines. Society's oppression and rejection of Elsa, an insecure girl searching for truth, enhances the poignance of her plight, both before the arrival of her champion and after. Keeping her vow to Lohengrin means she is responsible for her country's welfare as well as her own fate. Elsa realizes she can no longer shoulder those burdens. How can she, without knowing the man who, in the biblical sense, is about to know her?

1982 PHILIPS (VHS / LD)

(Stage Performance, Stereo, Color, Subtitled) 199 minutes

Karan Armstrong (A), Elizabeth Connell (B), Peter Hofmann (C), Leif Roar (D), Bernd Weikl (E), Siegfried Vogel (F), Bayreuth Festival Chorus and Orchestra—Woldemar Nelsson

Bayreuth Festival: Götz Friedrich (stage director), Brian Large (video director)

Götz Friedrich's somber 1979 production, one of Bayreuth's better efforts during the past two decades, deepens one's understanding of *Lohengrin* and touches the heart. Well documented by Brian Large, it is presented by Philips with high production standards. Friedrich's premise—that *Lohengrin* is Wagner's saddest work and a twin tragedy—results in staging that embraces realistic action and conceptual myth in bleak steel and black settings (by Gunther Uecker) where the sun never shines. The action takes place in the space between two large wooden grandstands (Winifred Wagner said it all looked like a football stadium), a setting that insures the identity of Saxons and Brabantines, each and together the image of an uncommonly straight-laced society. An upstage wall, seen at the beginning of Act II, rises for the Münster scene. The bridal scene, dominated by a bed shaped like a large tomb with a glistening swansdown coverlet, is soiled and molting in the final scene.

The musical performance, apart from the thrilling Bayreuth chorus and Weikl, an ideal Herald, never seemed anything remarkable (as heard on three still-available CBS / Sony CDs), but when seen *and* heard the principals make a stronger impression. Particularly Armstrong, who, notwithstanding some intonation problems and occasional insecurity in sustained notes above the staff, has what Elsa requires—the ability to convey in tone, appearance, and manner the illusion of purity and innocence. Hofmann, visually the ideal Swan-knight, brings uncommon humanity to his portrayal. His Lohengrin falls in love with the object of his rescue mission, heightening the poignance of the hero's dilemma. Hofmann, vocally more comfortable in the role than in the Met production four years later, sings with increasing ease and warmth, reaching distinction in the bridal chamber scene. Connell, a mezzo soon to take soprano parts, undaunted by Ortrud's challenging high tessitura, would more ably fulfill her role were she to offer more of her character's malevolence. Like Hofmann, Roar is better here than in the subsequent Met engagement, reaching high notes with less vocal strain and playing a righteous, paranoid, but insufficiently prideful Telramund. Vogel, without the compact sound or strong low notes of a memorable King Heinrich, nevertheless offers a sympathetic portrayal. The conductor, Nelsson, does not suggest uncommon musical sensitivity, but he molds the big ensembles effectively, provides good timing between stage and pit, and keeps the show moving.

1986 PARAMOUNT (VHS) / PIONEER (VHS)

(Stage Performance, Stereo, Color, Subtitled)
220 minutes

Eva Marton (A), Leonie Rysanek (B), Peter Hofmann (C), Leif Roar (D), Anthony Raffell (E), John Macurdy (F), Metropolitan Opera Chorus and Orchestra—James Levine

Metropolitan Opera: August Everding (stage director), Brian Large (video director)

August Everding seems to have had no coherent point of view in staging this opera. Because he has permitted an indeterminate acting style that gives the principal characters no more than vague psychological profiles, their interaction lacks intensity. The physical production (sets by Ming Cho Lee, costumes by Peter J. Hall), brutal in conception and colorless, has a raked central playing area bounded by overhanging docks, one much larger than the other, with low reeds and rushes at the front of the stage. As in Bayreuth, a wall (this one with a balcony and an entrance) divides the opening scene in Act II. Even with more imaginative lighting the set would appear deficient in mythological atmosphere and not an appropriate space for the kind of old-fashioned operatic acting often on view. Most set numbers are rendered in the style of stand-and-deliver, innocent of any contact with others onstage. As an example, Lohengrin sings his Grail narrative, presumably facing the river Scheldt, with his back to the King, Elsa, and the crowd of armed men and townsfolk.

The cast leaves mixed feelings. Marton's bold soprano sounds fresher and steadier than it has in recent years, but its tone is insufficiently pure to suggest Elsa's innocence and vulnerability. Rysanek hoots a bit, hams a bit, but never loses her dramatic concentration. In dialogue, like the committed singing actress she has ever been, Rysanek maintains vivid contact with whomever she is addressing. Hofmann looks as good as he did at Bayreuth, but his vibrato has loosened and he is increasingly troubled with problems of accurate intonation. Roar's portrayal of Telramund is much the same as before, but here his highest notes are uncomfortably close to yelps. Macurdy's bass, never the orotund sound one desires for King Heinrich, is worn, but his professionalism sees him through. The Herald is a disappointment; Raffell has a dry voice and pronounces German poorly.

In the big ensembles, the Metropolitan Opera Chorus sings impressively, even the boys in the Münster scene. The orchestra plays with beautiful tonal quality and color under Levine, whose attention to Wagner's dynamic indications and to judicious balancing of sonorities exposes plentiful, but often obscured detail. His pacing and shaping of large musical paragraphs is not always satisfying. In the overture and in some other episodes, for all his sensitive molding of phrase he is unable to sew them together to create a continuous tissue and a sense of inevitable continuity.

Brian Large's camera work is unobtrusive, withholding no essential action. Color saturation and picture quality are just above adequate. The audio engineering offers disappointing sound—too resonant, grainy, and annoyingly monitored.

1989 PHILIPS (VHS / LD)

(Stage Performance, Stereo, Color, Subtitled) 214 minutes

Cheryl Studer (A), Gabriele Schnaut (B), Paul Frey (C), Ekkehard Wlaschiha (D), Elke Wilm Schulte (E), Manfred Schenk (F), Bayreuth Festival Chorus and Orchestra—Peter Schneider

Bayreuth Festival: Werner Herzog (stage director), Brian Large (video director)

Before he was engaged as producer of the 1987 Bayreuth *Lohengrin*, Werner Herzog's most memorable association with opera was his movie *Fitzcarraldo* (about a man obsessed with building an opera house in the Amazon jungle). And it shows. In this 1989 edition of the 1987 staging, filmed without an audience in the Festspielhaus, Herzog, like most film directors, is at a loss attempting to make coherent the movements of a large ensemble. Even worse, he seldom finds solutions that help the principal players animate their characters.

To its credit, this production has many arresting stage pictures, thanks to designs by Henning von Gierke, magically lit by Manfred Voss; but their beauty is their own reward. Few seem relevant to Wagner's instructions.

The first act and finale take place on a frozen, boulder-strewn Scheldt river, before a dark sky in which a pale sun is intermittently seen. The river's moonlit waters noisily lap the shore throughout the second act's first scene, only to vanish mysteriously by the next (Ortrud's black

art or low tide?), during which no one seems to find a dried-up Scheldt unusual in any way. Equally indefensible, even risible, is the bridal chamber scene: a bed, a tin-foil-colored coverlet, and, for a headboard, a swan, wings spread, placed on a rocky knoll against a background of distant mountains.

Musical substance is of higher quality than the dramatic. Although Peter Schneider offers no revelations, his professionalism, not all that common these days, is not to be despised. The orchestra's sonorities are radiant; the chorus, trained by Norbert Balatsch, is, as ever, beyond anyone's encomiums.

The cast leaves a mixed impression. Distinctly on the plus side is Studer, who launched her international career at Bayreuth with Elsa, here finely controlled and sweetly sung (vocally even more secure, certainly better costumed, and visually more attractive than in the Viennese video). Praise is also due the young Schulte, an excellent Herald and a most promising Wagnerian baritone. Only occasional vocal strain mars Frey's sensitively phrased and sympathetic portrayal of the Swan-knight. With more vocal heft than his other video rivals, Manfred Schenk, apart from some weakness in his lowest notes, is a worthy King.

On the strength of his Alberichs and Klingsors, one expected more from Wlaschiha than the brusque, minimumly detailed Telramund he offers. Nevertheless, his sound is more tolerable than that of Schnaut, whose many *fortes* above the staff are not too far from those of a factory whistle. Moreover, her acting, no less than her singing, of Ortrud is crude (in the "I'm a devil, I'm a devil" style, as Bernard Shaw once described Edouard de Reszke's Méphistofélès in *Faust*).

Brian Large's video direction of this spectacle is up to his usual high standards. Philips provides first-rate sound and picture.

1990 KULTUR (VHS)

(Stage Performance, Stereo, Color, Subtitled) 180 minutes

Cheryl Studer (A), Dunya Vejzovic (B), Plácido Domingo (C), Hartmut Welker (D), Georg

Tichy (E), Robert Lloyd (F), Vienna State Opera Chorus and Orchestra—Claudio Abbado

Vienna State Opera: Wolfgang Weber (stage director), Brian Large (video director)

Even with outstanding singing in the two leading roles and better pacing in the pit, the Vienna State Opera's *Lohengrin* resembles that of the Met. It is another case of a whole that is less than the sum of its parts.

The Viennese production has even less dramatic focus than the Met's. That it has been staged with no particular concept in mind, excepting the Ortrud-Telramund scene, is continually betrayed by direction either bland or wrongheaded, as in the Lohengrin-Telramund duel. Wagner specifies a fight with swordplay, not one that permits Lohengrin to vanquish Telramund without striking a blow. Such action undercuts Lohengrin's mystery and Elsa's doubts. How could her faith be undermined when she has seen Lohengrin defeat his opponent without physical struggle?

The sets and costumes not only reveal conceptual indecision but are unevocative. Elsa's Act I costume is so unattractive it militates against any illusion of youth and restrains a viewer's sympathy.

The musical performance is, however, decidedly more rewarding. Abbado's pacing and shaping of the score is superior to that of his rivals; and, all told, execution by the Viennese forces is unsurpassed. Studer, a somewhat insecure balcony serenade aside, is tonally bright and beautiful. Expressively, she is a trifle generalized; her voice tells less than her face.

Wagner's wish for a Lohengrin capable of singing legato is fulfilled in the vibrant, easeful singing of Domingo. No other postwar tenor has sung the part as effortlessly as he; even though, on this occasion, there are some uncomfortable moments and a seeming loss of concentration in "Im fernem Land." Here and elsewhere, Domingo conveys no sense of his mystical mission; at best, he is just a guy in love. Despite a voice of no particular opulence, Welker pleases for his effort to humanize Telramund, his lack of bluster, and his excellent diction. Vejzovic is a steely-voiced Ortrud, dramatically ham-fisted, singing in a not-easily-recognizable language. Like most of his rivals, Robert Lloyd has a bass too light for the requirements of King Heinrich, but he sings with fervor and dignity. Tichy is a routine Herald.

Except for too many transparently monitored *fortissimos*, the sound of this performance is persuasive. The video, on the other hand, is far from crisp. Confronted with such an uninteresting *mise-en-scène*, the video director has had to rely too heavily on close-ups to convey the complexity of *Lohengrin*'s action.

––––––––––

One searches in vain for an entirely rewarding *Lohengrin*. The 1982 Philips will be the choice of those looking for the most illuminating production; Götz Friedrich's strikes me as both fresh and touching. Kultur's has the best realized musical performance and some excellent singing.

C. J. LUTEN

Tristan und Isolde (1865)

A: Isolde (s); B: Brangäne (ms); C: Tristan (t); D: Kurwenal (bar);
E: King Marke (bs)

That there are but two videotapes of *Tristan* available says much about the state of Wagnerian singing today. One of the tapes was made thirty years ago, and the other features attractive singers whose voices are palpably too light for their roles. Of the aural recordings since the days of Nilsson and Windgassen, only two feature a major Tristan (Vickers) or Isolde (Behrens). Even Wolfgang Wagner admits that he has had to "make do" with his Bayreuth casts, and the Met has not given *Tristan* in seven years.

In the theater, with the right voices, *Tristan* can be a mesmerizing spiritual experience. I missed Traubel, Melchior, and Mödl, but I did see Flagstad and Vinay, Windgassen and Nilsson, and Vickers in the opera. Each of these had his shortcomings, however minor, but at least one did not fear that the performance would kill the protagonists before the composer did. One got a viable *Tristan und Isolde*. People still speak of "Callas orphans." There are also, now, "*Tristan* orphans." As for those people who saw Callas in one of her three Genoese performances of *Tristan* in 1948. . . .

1967 LEGATO CLASSICS (VHS)

(Stage Performance, Mono, Black and White, Not Subtitled) 206 minutes

Birgit Nilsson (A), Hertha Töpper (B), Wolfgang Windgassen (C), Hans Andersson (D), Hans Hotter (E), Osaka Festival Chorus and Orchestra—Pierre Boulez

Osaka Festival: No director credited

What is one to say of this? Black and white, no subtitles, poorly filmed, variably sung, and, as here taped, embarrassingly costumed and set. Nevertheless, for some it is indispensable.

Nilsson had not the warmth of Flagstad nor the erotic anguish of Marthe Mödl, but she could be electrifying in the theater, and Windgassen was impressive in that he knew exactly what to do with his limited means. So it is here. Nilsson begins with an intimate quality not usually associated with her and then builds to a brilliant climax, laserlike, absolutely on pitch, without shadows. She continues thus in the love duet: often soft, often glorious, coldly ecstatic in tone. The Liebestod ends with a lovely soft final note. Windgassen is at first almost done in by the sound quality. The noble ring in his tone seems to have disappeared: only the steady emission and the fine phrasing remain. Act III is better recorded: the lyric quality returns, and he builds the long monologue with both technique and sensitivity. Of the others, Töpper is a knowing but sometimes harsh, sometimes pale Brangäne, and Andersson a decent enough Kurwenal. Hans Hotter is a special case: the voice wobbles, but he is in other ways a magnificent Marke. His sound is drenched in sorrow but not sentiment, and he looks splendidly regal in the role. Boulez is a speedy, efficient, and cold conductor.

Visually the tape is nothing more than a minimal record of the production. Nilsson seems to be bound in leather, and Windgassen looks like a Viking businessman in drag, his Act II costume hanging in wrinkles around him. The bare, symbolic settings, perhaps impressive in the theater, lose all their grandeur when deprived of color and reduced to two dimensions. The stage direction is often awkward.

There you have it. There are elements of grandeur here, and dross, too, but in many ways it is the record, however faulty, not only of a specific performance, but of an era, too. To some, that will decide the matter.

1983 PHILIPS (VHS / LD)

(Stage Performance, Stereo, Color, Subtitled) 245 minutes

Johanna Meier (A), Hanna Schwarz (B), René Kollo (C), Hermann Becht (D), Matti Salminen (E), Bayreuth Festival Chorus and Orchestra—Daniel Barenboim

Bayreuth Festival: Jean-Pierre Ponnelle (director)

Ponnelle sets this as a romance rather than the all-engulfing tragedy that Wagner envisioned. Act I is dominated by a diaphanous white sail through which Tristan can be seen, Act II by a gigantic tree with glittering leaves, and the Act III by a bare, split tree trunk reaching up to heaven. The lovers' voices (and indeed the vocal approach) are light, and the lovers themselves reasonably youthful, handsome, and agile. Tristan never really dies; he joins Isolde in a state of suspended animation. In a world without chairs the lovers spend a lot of time on their knees drawing strength from the earth or gazing into one another's eyes. (In Flagstad days they used to sit on a bench as if waiting for a bus.) It's nearly all quite lovely, and there are fewer tricks than one feared, although several events and moods are crudely given the official Ponnelle stamp of recognition. Isolde, always dressed in white, first appears crouched on the floor, weighed down—entrapped—by her enormous royal cloak. She also wears the notorious splinter from Morold's sword on a chain around her neck. At the moment the lov-

ers drink the potion all of the stage lights go out. As Isolde finally bows to Marke at the close of the first act, her huge white crown falls off: one assumes that this is an ironic comment and not an accident. In Act II, as she lights that torch for Tristan, half of those glittering leaves turn metallic orange. Some of these glosses are amusing; others are intrusive. The total visual effect is seductively pretty.

What's missing is the essential element of soul-wrenching tragedy. Johanna Meier is a fine-looking Isolde—womanly and passionate at once, she acts with magnetic intensity. She also handles her voice well throughout the four-and-a-half hours, but it lacks the vast range of colors necessary for a true Isolde. That was more obvious in the theater, where she didn't have the advantage of close-ups to supply what baleful thrust might be missing from the voice, but it is clear even here. René Kollo is a romantic Tristan and plays the role gracefully. The voice is sweet, agile, and firm on all but a few top notes, but he cannot quite deliver the full agony of Act III.

The others are fresh-voiced, resonant, and attractive, and Barenboim's conducting is persuasive throughout. The camera work and editing are also satisfying, though the battle in Act III is botched: it's not quite clear who kills Kurwenal. This is, then, a *Tristan* attractive to watch and pleasing to hear, and cast with intelligent, sensitive singers. Not quite the genuinely profound article, but touching in its own right and, in all, superior to any *Tristan* I can think of since the early seventies.

The 1983 Bayreuth is recommended as, in the main, enjoyably produced, pleasingly sung, and acted with intensity, even if it not quite the profound tragedy Wagner intended. The 1967 Osaka Festival performance, with Nilsson, Windgassen, and Hotter, will be required by some, but its technical and artistic limitations should be seriously noted.

LONDON GREEN

Die Meistersinger von Nürnberg (1868)

A: Eva (s); B: Magdalene (ms); C: Walther von Stolzing (t);
D: David (t); E: Hans Sachs (bar); F: Sixtus Beckmesser (bar);
G: Fritz Kothner (bs-bar); H: Veit Pogner (bs)

Wagner's comedy creates its own distinctive world, just as each of his other operas does. Nuremberg on this particular St. John's Eve and Day is filled with memorable and lovable (even when misguided) people, and a successful production must bring them to life as fully onstage as one imagines them when hearing or contemplating the score by itself. It's also a very long opera, which means both that it's an arduous piece of singing for several of the principals and that Wagner has taken the time to render everyone at length with full, varied characterizations. So if by some miracle all the principals are up to their roles vocally, they may still disappoint if they or the director renders them with fewer dramatic dimensions than Wagner has provided.

But even a less than ideal performance can leave one feeling glad to live in a world that contains such enriching art. What other opera predicates its entire denouement on the creation of a piece of music of such transcendent beauty that everyone will accept it as a masterwork—and then completely rises to the challenge?

1984 PHILIPS (VHS / LD)

(Stage / Studio Performance, Stereo, Color, Subtitled) 269 minutes

Mari Anne Häggander (A), Marga Schiml (B), Siegfried Jerusalem (C), Graham Clark (D), Bernd Weikl (E), Hermann Prey (F), Jef Vermeersch (G), Manfred Schenk (H), Bayreuth Festival Chorus and Orchestra—Horst Stein

Bayreuth Festival: Wolfgang Wagner (stage director), Brian Large (video director)

It takes some time to realize that this production (taped for Unitel without an audience present) is set in the nineteenth century. The locations in Nuremberg remain the same as ever, and the formal church wear does not send out immediate signals of anachronism. The apprentices and masters may raise some doubts, but Beckmesser's business suit is the first real tip-off. In fact the updated attire never becomes really obtrusive (at times it seems that Reinhard Heinrich's designs are aiming for a fanciful mixture of the two periods). It offers the advantage of making social distinctions clearer (and, for those bothered by such things, fitting the style of Wagner's music), and the disadvantage of putting well-known historical figures and practices into a time in which they don't fit. More serious is the general lack of imagination in Wolfgang Wagner's direction and scenic design. Some of the characterizations carry conviction, but the variation in completeness from one performer to another is so wide that one must surmise that personal input had a great deal to do with it. Of a true ensemble feeling, of scenes being played by a stageful of living people there is little.

Weikl has become known for his portrayal of

Hans Sachs, and he shows why here: though the voice is definitely a baritone, without the bass underpinnings valued in the classic interpretations of the role, it has warmth and color, and he portrays a relatively youthful and humorous shoemaker, devoid of wise-old-man stereotypes and the better for it. What he lacks is the resources to make the whole performance a memorable and soul-stirring one—which Sachs (participating in one scene and solo after another) can do. Weikl remains solid and sensible, avoiding clichés and vocal distress; it's ungrateful but essential to hope for more. For those who have long hoped to see Beckmesser sung beautifully and acted without buffoonery, Prey's performance is an example of "Be careful what you wish for, you might get it." His lyric baritone sings the role smoothly and easily, he doesn't exaggerate or spoof the character—but the old-style comedy gimmicks were at least effective in their way, whereas Prey doesn't offer anything in their place. His familiar genial presence comes off as a personal appearance, and there is really no characterization at all.

Jerusalem comports himself well, looks good (if about the same age as Sachs), and sings the role very musically, with rich flowing tone up to a pitch just short of the necessary climactic ones, which turn strained and juiceless. This adds up to a Walther better than many another, but still not quite enough to lift the spirit at the crucial moments. Häggender contributes some lovely singing and a positive stage presence devoid of false simpering. Clark, caught before his transformation into a piercing character tenor, renders David with a pleasant light voice and acts him expertly, without resorting to the traditional "young and perky" business. He is well matched by Schiml's delightful Magdalene, likewise solidly sung and not fussing about her character's age either way. Schenk sings and acts solidly and builds his big solo excitingly; the other Masters are quite strongly cast.

The Bayreuth orchestra sounds its expected distinguished self under Stein's baton. He doesn't ask for anything special in terms of pacing or balance, tending toward the traditional middle of the road; but there is nothing wrong with that, and he accompanies attentively and

well. The chorus, under the direction of Norbert Balatsch, sounds magnificent in its many important scenes, and its "Wach auf!" greeting to Sachs captures more of an authentic thrill than anything else in the performance.

c. 1990 KULTUR (VHS)

(Stage Performance, Stereo, Color, Subtitled) 277 minutes

Helena Döse (A), Rosemary Gunn (B), Paul Frey (C), Christopher Doig (D), Donald McIntyre (E), John Pringle (F), Robert Allman (G), Donald Shanks (H), Australian Opera Chorus, Elizabethan Opera Orchestra—Charles Mackerras

Australian Opera: Michael Hampe (stage director), Peter Butler and Virginia Lumsden (video directors)

While it would be wrong to call this production "provincial," it gives the effect of a willing and enthusiastic company stretched to its limit by the demands of this work. The singers execute the blocking, but mostly haven't filled out their stage time so as to seem continuously alive and involved; the scenery and costumes (respectively by John Gunter and Reinhard Heinrich) supply the minimum requirements and little more; the actions are those prescribed by the libretto; and the reactions are the standard operatic gestures. All this could be overlooked and enjoyed in the context of a live production making the most of local community resources, but is harder to accept for home viewing.

The three singers with international reputations show their experience in the way they handle the staging (likely incorporating ideas of their own from past productions) and create more complete characters. Döse has a bright full-bodied lyric voice apt for Eva, revealing a lack of focus only in the Quintet; her placid stage demeanor hampers her effectiveness, but she comes to life in the more extreme emotions of the workshop scene. Frey's knightly appearance and bearing serve him well, and his ideas about the music are lyrical and persuasive; unfortunately his voice keeps slipping into a whiny overbrightness when the musical demands mount. McIntyre creates a very complete and human Sachs, doing justice to both the character's nobility and his weakness. He looks just right for traditional conceptions of the character and has admirable ideas about how to shape the music and release its eloquence. Only the voice itself hampers him, refusing to expand or warm when it must.

Of the others, Pringle supplies an irritable and pedantic Beckmesser with both humorous and touching moments honestly earned, thoughtfully rendered, and adequately if unmemorably sung. The others make no special impression for good or ill, a quality they share with the chorus (a good enthusiastic group if falling short of unanimity at times). Hampe's direction attempts little beyond the basics of moving the characters around as required.

There is nevertheless an element of greatness in the performance, and it comes from Mackerras, whose conception of the score is exceptionally complete. He can be broad and expansive, but he also has his fine orchestra responding with snap and vivacity at appropriate times, and his skill at keeping the overall shape of scenes in line while doing justice to detail results in a flow that is irresistible. To hear him conduct this opera is to receive lessons in understanding its greatness.

———

Mackerras's conducting is a great temptation toward acquisition of the Kultur set. But little else in that production is on his level, and the Philips Bayreuth performance adds up as the more recommendable, though itself less than ideal.

JON ALAN CONRAD

DER RING DES NIBELUNGEN:
DAS RHEINGOLD (1869)

A: Fricka (ms); B: Erda (c); C: Loge (t); D: Mime (t); E: Wotan (bs-bar); F: Alberich (bs-bar); G: Fasolt (bs); H: Fafner (bs)

The musical challenges of Wagner's tetralogy are obvious and need no new listing. The additional task of making it all consistently coherent, believable, and communicative onstage is so daunting that one wonders how often it has been even relatively successfully met. One thinks first, perhaps, of the technical demands: Rhinemaidens swimming above Alberich's head, visible transitions from river depth to mountaintop to subterranean cavern, transformation of dwarf into dragon and toad, a navigable rainbow bridge. But just as challenging, and in the end more fundamental, is the task of drawing us into the story—making the characters and their goals clear, and making us see ourselves in all of them and care about the outcome. Many approaches to the challenge have been tried, and the first video to be considered amounts to a counterrevolution, with the first revolution and the original regime not available for viewing.

1980 PHILIPS (VHS / LD)

(Stage / Studio Performance, Stereo, Color, Subtitled) 164 minutes

Hanna Schwarz (A), Ortrun Wenkel (B), Heinz Zednik (C), Helmut Pampuch (D), Donald McIntyre (E), Hermann Becht (F), Matti Salminen (G), Fritz Hübner (H), Bayreuth Festival Orchestra—Pierre Boulez

Bayreuth Festival: Patrice Chéreau (stage director), Brian Large (video director)

This production changed *Ring* cycles at Bayreuth forever. Wieland Wagner's staging in the first season at Bayreuth under his artistic direction in 1951 had established a new possibility: not trying to emulate then standard realistic staging, nor following all of Wagner's stage directions literally, but creating a symbolic world in which the story's events could occur and insinuate themselves into the imagination. In 1965, another Wieland Wagner *Ring* went even further in probing psychological undercurrents through abstraction and suggestion.

It is in reference to this background that this *Ring*, new in 1976, was such a shock. Heavy, realistic scenery was once again to be seen (scenic design for the whole cycle by Richard Peduzzi, costumes by Jacques Schmidt), but it was not remotely what Wagner had specified in his score. Instead (so ran the rationale), audiences were invited to think about the meaning of the work in relation to Wagner's own time and the years since, to question the meaning and validity of each action, to ponder Wagner's own motives in writing the work. In a way, the production became a kind of lecture or symposium, questioning the operas even while performing them. The aesthetic debates raised by such a mode of presentation—including whether it falls within what has previously been thought of as "performance" as opposed to commentary—are with us still, and not just for the *Ring*.

So the first scene gives us the Rhine, all right, and the Rhinemaidens are there to tempt and tease passers-by—but the river is industrialized, with a hydraulic dam (a gate swings down to show the gold), and the maidens are Victorian-era tarts. When the dam revolves to transport us to Scene 2, Valhalla is a solid facade right at the back of the stage, just beyond a scrim and trench, and the gods wear clothes of Wagner's era (Wotan himself being explicitly identified with Wagner). Other devices that were to appear more and more in stagings of the *Ring* and other operas are the addition of silent onlookers and the arrival of characters well before their scripted entrances: a crowd of Nibelungs are onstage from the start of Scene 3 (the latter partly for a practical purpose—to facilitate Alberich's magical disappearance), and Wotan's two brothers-in-law show up long before they have anything to say. The Nibelungs, in a welcome novelty, are adult laborers, not children, and the giants are visibly and rather convincingly gigantic. There is plenty of smoke, or a stage substitute, but no attempt at a rainbow. And the closing moment is the sort of nonidea that's become a cliché of contemporary theater: the disruptive character—Loge in this case—pulling the curtain closed at the end, leering at us in complicity as if to say that he and the others are just like us.

Boulez secures balance, transparency, and timbral subtlety in masterful fashion, to a great extent disregarding traditional textural ideas in the work in favor of making his own decisions from the score. As he seems uninterested in any musical shaping that might have only a dramatic justification, the singers are left to fend for themselves, and unfortunately they're not a vocally overwhelming lot. McIntyre has an authority of carriage and movement that does not carry over into his labored and inexpressive singing. Becht applies a decent character baritone with middling success to the considerable demands of Alberich and is required to emote at the camera embarrassingly after his curse.

Zednik acts a convincing Loge, well-sung in the character-tenor vein, his characterization aided by the nonmythological costuming. Schwarz brings regality, if insufficient vocal "oomph," to Fricka, and Wenkel does well to maintain dignity as Erda while singing under a white tablecloth. The others fade from memory quickly, both vocally and histrionically.

1981 DEUTSCHE GRAMMOPHON (LD)

(Film, Stereo, Color, Not Subtitled) 145 minutes

Brigitte Fassbaender (A), Birgit Finnilä (B), Peter Schreier (C), Gerhard Stolze (D), Thomas Stewart (E), Zoltán Kélémen (F), Gerd Nienstedt / Karl Ridderbusch (G), Louis Hendrikx (H), Berlin Philharmonic Orchestra—Herbert von Karajan

Herbert von Karajan (director)

This film comes with very little information. Some of the designs bear a vague resemblance to Karajan's well-known cycle seen at Salzburg and then at the Met (designed by Günther Schneider-Siemssen), but they are uncredited. And although subtitles are promised in the packaging, none are present. The film itself is an odd mixture, beginning with an attempt at filming the first scene literally underwater. Unfortunately, whether due to limitations of technology or budget, the results resemble a home movie made in a giant aquarium; what with the murk, lip-synching that is half-hearted when it is even attempted, and an Alberich who is rarely in the same shot as the Rhinemaidens (fishlike, bare-breasted creatures with voices supplied by Eva Randova, Edda Moser, and Liselotte Rebmann—a listing that is surely upside-down), the scene doesn't register at all.

The second and fourth scenes, by contrast, are almost semi-staged oratorio, soloists isolated (very infrequently do we see as many as two or three at a time) in a very television-studio sort of mountaintop set (irregular rocky floor against a plain sky background). At each vocal entrance, the camera cuts to the new singer, generally with no indication of spatial relationships among the protagonists, or how newcomers arrived on the scene (at such moments it's easy to believe that the crediting of the film's direction to Karajan is literally accurate, so innocent is it of basic film syntax). Occasionally a camera tracks a character's movement, as with Loge's entrance (though again we don't see how he arrived). The only occasions when film techniques are used to substantial advantage are the trips to and from Nibelheim, when we move through rock strata with periodic glimpses of activity in nearby caverns, just as score and libretto suggest. But other moments when freedom from stage constraints should allow an advantage misfire: the aging of the gods is as ever a matter of mist rolling in, Valhalla is reminiscent of an out-of-focus photograph of Superman's Fortress of Solitude, and there's no crossing of the rainbow bridge. Alberich's transformations are handled with some ingenuity (the dragon has a human face) but little real surprise; perhaps we have been spoiled by movie magic of the "morphing" sort since this was made.

The gods have the best chance to make individual impressions, given the stand-and-sing handling of their scenes. Stewart and Fassbaender both sound splendidly authoritative and comport themselves with dignity. Schreier comes across best of all, the close-ups flattering his casual and ironic interpretation. Jeannine Altmeyer is suitably blonde and statuesque as Freia, though nearly as tall as the giants who menace but don't really pursue her. Kélémen, once past the obstacles put in his way in the first scene, is a potent and subtle actor and singer of Alberich, and Stolze makes a gripping Mime (the hyperactivity that so disfigures his audio recordings of the *Siegfried* Mime are easier to take as part of the total dramatic package). Erda is adequately voiced by Finnilä, but the character's materialization as a transparent head filling the screen reduces impact to a minimum.

Probably most *Ring* fans have dreamed of a cinematic version that would, just once, forget stage necessities and dazzle with visual illusion, but this effort isn't it.

1990 DEUTSCHE GRAMMOPHON (VHS / LD)

(Stage Performance, Stereo, Color, Subtitled)
163 minutes

Christa Ludwig (A), Birgitta Svendén (B), Siegfried Jerusalem (C), Heinz Zednik (D), James Morris (E), Ekkehard Wlaschiha (F), Jan-Hendrik Rootering (G), Matti Salminen (H), Metropolitan Opera Orchestra—James Levine

Metropolitan Opera: Otto Schenk (stage director), Brian Large (video director)

The Metropolitan Opera *Ring*, sets designed by Günther Schneider-Siemssen, costumes by Rolf Langenfass, is part of a series of Wagnerian productions undertaken there that attempt to restore a Romantic realism congruent with the music, while using modern stage techniques. The result reveals one reason why this is so seldom attempted these days: as painted flats and bare floors are no longer routinely accepted as representations of nature, everything has to be built in three dimensions, including a new stage surface for each scene. In other words, the whole operation is incredibly expensive. For those who have dreamed of seeing the saga look like their visions of mythology, the results may be worth it. Not all the effects come off (aside from the fact that Gil Wechsler's lighting had to be adjusted for the cameras, and some effects thus compromised): despite the provision of a bilevel Rhine floor, the Rhinemaidens are just running around waving their veils, not swimming, and there's no obvious reason why Alberich can't reach them. But the mountaintop prospect with Valhalla in the distance is undeniably stirring, it acquires a visible if not navigable rainbow bridge, and the production doesn't get in the way of whatever the performers have to offer.

This can be considerable in vocal terms, though they have not been united in any particular interpretation of the work. This has its good side (no limiting distortion leaving out whole sides of the piece) as well as bad (no moments that strike home with personal relevance). Much of the time, the performers are simply neutral dramatically, forming the right general picture but without the specific intent and impact of the two Bayreuth productions.

Morris makes a most impressive Wotan, the role sitting ideally on his mellow high bass, his rendition of the music eloquent and stirring. Of any of the singing in all these *Rheingolds*, his comes the closest to classic stature. Also first-rate are Mari-Anne Häggander's fresh, youthful Freia; Wlaschiha's sinister, bitingly vocalized Alberich; and Zednik's always characterful and musical Mime. Jerusalem, reptilian in costume, has more voice for Loge than the secondary tenors generally alloted to the role, along with some command of behavioral subtlety; if not outstanding in either respect, he is more than adequate at both, and does justice to his role. Ludwig, nearing the end of her stage career, remains a major artist; she looks regal and for the most part sounds it. The giants are a strong pair, singing beautifully as well as ruggedly. The Rhinemaidens (Kaaren Erickson, Diane Kesling, Meredith Parsons) make a harmonious and convincing trio. Levine provides a spacious framework that makes much of motivic unfoldings and musical developments and allows the orchestra to sound the magnificent group it is.

1991 TELDEC (VHS / LD)

(Stage / Studio Performance, Stereo, Color, Subtitled) 153 minutes

Linda Finnie (A), Birgitta Svendén (B), Graham Clark (C), Helmut Pampuch (D), John Tomlinson (E), Günter von Kannen (F), Matthias Hölle (G), Philip Kang (H), Bayreuth Festival Orchestra—Daniel Barenboim

Bayreuth Festival: Harry Kupfer (stage director), Horant H. Hohlfeld (video director)

This production was first seen at Bayreuth in 1988, and was videotaped for Unitel (without an audience) toward the end of its five-summer run. Kupfer's direction is of three alternating kinds. Most frequent, fortunately, is his best side: unusually insightful handling of character and interaction, rendered with remarkably consistent success by a cast who all seem to blossom as actors under his tutelage. (And, be it said, captured in by far the best video direction of the three *Rings*, with a reasonably complete stage picture and less reliance on close-ups.) And then at unexpected moments things will go overboard in one of two directions: becoming either so inexplicably symbolic as to elicit only bewilderment, or so extreme in terms of realistic detail as to be off-key with the rest of the production (this is often a scenic matter—stage designs are by Hans Schavernoch, costumes by Reinhard Heinrich—but surely at the director's behest). *Rheingold* has examples of all three. The puzzling side comes at the very start, with crowds of people clustered on the vast stage, drifting away as the prelude begins (possibly to suggest that the cycle does indeed represent a historical cycle: its events happen again and again in the course of human history). Then the prelude starts, green lasers create a tunnel leading from the proscenium back to a distant vanishing point, and grotesque Rhinemaidens dive in and out of the glowing "floor" thus created.

Some of Kupfer's ideas create witty and workable analogues: Valhalla is a plexiglass skyscraper (it will light up in rainbow neon at the end), and the whole godly family is onstage from the start of Scene 2, in traveling clothes and carrying suitcases as they prepare to move into their new home. But the giants are another unworkably literal idea: huge conical constructions with a tiny human head sticking out of the top, and floppy arms that are clearly no threat (Freia has to run straight into them to be captured).

The best side of Kupfer's direction comes to the fore in this opera mostly in the clear delineation of the gods as a basically loving and close family even during this stressful day. The most impressive vocal elements are Von Kannen's dark and authoritative Alberich, Kurt Schreibmeyer's elegant Froh, and Finnie's aptly matronly and concerned Fricka. Tomlinson has plenty of sound without much elegance or real shaping of the line; he's also an involving actor, good at both physical activity and stillness. Clark's incisive character tenor, reminiscent of the Stolze approach, combines with refined acting skills to create a sardonically detached Loge.

Svendén, popping up at the very front of the stage, makes a vocally firm if young-sounding Erda (as she did for Levine). Pampuch, as on Philips relegated to only the Mime while the tenor who will take over in *Siegfried* does Loge, does a vivid piece of acting—again, a detailed delineation of his nature is one of the strengths of this production. The giants are handicapped by their costuming and make little vocal effect. Barenboim's conducting does not run to extremes of speed or dynamics; he's moderate in his choices, inclined to a dark weightiness of texture but willing to charge ahead energetically when appropriate, and with the advantage of an excellent orchestra. But then all the video *Rings* are fortunate orchestrally.

―――――――――

1981 DG can be left out of consideration except for those who must have everything Karajan ever did. 1990 DG offers the best matching of visual evocation to aural, and overall the most distinguished singing. Philips and Teldec have more going on dramatically, though in both cases within a questionable overall concept; the latter comes off better in this respect.

JON ALAN CONRAD

DIE WALKÜRE (1870)

A: Brünnhilde (s); B: Sieglinde (s); C: Fricka (ms); D: Siegmund (t);
E: Wotan (bs-bar); F: Hunding (bs)

After the stageful of nearly equal leading roles in *Das Rheingold, Die Walküre* makes rather different demands: scenes predominantly for two or occasionally three characters, the sparseness relieved only just before and after the second intermission. For long stretches the action is interior, concentrating on momentous changes in thought and feeling. A performance that does justice to the work will involve its audience in just such processes and will therefore depend less on a striking production concept than on vivid realization of character development and interaction. As a central component of such dramatic progress, great singing becomes even more essential than in *Das Rheingold*.

1980 PHILIPS (VHS / LD)

(Stage / Studio Performance, Stereo, Color, Subtitled) 216 minutes

Gwyneth Jones (A), Jeannine Altmeyer (B), Hanna Schwarz (C), Peter Hofmann (D), Donald McIntyre (E), Matti Salminen (F), Bayreuth Festival Orchestra—Pierre Boulez

Bayreuth Festival: Patrice Chéreau (stage director), Brian Large (video director)

Die Walküre's dramatic focus on a small number of characters who live in isolation can (at least initially) make specifics of time and place in a particular production relatively invisible, and so it happens in the continuation of

Chéreau's cycle. Sieglinde in a nineteenth-century housedress is not so very different from a woman of timeless legend, and the same goes for Siegmund in his outlaw tatters. More novel is Chéreau's decision to have Hunding accompanied at all times by a band of henchmen; as so often happens with such unscripted onlookers, the other character's failure to acknowledge their existence becomes distracting enough to outweigh any benefit of such a choice (presumably, the depiction of Hunding's boorishness and power). Greater surprises are to come, with the first part of Act II taking place in a room that contains a mirror and a Foucault's pendulum (for Wotan to stop at "Das Ende!"). The scene changes to something more conventional for the Wälsungs' entrance; then Act III brings another surprise, the mountaintop including a ruined shell of some small building.

The personal relationships among the characters who inhabit these scenes are rendered very specifically, with Wotan especially human and touching in his pain and anger. Complete realization of the characters is limited by the lack of vocal means to convey the singers' choices. Hofmann and Altmeyer both have colorful, substantial instruments under limited control: they can sing out with some effectiveness but are under duress when it comes to controlling a gentle lyric line; in company with their striking visual qualities and willing, if not refined, histrionic involvement, this makes for an appealing but incomplete Wälsung pair. Both are at their best with the passionate requirements of their respective final scenes.

McIntyre conveys a strikingly varied and subtle visual image of Wotan, and his musical ideas are interesting too; but the dry and unvaried voice limits his success. The same might be said of Schwarz, with a fine voice a couple of degrees too light for Fricka; her dramatic intentions are so clear and telling that she puts her scene across anyway. Salminen has the biggest and most aptly cast voice in the production; puzzlingly, his overall performance is not particularly memorable—perhaps because he must share all his stage time with his tribal colleagues. Finally, there is Jones, a magnetic stage presence and an exceptionally insightful musician, with a voice that a few years before had been of beautiful quality but was much deteriorated by the time of this taping. With her difficulty in focusing and timing her pitches, her whole aural performance becomes a constant balancing act between what she wants to do and what she is able to do, and it is often hard to listen to. Her performance achieves some gripping moments when the musical demands are modest or momentarily congenial, or when she is not singing at all; certainly she makes a more positive impression than when merely heard, on the separately released sound track of the cycle.

1989 DEUTSCHE GRAMMOPHON (VHS / LD)

(Stage Performance, Stereo, Color, Subtitled) 244 minutes

Hildegard Behrens (A), Jessye Norman (B), Christa Ludwig (C), Gary Lakes (D), James Morris (E), Kurt Moll (F), Metropolitan Opera Orchestra—James Levine

Metropolitan Opera: Otto Schenk (stage director), Brian Large (video director)

This performance happens to reunite the cast of Levine's studio recording, and it maintains a higher average of vocal sumptuousness than the other *Walküre* videos. The visual aspect is aptly primeval though not really distinguished (*Rheingold* and *Siegfried* are the best achievements of this cycle in terms of overall design).

Hunding's house, for instance, is merely a plain log cabin, defensible in mundane terms but helpful neither to the staging nor to the imagination.

Norman and Lakes are well matched in the sense that both deliver stately, tonally attractive, musically well-shaped performances that might just as well be oratorio solos. One respects the quality of their work while missing the kind of dramatic excitement generated on the other videos. Moll, though, is the real thing: a dark bass who has definite ideas about Hunding—a limited but not intentionally evil man of his time who considers himself the wronged party in these dealings—and can convey them though both his acting and the refined flow of his singing. Ludwig's veteran status shows in a widened vibrato and traces of shrillness; but she is still a whole-hearted and noble artist, and even if others have brought more delicacy to the part and delineated its progress with more detail, hers is a memorable Fricka.

Morris's possession of the vocal goods for Wotan again puts him in a class of his own in the video cycles; he could communicate a more specific comprehension in great solo opportunities like his Act II monologue, but the roomy voice encompasses the music so beautifully and luxuriantly that there's no point complaining. Behrens has a challenge fitting her medium-sized and lyrically inclined voice to Brünnhilde's music. In several passages that lie congenially for her, she succeeds; elsewhere there is compromise of one sort or another. A committed and energetic actress, she manages to make this mixed vocal success work in the context of her whole performance. Levine's conducting sounds determined to be slow, whatever the needs of his cast. His orchestra is a superb one, and many striking orchestral moments result, but the overall impression is neither unified nor convincing.

1991 TELDEC (VHS / LD)

(Stage / Studio Performance, Stereo, Color, Subtitled) 238 minutes

Anne Evans (A), Nadine Secunde (B), Linda Finnie (C), Poul Elming (D), John Tomlinson

(E), Matthias Hölle (F), Bayreuth Festival Orchestra—Daniel Barenboim

Bayreuth Festival: Harry Kupfer (stage director), Horant H. Hohlfeld (video director)

The basic set for the Kupfer *Ring*, a dirt road leading off into infinity in a black void, becomes more visible in this installment, being used almost unadorned in Acts II and III. It is also seen at the very start, the prelude serving to accompany Siegmund's journey through the storm; then the front of the stage tilts up and he swings down through a hole (around a bulbous metallic tree) to find himself in a chrome-and-black dining room. He and Sieglinde feel their mutual attraction strongly from the start, and all three actors in this act sense the mysterious connection, without yet knowing what to make of it. The pair return to the outdoors for their love scene, staged most beautifully and evocatively as they luxuriate in their surroundings and the spring night.

In Act II as well, the prelude is staged, with exceptional success and relevance to musical progress: the sleeping lovers awaken and flee fearfully; Wotan runs in, thrilled with his success; and Brünnhilde joins him for some father-daughter sparring. "Hojotoho," it turns out is what she sings while pinning him to the ground in their regular wrestling matches. Seldom has this scene seemed so natural or touching (and few *Ring* productions have demanded so much active physicality from its participants). Wotan's ensuing argument with Fricka carries an unusually strong sense that they once loved each other, and on some level still do. Such interactions are so movingly right in this production, again and again, that it comes as a shock when Kupfer then perpetrates his Ride of the Valkyries, with clusters of ghostly souls sliding around the stage while the warrior maidens run down a giant fire escape that unfolds from the sky. Other oddities emerge in the scene between father and daughter. When Wotan announces "Das Ende!" a triangular chasm suddenly appears, for no apparent reason (Siegmund will later fight and die there). And the final scene between the two, begun quietly and grippingly

(they sit on the ground, facing away from each other) is built with fine psychological insight; but at the moment of musical climax they forget about interaction and throw themselves face down on the ground, side by side. A farewell to Earth?—only Kupfer knows. The final image, Brünnhilde surrounded by a red laser cube, is by contrast an impressive and convincing rethinking of the wall-of-fire idea in terms of this production.

Tomlinson's strong middle and rough top remain as before, likewise his histrionic and athletic confidence; vocally, he impresses most in the detailed way he lives his Act II monologue, least in his unlyrical farewell (where Barenboim's generally solid conducting also is at its weakest, with no real cantabile surge). Poul Elming makes an appealing first impression as Siegmund but accumulates demerits as he proceeds; his voice sounds seriously strained by the writing, and his acting turns out to be of the bug-eyed nostril-flaring variety. Secunde's large, hauntingly colored soprano, marginally off its best form, is used most musically, and she is also a subtle and responsive actress. Hölle is a real presence, menacing and black-toned, as Hunding. Finnie at first sounds like an underpowered oratorio-style alto, but her voice frees up as the scene proceeds and in the end rings out sufficiently to support her well-projected characterization of Fricka as a wife with legitimate grievances. Evans displays a bright, well-schooled soprano that does not sound more than lyric in weight; but like others who have learned their Wagner with Reginald Goodall at the English National Opera, she sustains her music with concentration and lyricism, never forcing, and in the end convinces as a valid Brünnhilde who matches her colleagues in dramatic understanding and physical prowess.

One might turn to DG for Morris or the general visual conception. But the production that makes the human drama real and involving is Teldec.

JON ALAN CONRAD

RICHARD WAGNER

SIEGFRIED (1876)

A: Brünnhilde (s); B: Erda (c); C: Siegfried (t); D: Mime (t);
E: Wanderer (bs-bar); F: Alberich (bs-bar)

When it comes to *Siegfried*, with all respect to the many important participants in a successful performance, it really comes down to one role. If the Siegfried of the performance is having difficulty, the audience is in for a difficult time as well. In addition, one hopes for a tenor who will not too hopelessly contradict visually the image of youthful inexperience so essential to the story, and who can lead us toward the dramatic meaning of his character's progress. Then there *are* the other characters, after all. Brünnhilde, for all that her role encompasses only one scene, has an exposed and delicate challenge, needing large-scale singing that is lyrical in character and centered higher than in her other two operas. The conductor has to maintain continuity and sense through some very long scenes for only two characters, which do not build to the sort of lyrical setpieces that can help "sell" the similar scenes in *Die Walküre*. If all these and other improbabilities are fulfilled, the rewards of a successful *Siegfried* performance can be commensurately great, but the challenge is a real one.

1980 PHILIPS (VHS / LD)

(Stage / Studio Performance, Stereo, Color, Subtitled) 225 minutes

Gwyneth Jones (A), Ortrun Wenkel (B), Manfred Jung (C), Heinz Zednik (D), Donald McIntyre (E), Hermann Becht (F), Bayreuth Festival Orchestra—Pierre Boulez

Bayreuth Festival: Patrice Chéreau (stage director), Brian Large (video director)

This is the opera where Chéreau starts creating a fundamentally different story from the one Wagner thought he was telling. In Wagner's terms, Wotan, having failed to create a "free hero" with Siegmund, is succeeding with Siegfried by staying out of his life and doing nothing to help him. For Chéreau, Wotan is still manipulating and lying. Having played his riddle game with Mime, he leaves an automatic forge as a farewell gift. The contraption scares Mime (nicely motivating his "fear" music at this point) and fascinates Siegfried—though they never mention it to each other, having no text for the purpose—and it does the job of forging the sword while Siegfried sings his song. (This leaves the notated hammer sounds to be supplied by a percussionist.) In the forest, Siegfried finds the forest bird (a real one) in a cage, and he releases it to show him the way to Brünnhilde. The dragon is a detailed model on wheels, laughable rather than impressive or scary. (When dying, he becomes Fafner again—an idea that has become almost traditional in recent stagings.) All through, then, Siegfried is still Wotan / Wagner's puppet, and I'm not sure how he nevertheless breaks the old man's spear as the plot requires he must.

Boulez's light, airy conducting seems more to

the point here than in the earlier segments, and more attuned with what his singers can do. Zednik is certainly a major-league Mime, enacting Chéreau's neurotic, slimy take on the character with skill and specificity, and singing the role honestly with his characterful if unlovely voice. Siegfried himself sounds more a Mime voice (indeed he undertook that role in the 1994 Bayreuth production). Not despicable or totally hopeless, Jung is still sorely lacking in tonal fiber and variety for such a long and demanding role. Unfortunately, his mediocre vocalism is not balanced by any appeal on the visual or histrionic front; even after considerable experience in the production, he looks like an unrehearsed understudy unable to convey any intention convincingly. McIntyre sounds more at ease with the Wanderer than the earlier Wotans, though still not truly beautiful or lyrical; he and Zednik make their riddle scene the most successfully realized passage in the opera, playing a real dramatic interchange. As Alberich and Erda, Becht and Wenkel are more striking visually than aurally: he dressed almost identically to the Wanderer and thus underlining the parallel between them; she again wrapped in a shroud, which eventually pulls away to reveal her decrepit and bald. Jones is a trial from the start, with all sorts of control troubles, though she has impressive individual moments along the way. Her beauty, magnetism, and intensity retrieve part of the deficiency, but only part, and she and Jung serve up a painful final half-hour.

1990 DEUTSCHE GRAMMOPHON (VHS / LD)

(Stage Performance, Stereo, Color, Subtitled) 253 minutes

Hildegard Behrens (A), Birgitta Svendén (B), Siegfried Jerusalem (C), Heinz Zednik (D), James Morris (E), Ekkehard Wlaschiha (F), Metropolitan Opera Orchestra—James Levine

Metropolitan Opera: Otto Schenk (stage director), Brian Large (video director)

Siegfried Jerusalem first undertook his heroic namesake in the Kupfer production at Bayreuth, which he had not yet committed to video

at the time he joined the Met production captured here. Very likely he carried over some of his Bayreuth groundwork here, for though Siegfried seems conceived as a conventionally "sympathetic" hero-figure in the Schenk production, Jerusalem impresses as continuously alert and alive in the part. It is easy to hear that his voice (always a lyric tenor with some juice in the middle and a chancy top) is not the ideal instrument for Siegfried, and that it can turn tight under the pressures of the role, but given the rarity of acceptable Siegfrieds we can be grateful that a video production preserves one who looks the part, is a strong musician with a good (if not the right) voice, and manages to maintain his poise and keep us on his side throughout. Zednik plays a good Mime opposite him, singing well and not going overboard on shtick; he's a less specific and controversial figure here than with Chéreau, but well matched to this production. Morris's voluminous, lyrical Wanderer adds substantially to the tonal pleasures of the performance.

So does Behrens when she wakes up on the mountaintop. She can adapt her less-than-heroic voice to some of the requirements here—the important lyrical passages have some balance and beauty, and she gets going effectively on some of the heavier stretches when they sit moderately high. For the rest, she manages with intelligence, and it's unfortunate that the video cameras disclose so faithfully the strain that she almost hides aurally but can't quite disguise visually.

Wlaschiha and Svendén remain strong supporting presences, he almost unexceptionable, she tonally appealing if lightweight—and visually, an unusually sexy earth goddess. Matti Salminen gets off some good roars as Fafner (more of an octopus than a "Wurm" in this conception), and Dawn Upshaw's clear soprano is well cast as the Forest Bird. Levine is always a major musician leading a great orchestra, but his commitment to a monumental broadness sometimes causes him to miss some of the simple obvious effects that are equally important, and he could do more to help his less-than-heroically endowed leading couple than he does.

Schneider-Siemssen and Langenfass's

designs are here among their most evocative in the cycle, with apt glimpses of endless primeval forest, a lowering mountain gorge for the crucial intergenerational confrontation, and a mountaintop from which one could almost touch the sky. Schenk's virtues are largely those of restraint and good sense rather than the encouragement of compelling behavior. But as Zednik, Jerusalem, and Behrens generate some personal life in their scenes, much of the opera goes well. The considerable effect of the final duet is much aided by the scenic realization (including Gil Wechsler's lighting, however modified for the camera), progressing from dawn to a blazing noon.

1992 TELDEC (VHS / LD)

(Studio / Stage Production, Stereo, Color, Subtitled) 243 minutes

Anne Evans (A), Birgitta Svendén (B), Siegfried Jerusalem (C), Graham Clark (D), John Tomlinson (E), Günter von Kannen (F), Bayreuth Festival Orchestra—Daniel Barenboim

Bayreuth Festival: Harry Kupfer (stage director), Horant H. Hohlfeld (video director)

Kupfer again shows a highly musical ear in his staging of music designed as preludes; the beginning of the opera suspensefully presents the three-way plotting and spying of Mime, Alberich, and Wotan as the impetus for Mime's opening lines. Mime has raised Siegfried in a half-buried metal tube with a furnace (this opera presents most clearly of all the cycle's production premise of a future world built on the ruins of our own), and Fafner lurks in the ruins of an underground structure. By contrast, the "eternal road" ("History Street," as the accompanying essays would have it) looms unadorned in Act III, and the surrounding black void belies Brünnhilde's salute to sun and sky. Act II encompasses a dubious piece of revisionism: the bird is operated and controlled by Wotan, who is thus lying whenever he claims that Siegfried is a free agent.

The personalities and relationship of Mime and Siegfried are presented with unusual com-

pleteness and detail: even Mime's worst actions are seen to emerge from his omnipresent fear and self-loathing, and Siegfried, though physically adult, is emotionally a child—one who still turns to his foster-father Mime for comfort at times despite his impatience with him. The effect is aided by Clark's acting skill, his voice used as musically as its unvaried metallic quality will allow. Alberich disappoints a bit, for though vocally equal to the part Von Kannen plays him as a broad villain rather than a comparably conflicted, complex individual. Philip Kang's light bass, not down to the descents required of him, hurts the impact of Fafner's scenes.

Jerusalem here delivers the most satisfying of his three preserved Siegfrieds (the other two being DG video and EMI audio); the voice is of course not of heroic proportions, but it is pitched compatibly with the role's demands, and he surmounts the big moments with minimal strain. Further, his experience in this production (the one for which he first assumed the role) results in a convincing visual portrayal as well, even when one disagrees with some of the directorial decisions. Evans finds this Brünnhilde a reasonable match for her likewise nonheroic voice, and the two overcome their gloomy surroundings in the finale to rather uplifting effect. Tomlinson's task, too, is eased by the Wanderer's lower tessitura, and if his singing is mostly loud and unsubtle, he delivers the basics vocally and complements them with the light and shade of his characterization. Barenboim's leadership is as before, solid and not tending to extremes, firmly drawn and very well played.

––––––––––––––

There is no true Siegfried among these presentations, but certainly Jerusalem takes a better shot at it than Jung. With Teldec / Barenboim he presents a more complete character (as do his colleagues) and is in better voice; with DG / Levine he has more evocative visual surroundings.

JON ALAN CONRAD

RICHARD WAGNER

GÖTTERDÄMMERUNG (1876)

A: Brünnhilde (s); B: Gutrune (s); C: Waltraute (c); D: Siegfried (t)
E: Gunther (bar); F: Alberich (bs-bar); G: Hagen (bs)

In *Götterdämmerung*, the singing demands become still more acute than in *Siegfried*. They are more spread out among a sizable cast, less concentrated in a single role, and yet even more insistent on heroic timbre and projection (tenors and sopranos able to survive the *Siegfried* roles have been known to meet their match with these). Shorter parts like Waltraute and the Norns are less obviously arduous, yet voices that can "manage" them may still lack the command and variety to do them justice, leaving the audience with an exceedingly boring half hour for each of these crucial scenes. And then, even if all the vocal and musical demands are approximated, there is still the challenge of making the performance work as a whole: a new set of crucial characters introduced just as the cycle is drawing toward a close, a shift in musical style (due to Wagner's interruption of composition between Acts II and III of *Siegfried*), and a finale that can seem unmotivated, however impressive, unless particular care is taken in production.

One *Götterdämmerung* video, though containing only a few scenes and not stemming from a stage performance, must be mentioned: "The Golden Ring," a 1965 BBC film (London, black-and-white, narrated and directed by Humphrey Burton) documenting the recording sessions for Georg Solti's recording of the opera. Along with interviews and behind-the-scenes material, the film offers the chance to see Dietrich Fischer-Dieskau, Gottlob Frick, Wolfgang Windgassen, and particularly Birgit Nilsson in substantial scenes that confirm their stature in this music—singing on a level beyond almost anything to be encountered in these complete videos.

1979 PHILIPS (VHS / LD)

(Stage / Studio Performance, Stereo, Color, Subtitled) 250 minutes

Gwyneth Jones (A), Jeannine Altmeyer (B), Gwendolyn Killebrew (C), Manfred Jung (D), Franz Mazura (E), Hermann Becht (F), Fritz Hübner (G), Bayreuth Festival Chorus and Orchestra—Pierre Boulez

Bayreuth Festival: Patrice Chéreau (stage director), Brian Large (video director)

Like some *Ring* directors, Chéreau seems to have focused on the possibility to critique "civilization" in *Götterdämmerung*. The Gibichungs live in an elegant palace on the waterfront, spending their days in stylish lounge outfits (Hunding, as the bastard half-brother, spends his time in a shabby suit, shirt unbuttoned at the neck). Siegfried gets more and more up-to-date clothes in each successive scene, getting married in a tuxedo. Gunther himself is subject to revisionism: not the passive youngster of tradition but a cowardly and aging predator who buys power over others and who displays his warrior bride as a wounded trophy. This Gutrune, if not as actively culpable as her brother, is certainly knowing enough to understand the cost of her conquest of her own hero-spouse.

As with Siegfried's forging scene, Chéreau chooses to eliminate a favorite stage effect of Wagner's, the onstage playing of an instrument: Hagen makes no pretense of playing any kind of horn when he summons the vassals, and the prescribed notes are simply heard while he sings. The Rhinemaidens reappear on their dam, it and they now dried up; Siegfried has one of his more endearing moments as he sings to them from the bridge above, dangling his feet over the edge like a schoolboy. The funeral march interlude is a tribute procession in which the whole chorus walks by in front of a forecurtain, and Gutrune addresses her nightmare soliloquy to the crowd as it disperses. At the end, the same throng, adopting a favorite bit of twentieth-century dramaturgy, turns to stare accusingly at the audience.

This taping took place a year before the others in this *Ring*, and it seems to have caught Jones in significantly better voice: the wobble is less omnipresent, and she occasionally has some choice in her vocal effects and can express some of her vocal characterization voluntarily. Much of the time, her assured command of the stage puts her in a class of her own in this cast, and she can generate involvement that galvanizes a whole scene—until a strenuous vocal passage takes her out of her comfort zone, which happens more and more often at the ends of the latter two acts. Jung is unfortunately not similarly helped by being captured at an earlier date, jumping beats and unvaried of expression. Becht and Hübner are doing the best they can with unremarkable instruments. Mazura's assured stage command stands him in good stead for the particular Gunther required of him, and Altmeyer, though no actress, has more voice and physical presence than Gutrune normally does; these two do a good deal to keep their long scenes eventful. The most noteworthy member of the cast, though, is Killebrew: a voice full of color and mystery, and a filled-out conception of Waltraute's crucial scene that makes it a high point of this performance.

Boulez seems to be conducting his own orchestral tone poem alongside this highly uneven vocal parade. There are plenty of intricate textural overlays for him to unravel here, as well as sparkling nature music and many challenges of tuning and ensemble to conquer. But it seems to have little to do with the human drama we're being asked to involve ourselves with. The video production has some odd touches: for scene changes, the stage recedes in the distance until it's a tiny square, the image changes almost undetectably, then swells gradually back to fill the screen.

1990 DEUTSCHE GRAMMOPHON (VHS / LD)

(Stage Performance, Stereo, Color, Subtitled) 281 minutes

Hildegard Behrens (A), Hanna Lisowska (B), Christa Ludwig (C), Siegfried Jerusalem (D), Anthony Raffell (E), Ekkehard Wlaschiha (F), Matti Salminen (G), Metropolitan Opera Chorus and Orchestra—James Levine

Metropolitan Opera: Otto Schenk (stage director), Brian Large (video director)

Last things first: the final cataclysm is just about perfect here (though the video framing and editing doesn't quite do justice to its seamlessness in the theater). The Gibichung hall collapses, the Rhine rises to reveal the Rhinemaidens playing with the gold and drowning Hagen, it recedes again to show Valhalla in flames, rises once more to engulf it, and finally subsides to show us a new generation waiting to start a promising new world. All just as Wagner wanted, as his music suggests, and as we otherwise never see it. Such an achievement more than makes up for some indifferently realized sections earlier on, with greater reliance on painted backdrops than earlier in the cycle, and unevocative costuming for the Gibichungs. There are some valuable ideas too: the angled presentation of the Gibichung Hall exterior, for instance, is a helpful solution to the problems of placing the action of Act II. In general, more imagination seems to have gone into the design than into the behavior that goes on within it. Behrens is the most successful at generating character on her own, Jerusalem is certainly willing, and Ludwig has her considerable authority to see her through her scene; but the others are sometimes left hanging, trying to act "natural" without instincts or training to tell them how.

Levine's pacing is problematic here, too, striving for a monumental broadness such as other conductors have achieved, without the constant eventfulness along the way to enliven and justify it. Behrens shows herself a skillful vocal tactician, using her modest means to their maximum effect and finding certain scenes (the Immolation among them, fortunately) workable in their particular demands; but she clearly is stretched beyond the bounds of comfort or good sense by what is required of her in other sections. Jerusalem's clever phrasing and his ability to present himself effectively visually just about disguise his vocal problems with the part, though the highest notes are more indicated than sung and it sounds as if the proximity of microphones is helping him.

Raffell and Lisowska are utility casting for the royal Gibichungs, rather less than that for an international house preserving its best work for telecast; neither vocally nor visually do they offer anything exceptional or evocative. Salminen has the vocal goods for Hagen, in the stentorian-roar vein, although his incessant smirk could not be more inappropriate for the notoriously humorless half-Nibelung. Ludwig, even near the end of her stage career, gives the occasion its chief vocal distinction, her mezzo retaining its plush and excitement and her bearing movingly intense and intimate. The Norns are also a well-above-average group (Gweneth Bean, Joyce Castle, Andrea Gruber), and the chorus is splendid.

1991 TELDEC (VHS / LD)

(Stage / Studio Performance, Stereo, Color, Subtitled) 270 minutes

Anne Evans (A), Eva-Maria Bundschuh (B), Waltraud Meier (C), Siegfried Jerusalem (D), Bodo Brinkmann (E), Günter von Kannen (F), Philip Kang (G), Bayreuth Festival Chorus and Orchestra—Daniel Barenboim

Bayreuth Festival: Harry Kupfer (stage director), Horant H. Hohlfeld (video director)

Kupfer has opted for a breach in visual style for his *Götterdämmerung*. The sides and back of the void surrounding the long road are now walled in, by screens for projections at the side and by a large X-shaped support at the back. This apparently represents the encroachment of civilization; after seeing the ruins of previous cultures in the earlier operas, we now encounter this era's upper class. And they are presented in overfamiliar contemptuous terms: Gunther wears a brocade dressing gown over dishevelled formal clothes, while Gutrune is a Jean Harlow siren in white. Metallic structures dominate Acts II and III: respectively, a high rostrum with steep stairs running up to it from several sides, and a kind of hamster habitat in the Rhine in which the Rhinemaidens have learned to live. Earlier, we have seen the Norns spin their rope in a forest of television antennas, and Siegfried and Brünnhilde live in an underground cave that rises in cross-section from below (another bit of excessive realistic detail from Kupfer).

Kupfer's most questionable dramatic ploy, though, is his staging of the very end, in which worldwide destruction is accompanied by the arrival of trendily dressed contemporaries of ours (so much for the otherwise consistently maintained premise that this all happens in a mythological future) watching it all on video monitors. Our culture no doubt deserves such a jab, but this particular musical moment offers no room to make it coherently; and it is any case topped by a worse piece of kitsch, a young boy leading a girl (upset at the shallowness around her, apparently) off to some better place as the curtain falls and Alberich looks on. What all this has to do with Wagner's drama, or with Kupfer's generally insightful handling of it earlier, is anybody's guess.

In among this nonsense lurks some fine direction of individual actors and their interactions, but less of it than in the previous installments; the absence of Wotan and his immediate family seem to have removed most of Kupfer's objects of empathy. It is perhaps symptomatic that the most memorable moment in the performance is an unscripted one. Siegfried's body is left onstage during the funeral march, and it sinks into the now-familiar triangular chasm; as the tragedy of the music mounts, Brünnhilde and Wotan appear on opposite sides of the canyon, stare into it at the loved one they have lost, and then look at each other. Wotan is of course not even scheduled to appear in this opera, but I'm not going to complain about the one true goosebump moment in the show.

Evans's resourceful handling of her voice gets her through her heavier moments better than one would expect, and she generates excitement through both visual and vocal means. Jerusalem sounds consistently better here than at the Met (probably partly due to it not being a continuous live performance, partly because he was in better voice) and acts a more consistent and involved character. Meier brings all her star presence to bear on Waltraute's dilemma and succeeds in riveting us with her narrative, even though her voice is centered too high up the scale for optimum results. Gunther and Gutrune are again undercast, in addition to being undercut by simplistic directorial ideas about them. Barenboim does a solid job without running to extremes in any direction and without molding anything special with any of his singers; he has a superb orchestra and chorus to work with.

Both Chéreau and Kupfer fall below their own standard in their final installment, which leaves Levine as the preferable choice by default.

JON ALAN CONRAD

PARSIFAL (1882)

A: Kundry (s); B: Parsifal (t); C: Amfortas (bar); D: Klingsor (bs-bar);
E: Gurnemanz (bs); F: Titurel (bs)

arsifal is disturbing. Is this our heritage, this contraption of ancient Manichean dualities, of fertility myths and god-eating rituals, half-digested Buddhist doctrine and alchemical superstition, torn by sexual compulsions and phobias, all hammered and mortared into the blood-obsessed underside of Christianity? Yes, it is. As anyone knows who has ever poked a toe into the Matter of Britain past the level of a childhood Tennyson stanza, it's as magnetic as it is scary; its hold has never loosened. Worse yet, there's one miracle we can all agree on: Wagner's music, infected with, and exalted by, mystical fever. Andrew Porter, in his note for the Teldec release, speaks of the score's "suppleness," of the apparent absence of beat in those opening bars. Exactly—this sound world seems to simply breathe itself into existence, its techniques so concealed, its progression of events so subtly guided, that they appear features of a natural landscape. One of civilization's supreme artists, in total command of his craft and with his inspiration and passion at their height, has taken the whole tortured mystery and burned it into us, forced us to feel it and acknowledge it as ours. That is upsetting. True, most performances of the work are reluctant to push beyond ritual, or unable to—they distance the extremes, the sickness, and try to slip by on reverence and benignity. They become ordeals of complacency. And that's upsetting, too.

1981 PHILIPS (VHS / LD)

(Stage Performance, Stereo, Color, Subtitled) 232 minutes

Eva Randova (A), Siegfried Jerusalem (B), Bernd Weikl (C), Leif Roar (D), Hans Sotin (E), Matti Salminen (F), Bayreuth Festival Chorus and Orchestra—Horst Stein

Bayreuth Festival: Wolfgang Wagner (stage director), Brian Large (video director)

A first-on-the-market accident, one presumes, that of all Bayreuth *Parsifals*, this is the one given us on video. Musically it is not negligible, but it is pulverizingly dull to watch. Wolfgang Wagner has done nothing but make some predictable visual arrangements and control traffic—and in this Kingdom of the Grail, the traffic's mighty sparse: your dawdling litter now, a plummeting swan a half-hour hence, and another thirty minutes along, the shuffling all-male congregation.

The set is unfriendly terrain for performers and depressing for viewers, semi-abstract splotches and geometric collations, ill-lit for television, with sullen blues and orangish reds that saturate. 1950s suburban modern is the feel. Obviously under Temple on the Mount constraints, Brian Large is unable to do anything with this except let the camera run and try to be judicious about who gets the lengthier close-ups. A couple of timid dissolves end in a pulpy mess because of the poor video quality, and there's one fetching Goodyear blimp shot during the first Grail Scene. That's it.

The acting is what one would expect under such *régie*. Randova and Jerusalem make energetic efforts of the sort that, in the theater, slip past as generalized struggle, but with the camera in close on the hunched shoulders, the shaking and flailing, don't. In more relaxed moments, Jerusalem resembles Gene Wilder in middle-period Mel Brooks, which at least brings a smile. Weikl conveys a sort of stupefaction, but little of the king's agony or self-loathing, and Sotin conveys nearly nothing in Gurnemanz's narrations, which have the air of that last exhausted stump speech when you know the election's lost.

Granted that Klingsor has his actions laid out more clearly than the other characters, it's still true that Leif Roar is the only principal able to sustain an intention and keep his character going. Large gives him close attention.

The musical performance will not rank among memorable *Parsifals*, but the ear fares much better than the eye. Sotin and Weikl have voices of warmth and some beauty, in good condition here. Neither is interpretively gripping, but both are reliably listenable. Roar's baritone is on the light side for Klingsor, but he's in command of the music. Randova, like most mezzos, has to keep driving to cross the finish line with Kundry (tough writing, this) and resorts to G's and A's in open chest that must have gladdened the heart of every laryngologist in Bavaria. But the voice is round, the top is there, and she's certainly not hedging. The musically intelligent Jerusalem, with his nice midrange and overly open technique, has no means of surmounting Act II without drying out. He recovers well in Act III, however, and finishes strongly.

Stein's reading is not of the profound or incandescent sort, and at points (e.g., the Act III prelude) strikes me as pushed. But moving the score along smartly is, under the circumstances, a quite wonderful idea.

1982 KULTUR (VHS)

(Film, Stereo, Color, Subtitled) 255 minutes

Edith Clever / Yvonne Minton (A), Michael Kutter and Karen Krick / Reiner Goldberg (B), Armin Jordan / Wolfgang Schöne (C), Robert Lloyd (D), Martin Sperr / Hans Tschammer (E), Prague Philharmonic Choir, Monte Carlo Philharmonic Orchestra—Armin Jordan

Hans-Jürgen Syberberg (director)

This is, as they like to say, a "response" to *Parsifal*, yet another Hail-Mary pass at digesting the cultural past in the literal, alimentary sense, at demolishing our monuments while continuing to occupy them, since we have nothing remotely comparable to build on their sites. Every shot is a deconstructive term paper aborning.

The film uses a studio set that makes no attempt at illusion—the materials are undisguisedly artificial and the groupings purely emblematic. The actors (except for the Kundry and Klingsor) immerse themselves in that adolescent Continental anomie that has somehow remained contemporary all the way from *Bonjour, Tristesse* to *Wings of Desire*, and whose relationship to the music is that of eraser to blackboard. Their physical and vocal actions are in constant contradiction. Alongside them are puppets and dolls, à la *Perceval*, Eric Rohmer's quixotic telling of the tale. There are tourist-trash minibusts of Wagner, Karl Marx (I think), and others I doubtless should recognize. To the quantity of fallen statuary that has bestrewn our opera stages the past two decades—surely the equivalent of Greece and Rome combined—Syberberg adds a fresh load. Much action takes place in steamy clefts of imitation rock, and the Grail sanctuary is approached down a corridor of nationalist pennants and banners that includes eagles, iron crosses, and swastikas.

Our "Feminine Principle" shall save us (a proposition advanced in several Wagner operas, but not this one): there are women at the Grail ceremony; Parsifal One (don't ask me to explain) is a softly beauteous lad, and when he's reborn as Parsifal Two, it's a she. Both P1 and P2 feature a wheedling goody-goody gaze that will have you itching to punch out your picture tube.

No point in going on. If it's the sort of thing that intrigues you, by all means check it out. For my part, I'm sorry the century has been such a mess; that the loftiest in German art and the basest in German crime are in such intimate congress; and that so many gifted European artists and intellectuals still can't stop "responding." But I'm bored and angry with the whole desperate set of arguments and evasions. Time to move on. Please: no more movies till you come out the other side, OK? *Vielen Dank.*

Happily, the musical performance, available separately, has things to offer. Jordan's reading is fairly brisk but not without weight (the timing cited above is bloated by some vaudeville with credits), and it is strongly structured. The chorus is only fair (smaller groupings don't sound very firm), but the orchestra plays well. There's the consistently expressive, if sometimes mushy, Gurnemanz of Robert Lloyd, often reminiscent of Hans Hotter's, and an Amfortas (Wolfgang Schöne) of whom similar things could be said.

While Reiner Goldberg is not one to freshly illuminate his music, he brings it a focus and proclamatory ring not commonly encountered. Unfortunately, his most tentative patch coincides with his most important pure singing, the "Nur eine Waffe taugt." Tschammer is unusually imposing as Titurel, and Haugland sings a clumsy but powerfully inflected Klingsor. Yvonne Minton's cool vocal color and classical musical temperament would work in this role if allied to an engulfing, settled voice (Frida Leider's, say), but her pleasing mezzo is of only medium caliber, and not always secure in the lower octave. One respects her work without being finally convinced.

The video quality here is fine, but the audio is a bit edgy and congested. The subtitles trade in thee's and thou's, which I like, but are often unreadable against these backgrounds, and the "synch" is far enough off to make a joke of every utterance—I suspect that's part of the plan.

1993 DEUTSCHE GRAMMOPHON (VHS / LD)

(Stage Performance, Stereo, Color, Subtitled)
266 minutes

Waltraud Meier (A), Siegfried Jerusalem (B), Bernd Weikl (C), Franz Mazura (D), Kurt Moll (E), Jan-Hendrik Rootering (F), Metropolitan Opera Chorus and Orchestra—James Levine

Metropolitan Opera: Otto Schenk (stage director), Brian Large (video director)

If you believe no *Parsifal* can ever be too slow, take this one out for a spin. True, there have been conductors capable of sustaining the movement and tension of such vast structures at very slow tempos (though sixteen minutes longer than Knappertsbusch, Bayreuth '62, is pushing it). Levine does not have this gift. Indeed, he apparently does not have this intention. Space precludes much detail here, but in general we're dealing with a combination of tempo (slow), accent (softened), and the discrete musical gestures themselves, which seem always to aspire to clarity and loveliness rather than drama. I'm not talking about such gross, overt intrusions as the first entrances of Kundry and Parsifal, which are vigorously addressed, but of the subtler potential dramatic events of the long stretches between. Essentially, there aren't any—at least, that's how it feels. Instead, there is endless mediation. Double bar, key change, tempo marking, entry of new voice or choir: we just slip seamlessly through, over and over. But the music already does what Levine is trying to make it do: Wagner succeeded in subsuming a thousand subtle but vital signs of life into a span that suggests eternity itself, at a pace that suggests that of evolution itself. The performers' job is to reawaken the thousand signs. The orchestra plays superbly and the chorus gives a sturdy repertory account; there are many exquisite sounds.

Hand-in-glove with Levine's approach is the Gurnemanz of Kurt Moll. Like Levine's conducting, it is much admired, and for similar reasons. It is, vocally and musically, extremely stable and smooth. Though the voice's timbre, always rather bland, has grown drier, its technical solidity and intonational accuracy are unimpaired. The low notes are still wonderful. Hats off. But this is Gurnemanz in the guise of that quiet neighborhood fellow, retired from some honest trade, who's reluctantly agreed to substitute at Sunday School. There's no investment in the knights' predicament, no excitement in telling the stories, and our eyes glaze as the narrations drone on. His presence is mountainous but not imposing—that Act III hermit is doing awfully well on his diet of herbs and berries. When we add Weikl, unchanged from Bayreuth '81 save for some serious vocal erosion (tone sometimes wobbly, often straight, pitch frequently flat), and Jerusalem, unchanged from Bayreuth '81 save for some added leather in the timbre, we begin to discern a landscape without a horizon.

Meier is better: light of voice for the part but managing it, far more stage wise and aware of histrionic responsibilities. Her performance is melodramatic and conventional, though, and because she's more interesting to watch than the others, Large uses her to tell the story with reaction shots and Avedon portraits—a huge obligation. Mazura's sound for Klingsor can barely be classed in the singing category, but at least he uses it to energize his extravagant old-school characterization, and one is grateful for the effort.

The physical production is a pale version of the traditional representational approach, looking quite murky and flimsy on video. Flowers are big: the *Blumenmädchen* are out of 1890s calendar art, and there are dainty blossoms in Kundry's locks. Then there's Good Friday. Consider the lilies of the field, how they grow. These sprong on their sprockets like drunken Jacks-in-the-Box when brushed by the hem of a passing robe. Purest ore from the rich lode of horticultural humor the Met has been mining with *Parsifal*, though perhaps not equal to the previous production's thrillingly engorged pistils and stamens of the Magic Garden.

1993 TELDEC (VHS) / (LD)

(Stage Performance, Stereo, Color, Subtitled)
244 minutes

Waltraud Meier (A), Poul Elming (B), Falk Struckmann (C), Günter von Kannen (D), John Tomlinson (E), Fritz Hübner (F), Chorus of the Deutschen Staatsoper, Berlin, Staatskapelle Berlin—Daniel Barenboim

Deutschen Staatsoper, Berlin: Harry Kupfer (stage director), Hans Hulscher (video director)

Having known Harry Kupfer only by reputation, and not having cared much for the little of Barenboim's Wagner I had previously heard, I opened the Teldec box in a skeptical mood. But this production is riveting from start to finish, and the reasons are worth noting, since a description (vaguely futuristic set dominated by a heavy bank-vault door, Amfortas floating on a levitating space-age kayak, the Flower Maidens on TV, etc.) might just as well describe any of the dozens of "conceptual" productions we have learned to loathe. But, although it uses many of the design devices of postmodern production, its concept returns to the older theatrical meaning of that word: the through-line, or spine, of a stagework, and the physicalization of its themes, as interpreted from the evidence of the work itself. And that evidence resides not so much in its intellectual content (a set of symbols, for example) as in the strivings of its characters. That's where its life is to be found.

This is far and away the best-acted performance of any Wagner opera I have seen—the only one, in fact, to consistently pursue its characters' lives, and to let that pursuit determine the outcome. Best of all, it only occasionally looks "directed." The opening scenes, meekly surrendered to exposition and descriptive narrative in most productions, crackle with life: Gurnemanz as gung-ho field sergeant, wholly and naïvely invested in the brotherhood and his duties for it, obsessed with the return of the relic and nearly crazed by his powerlessness; the esquires scapegoating Kundry with a vicious self-righteousness; everyone with vital tasks to carry out; everyone on edge because their perfect kingdom has something rotten at its core. The promise of these scenes is pursued with extraordinary success throughout the performance. Such a pursuit leads down many interpretive paths whose merits could be debated. That's not the point. "Choices" work best when they aren't choices—when they're arrived at, rather than decided upon. These are, and so we believe them. It's an astonishing thing to see in a Wagner opera, of all places.

Barenboim has found the musical analogue to this genuinely dramatic staging. His reading is for stretches as slow as Levine's, but has nothing in common with it. There's solid rhythmic bone here—the hearty Protestant recessional at the end of the first Grail Scene, for example, really takes off; the splendid orchestra plays not only with great beauty, but with intent and pungency. The phrases have not just sculptural form and finish, but dramatic destination. The long arc is maintained, but the events along it really happen, and they happen as a unity with stage events. This is profound work, worthy of its subject. Meier leaves her Metropolitan self behind like a discarded skin. Her voice is still her voice, a full lyric mezzo that in a sane operatic world would be singing the Strauss pants parts, Dorabella, some French roles, and a bit of Handel. (Why are these Kundrys all mezzos? Why do their voices have less depth and darkness than the dramatic sopranos who once sang the role?) But her use of it, and of her physical self, is so much more specific and vibrant as to utterly transform her work. Watch her in "Ich sah das Kind," a seductress so experienced and intelligent, so secure in her sexuality, that she can be the sort of woman (maternal, almost modest, her own needs subtly showing through) who might really tempt Parsifal without terrifying him. She becomes Herzeleide—the ultimate guilt trip.

As I've suggested, Tomlinson actually makes Gurnemanz a passionate man, simple in his belief but complex in his confusion. The voice is a good one, though technically erratic at the top and not always stable under the vehemence of his attack. Poul Elming, a less experienced performer, doesn't always succeed in making the behavior entirely his own, but he's still way ahead of most Parsifals, and is often touching. His fine voice is steady and of real quality for three-quarters of the range. But he, too, is uneven in his approach to the top, which tends to cut off disappointingly. He sings blandishingly in the Good Friday scene. Struckmann has a dark, steady baritone that doesn't quite extend to the required top G. Even more restricted physically than most Grail kings by his hang-glider cot, he has at least some of the internal intensity called for. Von Kannen has an interesting take on Klingsor, but there isn't quite enough authentic singing in his scene, from either principal. The Flower Maidens, who seem a good group, are musically cheated by their setup, but the male chorus sings with fine tone and fervor, and both they and the supporting soloists make valuable acting contributions.

The video direction is alert and subtle, thoroughly integrated with the musical and stage rhythms. Finally, the quality of both the video and audio tracks is very high.

———

There is no contest, and should be no hesitation. The Kupfer / Barenboim collaboration is a memorable one, as far removed from the others as the Realm of the Grail from your local Urban Enterprise Zone, and it is expertly preserved on the Teldec taping.

CONRAD L. OSBORNE

DER FREISCHÜTZ (1821)

A: Agathe (s); B: Ännchen (s); C: Max (t); D: Ottoker (bar);
E: Caspar (bs); F: Hermit (bs)

*G*erman tales of the cursed hunter casting magic bullets reputed always to find their mark originated centuries before Weber. In his time, indeed, several plays and musical extravaganzas on the subject had already been produced. His librettist, Friedrich Kind, however, further clarified and romanticized the story. Its love, faith, and terror in the face of evil defined in large part the Romantic movement, and his characters all symbolized vibrant national types even as Weber's music individualized them. Agathe, for example, has roots in Mozart's Pamina and descendants in Wagnerian maidens from Senta to Gutrune, and yet her music distinguishes her in passionate purity from all of them. These elements, together with the domestic, the natural, the supernatural, and the possibility of redemption gained the work a lasting place in German culture.

Ironically, in our day, the work itself is an easy mark. For current audiences a genuine sense of the supernatural in the theater or on videotape is difficult to achieve, and any cheap satiric bullet can shoot the drama dead—*but* the music always rises in generous rebuke and offers the possibility of theatrical redemption. Let us pray.

1981 HOME VISION (VHS)

(Stage Performance, Stereo, Color, Not Subtitled) 146 minutes

Catarina Ligendza (A), Raili Viljakainen (B), Toni Krämer (C), Wolfgang Schone (D), Wolf-gang Probst (E), Roland Bracht (F), Chorus and Orchestra of Wurttemberg State Opera—Dennis Russell Davies

Wurttemberg State Opera, Stuttgart: Achim Freyer (stage director), Hartmut Schottler (video director)

Thank heaven that there are no English subtitles *and* plenty of dialogue in this performance. That should scare a gratifying number of buyers away, for this is a colorful, "clever," and altogether dreadful production of *Der Freischütz*. It is conceived by designer-director Achim Freyer as, I would guess, a series of children's book illustrations—an idea that sounds *much* better than it plays. The sets are all vividly painted flats and cutouts. The women are all in doll-like whiteface with red lips and spots of rouge, and most of the men in dusty brownface. Their costumes vie with each other in childlike brightness. There are platforms for the chorus, and the main characters all sing either directly to the audience or directly upstage and gesture demonstratively: for example, when Ännchen mentions Kuno's picture falling from the wall, she herself, puppetlike, falls forward. Head-clutchings and many other elements satiric of the Romantic school of acting here become "style." The Wolf's Glen is a brightly lit place with some supers clomping about in cartoonish costumes that suggest neither wit nor menace. As involving experiences, this and the final scene are completely botched. Stills from the production suggest something rather charming, but after five minutes of observance, its conventions become dull and then annoying. The theatrical event denies the music and in fact almost entirely lacks emotional vitality.

Musically, things are uninspiring. Conductor Dennis Russell Davies does provide suavity, strength, and proportion, but his singers are struggling with not only the production but the score. Toni Krämer, handsome but awkward, is vocally strained and leatherbound—a particular disadvantage, since in this production his character is conceived as psychotic. Among the other men, Wolfgang Probst is a decent Kaspar, though his doll-like stances deprive the character of the gravity central to the tale. Catarina Ligendza hasn't quite the purity of tone for Agathe. You know instinctively that someone has engaged or will shortly engage that dark, slightly tremulous lyric soprano voice for Isolde, and that will be the end of that.

Anyone wanting to experience the wonder of *Der Freischütz* is referred to audio recordings. I agree strongly with the conclusions of C. J. Luten in *The Metropolitan Opera Guide to Recorded Opera* that the one to buy is the CD reissue on Allegro of the 1959 Keilberth recording, with Elisabeth Grümmer and Lisa Otto, save to add only that the Erich Kleiber broadcast of 1955, with Elisabeth Grümmer and Rita Streich, is also quite fine and available from time to time.

LONDON GREEN

FRANCESCA DA RIMINI (1914)

A: Francesca (s); B: Paolo (t); C: Malatestino (t); D: Gianciotto (bar)

While hardly a repertory piece, *Francesca da Rimini* is Zandonai's most durable opera, and it continues to be performed from time to time in Italy. Elsewhere, the work, if it is known at all, is generally held in disdain by the cognoscenti, for whom the entire unfashionable corpus of early twentieth-century Italian *verismo* opera is still beneath contempt. Admittedly, *Francesca* exudes a distinct aura of *fin de siècle* decadence, a sweetly scented perfume that some sensibilities find offensive, if not positively noxious. But that is precisely what this extravagant libretto requires, a reworking of the tragic Paolo-and-Francesca affair by Gabriele D'Annunzio in language of such gaudy grandiloquence and so drenched in the poet's cult-of-the-beautiful aesthetic that even Italians find much of the text incomprehensible. Yet Zandonai responded eagerly to the material, creating a masterly score notable for its delicate mood painting, graphic depiction of the drama's brutal passions, and sensitivity to the voice's unlimited capacity for soaring lyrical expression.

1984 PARAMOUNT (VHS) / PIONEER (LD)

(Stage Performance, Stereo, Color, Subtitled) 155 minutes

Renata Scotto (A), Plácido Domingo (B), William Lewis (C), Cornell MacNeil (D), Metropolitan Opera Chorus and Orchestra—James Levine

Metropolitan Opera: Piero Faggioni (stage director), Perio Faggioni and Brian Large (video directors)

The Metropolitan's 1984 production of *Francesca* was part of James Levine's program at the time to explore representative works from areas of the repertory that the company had lately either neglected or ignored altogether. Much thought must have gone into the project and, thankfully, no expense was spared; if one element in preparing this hothouse creation is slighted—sets, costumes, casting, conducting, or direction—then the entire illusion will inevitably collapse. Luckily, the physical production turned out to be gorgeous and ideally representative of the material. Ezio Frigerio's intricately decorative sets conjure up an exquisitely romanticized pre-Raphaelite vision of thirteenth-century Rimini—a flowery courtyard, an awesome citadel armed for battle, richly furnished castle apartments—while Faggioni's direction strikes a delicate balance between veristic stage action and stylized movement that is almost choreographic in its grace and poetry. Faggioni's touch is also evident in the fluid camera work, which includes details necessarily unseen in the house. An especially effective embellishment comes at the end of Act II as the faces of the Malatesta brothers materialize, one by one, on the juggernaut that hurtles toward the audience, a powerful symbol of the three men whose sexual obsession with Francesca cause her ruin and death.

It was getting late in the day by the time

Scotto sang Francesca, and her soprano tends to sound increasingly thin and edgy as it rises in pitch and volume. Even at that, the fascinating chiaroscuro of her timbre and the vibrancy of her special stage personality combine to create a glowing portrayal. She and Domingo make a handsome couple, and the tenor, in optimum vocal condition, could hardly be a more attentive or passionately committed suitor. Lewis is a properly slimy Malatestino, MacNeil roars like a wounded animal as the betrayed Gianciotto—not at all an inappropriate approach to the role—and the many smaller parts are all cast from the Met's apparently inexhaustible store of excellent comprimarios. Levine obviously adores the score, which he conducts as much out of love as duty, judging from the luscious instrumental colors and throbbing accents he draws from the orchestra. A competing version of *Francesca da Rimini* will probably not appear any time soon, but if one does it is unlikely to outclass such an outstanding achievement.

PETER G. DAVIS

BERND ALOIS ZIMMERMANN

DIE SOLDATEN (1964)

A: Marie (s); B: Comtesse de la Roche (s); C: Desportes (t);
D: Wesener (bs)

Zimmermann (1918–1970), a man of wide dramatic and musical enthusiasms, taught composition and also headed the department of radio, film, and stage music at the Cologne Musikhochschule for the last thirteen years of his life. His work shows a variety of influences, from German social realism to Büchner, Berg, and dramatic expressionism. The eighteenth-century Jacob Lenz play upon which his opera is based was intended as a societal lesson for all classes: the carefully observed, impassioned but rationalistic chronicle of an innocent woman's moral downfall in a barbarian society. Lenz was a Shakespeare enthusiast and mixes dramatic genres and class usages; the effects are far more various than in the opera, where a distraught expressionism and continual Berg-like intensity of response create the relentless impression of a madhouse. The composer has gained something of a posthumous reputation as the most provocative of Berg's followers, but the real interest in the opera may lie more in the academic game of finding the influences than in its emotional or intellectual vitality.

1989 KULTUR (VHS)

(Stage Performance, Stereo, Color, Subtitled)
111 minutes
Nancy Shade (A), Ursula Koszut (B), William Cochran (C), Mark Munkittrick (D), Stuttgart State Opera Chorus and Stuttgart State Orchestra—Bernhard Kontarsky

Stuttgart State Opera: Harry Kupfer (stage director), Axel Bornheimer (video director)

Kupfer's production capitalizes on what Zimmerman gives him. We have a two-level set for the many scenes, furnished in an eclectic style mixing realism and symbolism: there are real sofas and pub tables, but the onstage rape takes place in what looks like a plastic cube. Costumes verge on the bizarre, makeup and some of the blocking suggest the expressionistic, and the characterizations borrow much of their intensity from the theater of the grotesque. Zimmermann's score is generally in the assault mode; though it suggests Berg, the range of emotional effects is far narrower and the overall impression much noisier and at the same time much less penetrating. Given a score that breaks voices and destroys the depth and variety of the play on which it is based, the singers are defenseless. They seem to have been chosen for voices characterized by a penetrating harshness capable of driving them through to the final curtain. William Cochran, once a respectable Wagnerian tenor, exemplifies the first type; he's tonally unbearable. Nancy Shade has a healthier sound, but it's monochromatic; there is little chance for vocal coloring here. The lower voices are all worn and wobbly—and hence inexpressive. The singers perform their complicated and sometimes remarkably awkward blocking efficiently. For all the effort, and the work's incidental interests, the presentation is in the end simplistic, insensitive, and tiresome. Read Lenz's play.

LONDON GREEN

CONTRIBUTORS

BRUCE BURROUGHS received the ASCAP–Deems Taylor Award for his work as editor-in-chief of *The Opera Quarterly*. He is currently writing the biography of Zinka Milanov.

JON ALAN CONRAD is an assistant professor of music at the University of Delaware. He writes for *The New York Times* and *Opera News* and contributed to *The Metropolitan Opera Guide to Recorded Opera*.

PETER G. DAVIS has been the music critic for *New York* magazine since 1981 and contributed to *The Metropolitan Opera Guide to Recorded Opera*.

CORI ELLISON writes and lectures frequently on vocal music.

SHIRLEY FLEMING was the editor of *Musical America* and the music critic for the *New York Post*. She has written for *The New York Times*, *Opera News*, and many other publications.

LONDON GREEN taught dramatic literature and film and directed plays at Bishop's University for twenty years. He writes for and sits on the editorial board of *The Opera Quarterly* and contributed to *The Metropolitan Opera Guide to Recorded Opera*.

DAVID HAMILTON writes often for *Opera News* and *The New York Times*. He is the editor of *The Metropolitan Opera Encyclopedia*, co-producer of the Metropolitan Opera Historic Broadcast recordings, and contributed to *The Metropolitan Opera Guide to Recorded Opera*.

ALBERT INNAURATO has written articles and reviews for *The New York Times* and *Opera*

News. He has recorded several of the Metropolitan Opera Guild's "Talking About Opera" tapes and is a frequent guest on the Texaco / Met intermissions. His plays include *Gemini* and *The Transfiguration of Benno Blimpie*.

C. J. LUTEN has reviewed recordings for *Opera News* for many years. He contributed to *The Metropolitan Opera Guide to Recorded Opera*.

CONRAD L. OSBORNE has written for many publications, including *The New York Times*, *Opus*, *High Fidelity / Musical America*, and *Opera News*. He has published a novel, *O Paradiso*, performs as an actor and singer, and teaches voice. He contributed to *The Metropolitan Opera Guide to Recorded Opera*.

BRIDGET PAOLUCCI lectures extensively for the Metropolitan Opera Guild and has written several of the Guild's "Talking About Opera" cassettes. She is a music correspondent for National Public Radio and contributed to *The Metropolitan Opera Guide to Recorded Opera*.

HARVEY E. PHILLIPS has written for *Opera News*, *The New York Times*, *New Republic*, and *National Review*, and he has worked for many years as a qualitative market researcher.

HARLOW ROBINSON is the author of *Prokofiev* and *The Last Impresario*. He is a contributor to *The New York Times* and *Opera News* and is chairman of the Department of Modern Languages at Northeastern University.

RICHARD TRAUBNER is the author of *Operetta: A Theatrical History* and is a frequent contributor *The Economist*, *Opera News*, *The New York Times*, and *Stagebill*.

Index of Performers

Index of Directors